Health Program Planning

Health Program Planning

AN EDUCATIONAL AND ECOLOGICAL APPROACH

FOURTH EDITION

Lawrence W. Green

Marshall W. Kreuter
Rollins School of Public Health of Emory University

Boston   Burr Ridge, IL   Dubuque, IA   Madison, WI   New York
San Francisco   St. Louis   Bangkok   Bogotá   Caracas   Kuala Lumpur
Lisbon   London   Madrid   Mexico City   Milan   Montreal   New Delhi
Santiago   Seoul   Singapore   Sydney   Taipei   Toronto

Higher Education

HEALTH PROGRAM PLANNING: AN EDUCATIONAL AND ECOLOGICAL APPROACH

Published by McGraw-Hill, a business unit of The McGraw-Hill Companies, Inc., 1221 Avenue of the Americas, New York, NY, 10020. Copyright © 2005, 1999, 1961 by The McGraw-Hill Companies, Inc. All rights reserved. No part of this publication may be reproduced or distributed in any form or by any means, or stored in a database or retrieval system, without the prior written consent of The McGraw-Hill Companies, Inc., including, but not limited to, in any network or other electronic storage or transmission, or broadcast for distance learning.
Some ancillaries, including electronic and print components, may not be available to customers outside the United States.

This book is printed on acid-free paper.

7 8 9 0 DOC/DOC 10 9 8 7 6 5 4 3 2

ISBN-13: 978-0-07-255683-4
ISBN-10: 0-07-255683-8

Publisher: *Emily Barrosse*
Sponsoring editor: *Nicholas Barrett*
Developmental editor: *Gary O'Brien*
Senior marketing manager: *Pamela S. Cooper*
Media producer: *Lance Gerhart*
Project manager: *Jean R. Starr*
Senior production supervisor: *Carol A. Bielski*
Designer: *Marianna Kinigakis*
Media project manager: *Kathleen Boylan*
Art editor: *Emma C. Ghiselli*
Art director: *Robin Mouat*
Permissions editor: *Marty Granahan*
Typeface: *10/12 Palatino*
Compositor: *TBH Typecast, Inc.*
Printer: *Quebecor World Fairfield Inc.*

Library of Congress Cataloging-in-Publication Data

Green, Lawrence W.
    Health program planning : an educational and ecological approach / Lawrence W. Green
Marshall Kreuter.—4th ed.
      p. cm.
    Previous published with title: Health promotion planning.
    Includes bibliographical references and index.
    ISBN 0 07 255683 8 (alk. paper)
    1. Health education—Planning. 2. Health promotion—Planning. 3. Health planning. I.
Kreuter, Marshall W. II. Green, Lawrence W. Health promotion planning. III. Title.
RA440.G725 2005
613'.0973—dc22

            2004044976

www.mhhe.com

To the next generation of health professionals who will plan the programs that protect and promote the health of us all and to their collaborators in health and social sciences whose research will provide the evidence and theory on which better health programs can be planned.

BRIEF CONTENTS

CONTENTS

PREFACE

The periods between successive editions of this book have given us rich opportunities to field test and critique our ideas and learn of their strengths and limitations with the changing circumstances of planners. It has been each time a stimulating and rewarding challenge to fine tune both the causal logic and procedural details of the Precede-Proceed Model, guided by (1) advancements and innovations reported in the literature, (2) constructive feedback from university professors, students, and researchers, and (3) reports from practitioners, managers and planners applying the model in the field.

The first edition (1980) was inspired by the first applications of the model used to guide cost-benefit evaluations of health education,[1] and by our teaching applications and randomized-controlled trials testing the model in clinical and community settings.[2] Conceptually, the model was grounded on research and demonstration findings from health services research,[3] family planning,[4] and immunization programs,[5] and on well-established theories applicable to change processes in chronic diseases and health behavior.[6] The first edition presented the framework as a planning and evaluation logic model and procedural model for health education programs in various settings, and it coined the acronym PRECEDE (for predisposing, reinforcing, and enabling constructs in educational diagnosis and evaluation).[7]

The second edition more than a decade later followed on a period in which we had separate but overlapping opportunities to apply the model in our work with state, federal, and international agencies in health policy and program planning, implementation, and evaluation. Its application was expanded from PRECEDE to PROCEED with the addition of the *p*olicy, *r*egulatory, and *o*rganizational *c*onstructs in *e*ducational and *e*nvironmental *d*evelopment, which took health promotion beyond a more confined health education.[8]

The third edition *strengthened the ecological approach* reflected in the social-environmental aspects that were increasingly relevant to the emerging infectious diseases and problems of lifestyle and social conditions surrounding the development of chronic diseases.[9] As we now approach the fourth edition in a new century, we find that the 950 published applications of the Precede-Proceed Model increasingly have ranged beyond what many of its users think of as health education or even health promotion. The model has found increasing application in public health, community health, and population health planning and evaluation. At the same time, the Institute of Medicine (IOM) has issued two recent reports on the future of the public's health in the 21st century that have urged the wider application and teaching of ecological and participatory approaches in public health,[10] the two cornerstones of our "educational and ecological approach" to PRECEDE-PROCEED for health program planning.

This edition takes its inspiration from the realization that the cornerstones of health education and health promotion planning and evaluation have come of age sufficiently to offer the Precede-Proceed Model as an educational and ecological approach to broader public health and population health planning.

This expansion of the scope of application and range of potential users makes the model no less useful to health educators and those who seek to apply the approach to more strictly defined health promotion issues. We seek mainly to adapt the model in this edition as needed to respond to the challenges of the IOM report on the future of public health. If health educators and other health promotion professionals can provide the leadership within the health professions to help bring these educational and ecological approaches to bear on broader health planning and evaluation, more power to them, and, not inconsequentially, more power to health education and health promotion.

A major feature in this edition is the link to the Precede-Proceed web site: http://www.lgreen.net. To make this web site truly complementary and of added value to the print version of the book, we provide the full citation of references cited in the chapter endnotes, and we hyperlink many of them to their online abstract or full text. This inclusion of the full references *with* the chapter endnotes makes the lookup process more efficient for readers, who can read the book side-by-side with the web site, without having to flip pages to the endnotes and again to the references. The added value, then, is being able to link from many of the references cited in the endnotes and bibliography to the Medline or PubMed abstract, publisher's abstract or table of contents, our own abstract or notes, or for some the full-text online version of the article, book, report, chapter, or manuscript. This feature will be of particular value to scholars and other readers who want to go deeper on a given topic, and it saves them having to type in the URL for each bibliographic link they wish to pursue.

From within each chapter of the book, the reader can go to our home page at http://www.lgreen.net and navigate from there to any chapter, or enter the URL that links directly to the endnote pages for that chapter. Thus, for the endnote pages for Chapter 9, the user could enter the suffix to the home page, or type the full URL as follows: http://www.lgreen.net/hpp/Endnotes/Endnotes .htm, and click on Chapter 9. The user will soon become familiar with the web pages and navigating among them.

An Instructor's Resource CD will contain some of the web site material and some intended only for instructors, such as a testbank and PowerPoint presentation for each chapter.

One other significant addition to this edition is a specific place for genetic factors, alongside the environmental and behavioral determinants of health. We have skirted their inclusion in previous editions because of the limited range of interventions and the ethical challenges that could be anticipated for attempts to address genetic predispositions. Now, with the advances under the banner of the Human Genome Project, and the increasing attention public health is giving to genetic factors, we are better prepared to make at least some conceptual space for genetics in the model and to suggest some directions for their inclusion in epidemiological diagnoses and program planning.

Some Contraction to Compensate for the Expansions

By expanding the breadth of applications of the model in this edition, we were obliged to do some trimming back of material found in previous editions. First, we undertook a severe excision of older bibliographic references, saving a few "classics" and landmark citations, but mostly replacing older references with at least one new reference of post-1998 vintage, the year the previous edition went to press.

Second, we chose to set aside the first 18 or so pages of the third edition that attempted to define the emerging field of health promotion out of its roots in health education, social and behavioral sciences, and philosophical orientations. We are by no means disavowing our commitment to that history and conceptualization. Rather, having recorded it, we are building on the application of that history in an effort to add new dimensions to the larger domain of health planning and evaluation.

A third means of contracting the length of the text is the condensing and blending of three chapters from the third edition into other chapters in the fourth edition. Chapter 7 in the previous editions was a stand-alone chapter on evaluation. We were always somewhat uncomfortable with the placement of evaluation in this late position, considering our belief that evaluation begins with the first formulation of vision and goals in the planning process and the first collection of diagnostic baseline data to assess needs. We have chosen, therefore, in the fourth edition to combine the essentials of evaluation in each of the other chapters. Similarly, much of the material found in Chapter 12, "Technological Applications," in the third edition has been integrated throughout the other chapters. Robert S. Gold and Nancy L. Atkinson were the architects of that chapter, and we remain indebted to them. Thanks to their insights and those of other scholars like them, technological aspects of health program planning have, appropriately, become ubiquitous.

Chapters 3 and 4 in the third edition were both about epidemiology. Chapter 3 was called "Epidemiological Assessment" ("Epidemiological Diagnosis" in the first edition), Chapter 4, "Behavioral and Environmental Assessment" ("Behavioral Diagnosis" in the first edition), but the content and methods of Chapter 4 were just as epidemiological as they were in Chapter 3. Chapter 3 assessed the extent and distribution of health problems in the community or population; Chapter 4 assessed their etiologies in behavioral and environmental causes or determinants. Etiology of health problems is a matter of epidemiology, too, so we have combined Chapters 3 and 4 into a single Chapter 3 in this edition. This also achieves a more efficient and even flow in the phases. On the matter of efficiency, the algorithm provided at the beginning of Chapters 2–5 provides some short-cutting of the phases if the planner has reasonable confidence in the assumptions and prior decisions that have determined that the planning should start at the level of selected health problems, health behaviors, environmental problems, or other determinants. From phase 4 onward, we number the phases differently from one graphic representation of the model to another, depending on the level of detail or blending of implementation steps intended.

Literature and resources cited in chapter endnotes

In the third edition, we made the assumption that readers would prefer to have the new citations and the citations from previous editions in one place. The result was overloaded endnotes and a bibliography that did not discriminate well between important studies of the past whose findings remain unchallenged and studies that have since been displaced or superceded.[11]

Accordingly, references cited in the endnotes and listed alphabetically in the bibliography of this edition are mostly from 1998 (when the previous edition went to press) or later. We have deleted most of the earlier references cited in the third edition, replacing them with later citations. We have taken some pains to cite the latest review of literature on the topic to ensure access to that earlier literature, and to cite at least one contemporary case example to illustrate the point more concretely for the reader interested in digging deeper into that point. We also have moved some of the references deleted to our web site, so that they may be accessed there, if not in your personal copy of the previous edition. Where we retain earlier references, it is usually with a notation in the endnotes that these are classic touchstones or benchmarks or turning points on the topic, or that the reference cited was a notable or quotable study or influential commentary on the topic. Some have the explicit purpose of specifying the early work on testing, validating, adapting, describing, critiquing, or applying variations of the Precede-Proceed Model. These PRECEDE-specific references are marked with asterisks in the Bibliography, and in the Web pages for each chapter.

Acknowledgments

The participatory and ecological foundations of the Precede-Proceed Model hold true for its creation and ongoing development. From the outset we have been, and continue to be, motivated by the good work and inspiration of our teachers, colleagues, and students. Many of them have been acknowledged in previous editions.

In addition to the students, Fellows, and colleagues we acknowledged in the first three editions, we are indebted to the following, among others, for additional insights, helpful suggestions, and feedback from their experience with the Precede-Proceed Model: Collins Airhihenbuwa, John Allegrante, Kay Bartholomew, Charles Basch, Allan Best, Jim Burdine, Bob Cadman, Margaret Cargo, Mike Chiasson, Donna Cross, Mark Daniel, Nicole Dedobbeleer, Willy

de Haes, David DeJoy, Sherry Deren, Mark Dignan, Jacqueline Ellis, Jack Far-
quhar, Stephen Fawcett, Edwin Fisher, Vincent Francisco, C. James Frankish,
Nick Freudenberg, Anne George, Gary Gilmore, Robert Goodman, Nell Gott-
lieb, Carol Herbert, Alice Horowitz, Laura Kann, Chris Lovato, Marjorie Mac-
Donald, Karen Mann, Ken McLeroy, Shawna Mercer, Bobby Milstein, Gary
Nelson, Elan Paluck, Guy Parcel, Rena Pasick, Louise Potvin, Lise Renaud,
Lucie Richard, Lori Rolleri, Julie Shepard, Jean Shoveller, Bruce and Denise
Simons-Morton, David Sleet, Joan Wharf Higgins, Abraham Wandersman, and
Mark White.

We owe a particular debt to those professors who used the third edition of
this book and took the time to offer us constructive feedback from their
courses: Laura Linan at the University of North Carolina School of Public
Health, Andrea Gielen at the Johns Hopkins University Bloomberg School of
Public Health, Rima Rudd at the Harvard School of Public Health, Edith
Parker at the University of Michigan School of Public Health, Susan Butler and
Richard Crosby at the Rollins School of Public Health at Emory University,
Donald Morisky at the UCLA School of Public Health, Matthew W. Kreuter at
the St. Louis University School of Public Health, Theresa Byrd at the Univer-
sity of Texas at El Paso, Les Chatelain and the late Richard Dwore at the Uni-
versity of Utah, Kathleen Young at California State University at Long Beach,
and C. James Frankish and Chris Lovato at the University of British Columbia
School of Medicine.

As with most revisions, the publisher commissioned anonymous reviewers
to provide critical chapter-by-chapter assessments of the previous edition.
McGraw-Hill gave us the benefit of reviews, we know now, by Jill English, California State University at Fullerton; Ches Jones, University of Arkansas; and
Barbara L. Michiels Hernandez, Lamar University.

We are indebted to our colleagues Grant Baldwin and Eric Archueta for
their kind work and insights in helping to create the chapter test questions contained in the Instructor's CD that accompanies this edition.

We are grateful to Xanthia Berry at the Rollins School of Public Health at
Emory University for her help in updating our web site. And we are especially
indebted to Gary J. O'Brien and Jean Starr with McGraw-Hill. Their editorial
insights and experience, coupled with their enthusiastic support helped to
bring this edition to production.

As always, we are deeply indebted to our patient and always supportive
spouses, Judith M. Ottoson and Martha Katz, both of whom could legitimately
claim a degree of co-authorship.

Lawrence W. Green

Marshall W. Kreuter

1. *First publication of the model:* Green, 1974.
2. *Initial randomized trials testing the model:* For example, Green, Levine, & Deeds, 1975; Green,
   Levine, et al., 1979; Green, Werlin, et al., 1977; Levine, Green, et al., 1979; Morisky, et al., 1980,
   1981, 1982, 1983.

3. *Health services research origins of components of PRECEDE:* Anderson, 1968; Green, 1970c; Rosenstock, 1974.

4. *Family planning program origins of components of the model:* Green, 1970a; Green, Fisher, et al., 1975; Green & Jan, 1964; Green & Krotki, 1968; Stycos, 1955.

5. *Immunization program sources of components of the model:* Hochbaum, 1958; Rosenstock, Derryberry, & Carriger, 1959; Green, 1970c.

6. *First theoretical applications in analyzing forces in chronic diseases:* Green, 1975a, 1976a, b; Green & Roberts, 1974.

7. *The first edition:* Green, Kreuter, et al., 1980.

8. *The second edition with expansion to include policy, regulatory, and organizational aspects of environmental change:* Green & Kreuter, 1991. For detailed discussions of the events and experiences that influenced the migration from PRECEDE to PRECEDE-PROCEED, and the arguments both for expanding the model to encompass the environmental determinants and in defense of retaining the educational-behavioral, see Dwore & Kreuter, 1980; Green, 1980; 1983; 1984, 1985a,b, 1988b, 1991; Green & Kreuter, 1990, 1991 (esp. Chap. 1), 1992; Green & McAlister, 1984; Green & Raeburn, 1990; Green, Wilson, & Lovato, 1986; Green, Wilson, & Bauer, 1983; Kreuter, 1984; Kreuter, Christenson, & DiVincenzo, 1982; Kreuter, Christianson, et al., 1981.

9. *Ecological emphasis of the Third edition:* Green & Kreuter, 1999b; for our background work and commentaries on the new issues emphasized in the Third edition, see Green, 1992, 1994, 1996, 1998; Green & Frankish, 1996; Green, Glanz, et al., 1994; Green & Johnson, 1996; Green & Kreuter, 1999a; Green, Richard, & Potvin, 1996; Green & Shoveller, 2000.

10. *IOM reports emphasizing need for ecological and participatory approaches in public health:* IOM, 2002, 2003.

11. *Book review of previous edition:* Glanz, 2000.

1

A Framework for Planning

The really powerful forces which determine population trends are deep currents of which we know little, the fundamental physical and biological laws of the world, the habits and beliefs of mankind with their roots deep in the past.

—René Dubos

Planned actions are usually grounded in goals and principles. Losing sight of those goals and principles can lead programs into problems that might have been avoided. We begin this chapter with a clarification of three principles that you will find emphasized throughout the book: (1) population-based health programs, (2) an ecological and educational approach, and (3) respecting context. The chapter concludes with an introductory walk though the steps of the Precede-Proceed health program planning process including a discussion of some of the hallmarks of the process and the product.

KEY CONCEPTS

A "Population Health" Program

The word *program* has several meanings. It denotes the sequence of codes that guides and enables a computer to interpret and organize fragments of information. It also refers to a description and direction of the sequence of events that will occur during a meeting or a theatrical performance. The notions of "guidance," "organization," and "direction" in these two interpretations are also evident when **health program** is defined as: *a set of planned and organized activities carried out over time to accomplish specific health-related goals and objectives.*[1] Metaphorically, this simple definition of *program* serves as a compass that reminds us to keep our planning energies focused on a specific destination: health improvement. Like most journeys, however, those we take in pursuit of health will inevitably bring us face to face with complex challenges, many of which arise without notice. The principles and strategies described in this book are designed to give planners the tools they need to (1) anticipate those challenges, and (2) to resolve them successfully.

Population health program planning seeks to improve the health and quality of life among groups identified by the place where they live, work, go to school, or seek health services. This **settings approach** is more than merely identifying people by the venue of their congregation for purposes of finding captive audiences.[2] If asked to depict our traditional view of health graphically, a photographer would likely provide a close-up of a patient being treated by a physician for a disease or symptom. To get a population perspective of health, that photographer would have to change the lens, step back, and take a wider shot. This broader perspective would take us beyond the clinical, one-on-one aspect of acute health care and enable us to view the connections that people have with specific aspects of both their physical and social environments. A focus on population health is in no way intended to disparage the importance of the health care of individuals; both are necessary to achieve improvements in health. Programs of individual care and population health should be viewed as complementary and essential components of any **health system.**

The Ecological and Educational Approach

Ecology is typically defined as the study of the relationships among organisms and with their environment. The key to that simple definition is the phrase "study of relationships." It is well documented that health status and quality of life are most influenced by a combination of our genetic predisposition, the actions we do or do not take as individuals and groups, and a wide range of social and environmental factors often referred to as **social determinants of health.** This latter grouping would include factors like history and culture, levels and distribution of employment and education, housing, the availability and cost of health insurance, and the safety of neighborhoods.[3] The ecological approach to health program planning recognizes that any serious effort to improve the health status and quality of life of a population must take into account the powerful role played by the ecosystem and its **subsystems** (such as family, organizations, community, culture, and physical environment).[4] The **health care system** and the **public health system,** for example, are subsystems of the system that influences health. The health system, in turn, is part of a broader ecosystem consisting of other sectors and other aspects of community and society that bear on health, even though they are not designed or directed primarily at health.

The ecological perspective in the context of health is not new. In 1848, Rudolf Virchow, the father of modern pathology, identified socioeconomic factors such as poverty as key elements affecting disease, disability, and premature death.[5] Florence Nightingale, the mother of professional nursing during the same era, drew maps to associate patterns of patients' illnesses with their social conditions of living, and later in that century promoted home visiting by "health nurses" to complement the work of "sick nurses." From their earliest formulations and applications, the methods of public health and related disciplines embraced ecological concepts.[6] They were influenced by the 19th-century development of biological (especially Darwinian), concepts of the "web of life" and the role of the environment and adaptation in the survival of species. John Snow's removal in 1854 of London's Broad Street pump handle to prevent people from using cholera-contaminated water is heralded as the first classic epidemiological study. By mapping the sources of drinking water among those who died of cholera, Snow demonstrated that his ecological analysis of the problem enabled him to develop an effective intervention 30 years before Koch isolated the cholera organism. In developed countries, epidemiology remained almost exclusively preoccupied with the physical, chemical, and biological environments until the 1960s when it became evident that noncommunicable diseases and injuries were replacing communicable diseases as the leading causes of death, disability, and impaired quality of life. It was during that era that René Dubos,[7] in his classic book, *Mirage of Health: Utopias, Progress, and Biological Change* observed:

> Modern man [*sic*] believes that he has achieved almost complete mastery over the natural forces which molded his evolution in the past and that he can now control his own biological destiny. But this may be an illusion. Like all other things, he is part of an immensely complex ecological system and is bound to all its components by innumerable links. Moreover . . . human life is affected not only by the environmental forces presently at work in nature but even more perhaps by the past.

Dubos' comment rings true for those grappling with the complex health problems that dominate the contemporary landscape. Ecological approaches, however, have proven difficult to evaluate because the units of analysis do not lend themselves to the random assignment, experimental control, and manipulation characteristic of preferred scientific approaches to establishing causation. Although the linear, isolatable, cause-effect model of scientific problem solving remains as the point of departure for the training of health professionals, practitioners find that ecological perspectives insinuate themselves into their consciousness; like the photographer's wide-angle shot, they cannot ignore the contextual reality that health status is unquestionably influenced by an immensely complex ecological system. It is not surprising that community health and public health textbooks and the National Academy of Sciences' report on "Who Will Keep the Public Healthy" make ecology one of the four or five scientific foundations on which they build the community or population approach to health analysis and planning.[8]

The ecological systems around us are constantly, usually imperceptively, changing. To address those systems in our planning, we must first be able to *see* them. Table 1-1 provides some simple examples of how rather subtle changes in ecological systems trigger events that influence health and quality of life.

By definition, ecological sub-systems do not operate in isolation from one another. Therefore, the patterns illustrated in Table 1-1 present only part of the picture. The other part is more complex. It pertains to how the ecological sub-systems interact with each other to influence health. Suppose we undertook the

TABLE 1-1 How Changes in Ecological Subsystems Can Influence Health Status

Ecological/ Social Change	Increases the Probability of . . .	Can Result in . .	Leads to . . .	Can Contribute to . . .
Higher cost of living	Both parents working, possibly longer hours or on multiple jobs	Less time to prepare healthful meals and an increased demand for fast foods	Increased consumption of fats and carbohydrates	Overweight and obesity
Suburban sprawl	Not being able to walk to work or school	Increased use of motor vehicles and public transportation	Decreased levels of physical activity	Lower levels of cardiovascular fitness; higher rates of obesity
Introduction of walking trails and bike paths	People having access to multiple means of physical activity	Increases in the proportion of the population that walks, jogs, or bikes	Increases in levels of physical activity	Increased cardiorespiratory fitness; improved mental health; lower levels of obesity
Higher rates of unemployment and poverty	Lack of access to health services, good nutrition; adequate and safe housing	Deficiencies in preventive services; poor or undernutrition	Multiple risk factors	Disproportionately high rates of chronic diseases; violence; mental illness; poor school performance
Public denouncement of second-hand smoke	Laws and regulations to protect air quality	Less exposure to tobacco smoke	Decrease in asthma triggers	Improved quality of life of children with asthma

task of developing a population-based strategy aimed at reducing a disportionately high rate of cardiovascular disease mortality (CVD) among men in a given community. As a first step, we constructed a list of all of the factors and conditions of living in the target community that could contribute to that high rate of CVD mortality. Suppose we then carried out an exercise wherein we arranged those factors and conditions of living on a piece of paper and drew lines to show: (1) how each was connected to the high rates of CVD and (2) how the various factors were related to one another. The result would be a kind of ecological map or "web" or a "systems model"[9] enabling us to visualize the network of relationships that need to be taken into account as we plan our intervention strategy tailored to the unique circumstances of the target population and the place where they live and work.

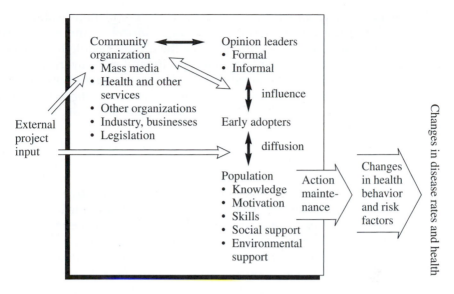

FIGURE 1-1 The North Karelia Project in Finland characterized its web of ecological relationships as shown here, reflecting in part the relationships among
organizations or sectors at the community level, the relationships among people
whose behavior was affected by the program over a 25-year period, and the relationships among variables that needed to change to affect disease rates and
health.
Source: Puska, P., & Uutela, A. (2000)."Community intervention in cardiovascular health promotion:
North Karelia, 1972–1999." In: Schneiderman, N., Speers, M. A., Silva, J. M., Tomes, H., Gentry, J. H., eds.
Integrating Behavioral and Social Sciences with Public Health. United Book Press, Inc., Baltimore: American
Psychological Association, 73–96.

Pekka Puska and his colleagues undertook such a process in developing
what has come to be considered one of the seminal community health promotion success stories: the "North Karelia Project." Numerous published descriptions of the North Karelia project made it clear that the project team took steps
to uncover the salient social, environmental, and economic factors contributing
to the high rates of CVD mortality in Finland.[10] In the process they established
close communications with key leaders in many sectors. They met face to face
with leaders in the Finnish dairy industry as well as with butchers and bakers
in communities—collectively they explored ways in which they could produce
healthful products while maintaining a productive economy. Insights from
these efforts informed the development of their program logic model (Figure
1-1). Note the sequence of the model. First, at the left, actions are undertaken to
engage, and heighten the awareness of, macro forces like business, industry,
and legislators as well as health services. This formative process serves to facilitate planned efforts to influence formal and informal opinion leaders for both
environmental change and population behavioral change. Then, once this
larger, supportive context has been established, combinations of CVD risk
reduction strategies are carried out to facilitate the diffusion of their influence
and to lower the unacceptable rate of CVD mortality.

The commitment to an educational approach to population health planning is both empirical and philosophical. It is empirical to the extent that awareness, knowledge, and skills do influence the actions people take, which in turn shape the social and environmental capacity and systems in any community. It is philosophical to the extent that health professionals remain committed to the principles of informed consent, volitional participation, and cultural sensitivity and competence as they formulate programs for health improvement.

Without education and a commitment to the open exchange of ideas, biases, and assumptions, the process of planning runs the risk of becoming a manipulative, social engineering enterprise. Without the policy supports for social change, on the other hand, educational efforts, shown to be effective on an individual basis, often prove to be too weak to yield a population-wide benefit.

Nancy Milio captured this point when she indicated that even though policy, organizational, economic, regulatory, and other environmental interventions are necessary to accomplish the goals of population health, we cannot justify abandoning health education as a critical channel for democratic social and behavioral change.[11] Planners who take an approach that is at once ecological and educational will have a heightened sensitivity to the dynamic forces that influence health and will also be more likely to be committed to a policy of open, transparent communication with stakeholders.

Respecting Context and People
in the Adaptation of "Best Practices"

Population health programs occur in places: workplaces, health care facilities, schools, and communities. The ecological approach inherently recognizes context, and the educational approach recognizes that each place has its own history, has learned its own traditions, enables people to perform their responsibilities, and reinforces its own way of doing things. A planner's sensitivity, or insensitivity, to these contextual characteristics can sometimes have a profound impact on the progress and effects of a program. Here's an obvious example. Suppose a group of practitioners in Long Beach, California is planning a tobacco control program for a segment of their community. They identify a promising combination of strategies documented in the Centers for Disease Control and Prevention's publication *Best Practices for Comprehensive Tobacco Control Programs* as being effective in reducing tobacco sales and consumption in several states in the United States.[12] Unlike the states where those strategies had been successfully applied, however, their community of interest consists primarily of first and second generation immigrants from Vietnam. In that Vietnamese population, 56% of men were smokers. It goes without saying that the planners would need to take steps to adapt the proposed program strategies, taking into account nuances of Vietnamese language and cultural traditions and beliefs. Such adaptation has at least two benefits: (1) it increases the probability that the population will see the intervention as relevant to their needs, and (2) the concern for cultural differences would be a manifestation of respect and a step toward building trust.[13] Beyond these, the practical values of linking program planning to cultural differences lie in assuring that the interventions selected or designed for the program will be culturally appropriate to the population, and therefore more likely to affect their behaviors and environments.

Not all contextual factors are so obvious. For example, like most bureaucracies, the organizational infrastructure of state health departments or health ministries is typically divided into categorical units or divisions. Inevitably, several of these will have interests in the same health issues. If not coordinated, these common interests can result in territorial struggles and counterproductive competition. In such cases, leaders are disinclined to be cooperative, especially if limited resources are allotted to one division or unit at the expense of the others. Left unchecked, such circumstances can lead to a quiet, downward spiral of mistrust, making subsequent collaboration almost impossible. Imagine yourself as a new employee, unaware of that context, being given the task of developing a cross-division collaborative effort! Sensitivity to the context is, in large part, a combination of one's understanding that places are unique and a belief (or attitude) that the characteristics that make them unique strongly influence what happens in that place.

Of course, the scenario just described can occur in reverse. The several divisions may well have a rich history of collaboration, linked by effective channels of communication. They may even have a flexible budgeting and accounting system that enables them to share and track resources and personnel. For a new employee, that context would constitute a substantial asset, but that new employee must move forward carefully to avoid appearing to devalue this finely honed collaborative structure. Although contextual sensitivity seems to come more naturally for some than for others, it cannot be left to chance. In the first phase of the Precede-Proceed Model or the planning and evaluation framework presented in this book,[14] emphasis is placed on an assessment strategy called "social diagnosis and situational analysis." Planners will find the social diagnosis a sensitizing tool for cultural awareness through participatory approaches to planning, and the situational analysis will heighten sensitivity to other contextual characteristics, including strengths and assets of the organization or community.

THE PRECEDE-PROCEED MODEL

What Are the Phases of the Precede-Proceed Approach to Population Health Planning?

Besides the ecological and educational approach that simultaneously respects context and people, the salient features of this model of program planning and evaluation are found in the phases and procedures that follow a sequence of steps aligned with a generic logic model or systems model of causes and effects. The primary purpose of implementing a population health program follows a straightforward and unambiguous formula: enhance quality of life and health status by doing what is necessary to prevent or short-circuit illness and injury. Population health programs may operate at one or a combination of three stages of prevention: primary (hygiene and health enhancement, and health protection through environmental controls), secondary (early detection and treatment of known risk factors), or tertiary (therapy to prevent sequelae or recurrence). Regardless of the stage that defines the scope of their work, planners will be faced inevitably with myriad potential factors and conditions that are likely to have some degree of influence on health and quality of life. In most instances many, but not all, of those factors and conditions will be amenable to change through planned programs. Health programs must also acknowledge that among the myriad factors are relatively intractable factors of genetic predisposition, aging, or one's place of residence, which can have strong influence on health and quality of life, but they are not (in a programmatic context) "changeable" in the same sense that policies, services, environments, or behaviors are amenable to change.

Let's start with a quick quiz. What does the phrase: "faced with myriad potential factors and conditions" conjure up in your mind?

A. Complexity?

B. Confusion?

C. A lot of factors to juggle?

D. An overwhelming situation?

E. All of the above?

Complexity is the price one pays for embracing an ecological approach to health planning. If we accept the notion that everything influences everything else and carry that notion to its logical extreme, one might argue that an average health practitioner would have good reason to shake his or her head and circle "D" above! There is no getting around the reality that crafting an effective health program will almost always require you to sift and sort through many factors. But, with the right tools, that process, instead of being confusing and overwhelming, can be a productive undertaking and rewarding challenge. One of the key features of the Precede-Proceed planning process is that it provides planners with a simple but effective way to carry out that sifting and sorting process. It has a built-in mechanism that acts like a sieve—the factors with little or no relevance to your goal fall through the perforated openings. Those remaining will be those that: (1) have the greatest influence on health and quality of life and (2) are most amenable to modification.*

The framework has two components. The first set of phases consists of a series of planned assessments that generate information that will be used to guide subsequent decisions. This series of phases involves considerable sifting

---

* The procedures for implementing this delimiting process, so critical to the effective application of the Precede-Proceed framework, are described for each of the first three phase in Chapters 2, 3 and 4.

and sorting and is referred to as **PRECEDE** (for *p*redisposing, *r*einforcing, and *e*nabling *c*onstructs in *e*ducational/*e*cological *d*iagnosis[15] and *e*valuation). The second component is marked by the strategic implementation of multiple actions based on what was learned from the assessments in the initial phase. This second component is named **PROCEED** for *p*olicy, *r*egulatory, and *o*rgani-zational *c*onstructs in *e*ducational and *e*nvironmental *d*evelopment. Evaluation is an integral part of both phases and serves as the primary vehicle to ensure the quality of the planning process. In PRECEDE, evaluation emerges immedi-ately in the form of quantitative and qualitative information about quality of life and continues as information is gathered about population health status indicators, factors associated with those indicators, including social, economic, cultural, environmental, and behavioral factors. All four phases of PRECEDE may be viewed as **formative evaluation** in which diagnostic and assessment data serve to set program priorities, goals, objectives, and targets, and also as baseline measures for later **summative evaluation.** In the PROCEED compo-nent and phases, this prior information serves as the source of baseline data and standardization of measures for monitoring progress toward or achieve-ment of program goals and objectives, adjusting the objectives and course of action, and shifting resources accordingly.[16]

PRECEDE and PROCEED[17] work in tandem, providing a continuous series of steps or phases in planning, implementation, and evaluation. The identifica-tion of priorities generated in the Precede component leads to quantitative objectives that become goals and targets in the implementation phase of PRO-CEED. These goals and targets become the standards of acceptability or criteria of success for the evaluation of the program.

How Does the Precede-Proceed Model Work?

Working through PRECEDE and PROCEED is like solving a mystery. Using it requires a combination of inductive and deductive logic, starting with a vision of the desired ends and working back to discover the forces that influence the attainment of that vision. Six basic phases comprise the procedure (see Figure 1-2). A final series of three levels of evaluation may be seen as phases following implementation, for example in demonstration programs that have an end-point, but for most ongoing programs we view these as parts of the implemen-tation, monitoring, and continuous quality improvement process. We refer the reader to separate texts on evaluation and research for the technical issues in conducting evaluations for purposes other than quality control in program implementation. As you review these individual phases, keep in mind that they are truly interdependent parts of an ecological planning system.

Phase 1: Social Assessment and Situational Analysis.   Combined, these two processes signal a commitment to engagement of the population of interest and, as a consequence, insights into the cultural and social circumstances unique to that population. An assessment of general hopes and problems of concern to the target population (patients, students, employees, residents, or

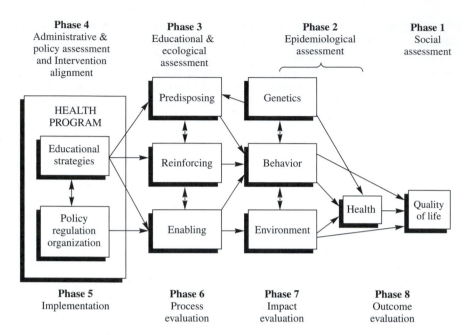

FIGURE 1-2 This generic representation of the Precede-Proceed Model for health program planning and evaluation shows the main lines of causation from program inputs and determinants of health to outcomes by the direction of the arrows. It shows the opposite sequence of analysis in planning and development for implementation and evaluation in the first four phases. This rendition of the model does not show the feedback processes inherent in the systems theory and specific social science theories underlying the model.

consumers) is the starting point for obtaining indicators of quality of life. Specific methods designed to unveil quality of life indicators are described in detail in Chapter 2. Some of the indicators of these subjectively defined problems and priorities are listed in Figure 1-3 as social indicators. Regardless of the methods employed, we urge planners to involve people in a self-study of their own needs and aspirations. Not only do the kinds of **social problems** a community experiences offer a practical and accurate barometer of its quality of life, they also can illuminate critical social and economic determinants. In turn, these insights can lead to creative intervention strategies.

Program success will be in part dependent upon a combination of the organizational strengths and weaknesses, and the degree to which those with a stake in the program activities, and its outcomes, are engaged. Furthermore, these factors tend to vary considerably between populations. The application of situational analysis tools during this phase will help planners detect the unique variations that require attention in the population they are serving.

Phase 2: Epidemiological Assessment. The initial task in Phase 2 is to identify the specific health goals or problems that may contribute to, or interact

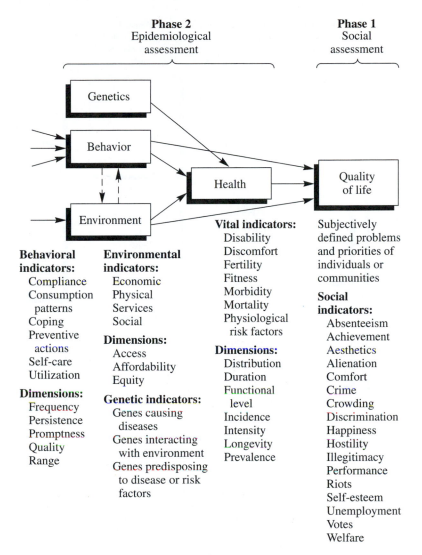

FIGURE 1-3 This more detailed representation of the output end of the model suggests relationships, indicators, and dimensions of factors that might be identified in Phases 1 and 2 of the Precede assessment process, or evaluated as outcomes in Proceed Phases 6, 7, and 8.

with, the social goals or problems noted in Phase 1. The use of available health data about the population enables the planner to rank several health problems or needs according to their importance and changeability. Examples of vital indicators and measures of health factors and dimensions from which they might be ranked are shown in Figure 1-3. This analysis yields information giving planners a rationale when they are faced with the decision of discerning

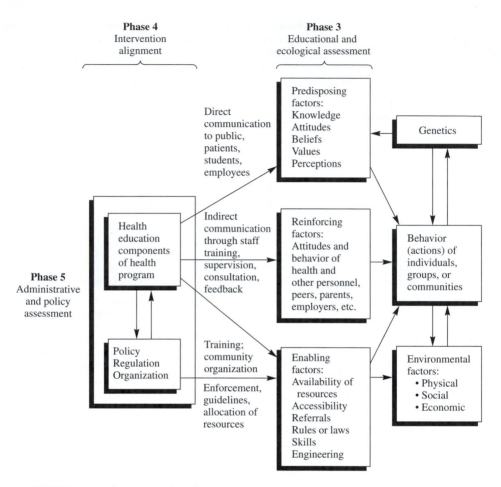

FIGURE 1-4 Phases 3 and 4 of PRECEDE address the strategies and resources required to influence the predisposing, reinforcing, and enabling factors influencing or supporting behavioral and environmental changes.

which specific health issues or problem(s) are most deserving of scarce resources.

A second task in the epidemiological assessment is the identification of etiological factors, or determinants of health in the genetics, behavioral patterns, and environment of the population. These three sets of determinants account for all premature deaths, as shown in Figure 1-4, and similar distributions of illness, injury, and disability.[18]

At this point, we need to pause for a reality check. Often, especially early in their careers, health program planners will be in situations where Phases 1 and 2 (or aspects thereof) have already been undertaken. To varying degrees, local governmental and nongovernmental health organizations will use information similar to that called for in Phases 1 and 2 as a part of their long-term planning.

In those instances, health professionals are typically asked to develop a program aimed at a predetermined health issue or problem or risk factor: diabetes, injuries, physical activity, or drinking and driving. Thus, the user of PRECEDE-PROCEED would essentially be thrust past the first one or two phases of the framework into Phase 2 or even 3. We strongly urge practitioners who find themselves in this situation to invest the time to ascertain what assumptions were made in relation to the cause-effect linkages implied in the first two phases, and to identify who was involved [or consulted] in the process. This will be time well spent for at least three practical reasons. First, it will lead to a better understanding of assumptions upon which the priorities were based. Second, the practitioner will get a sense of who the stakeholders are and the extent to which they have been, or want to remain, engaged. Finally, the review may reveal some deficiencies in Phase 1 or 2 that, left unattended, might threaten the success of the program.

For example, suppose your are employed by a local health department and the director gives you the assignment of planning a community-wide breast and cervical cancer screening program aimed at populations known to be at high risk. For this planning endeavor, you are given some modest staff support and a budget for 1 year with continued funding contingent on progress made in that first year. In your initial assessment you find that the program is strongly supported by local health data, and it is apparent that members of the at-risk population and their constituencies have been actively involved in the process. You also discover, however, that local physicians have not been involved and, consequently, are unaware of the proposed program. Trying to move a cancer prevention program forward without engaging the input and support of the medical community could be problematic. On the other hand, their active support could have multiple benefits, including their endorsement of funding support to sustain the program in future years.

A second part of Phase 2 is the assessment of the determinants of health, generally associated with the etiological work of epidemiology, and a natural outgrowth of the preceding descriptive epidemiology. Mindful of the ecological principles described above, this phase focuses on the identification of those specific health-related genetic, behavioral, and environmental factors that could be linked to the health and social problems chosen as most deserving of attention. In some instances, planners may strategically decide to intervene directly on a social or quality-of-life factor as an indirect means to influence health. In such a strategy, the outer arrows connecting lifestyle and environment to the quality-of-life box become the focus of this phase (see Figures 1-2 and 1-3). Chapter 3 provides an innovative example of this kind of application. The process of setting priorities on the basis of causal importance, prevalence, and changeability is important in each phase. Failure to establish priorities in the early phases of the planning process is likely to lead to an unwieldy number of causal factors in the subsequent phases.

Genetic factors are a new addition to this edition of the Precede-Proceed Model, recognizing the gigantic leap in the science available for future application and the rapid strides being made to isolate the genetic predispositions associated with various illnesses, risk factors, and biological conditions. Many of these associations are complex interactions of genes with behavior and the environment, so they will seldom be treated as independent effects on health, except in a few genetic diseases such as phenylketonuria (PKU), sickle-cell anemia, cystic fibrosis, and Tay-Sachs disease. For most of the gene-gene, gene-environment, and gene-behavior interactions, the science is not yet developed sufficiently for widespread application, but it is developing fast now that the genome has been unraveled. This section of the model will become more explicit as more knowledge of applied genetics develops in the years immediately ahead. The interaction of genetics with the other two classes of health determinants, behavior and the environment, are indicated by the vertical arrows connecting these three sets of determinants in Figures 1-2 and 1-3. Most controls on the gene-environment interactions depend on the behavior of individuals and populations in their exposure to environmental risks, so we place behavior between genetics and the environment.

Behavioral factors refer to the patterns of behavior (and together with social circumstances, lifestyle) of individuals and groups that protect or put them at risk for a given health or social problem.[19] They also include the behaviors and actions of others. For example, the behavior manifested by health care workers, parents, friends, or co-workers may influence the health status of a target population either in the aggregate as social norms or individually as the exercise of social power over the behavior of individuals. So could the collective social action (e.g., campaigning for votes) for or against relevant health policies. Environmental factors are those determinants outside the person that can be modified to support behavior, health, or quality of life. These overlap with the behavioral when behavior is taken in the aggregate as the social environment. Being cognizant of such forces will enable planners to be more realistic about the limitations of programs consisting only of health education directed at the personal health behavior of the public. It also enables them to recognize that powerful social forces might be influenced when the principles of *PROCEED* are translated into organizational strategies applied by coalitions on the community, state, or national level.

Phase 3: Educational and Ecological Assessment.   On the basis of cumulative research on health and social behavior, and on ecological relationships between environment and behavior, literally hundreds of factors could be identified that have the potential to influence a given health behavioral or environmental factor, or interaction of genes with behavior and environment. In the *Precede* component, these causal factors are grouped into three, manageable categories according to the educational and ecological approaches likely to be employed in a population health program. The three broad groupings are predisposing factors, reinforcing factors, and enabling factors (Figure 1-4).

Predisposing factors include a person's or population's knowledge, attitudes, beliefs, **values,** and perceptions that facilitate or hinder motivation for change. Figure 1-4 also shows how predisposing factors interact with genetic predisposition. Predisposing factors also include the early childhood experiences that created the attitudes, values, and perceptions in the first place. When childhood nurturing is incorporated as a part of a long-term, comprehensive population health program, it could be useful to include it among social factors under Phase 1 of the Precede model. Such positioning would enable planners to direct related arrows to the social goal of "childhood nurturing" because it is likely to enhance health and quality of life reciprocally in the long run.

Reinforcing factors—that is, the rewards received and the feedback the learner receives from others following adoption of a behavior—may encourage or discourage continuation of the behavior. Reinforcing behavior produces lifestyles (enduring patterns of behavior), which in turn influence the environment through social norms, political advocacy, consumer demand, or cumulative actions.

Enabling factors are those skills, resources, or barriers that can help or hinder the desired behavioral changes as well as environmental changes. One can view them as vehicles or barriers, created mainly by societal forces or systems. Facilities and personal or community resources may be ample or inadequate, as might income or health insurance, and laws and statutes may be supportive or restrictive. The skills required for a desired behavior to occur also qualify as enabling factors. For example, providing sphygmomanometers for a hypertension self-care program would have minimal value if the participants lacked the skill and/or capacity to use the device to take their blood pressure readings. We have found it helpful to think of enabling factors as those that *make possible* a change that people want in behavior or in the environment.

In summary, the primary tasks of the third phase involve sorting, categorizing, and selecting the predisposing, enabling, and reinforcing factors that seem to have direct impact on, and therefore the greatest potential to change, the behavioral and environmental targets generated in previous stages. Successful completion of these tasks will reveal which of the factors, or combination thereof, deserve highest priority as the focus of intervention.

Phases 4, 5, and 6: Intervention Alignment, Administrative and Policy Assessment, and Implementation.   Armed with the information generated in the first three phases, the planner is poised for the final assessments of the Precede component and the first phase of PROCEED. In practical terms, this assessment is designed to answer the questions: What program components and interventions are needed to affect the changes specified in previous phases? and Does this program have the policy, organizational, and administrative capabilities and resources to make this program a reality? Phase 4's "intervention matching, mapping, and patching" are procedures we outline in the first part of Chapter 5. Phase 5's organizational readiness (resources, policies, abilities, and time) is assessed by applying the methods described in the second part of Chapter 5. Inherently, most organizational entities will have limitations in their readiness or capacity to bear the full weight of a program that attempts to intervene on the wide range of forces influencing the determinants of health. Some of these limitations can be offset by cooperative arrangements with other local agencies or larger organizations at state, provincial, or national levels or through the development of coalitions and political alliances at the local level.

Phases 4 and 5 provide a practical illustration of why planners need a good conceptualization of the entire Precede-Proceed model before initiating the planning process. In the earliest stages of development, experienced planners will have an eye on Phases 4 and 5. From the outset they will rely on their experience with the range of possible interventions and their sensitivity to the mission, capacity, and readiness of their agency. Potential interventions and sensitivity to the sponsors' policies, capacity and readiness will serve as important parameters to consider as they scale their programs in the earlier planning phases. But the policies, capacity, and readiness of one's own institution need not be the only parameters of consequence. Information derived from their situational analysis in Phase one may yield insights into the probability of obtaining support from other organizations within their locality or resources from outside the community.

The planning and launching considerations specific to each of the major settings for health promotion—communities, work sites, schools, and health care settings—will be discussed and illustrated in Chapters 6 through 9, respectively.

Chapter 5 also launches the program into PROCEED, providing a focal point for the description of principles and methods of management and evaluation of programs, applying the Precede-Proceed framework in a continuously iterative process of monitoring and adjusting program components to fit the objectives, the changing circumstances, and the various population segments. It also provides guidelines and examples for the presentation of evaluation results. Indeed, PRECEDE was first developed as an evaluation model to aid practitioners in their efforts to document the cost-benefit effects of demonstration programs.[20] With the addition of PROCEED, it has evolved into the comprehensive planning framework presented in this book.

Throughout this edition we emphasize that in the context of health program planning, evaluation is an integral and continuous part of planning that is inseparably tied to measurable objectives generated from the beginning of the first steps of the process. For example, the expositions of the social assessment in Chapter 2 and the epidemiological assessment in Chapter 3 emphasize the importance of stating program objectives early on and routinely throughout the planning process. Figure 1-5 presents a rendition of the Precede-Proceed Model that highlights how evaluation is integrated into the overall process. The primary evaluation task is one of *documenting* (through measurable objectives and other data and information deemed relevant) baseline indicators. As one turns the corner from PRECEDE to PROCEED in Phase 5 and moves into implementation, the principal evaluation task is one of *using* the information gained from monitoring those indicators to make program adjustments and to inform stakeholders of program progress.

For those practitioners and researchers faced with the task of carrying out a demonstration program or research project to test the effects of a given innovation or strategy, PRECEDE-PROCEED provides a generic framework and logic

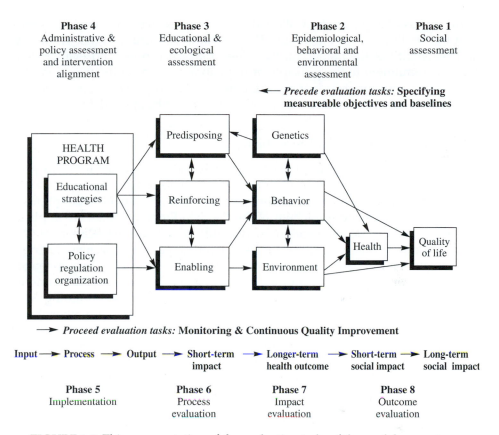

FIGURE 1-5 This representation of the evaluation tasks of the model suggests dimensions of factors that might be identified in the Precede assessment process (see Figure 1-3) or evaluated as outputs and outcomes in Proceed Phases 6, 7, and 8.

model. The markers for that framework are reflected in the continuum at the bottom of Figure 1-5 beginning with "input" and ending with "long-term social impact."

HALLMARKS

For three decades, the Precede-Proceed Model[21] has guided planning efforts addressing countless health issues in communities, schools, health care settings and workplaces in every continent in world. It has served as a successful model in the planning of numerous rigorously evaluated field trials.[22] This rich "field experience" has served as the primary means for the ongoing refinement and modification of the framework and its process. It has also helped us identify those characteristics of the model which, over time, are consistently associated with successful applications. Collectively, these enduring characteristics represent the "hallmarks" of the model: Those hallmarks include (1) the flexibility and scalability of the model, (2) its evidence-based process and evaluability, (3) its commitment to the principle of participation, and (4) its provision of a process for appropriate adaptation of evidence-based "best practices" to the populations and circumstances in which these would be applied.

Hallmark: Flexibility and Scalability

Whether one is involved in planning a large-scale, multinational health program, an integrated school health program, an immunization program for a specific population, or a patient education program for a small target population, the principles and guidelines of the Precede-Proceed Model are applicable. Considerable documentation is available about the application of the Precede-Proceed planning process across a wide range of populations, settings, disease prevention, and health promotion issues, to specific disease management and even to planning and evaluation in problem-solving situations in which health outcomes were not an immediate issue, such as continuing education and staff development issues. Local health departments and others have used it as a guide to developing programs subsequently adopted by several state health departments, and adapted into guidelines by national organizations.[23] It was widely distributed as a federal guide to the planning, review, and evaluation of maternal and child health projects.[24] It has been applied as an analytical tool for health policy on a national and international scale.[25] Adaptations of it have been published and recommended by the National Committee for Injury Prevention and Control for planning and evaluating safety programs,[26] by the American Lung Association as a *Program Planning and Evaluation Guide for Lung Associations*,[27] and by the American Cancer Society and the National Cancer Institute as the framework for a school nutrition and cancer education program.[28] It has served as an organizational framework for curriculum development, continuing education, dissemination and translation of research for nurses,[29] pharmacists,[30] allied health, behavioral medicine, and public health professionals and lay volunteers,[31] and most extensively among physicians.[32] Other applications and validations of the model will be cited or illustrated in subsequent chapters. You can visit our web site (www.lgreen.net) for a searchable bibliography of these among the more than 950 published applications, extensions, descriptions, and reviews of the model as related to hundreds of varied populations, health issues, and contexts.[33]

Hallmark: Evidenced-based and Evaluable

The Precede-Proceed process requires planners to begin with a clear picture of the desired final outcome. That is, the first questions asked are: What is the ultimate concern or aspiration here? and What do we want to accomplish in relation to that ultimate concern? The desired goal of the program is articulated first as a vision or mission statement, then increasingly during the planning is

spelled out in the form of a measurable objective that includes quantitative estimates of the magnitude of the desired effects and time anticipated to achieve
those effects.[34] Once the broad goal or vision has been agreed upon, planners
turn to a series of assessment tasks designed to uncover the salient factors and
conditions that, independently or in combination, influence the desired outcome. These are ranked or stratified in order of their causal importance, their
prevalence in the population, and the evidence supporting interventions to
affect them. Once those critical factors and conditions are identified, again in
measurable terms, planners will be in good position to ask and answer the next
question: What actions are most likely to yield a desired outcome?

The complex, ecological nature of population health challenges means that,
from the outset of planning a program through to its implementation, changes
are likely to occur that require adjustments or modifications. Because of the
commitment to use measurable objectives throughout the planning process, the
Precede-Proceed Model acts as a kind of "learning system" with a built-in evaluation mechanism. This evaluation capacity provides an ongoing source of
feedback that alerts planners to events or changes that might otherwise go
undetected. In less rigorous planning efforts, these undetected events often surface as problems after the program has been implemented—hence the term
unanticipated effects.

Hallmark: Participation

In the context of a population health program, **stakeholders** are those people or
groups with a vested interest in that program or aspects of it. Those who participate in or receive program services are stakeholders. Those who participate
in the planning and implementation of the program, and leaders in the organizations they represent, are also stakeholders. In the Precede-Proceed planning
process, the participation is central to both of these categories of stakeholders.
If health programs were a business, the former would be thought of as customers and the latter as the retail workforce or representatives of the company,
the product, or the services, who interface with the customers.

Consider those for whom a program is designed. Population health programs seek to redress a wide range of health issues from noncommunicable diseases, HIV/AIDS, and injuries, to bioterrorism, environmental pollution, and
malaria. These health concerns, and their behavioral and environmental precursors, are value laden and, to varying degrees, culturally defined. Intervention
strategies, including policy dictates from a distant central government, especially in pluralistic, democratic societies, will have little chance of being effective without the participation and understanding of those who will be affected
by the policy.[35] Many issues such as sexual behavior, obesity, and domestic violence, are not amenable to traditional surveillance and regulation. The constitu-
tional and civil rights of citizens protect most individual behaviors, including
bearing arms in the United States, the sexual practices among consenting
adults, advertising unhealthful products, or even producing pornography.
Governments such as those of Australia, Canada, and the United States limit

the powers of central government in favor of state or provincial rights to govern matters of health. Most of these powers are ceded to local governments.[36]

The most appropriate center of gravity for population health programs is usually the community.[37] State and national governments can formulate policies, provide leadership, allocate funding, and generate data for health promotion. At the other extreme, individuals can govern their own behavior and control the determinants of their own health, up to a point, and should be allowed to do so. But the decisions on priorities and strategies for *social* change affecting the more complicated lifestyle issues can best be made collectively as close to the homes and workplaces of those affected as possible. This principle ensures the greatest relevance and appropriateness of the programs to the people affected, and it offers the best opportunity for people to be actively engaged in the planning process themselves. An Institute of Medicine committee on *Improving Health in the Community* recognized, however, that

> there are limitations in a community-based approach to health improvement. Some of the factors affecting health in a community will originate elsewhere and may not be modifiable by efforts within the community. "Outside" influences are also a factor because of the geographic mobility of the population of most communities. Current health status in any given community reflects the combined and cumulative effects of factors operating over time in many other communities.[38]

Participation is also a critical factor for those with a stake in planning, implementing, and evaluating the program (which also may include those participants mentioned above). After three decades of evolution and application, the Precede-Proceed Model bears the fingerprints of many professional disciplines. These include epidemiology, health education and health promotion, anthropology, sociology, psychology, social psychology, political science, economics, health administration, health communication, and management sciences.

Given the multidisciplinary nature of the challenges facing health program planners, they can not afford to go it alone. Philosophers[39] have often reminded us what we know intuitively: that there are different ways of knowing and different interpretations of reality. Participatory research[40] in public health has taught us that an epidemiologist, an anthropologist, a health educator, and a layperson are likely to view a given problem through different lenses. Because each is quite likely to detect a glimpse of reality that the others may miss, it is in the planner's best interest to support multidisciplinary input into the process. In the Precede-Proceed approach to planning, practitioners, epidemiologists, and social, behavioral, economic, and political scientists (and certainly those they seek to serve) are expected to explore jointly how their various views of reality can be combined to generate a sound and effective program. Furthermore, planning cannot be limited to tidy boundaries of health institutions, for much of what relates to the health of human populations happens in other sectors, such as schools, industry, social services, and welfare. Participation will be productive to the extent that: (1) it occurs at the outset of the planning process, (2) time is dedicated to allow such discourse to occur, and (3) those discussions are carried out in an atmosphere of mutual *respect and trust.*

Participation is more than a philosophical principle. Evidence from decades of research and experience on the value of participation in learning and behavior indicates that people will be more committed to initiating and upholding those changes they helped design or adapt to their own purposes and circumstances.[41]

Hallmark: A Platform for Evidence-Based "Best Practice"

Within the field of health, the term *best practices* has generally referred to specific medical interventions that, under controlled experimental conditions, have been shown to be effective across the human species. That is, other than minor adjustments of dosage by age and sex, a best practice should be effective regardless of culture, socioeconomic condition, or historical precedent in social customs, laws, and policies. Experimental studies that yield bonafide best practices must rely heavily on the ability to control factors in the environment that may in any way confound the results. Immunization is often held up as the *sine qua non* of best practice in public health. Consider how vaccines are developed. The process begins with laboratory experiments, followed by carefully controlled animal studies, and eventually randomized controlled clinical trials among humans. The only difference between the experimental and control samples of the population being studied is that members of the experimental group receive the actual vaccine while members of the control group receive a placebo. Only after the evidence shows that virtually every administration of the vaccine will prevent the deleterious effects of the microbe in question, with minimal or no danger of side effects, do scientists declare the vaccine to be safe and efficacious for distribution to the public. It is precisely this kind of scientific rigor that has led to the prevention and control of many infectious and communicable diseases.

Ironically, bringing communicable diseases under control contributed a shift often referred to as the epidemiological transition. It is a process of substitution wherein infectious diseases as the primary cause of death—especially premature deaths—are replaced by a predominance of the chronic and degenerative diseases and includes many related shifts associated with epidemiological methods.[42] The preponderance of health problems shifts from the younger groups to adults and the elderly, and suffering is no longer a short, acute process—it becomes a part of daily existence.[43] As emphasized earlier in our discussion of the ecological approach in this chapter, the underlying causes of these new health priorities are embedded in the social, economic, cultural circumstances where people live and work. Because these conditions vary considerably from place to place, a program shown to be effective in redressing a health problem in one community may not fit the circumstances of another community with the same health problem.[44] In short, the creation of effective, generalizable, population health interventions is an illusion.

In the context of population health program planning, this book contends that the notion of best practice should be viewed as a process of careful, evidence-based planning that enables planners to *tailor* strategies and methods to the unique circumstances of a given place or population.

We recognize that generalizability or external validity is clearly one of the criteria of good science. Accordingly, research into population health programming can promise to produce reasonably reliable guidelines for *good* practices, but more importantly, population-based research will produce findings that can guide a generalizable *process for planning,* not a generalizable *plan.* The products of such research should be generalizable in ways of engaging the community, assessing the needs and circumstances of the community or population, assessing resources, planning programs, and matching needs, resources, and circumstances with appropriate interventions. The Precede-Proceed Model provides a platform for such a process.

SUMMARY

This chapter introduces a model of health program planning and its key features of blending ecological and educational approaches to a community diagnostic and capacity-building strategy for population health programs. It explains how the model frames the planning process such that practitioners are well positioned to adapt and employ evidence-based "best practices" to make them sensitive to the contexts and settings where they would be applied (which are usually different from those where the experimental studies that established the efficacy of these best practices were conducted). Health programs, especially those applied in community or population settings must consider the many ecological levels and relationships between environmental and behavioral determinants of health, and must therefore combine numerous interventions, each of which may have a different evidence base.

An overview of the Precede-Proceed Model summarizes six initial phases: (1) social assessment and situational analysis, (2) epidemiological diagnosis, (3) ecological and educational assessment of the highest priority health problems and determinants identified in phase 2; (4) alignment of interventions with the highest priority predisposing, enabling, and reinforcing factors identified in phase 3; (5) administrative and policy assessment of the resources and organizational changes required to coordinate, deploy and maintain the interventions identified in phase 4; and (6) the implementation and initial process evaluations required to launch the program of interventions and to take them to scale in a population. Evaluation is not viewed as a separate enterprise. Rather, it is integrated as a basic component throughout all phases of the Precede-Proceed Model. Integrated evaluation activities within each of the first six phases include formative evaluation of the priorities, determinants, and potential interventions; establishing baseline measures and quantitative targets as part of the setting of objectives in each phase; and in phases 4 and 5 evaluation insights help planners assess the match or fit of potential interventions with the priority changes they are required to affect. In Phases 6–8, during and after the implementation of the program, ongoing monitoring serves as the basis for both continuous quality improvement and for evaluation of the output and outcomes of the program.

The chapter concludes, based on over three decades of documented feedback on the application of the model, with Hallmarks of PRECEDE-PROCEED. These notable features include its flexibility and scalability to various ecological levels and in various settings and populations; its provision for participation of stakeholders in the planning process; and its incorporation of evidence-based practices and evaluation of those interventions that need be included in the program without as much supporting evidence.

EXERCISES

1. What trends have you noticed in recent years, in your community or among your friends, in health behavior, conditions of living, and health concerns? Can you find any objective data to support your observations? If not, how would you go about verifying your subjective view of these trends?
2. Identify at least three national or international health campaigns or programs spanning several years. How do you account for the public concern with these different health problems at different times? What were the major features of these programs? Why have different problems at different times required different health program methods?
3. Identify and describe the demographic characteristics (geographic location, size, age and sex distribution, etc.) of a population (students, patients, workers, or residents) whose quality of life you would like to improve. Follow the population you choose through most of the remaining exercises in this book. Look ahead at the upcoming exercises and make sure the population you choose is appropriate for the assessment and planning steps that will be required in later chapters.

NOTES AND CITATIONS

(Go to www.lgreen.net/hpp/Endnotes/Chapter1Endnotes.html for links to organizations, references, abstracts, and full-text online versions of many of the sources cited in these endnotes.)

1. *Program refers in this edition to the full range of components required to bring about the intended changes in health and social outcomes. In previous editions, program referred to the health promotion components of broader community, school, work site, or clinical programs.* Much of the historical discussion of health education and health promotion that was in Chapter 1 of the third edition has been removed from the fourth edition. A publication on which much of that historical review was based was still in press at the time the third edition went to the publisher (Green, 1999). A further extension of these 10 lessons from the 20th century to the directions in which we need to go in the 21st century are outlined in Green & Frankish, 2001. A chronicle of the evolution of the Precede-Proceed Model and its applications in health education, health promotion, and increasingly in broader community health organization and public health administration is available in endnote 14.

2. *The meaningfulness of a settings approach* to ecological, population, or community health is consistent with the findings of a recent study that showed *locus* to be the most frequently cited of 17 dimensions of the notion of *community* (MacQueen, McLellan, et al., 2001). See also Green, 1998; Green, Poland, & Rootman, 2000, esp. pp. 18–20.

3. *Social determinants of health:* Berkman & Kawachi, 2000; Green & Potvin, 2002; Last & McGinnis, 2003; Marmot, 2000; Marmot & Wilkenson, 1999.

4. *Role played by the ecosystem and its subsystems (such as family, organizations, community, culture, and physical environment):* Goodman, Wandersman, Chinman, Imm, & Morrisey, 1996; Institute of Medicine, 2003; Karpati, Galea, Awerbuch, & Levins, 2002; Kickbusch, 1989; McLeroy, Bibeau, Steckler, & Glanz, 1988; Powell, Mercy, Crosby, Dahlberg, & Simon, 1999; Rainey & Carson, 2001; Richard, Gauvin, Potvin, Denis, & Kishchuk, 2002; Simons-Morton, B., Brink, Simons-Morton, et al., 1989.

5. *Ecological approaches not new to public health and related disciplines:* Ackerknecht, 1953; Green, Poland, & Rootman, 2000, Green, Richard, & Potvin, 1996.

6. *Social determinants of health in nursing history:* Bullough & Rosen, 1992; DeFries, 1940; Green & Ottoson, 1999, chap. 2; Green, Poland & Rootman, 2000, esp. pp. 12–16; Rogers, 1960; Rosen, 1993, p. 252; Sydenstricker, 1933; Winslow, 1920.

7. *Limits of human mastery over nature and environment:* Dubos, 1987, pp. 219–20 (originally published in 1958).

8. *Ecological approaches as foundational to public health:* Elder, Talavera, Gorbach, & Ayala, 2003; Green & Raeburn, 1990; Green, Richard, & Potvin, 1996; Institute of Medicine, 2003; Minkler, 1989.

9. *Systems models:* Checkland, 1999; Flood, 2001; Midgley, 2000. Such complexities can be at least partially reflected in a "logic model" that attempts to show the causal chain of relationships in a linear fashion, usually limiting the feedback loops that would be found in an ecological or systems model (e.g., Renger & Titcomb, 2002). Such models are distinguished in planning as *effects models* showing how the interventions are expected to influence the outcomes. These may be distinct from, or combined with (as in the case of the Precede-Proceed Model) *stage models* showing how the planning and program would be carried out (e.g., Andersson, Bjaras, & Ostenson, 2002).

10. *North Karelia long-term results illustrate ecological effects and interactions:* Puska, 2000; Puska & Uutela, 2000. Puska P, Vartiainen E, Tuomilehto J, Salomaa V, Nissinen A: Changes in premature death in Finland: successful long-term prevention of cardiovascular diseases. Bulletin of the World Health Organization 1998, 76:419–425; Vartiainen E, Paavola M, McAlister A, Puska P: Fifteen-year follow-up of smoking prevention effects in the North Karelia Youth Project. Am J Public Health 1998;88:81–85.

11. *Necessity of combining ecological and educational approaches:* Milio, 1983.

12. *Example of drawing on "best practices" from previous research and statewide experiences:* Centers for Disease Control and Prevention, 1999.

13. *Limitations of best practices when applied in different populations:* Green, 2001b.

14. *History of the Precede-Proceed Model summarized in this endnote:* The model originated as a cost-benefit evaluation framework (Green, 1974) from converging streams of research and experience in public health (Rogers, 1960), medical care (Andersen, 1968), family planning (Green, 1970a), psychological (Green, 1970b) and social factors in health behavior (Green, 1970b), diffusion and adoption theory (Green, 1970a, 1975), other models of change (Green, 1976), and the demands of that period on health programs to demonstrate their effectiveness through evaluation in cost-effectiveness and cost-benefit metrics. The model was applied systematically in a series of clinical and field trials that confirmed its utility and predictive validity as a planning tool as well as an organizing framework for the variety of social, behavioral, epidemiological, and administrative sciences bearing on the planning and evaluation of programs (e.g., Green, Levine, & Deeds, 1975; Levine, et al., 1979; Morisky, et al., 1980, 1981, 1982, 1983). The first edition of this book appeared in 1980 with the coinage of the acronym, PRE-CEDE (Green, Kreuter, Deeds, & Partridge, 1980). The further history of the model can be traced in the successive editions (Green & Kreuter, 1991, 1999a,b) and in the evolution of the PROCEED components of the model (Green & Kreuter, 1992).

15. *Whether to refer to the phases as diagnoses or as assessments?* In the first and second editions of this text we used *diagnosis* to describe each stage of the Precede planning process (e.g., social diag-

nosis and epidemiological diagnosis). In the third edition, we replaced diagnosis with *assessment,* mainly in response to users who felt uncomfortable with the term *diagnosis.* Though we still consider *diagnosis* to be an appropriate denotation for the processes described in each phase, its connotation tends to associate the model, uncomfortably for some, with clinical procedures. For some, it also tends to imply that all the assessments must start with or find a problem. Positive approaches to health and assets-based community assessment call for at least part of the planning process to be concentrated on aspirations, assets, and strengths, not just on needs, weaknesses, deficits, problems, and barriers. We will use the terms interchangeably in this edition, using *diagnosis* when a problem focus is intended, *assessment* when a more assets-based assessment or combined assets-and-problems assessment is intended.

16. *Integrating evaluation into the early phases and implementation phase, rather than deferring to a later chapter:* In previous editions, a separate chapter was devoted to evaluation. In this edition, we integrate the evaluation considerations into each chapter, reminding the planner that evaluation should be part of the planning process, not left to evaluators after the planning is completed. Whereas previous editions have represented the model with nine phases, the last three of which were evaluation, formative evaluation is now incorporated into the Precede phases; process, impact, and outcome evaluation are incorporated into the implementation phase of PROCEED.

17. *Rationale for all capital letters versus "Precede-Proceed" in the acronym:* We use all capital letters when the terms PRECEDE and PROCEED stand alone as acronyms. Elsewhere, to relieve their obtrusiveness in the text, we drop to an initial capital letter only when the terms are used as adjectives with other nouns, such as Precede-Proceed Model and the Precede phases.

18. *Combining of epidemiological, behavioral, and environmental assessments and, from the 3rd edition, Chapters 3 and 4 into one epidemiological diagnosis:* In previous editions of this text, and in other previous representations of the Precede-Proceed Model, Phase 2 consisted only of the epidemiological assessment of the health problems of a population and their causal relationship to the social problems. We have now combined this epidemiological task with the etiological assessment of the determinants of health. Chapter 3 now encompasses what was previously also in Chapter 4 under behavioral and environmental assessments. For further discussion of this amalgamation, see the preface to this edition.

19. *Behavior, environment, and genetics combine to put people at greater or less health risk:* Aday, 2001; Berkman & Kawachi, 2002; CDC, 1999a; Fiscella, et al., 2000; French, Story, & Jeffrey, 2001; IOM, 2002; Kawachi, et al., 2002; Korenbrot, et al., 2000; McGinnis, Russo, & Knickman, 2002; Panter-Brick & Worthman, 1999; Rodgers, 2002; Soobader & LeClere, 1999; Thomas, 2001; Williams & Collins, 2001.

20. *Precede Model's original formulation as an evaluation model:* Green, 1974.

21. *Theory, model, or framework?* Early in the evolution of PRECEDE, we referred to it exclusively as a framework. This was a caution against claiming too much for it as a model or a theory. A theory is "a set of interrelated constructs (concepts), definitions, and propositions that presents a systematic view of phenomena by specifying relations among variables, with the purpose of explaining and predicting phenomena," from Kerlinger, 1986, p. 9. The primary purpose of PRECEDE was not to explain and predict phenomena, but to organize existing, multiple theories and constructs (variables) into a cohesive, comprehensive, and systematic view of relations among those variables important to the planning and evaluation of health programs. Given the extensive application and validation of the framework in practice and in research during the 1970s and 1980s, we have felt confident in calling it a model for the past two decades. It might qualify as a "theoretical model," or at least a "causal model," in some of its applications (Sussman & Sussman, 2001). For further discussion of models, theories, and emerging theories in health program planning and evaluation, see Crosby, Kegler, & DiClemente, 2002; Glanz, Rimer, & Lewis, 2001, pp. 22–31; Green, 1986f; Green & Lewis, 1986, pp. 55–74; Kegler, Crosby, & DiClemente, 2002; Lorig & Laurin, 1985; P. D. Mullen, Hersey, & Iverson, 1987.

22. *Some of the early trials that helped validate and shape the representation of the model* included applications by Cantor, et al., 1985; Green, 1974; Green, Fisher, Amin, & Shafiullah, 1975; Green, Levine, Wolle, & Deeds, 1979; Green, Wang, & Ephross, 1974; Hatcher, Green, Levine, & Flagle, 1986; D. M. Levine, et al., 1979; Mamon, Green, Gibson, & Mackenzie, 1979; Morisky, et al.,

1980, 1983, 1985; Morisky, Levine, Green, & Smith, 1982; Rimer, Keintz, & Fleisher, 1986; Sayegh & Green, 1976; Wang, et al., 1979. Some of the more recent trials and other tests and applications of the model will be cited or described in later chapters of this edition. For the bibliography of some 950 published applications and adaptations of the model for various purposes, go to www.lgreen.net/bibliographies.

23. *Applications of the model in local and state health agencies:* Brink, Simons-Morton, Parcel, & Tiernan, 1988; Eriksen & Gielen, 1983; Gielen & Radius, 1984; Health Education Center, 1977; Hutsell, et al., 1986; C. F. Nelson, Kreuter, Watkins, & Stoddard, 1987; Newman, Martin, & Weppner, 1982; PATCH, 1985; Taylor, et al., 1996, 1998; U.S. Department of Health and Human Services, 1996b. The U.S. federal adaptations evolved from PRECEDE to PATCH to APEX(PH) to the latest adaptation, MAPP, currently under development and testing by the National Association of County and City Health Officials, 2000 (http://www.naccho.org/tools.cfm, accessed 8/12/03), in collaboration with the Centers for Disease Control and Prevention (www.phppo.cdc.gov, accessed 8/12/03).

24. *Applications of the model in maternal and child health:* Green, Wang, et al., 1978. The initial Precede study on asthma education (Green, 1974) was first replicated with children in a trial by Cohen, Harris, & Green, 1979 that produced results with approximately the same 1-to-7 cost-benefit ratio in reduced emergency visits. More recent adaptations of the model in relation to maternal and child health have included studies and projects on *chronic diseases* (e.g., Bartholomew, et al., 1989, 1994, 1997, 2000; Chiang, et al., 2003; Downey, et al., 1987, 1988, 1989; Fisher, et al., 1995); *prenatal care* (e.g., Covington, et al., 1998; Donovan, 1991; Fraser, et al., 1997; Olsen, 1994; Sword, 1999; Windsor, et al., 1985, 1993, 2000); injury prevention (e.g., Farley, 1997; Eriksen & Gielen, 1983); *dental health* (e.g., Frazier & Horowitz, 1990; Horowitz, 1998); *breast-feeding studies* (Burglehaus, et al., 1997; P. Williams, et al., 1999), *child immunization* (e.g., Deeds & Gunatilake, 1989; Freed, et al., 1993), and a variety of *school health* and other applications for youth (see Chapter 7) including a model for *physical activity* promotion (Welk, 1999). It is notable that Windsor, et al. (1985, 1993, 2000) obtained a similar 1-to-7 cost-benefit ratio for smoking cessation interventions for women in public prenatal clinics that had been found in the early asthma education interventions with both adults and children.

25. *Applications of the model in developing or reviewing national policies in health promotion and disease prevention:* Danforth & Swaboda, 1978; Green, 1978a, 1980, 1983, 1986d; Green, Wilson, & Bauer, 1983; Kreuter, 1992; Mercer, et al., 2003; U.S. Department of Health & Human Services, 1981, 1988, esp. section D.

26. *Applications of the model in injury prevention and control:* National Committee for Injury Prevention and Control, 1989; Gielen & McDonald, 2002; Gielen & Sleet, 2003. For specific applications in child injury prevention and control, see H. Becker, et al., 1998; Eriksen & Gielen, 1983; Farthing, 1994; Gielen, 1992; Gielen & Radius, 1984; Hendrickson & Becker, 1998; Howat, et al., 1997; Jones & Macrina, 1993; for a study of recreational injury applying the model, Cadman, 1996; for studies and interventions in occupational settings, see Calabro, et al., 1998; Dedobbeleer & German, 1987; DeJoy, 1986a,b,c, 1990, 1996; DeJoy, et al., 1995; Reichelt, 1995; and for applications in automobile injury prevention, Simons-Morton, Brink, Simons-Morton, et al., 1989; Sleet, 1987. For a review applying the model to the classification of studies on suicide prevention among indigenous youth, see V. Clark, Frankish, & Green, 1995.

27. *PRECEDE as a guide for lung associations:* Green, 1987a. *Other published applications of the model on prevention and control of chronic lung diseases* include Deeds, Apson, & Bertera, 1979; Doyle, Beatty, & Shaw, 1999; Iverson & Scheer, 1982; Wang, Terry, Flynn, et al., 1979.

28. *Applications of the model in planning and evaluation of the American Cancer Society's and National Cancer Institute's "Changing the Course" nutrition education curriculum and broader youth education:* Contento, et al., 1992; Light & Contento, 1989. See also the broader ACS Plan for Youth Education: Corcoran & Portnoy, 1989.

29. *Applications in development of curriculum for nurses' education and standards, and assessment of primary care practices for purposes of planning continuing education and training for nurses and allied health personnel:* (Bennett, 1977; Berland, et al., 1995; Canadian Council of Cardiovascular Nurses, 1993; Cretain, 1989; DeJoy, Murphy, et al., 1995; Macrina, et al., 1996; Mahloch, et al.,

1993; Mann, Viscount, et al., 1996; Miilunpalo, et al., 1995; Morrison, 1996; Shamian & Edgar, 1987; Shine, et al., 1983; Simpson & Pruitt, 1989; Smith, Danis, & Helmick, 1998; Whyte & Berland, 1993.

30. *Applications of the model with pharmacists and pharmacy interventions* Fedder, 1982; Fedder & Beardsley, 1979; Hill, 1990; Mann, Viscount, et al., 1996; Opdycke, et al., 1992; Paluck, 1998; Paluck, Green, et al., 2002; Paluck, Haverkamp, et al., 2004; Wallenius, 1995.

31. *Applications of the model in training for behavioral medicine:* Altman & Green, 1988; Glanz & Oldenburg, 1997; D. M. Levine & Green, 1981; *school health:* Fisher, Green, McCrae, & Cochran, 1976; Higgins & MacDonald, 1992; MacDonald & Green, 2001; Simpson & Pruitt, 1989; *dieticians:* McKell, 1994, 1996; *other allied health:* Bennett, 1977; Goldenhar, et al., 2001; Mann, et al., 1996; *public health personnel:* Green, 1981; Ottoson, 1995, 1997, 1998; U.S. Department of Health and Human Services, 1996; *and volunteers:* Adeyanju, 1987–88; Bird, et al., 1996; DePue, et al., 1987; Ward, Levine, et al., 1982.

32. *Applications of the model with the study of physicians' behavior:* Battista, et al., 1986; Burglehaus, et al., 1997; Cheng, et al., 1999; Costanza, 1992; Desnick, et al., 1999; Donovan, 1991; Green, 1999b; Heywood, et al., 1996; Hiddink, et al., 1995, 1997a–d, 1999; Laitakari, et al., 1997; Langille, et al., 1997; Mann & Putnam, 1989; 1990; Mirand, et al., 2002; Walsh & McPhee, 1992, *continuing medical education, dissemination, and translation:* Bertram & Brooks-Bertram, 1977; Davis, Thomson, et al., 1995; Lomas, 1993; Mann, 1994; Mann, Lindsay, et al., 1996; Mann, Putnam, et al., 1990; Wang, et al., 1979; and *guidelines for physician action in preventive health care practices:* Bartlett, 1982; Clearie, et al., 1982; Cooke, 1995; Downey, Cresanta, & Berenson, 1989; Green, 1987a, 1999b, Green, Cargo, & Ottoson, 1994; Green, Eriksen, & Schor, 1988; Haber, 1994; Herbert, 1999; Levine, et al., 1979, 1987; Li, et al., 1984; Maiburg, et al., 1999; Makrides, et al., 1997.

33. *The web site* at http://www.lgreen.net also organizes these endnotes in such a way that the reader can use the web pages side by side with this book to look up references via links rather than having to page back and forth between text, endnotes, and references. Many of the references are also hyperlinked in this web site to their abstract or online full text. Many other hyperlinks are found in the web site but are not listed in this book to minimize the problems of broken links (URLs that change) and the need for the reader to type in complicated URLs.

34. *Quantified health objectives:* The most widely known and influential of such objectives have been the exercises undertaken in several countries (e.g., for the U.S., Australia, and the U.K., see McGinnis, 1990; Nutbeam, Wise, et al., 1993; Nutbeam & Wise, 1996; Green, 1980) to specify national health priorities in the form of goals and targets. The U.S. version of these (U.S. Department of Health and Human Services, 1981a, 1991, 2000) has been the most dynamic and durable, having been first formulated in 1979–81 as part of the "Healthy People" initiative, following on the broad goals set in the first *Surgeon General's Report on Health Promotion and Disease Prevention* (McGinnis, 1982; U.S. Department of Health, Education and Welfare, 1979). Buchanan (2000, pp. 37–42) discusses the logic of the U.S. objectives, as "originally articulated" in a variation of the Precede-Proceed Model (Green, 1980, 1991; Green, Wilson, & Bauer, 1983). In a later chapter, however, Buchanan takes sharp issue with this approach to health, recommending instead a participatory and values-based approach, but failing to acknowledge that the two are not mutually exclusive (Buchanan, 2000, esp. pp. 133–138). The Precede-Proceed Model, as our next chapter will emphasize, begins with, and retains throughout (as did the Healthy People process in each decade; e.g., U.S. Department of Health and Human Services, 1981b), a participatory approach, while also striving for an objective specification of goals and targets. Another critique of the goals and targets approach as represented by the Healthy People series in the United States is the proliferation of objectives (226 in the 1980–1990 round, now several hundred more in the 2000–2010 round). Sultz & Young, 2004, p. 55, take particular issue with the continued growth in the number of objectives even as we failed to meet 85% of the Healthy People 2000 targets.

35. *Importance of participation of ultimate recipients or beneficiaries of programs in planning those programs or adapting them to their localities and culture:* Chavis & Wandersman, 1990; Church, et al., 2002; Green, 1986c; Green & Shoveller, 2000; Kreuter, 1984; Macrina & O'Rourke, 1986–87; Wandersman & Florin, 2000; Wharf Higgins, 2002; Wharf Higgins, et al., 1999. Some good examples of the application of the principle of participation employing the Precede-Proceed

Model include Cain, et al., 2001; Castilla y Leon, 1993; Dewar, et al., 2003; Fisher, et al., 1995; Herbert & White, 1996; Howat, et al., 2001; Renaud & Mannoni, 1997.

36. *Federalism, state or provincial rights, and local authority in regulating health matters:* Green & Ottoson, 1999, pp. 589–593.

37. *Community as most appropriate center of gravity for planning health programs,* but not to the exclusion of state and national levels of support needed to communities, or of institutional and family levels of support to individuals: Bracht, 1998; Green, 1990; Green & Raeburn, 1990; Halverson, et al., 1996; Mays, Miller, & Halverson, 2000; Patton & Cissell, 1989; Rivo, et al., 1991; Roussos & Fawcett, 2000; Sanchez, 2000; Wickizer, Wagner, & Perrin, 1998.

38. *Limitations of community:* Institute of Medicine, 1997, pp. 25–26.

39. *Ways of knowing and interpretations of reality:* Wilber, 1998.

40. *Participatory research:* Boston, et al., 1997; George, et al., 1998–99; Goodman, 2001; Green & Mercer, 2001; 2004; McGowan & Green, 1995; Minkler, 2000; Minkler & Wallerstein, 2003; O'Fallon & Dearry, 2002.

41. *The principle of participation in peoples' learning and commitment:* Bjaras, et al., 1991; Green, 1986c; Schiller, et al., 1987; Wandersman & Florin, 2000.

42. *Epidemiological transition, applicable in developing countries?* M. S. Carolina, & L. F. Gustavo, 2003; Hackam & Anand, 2003.

43. *From acute to chronic, the epidemiological transition:* Sepúlveda, 1998.

44. *Applying evidence from previous research together with assessment of local circumstances:* Green, 2001b. Full text online at http://www.ajhb.org/2001/number3/25-3-2.htm.

2

Social Assessment, Participatory Planning, and Situation Analysis

We do not see things as they are; we see things as we are.
—Anais Nin

The whole of science is nothing more than a refinement of everyday thinking.
—Albert Einstein

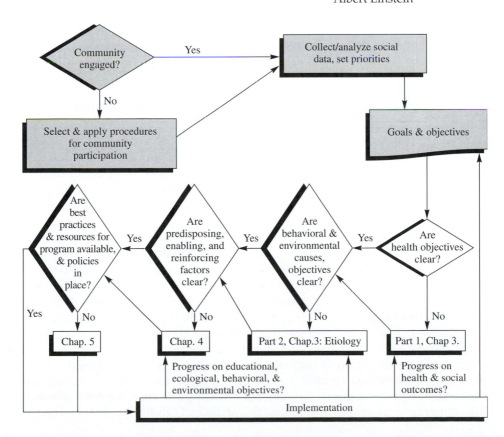

This chapter begins with the rationale and assumptions that justify social assessment and participatory planning. It describes the reciprocal relationship between health and the **social indicators** and **social determinants** that reflect or affect health and quality of life. It explains the importance of interpreting "health" as an instrumental rather than ultimate value. The chapter also describes tested methods and tools for conducting a social diagnosis and for promoting participation in planning and in the research that produces better planning, and an assessment of assets. Finally, it suggests ways of combining these to produce a **situation analysis** that "precedes" and, if urgency necessitates, bypasses, the additional technical and science-driven health planning processes to be presented in the two chapters to follow. Situation analysis thus can serve either to aid in the rest of the planning or to justify a shortcut to "proceed" with action.

SOCIAL DIAGNOSIS AND PARTICIPATION: THE RATIONALE

Health programs do not spring from a social vacuum. They typically emerge in community or organizational settings that require policy decisions to support them.[1] The *ecological* perspective tells us that the policies and other factors influencing a population's health status and perceptions are shaped, modified, and maintained by people's interaction with the community or organizational environments in which they live. The *educational* perspective tells us that people learn continuously from their environmental and social surroundings and can develop, individually or collectively, the knowledge and skills to modify them. These two perspectives point us to the central themes of this book and the Precede-Proceed Model: that people and their environments interact with reciprocal effects on each other. That is, people influence their social and physical environments through their attitudes and behavior, and they are influenced *by* their environments and their behavior. An essential starting point, then, is engaging people in defining their social conditions and quality-of-life concerns so that we can know what is important to them, beyond our relatively narrow health perspective.

Understanding the social context of communities and organizations from the perspective of those who live or earn their living there is both a pragmatic and a moral imperative. It is pragmatic because the actions necessary to resolve contemporary health problems or to pursue health goals require joint participation from multiple community institutions and individuals. It is also pragmatic insofar as people living day-to-day with the issues to be addressed will have knowledge and insights that professionals might not have. Without some mutual belief that the issue at hand is worthy of attention, time, and effort, joint participation is unlikely. The imperative is moral, based on the principles of informed consent and respect. People should be informed and their views acknowledged, if not honored with application. Chapter 1 stamped this imperative as one of the hallmarks of PRECEDE-PROCEED. Failure to attend to it would be both undemocratic and disrespectful, denying people the opportunity to register their concerns on matters that affect their health and quality of life.

Grounded in these two imperatives, **social diagnosis** is a first step in health program planning, but aspects of it are repeated throughout.. We define it as the application, through broad participation, of multiple sources of information, both objective and subjective, designed to expand the mutual understanding of people regarding their aspirations for the common good. The measurement of these sources of information for this first phase of planning is generally based on social and economic indicators for the population and on quality-of-life indicators for individuals. By self-definition, health planners seek to uncover those indicators that influence health. One purpose of the social diagnosis is to help these planners expand their view by taking note of aspirations and social goals that could benefit *from* health and those that might compete with health for resources and attention. Health planning must seek ways to link health to those potentially competing social and quality-of-life goals, showing how health improvements can contribute to them, or harmonizing health goals with them so that health and social or quality-of-life benefits are seen as complementary. This chapter's phase of Precede-Proceed planning is concerned particularly with this understanding and with the situation analysis that flows from a mutual understanding of what is important, and what resources are available, to guide the health program planning, implementation, and evaluation process.

Social and Health Conditions: A Reciprocal Relationship

Diagrammatic representations of the Precede-Proceed Model usually present it as a linear, cause-and-effect process where *inputs* (health education, policy, regulation, and organization) cause certain changes that will eventually lead to *outcomes* (health and improved quality of life). Of course, some of these linkages, especially the relationships between health and the social or personal quality of life, are not actually one-way streets. A more realistic view is suggested in Figure 2-1, representing the relationships between health problems and quality of life at the individual and community levels. The arrows indicate that health problems influence quality of life at the same time that quality of life and the social factors associated with it affect health.

Social determinants of health include the cumulative effects of current, or even a lifetime of exposure to conditions of living that combine to influence health status; many of these conditions of living are beyond the control of the individual. These determinants also lie beyond the purview of the health fields as conventionally defined, but they cannot be relegated entirely to other fields outside the health sector. Within the health professions, greater attention to these social determinants and quality-of-life outcomes is needed from professions typically limited in their scope to medical care settings and health outcomes.[2] The top arrow in Figure 2-1 implies that social conditions and quality of life can lead to health problems or the capacity and will to cope with health problems. Health workers can effectively address this aspect of the reciprocal

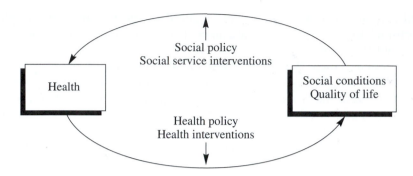

FIGURE 2-1 The relationships between health and social conditions are reciprocal.

relationship mainly in cooperation with social workers, housing and recreation professionals, law enforcement, and those in other sectors who shape social policy and social service programs. This reality has stimulated a large part of the growth in emphasis on community coalitions to facilitate the collaboration and shared resources needed across sectors and organizations.[3] This collaborative and capacity-building emphasis in community health has led in turn to a growing emphasis on **social capital** in the health literature, with its notions of interorganizational trust and cooperation to bond and bridge the complementary rather than competing capabilities of different sectors and organizations.[4]

The bottom arrow in Figure 2-1 indicates that social conditions and quality of life are themselves influenced by health problems or concerns amenable to modification by policies and interventions for health improvement or maintenance. PRECEDE-PROCEED, at this stage, emphasizes this aspect of the reciprocal exchange represented by the bottom arrow. At later stages of the planning process, we will address the organizational, policy, and regulatory ways in which health programs can alter social determinants of health. Meanwhile, recognizing at this stage the feedback loop in Figure 2-1 from quality of life produced by health can make the job of the health professional easier. That is because people will appreciate and support health innovations and policies, even regulations, if they can see clearly how such efforts address their social and economic concerns or contribute to their quality of life, in addition to their health.[5]

Health as an Instrumental Rather Than Terminal Value

More than a step in a planning and evaluation framework—the social diagnosis phase of the Precede-Proceed Model is also a way of thinking. This becomes evident when we ask, Among the many things in life we value, where does health fit? Health is certainly a good thing. Music, art, work, and play are also good, as are parenting or friendship, as well as eating. We value many good things in life, things that compete with each other for our investment of time, interest, and energy. In day-to-day affairs, it is probably rare for people to engage in a given "health-related behavior" primarily because they believe the behavior is going to make them live longer lives. More likely, actions we deem to be healthful[6] can be explained in terms of how those actions make us feel, function, or look. In some cultures, health behaviors are tied to religious and spiritual tenets. Generally, health seems to be cherished because it serves other ends. The 1986 Ottawa Charter for Health Promotion put it this way: "Health is seen as a resource for everyday life, not the objective of living."[7] Last's *Dictionary of Epidemiology* added, "it is a positive concept, emphasizing social and personal resources as well as physical capabilities."[8] The sociologist Talcott Parsons defined health as "the ability to perform important social roles."[9] These functional views of health see it as a means to other ends and define health in terms of a person's ability to adapt to social and environmental circumstances. This puts it squarely into an educational and ecological perspective, especially if one adds: "and to influence their environments, individually or organizationally."

Planners who acknowledge that health is an instrumental value use that insight quite practically, whether at the population or the individual level. When seeking collaboration with nonhealth organizations, health planners first identify the priority values of those organizations and then show how strategic health improvements can enhance those values. For example, corporate decision makers are more likely to support health initiatives for their employees, or even for their communities, if they can see how those initiatives relate to their corporate missions. They respond most readily to those health programs that might affect their priorities such as performance, absenteeism, or excessive medical claims.[10] Similarly, school officials are more likely to support integrated school health programs when they are presented with evidence that such programs reinforce their educational mission.

Through the application of "tailored communications," computer technology has given health professionals the opportunity to apply our understanding of ultimate and instrumental values at the individual level while taking a population approach.[11] In tailored health communications, a computer generates specific, personalized messages based on an assessment of an individual's characteristics, sometimes including those things he or she values and enjoys.[12] For instance, suppose a large work site wants to implement a health promotion program, a part of which includes a tailored communication component designed to increase the level of physical activity across the entire workforce. Brief questionnaires are given to 450 employees. Communication messages are created for various combinations of responses to the questions. The responses of one of those employees, a 32-year-old woman named Ellie Watson, reveals that she has a keen interest in classical music and a passion for gardening. Among the hundreds of messages designed for the subsequent communication back to the 450 employees, Watson will receive those framed within the context of her self-declared interests: listening to classical music while exercising and earning physical activity points through gardening. In contrast to messages encouraging Watson to increase her level of physical activity because science says it will give her cardiovascular benefits over time, tailoring constitutes a planned effort to connect the *ultimate values* of music and gardening with the *instrumental values* of physical activity and health.

QUALITY OF LIFE:
AN EXPRESSION OF ULTIMATE VALUES

An ultimate or terminal value usually goes beyond health. When people undertake efforts to be healthy, creative, and productive and try to make their conditions of living safe and enjoyable, they are seeking to improve some quality of life that is attached to their values. Health *is* one quality of life, but it usually has other purposes, each of which makes health a means to some other end. People seek health in order to be more effective, attractive, or productive, a better parent or lover; to live longer, livelier, more independent, comfortable, and respected lives. Like most concepts, **quality of life** is measurable to the extent that it can be operationally defined; but unlike most concepts, this one is elusive. We define it as the perception of individuals or groups that their needs are being satisfied and that they are not being denied opportunities to pursue happiness and fulfillment.[13]

Eliciting Subjective Assessments
of Community Quality of Life

Assessments that elicit information from community members about their subjective quality-of-life concerns provide the yeast for health planning. Surveys, structured interviews, or focus groups are frequently used to gain insight on such concerns. The subjective assessment of quality of life through participatory research methods offers a view of a particular situation through the eyes of the community residents themselves,[14] who share what matters to them and show where health lies in the context of their lives. Health promotion seeks to promote healthful conditions that improve quality of life as seen through the eyes of those whose lives are affected. Although health might have instrumental value in reducing risks for morbidity and mortality, its ultimate value lies in its contribution to quality of life.

For example, when the Kaiser Family Foundation staff and members of the governor's office conducted a social reconnaissance (see description of this method later in this chapter) with the state of Mississippi, prior to making health promotion grants in that state, they conducted structured interviews in local communities. These revealed that the main concerns of the population centered on quality of housing and economic development, which they related in part to the quality of schooling. These became central themes in the subsequent analysis of health problems and led to the coordination of planning with the housing and economic development sectors of the state government and with the school boards of local communities.[15]

> **BOX 2-1** Questions Used to Measure Health-Related Quality of Life (Healthy Days Measures)
>
> 1.   Would you say that in general your health is:
>   (a) Excellent?   (b) Very good?   (c) Fair?   (d) Poor?
>
> 2.   Now thinking about your physical health, which includes physical illness and injury, for how many days during the past 30 days was your physical health not good?
>
> 3.   Now thinking about your mental health, which includes stress, depression, and problems with emotions, for how many days during the past 30 days was your mental health not good?
>
> 4.   During the past 30 days, for about how many days did poor physical or mental health keep you from doing your usual activities, such as self-care, work, or recreation?

Measuring Quality of Life

A variety of questionnaires or tools have been used to assess quality of life as it pertains to specific health outcomes,[16] pain management,[17] functional disability and physical therapy outcomes,[18] leisure activities,[19] mental health,[20] unemployment rates, and descriptions of such environmental features as housing density and air quality. Some quality-of-life scales are designed for individual assessment based on the assumption that quality of life can only be determined by each person's unique values and experiences. The Ferrans and Powers Quality of Life Index is such a scale. It measures four quality-of-life domains: health and functioning, psychological and spiritual, social and economic, and family.[21] Ware reports on 20 years of validation studies for the SF-36, a widely used instrument for assessing patients' views of physical and mental well-being and ability to function.[22] In medical or nursing care, the counterpart of community social indicators or quality-of-life measures is health outcome measures other than biomedical. These may include ability to perform tasks of daily living, the tolerance for side-effects of medications, energy level, and other indicators of well-being associated with but not identical to the medical condition.[23]

The Behavioral Risk Factor Surveillance System (BRFSS) contains a module of questions that provides a valid and reliable measure called Health-Related Quality of Life (HRQOL). The estimate of HRQOL is based on self-reported responses to the four questions that appear in Box 2-1, labeled "Healthy Days Measures." These measures have been an integral part of the BRFSS since 1993 and were added to the National Health and Nutrition Examination Survey (NHANES) in 2000.

Relevance of an Ecological and Environmental Approach.   An ecological approach to planning stimulates our search for relevant connections and

HEALTH-RELATED QUALITY OF LIFE

The Behavioral Risk Factor Surveillance System (BRFSS) contains a module of questions that provide a valid and reliable measure called Health-Related Quality of Life (HRQOL). The estimate of HRQOL is based on self-reported responses to the four questions that appear in Box 2-1 labeled "Healthy Days Measures." These measures have been an integral part of the BRFSS since 1993 and were added to the National Health and Nutrition Examination Survey (NHANES) in 2000.

Collected annually by most states, and in some larger population areas within states, HRQOL provides planners with a concrete means to show how health problems in adult populations (age 18 and older) also compromise the quality of life of those populations. Unhealthy days are an estimate of the total number of days during the previous 30 days when the respondent felt that either his or her physical or mental health was not good. That number is obtained by combining responses to questions 2 and 3 in Box 2-1. Thus, a person who reports 3 physically unhealthy days and 2 mentally unhealthy days would be assigned a value of 5 unhealthy days. Based on the analysis of national data, here are examples HRQOL findings:

- Americans said they feel unhealthy (physically or mentally) about 5 days per month.
- Americans said they feel "healthy and full of energy" about 19 days per month.
- Nearly one third of Americans say they suffer from some mental or emotional problem every month—including 9% who said their mental health was not good for 14 or more days a month.
- Younger American adults, aged 18–24 years, suffered the most mental health distress.
- Older adults suffered the most poor physical health and activity limitation.
- Native Americans and Alaska Natives have reported the highest levels of unhealthy days among American race/ethnicity groups.
- Adults with the lowest income or education reported more unhealthy days than did those with higher income or education.

anticipates the potential impact of those connections. For example, health administrators who are unaware of the rationale for focusing on the association between health and quality of life may resist contributing their organizational support to broader social programs, because they believe that finite health resources will be spent on nonhealth objectives, which they may perceive as a bottomless pit. The ecological model and the educational approach to planning in this instance should prompt planners to employ educational effort to increase agency directors' and all health stakeholders' understanding that health programs addressing the increasingly complex social and behavioral determinants of health will depend on the cooperation of other sectors. Unless the health sector can buy into the broader social goals of primary concern to the community and the other sectors, one may find one's agency on the sidelines of the mainstream of community action and energy, isolated from community resources. If health programs are unable to attract the interest of the community, and unable to gain the trust and cooperation of nonhealth organizations, they stand a diminished chance of success in today's social web.

Limitations of Data.   Some worry that efforts to make explicit and to generalize perceptions of quality of life will necessarily ignore the subtle differences in perceptions among individuals within a population. They rightfully contend that it is inappropriate to impose one person's perception of wellness and satisfaction on another whose values and priorities are different. Aggregating individual data and reporting averages can seem to suck the soul out of what is most precious in people's lives. Respect for the diversity inherent in communities justifies seeking greater insight about local values and interests through a social diagnosis phase of planning for health programs and policies. At the individual level, we have tools that enable us to identify individual interests and perceived quality of life. At the group or community level, we have access to numerous sources of information and methods that allow people the opportunity to hear each other and increase the chances of identifying priorities that reflect the common concerns of all and the variability of concerns among individuals and groups. Not all of these, to be described in the last sections of this chapter, produce quantitative data. The social diagnosis phase of PRECEDE-PROCEED is designed to help planners with two tasks:

- To identify and interpret the social conditions and perceptions shared at the community or organizational level, and
- To make the connection between those conditions and perceptions and the diversity of health program strategies that will be needed to accommodate the diversity of values and needs

THE PRINCIPLE AND PROCESS OF PARTICIPATION

Social diagnosis, as a step that "precedes" the more "objective" indicators of need, applies the principle of participation to ensure the active involvement of the people intended to benefit from a proposed program. The importance of this principle, echoed for decades in various applied social sciences, has been confirmed in community experience in several fields. Notable among these for our application are the general literature on technical assistance, including public health (especially health education), health care services, family planning, and agricultural extension.[24] This literature has been most extensively reflected in community and rural economic development and participatory research from around the world, because the gaps between the technical assistance and research agencies and the communities they seek to help seem greatest in underserved rural and inner city areas and in developing countries.[25] A

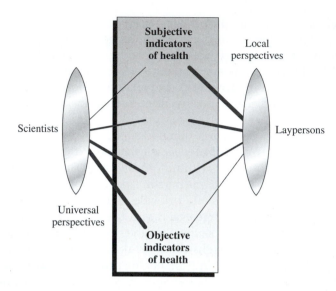

FIGURE 2-2 Scientists view health through a different set of lenses than do people viewing their own health or that of their community. The scientists' lenses have greater acuity at the objective end of the spectrum of health. The public views the subjective aspects of health more clearly.

third body of literature concerns community involvement through *concientación*,[26] a process largely of Latin American origin in the 1960s and early 1970s.

Figure 2-2 presents one rationale for participation based on the differing perspectives scientists and laypeople have concerning health.[27] Scientists tend to have a sharper focus on the objective indicators of health, whereas laypeople tend to have a more diffuse perception of health, with greater emphasis on subjective indicators. Their view is textured by aspects of their lives other than the strictly biological, such as social, emotional, and metaphysical or spiritual dimensions of health. *Objective* should not be equated with *actual,* any more than *subjective* indicators should be discarded as meaningless. The objective data may be less "biased" by personal perceptions of those taking the measures, but they are only as accurate a reflection of reality as the investigators' perspicacity in knowing what to ask or what to look for. Health professionals who work more intensively with the community can help bridge these alternative worldviews.

Forms of Participation

Freire contrasted the extreme forms of participation as two theoretical approaches to community change. He characterized the first as "cultural invasion," the second as "cultural synthesis." In cultural invasion, the actors draw the thematic content of their action from their own values and ideology; their starting point is their own world, from which they enter the world they invade. In cultural synthesis, the actors who come from "another world" do not come as invaders. They come not to teach or transmit or give anything, but rather to learn about this new world along with the people in it.[28]

He contended that those who are "invaded," irrespective of their level in society, rarely go beyond or expand on the models or innovations given them, implying that there is little internalizing, little growth, and seldom much adoption, adaptation, and incorporation into their social fabric. In the synthesis approach, there are no imposed priorities: Leaders and people collaborate in the development of priorities and guidelines for action.

According to Freire, resolution of the inevitable contradictions between the views of leaders or outsiders and the views of the local people is only possible where the spirit of cultural synthesis predominates. "Cultural synthesis does not deny differences between the two views; indeed it is based on these differences. It does deny invasion of one by the other, but affirms the undeniable support each gives to the other."[29]

The differences between cultures will not be as great when the collaborative planning or participatory research is between health professionals of two or more organizations within the community, or between university or state scientists and local professionals. But cultural differences should never be ignored, undervalued, or underestimated.[30]

Participation in Setting Priorities

Because resources for health are finite, planners must set priorities to avoid the debilitating bind of trying to do too much with too little. The needs to engender community participation and to set program priorities constitute mutually reinforcing reasons for putting the social diagnosis at the beginning of the Precede-Proceed process. As you will discover in the next chapter, the careful analysis of epidemiological data on mortality and morbidity plays an important part in determining how resources will be allocated for health improvement efforts at the national, regional, provincial, state, or local level. Political experience demonstrates, however, that priorities will not be based solely on statistical analyses indicating the pervasiveness of the problems, or even on their human burden and economic costs. If planners set priorities based on objective health data without involving the community in the process, some of the priorities, judged to be "lower" based on statistical criteria, will come back to haunt them on the grounds that the public's perceptions of what constitutes a priority was ignored. It would have been folly, for example, to ignore the anthrax concerns of the American public in 2001, even though only a handful of people had been exposed or suffered any health effects. The relatively enormous numbers dying of heart disease, cancer, diabetes, automobile injuries, and other leading causes of death notwithstanding, the public's concern had to take priority for at least that brief time.

The community will not often ask, Why are you doing A or C? They *will* ask, Why aren't you doing P? (Figure 2-3). We are not calling for the abrogation

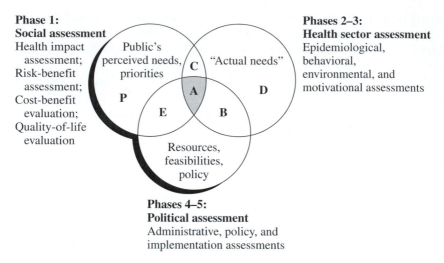

Phase 1:
Social assessment
Health impact
    assessment;
Risk-benefit
    assessment;
Cost-benefit
    evaluation;
Quality-of-life
    evaluation

Public's
perceived needs,
priorities

"Actual needs"

Phases 2–3:
Health sector assessment
Epidemiological,
behavioral,
environmental, and
motivational assessments

P   C   A   D
    E   B

Resources,
feasibilities,
policy

Phases 4–5:
Political assessment
Administrative, policy, and
implementation assessments

FIGURE 2-3 Finding the common ground among the public's perception of needs, the health sector's measurements of needs, and policy makers' perceptions resources and feasibility of meeting needs.

of scientific evidence and professional judgment in favor of incorrect public understanding. Nor are we advocating political decisions by public polls. We *are* advocating a sincere synthesis and search for common understanding.[31]

Public Perception and Professional Diagnosis: Common Ground

Figure 2-3 illustrates the need to discover "common ground" (area A) by bringing together the three key perceptions or assessments that influence planning: the public's perceived needs, health professionals' perceived "actual" needs as indicated by scientific data, and policy makers' perception of resources, feasibilities, and policy. It is in area A where action is most likely, because it is here that policy makers and others who allocate resources see the greatest convergence of public sentiment and scientific data. The task of social diagnosis and the subsequent steps in health program planning is to bring the three spheres of perception into closer alignment, as shown in Figure 2-4.

Usually, the public perceives its needs in ways that only partially accord with what epidemiologists and other health scientists and professionals might view as "actual needs" (Figure 2-3, area C). Yet, the view through the lay lenses often carries as much if not more weight (area E) with policy makers (elected legislators, appointed officials) than do the scientific data brought to the table by health professionals (area B). Priorities expressed by the public, who comprise political constituencies, will influence politicians in bringing resources to bear on issues of common concern and requiring organizational, policy, or regulatory action (area A). This is why public health education and media advocacy efforts to create an informed electorate are so important, even when the

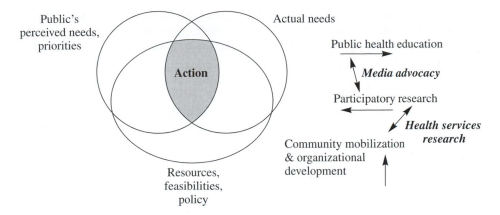

FIGURE 2-4 Bringing the three woldviews into closer alignment through public health education, participatory research and planning, media advocacy, health services research, and community mobilization of resources enlarges the area of potential action.

actions to be taken are not individual health behavior, but policy and regulatory actions by politicians.[32]

The arrows in Figure 2-4 indicate the directions each of the strategies in health program planning and development can pull the three spheres. Public health education helps pull the public's perception in the direction of what science has deemed to be the actual needs (area D). Media advocacy, a more politicized form of health education directed both at the public and at policy makers, usually employed by interest groups, seeks to pull the public's views and the policy makers' views into greater alignment, to enlarge the area of action (A). Participatory research engages the professional and scientific community in greater dialogue with the public on general community concerns or specific issues, pulling area D into greater alignment with area P, thus enlarging areas C and A. Finally, various strategies of community organization, mobilization of resources, grant writing, organizational development, and strategic planning drawing on health services research pull the southern sphere of policy and resources northward, further enlarging areas of common ground and enabling action.

Health program planning at national and state levels is generally broader in scope than planning at the local level and tends to rely more heavily on quantitative, epidemiological health information.[33] One might therefore assume that the principle of participation, so critical at the local level, is of lesser or even no importance at these more central levels. Not so. When policies and priorities set at one level depend on implementation or compliance by persons or institutions at another, planners must make every effort to solicit active participation, input, and even endorsement from that second level. Without such collaboration vertically, as well as horizontally within levels, the support and cooperation needed from the second level will be developed more reluctantly and cautiously, if not defiantly.

Inattention to this simple principle, even at the highest levels, is at once a foolish and serious oversight. It is foolish because participation requires mostly simple acts of courtesy and respect, along with the time needed to foster dialogue and, ultimately, trust. The oversight is serious because it often produces a threat to the proposed program. Continued failure to consult and reconcile differences fosters mistrust and undermines collaboration. Such mistrust explains much of the tension frequently observed between agencies at the national and state or state and local levels[34] and the cynicism of "street-level bureaucrats" employed by central levels to work at local levels. It is also what marks a weakened democracy, as Rose described the function of open debate:

> more public information and debate on health issues is good, not just because it may lead to healthier choices by individuals but also because it earns a higher place for health issues on the political agenda. In the long run, this is probably the most important achievement of health education . . . [that] in a democracy the ultimate responsibility for decisions on health policy should lie with the public.[35]

THE CAPACITY-BUILDING AND SUSTAINABILITY CASE FOR PARTICIPATION

The arguments for participation just made emphasized notions of cultural synthesis, cooperation, and facilitation of a democratic process of planning. Another set of arguments center on the pragmatic goal of transferring not only power of expertise and resources to local groups and organizations, but also the capacity to carry on after the external grants have expired—the sustainability case for participation.

Figure 2-5 presents an admittedly ideal characterization of health program planning. Although ideal, it is meant to provide a graphic vision of what health planners are trying to achieve through participatory planning. The steps fall into two broad categories of actions separated by the vertical divider: community functions and official agency functions. In this instance, we view *community functions* as those closest to where the people whose needs are in question live or work. This could be a work team in a factory, a department, or a floor of workers in an office building, industrial plant, classroom, school, neighborhood, town, county, or district. *Official agency functions* refer to those taken by organizations operating under the auspices of government policies or public mandates at either the local, state or provincial, or national levels. Most often, this will be an official health agency or department, but it may also include a foundation or the headquarters of a private or voluntary health organization. Ideally, the needs and interests expressed at the local or subunit level would trigger the entire sequence. But because of the concentration of resources at higher levels of government or more central offices of other organizations, the process too often starts as a top-down process at step 4.

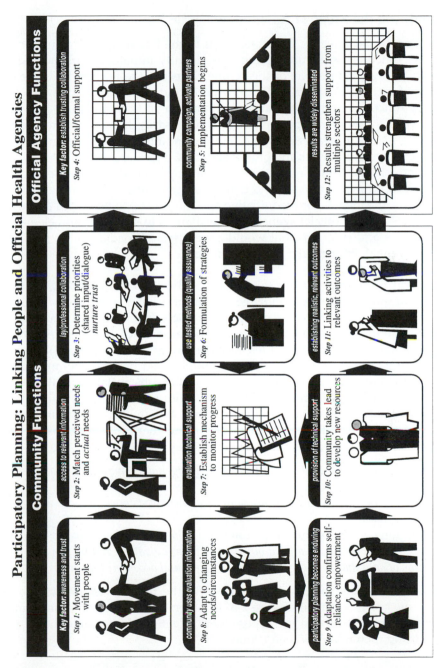

FIGURE 2-5 An ideal sequence of steps in a system and process of community social assessment and health planning, leading to official agency or centralized support, intersectoral cooperation, a cycle of continuous capacity building in the community (Steps 7–10), and ultimately greater self-reliance.

Source: Adapted from Green, L. W. (1983). New Policies in education for health, *World Health* (April–May): 13–, with permission of the World Health Organization.

Examining the Steps of Assessment

Two Functional Levels.   The three steps to the left at each stage under community functions in Figure 2-5 are those ideally initiated, implemented, and controlled by local people, or the people closest to the felt needs. These community functions are graphically drawn horizontally, side by side with official agency functions, rather than at the bottom of a vertical structure. This depiction seeks to avoid the perception of a necessarily hierarchical relationship characteristic of bureaucracies and levels of administration. The relationship between the communities and official agencies, regardless of their "level," need not (and ideally would not) be viewed or approached as bureaucratic, with implicit top-down command and bottom-up reporting. In planning for health programs, the ideal is for the initiative and the control to be vested at the most local level and for official agencies or legislatures to seek common elements of local needs and priorities that would benefit from broader policy, regulatory, organizational, financial, or technical support.

Technical Support.   All this talk about local initiative, autonomy, participation, and empowerment would seem to imply that the necessary skills and technical knowledge to carry out a systematic social diagnosis and planning process are extant in the local group or community. Clearly, communities do possess many of the skills and resources (although often untapped) needed to plan and implement an effective community-based health program.[36] At the same time, however, gaps exist, sometimes quite substantial, in local capacities and skills.[37] With sufficient searching and encouragement, one can find indigenous skills and resources in the community, but they may remain dormant without concerted efforts to identify and bring them into play. When health planners nurture community participation, they

- Predispose the community by *arousing indigenous community awareness, concern, and initiative,*
- Enable the community by *providing technical assistance to those who wish to take initiative,* and
- Reinforce the community by *connecting them with the sources of moral and tangible support needed from other levels of organization and by generating systems of data that provide feedback on progress and accomplishments*

These are implicit, roughly in this order, in the three levels depicted by the three rows of the chart in Figure 2-5. In other words, the community moves gradually from steps that predispose them to action, then enable them to take action, and then reinforce their action.

Tasks Common Across Precede Phases.   In Figure 2-5, the community functions are expressed in 12 steps. Cutting across all 12 are three essential elements that are applied, with some variation, in the first three phases of PRECEDE (this and the next two chapters)—the social diagnosis, the epidemiological diagnosis (including the health, behavioral, and environmental assessments), and the educational and ecological diagnosis. Those three steps are:

1. Self-study by the community (with or without technical assistance) of its needs, aspirations, and resources or assets (column 1)
2. Documentation of the presumed causes of the needs, or determinants of the desired goals (col. 2)
3. Decision on the priorities to be assigned among the problems, needs, or goals, based on perceived importance and presumed changeability, and formulation of quantified goals, objectives, and strategies (col. 3)

More technical skills are required for these three tasks in the epidemiological and the educational-ecological assessments (the next two chapters of this book). For example, the work a professional planning staff must do in reviewing the scientific literature to document the causes or determinants of health increases in the phases after social diagnosis. This is because the answers lie more in scientific fact than in values and local insight, which predominate at the level of social and quality-of-life diagnosis. Failure to engage the community actively in these three steps in the social diagnosis phase, however, can be costly in the long-term acceptance, effectiveness, and viability of the health program.

Step 3 in Figure 2-5 will reveal a good deal about the level of collaboration between professionals and lay participants. Hawe notes that planners can take two routes to change.[38] They can either base a proposed change on the needs of the community or consumer, or they can focus primarily on the needs of the managers or organization(s) they serve. This distinction made, Hawe warns those who are engaged in community-based planning of the political temptation to seek community "endorsement" to support the planner's agenda. "They should recognize the danger in sublimating community interests in an orchestrated process of consensus building and priority setting, which has a high risk of having its deliberations ignored."[39]

Equipped with factual data on a community's problems and trends, professionals will come face-to-face with the felt needs of community members and their natural desire to acknowledge the strengths, not just the problems, of their community. Often the felt needs will rank low, if at all, on routine data listings of leading causes of mortality or morbidity. Reconciling these differences is central to the educational approach to health program planning featured in this book and the Precede-Proceed Model.

Official Functions.   In Step 4, an official health organization formalizes the plans or proposals submitted by one or more local community groups and generates a strategic plan for allocating its resources. Official agency resources include funding, material support, transfers of necessary authority, and technical assistance. Step 5 suggests the need for centralized agencies to coordinate their assistance to communities or subcommunities so that a harmonized flow of resources reaches the community proportionate to the distribution of the needs to be met by programs. Too often, the state and national organizations seeking to carry out their separate missions at the local level compete unwittingly for the time and effort of precious talent and energy in needy communities. Intersectoral and interagency coordination at the central levels helps reduce the confusing and often redundant signals communities receive.

Implementation and Evaluation.   Steps 6 through 8 require central agencies to return selected implementation and evaluation functions to the community. Information and technical assistance number among the resources communities need to be able to carry out these functions, as in some of the earlier assessment and planning functions. We are going beyond the social diagnosis phase here, but it should serve you at this stage to have a picture that anticipates how the whole process of community organization and development for health might play out.

The Capacity-Building, Self-Reliance, and Sustainability Cycle.   Steps 7 through 10 engage the community in a progressively greater degree of responsibility for managing and evaluating their own progress. By Step 10, the "competent community"[40] will have unearthed or developed its own indigenous resources to maintain the program[41] or to move on to solve other problems on its priority list.[42] Rather than turning back to central agencies for more support at that point (Step 10), the community is "empowered"[43] with its own "collective efficacy"[44] and returns to Step 7, continuing the self-reliance and sustainability cycle outlined in Figure 2-5.

Evaluation, Demonstration, and, Diffusion.   Often, the payoff of central support to local community projects, from the point of view of the official or central agencies, is not only solving a local problem, but also demonstrating the problem-solving process by a typical community. The hope of most grant-making organizations is that their grants will inspire other communities or groups to emulate the example demonstrated by the grantees. To maximize this potential, evaluation of project impact and outcomes (Step 11) becomes a central priority. Evaluation results can inspire other communities. They can also help the funding organizations by providing documented examples of how they can improve their coordination with other central organizations (Step 12) and their technical assistance and support to other communities. Such demonstration, evaluation, and documented experience serve as powerful complements to the diffusion of "best practices" from formal research studies. The latter carry some limitations of credibility by themselves because community practitioners view the experimentally controlled study circumstances from which "best practices" are derived as unrepresentative of their own circumstances.[45]

Keeping Perspective on Participation and Partnership

Total community participation in developing good polices or plans should be neither expected nor targeted. As George Bernard Shaw put it:

> Every citizen cannot be a ruler any more than every boy can be an engine driver or a pirate king. . . . If you doubt this—If you ask me "Why should not the people make their own laws?" I need only ask you "Why should not the people write their own plays?" They cannot. It is much easier to write a good play than to make a good law. And there are not a hundred men in the world

who can write a good play enough to stand the daily wear and tear as long as a law must.[46]

Nevertheless, broad participation through a representation process should be sought in the diagnosis of needs, because some of the people least "skilled" at planning or "making laws" will bring other valuable assets to the planning table.

Although professional health practitioners and planners can take great pride in working collaboratively and responsively with their patients and communities, they should not lose sight of the technical insights and scientific data and skill they can share with communities. Counsel offered in the 1983 WHO Expert Committee Report remains valid in the new millennium.

> While health care workers should not compel communities to accept the health technologies they propose, they should also not allow themselves to be forced into a situation where they have to abdicate their views on technical matters. The common ground between the two groups should serve as a basis for fruitful dialogue, which may lead to change, provided health workers keep in mind that sociocultural factors and beliefs are not necessarily obstacles to development; in fact they can be points of departure for development.[47]

Professionals should take care not to abdicate their responsibilities while engaging the community in dialogue. In working hard to avoid being manipulative, health professionals can go too far and be so fearful of falling into Freire's "cultural invasion" trap of imposing their own agenda that they fail to offer constructive assistance. As a planner, you can do two things to avoid this situation. First, keep in mind the fact that you, the lay community, and your collaborators in other agencies and sectors are *partners*. Each can contribute technical or cultural experience and capacities to the task of making a difference. Second, make every effort to ensure that all the partners understand what you do and whom you represent. People are more willing to collaborate with you when they know what agency or group you represent and what its mission or agenda is. They need to understand what you can and cannot do—the technical capacities you have to offer as well as the limitations placed on you by your agency or employer. An understanding of these issues, which at first glance may seem irrelevant, helps all parties clarify boundaries and roles and set realistic expectations.

Partnership implies complementarity of roles and contributions. Each partner can magnify the contribution of others and through the partnership can leverage his or her own capabilities and resources. In the end, the partnership should evolve into "delegated power," relinquished by the outside helping agencies, and eventually into full control by the community and its own professional and lay leadership. This will not happen easily if the partnership starts out with a "senior partner" from the outside, with the community in the role of "junior partner."

In summary, social diagnosis should begin with more than token participation from the community, and it should lead ideally toward as much community control of the process as the community capacity and readiness warrants,

LAYERS OF COMMUNITY INVOLVEMENT IN A WORKSITE PROGRAM

A highly trained team of Minnesota professionals and University of Minnesota investigators carried out a systematic application of PRECEDE-PROCEED to reduce wood dust exposure in woodworking shops. They formed a planning committee consisting of "small wood-working shop owners, government officials, technical college instructors, health and safety professionals, and trade association representatives." They acknowledged that a "limitation of this study was the lack of involvement of employees in our planning activities other than as participants in a small focus group."[48] Results of the study showed significant increases in worker awareness, increases in stage of readiness to change, and actual behavioral changes consistent with dust control. But the change in dusty concentration fell short of statistical significance with a 10.4% reduction. The authors attribute the shortfall on outcome to problems of measurement and the resistance of employers to expensive environmental controls or equipment;[49] but would a more significant engagement of employees possibly also have produced more substantial commitment and change in both employees and employers? Would more attention to the financial and related concerns of employers have produced greater effort on their part to obtain equipment for dust control?

with helping agencies providing information and technical assistance as requested by the community.

METHODS AND STRATEGIES FOR SOCIAL DIAGNOSIS AND SITUATION ANALYSIS

For specific methods to plan, implement, and evaluate health programs, one should look to the continually evolving print and World Wide Web literature of public health, epidemiology, social and behavioral sciences, community development, nursing, health services research, health promotion, and health education as the first and continuing resources. By examining the findings and methods of others, one gains techniques, insights and sharpens one's thinking on social diagnosis.[50] The literature illustrates the ways diverse methods of data collection have been used in social diagnoses and other phases of health program planning, including key informant interviews, community forums, focus groups, nominal group process, and surveys. Because time and resources are precious, it is wise to retrieve existing information whenever possible; most sources of routinely collected data are governmental, so most of these are in the public domain and relatively accessible. A thorough social diagnosis and health program planning process, however, will usually require at least some new and tailored information, or it will tend to reinforce the status quo.[51] We offer the following descriptions of procedures and methods as options for obtaining such information.

Assessing Urgency and Assets: Situation Analysis

Having assessed the community's priority concerns or aspirations for social change in the previous steps, the planning group comes now to a critical junction. They must decide the urgency of the problem or need and the availability of resources to *proceed* immediately to application and action, or the need and opportunity to continue through a more systematic planning process that would *precede* action. Even if the ideal latter route is chosen, this situational consideration will arise in each of the next three phases of the planning process. A conscious decision can be made in each phase whether the patience and fortitude of the planners will permit a further refinement and scientific grounding of the plan through further epidemiological, educational, and ecological diagnoses. The alternative at each phase is to make assumptions about causation and draw heavily on strategies and methods for interventions that have been tested elsewhere but may or may not be optimal for this situation. Each additional phase of the Precede Model will further refine and verify the causal assumptions on which the right selection of methods can be made. But the ideal should not drive out the good or even the adequate and practical actions that have some prospect of ameliorating the problem, preventing the threatened problem, or advancing the community toward its goals.

Communities and populations differ on virtually any demographic or sociocultural or economic parameter one can think of: population size, ethnicity, culture, history, industry, employment, geography, and so on. Communities also vary in their resources and capacities, including past experience with implementing community-based health programs. Together with the highest priority problems or aspirations of the community, and the goals and resources of the planning agency, these constitute the elements of a **situation analysis.**[52]

Analysis of 25 years' data and experience of the North Karelia Cardiovascular Disease Prevention Project and the rest of Finland revealed that the combination of their multiple intervention strategies achieved a 50% decline in cardiovascular mortality among Finnish men.[53] In an early publication describing their methods and strategies, the investigators offered this advice: "To the greatest extent possible, the community analysis ('community assessment') should provide a comprehensive understanding of the situation at the start of the program."[54] Adhering to the principles of social diagnosis, they systematically obtained data to understand better the people's perceptions about the problems and how they felt about the possibility of solving those problems, but they did not stop there.

> Because the program would depend upon the cooperation of local decision-makers and health personnel, these groups were surveyed at the outset. *The*

community resources and service structure were also considered before deciding on the
actual forms of program implementation.[55] [Italics ours]

The italics highlight the commonsense notion that before taking action, one should determine what resources critical to the planning process and to the eventual implementation of a program one has at hand. Travel anywhere in the world and you will see this simple truth played out in architecture—wooden structures predominate in forested regions, rock structures prevail near quarries, and igloos dot the arctic. The results of a "situation analysis" give planners useful information about the resources (human and economic) and conditions currently in place. By taking stock of what is understood, and what resources can be brought to the situation, the situation analysis can provide a basis for streamlining and shortcutting the planning process, or for giving greater emphasis to early or middle phases of the process.

One of the early criticisms of PRECEDE from systematic evaluations of its applications in the Planned Approach to Community Health (PATCH) in Maine was that the systematic assessment steps could delay program action by 18 months or more if the community had to collect original data at each phase.[56] Some of the authors of that evaluation went on to define dimensions and measures of community capacity[57] and community coalitions,[58] and to examine more critically the participatory research dimension of the planning process.[59] CDC and state health departments responded by trying to provide more efficient ways to make state surveillance data usable at community levels and by providing technical assistance to communities in compiling and using existing data.[60] We responded, as authors of the Precede-Proceed Model, with revisions in the third edition of this book and in software aids to their application that sought mainly to provide stronger evidence of the importance of, and tools to apply to, each phase in the planning process. Older and wiser, we now yield to the practical realities faced by community planning groups, especially with the often voluntary involvement of community members who are at the table, unpaid, because they want to see *action* on the problems identified. What has given us the courage to short-cut some of the intermediate assessment phases of PRECEDE is the growing scientific literature on the types of problems communities frequently identify as priorities. This rapidly growing literature analyzes the causes, down to the motivational and enabling factors for change in specific behaviors and environments. It increasingly provides theory-guided and evidence-based meta-analyses of the "best practices" that have been shown in systematic evaluations to produce the necessary changes in specific behaviors, environments, or health problems.

We retain some skepticism, however, and caution the planners who would short-cut the planning process too readily for the sake of expediency that the "best practices" for action derived from studies conducted elsewhere under very different circumstances may not fit the situation of your community or population.[61] The steps outlined in the next two chapters would help ensure that the causes identified for the highest priority problems of your community are indeed the ones that lead you to the right selection of "best practices." On the other hand, it would be wasteful of community resources and participation

TABLE 2-1 Situation analysis: some key questions to be addressed before planning

Stakeholders
  (all those who have an investment in the health of the community organization)
    1. Who are they?
    2. Are they aware of the program?
    3. Are they supportive or apprehensive?

Potential Organizational Collaborators and Key Informants
    1. Who are they?
    2. Have they been invited to participate?
    3. Are they supportive or apprehensive?

Staff/Technical Resources
    1. Are experienced personnel available for this planning?
    2. Will the staff require special training for planning?
    3. What existing data and systems resources are available to plan a program or strategy?

Budget
    1. Have planning costs been estimated?
    2. Are the facilities and space necessary to conduct the program available?
    3. Are there opportunities to apply for funds to meet staff, equipment, and space needs?
    4. What is the timeline for the planning process before the program must begin?

to belabor the intermediate planning steps just for the sake of fashioning a homegrown solution that has little grounding in prior research or evaluation, or that could have been deemed adequate in the first phase of planning.[62] Avoiding these traps on either side of the short-cutting or the belaboring of the planning process can be aided by the situation analysis, which begins with asking the questions posed in Table 2-1.

Assessing Capacity: Community Competence and Readiness

In their critical examination of the determinants of health, Evans, Barer, and Marmor asked the simple but provocative question: "Why are some people healthy and others not?"[63] Changing the focus from individuals to communities, we pose a similar question: Why are some communities healthier than others? The answer is not simply that the members of the healthier population are genetically or biologically or even economically equipped for better health, though these factors, as Evans et al. and many others have shown, do account for a significant proportion of the variance in individual health. The answer lies also in the community's competence and readiness for dealing with emerging health issues that affect whole populations. Studies testing the effectiveness of community-based public health programs reveal that, even with the application of sound theory-tested methods that are adequately supported, some programs may fall short of their expected goals. At least some portion of so-called

TABLE 2-2 The 10 categories of the Civic Index are measured by the National Civic League

Citizen participation	Civic education
Community information sharing	Capacity for cooperation and consensus building
Community leadership	Community vision and pride
Government performance	Intercommunity cooperation
Volunteerism and philanthropy	Intergroup relations

Source: National Civic League. http://www.ncl.org/

program failures is likely to be attributable to preexisting social factors that mediate the planning and execution of those programs. One such factor may be a given community's past experience and capacity—its social capital.[64] We define **social capital** as the processes and conditions among people and organizations that lead to accomplishing a goal of mutual social benefit. Those processes and conditions are manifested by four interrelated constructs: trust, cooperation, civic engagement, and reciprocity.

Effects of Social Capital on Community Health. The practical implication for determining a community's level of social capital is that a sound plan and the resources to implement it will be more likely to materialize in communities with high levels of social capital. Those with lower levels of social capital would likely require a focused, preplanning effort to strengthen their existing collaborative capacities. Low levels of social capital should not be used as a qualification to apply for grants or worthiness for technical assistance to tackle the community's problems. Indeed, lower social capital will tend to mark the communities most in need of outside assistance in tackling their problems.

The constructs, or components, of social capital (trust, civic participation, social engagement, and reciprocity) have been independently measured.[65] The *Civic Index*[66] offers a practical approach that gives planners a sense of the level of a community's capacity for undertaking a community-based health program. Devised by the National Civic League and applied in numerous settings,[67] the Civic Index addresses 10 categories, each of which has just a few questions or probes designed to elicit information about the community's strengths and weakness for that domain (see Table 2-2).

Asset Mapping

Much of social and health policy seems to be driven by a focus on health problems, with outsiders and professionals calling attention to "deficiencies." This problem-oriented approach is inherently negative, especially for low-income populations. To balance this perspective, McKnight and Kretzmann[68] advocate a strategy called *asset mapping*, which is an assessment of the capacities and skills of individuals and the existing assets in a neighborhood or community. The process of asset mapping is divided into three tiers called primary building

TABLE 2-3 The primary and secondary "building blocks" of a community represent assets that can facilitate planning and should be acknowledged in the planning process to balance the negative connotation associated with assessing needs or problems

PRIMARY BUILDING BLOCKS	
Individual Assets	**Organizational Assets**
Skills, talents, and experiences of residents	Associations of businesses
Individual businesses	Citizens associations
Home-based enterprises	Cultural organizations
Personal income	Communications organizations
Gifts of labeled people	Religious organizations
SECONDARY BUILDING BLOCKS	
Individual Assets	**Organizational Assets**
Private and nonprofit organizations	Public institutions and services
Institutions of higher education	Public schools
Hospitals	Police
Social services agencies	Libraries
	Fire departments
	Parks

Physical Resources

Vacant land, commercial and industrial structures, housing

Energy and waste resources

Source: "Mapping Community Capacity," by J. L. McKnight and J. P. Kretzmann, 1997, in M. Minkler (Ed.), *Community Organizing and Community Building for Health,* New Brunswick, NJ: Rutgers University Press, pp. 163, 165.

blocks, secondary building blocks, and potential building blocks. The most accessible, primary building blocks can be discovered by assessing individual leadership capacities and those assets *controlled within the neighborhood or community.* Secondary building blocks refer to those assets located in the neighborhood or community but *controlled by those outside that area* (see Table 2-3).

Potential building blocks, which are the least accessible, refer to potential assets *located and controlled outside of the community.* Examples include state and federal grant programs, corporate capital investments, and public information campaigns. The lists of specific assets in a community can be visually reflected using the metaphor of a map, an architectural metaphor as suggested by the notion of building blocks or as a balance scale showing assets on one side and needs and problems on the other.

Given the diversity of communities and cultures, experienced health program planners may be inclined to devise their own simple surveys to identify community assets and individual abilities within the areas they serve. Before doing that, however, we urge them to review existing survey instruments such as the Civic Index, mentioned earlier, or the myriad tools and guidelines available now on the World Wide Web, such as the *Community Toolbox* web site.[69]

The Social Reconnaissance Method for Community Social Diagnosis

Social reconnaissance is a method for determining relevant aspects of the social structure, processes, and needs of a community using leaders (general, local, and specialized) as informants or interviewees. Developed by Sanders,[70] and elaborated on by Nix and Seerley,[71] social reconnaissance was adapted and applied by the Henry J. Kaiser Family Foundation for use in engaging state government and voluntary agencies in the southern region of the United States in a process of assessing community health needs and priorities.[72] The Kaiser staff recognized that in the poorest communities of the South, technical and financial assistance would inevitably have to come from outside the communities, thereby risking Freire's "cultural invasion." To engage the state workers in more of a "cultural synthesis," giving greater play to the needs and assets of communities with limited economic means, foundation officials insisted on a partnership in which their funds would be contingent on the state officials' participation in a social reconnaissance.

Foundation staff recognized that changes in the determinants of health must be preceded, as Nix had said a decade earlier, by changes in the "social structure . . . the prevailing attitudes, values, aspirations, beliefs, behavior, and relationships in the community."[73] The community in this case was the larger state community in which relationships between state- and local-level organizations had to be rebuilt to replace a legacy of suspicion and grievances, recognized two decades earlier during the civil rights initiatives of President Kennedy's New Frontier and President Johnson's War on Poverty. The host community was assisted in the social reconnaissance process, through its own agencies and organizations, to

1. Identify the felt needs or problems of the community (and other elements of social structure)
2. Rank in priority the needs and problem areas to be dealt with
3. Organize or mobilize the community to deal with chosen needs or problems
4. Study the identified needs or problems to determine specific goals or recommendations
5. Develop a plan of action to accomplish locally determined goals
6. Find the resources needed to accomplish goals
7. Act or stimulate action to accomplish goals
8. Evaluate accomplishments

Application at the State Level.   In this chapter, we shall focus on the first four of these objectives of social reconnaissance. The Kaiser Family Foundation's application of the reconnaissance method in the South engaged the governor's office, the state health department, other state-level social service agencies, state legislators, local or regional foundations, the United Way, the Chamber of Commerce, and other organizations in working through the first four functions. The foundation then provided a planning grant to a selected state agency or coalition to complete the process down to the community level, where projects would be developed (Step 5) and funded by grants from the foundation, other cooperating national and state organizations, and sometimes federal agencies (Steps 6–8). This process ensured greater support for the community projects from state-level organizations than would have materialized if Kaiser had funded community health promotion projects directly without state involvement or simply had made the grants to the states with the expectation that they would in turn distribute funds to local communities.

Application at the Community Level.   The same process and advantages apply at the community level and even within large organizations such as schools, work sites, or hospitals where health program planning calls for broad participation. The steps in applying the method can be delineated as follows:

Step 1: *Identify an entry point.* Choosing the point of entry to a host community can be crucial, affecting all subsequent information and relationships. The official health agency is the logical starting point, but in some communities that agency may be part of the community's suspected cause of some of the problems. The preferred entry point, where possible, is the chief executive official of the community: the governor, the mayor, the chair of the town council, the county board of supervisors. Usually, the chief policy maker is an elected official. Though an appointed official, the city manager tends to have the public's confidence. Entry at this level helps open doors at all levels and in all sectors. By making their first task to understand the structure and concerns of their community, planners can avoid a premature focus on health problems.

Step 2: *Identify local cosponsors.* An existing organization or an ad hoc group needs to support the study in one or more of the following ways, which various authors drawing on decades of experience in community development and participatory research have identified:
   1. Provide the opportunity for a representative group of local residents to participate in an initial session to explore common concerns and possibilities for collaboration and sharing of expertise and resources to study the issues.
   2. Organize representative sponsoring organizations or a community steering committee or "coalition" made up of representatives from different organizations and groups.[74]
   3. Support the participatory research group as they carry out the study. This support should include
      a. Assisting in the legitimization process
      b. Designing the instruments and sampling procedure for data collection

         c. Providing news releases that share the proposed study's pur-
             pose, sponsors, and schedule
         d. Contacting each person to be interviewed
         e. In some cases, schedule the interviews in a central place
     4. Pay for or share the cost of publication of the study
     5. Facilitate the public release of the findings through various
         media such as newspapers, public meetings, and distribution of
         the publication
     6. Ensure the use of the findings to stimulate study groups, pro-
         gram planning, policy decisions, and other community devel-
         opmental efforts

Step 3: *Development of research and briefing materials.* Background data usually need to be compiled from discursive sources in the community—data on its leaders, demography, and current affairs (based
on content analysis of newspaper stories). Such a compilation of
data provides an archival account of the community's structure,
assets, and trends. A summary of these analyses in a briefing book
to be shared with participants puts everyone on an equal footing
in regard to factual data. Ideally, this briefing book is produced by
the host community group. With this archival analysis, one can
formulate questions to be asked of community leaders and bring
them for discussion and pretesting before the sponsoring group.
These questions may form the basis of an interview schedule for
private meetings with community leaders or an agenda for public
meetings with community groups.

Step 4: *Identification of leaders and representatives.* Planners need to select
interviewees who can speak either for the community's power
structure or for the population at large and for segments of the
population, especially underrepresented segments. The **positional**
approach to identifying leaders selects those who hold key positions in government, political, business, and voluntary organizations. The **reputational** approach tends to identify the more
socially active among this same group of influential leaders; it also
picks up activists and opinion leaders who do not hold official
positions. A combination of these two is recommended, with a
careful eye to ensuring the inclusion of minority and women's
organizations and reputational polling among underrepresented
groups.[75]

Step 5: *Field interviews.* An intensive period of actual interviews and meetings with influentials, specialized leaders, subcommunity leaders,
and leaders of underrepresented categories comes next. Planners
should avoid spreading this phase out over too many weeks,
because local events could intervene to invalidate any comparisons between those interviewed early and those interviewed later.
The number of individuals who should be included in the sample

of leaders ranges from 50 to 125, depending on the size and diversity of the community. External helping agencies must restrain themselves from turning an assessment of needs and assets into an academic research project that the community may view as a distraction that merely delays the action they desire or as an unwarranted burden on their time and resources.[76]

Step 6: *Analysis, reporting, and follow-up.* Ideally, the local sponsoring group would carry out this step, with technical assistance as needed from the central helping agency. They would make their report public through open meetings, the news media, and broad distribution of the written report. Community organizations or groups are encouraged to select their own priorities among the broader community priorities defined; this leads to task groups that pursue specific issues of organizing a coalition or task force to pursue the interest to them and to mobilize resources in relation to those issues. Criteria and procedures for setting priorities among multiple needs (identified through the community self-studies) have been suggested in the health literature; these criteria, and variations thereof, will be applied in each of the next three chapters.[77]

Other Assessment Methods

Nominal Group Process.   The **nominal group process** is a method for assessing community perceptions of problems in a way that overcomes many of the difficulties arising from the usual unequal representation of opinions by those who are more vocal or who hold more power.[78] The method consists of a series of small-group procedures designed to compensate for the dynamics of social power that emerge in most planning meetings. Those who use the method should keep in mind that its central purpose is to identify and rank problems, not to solve them. It should be the method of choice when the task at hand is generating ideas, getting equal participation from group members having unequal power or expertise, and ranking the perceived importance of ideas or problems. Gilmore and Campbell provide a detailed description of the steps in applying the method specifically for health needs assessment.[79] Others provide examples of its use within their applications of the Precede-Proceed Model and participatory research.[80]

The Delphi Method.   The **Delphi Method** is also useful at the social diagnosis phase, especially if face-to-face meetings are impractical. Linstone and Turoff developed the method most fully.[81] In this method, one mails a series of questionnaires to a small number of experts, opinion leaders, or informants. Each successive questionnaire further refines the range of estimates or judgments based on responses to the previous questionnaire. This successive narrowing of the range of opinion simulates a consensus development process and produces a similar result. The Delphi Method offers several advantages. First, differences of opinion among various key people can be resolved by the planner without forcing confrontation. Second, the method enables planners to work from a distance with a variety of target-group representatives who are informed about the issue of concern. Third, large numbers can be managed at a relatively low cost, although having more than 30 respondents may not enhance results. Finally, throughout the process, participants remain anonymous, thus protecting the generated ideas from the influences of group conformity, prestige, power, and politics. Gilmore and his colleagues have provided a detailed description of the steps required to apply the Delphi Method in social assessments in health program planning.[82]

Focus Groups.   In recent years, **focus groups** have become the most popular qualitative interview strategy used in the application of social and behavioral sciences to practical enterprises. Focus groups last for one to one and a half hours. They are usually small in number (8 to 12 persons per group), with particular emphasis placed on recruiting people who represent the community or target group of interest. In a comfortable, informal session, a trained moderator asks representatives of a target population to discuss their thoughts on a specific issue or product. Focus groups are typically used as formative research to help planners zero in on what should be the content, delivery, and appeal of the message of a given program; but the flexibility of the method lends its use to assessing social concerns and consequences.[83] Recent published applications of focus-group methods applied this way in planning programs with the Precede-Proceed Model include work with families of children with cystic fibrosis,[84] with African American women and their breast cancer issues,[85] and on nutrition issues with urban adolescents in Canada and Brazil and with Vietnamese mothers.[86] Airhihenbuwa built on this approach in a series of studies of perceptions of nutrition, physical activity, and rest among African American workers to refine his PEN3 model of planning culturally sensitive programs, an extension of PRECEDE-PROCEED.[87] Krueger and Casey offer a practical step-by-step guide to conducting focus groups.[88]

Central Location Intercept Interviews.   **Central location intercept** interviews —or intercept interviews for short—offer the advantage of obtaining information relatively efficiently from larger numbers of people over the methods previously described. Such interviews are typically conducted where there are high levels of pedestrian traffic, such as at shopping malls, churches, and special community events. This method also provides a low-cost opportunity to obtain the opinions and interests of so-called hard-to-reach target populations.

Central intercept or location interviewing begins with the potential respondents intercepted and asked whether they are willing to be interviewed. Screening questions are then asked to see whether they meet the criteria of the target audience for the diagnosis. If so, they are taken to a quiet place or an interviewing station at the shopping mall or other site. Respondents are then asked a series of questions to get their opinions.

The respondents intercepted through central location interviews may not statistically represent the entire target population, but the sample is larger than that used in focus groups or individual in-depth interviews. Unlike focus groups or in-depth interviews, this method uses a highly structured questionnaire that contains primarily closed-ended questions. Open-ended questioning, which allows for free-flowing answers, should be kept to a minimum, because it takes too long for the interviewer to record responses. As in any type of research, the questionnaire should be tested before it is used in the field. An example of the combined use of data generated from mall intercept interviews and focus groups is found in uses of the Precede-Proceed model, among others, to develop the "5-a-day" national nutrition campaign.[89]

Surveys.   Health workers or any other group whose work requires a better understanding of the **beliefs,** perceptions, knowledge, and attitudes of the people they serve depend on surveys to fill the gaps in social indicators and health reporting systems such as registries and service reports. The quality of a survey is determined by the validity and reliability of the instrument (Does it consistently measure what it is supposed to?), how representative the sample is (Can you generalize your results to the entire community or group?), and how the survey is administered (Are the questions asked and coded in the same way for all the subjects interviewed?). Various texts offer practical descriptions of the steps and methods used to develop and implement a participatory community-based survey.[90]

Some notable examples of using survey methods for social assessments specifically within the context of applying the Precede-Proceed Model, include

An assessment in El Paso, Texas, on the perception of quality of life for those with bowel dysfunction among Hispanic and non-Hispanic whites[91]

Work site surveys of employees and managers prior to planning health promotion and disease prevention programs in occupational settings.[92]

An award-winning project in Houston, Texas, that used surveys and focus groups with adolescent patients and their parents concerning their lives with cystic fibrosis in the design and eventually the diffusion of programs[93]

Surveys of staff nurses in eight British Columbia hospitals and pediatricians in private practice concerning their perceptions of health promotion and disease prevention counseling in their professional roles and of the assets, resources, and needs of hospitals or private practice to support them in these roles[94]

Surveys with adolescents in Manaus, on the Amazon in Brazil, and with rural poor African Americans in North Carolina to assess social and economic aspects of their nutrition[95]

Both the U.S. and Canada federal governments applied the Precede-Proceed Model in expanding the range of variables included in their first national health promotion surveys beyond the usual health status and health risk factors[96]

Public Service Data. Data on perceived needs and problems are more readily available than one might realize. For example, rich sources of such data often overlooked are local broadcast media. The U.S. Federal Communication Commission requires television and radio broadcasters to ascertain community needs and concerns regularly and to offer public service programming to address such problems. Members of the print media along with radio and television broadcasters have formed coalitions with universities and foundations to conduct public opinion surveys periodically to identify the needs and problems of the population in their service area.[97] When asked to do so, most organizations will share their data unless they have proprietary value that they have not yet exploited or that another organization could use to competitive advantage against them.

USING DATA FROM A SOCIAL ASSESSMENT
AND SITUATION ANALYSIS
TO MAP THE PLANNING PROCESS

We have referred throughout this chapter to the importance of obtaining participation in accessing multiple sources of information to develop mutual understanding between professionals' and people's perceptions of needs. No matter how sophisticated, valid, or plentiful, information matters only to the extent that one uses it. To maximize the probability that data gathered will indeed be used, we offer the following practical guidelines.

1. *Participation is most important in the interpretation of the data.* One can engage the community in every phase of data collection, analysis, and interpretation, but involvement in some stages can become an unnecessary burden for volunteers from the community or for practitioners whose jobs do not provide much release time for data collection and analysis. Where their participation is essential, however, to ensure that the fruits of participation are carried forward to effective planning, is in the interpretation of the results. By bringing their understanding and their perspectives to bear on the interpretation of data drawn from their community about their issues and their assets, the program planning process stands to gain a large measure of relevance, credibility, acceptance, and ownership by the community.[98] Community participation in interpreting the data, however, will only be of interest to them if the data seem important, which may depend on their prior engagement in formulating the questions and pointing to some of the most important sources of data.

2. *Stay focused on the purpose.* Anyone with responsibility for collecting data, regardless of the subject area, should repeatedly ask and answer two simple questions: Why do we need this information? How will we use it? The purposes of the social diagnosis phase of the Precede-Proceed Model are to improve insight into:

- the ultimate values and perceived needs of a specific population; and
- existing human and resource assets, within a population, that would support a health program or strategy.

A third purpose is served by the situation analysis, which is to anticipate the program planning process, including organizational or policy barriers that might inhibit program planning or implementation.

When health planners gather only those data they need and can use, analysis becomes more efficient and less burdensome. We will extend this concept to the planning steps ahead, in search of efficiency in getting to action and outcomes and in the interest of minimizing the planning burden.

3. *Look for connections.* Social scientists use a method of analysis called *data source* **triangulation,** analogous to navigation and surveying. For one trying to locate one's position on a map, a single landmark can only provide the information that one is situated somewhere along a line in a particular direction from that landmark. With two landmarks, however, one can pinpoint one's position by taking bearings on both. We will propose some connections from this stage of social diagnosis and situation analysis to later stages of diagnosis that will help give a bearing on the phases of planning that must be pursued next and the phases that can be bypassed. But we seek here also to make use of data on the same issue from more than one source. If health program planners make judgments on a single piece of information, they run the risk that their source of information, and consequently their analysis, could be incorrect. Data source triangulation is possible when planners use different methods or reach different target groups to assess a common issue.[99]

4. *Identify themes and connect them to theory and research.* Once gathered, both objective data and information about perceived needs should be studied to identify the factors that constitute the most formidable barriers to a desired quality of life. Some objective indicators can be calculated, such as frequency counts, incidence rates, utilization rates, and frequency distributions. These quantitative data can be compared with previous measures of the same indicators to ascertain trends or changes. Information about personal opinions and interests based on open-ended interviews or focus groups are examples of qualitative data. Although some qualitative data can be characterized by measurement on a variety of categorical scales, the strength of such data lies in the descriptive richness, depth, and insight they provide. Qualitative data collected from open-ended questions are most often analyzed by seeking out categories of responses or recurrent themes. For example, Daniel and his colleagues used interviews, participant observation, and field notes as the primary sources of data in seeking to understand how Canadian Aboriginal people (in the rural Okanogan region of British Columbia) perceived the problem of type 2 (non-insulin-dependent) diabetes within the context of their cultural beliefs about health (see Box).

5. *Promote trust.* Bringing this advice full circle is the first point about participation: "Taking the temperature and pulse" of the community is a consciousness-raising activity for all. It builds trust through mutual understanding, not only for the planner, but also for others in his or her organization involved in the overall health program, as well as those engaged from other sectors, and for the patients, students, workers, or residents. For this reason, results of an analysis of information from the social diagnostic process, the assessment of assets, and the situation analysis should be translated and shared

PARTICIPATORY LESSONS FROM MORE DISTINCTIVE CULTURES FOR WORK WITH ANY LOCALITY

Daniel and colleagues organized and analyzed their data according to emerging diabetes-related themes and categories consistent with PRECEDE-PROCEED. These were linked to theory and evidence relevant to interventions appropriate to diabetes control in a rural native Aboriginal community.[100] In the end, however, the authors acknowledged that their "activation of the intervention community was insufficient to enable individual and collective change through dissemination of quality interventions for diabetes prevention and control. Theory and previous research were not sufficiently integrated with information from pre-intervention interviews. . . . Nor were qualitative results brought to bear on activation and intervention planning."[101] One lesson from this thoroughly evaluated demonstration project was that community involvement must be sufficient to allow the community to take the priorities for planning in directions other than the disease or health problem that brought the health officials or professionals to the community, and to solutions other than (or in addition to) those previously considered in the theoretical literature or previously tested in the empirical literature. Among Mark Daniel's recommendations from his dissertation research in this community were

- Theory should be integrated with Aboriginal logic and cultural concepts.
- The research and planning process should embrace the active involvement of Aboriginal people.

with the community. Ideally, the community would interpret and disseminate the information to promote consensus on the need for action. Through the sharing of such information, one strengthens the community's trust in taking the next collaborative steps to plan and implement a program, policy, regulation, organizational change, or some combination of these needed to address the issues raised.

During this important first phase in diagnosis and situation analysis, the main resources for health planners involve critical observation, cultural sensitivity, and good professional judgment. The final determination of quality-of-life concerns must be made by careful consideration of the available evidence, including the sentiments of community members—and especially those patients, students, workers, or residents who will participate in the health program.

Social Diagnosis and Situation Analysis "After the Fact"

Those responsible for planning health programs will sometimes receive that task *after* a social diagnosis, or something like it, has been done by someone else (if only in the minds of an administrator, legislative body, or decision-making

- Programs should be of an adequate duration to address the problems identified.
- Interventions should vary across different levels of implementation.
- Project management should ensure intensity of effort combined with appropriate adaptation at all phases of the participatory research and program planning process.[102]
- Program quality and implementation should be assessed by process evaluation.

The first two of these pertain to the social diagnosis and situation analyses that have been the subject of the current chapter. The other recommendations pertain to additional considerations that could account for the limited impact of the program in this study and that will be the subject of chapters to follow. Although a rural Aboriginal community might present more extreme contrasts with scientific theory and research from the mainstream culture, might these recommendations apply as well to any community that sees itself as having some unique features, some special circumstances, some particular history, some notable assets, or some local cultural distinctiveness? Wouldn't any community claim one or more of these distinctive characteristics? How should distinctive community features play into the social diagnosis, the assessment of community assets, the situation analysis, the subsequent planning and adaptation of interventions, and the evaluation process?

board) or bypassed altogether. Indeed, an epidemiological diagnosis, or at least some general aspects thereof, may also have been completed or presumed (see Chapter 3). In some instances, programs are instituted to address a need that has caused sufficient concern. For example, in schools, units or classes on alcohol and drugs or HIV/AIDS are driven by parents' or the public's judgment about the dangerous effects of these problems on society. National and international population and family planning programs receive money because funders expect them to help reduce the social maladies that often accompany overpopulation and problem pregnancies. Self-care programs are widely offered by managed care organizations and employers in the hope that program outcomes will include not only better health but also decreased medical costs, less sick leave from work, and increased self-esteem and personal control. In short, most health programs with any significant support from the general public or policy makers are likely addressing health problems already identified as potentially detrimental to quality of life or social conditions. Why, then, should one bother with a social diagnosis and situation analysis?

Program planners who find themselves assigned to plan a health program for which the social benefit is assumed or previously worked out should, if at all feasible, make it a priority to recapture and become familiar with the information used by others in that assessment process. Such a retrospective review provides the crucial information and orientation needed to keep perspective on the ultimate goal of the program. In addition, it may also reveal gaps that are not too late to fill, such as failure to engage the participation of the intended beneficiary population and key organizational partners. More often than not, the previous data and assumptions about the linkage of the assigned health problem to quality-of-life or social conditions will be from sources other than the population or community in which you will be working. Some backing and filling with data from other sources, in consultation with the community, will usually serve to validate or revise the assumptions and engage the community in seeing the convergence of the proposed health program with their values and needs. If it invalidates the assumptions, or collides with their values, priorities, and perceived needs, it is best to know early in the planning and to PRE-CEDE further planning by bringing the three circles of Figure 2-3 into closer alignment before PROCEEDing to implementation.

Situation Analysis:
Cutting to the Chase, Leaping Past the Obvious

Besides the backing and filling when your assignment is to start your planning in the middle of the PRECEDE phases (at Phase 2 or 3), your other challenge will be to know when to skip over or to short-cut one or more of these phases. Figure 2-6 shows a successive narrowing of focus in Phase 1 to a clear goal. That goal then leads to a repetitious narrowing of optional causes, determinants, priorities, and objectives associated with the goal and each of the determinants or points of intervention derived from assessments in Phases 2 and 3. Finally, the narrowed focus on key objectives or targets for change leads to a third level of analysis (Phase 4). In this phase the resources, policies, organizational capacities, and regulatory authorities will be assessed in relation to the literature on best practices and the theories of change that will guide the formulation of the program. One then reverses the direction of analysis during implementation and evaluation phases, drawing on the baseline data, assessments, and objectives formulated during the Precede phases.

As one takes stock of the situation analysis in Phase 1, derived from the considerations outlined in this chapter, one can project ahead to a plan for planning. Depending on one's familiarity with the science and the local circumstances, one might readily see a clear path from the social assessment's conclusions about the most important goal to the next steps required in analyzing the problem. One might even see a clear path to formulating the solutions because the problem has been so thoroughly analyzed before in the scientific and professional literature. The desiderata in justifying these leaps are outlined as a flow chart or algorithm in Figure 2-7. This algorithm also summarizes the major considerations, pathway, and product of Phase 1, the social diagnosis and situation analysis.

Phase 4: Administrative & policy assessment, PROCEED to action, formative evaluation

Phases 2–3: Epidemiological, educational, & ecological assessments

Phase 1: Social & quality-of-life assessments & situation analysis

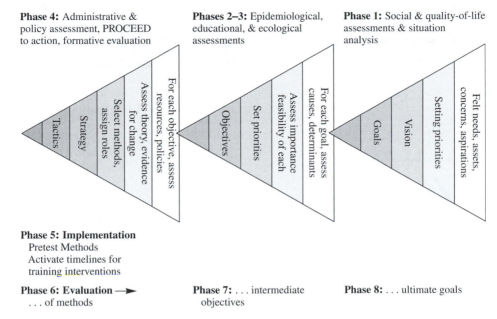

Phase 5: Implementation
Pretest Methods
Activate timelines for
training interventions

Phase 6: Evaluation ⟶
    . . . of methods

Phase 7: . . . intermediate
    objectives

Phase 8: . . . ultimate goals

FIGURE 2-6   Summary of the phases of PRECEDE-PROCEED. Three types and levels of analysis characterize the Precede phase, of planning and formative evaluation, and in reverse for the Proceed phase of implementation, process evaluation, and outcome evaluation. Depending on the clarity of goals, the strength of evidence, and the relevance of experience with previous attempts to address the same problems in similar populations and circumstance, Phase 2, 3, and 4 can be streamlined to get more quickly to action.

The first question at the end of Phase 1 is whether the social diagnosis, assets assessment, and situation analysis point so clearly to a particular health problem and goal for the focus of Phase 2 that the epidemiological analysis and procedures of Chapter 3 would be superfluous. If this is the case, then one can reasonably skip to Phase 3 (Chapter 4). This skip is the most likely of the three because epidemiological studies have been more extensively published and have greater generalizability across communities or populations than the types of data and conclusions called for in Phases 3 and 4.

The question one can ask upon entering Phase 3 is whether the etiology, that is, the behavioral and environmental determinants, of the clearly defined health problem or objective are so well established that one can simply draw down from the epidemiological literature. For example, if the health problem is malaria or West Nile disease, mosquitoes and their breeding places are clearly the environmental causes. People's use of protective clothing, netting, screening, and insect repellants, and their actions to eliminate standing water, are very well established as the behavioral determinants of the problem and the objective of reduced incidence of malaria or West Nile disease. Thus, one can skip planning Phase 3 for this health problem/objective, except to write clear

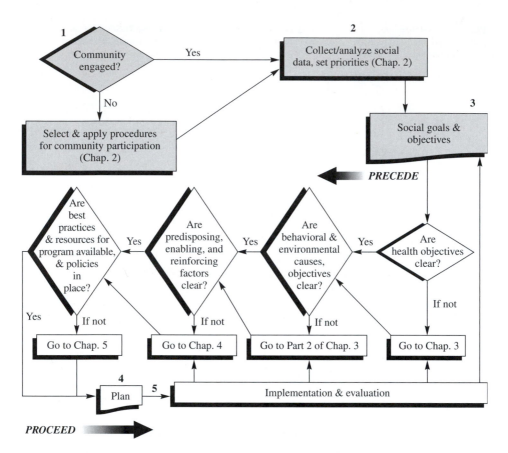

FIGURE 2-7 Flow diagram of skip patterns possible in applying PRECEDE-PROCEED. This algorithm offers a skip pattern for streamlining the Precede phases of planning in relation to specific situation analysis and goals verified from Phase 1.

objectives for one or more of these behavioral and environmental outcomes to sharpen the focus in Phase 4. Since data and scientific certainty are a little scarcer here than with epidemiological data on the health problem, but are more plentiful than those available at the next phase, we may anticipate a diminishing probability of justification for skipping Phases 3 and 4.

Skipping either of these phases in the planning process hastens the movement toward formulating the solutions and program or policy action. Such skipping carries with it, however, the liability of not establishing actual baseline data on the community or population for later use in evaluation. It also risks mistaking generalized scientific knowledge as necessarily applicable in the local situation and population. This second error is most likely when the research on which scientific knowledge is based has come from highly controlled situations unlike those in the local community.

We come then, either directly from Phase 1 by skipping Phase 2, or more systematically through two or more of the previous phases, to the messier, more complicated, more conjectural knowing of the most important causes or determinants of the selected behavioral and environmental problems or objectives. Even if theory pertaining to the specific types of behavior is strong, and the data pertaining to the behavioral and environmental risk status of the nation or state at large are good, data for this particular community become more important at Phase 3. It will be more difficult to satisfy the local constituents of the health plan that your assumptions for this population or community based on theories and data from other populations are locally appropriate.[103] They will tend to be more skeptical here and in the next Phase that their community is like others, and understandably so, for we are now into the more highly variable, more heterogeneous territory of beliefs, attitudes, perceptions, skills, resources, social support, and cultural norms. This heterogeneity is what makes the theory and the evidence more probabilistic and less deterministic in Phases 3 and 4. Because successful program development in Phase 4 depends so heavily on the clarity and validity of the targets of change chosen in Phase 3, we urge greater caution in skipping Phase 3.

Finally, there will be the temptation in Phase 4 to pull "off-the-shelf" packaged programs, commercially advertised products, and especially the scientifically verified "best practices" or "evidence-based practices" into a program design to streamline that phase. We encourage the use of these, especially the latter, and more especially as they become increasingly well founded in evidence that has grown out of multiple trials in widely varied communities or settings. The data and the tools for making the goodness-of-fit decisions at this stage have become more thoroughly delineated since our previous edition of this book.[104] They remain, however, part of an inexact science of matching and mapping often incompletely tested strategies to local circumstances and population characteristics that differ from those in which the research was done. The science often applies to interventions isolated from their imbedding in more complex programs, tested in relatively controlled studies that are uncharacteristic of the real circumstances in which they would be applied locally.

SUMMARY

Jointly identifying and analyzing, with a population or community, the social or economic problems, the communities' indigenous assets, and quality-of-life aspirations important to them is a valuable, if not essential, first step in thorough health program planning. Health is not an ultimate value in itself except insofar as it relates to social benefits, quality of life, or an organization's bottom line. Health takes on greater importance—both to those who must support the program and those expected to participate in it—when they can see clearly the connection between the health objective and some broader or more compelling social objective. This chapter has described a series of steps and a variety of strategies and techniques the planner can use to gather and analyze information about social problems and perceived quality of life, as well as to seek out maximum feasible participation and mobilize community assets.

One can summarize the objectives of social diagnosis (Phase 1 of health program planning) as follows:

1. To *engage* the community as active partners in the social diagnostic process
2. To *identify* ultimate values and subjective concerns with quality of life or conditions of living in the target population
3. To *verify* and clarify these subjective concerns either through existing data sources or new data from surveys, interviews, or focus groups
4. To *demonstrate* how social concerns and ultimate values can serve to heighten awareness of and motivation to act on health problems
5. To *assess* the capacities and assets of a community
6. To *make explicit* the rationale for the selection of priority problems
7. To use the documentation and rationale from social diagnosis as one of the variables on which to *evaluate* the program

The social diagnosis, combined with an analysis of the knowledge available in the literature on the issues identified by it, can produce a situation analysis that leaps over one or more of the other phases of planning in the chapters just ahead. An algorithm for doing so suggests considerations in making the jump. Getting as expeditiously to action and ultimately to outcomes is, after all, what planning is for. But the trade-offs between expediency and quality or effectiveness of the actions, and potential sacrifices in equity in the outcomes, must be weighed carefully before omitting steps in the systematic series of assessments that make up the additional planning processes in the chapters to follow.

EXERCISES

1. List three ways you could (or did)[105] involve the members of the population you selected in Exercise 3 of Chapter 1 in identifying their quality-of-life concerns and their resources or assets for addressing them. Justify your methods in terms of their feasibility and appropriateness for the population you are helping.
2. How did (or would) you verify or triangulate the subjective data gathered in Exercise 1 with objective data on social problems or quality-of-life concerns, and on assets or resources?
3. Display and discuss your real or hypothetical data as a quality-of-life diagnosis, justifying your selection of social, economic, and health problems to become the highest priority for a program.
4. Using the Precede-Proceed Model template in Chapter 1, draw a similar logic model of the presumed causal chain and objectives for each of the most important causes to identify gaps in understanding and next steps in planning.[106]

NOTES AND CITATIONS

1. *Definition of community:* We use the term *community* in most instances to refer to the larger geo-graphically and sometimes geopolitically defined aggregate of people (neighborhood, town, city, county, district, or occasionally, a whole state, region, or country). This is consistent with the most common current usage (MacQueen, McLellan, et al., 2001, in which locus was the most frequently cited of 17 dimensions of community cited by 4% or more of respondents). We will use it in later chapters to refer to organizationally defined communities (school, work site, industry, church, hospital, or nursing home) through which communication and deci-sions flow. (See the Glossary.) *Community,* however, appears as a secondary definition in most dictionaries as a reference to a group of people who share a common interest. This use may apply in patient education, self-help groups, and health programs for dispersed groups. Elec-tronic bulletin boards and satellite television open new possibilities for the interactive engage-ment of dispersed populations in health planning to address their common concerns. Such electronic meetings have been held, for example, to involve chief executive officers in discus-sions of the potential for work site health promotion programs in their industries. It is used currently to engage the community of health personnel across the United States in planning for antiterrorism preparedness in their local communities. For Web links on this and other ref-erences below, go to http://www.lgreen.net.

2. *Social determinants of health:* Bunker, 2001, p. 1266. For recent reviews, analyses, and commen-taries on social determinants of health, see Beaglehole, 2002; Berkman & Kawachi, 2000; Green & Potvin, 2002; Hart, 2002; Marmot, 2000; Marmot & Wilkenson, 1999; McDowell, 2002.

3. *Community coalitions:* Berkowitz, 2001; Berlin, Barnett, Mischke, & Ocasio, 2000; Butterfoss & Kegler, 2002; Chavis, 2001; Foster-Frisman, et al., 2001; Green, 2000; Kreuter, Lezin, & Young, 2000 (reviewed 68 published descriptions of coalitions and consortia); Lasker, Weiss, & Miller, 2001; Roussos & Fawcett, 2000; Sanchez, 2000; Wolff, 2001. The chapter by Butterfoss and Kegler builds on much of this literature, drawing from it seven theoretical constructs related to community coalition formation, structure, and processes, and another seven related to coalition interventions and outcomes. From studies of these they derive 23 propositions to for-mulate a theoretical model of community coalitions.

4. *Social Capital:* Hawe & Shiell, 2000; Kreuter & Lezin, 2002; Kreuter, Lezin, Young, & Koplan, 2001; Putnam, 2000.

5. *Reciprocal relationship of social/quality of life issues and health:* for example, Brown, Lipscomb, & Snyder, 2001; Centers for Disease Control and Prevention, 2000; Raeburn & Rootman, 1998, esp. Chap. 4, "Health and Well-Being in a Quality of Life Context," pp. 53–63; and Interna-tional Society for Quality of Life Research: http://www.isoqol.org; and International Society for Quality of Life Research: http://www.cob.vt.edu/market/isqols/.

6. *Health an instrumental value, not a terminal value:* We avoid the misnomer "healthy" in describ-ing actions, policies, or programs conducive to health (e.g., "healthy behavior" or "healthy public policy") because these objects of the adjectives are means, not ends; they are not living organisms that can be healthy. At best they can enhance health, and thus may be healthful, health promoting, health protecting, or disease preventing. Similarly, health is an instrumental value for quality-of-life ends.

7. *Ottawa Charter for Health Promotion, on health as a resource for living:* First International Confer-ence on Health Promotion, 1986, p. iii. See also Kreuter, Lezin, Kreuter, & Green, 2003, Preface, for the analogy of what a healthy squirrel looks like (from Kass, 1980), and how this applies to populations (also at http://www.lgreen.net).

8. *Definitions of health as functional capacity:* Last, 2000; see also Last, 2002, p. 520.

9. *Sociological definition of health:* Parsons, 1964, p. 433; for a discussion of "social health," see McDowell, 2002.

10. *Employers' criteria for outcomes beyond health:* Pelletier, 2001, p.114.

11. *Tailoring communications to individual and population segments' ultimate values:* for example, Nansel, Weaver, Donlin, Jacobsen, Kreuter, & Simons-Morton, 2002.

12. *Ultimate values as people's greatest enjoyments in life:* "Things people value and enjoy" can be measured using tools such as the Valued Life Activities (VLA) Index; Jette, 1993; or the STAR-LITE scale, Wilshire et al., 1997.

13. *Cultural considerations in ultimate values:* The phrase in the U.S. Constitution protecting "life, liberty, and the pursuit of happiness," acknowledges that happiness and fulfillment are highly individualized concepts. The wisdom of most philosophical systems suggests that we can help people find the freedom and capacity to pursue those elusive states, but we cannot expect to achieve them for others. Furthermore, happiness and fulfillment are *states* of being, not permanent *traits*. As states, they are variable and, therefore, can serve as positive and appropriate goals for promotion. The Canadian variation on the theme of "life, liberty, and the pursuit of happiness" is "peace, harmony, and good government." This phrase reflects a cultural difference in ultimate values that conditions how the people of neighboring countries might judge their quality of life and social conditions differently. For examples of the U.S.-Canadian differences in legislators' perceptions of policy issues in tobacco control and other public health matters, see Cohen, et al., 2001, 2002, Studlar, 2002.

14. *Participatory research to assess population's ultimate values and quality of life:* Doll, Berkelman, Rosenfield, & Baker, 2001; Green & Mercer, 2001; Minkler & Wallerstein, 2003; Olden, Guthrie, & Newton, 2001. Internet resources for participatory research approaches to community assessment and development are listed and linked at http://www.goshen.edu/soan/soan96p.htm and guidelines are online at http://www.ihpr.ubc.ca/guidelines.htm.

15. *Kaiser Family Foundation's Social Reconnaissance Method:* Butler, et al., 1996. COPC as approach to making clinical services relevant to population's perspective: For a current community-oriented primary care (COPC) project in the Delta region, funded by another foundation, go to http://www.dhep.astate.edu/, and for a history of the COPC approach from South Africa to the Mississippi Delta, see Geiger, 2002.

16. *Measuring personal health-related quality of life:* Fryback, Lawrence, Martin, Klein, & Klein, 1997; Lorig, Ritter, Stewart, et al., 2001; Ware & Kosinski, 2001. Some quality-of-life measures taken specifically within social assessments and studies using the Precede-Proceed Model are reported by Bartholomew, et al., 1997; Cramer, 1994; McGowan & Green, 1995. The notion originally articulated by Fries & Crapo, 1981, of adding life to years rather than merely years to life, or "compression of morbidity," is discussed in the context of using theory and models such as PRECEDE-PROCEED in patient education planning by Prohaska & Lorig, 2001. The most widely and consistently applied health-related quality-of-life measure now incorporated in most states of the United States is the CDC-designed Health-Related Quality-of-Life Measures. See endnote 20.

17. *Quality-of-life measures associated with pain management:* Lorig, Laurent, Deyo, et al., 2002.

18. *Quality-of-life measures associated with functional disability:* Haley, Jette, Coster, et al., 2002; Jette & Keysor, 2002.

19. *Quality-of-life measures associated with leisure activities:* Plante & Schwartz, 1990.

20. *Quality-of-life measures associated with mental health:* Holley, 1998, for contrasting Canadian and U.S. perspectives. For *environmental and health-related quality-of-life measures from a European perspective,* see the European Commission research at http://europa.eu.int/comm/research/quality-of-life/ka4/index_en.html (accessed Dec. 19, 2002). For a measure of "functional" physical and mental health at the population level, see Burdine, et al., 2000. For an example of the correlations of unemployment rates and other ecological measures with health, see Karpati, Galea, Awerbuch, & Levins, 2002. For the health-related quality-of-life and other specific measures used in the Behavioral Risk Factor Surveillance System (BRFSS), the years in which they were used, and whether they were in the core questionnaire or the optional (for states) modules, go to http://apps.nccd.cdc.gov/BRFSSQuest/ (accessed Oct. 18, 2003). *CDC's web site contains details on the 15 health-related quality-of-life measures* that have been used selectively in state BRFSS surveys since 1995. For other applications of the CDC-BRFSS quality-of-life measures, see Ahluwalia, et al., 2003; Mili, Helmick, & Moriarty, 2003; Moriarty, Zack, & Kobau, 2003.

21. *The Ferrans and Powers Quality of Life Index* is a 68-item instrument designed to measure satisfaction with and importance of health juxtaposed to psychological, spiritual, and family-life factors, and has been effectively applied cross-culturally. See Ferrans, 1996.

22. *Validations of the most widely used measure in medical care settings:* Ware & Kosinski, 2001. *Variations on the SF-36 instruments* are being tested now in 45 countries for cross-cultural validity and adaptation.

23. *Outcomes measured besides medical in SF-36:* Kosinski, Kujawski, Martin, Wanke, Buatti, Ware, & Perfetto, 2002; Manocchia, Keller, & Ware, 2001.

24. *Literature on technical assistance:* Church, Saunders, Wanke, Pong, Spooner, & Dorgan, 2002; Green, 1986f; Minkler, 1997; Wharf Higgins, 2002; and for classics on participatory approaches in health: Morgan & Horning, 1940; Nyswander, 1942; Steuart, 1965. For a recent Canadian review, go to http://www.hc-sc.gc.ca/hppb/healthcare/Building.htm.

25. *Participatory research in developing countries and underserved communities:* Eades, Read, & the Bibbulung Gnarneep Team, 1999; Green, George, Daniel, et al., 2003; Green, 2003; Minkler & Wallerstein, 2003. For an example from India of a project applying some of these principles, see The Gyandoot Project at http://www.unescap.org/rural/bestprac/gyandoot.htm. For similar projects addressing other aspects of rural development in developing countries, http://www.unescap.org/rural/bestprac/index.htm.

26. *Concientación* refers in this context to consciousness raising for a process whereby persons with limited means become conscious of the political realities and root causes of their situation and take collective action to address them. Shor & Freire, 1987.

27. *The history and international variations in taking these perceptions into account through participation in health program planning* was traced and developed into a formal theory of participation in Green, 1986f. It became operationalized subsequently in new forms of community coalitions, often required by funding agencies in the health fields to represent the diversity of perspectives and perceptions in the planning process. The coalition process, too, has been advanced to the status of a formal theory by Butterfoss & Kegler, 2002.

28. Freire, 1970, p. 181. For a discussion contrasting PRECEDE, adult education, and Freire's approaches, see Marsick, 1987, in which PRECEDE was "interpreted from a viewpoint of technical rationality even though it does not have to be so construed. Interpreted narrowly, PRECEDE would emphasize an accurate technical diagnosis of the problem [consulting] with clients and community leaders in problem setting, but the primary purpose would be to discuss the problem in order to develop the best professional solution" (p. 19). We would argue that the best technical or professional solution *is* one that addresses the felt needs of the community. For more recent applications of Freirian concepts in health, see Minkler, 2000, 2002; Wallerstein & Duran, 2003.

29. Freire, 1970, p. 183. See also Baum, Bush, et al., 2000; Parker, Lichtenstein, et al., 2001; Wallerstein, Duran, et al., 2003 for examples of contrasting, contradicting, and paradoxical perspectives in community studies, depending on levels of participation in community, socioeconomic variables, and inherent cultural, economic, and infrastructure needs and capacities of a community.

30. For a compelling and poignant account of *how the conflicting cultures and views of allied professionals and advocates for a common cause (the settlement with the tobacco industry) can undermine their planning and strategic positioning for policy change,* read Pertchuck, 2001. See also Schroeder, 2002. For a *cultural assessment framework* based in part on the Precede-Proceed Model, see Huff & Kline, 1999.

31. *Caveat:* We would temper this sentiment in areas of health protection such as water and food safety, as well as health services such as immunizations, where whole populations may be at extreme risk if the values and misunderstandings of a small but vocal group, or even a majority, were to override scientific evidence. This is not, however, to suggest that participatory approaches are more appropriate to health promotion and less important to health protection or health services. Indeed, two of the most significant contemporary initiatives in federal support for participatory research have come from the National Institute of Environmental Health

Sciences (O'Fallon & Dearry, 2002; Shepard, Northridge, Prakash, & Stover, 2002; and the whole issue in which these articles appear; see also the projects supported by NIEHS, online at http://www.niehs.nih.gov/translat/cbpr/proj2001.htm, accessed Oct. 18, 2003). The Indian Health Services and the Health Resources and Services Administration have applied participatory methods in Community-Oriented Primary Care (Nutting, 1990; Williams, 2002, APHA abstract online at http://apha.confex.com/apha/130am/techprogram/paper_49078.htm, accessed Oct. 18, 2003). Brown & Fee (2002), review the history of COPC and note that some recent initiatives seek "to jettison a prescriptive stepwise COPC model in favor of a more fluid and dynamic understanding that emphasizes community engagement and embraces socio-political objectives" (p. 1712).

32. *Importance of media in creating an informed electorate to support health policies:* American Public Health Association, 2000; Biglan, Ary, Smolkowski, Duncan, & Black, 2000; Chapman & Lupton, 1995; Green, Murphy, & McKenna, 2002; McLoughlin & Fennell, 2000; Mindell, 2001; Stead, Hastings, & Eadie, 2002; Stillman, Cronin, Evans, & Ulasevich, 2001; Wallack, Woodruff, Dorfman, & Diaz, 1999. To locate the media organizations in your area of the United States, go to http://capwiz.com/astho/dbq/media/ (accessed Oct. 19, 2003).

33. *Importance of participation at more central, as well as local, levels of decision making:* Green & Frankish, 1996; Green & Shoveller, 2000; Shoveller & Green, 2002. For descriptions of exemplary state and local actions addressing disparities in health, see National Association of County and City Health Officials, 2000.

34. *Tensions between national, state, and local agencies, and between centralized offices and local employees:* Ottoson & Green, 1987; Singh & Rajamani, 2003.

35. *Quotation:* Rose, 1992, pp. 123–124. *For a case example of these varied forms of participation* in health program planning, see Kreuter, Lezin, Kreuter, & Green, 2003, Chapter 3.

36. *Indigenous capacity and assets of communities:* McKnight & Kretzmann, 1997. The National Association of County and City Health Official's (NACCHO) Assessment Protocol for Excellence in Public Health (APEX*PH*), 1991, updated 2002, guides local health departments through an organizational capacity assessment and a community health assessment process. APEX*PH* '98 —software for the APEX*PH* process—is also available in CD-ROM or on a set of six disks. Go to http://www.naccho.org/tools.cfm. See also the Mobilizing for Action Through Planning and Partnerships (MAPP) instruments and the Protocol for Assessment of Community Excellence in Environmental Health (PACE-EH) at the same web site. Each of these CDC-sponsored community health assessment models builds on the previous one. MAPP and PACE-EH are elaborations or special applications of APEX*PH*, which was an extension of the Planned Approach to Community Health (PATCH, http://www.cdc.gov/nccdphp/patch/) and was based largely on the PRECEDE Model. During the same time, PRECEDE has evolved as PRECEDE-PROCEED to build on the experience of PATCH and the Kaiser Family Foundation's experience of applying a "social reconnaissance" approach to community needs and asset assessment (Green & Kreuter, 1997), and on subsequent experience with all of the assessment and planning models and instruments. Many of the assessment procedures in PRECEDE-PROCEED are illustrated in an interactive tutorial software package and manual called Expert Methods of Planning and Organizing Within Everyone's Reach (EMPOWER, see Gold, Green, & Kreuter, 1997; see also Chaisson, 1996; Gold & Atkinson, 1999; Green, Tan, Gold, & Kreuter, 1996; Lovato, Potvin, et al., 2003). Two other CDC community-grant programs that apply many of the same planning methods growing out of PRECEDE and PATCH are Racial and Ethnic Approaches to Community Health (http://www.cdc.gov/nccdphp/bb_reach/index.htm, accessed Oct. 21, 2003) and the Agency for Toxic Substances and Disease Registry's guidance to working with communities on environmental health issues such as toxic waste investigation programs (http://www.phppo.cdc.gov/phtn/envedu/crse-mat.asp, accessed Oct 21. 2003).

37. *Gaps in community assets:* Hawe, Noort, King, & Jordens, 1997; Kreuter & Lezin, 2002; Foster-Fishman, Berkowitz, Lounsbury, Jacobson, & Allen, 2001.

38. *Community-centric vs. agency-centric planning:* Hawe, 1996. For an example from mental health, see Blankertz & Hazem, 2002.

39. *Community endorsement of agency agenda is not same as community generation of agenda:* Ibid., p. 477.

40. *"Competent community"* was a term conceptualized generically by Iscoe, 1974, and Cottrell, 1976. Its applications in the health field have tended increasingly toward use of the term *"community capacity,"* e.g., Chaskin, Brown, Venkatesh, & Vidal, 2001; Crisp, Swerissen, & Duckett, 2000; Kalnins, Hart, Ballantyne, Quartaro, Love, Sturis, & Pollack, 2002; Ricketts, 2001; Smith, Baugh Littlejohns, & Thompson, 2001; and more recently, "social capital" or "community capital," e.g., Hancock, 2001; Kreuter & Lezin, 2002. For a commentary on the variations in the terms and concepts related to community capacity, see Poland, 2000.

41. *Tools and methods for asset identification and development:* Fawcett, Schultz, Carson, Renault, & Francisco, 2003; Minkler & Hancock, 2003; National Civic League, 1999, 2000; Puntenney, 2000; Sharpe, Greany, Lee, & Royce, 2000; Snow, 2001; Wang, 2003; Wang, Cash, & Powers, 2000. See also note 36 on asset mapping and Assets Based Community Development Institute of Northwestern University's Institute for Policy Research. ABCD's web site contains tools online at http://www.northwestern.edu/ipr/abcd.html.

42. *The notion of capacity building as being able to use the lessons of one program experience to solve other problems,* rather than the once popular notion of institutionalizing the funded program as the measure of success (cf. Green, 1989), is consistent with Senge's (1994) concept of the "learning organization." The most thorough review of the recent history and conceptual development of community capacity building in health is the chapter by Norton, McLeroy, Burdine, Felix, & Dorsey, 2002. See also the growing emphasis of schools of public health on this dimension of training and research: DeFrancesco, Bowie, Frattaroli, Bone, Walker, & Farfel, 2002.

43. *"Empowerment" as gaining confidence and skills for greater independence:* Fetterman, 2000; Minkler, Thompson, Bell, Rose, & Redman, 2002; Thompson, Minkler, Allen, et al., 2000; Wandersman & Florin, 2000; Zimmerman, 2000. For a detailed list of Internet resources, software, handbooks, and guides and related associations on participatory and empowerment evaluation to strengthen capacity building and self-reliance, go to http://www.stanford.edu/~davidf/empowermentevaluation.html.

44. *Collective efficacy:* Bandura, 2002.

45. *Dissemination value of demonstrations, as a complement to "best practices" from research:* Cameron, Jolin, Walker, McDermott, & Gough, 2001; Green, 2001b; Kahan & Goodstadt, 2001.

46. *Quotation:* Shaw, 1930, pp. xiv–xv.

47. *Public participation does not mean professional abdication:* World Health Organization, 1983, p. 17. See also Green & Mercer, 2001.

48. *Recognizing limits of participation of employees:* Brosseau, Parker, Lazovich, Milton, & Dugan, 2002, quotes from pp. 56 & 59, respectively.

49. *Recognizing limits of participation of employers:* Lazovich, Parker, Brosseau, Milton, & Dugan, 2002.

50. *Major print sources on health needs and asset assessments:* Gilmore & Campbell, 2003; Halverson & Mays, 2001; Lee, 2001; Melnick, 2001; Petersen & Alexander, 2001; Teutsch & Churchill, 2000.

51. *Need to supplement routinely collected data with tailored data:* Hawe, 1996.

52. *Situation analysis:* Gold, Green, & Kreuter, 1997.

53. *North Karelia Cardiovascular Disease Prevention Project:* Puska, Variainen, Tuomilehto, Salomaa, & Nissinen, 1998; Vartiainen, Jousilahti, Alfthan, Sundvall, Pietinen, & Puska, 2000. For contrast for the neighboring area of Russia, see Laatikainen, Delong, Pokusajeva, Uhanov, Vartiainen, & Puska, 2002.

54. *Social diagnosis and situation analysis in North Karelia:* P. Puska et al., 1985, p. 164.

55. *Surveys of community decision makers and health personnel:* Ibid., p. 165.

56. *Evaluation of PATCH revealed that needs assessment phase could take up to 18 months:* Goodman, Steckler, Hoover, & Schwartz, 1993.

57. *Defining and measuring community capacity:* Goodman, Spears, McLeroy, Fawcett, Kegler, Parker, Smith, Sterling, & Wallerstein, 1998.

58. *Assessing community coalitions:* Goodman, Wandersman, Chinman, Imm, & Morrisey, 1996.

59. *Caveats on participatory research dimensions of community planning:* Goodman, 2001.

60. *CDC's efforts to make surveillance data more usable by communities:* Remington & Goodman, 1998; Teutsch & Churchill, 2000, see esp. Chapters 3, 7, 11, & 12.

61. *Caveats on "best practices" research as a sole guide to interventions appropriate for communities other than those in which the research was conducted:* Glasgow, Lichtenstein, & Marcus, 2003; Green, 2001b.

62. *Caution against home-grown solutions that ignore "best practices" from previous research:* Green & Kreuter, 2002; Halfours, Cho, Livert, & Kadushin, 2002. For searchable access to the hundreds of guidelines and recommendations for best practices documented by the Centers for Disease Control and Prevention, go to http://www.phppo.cdc.gov/CDCRecommends/AdvSearchV .asp. This searchable web site provides *CDC Recommends: The Prevention Guidelines System,* which contains up-to-date and archived guidelines and recommendations approved by the CDC for the prevention and control of disease, injuries, and disabilities.

63. *Why are some people healthy and others not?* R. G. Evans, Barer, & Marmor, 1994.

64. *Social capital as community capacity:* Burdine, Felix, Wallerstein, Abel, Wiltraut, Musselman, & Stidley, 1999; Hawe & Shiell, 2000; Kreuter & Lezin, 2002; Putnam, 2000.

65. *Measures of the four constructs of social capital:* Kreuter & Lezin, 2002; Muntaner, Lynch, & Smith, 2001.

66. *A copy of the* Civic Index *can be obtained from the National Civic League:* 1445 Market Street, Suite 300, Denver, CO 80202, or online at http://www.ncl.org/publications/descriptions/civic _index_measuring.html (accessed Mar. 16, 2004).

67. For *a recent example of a city's application of the Civic Index,* go to http://www.memphiscan.info/ MemphisCan/CivicIndex/Index.cfm.

68. *Asset mapping:* McKnight & Kretzman, 1997. For recent updates, go to http://www.madii.org/ amhome/amhome.html. See also Painter, 2002, Chapter 2, for this and other community assessment tools, periodically updated. For an application example within the context of the community engagement process, go to http://www.cdc.gov/phppo/pce/part1.htm. In an example of a more specific application of asset mapping, Dato, Potter, et al., 2002, describe the development of inventories and a capacity map for public health workforce development, identifying training resources that could be tapped by health agencies.

69. *The "Community Toolbox" resource:* Fawcett, Francisco, Schultz, Nagy, Berkowitz, & Wolff, 2000. Maintained by the Work Group on Health Promotion and Community Development, The University of Kansas, Lawrence, Kansas, at http://ctb.lsi.ukans.edu/tools/tools.htm.

70. *Social reconnaissance method:* Sanders, 1950. See also the adaptations for participatory planning development for CDC in the 1970s: Nix, 1977.

71. *Later adaptations of social reconnaissance method:* Nix, 1970; Nix & Seerley, 1971, 1973.

72. *The Kaiser Foundation's experience with the social reconnaissance method* in the southern states was documented in annual reports of the foundation (1989, 1990), in the second and third editions of this book (1991, 1999), in an article in the *Council on Foundations* magazine: R. M. Williams, 1990, and in a full evaluation of the program by Butler, et al., 1996. Burdine, Felix, et al. (1999, 2000) have continued to refine the methods of leadership identification and other aspects of social reconnaissance, and have combined it with quality-of-life measures for a fuller social diagnosis. Braithwaite, Taylor, & Austin (2000), and Chavis (2001) have continued to draw on the reconnaissance experience of the Kaiser Family Foundation's Southern Strategy where they and their colleagues provided technical assistance (e.g., Mitchell, Florin, & Stevenson, 2002). It also provided some inspiration for the development and application of methods and guidelines for participatory research in Canada (Green, et al., 1996; McGowan & Green, 1995) and for the addition of the PROCEED components of the Precede-Proceed Model.

73. *Emphasis on social structural and relationship issues in social reconnaissance method:* Nix, 1977, p. 141. The Vancouver Foundation (1999) also adopted a variation of the social reconnaissance methods for social diagnosis and situation analysis in their community grant making.

74. *Coalition formation and development:* Berkowitz, 2001; Braithwaite, Taylor, & Austin, 2000; Butterfoss & Kegler, 2002; Chavis, 2001; Foster-Fishman, Berkowitz, Lounsbury, Jacobson, &

Allen, 2001; Goodman & Wandersman, 1994; Goodman, Wandersman, Chinman, Imm, & Morrisey, 1996; Green, 2000; Green, Daniel, & Novick, 2001; Green & Kreuter, 2002; Kreuter, Lezin, & Young, 2000; Hallfors, Cho, Livert, & Kadushin, 2002; Sanchez, 2000; Wolff, 2001.

75. *Applications of leadership analysis* within the context of Precede-Proceed assessments include Gold, Green, & Kreuter, 1997; Howat, Cross, et al., 2001; Michielutte & Beal, 1990; Taylor, Elliott, Robinson, & Taylor, 1998; and specifically, within the school context, Cottrell, Capwell, & Brannan, 1995; MacDonald & Green, 2001.

76. After reviewing their *funder's experience with decentralized planning models*, CDC concluded that the high expectations for a decentralized approach to HIV prevention community planning could be best achieved when a distinction is drawn between information-seeking tasks and decision-making tasks. They recommend that information-seeking tasks be centrally coordinated (provision of standardized data collection instruments and protocols, for example) and that decision-making tasks be decentralized. See Dearing, Larson, Randall, & Pope, 1998. This became a major debating point in the Robert Wood Johnson Foundation's "Fighting Back" program of grants to local communities for substance abuse prevention, in which the technical assistance providers left the communities a much greater degree of autonomy in developing their own "home-grown" interventions without insisting on some attachment to "best practices" from previous research (Green & Kreuter, 2002; Halfors, Cho, et al., 2002).

77. *Criteria and procedures for setting priorities among multiple needs:* For example, Conway, Hu, & Harrington, 1997. The same methods may apply to setting priorities on "liking" and "preferred" interventions or ways of pursuing a lifestyle or environmental change in later stages of the Precede-Proceed model, as demonstrated by McKenzie, Alcaraz, & Sallis (1994); and by Wang, Terry, & Flynn, et al. (1979) in one of the first full-scale applications and validations of the model. Wu (2000), applied the model to the economic analysis of insurance claims, fraudulent claims, claims-loss ratios, that would assist insurers in setting priorities for settlement of medical claims.

78. *Nominal Group Technique:* de Villiers, et al., 2003; Delbecq, 1983; Dewar, et al., 2003; Pololi, et al., 2003; C. C. Wang, et al., 2003.

79. *Descriptions of steps in applying the Nominal Group Technique:* Gilmore & Campbell, 2004, pp. 82–84 see also McDermott & Sarvela, 1999, pp. 234–235.

80. Examples of *applications of the Nominal Group process within PRECEDE and participatory research:* Adeyanju 1987–88; Green, George, Daniel, Frankish, Herbert, Bowie, & O'Neill, 2003; McGowan & Green, 1995.

81. *The Delphi Method:* Linstone & Turoff, 1975. See more recent adaptations for workplace settings (Leo, 1996) and discrete choice modeling in clinical priority setting (Farrar, Ryan, Ross, & Ludbrook, 2000).

82. *Steps in Delphi Method:* Gilmore & Campbell, 2004 (http://www.carolla.com/wp-delph.htm, accessed Dec. 26, 2002, for 10 specific steps in the process. Hunnicutt, Perry-Hunnicutt, Newman, Davis, & Crawford (1993), provide a *Precede-Proceed Model application of the Delphi Method* in planning a campus alcohol abuse prevention program. For an argument against its use on grounds that it may be used to squeeze out citizen or lay participation in favor of experts, go to http://www.icehouse.net/lmstuter/acf001.htm, (accessed Dec. 26, 2002).

83. *Focus groups:* See the boxed issue earlier in this chapter for a needs assessment example of focus group application, as well as anticipating intervention possibilities: Brosseau, Parker, Lazovich, Milton, & Dugan, 2002; Lazovich, Parker, Brosseau, Milton, & Dugan, 2002. For a comparative description of this and the other methods as applied in assessing the perceived efficacy of intervention methods, see Ayala & Elder, 2001. Our interest in this chapter, however, is primarily in the application of these methods in the earliest phase of assessing needs associated with more basic social and quality-of-life concerns. These findings from Phase 1 of PRECEDE-PROCEED will likely resurface as predisposing factors in Phase 4 (see, e.g., Young, et al., 2001).

84. *Focus group application with PRECEDE in cystic fibrosis:* Bartholomew, Seilheimer, Parcel, Spinelli, & Pumariega, 1989; Bartholomew, Czyzewski, Swank, McCormick, & Parcel, 2000.

85. *Focus group applications with PRECEDE in breast cancer and African American women:* Danigelis, Nicholas, et al., 1995; Eng, 1993; Paskett, Tatum, et al., 1999; Taylor, Taplin, et al., 1994.

86. *Focus group applications with PRECEDE on nutrition and related issues in urban adolescents, Vietnamese mothers, health professionals, and others:* Balch, et al., 1997; Cargo, Grams, et al., 2003; Doyle & Feldman, 1997; Mirand, Beehler, et al., 2003; Morris, Linnan, & Meador, 2003; Oliver-Vazquez, Sanchez-Ayendez, et al., 2002; Reed, 1996; Reed, Meeks, Nguyen, et al., 1998; Taylor, Coovadia, et al., 1999.

87. *Cultural context:* Airhihenbuwa, 1995; Airhihenbuwa, Kamanyika, & Lowe, 1995; Airhihenbuwa, Kumanyika, Agurs, Lowe, Saunders, & Morssink, 1996. Airhihenbuwa builds on the predisposing, enabling, and reinforcing factors in PRECEDE-PROCEED "in accounting for perceptions, resources/enablers, and significant others in health behavior outcome which for me occurs within broader social contexts with cultural interpretations and meanings" (personal communication, Jan. 4, 2002).

88. *Steps in focus group application:* Krueger & Casey, 2000. See also Gilmore & Campbell, 2003. Mwanga, Mugashe, & Aagaard-Hansen (1998) outline a procedure for video-recorded focus group discussion from a case study on schistosomiases in Magu, Tanzania.

89. Lefebvre, Doner, et al., 1995.

90. *Surveys:* Fink, 2002; Fowler, 2001. Especially relevant here are the growing numbers of participatory survey research projects, creating collaborative roles for representatives of community-based organizations and service providers, as demonstrated, e.g., by Schultz, et al. (1998).

91. *Quality-of-life surveys related to chronic diseases:* Zuckerman, Guerra, Drossman, Foland, & Gregory, 1996.

92. *Health-related quality-of-life surveys in occupational settings:* Bailey, Rukholm, Vanderlee, & Hyland, 1994; Bertera, 1990a, b, 1993.

93. *Quality-of-life surveys related to cystic fibrosis:* Bartholomew, Seilheimer, et al., 1989; Bartholomew, Czyzewski, et al., 2000.

94. *Surveys of staff nurses:* Berland, Whyte, & Maxwell, 1995; Cheng, DeWitt, Savageau, & O'Connor, 1999.

95. *Surveys on nutrition-related issues:* Campbell, Demark-Wahnefried, Symons, Kalsbeek, Dodds, Cowan, Jackson, Motsinger, Hoben, Lashley, Demissie, & McClelland, 1999; Doyle & Feldman, 1997.

96. *Federal health surveys incorporating quality-of-life measures:* Green, Wilson, & Bauer, 1992; Rootman, 1998. The Behavioral Risk Factor Surveillance System, a common survey conducted now by all 50 states, with coordination from CDC, has increasingly incorporated health-related quality-of-life and social health indicators in the telephone surveys (Centers for Disease Control and Prevention, 2000; and http://www.cdc.gov/nccdphp/brfss/ or http://www.cdc.gov/hrqol, accessed Dec. 31, 2002). See also community-level indicators, Karanek, Sockwell, Jia, CDC, 2000). These measures have been used also at the community level, e.g., in Canada, by Ounpuu, Kreuger, Vermeulen, & Chambers (2000), and http://www.oc.ca.gov/hca/public/healthbeat/2001_07.htm.

97. *Public service data:* For example, National Civic League, 1999, 2000; Washington Post/Kaiser Family Foundation/Harvard University Survey Project, 1996.

98. Flynn, 1995; Green & Mercer, 2000; Minkler & Hancock, 2003; Wang, 2003.

99. *Data triangulation:* For example, Thorpe & Loo, 2003; Wachtler & Troein, 2003. For PRECEDE examples, see Goodson, Gottlieb, & Radcliffe, 1999; Keintz, Rimer, et al., 1988; Morris, Linnan, & Meador, 2003; Wang, Terry, et al., 1979.

100. *Linking local assessment to theory and evidence from research literature:* Daniel & Green, 1995.

101. *Incomplete linking of community assessment with program planning decisions:* Daniel, Green, Marion, Gamble, Herbert, Hertzman, & Sheps, 1999.

102. *Lessons for use of theory and "best practices" literature vis a vis participation in planning:* Daniel, 1997. See abstract at http://www.ihpr.ubc.ca. These recommendations are discussed also in Daniel & Green (1999).

103. *The local skepticism about appropriateness of "best practices" from research for their community:* Green, 2001b.

104. *Growing science of aligning theory and research on "best practices" to population and community characteristics:* For example, Bartholomew, Parcel, Kok, & Gottlieb, 2001; Centers for Disease Control & Prevention, 1999; Fiore, Bailey, Cohen, et al., 2000; Friede, O'Carroll, Nicola, Oberle, & Teutsch, 1997 (updated regularly on CDC Recommends website: http://www.cdc.gov); Gilbert & Sawyer, 1995; Gregory, S., 2002; Harris, Zaza, & Teutsch, 2003; International Union for Health Promotion and Education, 1999; U.S. Department of Health and Human Services, 2000a; Wandersman, Imm, Chinman, & Kaftarian, 2000; World Health Organization, 2001, 2002, Chap. 5 (see also http://www.who.int/evidence for a regular update of CHOICE, CHoosing Interventions that are Cost Effective); Zasa, Sleet, Thompson, Sosin, Bolen, & Task Force on Community Preventive Services, 2001. For an alternative approach to the synthesis of quantitative evidence in arriving at "what works" for neighborhoods and communities, see Schorr, 1997.

105. *Exercises:* We suggest that these exercises be carried out on a real population accessible to the student or practitioner, in consultation with members of that population and service providers serving that population. If this is impracticable, the exercises can be applied to a more distant population using published census data, vital statistics, and data from surveys and other sources on the World Wide Web.

106. *For a three-step approach to building a Precede-Proceed logic model,* see Renger & Titcomb, 2002.

3

Epidemiological Diagnosis: Health, Behavioral, and Environmental Assessments

"The important thing is not to stop questioning."
—Albert Einstein

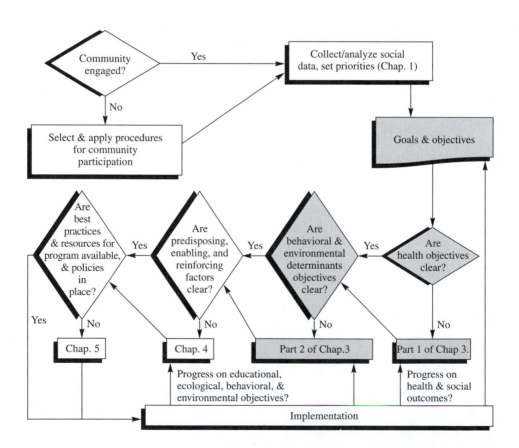

Ever mindful of the reciprocal relationship between quality of life and health status, we now turn our attention to the analytic tasks that will help planners focus their health programs on issues that are both important and amenable to change. Specifically, those tasks include (1) the identification of the health problems, issues, or aspirations upon which the program will focus, (2) uncovering the behavioral and environmental factors most likely to influence the priority health issues that emerged from the first task, and (3) translating those priority problems and factors into measurable objectives. Collectively, we refer to this phase of the Precede-Proceed Model as the "epidemiological diagnosis" because the problem-solving principles of epidemiology provide a sound and credible foundation to guide planners as they undertake those tasks.

THE EPIDEMIOLOGICAL, POPULATION-HEALTH APPROACH

Where's the Evidence?

It is well known that information is necessary, but insufficient, for the implementation of health programs that achieve their desired health goals. In the right circumstances and context, however, information can create a readiness that triggers action. To get a sense of this phenomenon, consider the following scenario that occurred during a 1999 plenary session at a national chronic disease prevention meeting. Dr. William Dietz, Director of the Division of Nutrition and Physical Activity at the National Center for Chronic Disease Prevention and Health Promotion at CDC, was giving a presentation about an emerging epidemic in the United States: obesity.

Prior to the meeting, co-workers at CDC had prepared a series of Power-Point slides illustrating how the proportion of residents in each state with a Body Mass Index (BMI) of 30 or greater had changed from 1985 through 1997. The data used in the slides were based on state-level annual prevalence rates obtained from the Behavioral Risk Factor Surveillance System (BRFSS). Prior to showing the slides, he explained to the audience what BMI meant: a height/weight formula used globally to assess a person's body weight as an accurate predictor of health risks that flow from overweight and obesity; the higher the BMI, the greater the risk of developing additional health problems. He clicked on the first slide, entitled, Prevalence of Overweight Among U.S. Adults (BRFSS, 1985). It showed a map of the United States with inserts for Alaska and Hawaii. Below the map were the color codes indicating the percentage of the population that had a BMI of greater than 30. If a state was colored yellow, the prevalence was 10% or less. Green indicated 10–15%. Those states with a prevalence of 15% or greater were colored blue. Some of the states were colored white indicating that obesity data were not available for that state in that year.

In the first slide, no state was blue. Seven were green, 12, were yellow and the remaining 31 were white. He clicked to slide 2, 1986. The number of yellow states increased to 16; there were no changes in the number of states colored either green or blue. In the slide for 1991, states colored yellow had dropped to nine, 36 were now green, and 4 were blue. With each click of the mouse key, the audience saw a gradual but persistent wave of blue enveloping the entire country. The final slide presented the data for 1997. None of the states were colored either yellow or white; 36 states were blue and the remaining 14 were green. The 12-year trends on data generated from the BRFSS told the story—no further explanation was needed.

Even in an audience of health professionals, the sense that they had heretofore not really understood the extent to which obesity had emerged as an epidemic was unmistakable. Subsequent to that event, updated versions of those data (including a new, red category indicating that 20% of the adults in a given state had a 30+ BMI) reflecting a continuing intensification of the epidemic have been presented in a wide variety of settings globally. One of those was testimony to the U.S. Congressional Budget Appropriations Committee hearing in 1999, by Dr. Jeffrey Koplan, then director of the CDC. The gasp was the same regardless of the audience.[1] In our continuing use of this set of slides, we sometimes end the series by reversing the order of the presentation to suggest a series of objectives for the future years in which we should hope to reduce the prevalence of obesity.

In Chapter 2, we emphasized that the planning process for health programs requires input from the perspectives held by a variety of stakeholders. As one of those stakeholders, the public health professional has the primary responsibility for ensuring not only that the planning process is informed by valid and reliable health data, but that those data, and their implications, are presented in a way that all stakeholders understand and can act upon them.[2]

Organization of the Chapter

The remainder of this chapter is divided into seven sections. The first addresses an issue we term "starting in the middle." Since the first formal applications of the Precede Model in the early 1970s, many of those trained in the use of the model have been asked to develop programs where the health problem has been predetermined and where its potential social impact may or may not have been established. This section describes how an understanding of the full Precede-Proceed Model benefits those who find themselves "starting in the middle"; it concludes by reinforcing the reciprocal connection between health and social problems. It also shows how the measures used for the comparisons in setting health goals and objectives in the planning process will also serve as measures for evaluation as the program PROCEEDs.[3]

The second section provides a background review of key principles and terms of *descriptive epidemiology*. Familiarity with these terms and principles will aid planners as they sort through data and as they undertake, in collaboration with other stakeholders, the process of identifying and setting priorities among the health problems upon which their program will focus. The third section describes the steps for identifying priority health problems and establishing program goals and objectives to address those problems.

The fourth section highlights the key terms and principles used in *etiological epidemiology*—identifying the major modifiable risk factors, risk conditions, and other determinants of health problems. Planners will find a working knowledge of these principles and terms and those reviewed in the second section to be of value not only in the program planning process, but also in communicating the rationale and purpose of the program to others. The fifth and sixth sections are extensions of the fourth section in that they outline the process and steps undertaken to identify and prioritize the behavioral (section 5) and environmental factors (section 6), factors deemed to be the most important and modifiable determinants of the identified health problem(s).

The final section, "Evaluation Summary" describes how critical elements of evaluation are by-products that naturally grow out of the combined processes of epidemiological, behavioral, and environmental diagnoses.[4]

STARTING IN THE MIDDLE:
A REALITY FOR PRACTITIONERS

Before examining the methods and procedures for carrying out the process of epidemiological diagnosis, we want to clarify what we mean by "starting in the middle." As a logic model, the Precede-Proceed process ideally begins with a social assessment that (1) yields insight into the quality of life for a given population, and (2) promotes collaborative actions designed to foster local participation in the planning and implementation process.

That assessment is followed by a delineation of the priority health problems relevant to the findings of the social assessment. The reality for a majority of practitioners and organizations, however, is that the health issue *is* the starting point, rather than the second phase of planning as the Precede-Proceed logic model on the title page of this chapter would imply. Thus, for many the task of planning is undertaken in a context where a health problem or issue is predetermined. Such would be the case at some level of predetermined health problems for a nurse in the office of maternal and child health at a local health agency; a health educator in the injury prevention and control division in a state or provincial health department; the tobacco control director for the American Cancer Society; and, often, the coordinator for a work site wellness program. Because the general health goal is a fait accompli in each of these cases, planning will logically start with an analysis of the various environmental and behavioral factors that loom as potential determinants of the predetermined health issue.

Three Reasons Why Planners
Should Know the Whole Model

One may ask, if "starting in the middle" is so often the norm, why bother having a command of both the social diagnostic and epidemiologic diagnostic phases of the Precede-Proceed model? We offer three very practical reasons.

Reason 1.   First, "often" isn't always. There are clearly circumstances when community and/or organizational health program planning efforts are initiated precisely for the purpose of establishing program priorities based on the unique social or economic needs and circumstances of a given population. In those instances the planning process is used to clarify and sort out multiple health and social issues and concerns and to establish mutually agreed upon priorities for program and policy action—ideal circumstances for the application of both social and epidemiological diagnoses. Recognizing this need, the National Association of County and City Health Officials (NACCHO), in collaboration with CDC, developed an online planning process called Mobilizing for Action Through Planning and Partnerships (MAPP). The MAPP process, which closely aligns with and complements many aspects of the Precede-Proceed process, provides a variety of tools and methods designed to help community health program planners in their efforts to establish local health priorities.[5]

Reason 2.   Sometimes, when the health problem is predetermined, that problem is viewed as the *end,* not a *means* to some other end. To avoid the mistake of casting health as an ultimate, rather than instrumental, value, planners will find it useful to look back over their shoulders to understand why this health problem or issue matters—to affirm the connection between the health status of a population and its quality of life. This connection has been formally established in the international public health community through the International Classification of Functioning, Disparity, and Health (ICF).[6]

Developed by the World Health Organization (WHO) and adopted by 151 WHO member countries, the overall aim of the ICF is to provide a standard language and framework for the description of health and health-related states. Functioning and disability are viewed as a complex interaction between the health condition of the individual and the contextual factors of the environment as well as personal factors. The ICF frames these dimensions as interactive and dynamic rather than as linear or static. It allows for an assessment of the degree of disability, although it is not a measurement instrument and it is applicable to all people, whatever their health condition. It has been designed to be relevant across cultures as well as age groups and genders, making it highly appropriate for heterogeneous populations. As a classification system, ICF systematically groups different domains for a person in a given health condition (e.g., what a person with a disease or disorder does or can do), and it serves as an organizational framework for assessment of a wide range of social and environmental issues or consequences related to health status. Those consequences are grouped into three categories:

Impairment (any loss or abnormality of structure or function)

Activity limitation (difficulties an individual may have in executing activities in manner or range considered normal)

Participation restriction (problems an individual may experience in involvement in life situations)

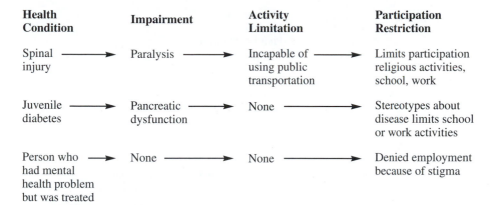

FIGURE 3-1 Examples of disabilities associated with three categories of functioning linked to a health condition
Source: Based on World Health Organization (2001). *International Classification of Functioning, Disability and Health.* Geneva: World Health Organization.

Figure 3-1 displays the sequence of the three categories as they are connected to the disease or disorder (health problem) and to social and quality-of-life outcomes. Although depicted in a linear progression, the relationships among the three dimensions are much more complex and interdependent, just as the association between health and social problems in the Precede-Proceed Model is reciprocal, as characterized in the previous chapter.

When planners explore the potential benefits that might accrue to the population if a program or policy accomplished its health improvement goals, they will be simultaneously addressing broader social concerns and issues. Sensitivity on the part of decision-makers and the general public to these potential social benefits can be instrumental in sustaining support for a program. For example, programs and policies that are effective in reducing youth violence will create a safer environment. In turn, safer communities will make it more likely that residents will walk in their neighborhoods and perhaps even create and promote the use of recreational facilities in those neighborhoods. Also, commercial enterprises are more apt to make investments in those places deemed to be safe.[7]

Reason 3. A third set of reasons for having a working understanding of both the social and epidemiological diagnoses is related to evaluation. In those cases where a given health problem or issue has been declared the focal point for a program, planners can get a head start on the evaluation process by thoroughly familiarizing themselves with any baseline data on the focal point of the program. Over time, evaluation strategies and program direction will be influenced by a working knowledge of the baseline indicators that were used to determine the health priority. That same *working knowledge* can help planners make program adjustments based on changes in demographic trends or technological advances. For example, categorical programs and surveillance systems focusing on the early detection and treatment of breast and cervical cancer

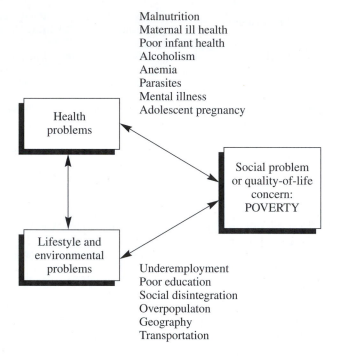

FIGURE 3-2 The examples here of health, lifestyle, and environmental factors interacting with poverty in reciprocal relationships support an ecological approach to assessment that cannot be rigidly linear or unidirectional in addressing causes and effects.

have served as the foundation for a more comprehensive approach to cancer prevention and control as the technical capacity to screen and treat other cancers has developed and improved.[8] Evaluation, as the middle part of the word implies, involves "valuing." The values placed on health relate to the social, economic, and emotional consequences of specific health outcomes, so evaluation has to take these into account and can do so more systematically if it can be based on a prior social diagnosis.

Maintaining a Reciprocal Balance

By definition, the reciprocal, ecological nature of health and social problems means that causation is multidirectional. The relationships in Figure 3-2 are supported by growing scientific evidence documenting the powerful influence that social, economic, and environmental factors have on health status.[9] It illustrates how poverty, health, lifestyle, and environmental factors can be viewed in an ecological perspective of reciprocal relationships. Such a categorization of factors can help planners gather relevant information that will provide the rationale, if not a mandate, for crafting programs directed at health-related factors that are framed within a broader social and ecological context. For example, migrant workers and their families might suffer from poor access to organized social support systems such as education and welfare. Poor roads or geographic isolation might contribute to poverty, as might lack of jobs. In addition, social biases regarding racial or ethnic minority status frequently contribute to social and health problems.[10]

Health programs undertaken by governmental health agencies are sometimes criticized for not placing greater emphasis on the social and economic factors. This lack of emphasis is in part a function of the way public health programs are funded. Planners are informed that their programs must focus on tightly defined categorical imperatives (specific diseases or risk factors), the appropriations for which have been made by federal or state legislators or local commissioners. Those mandates, coupled with the reality that the expenditure of tax dollars will be carefully audited, inhibit planners from using health agency resources to address social issues even though evidence of a connection may have been documented.

Participatory Research as Part of Participatory Planning

Effective planners can maintain the spirit of those regulatory realities and address the social dimensions connected to health problems by acting on one of the main points emphasized in Chapter 2: *that planning health programs inevitably requires the active participation and input from partners outside the traditional health sector.* Many of those partners will be associated with public, private, or philanthropic organizations whose missions and mandates focus on critical social or economic issues that the health agency would find difficult to tackle alone. For example, the Seattle Partners for Health Communities (SPHC) is a multidisciplinary collaboration of community agencies and interest groups that carries out participatory research aimed at improving the health of socioeconomically marginalized communities.[11] The stated goal of the SPHC is "to identify promising approaches through which communities and professionals can collaboratively address the social determinants of health" (p. 362). One of the SPHC projects focused on the problem of childhood asthma. Here is the list of collaborative partners with a key stake in the outcomes of that project:

- American Lung Association
- Center for Multicultural Health
- Community Coalition for Environmental Justice
- League of Women Voters
- Odessa Brown Children's Clinic
- Parent and Child Development Center
- Seattle Housing Authority
- Seattle Tenants Union
- Washington Toxics Coalition
- Seattle-King County Health Department
- University of Washington School of Public Health

The organizational diversity of this coalition creates the potential for leveraging resources, data, and support not only from the public and nonprofit health sector but also from other key sectors including justice, child develop-ment and education, cultural diversity, parent groups, political advocacy, and housing. It is evident that sustained and committed engagement of these part-ners in a health program will depend upon the extent to which they can see that the health goals of the program also contribute to and complement the goals and aims of their respective agencies and organizations. They will see that more clearly if they have participated in the formative research and evalu-ation process as part of the planning process.

KEY PRINCIPLES AND
TERMS OF DESCRIPTIVE EPIDEMIOLOGY

For planners and practitioners, the process of assessment and diagnosis is informed as they seek and obtain answers to five epidemiological questions:

1. What is the problem?
2. Who has the problem?
3. Why do those with the problem have it?
4. What are we going to do about it?
5. How will we know if our programmatic actions are having the intended effect?

The first three of these questions are addressed in this chapter. The third ques-tion is further examined in Chapter 4. The fourth question focuses on the devel-opment or section of intervention strategies and is specifically addressed in Chapter 5 and again in Chapters 6–9. Evaluation is at the heart of the fifth ques-tion, and it is integrated and addressed throughout the book. To illustrate, here are the five epidemiological questions reframed as evaluation questions:

1. How has the problem been affected subsequent to the introduction of the program?
2. Have the people who have had more of the problem benefited from the program (e.g., reduced disparities)
3. Have some of the determinants of the problem been reduced?
4. Have we effectively implemented the critical components of the program?
5. Can we attribute effects observed in the answers to questions 1–3 to the program?

Epidemiology: A Definition

Epidemiology is the study of the distribution and determinants of health-related conditions or events in defined populations and the application of this study to control health problems.[12] A closer examination of the components of this definition reveals why the principles of epidemiology are relevant for all phases of the Precede-Proceed planning process.

First, the word *study* implies a planned examination of health problems through a combination of methods: (1) observation and surveillance and (2) interpretive analysis. *Distribution* is an important concept because it highlights the reality that health problems are not distributed equally within or across populations. Not everyone is at the same risk of having, or eventually developing, a given health problem.

Determinants refer to those factors and conditions that influence health. Over time, we have come to use adjectives such as *physical, biological, social, economic, environmental, cultural, behavioral,* and *emotional* to make distinctions among a variety of different categories of determinants. These multiple determinants, many of which interact with one another, provide key insights for those responsible for health program planning and evaluation. These two dimensions, distribution and determinants, distinguish the two major parts of this chapter, the first addressing descriptive epidemiology and the second addressing the etiological analyses needed to identify relevant determinants.

Health-related conditions refers to specific, measurable events. Examples include diseases, injuries, disabilities, causes of death, behavior such as use of tobacco, or the provision and use of health services. *Specified populations* refers to those who either have, or are at risk for having, one or more health-related conditions. An example would be a population or subpopulation living in or around areas where environmental conditions may put them at risk (e.g., living in areas with high sun exposure increases the chances for skin cancers, or children with asthma living in roach-infested housing increases the likelihood of asthma attacks). Finally, the phrase *application to control* refers to the ultimate aim of epidemiology—using the information gathered as the basis for developing programs and policies to promote, protect, and restore health. In the examples that follow in this chapter we will see that epidemiology provides planners with rich descriptive insights that will help them not only as they sift and sort through various health indicators, but also in their efforts to explain the relevance of those indicators to others.

It has long been the tradition of the health professional to interpret local data in the light of medical and epidemiological knowledge about cause-and-effect relationships and the natural history and distribution of the health problems in the wider population. By showing the magnitude and distribution of health problems in the population, descriptive epidemiological data suggest the relative importance of the health problems as measured and compared by use of vital statistics such as fertility, morbidity, disability, or mortality. Such data also suggest how the health problems vary among subgroups of the population. Thus, a planner's ability to describe and quantify health problems in sufficient detail will help determine which health problems should receive priority attention.

In sum, the epidemiological analysis of health data is essential to the planning process because it

- Establishes the relative importance of various health problems in the target population as a whole and in population subgroups
- Provides evidence for setting program priorities among the various health problems and subgroups
- Identifies the relative importance of various determinants or factors, mainly in the environment, in people's behavior that are influencing the health problems

- Establishes markers and indicators essential for program evaluation, with data that represent before-program baseline measures against which data collected postprogram or during implementation of the program can be compared to assess progress toward objectives

What Is the Problem?

The classic indicators of health problems are **mortality** (death), **morbidity** (disease or injury), and **disability** (dysfunction). Sometimes, discomfort and dissatisfaction are added, making a list of "five D's" extending into quality-of-life measures. In addition, there are positive indicators of health status, such as health-related quality of life, life expectancy, and fitness.[13] Since 1982, mortality has been expressed increasingly in recent years as *years of potential life lost* (YPLL) to give greater weight to deaths at younger ages. This measure is more sensitive to the preventable mortality in children, youth, and the adult "productive" years.[14] Fertility measures among the vital statistics collected in virtually every jurisdiction in the world provide another measure used in health planning. Indirect measures of health, including environmental, behavioral, and social indicators, also serve in lieu of direct measures. These are becoming increasingly important as public health and medical care confront prevention issues related to chronic diseases for which direct measures may not show up for many years after the onset of the condition.

Comparative data on these indicators are available from a variety of sources, all of which have online web sites. These include the National Center for Health Statistics, Centers for Disease Control and Prevention, and other agencies of the Department of Health and Human Services (or the ministries of health in other countries). Local and state or provincial health departments and ministries, the Bureau of the Census (see the annual *Statistical Abstract of the United States*) and Statistics Canada, professional journals and associations, voluntary health associations, and the World Health Organization all have web sites with data. One can easily search these for statistical information on specific diseases, injuries, vital statistics, and survey data. Many of these sources include charts and graphs one can download to use in local planning meetings, bringing the data to life for community groups in much the same way as does the obesity example given at the outset of this chapter.

Rates

One can make data comparisons only between like data—apples with apples, oranges with oranges. For example, expressing rates of death and disease uniformly as "number per thousand population per year" allows direct comparisons between populations of different sizes within the same period and over time. It does not mean much to say, "In 2001, County Z had 48 fatal injuries, and its state had 1,712." Because the state is much bigger than the county and the size of neither is given, one cannot compare the numbers. One must first turn them into rates. A *rate* is the number of events (in this case, fatal injuries) for some common base population, usually per 1,000 or 100,000 population.

To generate rates in our example, one could do the following:

- First, divide the number of deaths in the county by the population of the county
- Then, divide the number of deaths in the state by the population of the state
- Finally, multiply the results by a multiple of 10 to obtain values preferably between 1 and 100

This calculation enables one to compare data with common properties: The injury death rate in County Z within the United States is 55.8 deaths per 100,000, and that of the state is 36.4 deaths per 100,000. Because the county has a higher rate of fatal injuries than does the state as a whole, further examination is warranted to determine what factors might explain the differences. For example, knowing that fatal injuries are more common among younger age groups, planners might want to see if the age distribution of the county might explain a portion of the difference observed. Summary descriptions of the epidemiological rates commonly used to support planning are presented in Table 3-1.

Specific and Adjusted Rates

Rates may need other kinds of statistical control or adjustment to make them equivalent for comparison. For example, data from different years or locations may need to be age specific and **age adjusted** to account for different age distributions in the populations. Figure 3-3 shows the age-specific overweight rates per 100 population in United States from 1960-2000 for three different age groups: 6–11, 12–19, and 20–74 years, respectively. Because the rates are age specific for a broader range of ages in the adults (20–74), they must also be age adjusted to a population standard so that changes in the distribution of ages during the 40-year span of this chart are taken into account. For children, overweight was defined as a body-mass index (BMI) at or above the sex- and age-specific 95th percentile BMI cut points from the 2000 growth charts for the United States. With these statistical controls on age, the trends for increasing overweight must be ascribed to some factor or factors other than the changing age structure of the nation.

If you were looking for the leading causes of death for white males, age 18–24, you would ask for an age-race-sex-specific rate. Comparing the rates of different groups can provide a clearer picture of the relative importance of health problems among or between those groups. If we examine the differences in cause-specific death rates among socioeconomic groups, we can identify causes of death that are more important for the poor or for the affluent. Comparison of rates within a group also can be instructive.

Incidence and Prevalence

Two rates deserve particular discussion: incidence and prevalence. Though both measure morbidity (disease or injury) in the population, they have important differences. **Incidence** measures *new* cases of the disease within a certain

TABLE 3-1 Common epidemiological measures for comparison purposes; their numerators, denominators, and multipliers for standardized expression of number at risk

Natality Measure	Numerator	Denominator	Expressed per Number at Risk
Crude birth rate	# live births reported during a given time interval	estimated total population at midinterval	1,000
Crude fertility rate	# live births reported during a given time interval	estimated number of women age 15–44 years at midinterval	1,000

Morbidity Measure	Numerator	Denominator	Expressed per Number at Risk
Incidence rate	# new cases of a specified disease reported during a given time interval	average or midpoint population during time interval	variable: $10x$ where $x = 2, 3, 4, 5, 6$
Attack rate	# new cases of a specified disease reported during an epidemic period of time	population at start of the epidemic period	variable: $10x$ where $x = 2, 3, 4, 5, 6$
Point prevalence	# current cases, new and old, of a specified disease at a given point in time	estimated population at the same point in time	variable: $10x$ where $x = 2, 3, 4, 5, 6$
Period prevalence	# current cases, new and old, of a specified disease identified over a given time interval	estimated population at midinterval	variable: $10x$ where $x = 2, 3, 4, 5, 6$

Morbidity Measure	Numerator	Denominator	Expressed per Number at Risk
Crude death rate	total number of deaths reported during a given time interval	estimated midinterval population	1,000 or 100,000
Cause-specific death rate	# deaths assigned to a specific cause during a given time interval	estimated midinterval population	100,000
Neonatal mortality rate	# deaths under 28 days of age during a given time interval	# live births during the same time interval	1,000
Infant mortality rate	# deaths under one year of age during a given time interval	# live births reported during the same time interval	1,000

Source: Adapted from *The Principles of Epidemiology,* 2nd ed. (Atlanta: Centers for Disease Control and Prevention), available from the Public Health Foundation at http://bookstore.pdf.org/prod12.htm or may be downloaded at http://www.phppo.cdc.gov/PHTN/catalog/pdffile/Epi_Course.pdf., accessed Dec. 3, 2003. The online epidemiology self-study course, SS3030 is at http://www.phppo.cdc.gov/PHTNOnline/registration/detailpage.asp?res_id=227.

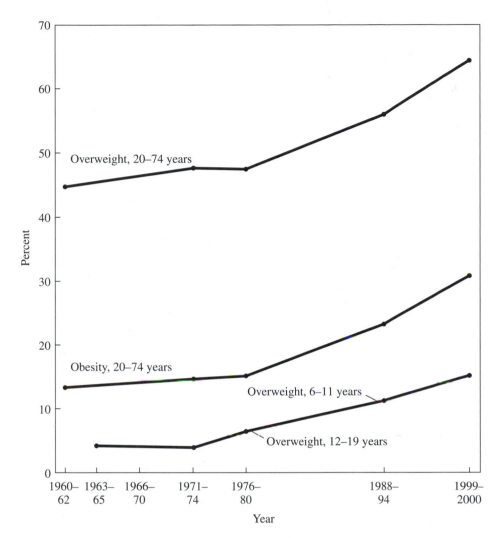

FIGURE 3-3 Overweight and obesity by age: United States, 1960–2000, with adult rates age adjusted.

Notes: Percents for adults are age adjusted. Overweight for children is defined as a body mass index (BMI) at or above the sex- and age-specific 95th percentile BMI cut points from the 2000 CDC Growth Charts: United States. Overweight for adults is defined as a BMI greater than or equal to 25 and obesity as a BMI greater than or equal to 30. Obesity is a subset of the percent with overweight.

Source: National Center for Health Statistics (2003). *Health, United States, 2003.* Hyattsville, MD: Centers for Disease Control and Prevention, U.S. Department of Health and Human Services, DHHS Pub No. 2003–1232, p. 38. Data from National Health Examination Survey and National Health and Nutrition Examination Survey.

period, whereas the **prevalence** of a disease (or a risk factor) is a measure of that portion of the population that represents cases at a particular *point* in time.

Incidence.   Although incidence rates for population groups are hard to find, especially for chronic diseases, they can reveal important insights for planners.

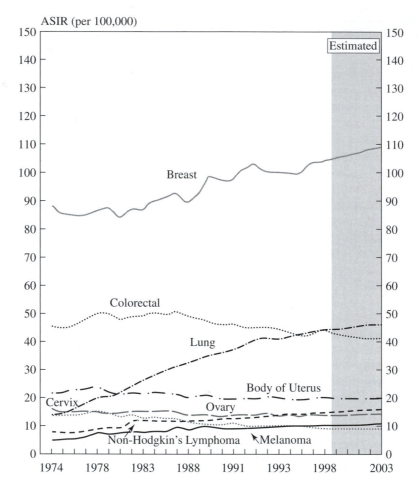

FIGURE 3-4 Age-Standardized Incidence Rates (ASIR) for Selected Cancer Sites. Females, Canada, 1974–2003

Note: Rates are standard to the age distribution of the 1991 Canadian population. For 2001, Quebec incidence is estimated.

Source: Surveillance and Risk Division, CCDPC, Health Canada

For example, Figure 3-4 shows the age-standardized incidence rates for selected cancer sites among Canadian women for the years 1974–2003. Figure 3-5 shows the age-standardized mortality among Canadian women for the same cancer sites over the same period of time. One notes that the incidence of breast cancer has increased (Figure 3-4) while the mortality from breast cancer has decreased (Figure 3-5). The increasing incidence rates for breast cancer coincide with public health screening efforts to enhance the detection of breast cancer. The declining breast cancer mortality rates are at least in part a manifestation of early treatment of breast cancer thanks to the effectiveness of those early detection efforts.

Prevalence.   Prevalence rates and incidence rates give health planners complementary, but different, information. Prevalence reflects both the incidence and

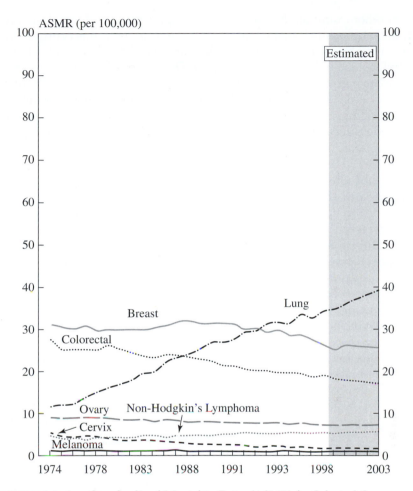

FIGURE 3-5 Age-Standardized Mortality Rates (ASMR) for Selected Cancer Sites. Females, Canada, 1974–2003
Note: Rates are standardized to the age distribution of the 1991 Canadian population.
Source: Surveillance and Risk Assessment Division, CCDPC, Health Canada

the duration of disease. Suppose Diseases A and B have equal incidence rates, but Disease A is mild and unlikely to be life threatening, while B is severe and causes early death. Disease A will have a higher prevalence in the population, because those who died from Disease B are no longer around to be counted when the prevalence survey is done! Just looking at the prevalence rates could mislead you in determining which disease affects a population most.

This is illustrated by comparing common allergies with AIDS. Because of both a higher incidence and a much milder disease course, allergies have a much higher prevalence than does AIDS. It would certainly be incorrect to deduce from the higher prevalence that allergies are more important, because here the one with the low prevalence causes death. When drug therapies proved effective in prolonging the lives of people with AIDS, the prevalence of the disease increased even though the incidence was declining.

In another example, the prevalence of Type 1 (insulin dependent, juvenile onset) diabetes is much higher today than it was early in this century, because improved treatment and self-management of the disease now allows those diabetics to live longer (and thus be counted). These examples illustrate that when one compares prevalence rates, one needs additional information about severity and duration to determine which diseases matter most. Although prevalence rates combine information about incidence and duration, and so must be interpreted with care, they are important for allocating resources and planning health programs.

Prevalence of Chronic Disease Rates: A Word of Caution.   Relying on the prevalence rates of chronic diseases, or of deaths, can be misleading in relation to setting health goals and priorities for the future. That is, prevalence data on chronic disease or even deaths this year may in fact be of limited utility for targeting health promotion priorities to prevent the future diseases and deaths that will be associated with current living conditions and behavioral trends. For example, we can say that "smoking is the number-one preventable cause of deaths" because we are reaping the lung cancers, lung diseases, and heart attacks of people who started smoking as many as 20 years ago. Considering the dramatic declines in smoking in advanced economies the past two decades, we might be more accurate in saying that "smoking that began 10 to 20 years ago is the number-one cause of deaths today." Ironically, our awareness of the prevalence of risk factors helps us counter the caveat just mentioned. Today's true main "causes of deaths," the ones that will cause the most deaths in the future, will in large part be explained by risk factors. Will tobacco remain a high priority, or will it be alcohol, poverty, social isolation, dietary fat, physical inactivity, or a combination thereof? We consider risk factors in greater depth in a later section of this chapter and in the next.

Surveillance

The word *surveillance* is derived from the French term *surveiller*, which means "to watch over." Hockin defines *health surveillance* as the "ongoing, systematic use of routinely collected health data to guide public health action in a timely fashion."[15] In the specific context of public health, surveillance data serve as critical indicators used by planners in developing health programs and policies. Most of the public health data systems that monitor health trends over time were designed many years ago for **surveillance** of communicable disease outbreaks. A substantial portion of such surveillance is based on information provided by physicians who (1) follow prescribed reporting guidelines for a "reportable disease" and (2) submit their findings through the appropriate channels. The emergence of severe acute respiratory syndrome (SARS) is evidence that, globally, infectious diseases continue to be an important cause of disease. At the same time, the early detection and containment of SARS confirms the importance of having an effective and responsive surveillance system in place.

As chronic noncommunicable diseases and injuries have steadily emerged as the predominant threats to health globally, health authorities are required to report some specific noncommunicable diseases and conditions associated with exposure to contaminants or toxic agents so that health officials can be alerted and better prepared to intervene on these emerging conditions. In the United States, surveillance began with, and continues to depend heavily upon, the National Vital Statistics System (NVSS). This system grew out of the need to meet two concurrent regulations: (1) state laws requiring that death certificates be completed for all deaths, and (2) federal law mandating national collection and publication of vital statistics data. State health agencies have the responsibility for maintaining a system that correctly documents the cause of death for every resident. Through cooperative activities of the states and the National Center for Health Statistics (NCHS), CDC, standard forms, and model procedures are developed and recommended for state use. Federal and state health agencies share the costs incurred by the states in providing vital statistics data for national use.

Thanks to continuous advances in epidemiological research into the etiology of health problems, combined with parallel advances in communications technology and the Internet, today's planners have ready access to sophisticated sources of health information and problem-specific surveillance data. For example, the Surveillance and Risk Assessment Division in Health Canada has a very user-friendly online web site that displays the chronic disease trends in Canada, and these trends are updated as new data are gathered. Users interact with the system and are able to examine chronic disease mortality across disease categories over time by province, age group, and sex. Data can be printed out using numerical formats, charts, or mortality maps.[16]

As survey tools to identify the prevalence of behavioral and environmental risk factors have developed, they too have merged into systems of surveillance. Notable examples in the United States include the Behavioral Risk Factor Surveillance System (BRFSS), the Youth Risk Behavior Surveillance System (YRBSS), the National Youth Tobacco Survey (NYTS), and the Youth Tobacco Surveys (YTS). Versions of these systems have been adopted for use in nations throughout the world.

Making Comparisons to Gain Insight

Throughout this section we have made references to comparing health data. Comparisons serve as one of the primary criteria used to determine the relative importance among several health problems, and the use of rates enables one to compare data with common properties. Planners can compare the data of interest in the community they are serving with those of other communities, the state, or the nation. They can also compare data for different health problems within the same community as well as for various subgroups of the community, based on age, race, or gender. Comparing data is equally fundamental to evaluation, as it is to planning; we will return to that point in the evaluation summary at the end of this chapter.

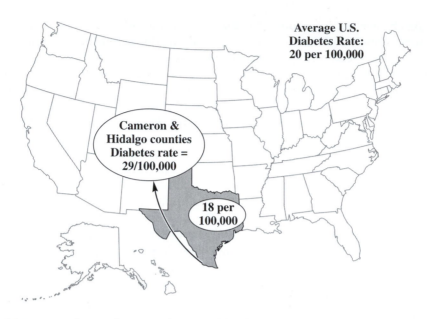

FIGURE 3-6 Comparing rates that reveal local health problems.
Source: National Center for Chronic Disease Prevention and Health Promotion, Centers for Disease Control and Prevention, 2004

Comparing data, especially those with common rates, helps us illustrate how given problems, in specific locations, and perhaps among specific populations, constitute a disproportionate, or higher than expected, health threat. For example, Figure 3-6 shows the year 2000 rates for diabetes at the national level for the State of Texas and the Texas boarder counties of Hidalgo and Cameron. Recalling the five epidemiological questions mentioned earlier in this chapter, we can say that one answer to the first question (What is the problem?) is diabetes. The stark differences between the state rate (18/100,000) and the rates in the two counties (29/100,000) clearly give us insight into responding to the second question: Who has the problem? Answer: selected residents in Hidalgo and Cameron counties. To get answers to the third question (Why do those with the problem have it?) planners will have to make some further assessments. Do the residents of Hidalgo and Cameron counties have the same level of access to affordable preventive services as do residents in those areas where the rates of diabetes are lower? Do residents have access to affordable and culturally acceptable foods known to lower the dietary factors associated with diabetes? To what extent does the built environment in those two counties promote physical activity? Interestingly, planners may already have insights about (if not answers to) questions like those based on findings from earlier social assessment activities they may have conducted, like *asset mapping* and/or a *situation analysis*. These two specific strategies are among the methods described under the heading: "Assessing Capacity: Community Competence and Readiness" in Chapter 2.

TABLE 3-2 Leading Causes of Death in Central Harlem, 2001

| | | | CENTRAL HARLEM COMPARED TO NYC AS A WHOLE | |
| | CENTRAL HARLEM | NEW YORK CITY | | |
	No. of deaths	Death rate (per 100,000 people)*	Death rate (per 100,000 people)*	Higher by	Lower by
All causes	1,465	1,065	736	45%	
Heart disease	418	303	304		5%
Cancer	305	226	167	35%	
AIDS	89	65	22	3 times	
Pneumonia and influenza	64	46	32	45%	
Stroke	61	45	24	90%	
Chronic lung disease	60	45	21	2 times	
Diabetes	55	40	22	85%	
Accidents and injuries	35	25	15	65%	
Drug-related	31	23	10	2 times	
Kidney disease	29	21	10	2 times	

* Age adjusted
Source: New York City Community Health Profiles, New York City Department of Health and Mental Hygiene. Website: http://www.ci.nyc.ny.us/html/doh/html/data/html, accessed Dec. 3, 2003.

Obtaining Data to Make Comparisons

Obtaining current and valid local area data for the purpose of developing health programs has long been a major barrier for planners. Advancements in Web-based technology, however, are helping to lower that barrier as planners are becoming more able to retrieve data electronically at virtually no cost. Globally, national, and state or provincial governments make a wide range of health, demographic, social, and economic data and information available in an equally wide range of formats. And in many cases, these kinds of data are available and accessible online through local government agencies as well.

The New York City Department of Health and Mental Hygiene, for example, has a web site that allows users to access data in easy-to-understand tables and graphics, enabling them to create a health profile based on a wide variety of health indicators, for any one of 38 communities within the five boroughs that make up New York City: Bronx, Brooklyn, Manhattan, Queens, and Staten Island.[17] In addition, the system has the added feature of enabling users to compare communities with one another or with the entire city of New York. For example, Table 3-2 presents the age-adjusted rates for the leading causes of death in the community of Central Harlem compared with New York City as a

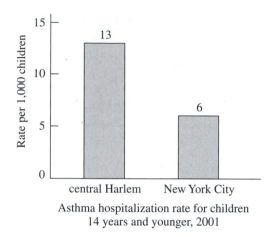

FIGURE 3-7 Severe asthma affects many children in central Harlem
Source: New York City Department of Health and Mental Hygiene. Website: http://www.ci.nyc.ny.us/
html/doh/data/data.html, accessed Dec. 3, 2003.

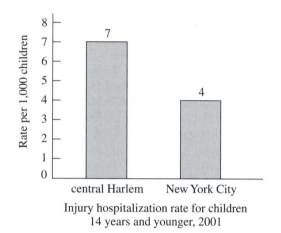

FIGURE 3-8 Children in central Harlem are nearly twice as likely as other New
York City children to be hospitalized with injuries
Source: New York City Community Health Profiles, New York City Department of Health and Mental
Hygiene. Website: http://www.ci.nyc.ny.us/html/doh/html/data/data.html, accessed Dec. 3, 2003.

whole. That comparison clearly reveals the health disparity experienced by the
residents of central Harlem. Figures 3-7, 3-8, and 3-9 show how that same
health disparity is maintained when comparing the children's health issues of
asthma, injuries, and lead poisoning for the same populations. It goes without
saying that such data provide a compelling call for actions to improve the social
and physical environment in which the adults and children of central Harlem
live, work, and play.

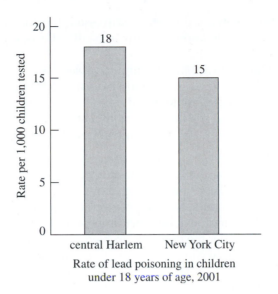

FIGURE 3-9 Lead poisoning—still a problem in central Harlem
Source: New York City Community Health Profiles, New York Department of Health and Mental
Hygiene. Website: http://www.ci.nyc.ny.us/html/doh/html/data/data.html, accessed Dec. 3, 2003.

SETTING PRIORITIES AND
OBJECTIVES FOR HEALTH PROGRAMS

In setting sound program priorities, the skilled planner will exercise his or her
skill in facilitating a process that balances the perceptions of stakeholder with
objectively constructed descriptions of prevailing health problems and how
they are distributed in the target population. The process of selecting one problem or a cluster of related problems for the focus of a program will be informed
as members of a planning team use the data and information they have gathered to seek answers to a series of questions:

Key Questions

1. Which problems have the greatest impact in terms of death, disease, days
   lost from work, rehabilitation costs, disability (temporary and permanent),
   family disorganization, and cost to communities and agencies for damage
   repair or loss and cost recovery?
2. Are certain subpopulations, such as children, mothers, ethnic minorities,
   refugees, indigenous populations, at special risk?
3. Which problems are most amenable to intervention?
4. Which problem is not being addressed by other organizations in the
   community?

5. Which problem, when appropriately addressed, has the greatest potential for yielding measurable improvements in health status, economic savings, or other benefits?
6. Are any of the health problems also highly ranked as a regional or national priority? (State health agencies develop priorities among health problems, often based on local epidemiological data.)
7. To what extent does the problem(s) as manifested in the community constitute a disproportionately high burden compared to other communities or the rest of the state?

The process of working through the health data and information not only enables planners to establish priority program targets, it has the added benefit of revealing early insights into how the program might incorporate the potential preventive, curative, and rehabilitative dimensions of their prospective program. For example, consider the complex problem of motor vehicle injuries.

Prevention efforts might consist of trying to reduce drunk driving, increasing the use of seat belts in combination with consistent enforcement of a legislated speed limit, or employing strategies to improve road markings and conditions in areas where crashes are most common. A curative program would emphasize immediate emergency medical services (including the transportation of injury victims to the appropriate facility). A rehabilitative effort would deal with disabilities resulting from injuries and with increasing the number of victims who regain productive lives and the speed with which they do so. Epidemiological information will provide insights on which facets of the problem will or will not yield to intervention and whether a preventive, curative, or rehabilitative focus should predominate.

Developing Health Objectives

When the health problem has been specifically defined and the risk factors identified, the next step is to develop the program objectives. This vital phase in program planning is often treated quite superficially, with unfortunate consequences for program implementation and evaluation.

Objectives are crucial. They form a fulcrum for converting diagnostic data into program direction and resource allocation over time. Health objectives should be cast in the language of epidemiological or medical outcomes and should answer the four questions of *who* will attain *how much* of *what* by *when*? At each of the phases of the Precede Model, the questions take a slightly different form on the "what," but at this stage it is specifically in relation to health benefits that should be achieved by the nascent program:

- *Who* will benefit from the program?
- *What* health benefit should they receive?
- *How much* of that benefit should be achieved?
- *By when* should it be achieved, or how long should it take for the program to produce a benefit?

> ## GRAFTON COUNTY MATERNAL
> ## AND CHILD HEALTH PLANNING TEAM
>
> A planning team for a maternal and child health unit in a predominately rural county agency is grappling with a range of issues related to the quality of infant care in their county. They have at hand the following information:
>
> - The area of interest is populated mainly by a low-income minority agricultural group with a high rate of teenage pregnancy.
> - The infant mortality rate in this area has remained at 24.9/1000 live births while there has been an overall decline in the state rate to 14.6/1000.
> - The identified pregnancy outcome problems include premature birth, low birth weight, respiratory distress at delivery, and failure to thrive.
> - The visiting nurse service also reports a high prevalence of maternal anemia and a high incidence of gastrointestinal infection and respiratory diseases in infants.
> - Many mothers are at risk because of age (a disproportionate number between ages 14 and 17), poor nutrition, lack of medical care, multiple pregnancies, and pre-eclampsia during pregnancy.
> - Childhood health is poor: Injuries are common, children look malnourished and report for school with handicapping conditions and no immunizations.
>
> While some observers feel that this problem reflects inadequate hospital equipment and facilities to care for neonates, the planning team believes that the data suggest that the real cause probably lies in poor prenatal care, poor maternal and infant nutrition, and lack of infant immunizations.

Consider the box entitled "Grafton County Maternal and Child Health Planning Team." The following program objective could be developed, based on those diagnostic data and consonant with the mission or resources of the given agency:

> The infant mortality rate in Grafton County will be reduced by 10 percent within the first two years and an additional 51 percent over the next three years, continuing to decline until the state average is reached.

The target population *(who)* is demographically implied (pregnant women) and geographically explicit (within Grafton County). *What* is reduced (maternal mortality)? *How much* benefit is to be achieved *by when* is stated in stages: a 10% reduction in two years, a 25% reduction over five years, to continue until the state average rate is achieved. (Note that the average rate for the state will probably go down concurrently, so the evaluation of the program will have to compare itself against a moving target.)

In developing program objectives, the planner should strive to set up the plan so that (1) progress in meeting objectives can be measured; (2) individual objectives are based on relevant, reasonably accurate data; and (3) objectives are in harmony across topics as well as across levels.

The third of these conditions implies *consistency*. It means that objectives dealing with various aspects of a health problem (for example, the objectives of a maternity program to improve nutrition, prenatal appointment compliance, weight and blood pressure control, and percentage of hospital deliveries) should be consistent with and complement each other in a hierarchy of objectives related to the presumed cause-and-effect relationships among them. The causal hierarchy will unfold more clearly as the logic model for the program plan unfolds in the phases ahead.

Objectives should also be *coherent* across levels, with objectives becoming successively more refined and more explicit, and usually multiplied from one level to the next. In the usual language of health planners, goals are considered to be more general than are objectives. For example, the maternal and child health program objective just presented serves a broader program goal of improved quality of life or social conditions caused by poor perinatal or infant health. It is in reality part of a hierarchy of concordant objectives consisting of an overall program goal, a set of more specific program objectives, and several even more specific objectives stated in behavioral terms, environmental, educational, administrative, and organizational terms. So far, we have covered the first two:

1. *Program goal:* The well-being of mothers, infants, and children will be raised through the optimal growth and development of children.
2. *Health objectives:*
   a. The maternal mortality rate within Grafton County will be reduced by 10% within the first 2 years and an additional 51% the next 3 years, with reductions continuing until the state average rate is reached.
   b. The infant mortality rate will be reduced to the state average within 10 years. Perinatal mortality rate will be reduced by 94%. Fetal death will be reduced from x to y percent in the same period.

The more specific behavioral and environmental objectives will emerge from the remainder as we address the behavioral and environmental diagnoses with other examples later in this chapter.

ETIOLOGY:
WHY DO THOSE WITH THE PROBLEM HAVE IT?

The indicators for the successful completion of the first phase of the epidemiological diagnosis just covered are as follows: the identification of health priorities, defined by clear goals and measurable objectives, through a collaborative process using the best health information and data available. We now turn to the next phase of the epidemiological diagnosis that helps planners address the third epidemiological question: Why do those with the problem have it? In this phase planners put into practice the etiological aspect of epidemiology: the analysis and clarification of those factors deemed to be the major determinants of the priority health problem(s) that constitute the focus of the health program.

Collectively, *determinants of health* refer to broad classes of factors that are considered powerful in their cumulative and aggregate effects on the health of populations, primarily because they are forces capable of becoming or shaping behavioral and environmental risk factors. As planners undertake the task of trying to determine which among these wide range of factors, or determinants of health, are most relevant to their health goal, we urge them to organize their analysis into two, parallel categories of factors: (1) the personal and collective *actions* most pertinent to controlling the determinants of health and/or quality-of-life issues selected in the preceding phases, and (2) the wide range of factors and *conditions* in the physical and social environment that may constrain or condition behavior or that may be directly influencing those same health and/or quality-of-life issues. We refer to the former as **behavioral diagnosis** and the latter as **environmental diagnosis.** Many of the factors that fall under the rubric of determinants of health are likely to surface as a part of the environmental diagnosis.

Regardless of where we formally start the planning process, whether with the identification of priority health problems and related social consequences or "in the middle," making a connection between the broadest statement of program mission to the most immediate and precise target, coherence is needed. By maintaining that coherence throughout the Precede-Proceed planning process, stakeholders will be able to see how the systematic achievement of each of the more specific and immediate objectives contributes causally to the achievement of the more general and the more distant objectives and goals.[18]

In the literature the general phrase "determinants of health" is usually preceded by an adjective to identify a specific category of determinants such as: *social* determinants,[19] *economic* determinants,[20] *environmental* determinants,[21] *cultural* determinants[22] and so on. From a technical perspective, we urge planners to keep in mind that the phrase "determinants of health" can be perceived by some as a misnomer insofar as most of the evidence linking so-called determinants with health outcomes is most often based on correlational or relative risk data. In most branches of science, such estimates do not achieve the status of "determinants." In a paper that examines the issue of socioeconomic inequality and health, Norman Daniels and his colleagues make precisely that point:

> Our health is affected not simply by the ease in which we can see a doctor—though that surely matters—but also by our social position and the underlying inequality of our society. We cannot, of course, infer causation from these correlations between social inequality and health inequality. . . . Suffice it to say that while the exact processes are not understood, the evidence suggests that there are social determinants of health.[23]

The implications of this issue for program planners are examined further in the discussion on ecological correlations later in this chapter. Having a good working knowledge of the concepts and terms used to characterize potential determinants of health will help planners as they (1) interpret the relevance, strength, and limitations of existing information about various determinants of health, and (2) ask technical experts to help them obtain data and information about determinants of health that may be potentially relevant.

In the context of public health, risk implicitly refers to several closely related aspects of probability. The "chance" aspect of probability is reflected in a question like: What is the risk of getting HIV/AIDS from an infected needle? Risk can also mean that a factor raises the probability of an adverse outcome. For example, malnutrition, poverty, and unsafe water constitute major risks to the health status of children.[24] Consequence is also an aspect of probability as in, what is the risk of driving while intoxicated? (Answer: being in a car crash that is potentially fatal).

Risk factor, a common term associated with determinants of health, is used to describe an action or condition which, based on evidence from epidemiological studies, has been shown to increase one's probability of developing a disease or health problem. Risk factors are characteristics of individuals; even if they refer to environmental conditions, when measured as a risk factor, they refer the exposure of the individual to that specific environmental condition. For example, exposure to tobacco, either by an individual's use of tobacco or an infant's exposure via tobacco in their environment, is a risk factor for several health problems. Age is a risk factor for a variety of health problems including lead poisoning, osteoporosis, cervical cancer, and injuries from alcohol-related auto crashes. In contrast to risk factors, we use the term *risk conditions* to refer to characteristics of the physical environment that are known to contribute or are strongly associated with health problems, disease, or injury. Lead-based paint constitutes a risk condition because it is highly toxic and, in the absence of early detection and treatment, can cause nervous system and kidney damage. Toxic waste sites, poorly lit roadways, and icy bridges are also examples of risk conditions.

Risk Factors: Finding Relevance for Planning

One of the purposes of epidemiology is to discover and calibrate the strength of risk factors for health problems. Findings from scientific studies serve as the basis for building consensus about the strength of the association between given risk factors and a specific health problem. Measures of risk-factor association relate individuals' exposure to a factor (a possible risk factor) to the development of the health problem of interest (e.g., disease or death) in the same people. The most commonly used measure is **relative risk,** which compares the risk of developing the health problem for people exposed to a factor and for people not exposed. This is done by dividing the incidence of the health prob-

TABLE 3-3 Relative risk for each of the major risk factors for coronary heart disease in middle-aged men are compiled from various sources

Risk Factor	Relative Risk
Smoking	2.0
Hypertension	2.4
Elevated serum cholesterol	2–3 (depending on level of elevation)
Diabetes	2.5
Obesity	2.1
Physical inactivity	1.9

Source: Compiled by Denise Simons-Morton, M.D. Relative risk estimates are from "Report of the Inter-Society Commission for Heart Disease Resources," by W. B. Kannel, et al., 1984, *Circulation, 70*(1), 155A–205A, and various U.S. government sources.

lem in the exposed population by that in the nonexposed to produce a simple equation:

$$\text{Relative risk} = \frac{\text{Incidence of the problem in those exposed to the risk factor}}{\text{Incidence of the problem in those not exposed to the risk factor}}$$

When the incidence of the disease is greater in the exposed group, the relative risk ratio will be greater than one. A relative risk tells you how many *times* greater the risk is in persons exposed to the risk factor. For example, the relative risk of developing coronary heart disease (CHD) in smokers compared with nonsmokers is about 2. This means that smokers have twice the nonsmokers' risk of CHD. Stated another way, they are 100% more likely to develop the disease than are nonsmokers.

The size of the relative risk indicates the comparative importance of the factor to the development of disease. If Factor A has a relative risk of 10 for a particular disease and Factor B has a relative of risk of 2, then you conclude that Factor A is the stronger risk factor. Table 3-3 shows the relative risks of developing CHD for several risk factors. Evidence that the risk factors have about the same impact on disease occurrence, and that the presence of more than one risk factor in the same people further increases the risk of disease, provides a rationale for interventions addressing multiple risk factors.

Relative risk can vary depending upon characteristics of the population being considered. Furthermore, a risk factor can have a variable impact on multiple health problems. Table 3-4 shows the relative risk ratio for smoking and mortality for seven types of cancers. Note that for males, the relative risk of smoking and lung cancer mortality is 22.4. Compare that level of risk with the relative risk of 2.0 for smoking and coronary heart disease for males of all ages in Table 3-3. Stronger epidemiological evidence that a factor increases risk is provided when there is a **dose-response relationship.** Such a relationship is

TABLE 3-4 Smoking and Cancer Mortality Table

		SMOKING AND CANCER MORTALITY TABLE	
Type of Cancer	Gender	Relative Risk Among Smokers	Mortality Attributable to Smoking
		Current	Percent
Lung	Male	22.4	90
	Female	11.9	79
Larynx	Male	10.5	81
	Female	17.8	87
Oral Cavity	Male	27.5	92
	Female	5.6	61
Esophagus	Male	7.6	78
	Female	10.3	75
Pancreas	Male	2.1	29
	Female	2.3	34
Bladder	Male	2.9	47
	Female	2.6	37
Kidney	Male	3.0	48
	Female	1.4	12

Source: Newcomb, P. A. & Carbone, P. P., The health consequences of smoking: cancer. In: Fiore, M. C., Ed. *Cigarette Smoking: A Clinical Guide to Assessment and Treatment.* Philadelphia, PA: WB Saunders Co, 1992, 305–331, *Medical Clinics of North America.*

shown in Table 3-5 for smoking and CHD death: the higher the number of cigarettes smoked per day, the higher the relative risk.

Risk ratio, *odds ratio* (OR), and *standardized mortality* or *morbidity ratios* (SMRs) are other terms used to refer to relative risk. These estimates of the relative risk are also used as measures of association, and they can be interpreted in the same way. Compared to measures of association, such as correlation coefficients, these measures of risk can be translated directly to a meaningful and quantifiable statement about how much more risk is incurred in a population (or by a leap of inference, for an individual) with increased exposure to the risk factor. A relative risk or odds ratio of 1.2, for example, is a 20% increase in risk.

Risk Factor Surveillance

As previously noted, relying on the prevalence rates of chronic diseases, or of deaths, can be misleading in relation to setting health goals and priorities for the future. That is, prevalence data on chronic disease or even deaths this year may in fact be of limited utility for targeting health promotion priorities to prevent the future diseases and deaths that will be associated with current living

TABLE 3-5 Relative risks for coronary heart disease death vary systematically by number of cigarettes smoked per day, shown here for men and women, 40–79 years old

Number of Cigarettes Smoked Daily	Relative Risk	
	Men	Women
Nonsmoker	1.00	1.00
1–9	1.45	1.07
10–19	1.99	1.81
20–39	2.39	2.41
40+	2.89	3.02

Source: Adapted from "Cardiovascular and Risk Factor Evaluation of Healthy American Adults," by S. M. Grundy et al., 1987, *Circulation, 97,* 1340A–1362A. Data are from "Coronary Heart Disease, Stroke, and Aortic Aneurysms," by E. C. Hammond and L. Garfinkel, 1969, *Archives of Environmental Health, 19,* 167–182.

conditions and behavioral trends. Knowledge of the prevalence of risk factors, especially those with measures of relative risk, will keep planners alert for changing trends that, left unchecked, might account for health problems that become prominent in the future. Earlier we mentioned several surveillance systems that focused primarily on documenting and periodically tracking health-related behaviors. Two are highlighted here.

The Behavioral Risk Factor Surveillance System (BRFSS) is a U.S. national, population-based household telephone survey, managed and conducted by individual states to assess the prevalence of health-related behavioral risk factors associated with leading causes of premature death and disability among adults aged 18 and over. Since its inception in the early 1980s, the primary focus of BRFSS data has been on state-level surveillance. Although most public health programs are planned to address health at the local level, most communities do not have good surveillance systems in place to monitor the risk factors on a continuous or periodic basis.[25] To address the need for better local-level risk factor data, more emphasis is being placed on oversampling selected specific population areas within states.[26]

The Youth Risk Behavioral Surveillance System (YRBSS), for example, was developed in 1990 as a national system to monitor the behavioral risk factors that contribute to the leading causes of death, disability, and social problems among youth and adults in the United States. The YRBSS consists of national, state, and school-based surveys of representative samples of students in grades 9–12. Items in the YRBSS address self-reported behaviors related to tobacco use, diet, physical activity, alcohol, and other drug use. Sexual behaviors and behaviors related to unintentional injuries are also included. The surveys, conducted collaboratively every 2 years by staff from the state departments of education and health, are designed to (1) ascertain the prevalence of health risk behaviors, (2) determine trends and changes in those behaviors over time,

TABLE 3-6 Population Attributable Risk (PAR) estimates for six risk factors in the State of Michigan

Risk Factor	Michigan Adult Prevalence, %	PAR Deaths Before Age 65	PAR Life Years Lost Before 65
Smoking	32.4	3,444	38,106
Drinking	7.5 (heavy) 20.5 (moderate)	1,751	51,493
Seat belts[a]	86.5+ (use less than always)	546	17,736
Hypertension	20.6 (uncontrolled)	1,422	15,549
Exercise	65.1 (no regular exercise)	1,024	10,647
Nutrition/weight	17.7 (120% of ideal) 15.0 (111–119% of ideal)	4,088	45,485
Total		12,275	179,016

[a] Before seat belt law took effect.

Source: Health Promotion Can Produce Economic Savings, by Michigan Department of Health, 1987, Lansing: Center for Health Promotion, Michigan Department of Health, p. 7; used with permission of the publisher.

(3) and examine the co-occurrence of behavioral risk factors. A more detailed Youth Tobacco Survey (YTS) on smoking and smokeless tobacco use has been launched in many U.S. states and in more than 90 other countries with the collaboration of CDC and WHO. State-specific data generated by both of these behavioral risk surveillance systems can be directly accessed through the web sites of each state health agency.[27] National and state-level data may also be obtained directly through interactive web sites at the CDC.

Population-Attributable Risk

A partial solution to the mortality-based and relative-risk priority-setting problem just described is provided by the prevalence of those risk factors in the particular population for which one is planning a health promotion program. Where the prevalence of risk factors is known or can be estimated, the projected number of deaths in the population can be estimated. Conversely, the number of deaths in each mortality category can be used to work back to an estimate of the number of those deaths attributable to each of the major risk factors. Table 3-6 illustrates a set of such calculations by the Michigan Department of Public Health's Center for Health Promotion. Take, for example, the smoking example in the first row of the table. A statewide survey showed that 32.4% of Michigan adults were smokers. As shown in Table 3-4, current female and male smokers have a 12 to 22 times greater risk of getting lung cancer and a relative risk of 2 of cardiovascular death, compared with nonsmokers. By combining the prevalence rate for smoking with the mortality from cancer, heart disease, lung diseases, stroke, and fires, each multiplied by a relative risk statistic, one generates

TABLE 3-7 Return on dollar invested in health risk-factor interventions over working lifetime (age 20–64) of those at risk, State of Michigan

Risk-Factor Intervention	$ Discount at 0%	$ Discount at 4%	$ Discount at 8%
Smoking	21.01	15.26	10.88
Hypertension	0.99	0.92	0.84
Nutrition/weight			
Moderate	0.34	0.26	0.18
Severe	0.62	0.48	0.36
Drinking			
Drinking/driving	1.40	1.30	1.19
Heavy drinking	3.17	2.68	2.24
Binge drinking	1.41	1.30	1.19
Sedentary (exercise)	0.42	0.35	0.27
Seat belt	105.07	105.07	105.07
Combined (nutrition/hypertension/exercise)	2.74	2.07	1.50

Source: Health Promotion Can Produce Economic Savings, by Michigan Department of Health, 1987, Lansing: Center for Health Promotion, Michigan Department of Health, p. 9; used with permission of the publisher.

a product known as Population Attributable Risk (PAR). This represents the mortality attributable to smoking. One can express this as the total number of deaths, the number of deaths before age 65 (responding to those policy makers who say, "Ya gotta go sometime"), or total years lost before age 65 (for those policy makers who worry most about "productive" years lost).

Cost-Benefit Analysis From PAR

Once the mortality data have been interpreted in relation to risk factors of known prevalence, the population attributable risk data can be related back to the social diagnosis in a form that has additional meaning to policy makers— namely, cost-benefit analysis. The health department, for example, knows the cost of starting and maintaining a smoking-cessation program. The cost-per-person-enrolled is easily calculated from the experience of the agency in maintaining such programs. On the benefit side, the medical costs associated with all diseases linked to a risk factor (e.g., smoking) and the lost income due to premature death before age 65 can be added up for a dollar estimate of the losses associated with each risk factor. These losses can be interpreted as the potential benefit of controlling the risk factor in question. To obtain a cost-benefit ratio, the potential benefits in dollars can be divided by the costs of interventions needed to achieve those benefits. As shown in Table 3-7, the ratio is expressed as the return on each dollar invested in the risk-factor intervention.

The bottom line on smoking, then, appears to be that smoking is important not just because of high current death rates for past smokers, as shown by the relative risk estimates from exposures in the past. PAR tells us also that with recent smoking prevalence and related death rates projected into the future, smoking could cause thousands of needless deaths and illnesses in the 21st century.[28] Cost-benefit analyses also tell us that because of all the attendant costs following from smoking, the preventable deaths and illnesses would cost 10 to 21 times more than the cost of interventions to prevent them.

Data: Follow the Signs

"All politics are local" and "not in my backyard" are sayings that imply that people will ultimately be most concerned with those matters that are, literally, closest to home. And so it is with health data. The Behavioral Risk Factor Surveillance System (BRFSS), which generates state-level risk-factor prevalence for the leading causes of death, disease, and disability, was launched about the same time as the publication of the first edition of this book. As more and more states joined the system and health officials used BRFSS to justify health program requests, it became apparent that policy makers in those states could no longer say "well those are national estimates and don't necessarily apply to us." And now, the priority for the BRFSS is to place more emphasis on local-level data within states. National and state-level data do paint an important big picture, and for planners at the local level, they can be a useful point of departure that leads to the kind of detail and local nuance needed to tailor programs to address local health priorities. Consider the following scenario.

A nurse educator with a district health department in southeast Missouri is a member of a small planning team. The team was asked by the local health director to prepare a draft proposal requesting resources from the state health department to address a high priority health problem in their region. Basically her assignment was to gather information that will help answer the first two epidemiologic questions: "What is the problem?" and, "Who has it?" She began by examining data according to selected demographic and geographic factors at a macro level. She noted the differences in Tables 3-8 and 3-9, showing the comparisons between Missouri and the United States for (1) the leading causes of death, and (2) selected risk factors and preventive services for adults and high school students. Although Table 3-6 showed that the comparative death rates for diabetes mellitus in Missouri and the United States are similar, further analysis of data from the health department's web site provided her with the kind of additional insight often used to identify program priorities.

Continuing her search, she discovered that in 2000, an estimated 261,000 adults in Missouri; and were diagnosed with diabetes; in 1999 diabetes accounted for 1,554 deaths in Missouri; and in that same year, rates of death from diabetes were 141% higher among African Americans than among whites. The data clearly suggested that African Americans who reside in Missouri were far more likely than whites to suffer major complications of diabetes, including blindness, amputation of limbs, kidney failure, and stroke. She also discovered that the statewide prevalence rates for the risk factors of "no leisure time activ-

TABLE 3-8 Causes of Death, Missouri Compared with United States, 1999*

	Missouri	United States
Diseases of the heart	302.9	267.8
All cancers	210.7	202.7
Stroke	66.1	61.8
Chronic obstructive pulmonary diseases	52.2	45.7
Unintentional injuries	43.8	35.9
Diabetes mellitus	26.6	25.2
Influenza and pneumonia	28.5	23.6
Alzheimer's disease	15.0	16.5
Nephritis and nephrosis	15.2	13.1
All other causes	193.0	189.6

* Deaths per 100,00, age adjusted to 2000 total U.S. population. Bootheel Region of Missouri is located in the southeast corner of the state. The poverty rate for this area is 20.4%, the highest rate among the state's regions. The state's poverty rate is 11.8%. The unemployment rate during 2002 for the Bootheel Region was 7.2%, much higher than the state's rate of 5.5%. The per capita income in the region was only $20,442 during 2001, compared with $28,221 for the state.
Source: CDC, Behavioral Risk Factor Surveillance System, 2000. CDC, Youth Risk Behavior Surveillance System, 1999. http://apps.nccd.cdc.gov/BurdenBook/tabdata.asp?StateID=26#DC.

TABLE 3-9 Risk Factors and Preventive Services, Missouri Compared with United States*

	Missouri	United States
Adults: Cigarette smoking	27.2	22.3
Adults: No leisure-time physical activity	28.8	27.5
Adults: Fewer than five fruits and vegetables	79.3	75.6
Adults: Overweight	56.4	57.3
HSS: Cigarette smoking	32.8	34.8
HSS: Not enrolled in PE class	49.6	43.9
HSS: Fewer than five fruits and vegetables	81.7	76.1
HSS: Overweight	7.8	9.9
APS: No mammogram in last 2 years	24.2	20.4
APS: No sigmoidoscope in last 5 years	73.4	66.3
APS: No fecal occult blood test in last year	82.5	79.2
APS: No health care coverage	13.4	16.4

* Percentage of population.
HSS: High school students   APS: Adult preventive services
Source: CDC, Behavioral Risk Factor Surveillance System, 2000. CDC, Youth Risk Behavior Surveillance System, 1999. http://apps.nccd.cdc.gov/BurdenBook/tabdata.asp?StateID=26#DC.

ity," "eating fewer than five servings of fruits and vegetables per day," and "overweight," were consistently higher for blacks than for whites.[29]

There is an old aphorism that says "in matters of observation, chance favors the prepared mind." Such is the case with our nurse educator. Aware that she was seeking information about health status in the southeast region of the state, a colleague called her attention to a well-documented unpublished formal report that was presented to the board of the Missouri Health Foundation a year earlier. Reading the report she found the following statement, supported by data, in a special section addressing health disparities in Missouri:

> Almost one out of every four African-Americans over the age of 45 in St. Louis, Kansas City, and the Bootheel Region has diabetes. This may be related to obesity: the African-American community over the age 45 has a rate of 40.9 percent; and white of the same age group, a rate of 24.1 percent.[30]

In their serious pursuit for greater insight about the nature and causes of a health problem, planners are often rewarded by uncovering valuable resources, information and/or perspectives of which they were previously unaware.

Ecological Correlations

In making considered decisions about program priorities, planners routinely take into account the relative strength of a given risk factor (if known) in relation to the health problem. To this point, most of the emphasis has been placed on the strength of known risk factors as they are associated with various indicators of health status. Ecological studies offer another means to estimate the relative strength of association between risk *conditions* in environments and rates of disease, injury, or death in populations without having data on individual risk factors. Ecological correlations require large numbers of census tracts, schools, or other local data units from which to draw aggregate data for comparison.

Advantages. Ecological correlations have the advantage of being relatively available through census and other routinely collected community-level descriptors of neighborhoods, political districts, census tracts, blocks, postal code zones, school districts, and so forth. One can produce ecological correlations by correlating aggregate statistics for a large number of population units with data on health status measures for the same group of units. An ecological correlation tells us the characteristics of the social or physical environment or aggregate behavioral norms of a place that are associated with the health measures of the same place. In effect, ecological analyses provide insight on "big picture" connections by illustrating the association between environmental conditions and population health outcomes.

For example, Kawachi conducted two ecological studies exploring the correlation of social capital with health status. In the first, he analyzed the relationships among income inequity, mortality, and measures of social capital based on state-level census data and results of population surveys. He concluded from his analysis that income inequality leads to increased mortality through the reduction (loss) of social capital. In the second study, Kawachi and his colleagues, again using national state-wide health data together with population data on trust and levels of group membership, found a strong inverse association between social trust and group membership and overall mortality (cardiovascular disease, unintentional injuries, and suicide). That is, the higher the former, the lower the latter.[31] Big picture findings from studies like these provide the empirical evidence to support the testing of program interventions designed to address factors in the social or physical environment and assess the extent to which strategic efforts to change those factors influence health.

Disadvantages.   The disadvantage of the ecological correlation is that it does not say whether individuals affected by a given feature of the place where they live are the same people who have the health problem associated with the feature. For example, carried to the extreme, the "fallacy of the ecological correlation" could lead us to conclude from such aggregate data that the people who died from lung cancer in one group of counties with high rates of beer consumption got their cancer because of their beer consumption. The correlation would tell us correctly that people drink much beer in areas where the disease rates are high, and this might be useful data for planning population-based programs. The correlation does not say, however, that those who died from lung cancer drank beer or that those who abstained from beer drinking did not develop lung cancer. Beer drinking might merely have been associated with the large numbers of blue-collar workers, who also had higher smoking rates and higher rates of exposures to carcinogens at their workplaces in neighboring counties. In short, ecological correlations can be useful and efficient ways of drawing attention to social and environmental conditions associated with health conditions. Planners should be cautious in their interpretation, however, to avoid misstating the nature of the association.

An Example: Coal Miners in Appalachia

The following is an example of the use of health status indicators and measures of association in an early project in which the behavioral and environmental assessment procedures of PRECEDE were applied very systematically.[32] The Mineworkers Union wanted to sponsor a health promotion program for a population of coal miners in two northern Appalachian counties of West Virginia. Population data clearly suggested that the incidence of lung disease in coal miners in this area was greater than in other areas of the state, a situation they wanted to change. An important risk factor for lung disease in this area was, not surprisingly, frequent exposure to coal mining.

The behavioral, environmental, and biological determinants of the health problem were studied. Certain epidemiological questions were pursued: Do all miners get lung disease? Who does and does not get lung disease? Are all mineworkers male? Do those who get lung disease have a family history of the disease? Answers to these "who has the problem" questions (age, gender, and family history) identified the high-risk groups.

In general, once one has identified the high-risk groups, one asks questions about behavioral and environmental factors: Is there a higher incidence of disease in workers exposed to different levels of coal dust because of working, for example, in different mine locations? Do some mines have better air circulation, associated with lower rates of lung disease? Is there a higher incidence of disease in smokers than in nonsmokers? These types of questions helped project leaders select the behavioral and the environmental factors warranting further attention.

"Protective" Factors

The effort to gain greater insight on the relationships between risk factors and disease is sometimes construed as negative, driven by a preoccupation with disease. This raises the concern of some who believe that too much attention to epidemiological aspects results in a disease or health-*problem* approach (negative) rather than a health and wellness (positive) approach. We wonder how valid or productive this concern really is.

Attention to and a working knowledge of the complex factors that compromise our health and quality of life do not dictate that the subsequent effort to resolve the problem has to be accompanied by a negative tone. The epidemiological data that pinpoint the causes of a health problem, or the points of intervention to achieve a health goal, need not form part of the message to the public about their role in improving their health.

Data drive policy, and policy generates resources. The use of "negative" information (AIDS is a disease caused mainly by unprotected sex and sharing of needles; smoking causes lung cancer and heart disease), has been instrumental in helping pry loose resources needed for comprehensive school, community, and work site programs. The availability of these resources has enabled wonderfully talented teachers, nurses, physicians, physical educators, and others to develop upbeat wellness programs in health care settings, schools, communities, and work sites.

On the positive side, epidemiological risk factor studies like the classic research of Belloc and Breslow can be turned around to emphasize the factors that can *improve* health. Analyzing data from large-scale surveys of adults in Alameda County, California, they found at least seven personal health practices that were highly correlated with physical health and cumulative in their effect. These included sleeping 7 to 8 hours daily, eating breakfast most days, rarely or never eating between meals, being at or near the recommended height-adjusted weight, being a nonsmoker, using alcohol moderately or not at all, and participating in regular physical activity. The ongoing series of analyses from this longitudinal study also showed a correlation between positive health practices and physical health, rather than the usual relationship between negative risk behavior and mortality and disease. Further analyses also showed that selected social determinants (social support and memberships in associations) accounted for a large part of the positive health profile.[33]

The California investigators followed up the people originally interviewed in 1965, examining mortality records 5.5 and 9.5 years later. They found, for both men and women in all age groups, that those who had practiced more of the health behaviors were less likely to have died than were those who practiced fewer of them. Indeed, at 9.5 years, men who were engaging in all seven practices in 1965 had experienced 72% lower mortality than those who practiced zero to three of the behaviors; for women, the figure was 57%. Most of these relationships held when adjusted for 1965 income level and health status.[34]

Health workers of all disciplines and professional roles share the long-term goal of improving the health and quality of life of the people they serve. To succeed, these workers must have the active and effective participation of such people. Behavior can be a pivotal variable in the relationship between professional or program interventions on the one hand and health or quality-of-life outcomes on the other. Virtually all members of a target population, other than terminally comatose patients, can play an active role in improving their health. Even bedridden, postsurgical patients can make a major difference in postoperative recovery outcomes by the *positive* action they take—for example, by following specific instructions for breathing, coughing, and moving while in bed.[35] At the other end of this continuum, some people participate in or donate to political action to bring about legislation for environmental reforms or enforcement of laws regulating tobacco advertising. Human behavior inescapably influences most of medicine and virtually all of public health.

BEHAVIORAL DIAGNOSIS

Three Levels or Categories of Behavior

In the Precede-Proceed Model, "behavior" surfaces as an important factor at three levels—proximal, direct actions influencing one's own health; actions influencing the health of others within one's immediate environment; and more distal actions on the organizational or policy environment. Based on the relative risk calculations discussed earlier, planners have good evidence showing the strength of a given behavioral risk (smoking) and a specific health problem (lung cancer). Thus, the behavioral action of smoking (or not smoking) has direct health consequences. Said another way, risk behaviors like smoking, or not wearing safety restraints while driving an automobile, are more proximal to the health problems of lung cancer or auto-related injuries than the other two categories. Within the specific context of carrying out a behavioral diagnosis, the focus is on this category of behaviors; that is, those actions (taken by individuals, or groups of individuals) that are known to have a *direct effect* on the health problem or issues in question—hence the term *behavioral risk factor*. In some instances, this definition may also include the actions of others. Examples would include mothers' breast-feeding their infants or the preventive actions of parents to ensure that their children are appropriately immunized.

A second category of behaviors are those actions, or inactions, taken by others that can directly influence the actions of an individual at risk. Although more distal from the health problem than risk behavior, this level of behavior can have a major impact the social or physical environment which, in turn, can result in the support of (or deterrence from) efforts to modify health risk

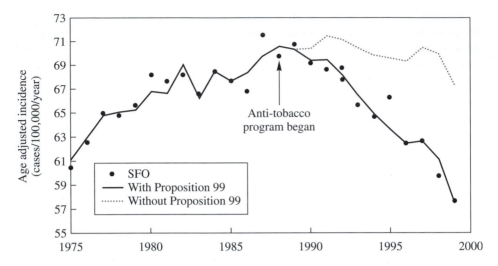

FIGURE 3-10 Lung cancer in the San Francisco area (SFO) before and after the launch of the comprehensive California tobacco control program (solid line), compared with the predicted trend (dotted line) based on other cancer registries in metropolitan areas outside California that had similar historical trends before 1988, but no comprehensive tobacco control program like California's after 1988. *Source:* J. Barnoya & S. Glantz. Association of the California tobacco control program with decline in lung cancer incidence. *Cancer Causes and Control* (in press), 2004.

behaviors. This level of behavior has an *indirect effect* on the ultimate health problem and is an important feature in process of educational and ecological diagnosis described in the next chapter. Examples include the actions of parents toward their children, caregivers toward their patients, teachers toward their students, peers with one another, and so on.

A third category or level of behaviors is represented by those actions taken by individuals or groups that could influence some dimension of the physical, social, or political environment which, in turn, could influence a specific risk behavior or the health problem directly. Even more distal from the health problem than behaviors in the first two categories, this level of behavior is manifested by those in positions where their actions and decision can influence or directly shape the perceptions, policies, regulations, and laws that influence the environments of organizations, communities, states, and nations. Examples include organized actions taken by advocacy groups, actions taken by city planners to create user-friendly environments, legislators passing a clean indoor act, or the board of a corporation instituting an employee wellness program.

Behavior change at this third level can be especially powerful because, in addition to providing an environment in support of healthful behavior, they can have a direct impact on the health problem itself. Such was the case in California when the actions of advocates led to the voter-approved tobacco tax and Health Promotion Act of 1988 (Proposition 99). Subsequent to the passage of that initiative, California experienced dramatic declines in tobacco consumption compared with the other 49 states, which led to parallel declines in California lung cancer rates and heart disease mortality[36] (Figure 3-10). A similar pattern of decline in smoking was observed in Massachusetts after it passed its tobacco tax and launched an even more aggressive tobacco control program, surpassing California's rate of decline, which more than doubled the rate of decline for the other 48 states. Behavior related to this third ecological level of organizational and policy change will be a subject of later chapters.

If planners focus *only* on risk behaviors, ignoring the importance of behaviors in the other two categories and nonbehavioral causes like exposure to hazards in the environment, genetic predisposition, age, gender, congenital disease, physical and mental impairment, and social or economic disadvantage, the programs they develop are likely to have two serious flaws. First, such an approach will inevitably place all of the responsibility for health improvement on the individuals whose health is threatened; programs limited to that narrow focus are likely to yield modest effects and potentially add to the burden of those at risk. Second, programs that focus only on the behavioral actions of those at risk will be not only vulnerable to the charge of "blaming the victim," but also missing the opportunity to address other powerful determinants of health. By keeping an eye on all three levels of behavior (as well as relevant nonbehavioral factors) planners acknowledge the ecological reality that most human health problems can be linked to the interaction between behaviors, environmental conditions, genetic variation, and other nonbehavioral factors, many of which are amenable to change through strategic intervention.

Genetics and Behavioral Interactions

The interactions of genes with behavior and the environment are inherently complex; consequently, they will seldom be treated as independent effects on health, except in a few genetic diseases such as phenylketonuria (PKU), sickle-cell anemia, cystic fibrosis, and Tay-Sachs disease. Applications of genetics to public health practice have already emerged in areas like diet and obesity and will become more useful as our understanding of the human genome grows. The practical implications specifically related to gene-behavior interaction are captured in this interesting passage from Matt Ridley's book, *Genome*:

> We instinctively assume that bodily biochemistry is cause whereas behavior is effect, an assumption we have taken to a ridiculous extent in considering the impact of genes upon our lives. If genes are involved in behavior then it is that they are the cause and are deemed immutable. This is a mistake made not just by genetic determinists, but by their vociferous opponents who say behavior is "not in the genes"; the people who deplore the fatalism and predestination implied, they say, by behaviour genetics. They give too much ground to their opponents by allowing this assumption to stand, for they tacitly admit that if genes are involved at all, then they are at the top of the hierarchy. They forget that genes need to be switched on, and external events—or free willed behavior—can switch on genes. Far from us lying at the mercy of our genes, it is often our genes that lie at the mercy of us. If you go bungee jumping or take a stressful job, or repeatedly imagine a terrible fear, you raise your cortisol levels and the cortisol will dash about the body busy switching on genes. (It is also an indisputable fact that you can trigger activity in the 'happiness centres' of the brain with a deliberate smile, as surely as you trigger a smile with happy

thoughts. It really does make you feel better to smile. The physical can be at the beck and call of the behavioural.[37]

The purpose of the diagnostic phases of PRECEDE-PROCEED is to generate valid information that can be used by planners in their efforts to tailor programs designed to meet the health needs of a given population. Insights into potential individual digenetic variations will enable local-level planners to develop programs and policies that take into account those variations. For example, the uniform dietary guidelines highlighted in the United States Department of Agriculture's (USDA) food pyramid constitute a national recommendation. While those guideline do not, per se, infer that all Americans are the same—culturally, socioeconomically, physiologically, and genetically, they leave little room for variability. Data from the human genome project and other studies show that genetic variation among individuals alters interactions among dietary chemicals that can either lead to health improvement or increased susceptibility to disease.[38]

Obesity has emerged as a serious global health problem. Not only has it reached epidemic proportions in the United States as highlighted at the outset of this chapter, obesity rates having increased threefold or more since 1980 in some areas of the United Kingdom, China, Eastern Europe, the Middle East, the Pacific Islands, and Australia.[39] The global obesity epidemic appears to be the result of modern life—which combines access to and consumption of high calorie foods with decreasing levels of physical activity. Many people appear to respond to this modern life environment by an imbalance that favors energy input over the expenditure of energy and results in overweight, while others do not. What accounts for these differences? Genetic research is beginning to offer some insights. For example, there is strong evidence for a genetic component to obesity. However, genes interact with one another (polygenic) and, collectively, those interactions work in combination with other factors like nutrients, physical activity, and smoking.[40]

Developed by the CDC's Office of Genetics and Disease Prevention, Box 3-1 juxtaposes a series of statements addressing what we know and what we don't know about issues for which genetic research may uncover important insights for prevention. Rapid strides are being made in the pursuit of a better understanding of how variations in our genetic makeup influence various illnesses, risk factors, and biological conditions. The capacity of health program planners will be greatly enhanced as they gain access to answers to questions about genetic variability like those raised in column 2 of Box 3-1.

The science for most of the gene-gene, gene-environment, and gene-behavior interactions is well underway, but not yet developed sufficiently for widespread application. This section on genetics is, therefore, essentially a space-holder for the anticipated opportunities likely to surface for health program planners in the near future. The interaction of genetics with the other two classes of health determinants, behavior and the environment, are indicated by the vertical arrows connecting these three sets of determinants. Most controls on the gene-environment interactions depend on the behavior of individuals and populations, including the behavior of community, national, and

BOX 3-1 Obesity and Genetics: What we do and don't know

What We Know:	What We Don't Know
Biological relatives tend to resemble each other in many ways, including body weight. Individuals with a family history of obesity may be predisposed to gain weight, and interventions that prevent obesity are especially important.	Why are biological relatives more similar in body weight? What genes are associated with this observation? Are the same genetic associations seen in every family? How do these genes affect energy metabolism and regulation?
In an environment made constant for food intake and physical activity, individuals respond differently. Some people store more energy as fat in an environment of excess; others lose less fat in an environment of scarcity. The different responses are largely due to genetic variation between individuals.	Why are interventions based on diet and exercise more effective for some people than others? What are the biological differences between these high and low responders? How do we use these insights to tailor interventions to specific needs?
Fat stores are regulated over long periods of time by complex systems that involve input and feedback from fatty tissues, the brain, and endocrine glands like the pancreas and the thyroid. Overweight and obesity can result from only a very small positive energy input imbalance over a long period of time.	What elements of energy regulation feedback systems are different in individuals? How do these differences affect energy metabolism and regulation?
Rarely, people have mutations in single genes that result in severe obesity that starts in infancy. Studying these individuals is providing insight into the complex biological pathways that regulate the balance between energy input and energy expenditure.	Do additional obesity syndromes exist that are caused by mutations in single genes? If so, what are they? What are the natural history, management strategy, and outcome for affected individuals?
Obese individuals have genetic similarities that may shed light on the biological differences that predispose to gain weight. This knowledge may be useful in preventing or treating obesity in predisposed people.	How do genetic variations that are shared by obese people affect gene expression and function? How do genetic variation and environmental factors interact to produce obesity? What are the biological features associated with the tendency to gain weight? What environmental factors are helpful in countering these tendencies?
Pharmaceutical companies are using genetic approaches (pharmacogenomics) to develop new drug strategies to treat obesity.	Will pharmacologic approaches benefit most people affected with obesity? Will these drugs be accessible to most people?
The tendency to store energy in the form of fat is believed to result from thousands of years of evolution in an environment characterized by tenuous food supplies. In other words, those who could store energy in times of plenty were more likely to survive periods of famine and to pass this tendency to their offspring.	How can thousands of years of evolutionary pressure be countered? Can specific factors in the modern environment (other than the obvious) be identified and controlled to more effectively counter these tendencies?

Source: Office of Genetics and Disease Prevention, Centers for Disease Control and Prevention, U.S. Department of Health and Human Services. *http://www.cdc.gov/genomics/info/perspectives/files/obesknow.htm.*

international decision makers, in the exposure of people to environmental risks; so we have placed behavior between genetics and the environment as a practical matter. This is also consistent with the inclusion of behavior within the use of the term *environment* in most of the genetics literature.

For instructional purposes the process of behavioral diagnosis (as well as the environmental diagnosis in the following section) has been delineated into four steps to highlight important nuances that help keep the process focused on the goal of the program. As planners have used the steps in practice, however, they have discovered that the process is indeed more than the sum or sequence of its parts, one step seamlessly merging with the next, but next steps sending the planners back to revisit and revise previous steps.

Step 1: Listing Potential Behavioral Risks for the Health Problem

Keep an eye on the literature.   The primary task for this step is to list those behaviors that are known to account for some portion of the specific health problem you are addressing. Experienced practitioners, especially those who work in a given health topic over time, are likely to have a good working knowledge of those risk behaviors. Regardless of experience, however, it is prudent to review the literature and current scientific reports of known risk factors for the disease or health problem in question. Since the inception of the Precede Model in the early 1970s, access to risk factor information has grown exponentially. For example "The Burden of Chronic Diseases and Their Risk Factors" is an interactive web site that provides users with access to the "prevention pathways" that link risk factors to specific chronic disease outcomes and the data on those risk factors for each state. The indicators were concluded based on a scientific consensus process undertaken by the Council of State and Territorial Epidemiologists, the Association of State and Territorial Chronic Disease Program Directors, and the National Center for Chronic Disease Prevention and Health Promotion, Centers for Disease Control and Prevention. The indicators were developed to facilitate the following:

- Collection, analysis, and dissemination of epidemiologic data
- Utilization of data and other scientific information for public health decision making
- Prevention and control of chronic diseases through public health action

Table 3-10 shows the risk factors (prevention pathways) for the leading causes of death.

Some of the risk factors under the heart disease category in Table 3-10, including smoking, alcohol abuse, high-fat diet, and sedentary lifestyle, immediately fall into the behavioral category and are clearly behavioral. Although not strictly behavioral, other factors—those associated with elevated serum cholesterol, obesity, and high blood pressure—serve as signposts calling our attention to behaviors like eating habits and inactivity.[41]

TABLE 3-10 The most common priorities for public health and other population-based prevention, health promotion, and health protection programs are the major risk factors and risk conditions associated with the leading causes of death.

Risk Factors and Conditions	Heart Disease	Cancers	Stroke	Injuries (nonvehicular)	Influenza, Pneumonia	Injuries (vehicular)	Diabetes	Cirrhosis	Suicide	Homicides	AIDS
Behavioral risk factors											
Smoking	•	•		•	•						
High blood pressure	•		•								
High cholesterol	•										
Diet	•	•					•				
Obesity	•	•					•				
Sedentary lifestyle	•	•	•				•				
Stress	•		•	•		•					
Alcohol abuse		•		•		•		•	•	•	
Drug misuse	•		•	•		•			•	•	•
Seat belt nonuse						•					
Handgun possession				•					•	•	
Sexual practices											•
Biological factors (e.g., genetics)	•	•	•				•	•			
Environmental risk											
Radiation exposure		•									
Workplace hazards		•		•		•					
Environmental contaminants		•									
Infectious agents		•			•						
Home hazards				•							
Auto/road design						•					
Speed limits						•					
Medical care access	•	•	•		•		•	•	•	•	
Product design				•							
Social factors[a]	•	•	•				•	•		•	•

[a] This category of social determinants of health includes a variety of less well-defined or circumscribed conditions of living related to social relationships, social support, social pressures, early childhood experiences, and socioeconomic status.

Source: Adapted from unpublished material, Centers for Disease Control, U.S. Department of Health and Human Services.

Systems thinking. Further review of the behaviors listed in Table 3-10 reminds us that some of the risk factors and their implicit behaviors are dependent on prior behaviors and on their interaction with environmental circumstances. For example, suppose a blood test reveals that a person, even after efforts to increase level of physical activity and control intake of fat, is found to have an elevated level of serum cholesterol. After an assessment, the physician prescribes a given medication and informs the patient that he needs to return after one month to get another test to confirm whether the initial prescription was working properly with no side effects. "Taking a prescribed medication," while a relatively discrete behavior, is logically influenced by other discrete behaviors such as seeking medical care, obtaining a prescription, and seeing that the medication is modified as necessary, as in the control of high blood pressure in addition to the cholesterol. This cycle of actions and interactions is an example of what is meant by the statement "health behavior is best understood a part of an ecological system." Experienced planners who work in clinical settings understand that this cycle could be sabotaged at many points along the way. For example, a patient may fail to keep an appointment at which prescriptions might be renewed or changed. Failure to keep an appointment could be a result of a variety of possibilities. One can create this kind of systems picture quite simply by asking, at each juncture, "but why?" Many of the answers can be linked to behaviors that might be added to the list you are compiling or could be deferred as a category of behavior taken by others.

Appointments aren't being kept.

But why?

Patients are dissatisfied.

But why?

In some instances they had a bad relationship with the caregiver; in other instances they had to wait 30–45 minutes after the scheduled appointment.

But why did they have to wait too long?

The clinic applied a policy that overscheduled appointments for patients.

Figure 3-11 provides a systems view of the "broken-appointment cycle." This kind of systems-level thinking helps planners identify and isolate concrete behavioral events, in the context of nonbehavioral and environmental factors, that enable them to be more precise in targeting program strategies. Training of staff, adjustment of appointment schedules, and child care or transportation provisions all could become relevant interventions identified by the behavioral assessment reflected in the broken-appointment cycle.

Case example: Roseville. Suppose you were assigned to coordinate the planning of a health program focused on the prevention of heart disease for the hypothetical community of Roseville. As a first step in your behavioral diagnosis, you share the risk factors listed under heart disease in Table 3-10 with the

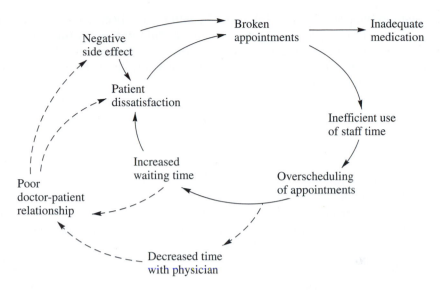

FIGURE 3-11 A systems view of the behavior of keeping appointments can be delineated as a broken-appointment cycle with a sequence of actions and reactions, decisions and choices, branching toward or away from further broken appointments.

other members of the planning team. Based on their collective experiences in Roseville, they think that five risk factors are especially relevant: overweight, cholesterol screening, screening for hypertension, physical inactivity, and smoking. After further discussion, members of the team want to add fruit and vegetable consumption because of its possible connection to overweight. Thus, the starting list included more specific risk behaviors embedded in the more general list of "risk factors":

- Reduce weight (fewer foods high in saturated fat; more fruits and vegetables)
- Get cholesterol screening test
- Get blood pressure screening for hypertension
- Increase physical activity
- Eliminate smoking

Step 2: Rating Behaviors on Importance

On the understanding that no program has sufficient resources to do everything that might be done, the extensive list of behaviors identified in Step 2 now needs to be reduced to a manageable length. This is done first by determining which behaviors are the most important and eliminating (or at least deferring) the least important. The broad criteria for determining the importance of a given behavior include evidence that it (1) is clearly linked to the health problem, and (2) is present (you can document that it occurs) and is prevalent in the population of interest. The latter point becomes especially critical in those situations where a given risk factor, although universally acknowledged to be important, has an unusually low prevalence rate. For example, smoking or drinking alcohol behaviors are not likely to surface as important factors in cultures where they are prohibited.

Continuing the Roseville Case.   To help planning team members weigh the importance of the behavioral factors they have identified, you call their attention to the information in Table 3-3. You point out that relative risk estimates for four of five risks factors on their current list fall within a range of 2.4–1.9, telling you that a person having any one of those risks essentially has twice the chance of developing CHD.

Then, you introduce them to some additional Roseville-specific risk factor information from two sources. The first source provides data from a behavioral risk factor survey of adults aged 18–64 gathered semi-annually over the past decade. Those data reveal the following trends:

1. There has been a steady decline in smoking from 36.8% to a current level of 17.8%.
2. The percentage of those who were not screened for hypertension in the last 2 years has declined and is now stable at 5%.
3. The percentage of those who have had their cholesterol checked in the past five years is 81%, exceeding the Healthy People 2010 objectives.
4. The percentage of the population reported to be overweight rose from 27% to 39%.
5. The percentage of persons reporting no leisure time activity increased from 21% to 30%.

The second source includes information and data gathered the year before in a joint effort carried out by the Roseville School District and the Roseville Health Department. It includes two school-based surveys (one of high school students and one of elementary students) and a short community survey and tobacco policy assessment.* In the survey of students in grades 9–12 they found that 40% of students surveyed indicated that they had used tobacco at least once in the last 30 days. The survey also showed that 11% of male and 8% of female students were overweight. In a companion survey of elementary schools, 13% of male sixth-grade students answered yes to the question: "have you used cigarettes in the last 30 days?" Twenty-four percent of male seventh-grade students answered yes to the same question.

Based on those local risk factor prevalence rates, the planning team concludes that in Roseville, behaviors related to overweight and obesity constitute important problems, especially in light of data showing declines in the levels of physical activity. Since the word *overweight* describes a condition rather than a behavior, the team decides to delineate three specific behaviors known to be

---

* Findings from the community survey and policy assessment will be addressed in the environmental diagnosis section that follows.

associated with the problem of overweight: (1) consumption of food high in saturated fats, (2) consumption of fruits and vegetables, (3) physical activity.

Although there is a very promising decline in smoking among adults, the planning team found the data on smoking among youth troubling and viewed it as a harbinger of things to come. They are aware of the literature indicating that the earlier one initiates smoking, the more likely one is to become a smoker as an adult—a clear sign that postponing the onset of smoking among youth will decrease tobacco use among adults.[42] The planning team was unanimous that smoking *among youth* should be specified as important. They also noted that the preventive behaviors associated with screening for cholesterol and hypertension were moving in the right direction and, for Roseville, may not need to be focal points for program intervention. So, the list of behavioral risk factors deemed to be important for the emerging heart disease prevention program in Roseville were

- Consumption of foods high in saturated fat
- Consumption of fruits and vegetables
- Physical inactivity
- Smoking among youth

The absence of the behaviors related to cholesterol and hypertension screening from this list provides planners with valuable information as they move forward in the planning process. The positive trend in screening sends a signal that prevention is working. It implies that those providing preventive services are doing a good job and that constitutes an asset in Roseville. When such assets are built into health programs as complementary components, they strengthen the comprehensive nature of that program.

Step 3: Rating Behaviors on Changeability

Having established the level importance of selected behaviors, the next step in this phase is to determine if there is reasonable evidence that the behaviors in question can be changed. Given the ongoing evaluation research activities testing the effectiveness of various intervention strategies, it is not possible to generate tables that will provide valid, reliable and up-to-date estimates of the changeability of a given risk behavior. For this reason, planners must take the responsibly to stay abreast of the current literature on evidence-based intervention strategies and use that information as the prime source of their rationale for making professional judgments about changeability.

With that caveat in mind, here are a few practical rules of thumb that will help planners begin the thinking process. A given behavior has a higher probability for change when

- It is still in the developmental stages or has only recently been established
- It is not deeply rooted in cultural patterns or lifestyles
- There is compelling theoretical rationale for its changeability

Most resistant to change, or subject to the highest relapse rates, are those behaviors that have an addictive component (tobacco, alcohol, drug misuse), those

TABLE 3-11 Relative changeability based on perceived attributes of selected preventive health behaviors, as illustrated here for heart-health behaviors

Health Behavior	Relevance	Social Approval	Advantages	Complexity	Compatibility with Values, Experiences, and Needs	Divisibility or Trialability	Observability
1. Quitting smoking	+	+	+	−	−	+	+
2. Controlling weight	+	+	+	−	+	+	+
3. Controlling blood pressure	+	+	−	−	−	+	−
Taking medication	+	+	−	−	−	+	−
Maintaining low-sodium diet	+	+	−	−	−	+	−
4. Maintaining low-cholesterol diet	+	+	+	−	+	+	+
5. Exercising	+	+	+	−	+	+	+
6. Having preventive medical examinations	+	+	+	−	+	−	+

Note: + = positive, − = negative. Changes since the first edition in 1980 reflect changes in social norms and technologies. The only change in a negative direction has been in the complexity dimension of having preventive medical examinations. This is a manifestation of decreased support for indigent care and inaccessibility of health services to the rural and disadvantaged segments of the population in the United States.
Source: Adapted from L. W. Green, "Diffusion and Adoption of Innovations Related to Cardiovascular Risk Behavior in the Public," by L. W. Green, 1975, in A. Enelow and J. B. Henderson (Eds.), *Applying Behavioral Sciences to Cardiovascular Risk,* New York: American Heart Association.

with deep-seated compulsive elements (compulsive eating, compulsive work), and those with strong family patterns or routines surrounding them (eating patterns, work, and leisure). Also, judgments about changeability should include careful consideration of the time factor. What expectations are being held as to when a change in a given risk factor will be manifested? Deeply rooted and widespread behaviors are likely to take a while to change, making the time factor quite important. This issue will be addressed in greater detail in the Evaluation Summary at the end of the chapter.

By testing behaviors for changeability, we come closer to an informed decision on which behaviors we should slate or recommend for intervention. In Table 3-11, the behaviors generated by the Roseville cardiovascular disease–prevention program planning team are among those listed in the rows; the four "rules of thumb" described above are expanded in the column headings of the table to include more specific attributes of health practices or tech-

TABLE 3-12 Assessing the Changeability of Risk Behaviors

Health Behavior	Documented Evidence for Δ	Still in developmental stages	Not deeply rooted in culture/lifestyle	Strong supporting theory
Consumption of foods high in saturated fat	Variable	Variable	Deeply rooted for some in Roseville	Modest
Consumption of fruits/vegetables	Variable	Variable	Deeply rooted for some in Roseville	Modest
Physical activity	Trends promising especially related to environmental strategies	For many, no	Not deeply rooted	Strong
Smoking among youth	Good evidence	Yes	Varies by sex and cultural and ethnic factors	Strong

nologies that predict their rate of adoption. Planners will find this kind of simple analysis helpful as they attempt to estimate the changeability of the risk factors being considered for program intervention. In this instance, the team has chosen to enter narrative assessments based on their reading of the literature and their collective experience.

After reviewing the information in Table 3-11, the Roseville planning team creates their own table, as shown above in Table 3-12. The planning team makes the following decisions: (1) smoking and physical activity were deemed changeable based jointly on findings from the literature as well as positive estimates on the matters of development stage and theory, and (2) the change ability rating of the two eating-related behaviors stimulated considerable discussion and debate.

Some members of the planning team indicate that the dramatic changes in the dietary habits documented in the famous North Karelia Cardiovascular Disease Prevention Project provided specific evidence that the consumption of high-fat foods could be reduced, and that the consumption of fruits and vegetables could be increased, through community-based interventions.[43] While acknowledging that evidence, others call attention to a report from Agency for Healthcare Research and Quality (AHRQ) indicating that even though behavioral research is being conducted to test numerous dietary interventions in a variety of populations, no clear understanding has emerged regarding which interventions are more efficacious in influencing dietary change and for which groups.[44] Thoughtful exchanges of this kind indicate that planners are engaged in a serious and caring examination of options; they also characterize a key element of health program planning: the continuous struggle to strike a prudent balance between scientific certitude and good judgment.

	More important	Less important
More changeable	High priority for program focus (Quadrant 1)	Low priority except to demonstrate change for political purposes (Quadrant 3)
Less changeable	Priority for innovative program; evaluation crucial (Quadrant 2)	No program (Quadrant 4)

FIGURE 3-12 The rankings of behaviors on the two dimensions of importance and changeability leads to at least four categories of possible action.

Step 4: Choosing Behavioral Targets

With the behaviors ranked on importance and changeability, the planning team is ready to select those risk behaviors that will constitute one of several strategic focal points in the total health program. To facilitate the selection process, we recommend that the ratings for importance and changeability be arranged in a simple fourfold table, as shown in Figure 3-12.

Depending on the program objectives, the behavioral objectives will most likely originate in Quadrants 1 and 2. Evaluation is crucial when one is uncertain about whether change will occur. Behaviors in Quadrant 3 will be unlikely candidates. Two exceptions to this might arise. One involves a political need to address a lower priority behavior. For instance, a community group representing the taxpayers who support the agency might insist on their preference for a behavior that scientific review has deemed less important. The other exception might arise when an administrator or steering committee needs to see "evidence" of some change before investing in more costly behavioral interventions. When such a need exists, the behaviors should be given priority on a temporary basis only, and only if the planner can proceed with assurance that no harm will be done. In some instances, it is possible that no behaviors will surface in Quadrant 1; this is most likely to occur because of limited evidence on changeability. If the health problem is urgent, then extensive educational and behavioral research and experimental program evaluation are justified. These procedures merely make explicit and systematic what most good practitioners and planners, agencies and foundations, do intuitively and implicitly in determining their own research or program priorities.

Using Figure 3-11 as a template, the Roseville example would likely place smoking and physical activity in Quadrant 1 and the two eating behaviors in Quadrant 2. Even though all of those actions are deemed important in preventing cardiovascular disease, the team was divided on the matter of whether there was sufficient evidence to support the idea that both are amenable to sustained change.

Step 5: Stating Behavioral Objectives

Once target behaviors have been identified, the final step in this stage is stating behavioral objectives. In this step, specificity is vital. The efficiency and effectiveness of health promotion efforts are jeopardized when behavioral objectives are too vague or generic. Given the scarcity of health promotion resources, vagueness is a luxury one cannot afford. Instances of "intangible" and claims of "unmeasurable" target behaviors generally reflect inadequacy in how the behavioral components of the health problem have been delineated. Phrases such as "improve health habits" and "increase the use of health services" cannot stand as useful behavioral objectives. Program efforts aimed at such diffuse targets will likely be scattered, with too little effort directed at any one behavior to make a difference for the individuals reached and with too few individuals reached to make a difference on the population level.

For this reason, when behavioral change is possible and appropriate, one must take the utmost care in stating the objectives with specificity. Each behavioral objective should answer the following questions:

- *Who?* The people expected to change
- *What?* The action or change in behavior or health practice to be achieved
- *How much?* The extent of the condition to be achieved
- *When?* The time in which the change is expected to occur

In the Roseville cardiovascular disease–prevention program example, one of the behaviors that surfaced was smoking among youth. As they consider crafting a behavioral objective, the planning team concludes that that the term *youth* is too general and imprecise. Based on the survey data available, it is clear that smoking is currently initiated sometime around or before the sixth grade and continues to accelerate through to high school. They decide that the "who" (for at least part of the program) would consist of all sixth-grade students in Roseville. The "what" will be a reduction in the incidence of the onset of smoking. "How much" will be established as 38%. (A decrease from 13% to 8% is a 38% reduction.) The planning team arrive at that estimate based on a report showing that between 1996 and 1999, the rate of cigarette use among sixth-graders in Massachusetts dropped from 16.5% to 7%. This represents a 57% decline.[45] "When" is defined as the proposed time of follow-up evaluation, which the planning team sets as 2 years. Concisely stated, then, the behavioral objective would read as follows:

"Sixth-grade students in Roseville will show a 38% reduction in the onset of cigarette smoking within 2 years of program implementation."

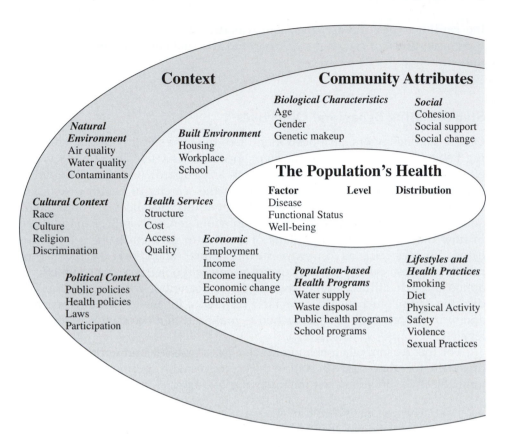

FIGURE 3-13 Influences on the population's health
Source: Shaping a Vision of Health Statistics for the 21st Century (NCVHS-2002)

ENVIRONMENTAL DIAGNOSIS

As we have repeatedly emphasized, risk behaviors constitute one among a complex array of multiple factors that influence health status. We now turn our attention to the examination of the social and environmental factors that influence the health and behavioral priorities already identified. Regardless of the health problem, the environment around us greatly affects our health status. The places where we live and work, the air we breathe and the water we drink, the physical terrain and climate, and the sources of transportation can all be healthful or pose potential risks. Similarly, our health is also affected by social factors that surround us. There is growing scientific evidence supporting what we know intuitively: that our health and well-being is likely to be enhanced when we are surrounded by social support in communities where good relationships are the norm.[46]

Figure 3-13 presents a model of health determinants taken from *Shaping a Vision of Health Statistics for the 21st Century*.[47] Although designed to illustrate the various indicators that are needed to assess the wide range of social and environmental factors that influence health and require attention in a national health statistics system, you will see the parallels with the diagnostic process discussed in this chapter. The health problem of interest is anchored in the center of the model; this is consistent with the task of epidemiologic diagnosis. The various determinants of that health problem are positioned in successive concentric circles. In the two outer concentric circles (Community Attributes and Context) factors in the subcategories entitled "social," "biological characteristics," "lifestyle and health practices," "cultural context," and "health services" are directly addressed by either the health or behavioral assessment. (Regarding the latter, recall the broken appointment cycle example cited earlier in this chapter.)

The subcategories of "population-based health programs," "economic," "natural environment," and "built environment" contain many factors that are likely to surface during an environmental assessment.* The "built environment" refers to that aspect of the physical environment that is manmade and is often the source of factors that surface in the environmental assessment. Our homes, schools, places of work, our streets and freeways, our sewers and parks —these make up the built environment. From a public health perspective, the way we go about building and shaping our environment has a direct and powerful effect on health.[48] Only one in nine children walks to school; one half are driven in a private vehicle and one third take a bus.[49] Strategies designed to enhance the built environment include those that (1) foster recreational activity, (2) provides and promotes safe, affordable, housing, (3) provide safe, reliable, and affordable means of transportation, (4) ensure safe, clean water, soil, air, and building materials, and (4) ensure a well-maintained, aesthetically appealing environment.

The physical environment makes its greatest impact on living conditions and directly on some risk factors for disease brought about by exposures ranging from air, water, soil, and housing to transportation and an absence of safe modes for walking and recreation. For example, Lee offers an interesting ecological analysis in his description of how indoor environments affect health status. He points out that the demographic shift from rural to urban lifestyle has led to a number of compounding risks. Work has become primarily an indoor activity to the point where the average person spends over 90% of their time indoors. Those indoor areas, built "air tight" to conserve energy, reduce the infiltration of air which, in turn, can lead to an increase in indoor air contamination.[50]

If the scope of environmental determinants on health becomes so encompassing and complex as to be impractical for the scope of the health program you are planning, we recommend concentrating attention on those aspects of the environment that are

---

* In the Political Context category, "participation" is a critical element not only in the social diagnosis, but throughout PRECEDE-PROCEED. The remaining indicators: "laws," "health policies," and "public policies," will surface as critical factors in Phase 5, administrative and policy diagnosis.

1. More social than physical (e.g., organizational and economic)
2. Interactive with behavior in their impact on health
3. Changeable by social action and health policy

Much of health promotion concerns the passage of laws and organizational changes to regulate or constrain behavior that threatens the health of others. We consider the initial stimulation of public interest and support for such legislation or to be, in large part, a function of the third category of behavior discussed earlier in this chapter: those planned behaviors and acts of advocacy taken by individuals or groups that influence some dimension of the physical, social, or political environment.

Step 1: Identifying Environmental Factors

This first step parallels Step 1 in behavioral assessment: list those environmental factors known to contribute to the health problem or goal directly or indirectly (through a high priority behavioral factor). Continuing with the Roseville example, recall that the planning team established the following as one of its behavioral objectives:

"Sixth-grade students in Roseville will show 38% reduction in the onset of cigarette smoking within 2 years of program implementation."

What factors in the social or physical environment are likely to have an influence on the attainment of that objective? After pondering that question, the planning team agrees on a short answer: tobacco! Their selection of smoking among youth was in large part based on the compelling evidence indicating that earlier initiation of smoking leads to becoming an adult smoker who is likely to be addicted. Insofar as purchasing tobacco is illegal for minors, a factor in the environment may be access to tobacco. Recall that during the behavioral diagnosis, the planning team used findings from surveys jointly carried out by the Roseville School District and the Roseville Health Department. That same effort included a brief community survey and tobacco policy assessment. Table 3-13 presents information combining findings from that community survey and policy assessment with two items from the youth surveys.

Step 2: Rating Environmental Factors on Relative Importance

The planning team concludes from these data that they may be able to achieve a substantial effect by focusing attention on the following as potential environmental factors related to the onset of smoking among sixth-grade students in Roseville.

- Merchants' selling tobacco to youth
- Merchants' verification of age prior to selling tobacco
- School policy banning tobacco use on school grounds

TABLE 3-13 Summary of Findings From Roseville Community Survey

Percentage of current smokers (middle school) who bought cigarettes at gas stations or convenience stores	63%[a]
Percentage of current smokers (middle school) who purchased cigarettes but were not asked to show proof of age	72%[a]
Number of restaurants that are entirely smoke-free	46% (17/37)[b]
Number of Longview merchants (clerks) who ask for verification of age before selling	62% (34/55)[b]
A formal program to train merchants about minors' access to tobacco	None[b]
School policy calling for a uniform ban on tobacco use for students, teachers, and staff not only on school grounds but at all school-related functions.	None[b]
Enforcement-related activities reported by police department	
• Inspections for signs?	No[b]
• Periodic compliance checks?	Yes[b]
• Citations?	No[b]
• Awards/letters for compliance?	No[b]
• Volunteers in tobacco enforcement?	No[b]

[a] Youth Tobacco Survey data
[b] Interview data
  (Numbers in parenthesis = number interviewed from total available.)

As with the behavioral assessment, the broad criteria for determining the importance of a given environmental factor include evidence that it (1) is clearly linked to the health problem, and (2) is present (you can document that it occurs) and is prevalent in the population of interest. Some of the factors will matter more than others because of one or both of the following criteria: (1) strength of the relationship of the environmental factor to the health or quality-of-life goal or problem; (2) incidence, prevalence, or number of people affected by the environmental factor. Based on the information they have in hand, the Roseville planning team judges all three of the environmental factors identified to be "important."

Step 3: Rating Environmental Factors on Changeability

With a list of important factors in hand, the task in this step is to select those that are most likely to yield to intervention through policy, regulation, or organizational change strategies. As was the case for assessing the changeability of specific risk behaviors, planners are urged to consult relevant literature for evidence that environmental factors can be modified. But even if there is compelling scientific evidence indicating that certain strategies are effective in creating environmental change, the implementation of those strategies may be impossible without public and/or political support. This reality provides further reinforcement for the ongoing need for planners to act on the critical principles of participation, stakeholder involvement, and situational analysis

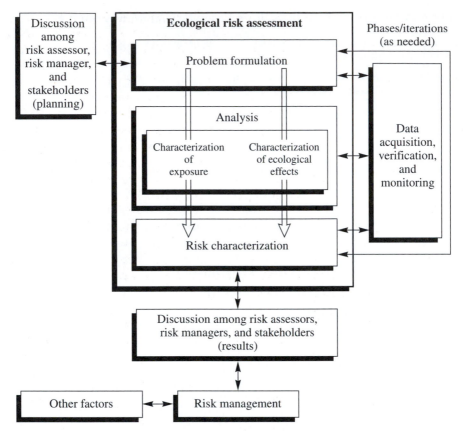

FIGURE 3-14 The Environmental Protection Agency's framework for ecological risk assessment was adapted by the Commission on Risk Assessment and Risk Management for the U.S. Congress to include the particular points at which public consultation or community "stakeholders" would be most important.

discussed in Chapter 2. We will return to these questions when we take up administrative, organizational, and policy diagnosis in Chapter 5.

Assessing political will to make changes is essential to changeability analysis, because environmental factors, like lifestyle factors, will often prove to be important to the community for purposes other than health. For example, a common dilemma is the occupational hazard that can only be eliminated at the risk of losing the industry that supplies jobs for the community. Recall the West Virginia mining example discussed earlier in this chapter. The lung disease might be largely attributable to the mining work, and so there might be no way to eliminate that hazard without eliminating the jobs. When the hazard cannot be eliminated, we usually resort to behavioral solutions, such as wearing protective equipment, stopping one's smoking, and going for periodic screening.

Figure 3-14 suggests that consultation by risk assessors (you, the planner) with risk managers (practitioners, policy makers, and others responsible for the environmental or ecological risks) and with stakeholders (the community) should occur at least at two points in the diagnosis and planning process. At the early point of formulating the problem or issue (upper left in figure) and at the point of analyzing the results (lower center), discussion should assess views of changeability as a matter of assessing political will and costs associated with change. Views of importance as a matter of subjective quality-of-life concerns and lifestyle priorities can be factored into these discussions, but most of the analysis of importance is part of the technical ecological risk assessment itself (center of figure).[51]

Here are some questions planners should consider as they assess the changeability of important environmental factors.

- Is there evidence that this factor is amenable to change? (This is not quite the same as a later step, in Chapter 5, in which the question becomes, "Is there evidence that interventions have worked to change this factor?")
- Is there public and political support for the proposed environmental change? If not, can that support be gained?

As the Roseville planning team discussed the issue of changeability, they once again agreed that merchants selling tobacco to youth, verification of age prior to selling tobacco, and school policy banning tobacco use on school grounds are all changeable. However, they also concluded that the behavior of the merchants was not likely to change without periodic compliance checks by law enforcement authorities. Members of the planning committee met with Roseville law enforcement officials, who indicated that they would be willing to add periodic checks to their workload contingent on their budget not being cut by the city council. Accordingly, the list of environmental factors then included

- Merchants' selling tobacco to youth
- Verification of age by merchants prior to selling tobacco
- Formal compliance checks by law enforcement including issuance of citations when not in compliance and letters of recognition when in compliance
- School policy banning tobacco use on school grounds

Note that the environmental changes needed often involve, as in this case, changes in the behavior of people who control the environment. We will return to this layering of behavioral changes in later chapters.

Step 4: Choosing the Environmental Targets

The same analytic method used in selecting behavioral targets is applied here. (See Figure 3-12.) The same four quadrants in the two-by-two table would yield a distribution of environmental factors that would be more or less important and more or less changeable. The policy implication for action on factors in each quadrant would pertain equally to the environmental factors.

The only exception might be the greater weight one could give to Quadrant 3, where the environmental factor is apparently changeable but relatively low in objective importance. As Slovic and others have pointed out in their research on risk perception, the subjective importance of an environmental factor for the community is often as important as the objective evidence for its relationship or causal link to the health goal or ecological problem—risk is not just a scientific construction, it is a social construction.[52] When public health professionals and community stakeholders grapple with problems simultaneously from an objective and subjective perspective, the problems cannot be resolved solely by applying traditional linear, cause-effect approaches to problem solving. Rather, these complex, environmental health problems (sometimes referred to as "wicked problems") are most likely to yield to a combination of the following: (1) the *combined application* of effective community health education skills (especially those focusing on stakeholder involvement and participatory research) and systems thinking, (2) a sustained commitment to sound environmental and epidemiological science, and (3) ongoing, transparent communication among all stakeholders and community residents.[53]

Step 5: Stating Environmental Objectives

With the priorities established among environmental factors to be changed, the final step in this phase of the assessment planning process is to state the objectives for environmental change in quantitative terms. Again, we urge planners to follow the same protocol recommended for crafting behavioral objectives with the exception that it would not be uncommon to see an absence of the "who." For example, in a health program with a focus on clean air in the environment, an objective might be

> *The amount of carbon monoxide released into the atmosphere in our community will be reduced by 20% by the year 2010.*

In the Roseville case for example, the planning team might state one of their environmental objectives as follows:

> *Student access to tobacco in Roseville will be reduced by 75% by 2 years after the launch of the program.*

The Roseville group chose to insert a specific "who," as in this version:

> *Merchants in Roseville gas stations and convenience stores will reduce their sales to minors by 100% by 2 years after the launch of the program.*

If the environmental or social change objective requires for its accomplishment the action of specific groups of people, behavioral objectives might be set for their actions as well. This relationship between environmental and behavioral objectives is reflected in the vertical arrows in the diagrams of the Precede-Proceed Model (see Chapter 1) and by the ecological acknowledgment of the overlapping spheres of lifestyle, environment, health, and quality of life in Figure 3-15. This latter representation of the model also suggests the complex-

Proceed: policy, regulating or resourcing, and organizing for . . .

Precede: predisposing, reinforcing, and enabling constructs in ecosystem diagnosis and evaluation

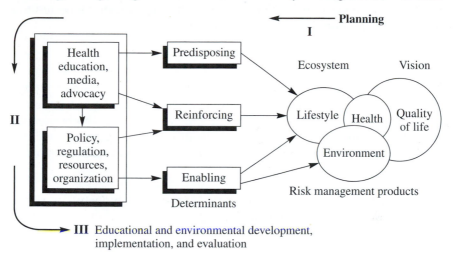

FIGURE 3-15 This representation of the Precede-Proceed Model acknowledges the overlapping spheres of behavioral, environmental, and health components.

ity that comprises these interacting spheres when viewed as an ecosystem. Within it, the combination of lifestyle and environmental risks found to be associated with the health and quality-of-life "vision," or goals, could be referred to as risk characterization (Figure 3-14) or risk management products (Figure 3-15) when they are specified as behavioral and environmental outcome objectives.

EVALUATION SUMMARY

As mentioned in Chapter 1, one of the hallmarks of the Precede-Proceed Model is that evaluation is built systematically into the planning process. Suppose a very capable planning team, with representatives from the relevant stakeholder groups, develops a community health program plan. The program goals and objectives are clearly stated and endorsed by the community. The proposed program appears to have adequate staff and fiscal support, and experienced professionals who have reviewed the program consider it to be well conceived and theoretically sound.

If we visited that program 2 years after it was launched, what are the chances that the program activities and strategies, staff roles, and budget lines we see will be exactly the same as those envisioned at the outset? Slim to none! The complexity of the changing social and economic forces and conditions that influence health, combined with the subtle nuances of human behavior, make it virtually impossible to plan any program that will not require adjustments along the way. The extent to which those adjustments are made, with minimal disruption or delay in pursuing the program goal, will depend on having an evaluation s> >tem in place that serves as a continuous sensor connected to key elements of «ie program.

Definition

Dictionaries generally define *evaluation* in two ways: to ascertain or judge the worth of something, and to examine carefully. The primary tasks for the evaluator are "carefully examining" and "judging the worth" of methods, personnel, materials, or programs. In the context of health program planning we define *evaluation* simply as "the *comparison* of an *object of interest* against a *standard of acceptability.*"

Objects (and Order) of Interest.   Objects of interest include any or all of the factors that one takes into account in applying the Precede-Proceed framework. The objects may be measures of quality of life; health status indicators; behavioral and environmental factors; predisposing, enabling, and reinforcing factors; intervention activities; methods of delivery; changes in policies, regulations, or organizations; level of staff expertise; or quality of performance and of educational materials. Any or all may be the objects of interest for evaluation. The interest in *program* evaluation per se lies in some *change* in the object that one can associate with some change in program activity or input. Each of the inputs, intermediate effects, and ultimate outcomes of health programs can be objects of interest in an evaluation. In PRECEDE-PROCEED, the planning moves from right to left. It begins with the identification of priority health and social problems followed by a systematic search for determinants, root causes of those problems. The findings from that search inform the subsequent selection of interventions designed to mitigate those determinants and root causes. Evaluation applies that same process *in its planning*, but in its *execution*, as with the implementation of the program plan, one moves from left to right—from immediate policies, activities, resources, and implementation, to intermediate effects, and then to ultimate health outcomes and social benefits. The objects of interest remain the same; the order of their examination and judgment is reversed.

Standards of Acceptability.   When we delineate the "how much" and "by when" estimates in the objectives developed through the planning process, we are specifying our standards of acceptability. Said another way, we are making a declaration of how we are expecting an object of interest to measure up. They also serve as targets, which, when attained or exceeded, signal success, improvement, or growth. For health programs, the standards will be the expected *level* of improvement in the social, economic, health, environmental, behavioral, educational, organizational, or policy conditions stated in the objectives. The matter of *standards of acceptability* will surface in each chapter as objectives are set and as interventions are selected, designed, and deployed.

Being an "Accountable Practitioner"

At the outset, planners establish measurable health goals that are linked to measurable enhancements in quality of life. Thereafter, they are asked to (1) delineate measurable objectives describing factors known to be relevant determinants of the health problem chosen, and (2) detail descriptions of the behavioral, social, or environmental actions designed to achieve those objectives. Collectively, the objectives, and the descriptions of activities designed to achieve them, constitute measurable program indicators. These indicators generate information that gives program managers and stakeholders tangible evidence about their program—what it is doing and how well it is doing it.

The continuous monitoring of indicators (program goals, objectives, and activities) has several practical benefits: (1) it provides quick access to tangible information that keeps stakeholders apprised of program status and progress, (2) it enables program managers and staff to detect potential problems early and to make midcourse modifications as needed, (3) it provides tangible evidence that those managing the program are accountable, (4) it establishes a "norm" wherein making program adjustments and midcourse corrections is viewed a strength, not a weakness, and (5) it provides documented insight about methods that others may wish to replicate.

The Precede-Proceed Model features three traditional levels of evaluation: outcome evaluation, impact evaluation, and process evaluation. The methodologies for detecting the indicators at each level (and the indicators themselves) will vary at each level (Figure 3-16).

Outcome Evaluation

The objects of interest for **outcome evaluation** are those health status and quality-of-life indicators that have been crafted in the earliest stages of the planning process. As evidenced by the crafting of the health goal and objective earlier in this chapter that focused on a reduction in infant mortality, health objectives typically are referenced in terms of mortality, disease, or disability rates for a given portion of the population. Social indicators such as hunger, unemployment, homelessness, perceived quality of life, school performance, or elderly people living independently can be measured by quantitative indicators and are often expressed as a percentage of the population. This is the first level at which evaluation is planned and usually the last level at which data will become available from the execution of the evaluation, especially if the outcomes sought are chronic diseases with a major lag between changing risk factors and detecting changes in vital measures.

Impact Evaluation

The second level, **impact evaluation,** assesses the immediate effect the program (or some aspect of it) has on target behaviors and their predisposing, enabling, and reinforcing antecedents or on influential environmental factors. Recall the

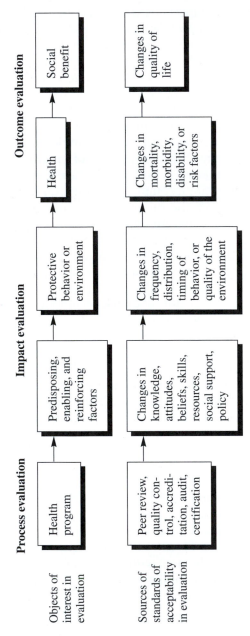

FIGURE 3-16 Three levels of evaluation for accountability suggest the objects of inter-est and the sources of standards of acceptability for each.

examples in the Roseville case where the behavioral objective called for a specific reduction in the onset of smoking among sixth-grade students and the environmental objective focused on a change in the environment that would lead to a reduction in the sale of cigarettes to minors. The clarity, specificity, and plausibility of the behavioral and educational objectives generated in Phases three and four of the Precede planning process provide the foundation for evaluating program impact. A full-scale health promotion program should expect to find some impact on behavior, but components of the program, such as mass media, might not yield palpable behavioral impact if evaluated in isolation.

Process Evaluation

Process evaluation focuses on matters of implementation of the program, that is, how it is being carried out. Most often, this is routinely done through observations and/or interviews with staff and participants. Questions might include the following. Are the methods described in the program planned going as expected? Is the intended population being reached? If not, why not? Has adequate time been allotted for the activity in question? To what extent is the level of support from the partner organization affecting the activities in the program? Is the time allocated for a given activity adequate? Although it is linked to the ultimate outcome being sought by the program, the goal of process evaluation is to understand and describe *how* an outcome was produced. In the summary to Chapter 2 several objectives of social diagnosis and assessment are highlighted including

- To *engage* the community as active partners in the social diagnostic process
- To *identify* ultimate values and subjective concerns with quality of life or conditions of living in the target population
- To *assess* the capacities and assets of a community

Evidence of the extent to which each of these objectives was attained represents a tangible example of process evaluation.

This chapter began by highlighting the process of epidemiological diagnosis through (1) examining the relationship between health problems and social problems, (2) reviewing methods by which health problems are quantified and prioritized, and (3) identifying plausible determinants of health. Emphasis was placed on describing health problems in detail, using data from local, regional, state, and national sources interpreted against a background of current epidemiological knowledge as reflected in the literature. By analyzing existing data on who is most affected (age, sex, race, residence), the ways they are affected (mortality, disability, signs, symptoms), planners gain the critical insight needed to develop programs that are targeted by specific objectives and, therefore, are amenable to evaluation. The chapter also guided readers through the process of behavioral and environmental assessments illustrating how to identify the most fruitful behavioral and environmental targets for intervention. Anticipating that each chosen behavior generates an educational assessment and each environmental factor generates an ecological assessment, the planner must be parsimonious in selecting problems. Thoughtful examination of the importance and changeability of each potential target behavior and environmental condition will cut down on the scope of subsequent diagnostic efforts. Finally, the concise statement of objectives not only leads to greater program specificity, but provides measurable indicators, linked to program goals and activities, that make evaluation an integrated part of the planning and implementation.

EXERCISES

1. List the health problems related to the quality-of-life concerns identified in your population in Exercise 3, Chapter 2.
2. Rate (low, medium, high) each health problem in the inventory according to
   a. its relative importance in affecting the quality-of-life concerns and
   b. its potential for change.
3. Discuss the reasons for your giving high-priority ratings to health problems in Exercise 2a in terms of their prevalence, incidence, cost, virulence, severity, or other relevant dimensions. Extrapolate from national, state, or regional data when local data are not available.
4. Cite the evidence supporting your ratings of health problems in Exercise 2b. Refer to the success of other programs and/or to the availability of medical or other technology to control or reduce the high-priority health problems you have selected.
5. Cite two uses for data generated by epidemiological assessments other than for program planning, and give an example of each.
6. Write a program objective for the highest-priority health problem, indicating who will show how much of what improvement by when, and how it will be evaluated.

NOTES AND CITATIONS

1. *The obesity epidemic trend maps:* Details of this event based on personal conversations with Dr. William Dietz, Director, Division of Nutrition and Physical Activity, National Center for Chronic Disease Prevention and Health Promotion, Centers for Disease Control and Prevention (CDC); and Jeffrey P. Koplan, Vice President for Health Sciences at Emory University and former Director, CDC. Interviews conducted on October 5 and 7, 2003. To review the Power-Point slides presenting obesity and diabetes trend data, see http://www.cdc.gov/nccdphp/dnpa/obesity/trend/maps/index.htm.
2. *Role of public health professionals in surveillance, monitoring, analyzing, and presenting health data:* Institute of Medicine, 2003.
3. *Starting in the middle:* The algorithm on the title page of Chapters 2–5 shows how the planner can locate the most appropriate place in PRECEDE to undertake data collection and planning.
4. *Evaluation as an integrated element of planning phases, rather than as a separate phase:* In previous editions of this book and earlier renditions of the Precede-Proceed Model, we have devoted a separate chapter and a separate phase to evaluation, following the diagnostic and implemen-

tation phases. We have discovered that a separate, end-of-planning evaluation chapter has had an unintended effect for some planners: putting off thinking about evaluation until the program is launched. This leads to the neglect of evaluation considerations in the earlier phases of planning where it is so essential not only for making inevitable midcourse corrections but also for establishing the baselines needed for measuring, monitoring, and documenting the important outcomes. As Carol Weiss (1973) so famously said, "The sins of the program are often visited on the evaluation" (p. 54).

5. *Web-based tools for linking social and epidemiological diagnosis:* MAPP is a refinement and extension of the CDC Planned Approach to Community Health or PATCH (which was based on the principles and methods of the Precede-Proceed Model) and Assessment Protocol for Excellence in Public Health (APEX/PH). For more details on the MAPP process, contact the National Association of County and City Health Officials, 1100 17th Street, NW, Second Floor, Washington, DC 20036. Phone: (202) 783-5550, Email: map@naccho.org. See endnote 36 in Chapter 2 for Web links. Related to the MAPP Web-based tools are other resources designed to tie local planning efforts to national health objectives as part of the Healthy People 2010 initiatives, e.g., U.S. Department of Health and Human Services, 2001, 2002.

6. *International example of linking health with social functioning:* First published by the World Health Organization in 1980, the WHO *International Classification of Functioning, Disability and Health, 2001,* is now available online at http://www.who.int/classification/icf/intros/ICF-Eng-Intro.pdf, and bundled with the companion *International Classification of Diseases* (ICD-10) in book and CD-ROM.

7. *Potential social consequences of health objectives:* For example, on youth violence, Rigby, 2003. On parental alcohol abuse, Christoffersen & Soothill, 2003.

8. *Working knowledge of trends, technologies, and recent evaluations of programs on similar health problems helps set up evaluation baseline measures:* For example, CDC, 2003, http://www.cdc.gov/cancer/ncccp/guidelines/index.htm

9. *Growing evidence of the social gradient in morbidity and mortality:* For example, Evans, Barer, & Stoddard, 1994; Smedley & Syme, 2000; Wilkinson, 1996. See also endnote 2, Chapter 2.

10. *Poverty, racial, and ethnic factors in health disparities:* For example, Stewart & Napoles-Springer, 2003; Whaley, & Geller, 2003; Zuvekas & Taliaferro, 2003.

11. *Participatory research engaging intersectoral collaboration on social determinants of health:* For example, Krieger, Cheadle, et al., 2002.

12. *Epidemiology definition:* Last, 2000, pp. 62ff. The definition and explanation of epidemiology has been paraphrased from several pages of Last, which he assures us was a committee product and never considered to be cast in stone (personal correspondence, Dec. 3, 2003). For variations on this definition, see Green & Ottoson, 1999, p. 70; Timmerick, 1998, pp. 2–3.

13. *Measures of quality of life:* For example, Centers for Disease Control and Prevention, 2000; see also Chapter 2, notes 5 and 16–22.

14. *Years of potential life lost (YPLL)* measure the impact of diseases and injuries that kill people before the customary age of retirement. It is computed as the sum of products over all age groups up to age 65, sometimes 75, each product being the annual number of deaths in an age group multiplied by the average number of years remaining before the age of 65 for that age group. See Centers for Disease Control, 1986; McDonnell & Vossberg, 1998; Fellows, Tosclair, et al., 2002.

15. *Definition of surveillance:* Hockin, 2002, p. 1171. Earlier definitions from the communicable disease era of public health had emphasized "continuous" rather than "ongoing" collection of data, but because surveillance of chronic diseases calls upon public health to have earlier warnings of emerging diseases than the symptoms that are detected in continuous reporting by doctors, surveys of population health practices and lifestyles have been required to detect risk factors like smoking or obesity that would predict oncoming epidemics like cancer and diabetes. Surveys usually cannot be done continuously, hence the shift in definition of surveillance.

16. *Canadian federal compilation of surveillance data:* Go to http://www.hc-sc.gc.ca/pphb-dgspsp/ (accessed Dec. 3, 2003).

17. *New York City Community Health Profiles,* New York City Department of Health and Mental Hygiene. Website: http://www.ci.nyc.ny.us/html/doh/html/data/data.html (accessed Dec. 3, 2003).

18. *Some applications of PRECEDE illustrating epidemiological assessments and setting of health objectives* include Antoniades & Lubker, 1997; Cadman, 1996; Cain, Schyulze, & Preston, 2001; Castilla y Leon, 1993; Clarke, Frankish, & Green, 1997; Farthing, 1994; Gielen, 1992; Green, Mullen, & Friedman, 1991; Green, Wilson, & Bauer, 1983; Howatt, Jones, et al., 1997; Livingston, 1985; Simons-Morton, Parcel, Brink, Harvey, & Tiernan, 1991; Stevenson, Jones, Cross, Howatt, & Hall, 1996; Stevenson, Jones, et al., 1996; Timmerick, 1998, pp. 338–340; Walter, Hoffman, Connelly, et al., 1985. See also Chapter 1, endnote 26.

19. *Social determinants of health:* For example, Karpati, Galea, et al., 2002; Marmot 2000; Marmott, & Wilkinson 1999; Wilkinson & Marmot, 1998.

20. *Economic determinants of health:* For example, Green & Potvin, 2002; Hart, 2002; Wilkinson, 1996.

21. *Environmental risks:* For example, Dannenberg, Jackson, et al., 2003; Wallerstein, Duran, et al., 2003; Wright & Fischer, 2003. See also Chapter 4, note 71.

22. *Cultural determinants of health:* For example, House, & Williams, 2000.

23. *"Determinants" might overstate the causal certainty of the connection, but not the consistent weight of evidence:* Daniels, Kennedy, & Kawachi, 2000.

24. *Risk, risk perception, risk assessment:* For a detailed review of these concepts and data related to them, see WHO, 2002, Chapters 3, 4, & 5.

25. *Limited surveillance capacity in most local jurisdictions:* For example, Ounpuu, Kreuger, et al., 2000; Remington & Goodman, 1998; Teutsch & Churchill, 2000.

26. *Making surveillance systems relevant to regional or local program planning:* McQueen, et al., 2003. See especially the analysis and interpretation of data from the BRFSS, Holtzman, 2003; and the bottom line, "Will they use it?" Ottoson & Wilson, 2003.

27. *Accessing state risk factor survey data:* The easiest way to access state-specific data for the BRFSS is to go to the web site for the Association of State and Territorial Health Officers at http://www.astho.com. Once in that site, go to the map of the United States and click on the state or territory for which you are seeking data. Most state health departments now have some of their *state data on health indicators* available on their respective web sites. One of the most thoroughly developed databases of health indicators is the IBIS-PH (Indicator-Based Information System for Public Health) of the Utah Department of Health. The following web site will link you to categorized and alphabetical listings of all indicators, with links from there to each of the corresponding databases: http://health.utah.gov/ibis-ph/. For an extensive *guide to compiling* such *data in the context of a Precede approach to planning,* see the guides and manuals for the CDC PATCH planning process online and downloadable: http://www.cdc.gov/nccdphp/patch/.

28. *Smoking-attributable risk:* The recent population-attributable risks and social costs for smoking are calculated for the United States in Fellows, Trosclair, et al., 2002. For a review of health-related costs, see Max, 2001. Software for calculating smoking-attributable mortality and economic costs for adults and for maternal and child health are available from the Office on Smoking and Health, CDC, 2002, and online at http://www.cdc.gov/tobacco/sammec.

29. These data were taken from Section IV Chronic Disease, Risk Factor, and Preventive Services, Missouri, The Burden of Chronic Diseases and Their Risk Factors: National and State Perspectives 2002; http://www.cdc.gov/nccdphp/statbook/statbook.htm (accessed Dec. 3, 2003). Any other state's data can be accessed from this site.

30. *The report to the Missouri Board of Health:* Missouri Foundation for Health, 2001, p. 20.

31. *Two studies on social capital and health,* both in Kawachi, et al., 1997.

32. *The Appalachian mine workers' lung disease project:* Terry, Wang, et al., 1981; Wang, Terry, et al., 1979.

33. *The Alameda County studies of protective health factors:* Belloc, 1973; Belloc & Breslow, 1972; Berkman & Breslow, 1983; see also the retrospective interview with Lester Breslow at age 89: Stallworth & Lennon, 2003.

34. *The longer-term follow-up of Alameda County cohort:* Breslow & Egstrom, 1980.

35. *Even bedridden, postsurgical patients can make a difference through participation in their care:* Devine & Cook, 1983; Hughes, Hodgson, et al., 2000.

36. *The declines in smoking, lung cancer incidence, and heart mortality rates in California following passage of Proposition 99:* Fichtenberg & Glantz, 2000; MMWR, 2000.

37. *Genetic-behavioral-environmental interactions:* Ridley, 1999, pp. 153–154.

38. *Genetic variations, food, and susceptibility or resilience:* The Pyramid Paradigm, Center of Excellence for Nutritional Genomics, University of California, Davis, http://nutrigenomics.ucdavis.edu.

39. *Global obesity epidemic:* WHO, 2002.

40. *Gene-gene, gene-environment interactions in obesity.* Froguel & Boutin, 2001.

41. *For examples of the application of PRECEDE in behavioral risk factor assessment in cardiovascular disease,* see Arbeit et al., 1992; P. H. Bailey, Rukholm, Vanderlee, & Hyland, 1994; Berenson, Harsha, et al., 1998; Bruce & Grove, 1994; Bush, Zuckerman, et al., 1987, 1989; Carlaw, Mittlemark, et al., 1984; Downey, Butcher, et al., 1987; Green, Lewis & Levine, 1980; Kok, Matroos, et al., 1982; Mantell, DiVittis, & Auerbach, 1997, pp. 199–203; Morisky, et al., 1981; Morrison, 1996; Nguyen, Grignon, Tremblay, & Delisle, 1995; Nguyen, et al., 1995; O'Loughlin, et al., 1995; Paradis, et al., 1995; Zuckerman, Olevsky-Peleg, et al., 1989.

42. *Teen smoking predicts adult smoking:* Jacobsen, Lantz, et al., 2001.

43. *For details on the North Karlia Project,* Pietinen, Nissinen, et al., 1992; Puska, 1992; Puska & Uutela, 2000; Puska, Vartiainen, et al., 1998; Vartiainen, Jousilahti, et al., 2000.

44. *Limitations of the evidence for best practices in dietary behavior change:* Agency for Healthcare Research and Quality, 2000: http://www.ahrq.gov/clinic/epcsums/dietsumm.htm.

45. *A source for Roseville's estimate of how much reduction they might expect:* Cigarette use among adolescents in Massachusetts in Grade 6, 1996–1999, Health and Addictions Research Inc., June 2000: http://www.state.ma.us/dph/mtcp/report/had.htm.

46. *Evidence of social-environmental factors in health:* Cannuscio, Block, & Kawachi, 2003; Kreuter & Lezin, 2003; Lochner, Kawachi, et al., 2003.

47. *Ecological vision of influences on the population's health:* National Committee on Vital and Health Statistics, 2002.

48. *The built environment:* For example, Dannenberg, Jackson, et al., 2003; Killingsworth, Earp, & Moore, 2003.

49. *Promoting safe walking and biking to school:* Staunton, Hubsmith, & Kallins, 2003.

50. *Indoor air example of emerging environmental threat:* Lee, T. G. 2003; Health and the Built Environment: Indoor Air Quality, Health and Well Being, Vital Signs Curriculum Project. http://arch.ced.berkeley.edu/vitalsigns/.

51. *Consulting with the community on environmental risk assessments:* Commission on Risk Assessment and Risk Management, 1996. A debate in the community-based participatory research literature, which has been stimulated by such environmental assessment issues, is whether community participants in the research effort need to be involved in every aspect of the research, or whether, as the commission suggests, they can be involved primarily in these two points in the formulation of the risk assessment research questions and the interpretation of the results. See, e.g., Green & Mercer, 2001.

52. *Risk assessment versus risk perception, subjective and objective considerations:* Slovic, 1999, 2001.

53. *Three ingredients for success in addressing "wicked" environmental problems:* Kreuter, Marshall, DeRosa, Howze, & Baldwin, 2004.

4

Ecological and
Educational Diagnosis

*Discovery consists of seeing what everyone has seen and thinking what nobody has
thought.*

—Albert von Szent-Györgyi

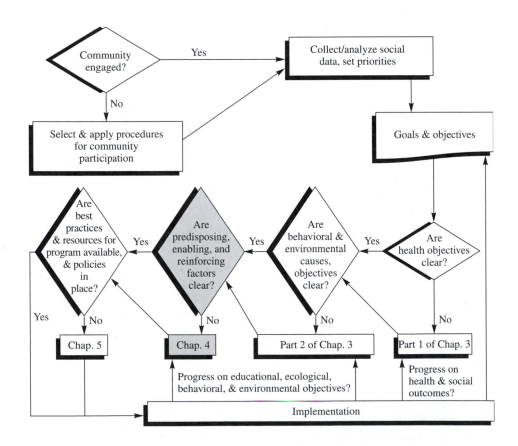

The foregoing sequence of social and epidemiological assessments produces a clear understanding of the behavioral and environmental actions and conditions of living affecting a population's aspiration, problem, or need. The next phase of the Precede Model—the educational and ecological assessment—examines the highest-priority behavioral and environmental conditions linked to health status or quality-of-life concerns to determine what causes them. The educational and ecological assessment identifies factors that require change to initiate and sustain the process of behavioral and environmental change. The determinants of health and social conditions identified in this phase will become the immediate targets or objectives of a program. Planners may see them as the processes of change that must be activated or set in motion if the necessary behavioral and environmental changes are to occur.

The educational and ecological assessment in population health is concerned with factors influencing the health-related behavior and conditions of living (and possibly genetic effects) identified in Chapter 3 as important in the health and quality-of-life outcomes identified in the previous chapters. It also begins a process of behavioral assessment on those people who can influence environmental conditions. This assessment phase of PRECEDE helps planners untangle the complex forces shaping health-related behavior and environmental conditions.

FACTORS INFLUENCING BEHAVIOR AND THE ENVIRONMENT

We begin by identifying three general categories of factors affecting individual or collective behavior: predisposing, enabling, and reinforcing factors. Each exerts a different type of influence on behavior, but all three are needed in some combination to motivate, facilitate, and sustain behavioral change. Behavior change, in turn, will influence the environment, but environmental change can also be supported and sustained independent of behavior through certain enabling factors directed at the environment.

Predisposing factors are antecedents to behavioral change that provide the rationale or *motivation* for the behavior.

Enabling factors are antecedents to behavioral or environmental change that allow a motivation or environmental policy to be realized.

Reinforcing factors are factors following a behavior that provide the continuing *reward* or incentive for the persistence or repetition of the behavior.

Inherent in these definitions is the understanding of a reciprocal relationship between behavior and environment. The predisposing and reinforcing factors are specific to a given behavior, and they vary in their power for different people. For program planning purposes we must think about them not so much in purely psychological terms as in social-psychological and socio-environmental terms. To make them operational at an organizational or community level, the environment usually needs to be altered through policy changes or changes in social norms that create a changed social environment.

The category of enabling factors also contains the resources necessary to make a behavioral or environmental change possible. These interactions are implied by the vertical arrows between behavior and environment and among the shaded boxes of the graphic representation of the model on the next page.[1]

The Theory Underlying This Part of the Model

Consistent with the notions of *collective causation* and *contributing causes*, one can explain any given behavior or environmental change as a function of the collective influence of these three types of factors. Rarely is any one behavior, or feature of the social or health environment, caused by just one factor. "'Tis a tangled web we weave" of causal factors, each increasing or decreasing the probability that the action will be performed or the environment will change, and each potentially affecting the influence of other factors.

Even so, there are exceptions. For example, a highly motivated behavior can sometimes overcome some deficit of resources and rewards. A highly rewarded behavior might occur in the absence of personal beliefs about its value or correctness. For the average person, however, the three conditions— predisposing, enabling, and reinforcing—must be aligned for the behavior to occur and persist. Any plan to influence behavior must consider not just one, but all three sets of causal factors. For example, a program disseminating health information to increase awareness, interest, and knowledge, without recognizing the influence of enabling and reinforcing factors, most likely will fail to influence behavior except in that segment of the population that has resources and rewards readily at hand—usually, the affluent. On the other hand, a program that simply offers a new immunization service in the local environment to *enable* people to get the necessary preschool immunizations for their children will fail to attract the uninformed, the unmotivated, and those fearful of vaccinations. Without attention to predisposing factors, the attempt to enable an unmotivated behavior will fall flat. It is not necessarily true that "if you build it, they will come." Even the motivated and the enabled will fail to follow through with booster shots unless they feel some reinforcement from the initial experience.

Of the many theories that attempt to explain human behavior, each explains a useful portion of reality for different purposes. No single theoretical model has been universally accepted as sufficient to encompass the range of human experience. Models undergo modification in response to new situations and changing conditions of living. The classification of predisposing, enabling, and reinforcing determinants of behavior offers a broad framework within which one can organize and apply more specific theories and research. The rationale of this framework is based on several common theoretical themes that have proven especially applicable and appropriate to health promotion.[2] PRECEDE merely organizes the multitude of precursors into three categories. Within these three categories, the various concepts and models can be used in

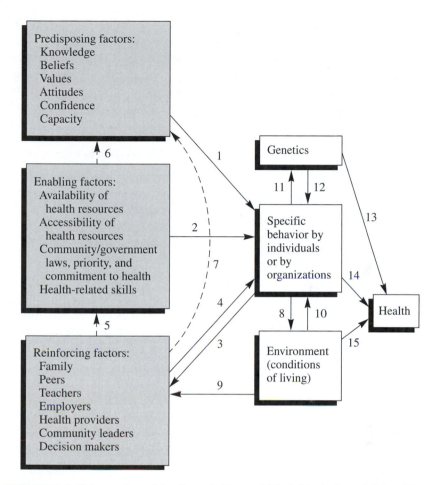

FIGURE 4-1 This portion of the Precede-Proceed Model includes additional lines and arrows to outline a theory of causal relationships and order of causation and feedback loops for the three sets of factors influencing behavior. In addition to the lines shown, an arrow from "enabling factors" to "environment" would elaborate the ecological aspect of factors that influence behavior indirectly through changes in the environment.

planning the details (e.g., messages, incentives, training, policies) of a particular component of a health program.

Figure 4-1 shows in more detail some relationships among the three types of factors, how these factors can influence behavior through various pathways, and how behavior can, in turn, influence the environment or genetics. For example, an adolescent may have a negative attitude toward smoking and believe that smoking is harmful (predisposing factors), which causes her not to smoke (Arrow 1 to the behavior); her nonsmoking may then be rewarded by her parents (Arrows 3 and 4 to and from reinforcing factors). Strong enforcement of local ordinances prohibiting the sale of cigarettes to minors may lead to unavailability of cigarettes in her immediate environment (Arrow 2, an enabling factor). On the other hand, an adolescent may perceive peer pressure to smoke in environments where smoking is common (Arrow 5, social norms as a reinforcing factor on enabling environments, and Arrow 7 reinforcing her perception that smoking is cool). She notices in some of these environments the availability of cigarettes in vending machines (Arrow 2, an enabling factor). This also can result in a more positive attitude toward smoking (Arrow 6, producing a predisposing factor). This changed attitude can then cause her to smoke (Arrow 1 to the behavior), which is then reinforced by her peers (Arrows 3 and 4, a reinforcing factor), while it is hidden from parents, teachers, and others who might disapprove.

Figure 4-1 illustrates how the three types of factors interact with the environment to affect behavior through various pathways. The interdependence of these factors and the circumstances and conditions of living defines the determinants of behavioral and environmental change as an ecological and educational process. At this point we are using the term *educational* to refer to the natural social learning process that occurs in everyday living, by which individuals make sense of and exercise some control over their environment, as distinct from the formal educational process that might occur in classrooms or training programs. As Albert Bandura describes it: "Personal agency operates within a broad network of sociostructural influences. In these agentic transactions, people are producers as well as products of social systems."[3] *Ecological* refers here to the reciprocal determinism of behavior and environment, where environment includes social and physical influences at several levels (family, peers, hangouts, nonsmoking policies). At a later point, we will refer again to educational and ecological approaches to indicate the organization of interventions into programs that seek to interrupt or strengthen selected aspects of these educational and ecological processes of influence on behavior and the environment.

The sequence would most typically proceed as follows: (1) A person has an initial reason, impulse, or motivation (predisposing factor) to pursue a given course of action. This first factor (Arrow 1 in Figure 4-1) in the causal chain may suffice to start steps toward the behavior, but it will not complete it unless the person has the resources and skills needed to carry out the behavior. The motivation, then, is followed by (2) the deployment or use of resources to enable the action (enabling factor). This usually results in at least a tentative enactment of the behavior, followed by (3) a reaction to the behavior that is emotional, physical, or social (reinforcing factor). Reinforcement strengthens (4) behavior, (5) the search for, mobilization, or commitment of future resources, and (6) motivation. The ready availability of enabling factors provides cues and heightens awareness and other factors predisposing the behavior. An Exercycle in your home will more likely prompt you to use it than will one at the YMCA. (7) Similarly, rewards and satisfactions from behavior make that behavior more attractive on the next occasion; today's reinforcing factor becomes tomorrow's predisposing factor. Finally, perhaps most relevant to the social ecological perspective of health promotion, (8) building up social reinforcement for a behavior through the (9) social environment (social norms) can lead to the enabling of behavior in the form of social support and assistance (Arrow 5). This sequence of developmental steps and presumed cause-effect relationships in behavior change and maintenance uses language and concepts related to, but distinct from, those of the Transtheoretical Model applied to populations,[4] the Health Belief Model (see later in this chapter), and other similar theories and models.

The Practical Uses of This Component of the Model

To uncover the factors that influence behavior (smoking in the recent example), planners must take into account the circumstances and conditions of the population of interest (e.g., adolescents). Fisher and his colleagues used the Precede-Proceed Model as the organizing structure for a community-based pediatric asthma-control program in a low-income African American neighborhood in St. Louis, Missouri. Key to their approach was the clear delineation of parental behaviors associated with selected preventive actions, the early detection of a potential asthma attack, and prompt seeking of appropriate care as needed. In selecting the predisposing, reinforcing, and enabling factors influencing the behaviors of interest, the planners were guided in part by existing data from the literature on surveys of parents of children with asthma. More importantly, they had data that enabled them to compare survey findings on a population of adult patients from a clinic that served their neighborhood population with data on patients from a predominantly middle-class, suburban practice. They found that patients in their target population, compared with the suburban patients, considered their asthma

> less of a concern and indicated that they were less careful to take their asthma medications, more satisfied with over-the-counter medications for asthma, and more likely to try to fight asthma attacks on their own without medical help. . . . These observations have led us to identify several key curricular concepts for the NAC education activities: (i) take asthma seriously, (ii) take asthma medications for asthma symptoms, (iii) when symptoms persist .or worsen, follow an asthma action plan developed with your doctor, (iv) when symptoms continue or worsen, get help.[5]

The St. Louis example illustrates very simply how the examination of predisposing, reinforcing, and enabling factors led to the formulation of messages for health communications. It also led them to other strategies that addressed the enabling and reinforcing factors.[6] Besides its theoretical value in explaining and predicting behavior, the classification of behavioral and environmental determinants into predisposing, reinforcing, and enabling categories makes it possible to group the specific features of the situation according to the types of interventions available in health programs. Most commonly these include

- *direct communications* to the target population to strengthen the predisposing factors;

- *indirect communications and policy change* through parents, teachers, clergy, community leaders, employers, peers, and others to strengthen the reinforcing factors; and
- *community organization,* political interventions or advocacy, regulation, organizational changes, and training to strengthen the enabling factors.

Educational and ecological assessment identifies the prevalence or intensity of specific factors of each type while keeping in mind that there may be complex interactions among the factors. These interactions need not be delineated in precise detail or for each person in a target population: The average or prevailing configuration of factors will suffice to plan an effective health program for the subpopulations making up relatively homogeneous groups such as residents, students, patients, or employees, grouped by neighborhood or organizational settings. In recognizing that personal factors differ among individuals, that each average has a range and a distribution of values within a population, and that these variations have their covariations or interactions with other factors, one can maintain a statistical or probabilistic perspective rather than a simple deterministic one. The eventual configuration of a program will consist of multiple interventions and some variations within interventions, some of which will reach some people, while others will reach other people.

A caveat for planners before plunging more deeply into specific determinants: For practical, program planning purposes, the exact placement of a factor believed to be important need not become a matter of paralyzing debate or indecision. As shown in the next section, some types of knowledge and skills may serve both predisposing and enabling functions in supporting different types of behavior. Further, as stated earlier, today's reinforcement becomes tomorrow's predisposition. The decision to place a factor in one category or another is less important than both ranking the factor as an influence on or determinant of behavioral or environmental change worthy of attention and also finding a way to address it in the program. It is preferable to think of the predisposing, enabling, and reinforcing factors as capacities to be strengthened, rather than deficits or problems to be corrected.

PREDISPOSING FACTORS

Among the many predisposing factors for any given behavior, some are of more immediate concern—including knowledge, attitudes, beliefs, values, and perceived needs and abilities. These relate to the motivation of an individual or group to act. Falling mostly in the psychological domain, they include the cognitive and affective dimensions of knowing, feeling, believing, valuing, and having self-confidence or a sense of efficacy. Personality factors could also predispose a given health-related behavior, but we set these aside in a special subcategory of predisposing factors that do not lend themselves readily to health program interventions (besides psychotherapy). Predisposing personality factors and deep-seated values may not yield to change within the context of a health program, but marketing companies use them in "psychographic" pro-files to pitch or "spin" the advertisement of products and services.[7] These less changeable factors may serve health programs similarly as planning indicators in the short run, but they might also indicate the need for early childhood inter-ventions and broad cultural change in the long run.

Sociodemographic factors—such as socioeconomic status, age, gender, eth-nic group, and family size or history—predispose health-related behavior through a variety of mechanisms.[8] Social status (based on income, education, occupation, area of residence, and other census data), age, and gender all can be used to segment a target population or individuals for planning purposes.[9] In planning short-term programs, though, we set these aside from the predis-posing factors that will become targets for change, because these cannot be readily and directly influenced by most health programs. The identification of socioeconomic and demographic factors can help the planner determine whether different interventions should be planned for different groups. For example, predisposing factors for smoking cessation in women include atti-tudes and concerns about weight control, whereas those concerns are not so important in men.[10] Without attempting to change these perceptions or the val-ues underlying them, a health program can take them into account when plan-ning different smoking-cessation messages and supportive services for women and men. In the long term, again, or at broad national or policy levels, these can and sometimes should be the targets of health and social programs.

Capacity-Building Cycle of Predisposing and Enabling Factors

Besides enabling behavior, existing skills and resources can predispose people to take action. This loop (shown in Figure 4-1 as Arrow 6) operates through the self-efficacy factor, which we shall examine later in this chapter. The extent to which people, organizations, or communities possess certain skills or capacities may predispose them to take certain actions, but for most purposes, we classify skills as enabling factors. Similarly, some types of knowledge could be seen as enabling, rather than predisposing, insofar as knowledge serves the individual or group less as a stimulus to than as a facilitator of action. Knowing where to go for a desired service, for example, enables one to obtain it. Generally, we can think of predisposing factors as the motivation, desires, or preferences that an individual or group brings to a behavioral or environmental choice or to an educational, political, or organizational experience. These preferences may pull the person or group either toward or away from specific actions.

These capacity-building processes, in the most basic Darwinian sense, pro-duce a natural history of health (Figure 4-2), whereby people adapt to their inherited environmental, biological, and health circumstances. Their successful adaptation results in learning through a process of reinforcement (a fast-track psychological counterpart to the slower genetic adaptation that occurs over generations). The learned behavior is reinforced, which means it repeats itself in response to further challenges or opportunities presented by the environ-ment and the biological aging process. This is the simple cycle of health and

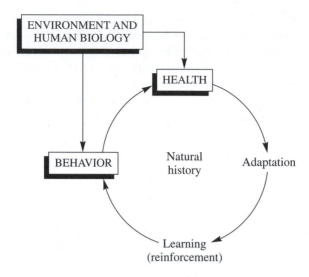

FIGURE 4-2 This representation of the natural history of health could be seen as the most primitive *system* of health before social organization, for better or worse. It places the learning process, however unconscious, as a response to successful adaptation to inherited environmental and biological circumstances as they affect health.

Source: Adapted from *Community and Population Health,* by L. W. Green and J. M. Otttoson, 1999, New York: WCB/McGraw-Hill; used with permission of the publisher.

health behavior that might apply to most species and might have prevailed in prehistoric human species before social organization.

Awareness, Knowledge, and Health Literacy

Cumulative cognitive learning results from exposure to an object, experience with it, and awareness of it, and these gradually produce recognition knowledge, then recall knowledge, and eventually analytic skills and wisdom pertaining to the object. An increase in knowledge alone does not always cause behavioral or organizational change, but positive associations among changes in these variables have been found in countless studies over decades of educational research. Health knowledge of some kind, at least some awareness of a need and an action that can be taken to meet that need, is probably necessary—but not sufficient—before a conscious personal health action will occur. The desired health action will probably not occur unless a person receives a cue strong enough to trigger the motivation to act on that knowledge. A threshold of knowledge may need to be met for some actions to occur (such as recognizing a symptom as abnormal before one will go for a medical check), but after that amount of knowledge or health literacy is attained, additional information will not necessarily promote additional behavioral change.[11]

Cognitive learning also accumulates as experience, which produces beliefs, which combine over time to produce values. Together with social influences,

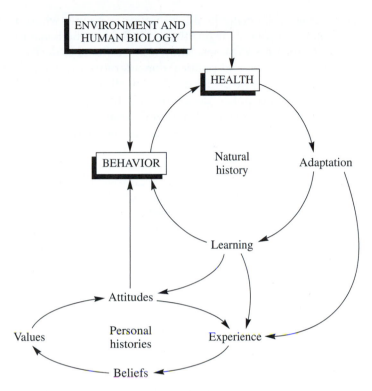

FIGURE 4-3 The development of predisposing factors shows the interaction of experience with learning in natural human history and with beliefs, values, attitudes, and behavior in personal histories.
Source: Adapted from *Community and Population Health,* by L. W. Green and J. M. Otttoson, 1999, New York: WCB/McGraw-Hill; used with permission of the publisher.

values in turn produce attitudes. Figure 4-3 shows these processes of shaping personal experience and behavior through the predisposing factors; we shall unfold this process more fully in the sections that follow.

The specific knowledge requirement for the person or population to carry out an intended behavior can often be identified through simple logic. Before people will act voluntarily, they need to know *why* they should act, *what* actions are needed, *when* or under what circumstances, *how* to act, and *where*. For example, some essential informational components of asthma education include

- How to recognize asthma symptoms and their severity
- When to administer medications (recognize symptoms, know how to measure airflow)
- What avoidance strategies to employ and what minimum of medication to use
- Where to avoid allergens or triggers of asthma attacks
- How to maintain self-management and control through normal daily activities[12]

The same factors influencing health behavior in people whose health is at risk or who seek to improve their health also influence the behavior of health professionals and even organizations. Knowledge influences decisions by those in charge, but other strategic and political considerations must come into play in the implementation of those decisions. The applications of PRECEDE-PROCEED to professional and policy decisions and to regulatory and organizational behavior will be addressed in Chapter 5. That chapter also will address how to use the results of the foregoing stages of the planning process to produce the final plan for implementation.

Motivation usually comes from sources other than, or in addition to, factual knowledge. School health curricula, for example, are frequently justifiable by reference to the simple, commonsense notion that knowledge is the best road to good health. Opponents argue that educational goals of knowledge are too soft and intangible to be used as criteria for program effectiveness in school health curricula. They also view students as bored by facts. A more accurate assessment might be that students are turned off not by facts, but by moralization, superficial coverage of subject matter, scare tactics, and tedious methods of presenting facts. Some health teachers may be abandoning information and facts in favor of armchair moralization about how one should behave to be healthy, or appeals to fear, or attempts to build resistance to peer pressure. We believe that *both* colorfully presented facts and sensitivity to values, such as those reflected in the social and quality-of-life assessment, are essential to predisposing behavioral change. Other factors that enable and reinforce the behavior will suggest the need for additional interventions in sections and chapters to follow.

To say knowledge makes no difference is as ludicrous as to say it makes all the difference. A more balanced perspective is that knowledge is a necessary but usually not sufficient factor in changing individual or collective behavior.[13] The same could be said for every other factor in the predisposing category. To recapitulate: A *combination* of factors define motivation, a combination of motivation with skills, resources, and reinforcements defines behavior and behavioral change, and combinations of interventions define a health program.

Like any other change in the complex system of predisposing factors, a change in awareness or knowledge will affect other areas because of the human drive for consistency.[14] Behavior may not change immediately in response to new awareness or knowledge, but the cumulative effects of heightened awareness, increased understanding, and greater command (recognition and recall) of facts will seep into the system of beliefs, values, attitudes, intentions, self-efficacy, health literacy, and eventually behavior.

Beliefs, Values, and Attitudes

Beliefs, values, and attitudes are independent **constructs,** yet the differences among them are often fine and complex. As this book is directed primarily to practice rather than research, we shall forgo technicalities and examine these factors in a practical way, trusting that those interested in more detailed analysis will look further in the theoretical research literature.[15]

Beliefs.   A *belief* is a conviction that a phenomenon or object is true or real. *Faith, trust,* and *truth* are words used to express or imply belief. Health-oriented belief statements include such statements as "I don't believe that medication can work"; "Exercise won't make any difference"; and "When your time is up, your time is up, and there's nothing you can do about it." If beliefs such as these are strongly held, to what extent will they interfere with good health? Can they be changed? Will changes facilitate health-promoting or health protecting-behavior?

The **Health Belief Model,** developed and widely employed over the past half century,[16] attempts to explain and predict health-related behavior from certain belief patterns.[17] The model is based on the following assumptions about behavior change:

1. The person must believe that his or her health is in jeopardy. For an asymptomatic disease such as hypertension or early cancer, the person must believe that he or she can have it and not feel symptoms. This constellation of beliefs is referred to generally as *belief in susceptibility.*
2. The person must perceive the *potential* seriousness of the condition in terms of pain or discomfort, time lost from work, economic difficulties, and so forth.
3. On assessing the circumstances, the person must believe that benefits stemming from the recommended behavior outweigh the costs and inconvenience and are indeed possible and within his or her grasp. Note that this set of beliefs is not equivalent to actual rewards and barriers, which fall under enabling and reinforcing factors in the Precede Model. In the Health Belief Model, these are *perceived* benefits and costs, anticipated or expected, but not yet realized.
4. There must be a "cue to action" or a precipitating force that makes the person feel the need to take action.

Specific applications and experimental tests of the Health Belief Model for **educational assessment** and evaluation can be found in studies of the following health actions or health problems,[18] with citations to the most recent publications found in each category:

- Breast cancer screening and mammography[19]
- Cervical cancer screening[20]
- Colorectal cancer screening[21]
- Prostate cancer screening[22]
- Skin cancer, sun exposure, and sun protection[23]
- Cardiovascular disease prevention and risk reduction[24]
- Diabetes prevention[25]
- Diet, exercise, physical activity, obesity, and weight control[26]
- Immigrants, minority, and cross-cultural health[27]

- Multiple risk behaviors[28]
- Osteoporosis[29]
- School and college health programs[30]

The Health Belief Model relates largely to the predisposing factors in the Precede-Proceed Model and serves as a useful tool to carry out that part of the educational assessment in PRECEDE.[31] Several authors have suggested ways of integrating this and other specific cognitive and affective models with PRECEDE-PROCEED.[32] Others have beliefs related to other predisposing factors in the Precede model without using the Health Belief Model,[33] or by working the Health Belief Model or the Precede-Proceed Model into other models for patient counseling.[34]

Fear.   Two of the dimensions of the Health Belief Model—belief in susceptibility and belief in severity of consequences—could be interpreted as fear of the disease, condition, or behavior. Protection Motivation Theory made this aspect of the susceptibility and severity beliefs more explicit in formulating a variation of the Health Belief Model that gave emphasis to the need for people to balance fear with a sense of self-efficacy if action is to occur. **Fear** is a powerful motivator that contains the additional dimension of anxiety beyond the belief. The source of such anxiety is the belief in susceptibility and severity *in combination with* a sense of hopelessness or powerlessness to do anything about a vague or diffuse threat. This combination produces a flight response that often manifests as denial or rationalization of the threat as unreal. Thus, arousal of fear in health education messages can backfire, unless the fear-arousing message is accompanied by an immediate course of action the person can take to alleviate the fear.[35]

Values.   The cultural, intergenerational perspectives on matters of consequence reflect the values people hold. Values tend to cluster within ethnic groups and across generations of people who share a common history and geography. They provide individuals ultimately the basis for justifying their actions in moral or ethical terms. Values underpin the right and wrong, the good and bad dimensions of people's outlook on specific behaviors. Consider this brief exchange between two people:

HE: Did I hear you say that you are going to try skydiving?
SHE: Absolutely not!
HE: Why not?
SHE: Because I value my life, that's why not!
HE: Then why do you smoke cigarettes?
SHE: Because I enjoy smoking and it helps me relax.
HE: If that's the case, can you honestly say that you really value your life?
SHE: Sure I can. It's not that I don't value my life and health but that I value other things too, among them the pleasure of smoking. What's wrong with that?

Obviously, personal values are inseparably linked to choices of behavior. In this scenario the person who values life and health—and cigarettes, too—reveals a conflict of values. Values often conflict with each other, as a former minister of health for Canada observed: "Most Canadians by far prefer good health to illness, and a long life to a short one but, while individuals are prepared to sacrifice a certain amount of immediate pleasure in order to stay healthy, they are not prepared to forgo all self-indulgence nor to tolerate all inconvenience in the interest of preventing illness."[36]

Health programs do not set out to *change* values, at least in the short term. They seek instead to help people recognize inconsistencies between their values (usually prohealth) and their behavior or environment (often antihealth). Recognizing deeply held values within ethnic groups, age groups, and other demographically defined subpopulations or settings also provides an immediate and efficient indicator of starting points for the analysis of predisposing factors in segments of the population.[37]

Attitudes.   After *motivation*, one of the vaguest yet most frequently used and misused words in the behavioral sciences lexicon is **attitude.** To keep matters short and simple, we offer two definitions that, in combination, cover the principal elements of attitude. In line with classical psychological conceptualizations of this construct, Mucchielli described attitude as "a tendency of mind or of relatively constant feeling toward a certain category of objects, persons, or situations."[38] In a more applied mode in line with his Health Belief Model collaborators, Kirscht viewed *attitudes* as a collection of beliefs that always includes an evaluative aspect.[39] Attitudes can always be assessed as positive or negative. They differ from values in being attached to specific objects, persons, or situations and being based on one or more values. In the hierarchy posited by Rokeach, values are more deeply seated and therefore less changeable than are attitudes and beliefs.[40]

These classical distinctions highlight two key concepts for assessment of predisposing factors: (1) Attitude is a rather *constant* feeling that is *directed toward an object* (be it a person, an action, a situation, or an idea). (2) Inherent in the structure of an attitude is *evaluation*, a good-bad dimension. We gain further understanding of the structure of an attitude by examining one technique frequently used to measure attitudes: the semantic differential.[41] In this technique, one responds to concepts by making a mark on a continuum between antonyms. Suppose we want to measure the attitudes toward skydiving and cigarette smoking expressed by the woman in the dialogue. Having heard her conversation with the man, we already have an idea about what her attitudes are, but let's measure them just the same.

Concept: Skydiving

good   : __ : __ : __ : __ : _X_ : __ : bad

pretty   : __ : __ : __ : __ : _X_ : __ : ugly

happy   : __ : __ : __ : _X_ : __ : __ : sad

Concept: Cigarette smoking

good   : __ : _X_ : __ : __ : __ : __ : bad

pretty   : __ : __ : _X_ : __ : __ : __ : ugly

happy   : _X_ : __ : __ : __ : __ : __ : sad

From the conversation and from her responses to the semantic differential, her attitudes toward skydiving and smoking are consistently in opposite directions. Insofar as they are constant, they are probably also strong. We can also see the woman's evaluation of the concepts (in terms of good and bad). The woman avoided neutral responses on the continuum.

Though not completely understood, the relationships between behavior and constructs such as attitudes, beliefs, and values exist, given the ample evidence of their association. Analysis will show, for example, that attitudes are to some degree the determinants, components, and consequences of beliefs, values, and behavior. This alone gives sufficient reason to be concerned with attitudes, beliefs, and values as interrelated predisposing factors. Let us now see how these personal psychological characteristics relate to behavior and to the more basic learning process suggested by the natural history of health in Figure 4-2.

Self-Efficacy and Social Cognitive Theory

The concept of self-efficacy as a determinant of behavior found early acceptance in health education and health promotion because of its emphasis on learning and on the empowerment of people to have a sense of control over their health. This concept from social learning theory, later called *cognitive learning theory*, has held a special fascination for those working in self-care education and health promotion.[42] The concept of self-efficacy was attractive probably because it expressed so succinctly the dominant purpose ascribed to health promotion by the Ottawa Charter as: "the process of enabling people to increase control over, and to improve, their health."[43] Self-efficacy had emerged as a central concept in Albert Bandura's social learning theory to describe a cognitive state of taking control, in which people are not just acted upon by their environments, but also feel they can act upon and help create and control their environments.[44]

This concept of reciprocal determinism is social cognitive theory's major departure from *operant conditioning theories*, which tend to view behavior as a one-way product of the environment. Reciprocal determinism, with its associated concepts of self-management and self-control, make social cognitive theory ideally suited to the integration of the Precede and Proceed frameworks of behavioral, environmental, predisposing, enabling, and reinforcing factors and to the development of an educational *and* ecological approach to health program planning.

Learning takes place through three processes: (1) direct experience, (2) indirect or vicarious experience from observing others (modeling), and (3) the storing and processing of complex information in cognitive operations that allow one to anticipate the consequences of actions, represent goals in thought, and weigh evidence from various sources to assess one's own capabilities. Out of this last process comes a situation-specific self-appraisal that makes the individual more or less confident in taking on new behavior in situations that may contain novel, unpredictable, or stressful circumstances. Self-efficacy, then, is a perception of one's own capacity for success in organizing and implementing a pattern of behavior that is new, a capacity based largely on experience with similar actions or circumstances encountered or observed in the past.

In addition to its influence on behavior, self-efficacy also affects thought patterns and emotional reactions that may alleviate anxiety and enhance coping ability. These interactions make self-efficacy particularly useful in studies of smoking cessation and other addictive, compulsive, or strenuous behavioral patterns where high rates of relapse are experienced, including physical activity and weight loss.[45]

The self-efficacy variable has proved particularly useful in planning health programs using mass media or school-based media with role models for the vicarious learning and modeling process and for instruction in self-control.[46]

Measurement instruments to assess self-efficacy have been validated for several health behaviors.[47] A review of the literature to identify the latest measurement advances is always advisable before one embarks on a survey to assess any of the predisposing factors.

Besides self-efficacy, other predisposing factors within social cognitive theory include

- *Expectations,* anticipated outcomes of a behavior
- *Expectancies,* the values that the person places on a given outcome.[48]

Other components of the theory will be found in the following sections on enabling and reinforcing factors.

Behavioral Intention

The pivotal predisposing factor in the theory of reasoned action and the theory of planned behavior is the concept of **behavioral intention.** The theory of *reasoned action* holds that the final step in the predisposing process, before actual action takes place, is the formulation of a behavioral intention. This step is influenced by other predisposing factors such as attitudes toward the behavior and by perception of social norms favorable to the behavior. These attitudes, in turn, are influenced both by beliefs concerning the efficacy of action in achieving the expected outcomes and by attitude toward those outcomes. Perception of social norms is influenced by beliefs about the strength of others' opinions on the behavior and the person's own motivation to comply with them.[49]

Applications of the theory of reasoned action in health behavior studies and health program planning can be found in a wide range of health issues.[50] A school-based smoking prevention project in the Netherlands specifically integrated the theory of reasoned action with PRECEDE to design interventions that proved effective in reducing the uptake of smoking.[51]

Like self-efficacy, the theories of reasoned action and planned behavior had natural appeal to health education because they seemed by their very names to place the emphasis on a thinking person's actions, informed by knowledge and guided by reason, all of which would lend credibility to an educational approach to behavioral change. They also gave credence to the social norms and to the perceptions of those norms, which set well with the community orientation of public health education and the social determinants interests of the health promotion movement. The limitation of both models, however, is that they did not feature the objective realities of resources required to *enable* the behavioral change. The Precede-Proceed Model seeks to encompass these several theories, recognizing the need to combine an educational approach with an environmental or ecological approach.

Precontemplation to Contemplation and Preparation

Another set of related predisposing factors that encompasses most of the foregoing concepts is organized within the early stages of change of the Transtheoretical Model by Prochaska and DiClemente. Among the five stages of change that grew out of their analyses of some 300 theories of psychotherapy[52] and empirical analysis of people who quit smoking on their own compared with those under professional treatment,[53] the first three align with the predisposing factors. These are the precontemplation and contemplation stages, and at least part of the preparation stage. The last three stages of preparation, action, and maintenance align more with enabling and reinforcing factors in PRECEDE.

During the first three stages, or in moving from one stage to the next, the predisposing factors we have reviewed above correspond roughly with constructs of the Transtheoretical Model (TTM): awareness and knowledge (TTM's "consciousness raising"), beliefs, values, and attitudes (TTM's "decisional balance" of pros and cons, benefits and costs of changing; its "dramatic relief" in experiencing the negative emotions of fear, anxiety, and worry that go with the old behavioral risks), self-efficacy (TTM's "confidence and temptation" balancing, and "self-reevaluation"), and behavioral intention (TTM's "contemplation and preparation" transition). What makes the TTM especially attractive as a diagnostic tool in the educational diagnostic phase of PRECEDE is its focus on the overarching predisposing factor of readiness to change and its association of these early and subsequent stages of change with specific interventions to alter or support these predisposing, enabling, and reinforcing factors, as shown in Table 4-1.

Various health studies and programs have specifically combined the Transtheoretical Model or its stages of change into Precede-Proceed needs analyses, program planning and development, evaluation, or proposed guidelines for practice.[54] Other recent applications of the TTM or its stages of change in health programs illustrate its range of potential use as a planning tool,[55] including assessment of organizational readiness for change.[56]

TABLE 4-1 The Transtheoretical Model's Stages of Change and Associated Interventions

Concept	Definition	Application
Pre-contemplation	Unaware of problem, hasn't thought about change	Increase awareness of need for change, personalize information on risks and benefits
Contemplation	Thinking about change, in the near future	Motivate, encourage to make specific plans
Decision/Determination	Making a plan to change	Assist in developing concrete action plans, setting gradual goals
Action	Implementation of specific action plans	Assist with feedback, problem solving, social support, reinforcement
Maintenance	Continuation of desirable actions, or repeating periodic recommended step(s)	Assist in coping, reminders, finding alternatives, avoiding slips/relapses (as applies)

Source: Glanz, K., & Rimer, B. (July 1995). *Theory at a Glance: A Guide for Health Promotion Practice.* Bethesda: National Cancer Institute, NIH Pub. No. 95-3896, Public Health Service, U.S. Dept. of Health and Human Services.

Existing Skills

A person may come to an educational situation already possessing the skills to take certain actions. Such skills may predispose the person to act in a particular way. For example, an experienced mother may already possess the skills for breast-feeding. When she gives birth to another child, those skills may predispose her to breast-feed that child. The mother has a high self-efficacy about breast-feeding because she has successfully breast-fed in the past; she has formulated a behavioral intention to breast-feed because of her prior acquisition of skills. Thus, existing skills or capacity are closely tied to self-efficacy, behavioral intention, and readiness to take action.

Self-confidence and self-efficacy can be linked to skills that are already present for a specific health-behavior situation and thus do not need to be learned. For example, the ability to resist peer pressure is associated with non-smoking in adolescents.[57] If a person does not possess the skills for a certain action, then the acquisition of those skills becomes an enabling factor for performing the action. Several smoking-prevention and drug abuse prevention programs have included skills training in resisting peer pressures to smoke or take drugs, to aid those students who do not already have those skills.[58]

ENABLING FACTORS

Mostly conditions of the environment, enabling factors *facilitate* the performance of an action by individuals or organizations. The absence of adequate enabling conditions inhibits action. These conditions include the availability, accessibility, and affordability of health care and community resources. They also include conditions of living that act as facilitators or barriers to action, such as availability of transportation or child care to release a mother from that responsibility long enough to participate in a health program. Enabling factors also include *new* skills that a person, organization, or community needs to carry out a behavioral or environmental change.

Enabling factors become the immediate targets of community organization or organizational development and training interventions in one's program. They consist of the resources and new skills necessary to perform a health action and the organizational actions required to modify the environment. Resources include the organization and accessibility of health care facilities, personnel, schools, and outreach clinics, or any similar resource. Personal health skills, such as those discussed in the literature on self-care and school health education, can enable specific health actions.[59] Skills in influencing the community, such as those used to promote social action and organizational change, can enable actions directed toward influencing the physical or health care environment.[60]

To plan interventions directed at changing enabling factors, the health promotion planner assesses the presence or absence of enabling factors in the community of interest. This calls for an organizational or ecological assessment of resources and an educational assessment of required skills. Together, these resources and skills may be referred to at a population level as **community capacity.** This term has gained legs in recent years with the growing interest in social capital and related notions of collective efficacy.[61]

The Health Care Environment

Enabling factors for health care or medical care behaviors include health care resources such as outreach clinics, hospitals, emergency treatment rooms, health care providers, classes or counselors for self-care, and other facilities, programs, or personnel. Cost, distance, available transportation, hours open, and so forth are enabling factors that affect the availability and accessibility of the health care services.

Suppose a well-intended educational effort were successful in appealing to the motivation of members of a target group to make greater use of medical services in their area, but the health care providers in the area were not consulted. If they had been, they would have warned that existing facilities were overcrowded and that providers were overworked and unwilling to take on more work without an expansion of facilities and additional personnel.

What will the outcome likely be? Deprived of services they need and were promised, participants in the program may become discouraged and feel they have been "let down." Because they were not considered and were made to look bad for not delivering promised services, health care providers may become angry and alienated from health education efforts. A broken-appointment cycle like that shown in Figure 3-11 would likely develop.

As emphasized throughout this book, a health behavior has many causes, so one-dimensional efforts to affect behavior rarely produce the desired results. In this example, health education for better use of medical services would fail to achieve its desired outcome because it paid no attention to the enabling factors for that utilization by the public. In his original formulation of predisposing and enabling factors that inspired the early version of the Precede Model, Ronald Andersen showed the variable influence of individual, family, and community resources as enabling factors in use of health care services for different needs, such as emergency medical care, preventive care, and dental care.[62] The Precede Model added reinforcing factors at a time when chronic diseases were throwing an increasingly intense spotlight on lifestyle behaviors that depended for their maintenance on continuing reinforcement.

Other Environmental Conditions That Affect Health-Related Behavior

Numerous environmental conditions encountered in everyday living influence health-related behavior. For example, the availability, accessibility, and low cost of unhealthful consumer products produce environmental cues to engage in behavior that affects health, for better or for worse. Negative examples include cigarette machines, which enable smoking by adolescents even where laws prohibit sale to minors; laborsaving and movement-reducing devices and machinery that foster sedentary lifestyles; "fast food," which is convenient but often high in salt and fat; and alcoholic beverages sold at sports events, which can put an intoxicated fan in the driver's seat on the road home. Examples of environmental enabling factors that can counteract such influences include the availability and low cost of smoking-cessation programs, exercise facilities, and healthful food, as well as the enforcement of laws prohibiting alcohol sales to minors or during the second half of a sporting event.

For each priority behavioral risk factor or capacity identified in the behavioral epidemiology assessment, one can identify environmental enabling factors. For example, many such factors have been found to affect smoking: cost of cigarettes, accessibility of cigarettes, smoking restrictions and bans, availability of smoking cessation and smoking prevention programs, and smoking cessation aids such as nicotine gum.[63] In one of these studies, instruments to measure predisposing (38 items), enabling (12 items), and reinforcing factors (14 items) were developed and tested, with a 93.1% accuracy of classifying (predicting) smokeless tobacco users and nonusers among adolescents.[64]

In a second example, the following enabling factors can discourage alcohol misuse among youth: leisure-time alternatives such as sports and recreation programs, after-school activities, and alcohol-free social events; adult supervision; and regulation of alcohol sales through retail outlets.[65] Project Graduation demonstrated that chemical-free graduation celebrations can reduce the number of fatalities, alcohol or drug-related injuries, and arrests for driving under

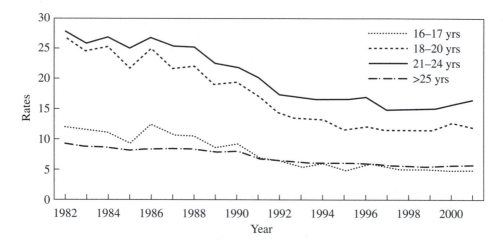

FIGURE 4-4 Rate* of drinking drivers in fatal alcohol-related crashes, by age group—Fatality Analysis Reporting System, United States, 1982—2001†
* Per 100,000 population
† Because of the unavailability of census data, crash rates for 2001 were calculated by using 2000 population estimates.
Source: Elder, R. W., & Shults, R. A. (2002)."Involvement by young drivers in fatal alcohol-related motor-vehicle crashes—United States, 1982–2001." *MMWR Morbidity and Mortality Weekly Report, 6;*51(48), 1089–1091. Web site: http://www.cdc.gov/mmwr/preview/mmwrhtml/mm5148a2.htm, accessed September 28, 2003.

the influence of alcohol.[66] The laws limiting blood-alcohol (BAC) levels in drivers on penalty of loss of driver's license have been another example of enabling factors contributing to the reduction of driving while drinking, or after drinking and concomitant reductions in alcohol-related crashes, injuries, and fatalities.[67] Fatal crashes involving drunk drivers decreased 46% from 1982 to 2001, with the most dramatic declines in teen drivers,[68] and much of this is attributed to laws enabling environmental controls, regulation, and penalties (see Figure 4-4).

This separate discussion of enabling factors could leave the impression that these factors represent an easier and more efficient pathway to health. We want to emphasize here that the successful passage of legislation, the public's assent or cooperation in responding to regulations promulgated by legislation or administrative policy, and the viability of legislation and regulation usually depend on building some degree of public awareness, outrage, or activation in support of the legislation and enforcement of the regulations and understanding the behavior required to comply with the regulations. These predisposing factors usually must precede passage of legislation or enforcement of regulations, and the reinforcing factors usually must be strengthened in conjunction with the enforcement of the regulations.[69]

For physical activity in adults, the following environmental enabling factors pertain: availability of programs that emphasize moderate exercise and increases in daily physical activity; accessibility of an exercise facility; low cost;

and environmental opportunities for physical activity.[70] Recent research has discovered numerous ways in which the "built environment," from the availability of sidewalks in suburban areas to residential density, land use mix, street connectivity, aesthetics, and safety, enables more physical activity, and some of these studies have shown corresponding differences in obesity rates.[71] Measures of these dimensions of enabling environments have been variously validated.[72]

New Skills

Skill refers here to a person's ability to perform the tasks that constitute a health-related behavior. Skills for health promotion include abilities to control personal risk factors for disease, skills in appropriate use of medical care, and skills in changing or controlling exposures to the environment. Examples include knowing how to use relaxation techniques, to exercise properly, to use the variety of medical instruments and diagnostic procedures frequently required in self-care programs, to apply insect repellant preventing mosquito bites and West Nile disease, and to tap one's voting power and potential for coalition building and community organizing to bring about change in one's neighborhood or community.

For each specific behavioral priority identified in the behavioral assessment, one should identify needed skills. For asthma self-management, such skills include environmental management and self-medication skills.[73] For substance abuse prevention, such skills include resisting peer pressures to experiment with alcohol, tobacco, or other drugs.[74] For physical activity, skills in flexible goal setting can increase adherence to an exercise program and to diet in obesity control.[75]

Health programs working to increase the ability of the people, individually or collectively, to change their environment need to know whether the people possess skills for influencing family, organizations, their environment, or their community. Such skills might include community organizing, coalition building, fund-raising, negotiating, working with the media, writing, and speaking.[76]

Assessing the extent to which members of the target population possess enabling skills can give the planner valuable insight into possible program components. Failure to consider the impact of enabling factors on the achievement of behavioral and environmental goals can lead to frustration when all the other program elements of motivation, resources, and rewards seem to be in place.

Reinforcing Factors

Reinforcing factors are those consequences of action that determine whether the actor receives positive (or negative) feedback and is supported socially afterward. Reinforcing factors thus include social support, peer influences, and advice and feedback by health care providers. Reinforcing factors also include the physical consequences of behavior, which may be separate from the social context. Examples include the alleviation of respiratory symptoms following the correct use of asthma medication and feelings of well-being or pain caused by physical exercise.

Social benefits—such as recognition, appreciation, or admiration; physical benefits such as convenience, comfort, relief of discomfort, or pain; tangible rewards such as economic benefits or avoidance of cost; and self-actualizing, imagined, or vicarious rewards such as improved appearance, self-respect, or association with an admired person who demonstrates the behavior—all reinforce behavior. That is, they make it more likely that the same behavior will be repeated and even maintained over long periods.

Reinforcing factors also include adverse consequences of behavior, or "punishments," that can lead to the extinction of a positive behavior. Rewards also can reinforce behavior that is *not* conducive to health. For individuals, these rewards might include the "high" that rewards the drug abuser, the relief of tension that rewards the smoker, or the masking of emotions that accompanies compulsive eating. For organizations, these might include the profits that accrue from promoting a harmful product or the savings that accrue from using a pollutant in the manufacturing process. Tax incentives that support nonpolluting products and penalties or fines that discourage polluting products can positively and negatively reinforce changes in organizational behavior, respectively.

For each of the priority behaviors from the behavioral diagnosis, important reinforcing factors can be determined. For example, for smoking cessation, one may seek support from peers and spouse or advice from health care providers.[77] Cigarette and alcohol advertising provides vicarious reinforcement for continuing to smoke or drink.[78] Family support and recommendations from health care providers reinforce adherence to physical activity programs.[79]

Social reinforcements, as well as social images created by the mass media, set up norms of behavior transmitted from one generation to another as *culture*. Culture shapes our institutions, which in turn organize themselves to meet our cultural expectations. By organizing resources institutionally, we can as communities and societies exert much more extensive and effective control over the environment. The cycle is thus closed with the third part of the cycle (shown in Figure 4-5), the "social history of health," as related to natural history and personal histories. Culture influences personal values, norms influence personal attitudes, and these influence behavior. Organizations directly affect the environment and indirectly through the environment affect behavior. Organizations also affect behavior more directly through the enabling and reinforcing factors discussed in the preceding pages.

One can anticipate reinforcement—negative or positive—prior to a behavior. Such *anticipated* reinforcement will influence the subsequent performance of the behavior. Social acceptance or disapproval, real or expected, thus can be a reinforcing factor. Some such factors that provide social reinforcement can become enabling ones if they generate ongoing social support, such as financial assistance or transportation, or even friendly advice. Reinforcement can also be

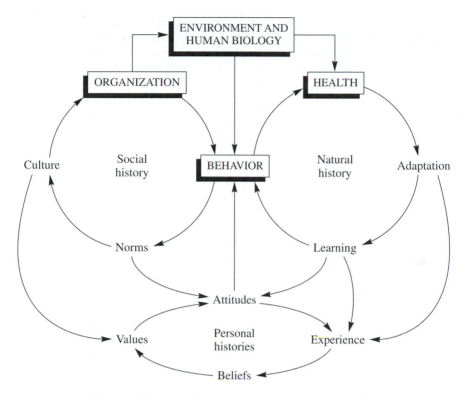

FIGURE 4-5 The social history of health includes the dimensions of social norms, culture, and organization because these influence behavior directly and indirectly through values, attitudes, and the environment.
Source: Adapted from *Community and Population Health,* 8th edition, by L. W. Green and J. M. Ottoson, 1999, New York: WCB/McGraw-Hill; used with permission of the publisher.

vicarious, in the form of modeling a behavior after a television personality, after an attractive person in an advertisement who seems to be enjoying the behavior, or after a parent or teacher.[80] These perceptions of the behavioral norms of other people, including misperception of behaviors as being more common than they are, contribute to the adoption of risky behavior under false assumptions that can be corrected.

In developing a health program, the source of reinforcement will, of course, vary depending on the objectives and type of program, as well as the setting. In occupational health programs, for example, co-workers, supervisors, union leaders, and family members may provide reinforcement. In patient care settings, reinforcement may come from nurses, physicians, fellow patients, and, again, family members. Reinforcement for the behavior of staff may come in either of those settings from other staff, supervisors, or higher-level administrators who control rewards.[81]

Whether the reinforcement is positive or negative will depend on the attitudes and behavior of significant people, some of whom will more greatly affect behavior than others. For example, in a high school health program, where reinforcement may come from peers, teachers, school administrators, and parents, which group will likely have the most influence? Research in adolescent behavior indicates that adolescent smoking, drinking, and drug-taking behaviors are most influenced by approval from friends, especially best friends. Parental attitudes, beliefs, and practices, especially those of the mother, hold second place among social influences affecting the health behavior status of adolescents.[82]

Incremental and easily reversible changes in behavior are more likely to be reinforced by success than are drastic changes. For example, to decrease sodium consumption, people tolerate small steps of a low-salt diet more easily, and these are more apt to be reinforced through their successful implementation than are large steps toward the goal. Consider, for example, the steps one can use for low-salt diets. The following could be added one at a time after success in the previous steps: salting only after tasting, cutting salt in cooking, eliminating table salt, buying low-salt food products, and, finally, eliminating cooking salt.

Behavior of policy makers that influences environmental or health care conditions also responds to reinforcing factors. Community or social support can reinforce their actions to influence these changes. Such support can be provided by community residents, health care provider associations, and media advocacy. The community change agent who does not have such support becomes discouraged, experiences "burnout," and consequently abandons his or her efforts.

Program planners must carefully assess reinforcing factors to make sure that program participants have maximum opportunities for supportive feedback, rewards, and public support for making changes in their behavior. Without such feedback, programs have a reduced chance of sustained momentum and eventual success. From the perspective of an agency's relationship to the community or population it serves, failing to address enabling and reinforcing factors, especially after building a high level of motivation in the population, can produce a backlash, or frustration, that can sour future attempts to affect change in the population.

SELECTING DETERMINANTS OF BEHAVIOR
AND ENVIRONMENTAL CHANGE

Selecting those predisposing, reinforcing, and enabling factors that, if modified, will help bring about the targeted health-related behavior and environmental change is the core of PRECEDE's educational and ecological phases. The three basic steps in this process are (1) identifying and sorting factors into the three categories, (2) setting priorities among the categories, and (3) establishing priorities within the categories. Specific factors selected by this process form the basis for both educational and organizational or policy objectives, which then lead to the selection of materials and methods for program advocacy and implementation. If the program is well designed and carefully implemented, the probability is high that objectives will be met, the needed behavioral and environmental changes will occur, and the eventual, consequent health and quality-of-life goals will be met.

Step 1: Identifying and Sorting

The list of causal factors initially identified for each behavior and environmental target should be as comprehensive as possible to help the planner avoid overlooking crucial determinants. Both informal and formal methods can be used to develop the list.

Informal Methods.   The team assigned the responsibility for designing the intervention plan usually has educated guesses and hypotheses about the reasons why people do or do not behave in a desired manner. At this point, it can be helpful to involve members of the group at risk (the consumers or target population) in the planning again. Their information and insight on their own behavior, attitudes, beliefs, values, and barriers to reaching the stated objectives are quite relevant. Intensive interviews, informal group discussions, nominal groups, focus groups, panels, and questionnaires can provide useful data.[83] Focus groups have been the most widely applied method for informal collection of perceived causes of the behavioral and environmental issues.[84] Brainstorming and nominal group process are useful techniques for generating data on barriers to behavioral change.[85]

The same methods of eliciting information can be used with staff who will be involved in the delivery of the intervention and with people in agencies providing related services. They might suggest potential causes of behavior based on insights from personal experience or unrecognized effects of agency or community resources, services, and operations. Planners must be critical in accepting health workers' assumptions about the predisposing factors of patients or clients. Some providers may judge behavior that differs from expectations as lazy, apathetic, or ignorant. Generalizations of this sort do not help explain the behavior at issue but merely describe it with value-laden pejoratives. "Blaming the victim" may arise out of misunderstanding, poor communication, burnout, or rationalization: The system may be at fault, rather than the population or patient.[86] On the other hand, "system blaming" may arise out of frustration with the organizations and management of services, and this can be just as unproductive as putting all the responsibility for change on individuals. The purpose of the assessment at this stage is not to fix blame or responsibility, but rather to take inventory of all the potential targets of change that might improve the situation.

A vital step in this phase of PRECEDE is sorting the predisposing, enabling, and reinforcing factors according to whether they have negative or positive effects. The negative effects must be overcome, and the positive effects can be built on and strengthened. Systematic recording of the data will make

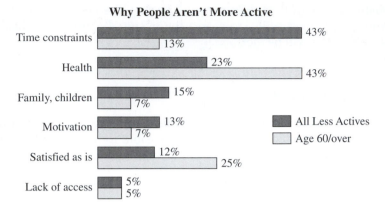

FIGURE 4-6 Reasons people give for not being more active, with contrasts between the 43% of the overall population who are less active and the population of older adults over 60 years of age.
Source: President's Council on Physical Fitness and Sports Medicine, U.S. Department of Health and Human Services. Web site: http://www.fitness.gov/american_att.PDF.

this information useful and retrievable. Probing for more specificity and delineation of differences in causation across subpopulations will help offset the tendencies toward stereotyping, overgeneralization, victim blaming, and system blaming.[87]

Formal Methods.   A search through relevant literature can yield information on cultural and social attitudes and descriptions of studies defining the causal importance of specific factors on health-related behavior or environmental change.[88] For example, assessments that examine those beliefs and perceptions of adults that may influence their physical activity typically find that (1) people are generally misinformed or confused about the frequency, intensity, and duration of activity needed to obtain a cardiovascular benefit; (2) one's doctor is the most important referent regarding exercise; and (3) people do not think health benefits of exercise are as critical as the intrinsic, psychological, or emotional benefits. Such a search may also yield items that can be used in surveys or a record-keeping system that will eventually become the basis for evaluation of the program. This is where the construction of a data-based profile of the population provides a baseline for subsequent evaluation of progress and achievements of the program.[89]

For example, a national study has shown the American public to express particular reasons why they are not more active (Figure 4-6). Among the least active segment of all adults (43% of the adult population), the most common reason given is time constraints, whereas for older adults (over 60), health is most frequently mentioned as the barrier (or excuse) for not getting more physical activity. Such survey data can provide guidance to the relative importance (see steps 2 and 3 below) of specific predisposing ("motivation," which isn't specific enough), enabling ("time constraints, health, family . . . lack of access"), and reinforcing ("family," "satisfied as is") factors that might point toward the selection of communication messages and other interventions (see next chapter). They also should provide baseline data against which objectives can be stated as to how a program should reduce these barriers or perceptions of barriers (see final section of this chapter). The question the local program planners must ask themselves is whether these national data from a survey conducted several years ago pertain to their own local population at this time.

Checklists and questionnaires are structured ways of collecting and organizing information from important individuals and groups within the local or "target" population. These can be used to measure knowledge, attitudes, and beliefs as well as perceptions of services. Numerous projects and programs have conducted formal surveys of the predisposing, enabling, and reinforcing factors associated with behavioral and environmental changes required to affect health outcomes. Their analyses illustrate the formal application of survey methods to the identification, assessment, and sorting process.[90] Most of these formal surveys applying the Precede Model were also used in the follow-up evaluation of the programs and can be used in future assessments as a source of developed survey instruments and comparative data with some degree of prior validation.[91]

Community organizations and planning agencies often compile directories of available community resources. These directories are particularly helpful when enabling factors are being examined. Utilization data from health care organizations and attendance records from agencies may also be available.[92] Surveys of community organizations can also be conducted, as recommended and detailed in a series of CDC and Peace Corps community intervention handbooks organized in relation to Precede-Proceed constructs[93] and in CDC manuals for implementation of the Planned Approach to Community Health.[94]

Correctness in deciding whether a factor influencing behavior is predisposing, enabling, or reinforcing is less important than listing it in whichever categories might apply. As you have seen, the three categories are not mutually exclusive; many determinants can appropriately be placed in more than one. A family may be predisposed to dieting, for example, and reinforce (negatively or positively) that behavior once it has been undertaken. We do not wish to define the categories so rigidly that PRECEDE becomes an academic debating point. The categories are meant to sort the causal factors into three classes of targets for subsequent intervention according to the three broad classes of intervention strategy: (1) direct communication to change the predisposing factors, (2) indirect communication and mobilization of support (through family, peers, teachers, employers, and health care providers) to change the reinforcing factors, and (3) organizational, developmental, regulatory, policy, and training strategies to change the enabling factors.

Later in the planning process, the specific educational and organizational activities and messages for each factor will be devised based on judgment of their importance as determinants of the desired outcomes. Then, the category in which the factor falls *will* make a difference. For example, the design of messages, learning opportunities, and organizational strategies directed at families

TABLE 4-2 An example of classifying the determinants of behavioral and environmental factors in relation to parents' actions on sore throat symptoms in young children

Behavioral objectives

Within three days of the initial manifestation of sore throat, 80% of the children in Hobbit's Preschool Program will have a throat culture done based on a swab taken by a parent.

The target group for the learning objectives will be the parents of the preschoolers, the parents' employers, relatives, and physicians, and the preschool personnel.

Predisposing factors

Positive	Negative
Attitudes, beliefs, and values: Mothers value child's health; mothers have been willing to use health services regularly. Knowledge: Mothers can read thermometers and determine temperatures; children are old enough to report sore throats.	Attitudes, beliefs, and values: Sore throats are not important; mothers feel that sore throats are temporary; mothers feel that sore throats do not have serious consequences and that there is no relationship between strep throat and sequelae.

Reinforcing factors

Positive	Negative
Teachers relate well to parents; physician has set up positive interaction with group; teachers and medical personnel encourage and support parents in taking throat swabs.	Mother's employers are not generous about time off for child's illness; grandmothers (or baby sitters) consider sore throats inconsequential and temporary.

Enabling factors

Positive	Negative
Mothers have thermometers in homes; clinic is close by; insurance reduces cost of follow-up visit. Throat swab kit for home use is available; clinic provides culture and analysis in three days; skill in swabbing is easily learned.	Cost of prescription penicillin regimen; teachers cannot take child to doctor; parent has to stay home with child or arrange for sitter because there is no preschool isolation room.

will differ according to whether a family seems most important in creating rewards to *reinforce* the behavior or in providing financial support to *enable* the behavior.

A list at this point might look something like the one in Table 4-2, which shows both positive and negative factors related to reducing the sequelae of streptococcal throat infections in a preschool population. At the end of this chapter, you will convert some of these factors into learning and resource objectives, which are statements of the immediate goals of a health promotion program. One must achieve such objectives in order to obtain behavioral and environmental changes, which are the intermediate goals of the program. In turn, one must meet the behavioral and environmental objectives if one hopes to achieve health improvements or improvements in quality of life—the ultimate goals of the program.

Step 2: Setting Priorities Among Categories

All the causes in a complete inventory for several behavioral and environmental changes cannot be tackled simultaneously. One therefore needs to decide which factors are to be the objects of intervention first and in what order the others need to be addressed by a program of interventions.

A first basis for establishing priorities among the three kinds of factors is logical development. For example, an HIV or cancer screening service must have its facility and laboratory in operation and services available before it creates a demand for the services. The organizational enabling factors that provide the services and make them accessible usually need to precede the educational efforts to predispose people to use them. Raising public expectations for a service that does not yet exist would be illogical in most cases and can be expected to create frustration and subsequent denial or rejection of further attempts to persuade the population. There will be instances, however, when raising public awareness and demand is necessary before the political support to fund the necessary services will be forthcoming. In such instances, the use of health education becomes an advocacy tool, as it has been in creating demand for HIV and breast cancer services, tobacco control, and programs for prevention of alcohol and drug abuse.[95]

For most health programs, an initial focus on the predisposing factors is the logical order. People will not adopt a set of behaviors to reduce a health risk if they are not aware that there *is* a risk. Belief in the immediacy of the risk and its implications will have to be developed for the enabling resources to be utilized. Finally, reinforcing factors cannot come into play until behaviors have taken place. Thus, for a community program, enabling, then predisposing, then reinforcing factors would be translated into interventions, in that order. Different situations may require a different order of development, depending upon the factors that already exist. The order of needs might also vary across a population. Underserved segments of the population will likely need more help with the enabling factors of access to resources, financial support, transportation, and child care before they can take advantage of services, whereas in the more affluent segments of the population, a little motivation (increase in predisposing factors) will stimulate actions unencumbered by resource barriers.

Some enabling factors may have to be developed over a long period by means of community organizational efforts, legislative pressure, and reallocation of resources. If so, the concerns of the highest priority group within the population may have to be postponed for months. In such cases, the population so predisposed might be mobilized to support legislation or organizational development to strengthen the enabling factors.

Some factors may be difficult to work with because of agency policies or mandates. An agency may be restricted to activities related to one set of factors. A hospital, for example, may not have the personnel to contact families at home and may have to depend on another agency to undertake that task. A school system may have to follow a board of education ruling that AIDS information can be taught only within classes on marriage and the family and that discussion and provision of contraception is not a school responsibility.

Work on several factors can and should proceed simultaneously, however. Cooperation with the appropriate agency to establish a rehabilitation service for alcoholics, for example, can coincide with the mounting of a general information campaign on the costs of alcoholism and the efficacy of treatment. By the time the service is operational, the climate is set for specific information about the type and availability of services.

Step 3: Establishing Priorities Within Categories

Within the three categories of determinants of behavioral and environmental changes, factors can be selected for intervention in a logical order of priority. One uses the same criteria as those used for selecting high-priority health-related behaviors in the previous chapter: importance and changeability.

Importance.   Importance can be estimated by judging *prevalence, immediacy,* and *necessity* according to logic, experience, data, and theory. **Prevalence** asks, How widespread or frequent is the factor? If the factor identified is very widespread or occurs often, it should qualify for priority consideration. For example, if 80% of the students in a school system believe smoking is glamorous, then addressing that belief in an antismoking campaign should have much higher priority than if only 10% of students hold that belief.

Immediacy asks, How compelling or urgent is the factor? Knowing the symptoms of a heart attack and what is needed to save a victim's life is one example of knowledge that has immediate consequences for people at high risk of heart attacks. Another type of immediacy has to do with how close the connection is between the factor and the group at risk. If a certain group of adults believes no connection exists between strep throat and rheumatic heart disease, changing that belief is a high priority if the adults are the parents of young children, who are at high risk. It is not a high priority if the adults are the parents of graduating seniors.

Necessity is based on the consideration of factors that have a low or high prevalence but still must be absent or present for the change in behavior or environment to occur. If an outcome cannot be achieved without a certain factor, that factor deserves priority. Knowledge is often necessary though insufficient to bring about an action. It is difficult to envision an intravenous drug user giving up drugs to avoid AIDS without understanding how dirty needles can transmit HIV. A person is unlikely to commit himself or herself to a patient role, for example, without at least a minimal awareness of the illness. Knowledge of the unavoidable need for exercise is necessary for a person to join an

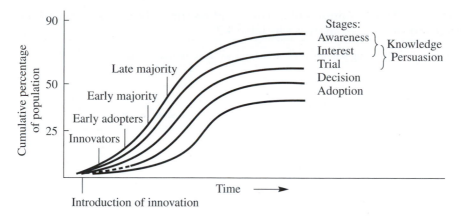

FIGURE 4-7 Five stages of adoption for four groups of adopters show increasing time lags among awareness, interest, trial, decision, and adoption stages as time passes from introduction of the innovation.

aerobics program in response to a physician's referral. Certain beliefs can also be considered necessary. People who are supposed to present themselves for medical services must have some belief (however faint) that the health professional can help alleviate the problem. A person who is attempting to stop smoking must believe smoking is harmful, at least, to his or her social relationships if not to health.

Changeability.   One can gather evidence of the changeability of a factor by looking at the results of previous programs or the trends in that factor's prevalence in a population over time. Assessments of changeability can also be made using techniques set forth in the literature. Rokeach, for example, posits a hierarchy in which beliefs are easier to change than are attitudes, and attitudes are easier to change than are values.[96] One also can analyze changeability and the priority of factors according to a theory on stages in adoption and diffusion of innovations. This theory is based on work in communications and extensive experience in agriculture, education, family planning, and public health.[97]

Behavioral change is analyzed over time, and the stages by which one adopts behavior are observed at the individual and societal levels. Individuals pass through stages labeled awareness, interest, persuasion, decision, and adoption. When these stages are charted in a population or social system, they follow a pattern of prevalence or cumulative diffusion that looks like a series of increasingly flattened S-shaped curves.

In Figure 4-7, the five stages of adoption and the four groups of adopters identify points in time when different communication methods and channels are more or less effective. Identification of the stages allows the health program planner to match the most appropriate intervention strategy with the stage of

TABLE 4-3 These examples of learning and resource objectives are based on predisposing factors analyzed in Table 4-2

Problem	Teaching parents to swab sore throats and submit swabs for throat cultures

Target Group: Parents

Knowledge	By the end of the program period, 90% of the parents will be able to 1. Identify sore throat and fever as potential strep throat 2. Identify throat swabs as necessary to determine whether strep accompanies sore throat 3. State the cure for strep throat 4. State that prescriptions are available at the clinic
Beliefs	By the end of the program, 80% of parents will believe 1. The consequences of strep throat can be serious 2. A cure is available 3. They can take action leading to identification and treatment of strep throat 4. This series of steps will reduce the potential for further illness
Skills	By the end of the program, 70% of the parents will be able to 1. Swab the child's throat 2. Return the swab to the clinic laboratory

the program recipient. For example, mass media are most efficient with **innovators** and **early adopters,** but outreach methods such as home visits are necessary with late adopters. Depending on the percentage of the population who have already adopted the health behavior at a given point in time, the relative changeability of the behavior in the remaining population is defined by this theory of diffusion.

Observability also influences changeability. If one can demonstrate the factor, one can set a climate for others and reinforce their efforts. As an example, consider the growing emphasis on nonsmoking in public meetings. Mass communications often can be utilized to promote reinforcing messages that support certain behaviors. The function of media, in such instances, is not to motivate but to reinforce.

LEARNING AND RESOURCE OBJECTIVES

Writing learning objectives and resource objectives is similar to writing behavioral objectives, as presented in Chapter 3. Learning objectives define the proportion of a population that should possess a predisposing factor or a skill by a particular time following the beginning of a program, or at the end of a program. Resource objectives define the environmental enabling factors that should be in place at a point in time after the start of a program, or, again, by the end of the program.

Table 4-3 shows examples of learning objectives. The predisposing and enabling factors analyzed in Table 4-2 have been restated in terms of learning

TABLE 4-4 These examples of learning and resource objectives are based on reinforcing and enabling factors analyzed in Table 4-2

Problem	Teaching preschool personnel to reinforce and enable parents to swab sore throats of children

Target Group: Preschool Personnel

Learning objectives for reinforcement	By the end of the program, 90% of the preschool personnel will 1. Verbally reinforce mothers for swabbing their children's throats within 3 days of the initial manifestation of sore throat 2. Verbally reinforce mothers for returning swabs to the clinic laboratory 3. Inquire of parents about the results of throat swabs 4. Inform parents that prescriptions are available at the clinic 5. Administer prescribed medication according to parents' and physicians' instructions 6. Inform other parents when a positive throat culture occurs in a preschool child
Resource objectives for environmental enabling factors	By the end of the program, 100% of the time the following will be made available by preschool personnel for parents' use: 1. Throat swab kits 2. Thermometers 3. Laboratory slips for throat cultures

objectives for parents. Note the variations in the "how much" in these examples. One can usually create a high level of knowledge. Often, over 90% of a given population can be made aware of a given fact. A smaller percentage of those who are aware will believe the fact is relevant, important, or useful. Not all of these will develop the requisite skill to carry out recommended actions. Hence, if 60% of the population is expected to adopt a behavior, it is necessary to develop skills in 70%, establish health beliefs in 80%, and to create knowledge of the problem or recommendation in 90% or more. This "leakage" of effect over the sequence of cascading cause-effect linkages provides a rough guide to estimating reasonable quantified objectives in the absence of complete baseline data.

One can develop learning objectives not only for the target population but also for those people who will reinforce the target population. For the example of throat cultures in preschool children, the preschool personnel might also be targets of intervention to teach them how to reinforce the parents. In addition, information about environmental enabling factors provides the basis for developing resource objectives.

Table 4-4 provides examples of learning objectives for reinforcement and examples of resource objectives for environmental enabling factors. Note that the objectives address the reinforcing and environmental enabling factors that were defined in Table 4-2. Learning objectives for reinforcers and resource objectives are important components of a health program that addresses all three categories of determining factors. Achievement of ongoing reinforcement and environmental resources can create a situation where the effect of the health program can continue even after the program ends.

SUMMARY

This chapter examines the factors affecting behavior and the environment as these relate to health. We call this phase of PRECEDE the educational and eco-logical assessment because we identify those factors on which health educa-tion, policy, and community organization can have direct and immediate influences and thereby an indirect influence on behavior or environment. Three sets of factors are identified—predisposing, reinforcing, and enabling. Each plays an important role in health-related behavior and organization. After identifying the factors, we suggest how to assess their relative importance and changeability. Use of these two criteria allows one to prioritize the various causes of health behavior. Then, related learning and organizational objectives can be stated so that health programs can focus where they will do the most good in facilitating development of or changes in behavior and environment.

Formulation of learning objectives follows from the identification of pre-disposing factors and skills; development of organizational and resource objec-tives follows from the identification of reinforcing and enabling factors.

EXERCISES

1. For one of the high-priority behavioral changes you selected in the previous chapter, make an inventory of all the predisposing, enabling, and reinforcing factors you can identify. For a priority environmental condition, list the enabling factors.
2. Rate each factor believed to cause the health behavior or environmental con-dition according to its importance and changeability. Give each factor a rat-ing of low, medium, or high on each criterion.
3. Write learning or resource objectives for the highest-priority predisposing factor, enabling factor, and reinforcing factor.

NOTES AND CITATIONS

1. *Reciprocal determinism of behavior and environment:* In previous editions, we have presented these concepts of predisposing, enabling, and reinforcing factors in separate sections for their influences on behavior and the environment. As the ecological approach has taken hold in program planning, the artificial compartmentalization of these by the disciplines that have nurtured the theories and research on each factor and its influence has given way to a trans-disciplinary view of their interaction and reciprocal determinism reflected in this discussion. For example, Best, et al., 2004; Halfon & Hochstein, 2002; Hertzman, et al., 2001; IOM, 2001; Jamner & Stokols, 2000; Keating & Hertzman, 1999; King, et al., 2002; Singer & Ryff, 2001; Stokols, 2000.

2. *Theoretical themes underlying the Precede-Proceed Model:* See endnote 14 in Chapter 1 and Chap-ter 1 of previous editions for earlier published references. For a searchable bibliography of some 950 published applications of the model, go to http://lgreen.net/hpp/precede apps/preapps.htm. The theoretical grounding and evolution of the model has been influ-

enced as much from its various applications and the theories brought to bear in those applications as in the original theories and research that led to the formulation of the model.

3. *Social learning, as distinct from formal educational process, and the individual as an agent of environmental change, not just a victim of or reactor to the environment:* Bandura, 2001, 2002.

4. *Stages of change and transtheoretical model applied at the population level:* Prochaska, 2001; Prochaska, et al., 2001; Sarkin, et al., 2001. For critiques of the theory and its application, see Bandura, 1997; Lechner, Brug, & Mudde, 1998.

5. *St. Louis community asthma project with African American low-income neighborhood:* E. B. Fisher, et al., 1996, p. 371. For *other Precede analyses of educational and ecological determinants of behavior and environments influencing asthma,* see W. C. Bailey, et al., 1987, 1999; Barner, et al., 1999; Bartholomew, Parcel, Kok, & Gottlieb, 2001, pp. 34–36 & Fig. 2.5; Boulet, Belanger, & Lajoie, 1996; Boulet, Chapman, Green, & FitzGerald, 1994; Chiang, et al., 2003; H. Cohen, Harris, & Green, 1979; Fireman, Friday, Gira, Vierthaler, & Michaels, 1981; Green, 1974; Green & Frankish, 1994; Hindi-Alexander & Cropp, 1981; Liu & Feekery, 2001; Maiman, Green, Gibson, & Mackenzie, 1979; Mesters, Meertens, Crebolder, & Parcel, 1993; Pujet, et al., 1997; Taggart, et al., 1991.

6. Bartholomew, Parcel, Kok, & Gottlieb, 2001, present *a graphic summary of the determinants of behavioral factors in asthma outcomes that also lists a set of environmental factors that interact with the behavioral factors* (Fig. 2.5, p. 35). We commend this to those planning asthma self-management programs, but would recommend directing the enabling and reinforcing factors listed under "educational diagnosis" at the environmental factors as well as the behavioral. Many of their enabling and reinforcing factors would influence behavior and health outcomes through the social and physical environmental determinants, whereas the graph as drawn implies that all of the direct effects of change in the enabling and reinforcing factors would be on behavioral change in the parents or children with asthma.

7. *Psychographics:* The use of marketing concepts and tools such as psychographics have found their way increasingly into health program planning, especially via social marketing and where the health program has a product or service to "sell" to the public, such as condoms: Gray, et al., 2001, or nicotine replacement treatments for smokers: Ling, & Glantz, 2002. Some other recent examples of psychographics in health planning include Stephenson, et al., 2002, in drug abuse prevention, and Candel, 2001, in studying consumer orientation toward convenience in meal preparation.

8. *Sociographics:* Demographic characteristics that predict and sometimes explain variations in health behavior serve in conjunction with psychographics to segment and target health communications and other program interventions. For example, Espy & Senn, 2003; Fernando, et al., 2003; Green & Potvin, 2002; Shoenberg, et al., 2003; Whaley & Winfield, 2003.

9. *PRECEDE examples of using sociodemographic information for health planning by examining cultural differences imbedded in the predisposing demographic variations:* Airhihenbuwa, 1995, esp p. 152 ff.; Bird, et al., 1996; Castro, et al., 1999, esp. pp. 139, 151; Dabbagh, et al., 1991–92; Doyle, et al., 1999; Doyle & Feldman, 1977; Farthing, 1994; Frankish, Lovato, & Shannon, 1999, esp. pp. 59–63, 67; Glanz, et al., 1999 (using Andersen's earlier classification in which reinforcing were part of enabling factors); Gutierrez & Le, 1999, esp. pp. 359–360, 367, 370; Hiatt, et al., 1996; Huff & Kline, 1999, esp. pp. 482, 495, see also pp. 76–78, 8–91, 383, 389–390, 504–506, 509, & 513; Maxwell, et al., 1998; Pasick, D'Onofrio, & Otero-Sabogal, 1996; Turner, et al., 1995; Ugarte, et al., 1992. Some applications of Precede analyses for planning programs cross-culturally have used participatory research methods with *native populations,* which have tended to draw them to a closer examination of demographic variations within what had been treated as culturally homogeneous populations: Daniel & Green, 1995; Daniel, et al., 1999; Kieth & Doyle, 1998; Macaulay, et al., 1997; McGowan & Green, 1995.

10. *Use of demographic variation in predisposing factors to plan programs: e.g., motivation to quit smoking vs. weight gain; males vs. females:* Riedel, et al., 2002. And further variation between African-American and white women, Pomerleau, et al., 2001.

11. *Examples of applied health-related awareness and knowledge acquisition, and relation of knowledge to behavior:* For example, Collins, et al., 2003; Jardine, 2003; Jungers, et al., 2003; some within the

Precede-Proceed framework of predisposing, enabling, reinforcing factors: Canto, et al., 1998, 2001; Chiou, et al., 1998; Daltroy, et al., 1993; Rudd et al., 2003, on health literacy.

12. *Knowledge requirements for asthma self-management actions:* Bartholomew, Parcel, Kok, & Gottlieb, 2001, p. 35, do not include knowledge as a necessary predisposing factor in asthma self-management, though they do include several skills needed by parents and children as enabling factors; cf. Boulet, Chapman, Green, & FitzGerald, 1994; McLean, et al., 2003; Meszaros, et al., 2003.

13. Awareness or new knowledge sometimes appears to be the only thing required to get a change in behavior in those situations where the other predisposing, enabling, and reinforcing factors are already in place. A case study of the Ford Motor Company's medical screening and surveillance program notes, "Although there is little evidence that information alone achieves behavior change . . . considerable evidence exists to indicate that, in some kinds of situations, information is all that is needed to provide behavior change. . . . This was such a case." Quotation from Ware, 1985, p. 321.

14. *Awareness and knowledge prevail over time in many cases because of the human drive for cognitive consistency:* The classic sources on this are Abelson, Aronson, McGuire, et al., 1968; and Festinger, 1957. Recent applications of the concept of cognitive consistency and cognitive dissonance in health include Offir, et al., 1993; Salovey, Schneider, & Apanovitch, 2000.

15. For reviews of the various theories of intrapersonal or psychological dynamics in health behavior, see Glanz, Rimer, & Lewis, 2002, pp. 45–159; esp. Rimer, 2002; B. G. Simons-Morton, Greene, & Gottlieb, 1995; K. Tones & Tilford, 1994, esp. pp. 87–103.

16. *The classic study that put the Health Belief Model on the map* was reported in Hochbaum, 1956, 1959 to explain why people sought screening X-rays for tuberculosis. The model soon changed shape when applied to seeking immunization. Hochbaum's colleagues substituted belief in susceptibility for belief that one could have a disease and not know it, which Hochbaum had found to be the most important belief accounting for getting screening examinations. See Rosenstock, 1974; Rosenstock, Derryberry, & Carriger, 1959.

17. *For a review of the origins, components, and applications of the Health Belief Model,* see Janz, Champion, & Strecher, 2002. *For a review and critique of studies testing the model,* see J. A. Harrison, Mullen, & Green, 1992. *For a validation of its predictive power in relation to other models, including PRECEDE, which encompasses the Health Belief Model,* see P. D. Mullen, Hersey, & Iverson, 1987.

18. *Most recent examples of Health Belief Model applications* are cited in the series of endnotes (19–30) to follow, by health issue, settings, or populations. For more extensive and earlier bibliographic references on applications and tests of the Health Belief Model in each of these and other areas, see the previous editions of this book: Green & Kreuter, 1991, 1999, endnote 17, or Harrison, Mullen, & Green, 1992; and Janz, Champion, & Strecher, 2002. For a critique of this and several other social cognition models used widely in health planning (theory of reasoned action, theory of planned behavior, and protection motivation theory), see Ogden, 2003.

19. *Breast cancer screening and mammography:* Allen, Bastani, et al., 2002; Oliver-Bazquez, et al., 2002; Parten & Slater, 2003.

20. *Cervical cancer screening:* Austin, et al., 2002; Kahn, et al., 2001; Lee, 2000; Michielutte, et al., 2001.

21. *Colorectal cancer screening exams:* Jacobs, 2002; Manne, et al., 2002, 2003; Rawl, et al., 2002.

22. *Prostate cancer screening exams:* Clark-Tasker & Wade, 2002.

23. *Skin cancer, sun exposure, and sun-protection behavior:* Cokkinides, et al., 2001; Grubbs & Tabano, 2000.

24. *Cardiovascular disease prevention, risk reduction:* Ali, 2002; Docherty, 2001.

25. *Diabetes prevention:* Burnet, Plaut, et al., 2002; Wdowik, Kendall, et al., 2000.

26. *Diet, exercise, physical activity, weight control,* usually related to the two previous categories of cardiovascular disease prevention, risk reduction, and diabetes control: Ali, 2002; Burnet, Plaut, et al., 2002; Chew, Palmer, et al. 2002; Murimi, 2001; Rosal, Ebbeling, et al., 2001; Shephard, 2002; Soto Mas, et al., 2000.

27. *Immigrants, minority, and cross-cultural health:* Burnett, et al., 2002; Hyman & Guruge, 2002; Lee, 2000; Poss, 2001; Soto Mas, Kane, et al., 2000.

28. *Multiple risk behaviors:* Chew, Palmer, et al., 2002; Docherty, 2001; Strecher, Wang, et al., 2002.

29. *Osteoporosis:* Murimi, 2001; Wallace, 2002.

30. *School and college health programs:* Wdowik, et al., 2000; Winnail, et al., 2002.

31. For example, Lux & Petosa, 1994; Wong & Seet, 1997.

32. Bartholomew, Parcel, et al., 2001; Neumark-Sztainer & Story, 1996; Skinner & Kreuter, 1997, esp. pp. 56–59. Street, Gold, & Manning (1997) recommend "an integrative framework for health promotion" such as Precede-Proceed to organize and expand the more specific theories and models, including Health Belief Model, Efficacy Theory (Social Cognitive Theory), Attribution Theory, the Theory of Reasoned Action, and the Transtheoretical Model.

33. *The Health Belief Model and other predisposing factors are sometimes incorporated into other needs assessment, communication, or patient education and counseling models:* Airhihenbuwa, 1995; Burnett, et al., 2002; Rosal, et al., 2001; Strecher, Wang, et al., 2002; Wong & Seet, 1997, although the use of the term *model* varies across these applications, where one model is often seen as a subset or component of another model, as with the Health Belief Model within the predisposing component of the Precede-Proceed Model. Some are mainly conceptual models to explain or predict, as with the Health Belief Model; others are that plus procedural or stage models for systematic application of the concepts, as with Precede-Proceed, Airhihenbuwa's PEN-3 (Person—Extended Family—Neighborhood) Model, and the Patient-Centered Counseling Model (Poss, 2001; Rosal, et al., 2001).

34. *Relating beliefs to other predisposing factors in the Precede Model without using the Health Belief Model:* H. Becker, Hendrickson, & Shaver, 1998; Risker & Christopher, 1995; Szykman, Bloom, & Levy, 1997: e.g., using *Protection Motivation Theory* introduced by Rogers (1975) and recently applied to genetic counseling by Helmes (2003), amblyopia: Norman, et al., 2003, and HIV-AIDS: Bengel, et al., 1996. This theory contains the same essential elements as the Health Belief Model, but adds a dimension of *self-efficacy* to the original HBM. Some of the architects of the evolving HBM later suggested adding self-efficacy to that model as well: Rosenstock, Strecher, & Becker, 1988.

35. *Fear as motivation, or as barrier to action if belief in self-efficacy is lacking:* Cho, 2003; Helmes, 2002; Norman, et al., 2003; van der Pligt, 1998.

36. *Competing values, pro-health versus non-health:* Lalonde, 1974, p. 8; see also Resnicow, Braithwaite, et al., 2002, esp. pp. 494–495 on *differing core values of cultural or ethnic groups,* and pp. 500–502 on *core values of individualism versus communalism,* and of *religiosity;* Franzini, et al., 2002, esp. pp 302–304, and Aguirre-Molina, et al., 2001, pp. 77–178, on how these values vary within Hispanic populations depending on their degrees of *acculturation and stage of life;* and Huff & Kline, 1999, for *cultural assessment frameworks and tools* to gauge values within cultural or multicultural settings.

37. *This approach to audience segmentation and analysis is central to the marketing and social marketing fields:* For examples of this application within the Precede Model, see Bonaguro & Miaoulis, 1983; De Pietro, 1987, esp. pp. 105–107; Glanz & Rimer, 1995; Hall & Best, 1997; Kotler & Roberto, 1989, pp. 282–294; Lefebvre, et al., 1995; Miaoulis & Bonaguro, 1980–1981; Sleet, 1987; J. A. Smith & Scammon, 1987. Recent reviews show a growing *convergence in the use of social marketing methods of formative research with the traditions of community health in participatory research and planning:* for example, Bryant, et al., 2000; CDC, 1999; Neiger, et al., 2003.

38. *Definition of attitude:* Mucchielli, 1970, p. 30.

39. *Relation of attitude to beliefs:* Kirscht, 1974.

40. *Relation of attitudes and beliefs to values:* Rokeach, 1970.

41. *The semantic differential as a tool to measure attitudes:* Osgood, Cuci, & Tannenbaum, 1961.

42. *Self-efficacy applied in health:* Baranowski, Perry, & Parcel, 2002; see from some of the earliest applications in patient self-care education: e.g., Bowler & Morisky, 1983; Green, Levine, & Deeds, 1975; Lorig & Laurin, 1985; and for broader school and community health education:

Parcel & Baranowski, 1981; Strecher, DeVillis, Becker, & Rosenstock, 1986, to recent applications in chronic disease self-management: e.g., Lorig & Holman, 2003, to risk-reduction and health promotion: Petosa, et al., 2003.

43. *Resonance of self-efficacy with health promotion's definition from the Ottawa Charter:* First International Conference on Health Promotion, 1986, p. iv.

44. *Albert Bandura's concept of self-efficacy from his original social learning theory, later named social cognitive theory:* Bandura, 1977, 1982, 1986, 2001, 2002, 2003. For a commentary on the significance of Bandura's work for the health field, see Green, 2003.

45. *Self-efficacy's cognitive dimensions in coping with relapse in complex behavioral changes:* For example, Ausems, et al., 2003; Dijkstra & Borland, 2003; Fiorentine & Hillhouse, 2003; McAuley, et al., 2003; Mermelstein, 2003; Scholes, et al., 2003.

46. *Self-efficacy variable in planning media-based programs:* For example, Levin, et al., 2002; Mermelstein, et al., 2003; Renger, et al., 2002.

47. *Measurement instruments for self-efficacy in health areas:* Brug, Glanz, & Kok, 1997; Love, Davoli, & Thurman, 1996; Lorig, Stewart, Ritter, et al., 1996; Shannon, Kirkley, Ammerman, & Simpson, 1997.

48. *Expectations and expectancies as related predisposing factors in social learning theory:* Bandura, 1986, as defined by Baranowski, Perry, & Parcel, 2002, p. 169; see their table showing implications of each of these and the other elements of social cognitive theory for the design of health program interventions.

49. *Behavioral intention and other predisposing factors from the theory of reasoned action and the theory of planned behavior:* First introduced by Fishbein, 1967, in the face of growing discontent with the inconsistencies of "attitude" as a construct to predict and explain behavior: e.g., Green, 1970b, he distinguished between attitude toward an object of behavior and attitude toward the behavior itself, which he reframed as "evaluation of behavioral outcomes" and "behavioral beliefs": Fishbein & Ajzen, 1975. In the Theory of Planned Behavior, Ajzen and colleagues added a dimension akin to self-efficacy, which they called "perceived behavioral control," a product of "control beliefs and "perceived power," to account for situations over which people do not have complete volitional control: Ajzen & Madden, 1986. For reviews of the evolution and early applications of this pair of theories in health, see Godin & Kok, 1996; Montano & Kasprzyk, 2002.

50. *Applications in health programs of the concepts from the theory of reasoned action and theory of planned behavior:* See previous edition: Green & Kreuter, 1999, p. 167, for a range of applications prior to 1999. Armitage & Conner, 2001, conducted a meta-analysis of 185 studies that had applied the broader theory of planned behavior and were published before 1997. More recent applications in health studies and programs, besides those on *HIV and STD prevention* reviewed in detail by Albarracin, et al., 2001 and by Montano & Kasprzyk, 2002, include *breast-feeding:* Gosken, 2002; *drug abuse:* Morrison, et al., 2002; *oral health:* Syrjala, et al., 2002; *physical activity:* Trost, et al., 2002); *smoking prevention:* McGahee, et al., 2000.

51. *Combination of the theory of reasoned action with PRECEDE:* DeVries & Kok, 1986. *Other applications of the behavioral intention concept within PRECEDE* include DeVries, Dijkstra, & Kuhlman, 1988; Keintz, et al., 1988; Kraft, 1988; Liburd & Bowie, 1989; P. D. Mullen, Hersey, & Iverson, 1987; Ostwald & Rothenberger, 1985; Padilla & Bulcavage, 1991; Salazar, 1985; J. A. Smith & Scammon, 1987.

52. *Origins of the theories of change and psychotherapy initially reviewed for the Transtheoretical Model:* Prochaska, 1979.

53. *Empirical studies of smokers to derive stages of change for the Transtheoretical Model:* DiClemente & Prochaska, 1982; Prochaska & DiClemente, 1983.

54. *Applications of the Stages of Change constructs with PRECEDE:* Grueniger, 1995; Grueninger, Duffy, & Goldstein, 1995; Haber, 1994; Hubball, 1996; Koivula & Paunonen, 1998; Neumark-Sztainer & Story, 1996.

55. *Other recent applications of the Transtheoretical Model in health behavior studies or program planning:* For a description of the model and recent reviews of its application in health, see Prochaska,

Redding, & Evers, 2002. More recent applications include condom use in HIV prevention: Gullete & Turner, 2003; hypertension control: Chang, McAlister, et al., 2003; mammography adoption: Champion & Skinner, 2003; physical activity: Schumann, Estabrooks, et al., 2003; self-management of pain: Habib, Morrissey, & Helmes, 2003; smoking cessation: Andersen, Keller, & McGowan, 1999.

56. *Stages of Change applied to organizational change:* J. M. Prochaska, Prochaska, & Lavesque, 2001.

57. *Existing skills in resisting peer pressure can predispose to not smoking:* for example, Engels, Knibbe, & de Haan, 1997; but success in changing these skills with resulting reduction in susceptibility to taking up drinking or other substance abuse is mixed: D. R. Black, et al., 1998; Clayton, et al., 1996; Dedobbeleer & Desjardins, 2001; Donaldson, Graham, et al., 1995.

58. *Programs that seek to build new health-related social skills in youth:* D. R. Black, Tobler, & Sciacca, 1998; Hermann & McWhirter, 1997. For reviews of the studies in this vein, see Allott, Paxton, & Leonard, 1999; Gerstein & Green, 1993, pp. 76–117; Midford, Munro, et al., 2002.

59. *Skills as enabling factors:* See, for example, the 12 behavioral outcomes described as skills needed by an asthmatic child, in Bartholomew, Parcel, Kok, & Gottlieb, 2001, Fig. 2-5, p. 35; or the 22 skills contributing to self-management ability in children and adolescents outlined by Thoresen & Kirmil-Gray, 1983. Some applications of PRECEDE in assessing needs for enabling skills include projects in asthma: Bailey, Richards, et al., 1987; Fireman, Friday, et al., 1981; Taggart, et al., 1991; cystic fibrosis: Bartholomew, Seilheimer, et al., 1989; preventing back pain: Daltroy, et al., 1993; professional continuing education and training for health practitioners: Bennett, 1977; Hubball, 1996; Lomas, 1993; Mann & Putnam, 1989, 1990; Mann, Putnam, et al., 1990; McKell, 1996; Ottoson, 1995; childbirth and parenting skills: O'Meara, 1993; child health and survival: Schumann & Mosley, 1994; alcohol: Villas, Mottinger, & Cardenas, 1996; smoking cessation in pregnant women: Windsor, 1986; negotiation skills for condom use among sex workers: M. L. Wong, Chan, Koh, & Wong, 1994–95, 1996, 1998, 2000; and breast self-examination skills: Worden, Solomon, et al., 1990.

60. *Social-action or collective action skills and capacity:* See Chapters 5, 7, and 8 for more on these social-action skills.

61. *Enabling factors at the population level expressed as collective efficacy, community capacity, and social capital:* For example, Chaskin, et al., 2001; Crisp, et al., 2000; Poland, 2000, and others cited in note 40 of Chapter 2.

62. *Andersen's original family and community resources as enabling factors with varying weights for utilization of services for different health care needs:* Andersen, 1969. For some of his more recent studies of health care utilization, occasionally with the Andersen-Newman adapted Model of Families' Use of Health Services, where enabling factors typically consist of income, insurance, and a regular source of care, see Andersen, Yu, et al., 2002; Barkin, et al., 2003; Dobalian, Andersen, et al., 2003; Goodwin & Andersen, 2002; Heslin, Andersen, & Gelberg, 2003a, b.

63. Center for Health Promotion and Education, 1987; D. G. Simons-Morton, Parcel, Brink, Harvey, & Tiernan, 1991. This and the other *CDC Handbooks* listed in subsequent citations each applied the Precede Model to the assessment of needs and the planning of interventions for selected health problems and target populations. They provide detailed procedural guidelines on collecting and analyzing the data necessary to arrive at efficient judgments about the behavioral determinants and the predisposing, enabling, and reinforcing factors for behavioral change. Other *applications of PRECEDE-PROCEED in assessing enabling factors in tobacco control include studies and program descriptions in adolescents and school-aged children:* C. Boyd, 1993; Canto, Drury, & Horowitz, 2001; Canto, Goodman, et al., 1998; Dovell, 2001; Fawcett, et al., 1997; Lipnickey, 1986; Parcel, Eriksen, et al., 1989, Parcel, O'Hara-Tompkins, et al., 1995; Polcyn, Price, Jurs, & Roberts, 1991; Reid, Harris, et al., 1983; Younoszai, & Lohrmann, 1999; *college students:* Hofford & Spelman, 1996; *disabled clients of rehabilitation workers:* Glenn, 1994; *clinical counseling on smoking:* Heywood, Firman, et al., 1996; Kientz, Rimer, et al., 1988; Kientz, Fleisher, & Rimer, 1994; *pregnant women:* Lelong, Kaminski, et al., 1995; *adult male populations:* Koivula & Paunonen, 1998; *community programs:* Paradis et al., 1995; Sanders-Phillips, 1996; *with mass media:* Secker-Walker, Flynn, & Worden, 1996; Secker-Walker, Worden, et al., 1997; Tillgren, Haglund, et al., 1995; *worksites:* Bertera, 1990; Bertera, Oehl, & Telepchak, 1990;

Gottlieb, Eriksen, et al., 1990; Gottlieb, Lovato, et al., 1992; Gottlieb, & Nelson, 1990; Pucci & Haglund, 1994; and *developing countries:* Smith, & Alpers, 1984; Sun & Sun, 1995; Zhang & Qiu, 1993.

64. *Validated measures of enabling and other factors (predisposing and reinforcing) determining smokeless tobacco use:* Polcyn, Price, Jurs, & Roberts, 1991.

65. B. G. Simons-Morton, Brink, Parcel, et al., 1989. Other applications of PRECEDE-PROCEED in *assessing enabling factors and other determinants of alcohol-related behavior* in youth include Canto, Goodman, et al., 1998; Dedobbeleer & Desjardins, 2001; Donovan, 1991; Fawcett, Lewis, et al., 1997; Higgins & MacDonald, 1992; Hunnicutt, Perry-Hunnicutt, Newman, Davis, & Crawford, 1993; Hofford & Spelman, 1996; Kraft, 1988; Newman, Martin, & Weppner, 1982; Stivers, 1994; Vertinsky & Mangham, 1991; Villas, Cardenas, & Jameson, 1994.

66. *Project Graduation demonstrated reduction in teen alcohol-related vehicle fatalities following provision of enabling factor of alcohol-free graduation parties:* Mowatt, Isaly, & Thayer, 1985.

67. *Laws enabling and reinforcing environmental controls on alcohol consumption before or during driving have reduced drunk driving, alcohol-related crashes, injuries and fatalities:* Holder, Gruenewald, et al., 2000; Senserrick, 2003; Shults, Elder, et al., 2001; Shults, Sleet, et al., 2002; Treno & Lee, 2002.

68. *Dramatic decline in alcohol-related fatalities from 1982–2001:* Elder & Shults, 2002.

69. *Enabling factors related to legislation and regulation usually depend on building the predisposing and reinforcing factors of an informed electorate and a favorable social climate:* For example, Bashford, 2003; Halperin & Rigotti, 2003; Lorence & Richards, 2003.

70. *Enabling factors contributing to physical activity:* Bauman, Smith, et al., 1999; Centers for Disease Control and Prevention, 2001; Craig, Brownson, et al., 2002; Ewing, Schmid, et al., 2003.

71. *The "built environment" of cities, suburbs, parks, and transportation enable more or less physical activity and can be designed to enable more:* Dannenberg, Jackson, et al., 2003; Hoehner, Brennan, et al., 2003; Killingsworth, Earp, & Moore, 2003; Saelens, Sallis, et al., 2003; Stokols, Grzywacz, et al., 2003.

72. *Measurement of the various enabling environmental factors that affect physical activity:* Emery, Crump, & Bors, 2003; Moudon & Lee, 2003.

73. *Skills as enabling factors in asthma self-management:* Bartholomew, Parcel, Kok, & Gottlieb (2001, p. 35) list several skills needed by parents and children as enabling factors; Boulet, Chapman, Green, & FitzGerald, 1994; McLean, et al., 2003; Meszaros, et al., 2003. See endnote 59 for applications of PRECEDE in analyzing skills required to enable change related to 10 types of health program outcomes.

74. *Skills to enable resistance to peer pressure to experiment with alcohol, tobacco and other drugs:* Recent studies of this enabling factor, related to the reinforcing factor of peer pressure, include Crone, Reijneveld, et al., 2003; Holm, Kremers, & de Vries, 2003; Wang, Tsai, et al., 2003.

75. *Skills in goal setting as an enabling factor in physical activity and obesity control:* Conn, Minor, et al., 2003; Nies & Kershaw, 2002; Ory, Jordan, & Bazzarre, 2002. A recently validated instrument for measurement of goal setting and other psychosocial and enabling factors in physical activity is presented in Nies, Hepworth, et al., 2001. Applications incorporating goal setting in analyses and program planning using PRECEDE include Bush, Zuckerman, et al., 1989; Cheng, DeWitt, et al., 1999; Mann, 1989; Mann & Sullivan, 1987; McMurry, Hopkins, et al., 1991; D. G. Simons-Morton, Parcel, et al., 1988.

76. *Assessing individual and community capacity or developmental skills for management of personal environments, or for community organization and community mobilization to collaborate in changing the environment:* Atkins, Oman, et al., 2002; Carr, 2000; Green & Shoveller, 2000; National Alliance of State and Territorial AIDS Directors, 2000. A survey instrument to measure some of these skills in adolescents has been validated by Oman, Vesley, et al., 2002, and applied variously to their *management of risks related to tobacco:* Atkins, Oman, et al., 2002; and *sexual activity:* Oman, Vesley, et al., 2003. Participatory research approaches to developing these skills while assessing them in youth and others have been the subject of recent projects: e.g., Cargo, Grams, et al., 2003; Minkler & Hancock, 2003.

77. *Seeking social support while trying to quit smoking:* For example, Franks, Pienta, & Wray, 2002. This effect can work against the behavior change when the source of social support is negatively inclined toward the change, such as a spouse who smokes: e.g., McLeod, Pullon, & Cookson, 2003. The influence of spouses and other family and peer support on quitting appears to be more positive for men than for women: Westmaas, Wild, & Ferrence, 2002, and women's perceptions of support from partners also tended to be less positive than the support male partners perceived themselves giving: Pollak, McBride, et al., 2001. These reinforcing factors could account for part of the difference in quit rates between men and women: Monso, Campbell, et al., 2001.

78. *Reinforcing influence of role models in product advertising on alcohol and tobacco consumption, violence, food choices, and other health-related behavior:* Green, Murphy, & McKenna, 2002; Hackbarth, et al., 2001; Ribisl, Lee, et al., 2003; Stebbins, 2001; Villani, 2001; Wakefield, Flay, et al., 2003.

79. *Reinforcement of physical activity by family, peers, and health care providers:* For example, Burke, Mori, et al., 2002; Mercer, Green, et al., 2003; Neumark-Sztainer, Story, et al., 2003; Painter, 2003; Satariano, Haight, & Tager, 2002. For examples of the *assessment of reinforcing factors for physical activity within the context of the Precede-Proceed Model,* see Allegrante, Kovar, et al., 1993; Furst, Gerber, et al., 1987; Hill, 1996; Hopman-Rock, 2000; Lian, Gan, et al., 1999; Nguyen, Grignon, et al., 1995; Paradis, O'Loughlin, et al., 1995; Singer, Lindsay, & Wilson, 1991. One that found the reinforcing factor of "need for social support" to be unimportant relative to predisposing factors in the adoption of a physical activity regimen was Hill, 1996. This supports the theoretical grounding of the reinforcing factors in *maintaining* a behavioral change more than in the initial adoption of the behavior.

80. *Vicarious reinforcement and learning of behavior:* Brown, Basil, & Bocarnea, 2003; Dye, Haley-Zitlin, & Willoughby, 2003; Peel & Dansereau, 1998; Thombs, Olds, & Ray-Tomasek, 2001; Tripp, Herrmann, et al., 2000.

81. *Role models as source of reinforcement and vicarious learning by professionals and other staff:* Elnicki, Kolarik, & Bardella, 2003; Kern, Thomas, et al., 1998; Wright & Carrese, 2003.

82. *Role models—peers and parents—for adolescent health-related behavior:* Galambos, Barker, & Almeida, 2003; Musher-Eizenman, Holub, & Arnett, 2003; Urberg, Luo, et al., 2003. In a review of the literature on peer influence on teen smoking, Kobus (2003) views the data through the various theoretical lenses of social learning theory, primary socialization theory, social identity theory, and social network theory, and notes that peer and family influence work to stimulate use in some and to deter it in others.

83. *Informal methods of data collection on factors influencing behavior and environment:* Gilmore and Campbell, 2004.

84. *Focus group methods in identifying perceived causes of behavioral and environmental problems:* Basch, 1987; Gilmore & Campbell, 2004. See Chapter 2 for more detail on focus-group methods and applications. For recent *examples in the context of applications of the Precede-Proceed Model,* including issues of *nutrition:* Balch, Loughrey, et al., 1997; Doyle & Feldman, 1997; Lefebvre, Doner, et al., 1995; Reed, Meeks, et al., 1998; *occupational health:* Brosseau, Parker, et al., 2002; *dental health:* Canto, Goodman, et al., 1998; *cancer screening:* Danigelis, Roberson, et al., 1995; Dignan, Michielutte, et al., 1990; *infectious disease control:* Larson, Bryan, et al., 1997; M. Taylor, Coovadia, et al., 1999; *primary care behavior of physicians:* Mirand, Beehler, et al., 2002; Mahloch, Taylor, et al., 1993; V. Taylor, Taplin, et al., 1994.

85. *Examples of brainstorming:* Doyle, Beatty, & Shaw, 1999, *and nominal group process:* Adeyanju, 1987–88, to generate insight and ideas on predisposing, enabling, and reinforcing factors in behavioral and environmental problems.

86. *Tendency of informal methods to produce "victim blaming" or "system blaming," or "fate" and other unproductive and stereotyping explanations:* for example, De Moura, Harpham, & Lyons, 2003; Green, 1994; Johnson, Mullick, & Mulford, 2002; Ogden, Bandara, et al., 2001. *Use of informal data to construct more formal questionnaire items to measure extent of misperceptions and myths about causation:* e.g., Walsh, Devellis, & Devellis, 2003.

87. *The stereotyping and victim-blaming tendencies extend beyond health professionals to policy makers and professionals in other sectors whose cooperation in addressing determinants of health will be*

needed: for example, Bensberg & Kennedy, 2002; de Almeida, Binder, & Fischer, 2000; Mittelmark, 1999; Raj & Silverman, 2002. *Attribution theory* suggests a tendency for observers to overattribute the behavior of others to predispositional variables and to underestimate the importance of situational determinants, but these tendencies diminish over time with greater familiarity (e.g., Truchot, Maure, & Patte, 2003).

88. For *examples of analyses of demographic correlates of health-related behavior and environments,* see Carpenter, 2003; Epstein, Botvin, & Diaz, 1998; N. H. Gottlieb & Green, 1987; O'Loughlin, Paradis, & Gray-Donald, 1998; Winkleby, Kraemer, & Varady, 1998.

89. *Diagnostic or assessment data as baseline data for subsequent program evaluation:* For example, Rossi, Lipsey, & Freeman, 2003, esp. Chapters 4–6.

90. *Examples of surveys constructed in line with PRECEDE's predisposing, enabling, and reinforcing factors to identify and assess determinants of behavioral and environmental changes* related to *asthma:* Pujet, J-C., C. Nejjari, et al., 1997; *breast self-examination, clinical breast examination, and mammography screening:* Danigelis, Roberson, et al, 1995; Desnick, Taplin, et al., 1999; Han, Baumann, & Cimprich, 1996; McPhee, Bird, et al., 1996; Morrison, 1995; Lee, Lee, & Stewart, 1996; Taplin, Taylor, et al., 1994; Zapka, Costanza, et al., 1993; Zapka & Mamon, 1982; Zapka, Stoddard, et al., 1989; *other cancer screening:* McPhee, Bird, et al., 1996; Mercer, Goel, et al., 1997; Neef, Scutchfield, et al., 1991; Ngtuyen, McPhee, et al., 2002; Wismer, Moskovitz, et al., 1998; 2001; Zuckerman, Guerra, et al., 1996; *cardiovascular diseases:* Bailey, Rukholm, et al., 1994; Mann & Putnam, 1989; McKell, Chase, & Balram, 1996; *childbirth and parenting:* O'Meara C., 1993; cystic fibrosis: Bartholomew, Seilheimer, et al., 1989; *fetal alcohol syndrome:* Donovan, 1991; *diabetes:* Daniel, 1997; Daniel, Green, et al., 1999; *gerontology:* Rimer, Jones, et al., 1983; *hospital infections:* McGovern, Kochevar, et al., 1997; Michalsen, Delclos, et al., 1997; *medication adherence:* Opdycke, Ascione, et al., 1992; *nursing and physician staff behavior related to prevention and health promotion:* Berland, Whyte, & Maxwell, 1995; Cheng, DeWitt, et al., 1999; Clearie, Blair, & Ward, 1982; Desnick, Taplin, et al., 1999; Donovan, 1991; Han, Baumann, & Cimprich, 1996; Laitakari, Miilunpalo, & Vuori, 1997; Mann & Putnam, 1989; Michalsen, Delclos, et al., 1997; Miilunpalo, Laitakari, & Vuori, 1995; Taplin, Taylor, et al., 1994; *nutrition:* Campbell, Denmark-Wahnefried, et al., 1999; Doyle & Feldman, 1997; Kristal, Patterson, et al., 1995; Lefebvre, Doner, et al., 1994; McKell, Chase, & Balram, 1996; *physical activity:* Lian, Gan, et al., 1999; *school health:* Cottrell, Capwell, & Brannan, 1995; Rubinson & Baillie, 1981; *sexuality education:* Rubinson & Baillie, 1981; *tobacco control: adolescent smoking:* Dovell, 2001; Flynn, Worden, et al., 1992; Sun & Ling, 1997; *adult smoking:* Koivula & Paunonen, 1998; Secker-Walker, Flynn, et al., 1996; *smokeless tobacco use:* Canto, Goodman, et al., 1998; *use of prosthetic devices:* Gauthier-Gagnon, Grise, & Potvin, 1998); *skin cancer prevention:* Glanz, Carbone, & Song, 1999; Miller, Geller, et al., 1999; *genetic testing:* Glanz, Grove, et al., 1999; *general health risks related to ethnic and other disparities in health:* Gottlieb & Green, 1984, 1987; McPhee, Bird, et al., 1996; Sanders-Phillips, 1991; Zuckerman, Guerra, et al., 1996; *worksite health:* Bertera, 1990; Daltroy, Iversen, et al., 1993; Kristal, Patterson, et al., 1995; McGovern, Kochevar, et al., 1997; Michalsen, Delclos, et al., 1997; Sun & Shun, 1995. Additional site-specific references to survey instruments using Precede-Proceed categories appear in later chapters.

91. *Formal surveys applying Precede constructs of predisposing, enabling, and reinforcing factors in educational and ecological assessments usually are also used in subsequent surveys to evaluate progress. More or less standardized instruments* are found in Green & Lewis, 1986; see esp. Chapter 6 for inventories and references on instrument selection and development, and Appendix C (pp. 331–341) for a questionnaire developed for the National Survey of Personal Health Practices and Consequences and adapted for community-level application. Other measures and exemplary survey instruments are found in Lorig, et al., 1996. See also Louis Harris and Associates, 1996; Lovato & Allensworth, 1989. Some of the *Precede measures have been adapted to various countries, languages, and cultures,* e.g., *Australia* (Cockburn, et al., 1989, 1997, on *sunscreen protection behavior;* Farr & Fisher, 1991, and Newman & Martin, 1982, on *smoking;* O'Meara, 1993, on *childbirth and parenting preparation;* Spillman, Harvey, et al., 1994, on *nutrition;* Stevenson & Jones, 1996, on *child injury prevention*); the *Netherlands* (deVries, Dijkstra, & Kok, 1992, on *smoking;* Hiddink, Hautvast, et al., 1995, 1997, on *physicians' nutrition guidance to patients;* Spruijt-

Metz, 1995, on *adolescent sleeping habits and snacking*). A *Canadian national survey,* based on the Precede factors, is described in Rootman, 1988. Nozu et al., translated to *Japanese* the Alteneder, Price, et al., 1992, instrument for measurement of Precede constructs in *HIV-AIDS* and tested its psychometric properties in a sample of senior high school students in Japan.

92. *Local sources of data:* see Phillips, Morrison, & Aday, 1998; Vissandjee, Barlow, & Fraser, 1997. *Such local sources of data can be most illuminating when contrasted with state or national data. A review of national data sources for the United States, organized according to the Precede Model's factors influencing behavior,* is provided by R. W. Wilson & Iverson, 1982, and various web sites (go to http://www.lgreen.net).

93. *CDC handbooks for conduct of community surveys and planning according to Precede-Proceed Model:* for example, Brink, Simons-Morton, Parcel, & Tiernan, 1988; Parcel, Simons-Morton, et al., 1987; B. Simons-Morton, Brink, et al., 1991; D. G. Simons-Morton, Parcel, et al., 1988. *The Peace Corps also adapted the Precede Model for its overseas training of volunteers, and for work in specific health campaigns,* e.g., Silverfine, et al., 1990, on *guinea worm eradication.*

94. *CDC's application of the PRECEDE Model in formulating the Planned Approach to Community Health (PATCH) program of technical support through states to community health planning with systematic local assessments of needs and resources:* Green & Kreuter, 1992; Hanson, 1988–1989; Liburd & Bowie, 1989; Nelson, Kreuter, et al., 1986; Steckler, Orville, et al., 1992. A similar *application of PRECEDE by CDC's HIV-AIDS prevention programs* was outlined in USDHHS, 1988. Although the PATCH program is no longer funded by CDC, many communities continue to apply its Guide for Local Coordinators (USDHHS, 1996; periodically updated at http://www.cdc.gov/nccdphp/patch/index.htm, accessed Sept. 29, 2003).

95. *Health education and media can raise public awareness, outrage, or demand as advocacy for the creation of community action or services:* Chapman & Lupton, 1994; Entman, 1993; Wallack, Woodruff, et al., 1999; *especially in breast cancer:* Braun, 2003; *HIV-AIDS:* Sowell, 2003; *tobacco:* Chapman & Dominello, 2001; Chapman & Wakefield, 2001; Durrant, Wakefield, et al., 2003; *cardiovascular disease prevention:* Schooler, Sundar, & Flora, 1996; *mainstreaming of the drug abuse problem:* Fan, 1996; and *alcohol:* Holder Lopez-Escobar, Llamas, & McCombs, 1998; McCombs, Shaw, & Weaver, 1997; Wallack, Woodruff, et al., 1999.

96. *A hierarchy of changeability among predisposing factors:* Rokeach, 1970.

97. *Diffusion theory:* Oldenburg & Parcel, 2002; E. M. Rogers, 1995. *More refined analyses of the rates of change and diffusion for the successive stages of change and for specific health innovations are suggested in* Crow, et al., 1986; Green, 1975.

5

Program, Administrative, and Policy Design: Turning the Corner from Formative to Process Evaluation, from PRECEDE to PROCEED

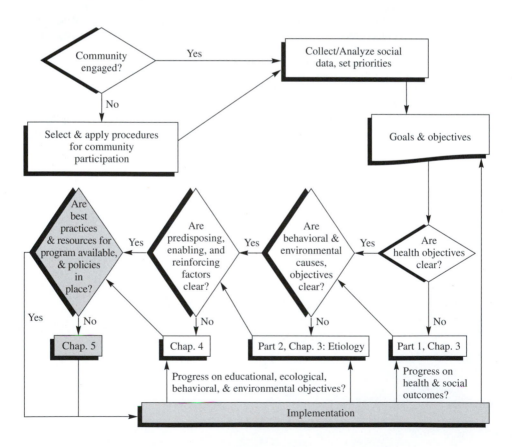

Having identified your program priorities, determinants of change, and objectives for change, you stand on the threshold of converting these assessment results into a program plan and from that into action. A first step in that conversion is to match program components with levels of individual, organizational, and community change, and to map specific evidence-based interventions to specific determinants identified as priorities in the previous phase. Unless it is a very homogeneous population, this will include provisions for variations on those interventions for varied population subgroups. Where evidence is lacking, theory must come into greater play. A second step is to pretest those elements that have not been tested before in the populations for which they will be used. The third step in this preimplementation alignment of program needs with program components is the strategic blending and sequencing of interventions into a cohesive and comprehensive program, taking administrative, organizational, regulatory and policy status, and needed changes into account.

The success of implementation is greatly enhanced when organizational and policy supports for, as well as barriers to, a proposed program have been clearly identified and appropriately addressed. Some of the barriers will be internal structures in the implementing organization (or several organizations if planning has involved a coalition). New policies, regulations, or administrative orders can overcome these barriers by reorganizing or reassigning responsibility within organizations. Other barriers may lie in the behavior or operating procedures of the implementing organization or other organizations whose cooperation is required. Here, the implementation of a health program might gain cooperation through educating decision makers or negotiating exchange agreements. In some instances, enforcement of existing agreements, rules, and laws or advocacy and promotion of new regulatory legislation may be required at the local, state, or provincial level.

The primary purpose of this chapter is to help you over the implementation threshold by calling your attention to some key theoretical, empirical, administrative, organizational, and policy factors, specifically:

- The selection and alignment of program components with priority determinants of change identified in the previous phase
- The resources needed and available to launch and sustain your program
- The organizational barriers and facilitators that can affect program implementation
- The policies you can use to support your program or that need to be changed to enable the program to proceed

This phase of the assessment and planning process will help you put the final touches on your formal plan with a timetable, an assignment of resources and responsibilities, and a budget. With these finishing touches, you turn the corner from PRECEDE to PROCEED, but remember that a program plan is never really finished. In this phase, you also identify the specific **settings** in which health promotion activities must take place, and each of those settings will have modifications of the plan to require or suggest. The implementing organization may itself provide a setting, such as a school or work site, for implementing the population focus of the program. Otherwise, the implementing or sponsoring organization, such as a public health department, must depend on other health organizations, and even other organizations outside the health sector, to share responsibility for implementation. This adds multiple dimensions of coordination and collaborative complications that must be considered in the plan. The setting dictates many of the specific methods, materials, and other intervention components. We shall discuss the more specific considerations for selecting appropriate methods to match the setting in alignment with the targets of change (predisposing, enabling, and reinforcing factors) in Chapters 6 through 9.

With a complete plan in hand, you PROCEED to implementation and process evaluation, which draws immediately on the findings from the administrative assessment. Even though evaluation is an inherent, built-in aspect of the entire Precede-Proceed planning framework, an evaluation plan also needs to be implemented and will require some level of similar policy, regulatory, and organizational support. *P*olicy, *r*egulatory, and *o*rganizational assessments (the "PRO" in PROCEED) are designed to reveal the *e*nabling constructs for *e*ducational and *e*cological *d*evelopment (the "CEED" in PROCEED).

SOME DEFINITIONS

A first distinction that will be helpful in the lexicon we need to employ for the complex field of health program planning is between **intervention** and **program.** Our use of these two terms tends to be somewhat interchangeable, but the term *intervention* will usually refer to a specific component of a more comprehensive *program.* A mass media message, for example, is an intervention within a more complex mass media campaign, and a media campaign is usually one component of a more complex program that may consist of media, organized facilities and services, and legislative initiatives for taxes or regulation of environments.

A second distinction that begins to take form in this chapter is between **formative evaluation,** which has been the subject of the previous phases and their culmination here into design of interventions and programs, and **process evaluation.** Formative evaluation is the use of systematic analysis of needs and the appropriate fit of past and potential interventions and programs to achieve the objectives in relation to meeting those needs. The previous chapters (2–4) have identified the needs and set objectives for meeting them, while also setting baselines and targets for impact and outcome evaluations of the eventual program. The first part of this chapter examines the processes by which the actual interventions (as program components) and programs themselves take shape.

Best practices refer to interventions and sometimes to whole programs consisting of multiple interventions that have been submitted to rigorous scientific evaluation, ideally in multiple settings and populations, and subjected to

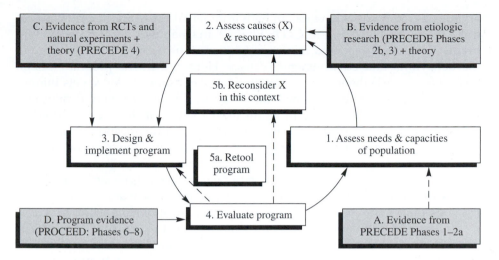

FIGURE 5-1 Types of evidence brought to bear at each point in the planning-evaluation cycle. Theory fills the gaps between evidence and the characteristics of the population, problem, or circumstances that differ from those in the studies from which evidence was generated.

critical analysis across multiple studies. These ideals of best practices are much easier to achieve in medicine, where the concept of best practices arose from the dozens and sometimes hundreds of randomized, controlled studies that would accumulate on specific medical practices. In communities, populations, and public health applications, however, the variations are far greater than for the biological organism on which medicine intervenes. Thus, we find ourselves using these notions of best practices more cautiously and preferring a notion of **best processes.**[1] The *processes* of assessing the population and the local circumstances for a program, as described in the foregoing chapters, provide a more appropriate basis for the selection of interventions than does the testing of specific interventions in dissimilar populations and circumstances. But together, *the combination of best processes of diagnosis* and *best practices of intervention* can produce the best *program* for a particular population and circumstance. These combined sources of data produce **evidence-based practice,** but the evidence is not limited to previous tests of the interventions in populations and circumstances other than those in which the program is being planned. It also includes assessments or diagnoses of the population and circumstances in which the "best practices" would be applied. Figure 5-1 shows the types of evidence brought to bear at several points in the planning-evaluation cycle.

Evidence-based practice brings evidence of a different type (identified by letters A–D in the shaded boxes) to each numbered step in this rendition of the cycle. Chapter 2 showed how evidence from the community itself is used in the social diagnosis, assets assessment, and situation analysis of PRECEDE Phase 1, part of Step 1 in this cycle. Chapter 3 showed how the epidemiological diagnosis of PRECEDE Phase 2 first brings surveillance evidence to an assessment of the health problems (of Step 1 in this cycle), and then etiological evidence to an understanding of behavioral and environmental causes or determinants of those (Step 2 in Fig. 5-1). PRECEDE Phase 3, in Chapter 4, further delved into predisposing, enabling, and reinforcing factors causing or affecting change in the behavioral and environmental causes. Here and in the program design (Step 3 of Fig. 5-1) theory comes into greater play as the evidence gets thinner for the particular context in which the program is being planned. Finally, evidence from evaluation of the program itself (Step 4 of the cycle) is used to adjust the program implementation (Step 5a), to call into question the assumptions about causation made earlier (Step 5b), and to adjust the selection of interventions accordingly. This chapter will concentrate on Steps 3–5 in this planning cycle, getting from "evidence-based practice" to *practice-based evidence*.

Evidence is a loaded term for many practitioners wary of the "more-rigorous-than-thou" ethic that creeps into their relationship with academia, government and foundation funding agencies, evaluators, and consultants. They tend to see the demand for evidence as a bottomless pit of demand for more data, for which they have few resources and little time to pursue. As it relates to a given practice or intervention method, however, we are reminded of the asterisk in each of the "best practices" documents from the Community Preventive Services Task Force sponsored by CDC, as they summarize the evidence in relation to that practice or intervention:

> A determination that evidence is insufficient should not be regarded as evidence of ineffectiveness. A determination of insufficient evidence assists in identifying (a) areas of uncertainty regarding an intervention's effectiveness and (b) specific continuing research needs. In contrast, evidence of ineffectiveness leads to a recommendation that the intervention may not be used.

As we argued in Chapter 3, "planners . . . characterize a key element of health program planning: the continuous struggle to strike a prudent balance between scientific certitude and good judgment."

Administrative assessment or diagnosis refers here to an analysis of the policies, resources, and circumstances in an organizational setting that either facilitate or hinder the development of the health program. **Policy** refers to the set of objectives and rules guiding the activities of an organization or administration. **Regulation** refers to the act of enforcing policies, rules, or laws. It applies in health particularly where existing policies are not being enforced to protect the health of some from the illegal behavior of others, such as in community actions against selling cigarettes to minors or drunk driving. It overlaps with **health protection,** but in health promotion it usually has more to do with behavior or the social environment than with the physical environment. **Organization** refers in this chapter to the act of marshaling and coordinating the resources necessary to implement a program. In Chapter 6, **community organization** will refer to the set of procedures and processes by which a population and its institutions mobilize to solve a common problem or pursue a common goal. **Implementation** refers here to the act of converting program objectives into actions through deployment of resources, policy changes, regulation, and organization, and coordination and supervision of activities in support of the planned interventions.

Additional definitions arise in the following consideration of some principles used to guide this phase of the Precede-Proceed planning process, matching interventions and program components and resources to predisposing, enabling, and reinforcing factors for change.

Some Principles.   The first principle that underlies the diagnostic, ecological planning approach of this book, and that justifies all of the steps that have preceded this one, is the **principle of intervention specificity.** One way of expressing it is with the proposition that *there is nothing inherently superior about any intervention method,* or any method of social change, for that matter. It always depends on the appropriate fit of the intervention with the person or population and their circumstances, and the delivery setting. The corollary of this principle is that individual change or social change should begin with an assessment of the problems calling for change, the circumstances, and the settings in which the change will need to occur. By pursuing the assessment or diagnosis of needs and capacities before prescribing the interventions to go into a program, one acknowledges this proposition and the principle of specificity. This principle is also expressed as **"tailoring"** of messages and other interventions to the individual, where possible, or matching multiple interventions to population segments when individualization is impracticable. Tailoring at the population level becomes **"segmentation"** of audiences and stratification or distribution of interventions accordingly.

A second principle telescoped by the foregoing reference to interventions *and* programs is that *no single method or intervention by itself can be expected to achieve lasting change.* At a minimum, as we have argued in Chapter 4, a program for change must combine interventions that address at least three theoretical constructs implicated in the change process: predisposing factors, enabling factors, and reinforcing factors. A corollary of this **principle of multiplicity and comprehensiveness** of interventions, then, is that social, group, or individual change must combine educational, organizational, economic, regulatory, and other environmental change components.

The right mix or blend of these components, and their sequencing, will depend, again, on an accurate prior assessment of their relative importance in determining the behavior, their logical order of effects on each other and on the change process, and the circumstances in which they will be implemented. The urgency and magnitude of the change sought, as reflected in the goals and objectives laid out in the previous phases of PRECEDE, also dictate the necessary blend of more voluntary to more coercive change processes and methods of intervention, from strictly educational to more aggressively regulatory and even punitive. The latter also apply when the behavioral changes required are ones in which the behavior of some affect the well-being of others. Hence, more regulatory and punitive interventions and policies are called for with drunk and reckless drivers, people who smoke in public places, employers who expose employees to hazardous work conditions, manufacturers or advertisers of dangerous toys, unsafe vehicles, addictive substances, and hazardous materials.

ALIGNING PRIORITY DETERMINANTS
WITH PROGRAM COMPONENTS

At least two levels of alignment from Phase 3 to Phase 4 must occur to make a program plan. One is at the broad macro level. Program components must be aligned with levels of policy, regulatory, or organizational change needed from groups of individuals up to organizations and whole communities (which may be states, provinces, or even countries). This we refer to as the *ecological level of alignment*. It sets the stage for putting the program into the broader environmental context in which the change must occur, and it recognizes the interdependence of levels in a social system. Each subsystem (such as a family) relates to a larger system (such as a community), and each system depends for its maintenance on multiple subsystems. The program components at this level are ones that might be referred to as strategic rather than tactical, organizational, and environmental in their initial manipulation, though often occurring with a behavioral change in large numbers of people as a secondary but purposeful effect. Changing the nonsmoking policies in a building, the food choices in vending machines of a school, and the carpooling lanes on a commuter's highway are examples of organizational and environmental changes that have secondary or ecological effects on the behavior of large numbers of people without necessarily trying to persuade their change through direct communication. These elements of a program operate primarily through enabling factors for environmental change to enable, in turn, behavioral change in whole populations, or to reduce exposure to environmental risks that could have a direct effect on the health of the population.

At more individual, behavioral, family, or other micro levels of social systems, the task of alignment is between specific predisposing, enabling, or reinforcing factors and the more specific program components, interventions, or methods for which evidence of their effectiveness has been derived from previous research. Such interventions to affect *predisposing* factors are applied directly to individuals, whether through mass media, classroom education, informal group sessions, patient counseling, parenting, or other methods of direct communication. To affect *enabling* factors, the interventions or program components may include facilitating action through monetary subsidies to make specific health resources more affordable or arranging services or transportation to make them more accessible. These tend to be directed at the environment. Finally, the reinforcing factors are addressed through interventions that usually are directed at the social environment of those whose behavior or lifestyle is changing. Thus, the parents, teachers, or peers of children and youth, the employers, friends, family, co-workers, or neighbors of adults, all have the potential to provide social rewards, approval, or disapproval of the behavioral changes sought by health programs. Some of them have the potential to offer financial incentives and rewards or to withhold scheduled rewards or benefits. In short, reinforcement is achieved by health programs using indirect communication through organizations and significant others to those whose behaviors need to change.

In previous phases of applying PRECEDE, you identified a population's priority social and health problems and objectives, priority determinants of the health problems among behavioral and environmental factors, and finally priority predisposing, enabling, and reinforcing factors for the needed behavioral changes, and enabling factors for the necessary environmental changes. Now you seek the right fit for program components and specific interventions that can affect the changes in predisposing, enabling, and reinforcing factors.

Alignment 1: Intervention Matching, Mapping, Pooling, and Patching

A series of initial alignments (1) *match* the ecological levels with broad program components, (2) then use the theories employed in Phase 3 to *map* specific interventions from prior research and practice to specific predisposing, enabling, and reinforcing factors, and finally (3) *pool* prior interventions and community-preferred interventions that might have less evidence to support them, but that might be needed to *patch* or fill gaps in the evidence-based "best practices." The terms *match, map,* and *patch,* align roughly with the planning models that use these terms as acronyms or analogies.

The Ecological Level of Matching.   The ecological approach calls first for a matching of types of interventions with the level at which—or channels and settings through which—they can have their effects. We will focus in this chapter on the levels, because we devote the next four chapters to the most likely settings and channels for health programs—community (including homes, restaurants, other public or commercial places, and mass media), schools, work sites, and health care institutions. We use the term *matching* for this level of alignment because a cogent model for aligning interventions or program components with ecological levels is one called MATCH—Multilevel Approach To Community Health.[2] It emerged as ecological approaches saw a renaissance in public health and health promotion, bringing renewed interest in risk *conditions* after a period of highly focused research and development on individual risk *factors.*[3] The conditions of particular interest in MATCHing program interventions to the levels of determinants are identified in Figure 5-2.

The health goals selection (Phase 1 in Fig. 5-2) was completed in Phase 2 of PRECEDE; but just in case it was skipped in the interest of expediting a program plan, the selection of health goals and objectives now can be tagged to statewide or provincial averages and trends if sufficient baseline data are unavailable at the local or regional level where your program is to be focused.[4] This estimation process follows the same rationale used by states and provinces in setting their goals and objectives against national data. They seek to rise at least to the national average, or they set challenge goals to surpass the trajectory of current trends within their jurisdiction. On our associated web site for this book, we will maintain the current Web addresses (URLs) for major sources of such data on health, behavioral, and environmental trends related to the most common and current health programs and priorities. By placing these

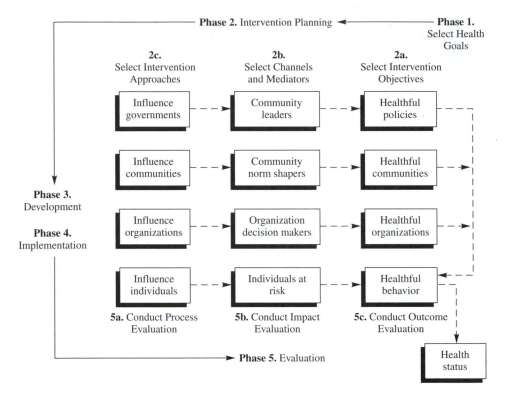

FIGURE 5-2 Multilevel Approach to Community Health (MATCH). This simplified rendition of Simons-Morton et al.'s model shows steps in aligning interventions with levels of an ecological system and with the objectives associated with each.
Source: Adapted from Simons-Morton, Greene, & Gottlieb, 1995.

Web addresses at your disposal on our Web pages, we can ensure that they are periodically updated and save you the hassle of typing in long URL addresses.

At Phase 2 in Figure 5-2, the matching process calls for the selection of intervention objectives for each level of the simplified ecological structure, from

- governmental objectives (policy, budgetary, and regulatory objectives, summarized as "healthful policy"),
- community objectives concerning infrastructure, resources, services delivered, and social norms,
- organizational objectives concerning facilities, environments, programs, resources, and the policies, to
- individual level, which is where the behavioral objectives meet the health status objectives.

These ecological levels and their separate objectives for change create a system of interconnected, dynamic, reciprocal relationships that could be shown by vertical arrows between and among them. The one arrow from the higher eco-

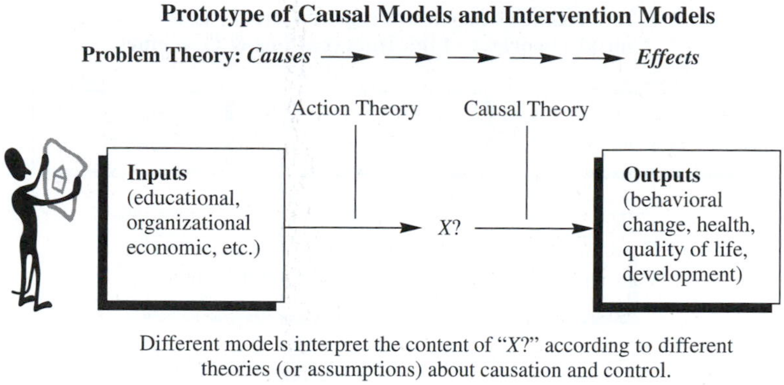

Prototype of Causal Models and Intervention Models

Problem Theory: *Causes* ⟶ ⟶ ⟶ ⟶ ⟶ *Effects*

Action Theory   Causal Theory

Inputs
(educational,
organizational
economic, etc.)

X?

Outputs
(behavioral
change, health,
quality of life,
development)

Different models interpret the content of "*X?*" according to different
theories (or assumptions) about causation and control.

FIGURE 5-3 Problem theory seeks to identify the causes of certain problems or
effects. **Causal theory** explains the causal relationship or mechanism by which
the "determinant" causes the effect. Such theories, in tandem, serve planning by
specifying the presumed link between what we can do by way of intervention
and what we hope to achieve as outcomes. This series of links is often expressed
as a complex "logic model" showing the pathways of influence assumed to be set
in motion by one or more interventions in a program.

logical levels to the individual level imply that this is a unidirectional causal
flow of influence, but we know from the literature discussed in the two previous chapters that these relationships are multidirectional and that the organizational, community, and higher governmental levels can moderate the effects of
individual characteristics on individual behavior.[5] We also know that the
higher levels of organization, that is, the physical and social environments that
they represent or encompass, do not affect health exclusively through behavioral change, but rather can have some direct effects on health independent of
the main behavioral effects.[6]

Mapping Causal Theory, Action Theory, and Program Theory.   Having been
drawn by the MATCH model of planning back into a discussion of causality,
we might pause to review some further distinctions that should serve to link
this chapter with the two that preceded it. Beginning with the reciprocal relationship between health and social outcomes in Chapter 2, and the etiological
emphasis of the second part of Chapter 3, through the discussion of theories
pertaining to the predisposing, enabling, and reinforcing factors as determinants of behavioral and environmental change, we have been preoccupied with
problem theory and causal theory. The place of these theories in PRECEDE-
PROCEED can be seen as specifying the *x* shown in Figure 5-3.[7]

Problem theory lends itself well to causal theory in matters of prevention,
insofar as the cause-effect relationship from etiological studies is usually the
same as the relationship that can be corrected to prevent disease, injury, or
death or to improve health by intervening on the cause. The focus of intervention is less consistently on causes with curative or therapeutic interventions

**Action Theory and Program Theory Use
Causal Theories to Link Interventions & Outcomes**

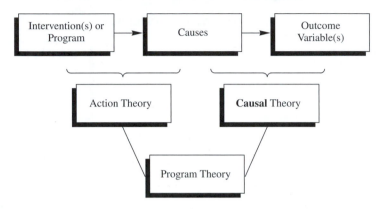

FIGURE 5-4 Action theory explains the link between proposed interventions and the mediators or intervening variables (identified as causes or determinants of the outcome variables). Together with causal theory, they form a logical model or program theory, usually more complex than this simple three-part model.
Source: Adapted from Suchman, 1967, pp. 84, 173; Weiss, 1970; Chen, 1990, p. 250; Donaldson, 2001, pp. 473–487.

and rehabilitation. Indeed, we first saw these graphic representations of the relationship of independent, intervening, and dependent variables in one of the first textbooks on evaluation in social services and public health by Edward Suchman in 1967. In that era of public health, these were commonly referred to, respectively, as primary intervention (prevention) where the focus was on the relationships between preconditions and causes; secondary intervention (detection and early treatment), where the intervention is on the causes (e.g., risk factors) to reduce the impact on health; and tertiary intervention (cure or rehabilitation), where the intervention is on the health effects or pathology to reduce complications and consequences (sequelae).[8] These distinctions have become blurred in the face of the increasing prevalence of chronic and degenerative conditions in which many health conditions and their risk factors are to be "managed," "controlled," or compensated for, rather than treated or cured.

The task now is to turn causal theory into action theory, and the two in combination into program theory (see Figure 5-4). We can do this first by specifying which interventions can be matched most fruitfully to which levels of the ecological structure, and, as implied by Phase 2b in Figure 5-2, to which channels or mediators within those structures or levels. The variations in causal theories are as wide as the science disciplines that spawn them, as suggested by the examples in Box 5-1. We might divide the theoretical approaches broadly into the macro and the micro. Macro-level theories such as sociological, political science, economics, and cultural anthropology seek to describe, explain, and predict phenomena at the aggregate level of societies, economies, ecologies, cultures, and organizations or groups. A middle range of theories among these,

> **BOX 5-1** Examples of Causal Theories on Which PRECEDE-PROCEED Is Based
>
> - Psychological theories in which X includes behavior and its antecedents such as attitudes, beliefs, perceptions, and other cognitive variables.
> - Sociological theories in which X includes organizational functioning and interorganizational exchange, social capital, and coalitions
> - Economic theories in which X includes consumer behavior and organizational response to consumer demand
> - Pathophysiological theories in which X includes organisms or environmental exposure processes

such as social psychology, microeconomics, organizational behavior, and group dynamics, seek to link the aggregate phenomena or social environments with individual behavior. At the micro level, intrapersonal theories of psychology and education seek to describe, explain, and predict individual variations in behavior within environments by assuming or holding relatively constant or common the environments among individuals.

Multiply the social environments by the multiple levels, channels, and settings in which intervention could occur (and ideally would occur for the sake of population-wide effects), and the possible intervention combinations to make up a program become vast. Multiply these again by the variability of the population segments for which programs might be planned and the number of possible intervention combinations approaches infinity. To the rescue comes evidence in the form of tested interventions packaged as "best practices." Alas, the range of populations and circumstances in which interventions have been tested is severely limited, especially the broader population or community-level interventions.

Where evidence-based best practices can be matched with the ecological levels, channels, and mediators for maximum effect, the pathway is clear toward achieving objectives and health outcomes, assuming adequate resources, strategic organization, and effective implementation, which we come to in the last half of this chapter. In most populations and circumstances, however, the planner will (a) have Type A evidence (see Figure 5-1) about the problem in the population for which the plan is intended; (b) hold a plausible causal theory for which there is ample evidence of Type B; and (c) have few, if any, best practices and most of which will be based on evidence generated in other populations. In the absence of evidence-based best practices for some of the important predisposing, enabling, and reinforcing factors, we turn to prior and existing interventions that can help patch the gaps in the comprehensive program with *practice-based evidence*.

Pooling and Patching Prior and Existing Interventions.   A program never starts from scratch. Seldom will your effort be the first time someone, somewhere, has tried to solve the problem or to address the need that your program plan addresses, nor does your plan start at time zero in this place. Other attempts elsewhere and here should be considered resources and guides. A step in the intervention selection process, then, should be to review and pool the best experience of prior attempts to address the problem and to build on the existing program activities related to the intervention targets.

Pooling information about prior interventions is a time-honored starting point for professionals of all stripes. Calling one's friends and colleagues, tapping into professional networks by phone or e-mail, and asking the question of others' experience on a Listserv, all have widespread use as ways to jump-start one's thinking about program interventions and to understand the reputability and the pros and cons of some of the more obvious options. D'Onofrio observed, however, that only one of six program planning models she cited, including PRECEDE-PROCEED and PATCH, had identified "examining other programs as a specific step in intervention development. . . . To date, no systematic procedures have been suggested for accomplishing this task as part of the program-planning process."[9] She identifies the following sources of information about prior interventions or programs, among others:

- Reports of specific interventions in journal articles, which are usually strong on evaluation methods, but usually skimpy on details about the interventions
- Overview reports or reviews of health programs addressing a particular problem or population, or reviewing specific methods or approaches to a class of problems
- Meta-analyses of multiples studies of programs addressing the same problem
- Sections of some professional journals devoted to brief reports from practitioners
- Books and monographs on specific projects or problems often containing much more detail or case study information about the interventions than in the published articles describing the same projects
- Technical reports containing official guidelines from government agencies or national advisory groups, based usually on consensus among experts and staff reviews of literature
- Conferences and professional meetings, providing presentations and descriptions of programs before they are published, but also not yet peer reviewed
- National clearinghouses and web sites for guidelines derived from systematic reviews and consensus of experts
- Funding agencies and their newsletters, and web sites, or grantees directly.[10]

Besides prior interventions from which ideas and inspiration and insight can be drawn, and bad ideas discarded, the community or setting in which the program is to be planned has ongoing programs and activities that will be part of any new program, whether they are preconceived that way or not. Unless they are purposefully discontinued, their existence in the same population will make them at least parallel, if not integrated, with the new program. Their existence should be acknowledged for purposes of avoiding conflicts and duplication, and to recognize confounding in the evaluation of either the old or the new programs. This is where continuing engagement of partner organizations and community participants in the planning can help. Many planning models emphasize this "coordinative" function of community partnerships, but others give as much emphasis to coalitions mobilizing the resources of other agencies in support of new programs.

The existing programs and activities in a community can also be a source of even richer information than prior interventions conducted elsewhere, because they are indigenous to the community or setting, and they were designed with the same population and more similar circumstances than most prior interventions. Here is where the PATCH adaptation of PRECEDE-PROCEED offered a useful "Existing Community Programs and Policies Matrix" available online and downloadable in Chapter 4, and a checklist in Table 2 of the PATCH toolkit.[11] The specific inventory identifies each ongoing program activity and the interventions with the settings (e.g., schools, work sites, health care, etc.) in which they occur, so we will defer further discussion of this aspect of the intervention planning and program development process to the chapters that follow.

For guidelines and specific checklists on choosing research-tested or prior intervention methods and approaches and adapting them to a new situation, see the National Cancer Institute's and Substance Abuse and Mental Health Services Administration's "Research-Tested Intervention Programs" (RTIPs) web site. Although intended for use with research-tested prior interventions, the guidelines apply equally, with additional caveats, to prior interventions that have not been formally tested.[12]

Alignment 2: Formative Evaluation and Blending Interventions Into Comprehensive Programs

Many of the foregoing and further steps that we recommend for the selection or design of interventions and their addition to a set that will make up a program can be called *formative evaluation*. We defined formative evaluation earlier as the use of systematic analysis of needs and of the appropriate fit of past and potential interventions to achieve the objectives for meeting those needs. Sussman has offered yet another program development guide that overlaps with and complements our integration of PRECEDE-PROCEED, MAPP, PATCH, MATCH, and the pooling of prior intervention information. His "Six-Step Program Development Chain Model" starts with the use of theory that considers antecedents of healthful or unhealthful behavior, as in PRECEDE Phase 3 (Chapter 4), and considers the mediation of the relations between antecedents and behavior.[13] The question of mediators is explicit in MATCH Phase 2b, but how to characterize mediators, and how to distinguish them from antecedents or causes, depends on the theory or theories chosen and on the definition of mediator. In MATCH, "Mediators are factors that are causally associated with

Mediating and Moderating Variables

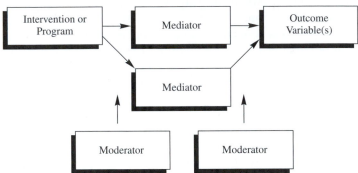

FIGURE 5-5 Mediators refer to the causal, intermediate variables through which interventions or programs can affect outcomes; moderators are the characteristics of the persons, settings, or circumstances of the intervention or the mediators that can enhance or depress the effect of interventions on mediators or of mediators on outcomes.

the target behavior,"[14] whereas for Sussman, "a mediator variable may potentiate or suppress/counteract the effects of the causal variable on the outcome variable."[15] A more common use of the term *mediators* is as media channels or go-between persons or settings, or characteristics of those persons or settings that modify, enhance, or suppress the effective flow of influence. This meaning is more consistent with Sussman's "moderator" variables, which "modulate the relation of the cause with the effect. They may or may not themselves have any influence on the effect variables (behavior or health consequence)."[16] We will split the differences and use **mediators** as causal or intermediate variables that can directly affect outcomes, and **moderators** as characteristics of individuals, settings, channels, and circumstances that can ameliorate or enhance the effect of program variables on mediator variables, or the latter on outcome variables. We are concerned here with the first type, whereas genetics could be seen as a moderator variable for behavioral and environmental influence on health in Chapter 3. These relationships are shown in Figure 5-5.

These definitions of mediators and moderators bring us back now to the "principle of intervention specificity" articulated at the beginning of this chapter. If mediators are predisposing, enabling, and reinforcing factors that we must influence in order to affect changes in behavior and the environment, and eventually health outcomes, then we must make the interventions specific to the high-priority predisposing, enabling, and reinforcing factors identified in the previous phase. We know, however, that the effectiveness of specific interventions varies among age groups, sexes, ethnic groups, socioeconomic groups, settings in which they are deployed, and other "moderator" variables. So we have a third level of intervention mapping that not only aligns interventions with the ecological level (2a in Figure 5-2), that is, the mediator variables they are intended to affect (2b), but also varies them according to the characteristics of people, settings, and circumstances (2c).

Each of the channels and mediators in column 2b of Figure 5-2 will have a different set of predisposing, enabling, and reinforcing factors (mediators) causing their behavior, or potentially causing it to change. To ensure an ecologically robust program, one should seek to influence the behavior of someone or a population in each of these categories or at each of these levels, unless the program is tightly confined to a specific setting and encounter, as in some clinical patient encounters. Within each setting or level, the predisposing, enabling, and reinforcing factors for that person's or group of people's behavior, as it might affect the outcomes, becomes the mediator variables for this stage of intervention mapping. Column 2c will consist of the interventions or components of an integrated, comprehensive program. Now we turn to three sources of guidance for the selection of interventions:

- "Best practices" from previous research and evaluation on the change objectives
- "Best experience" from previous programs with less formally controlled evaluation
- "Best processes" from theory, descriptive data, and local wisdom

"Best Practices."   If the previous research on interventions to affect the objectives through the mediators identified is extensive, strong, or both, it will likely be summarized in guidelines based on systematic review and synthesis of the research. These guidelines will likely provide sufficient detail down to intervention components directed at the key predisposing, enabling, and reinforcing factors. Examples of sources of such guidelines include those that are periodically updated and on the World Wide Web:

- The Community Preventive Services Guides (www.thecommunityguide .org)[17]
- The U.S. Preventive Services Task Force Reports (http://www.preven-tiveservices.ahrq.gov/)
- The Canadian Task Force on Preventive Health Care (http://www.ctfphc .org/)
- The Cochrane Collection of systematic reviews (http://www.cochrane.or)
- The National Guideline Clearinghouse for clinical guides (http://www .guideline.gov)
- Others published but not necessarily updated online.[18]

Within the "best practices" guidelines, the varied appropriateness of an intervention for different demographic or other moderator variables will be indicated if the research is based on sufficiently large and heterogeneous samples to recommend such variations. For example, intervention effectiveness often varies between males and females, between highly educated and less educated people, or between younger and older people. At the community level, some interventions will be more or less effective depending on mediator variables such as community resources, social capital, and ethnic composition.

"Best Experiences." When the scientific literature in relation to a given health problem, behavioral change, or predisposing, enabling or reinforcing factor falls short of the strength of evidence required to recommend for or against specific interventions for specific populations or types of individuals, the planners must draw more heavily on the prior experience of other practitioners, communities, states, or national programs in addressing the same issues. Best experiences can come from prior or existing programs and from the indigenous wisdom of the local community in which the program would be implemented. Sussman proposes as Step 2 in his Six-Step Program Development Chain Model, "Go to a resource that systematically pools and warehouses promising activities . . . pool activities from several sources, or create your own activities, and collect these plausible activities for potential testing."[19]

Following this pooling of intervention experiences, a further screening of the more promising alternatives can be accomplished by Sussman's Step 3: "Systematize a set of perceived efficacy studies that can screen among promising activities . . . for additional program development work."[20] Perceived efficacy studies also are referred to as "concept evaluation" and "pretesting" in communications, or "product-market fit" in social marketing,[21] or more generally, *formative evaluation.* Ayala and Elder define **perceived efficacy** as "the process of determining how well a given program or its components might fit into an existing structure of services, how well it will be received by the target population, and the extent to which the new program or its components might meet the needs of the community."[22] The first two of these purposes go beyond the best practices methods of assuming a fit to a local structure or system and acceptability to the population. To that extent, these methods are recommended even when the literature provides evidence-based best practices if the studies on which the recommended best practices are based were conducted in quite different populations, settings, or circumstances.

The methods recommended to pretest "best experiences" for their perceived efficacy include various "verbal methods," in which information is gathered from members of the population of interest by talking with them, including unstructured or semistructured interviews, key informant interviews, community forums, role-playing, and focus groups. The methods could be seen as **participatory research,** assuming that the members of the population of interest share a common desire and purpose for gathering the information. The data sought enable the inventory of pooled experiences or interventions to be assessed for their readability and comprehension if they are materials, their desirability if they are channels of communication, and their pros and cons, their relevance, and their potential for controversy, sensitivity, misunderstanding, or abrasiveness. In the end, some pooled intervention ideas are discarded, some given higher priority than others.

In addition to the pooling and patching of pretested experiences with specific interventions from other programs, another best experiences approach is to compare the data from community or statewide surveillance systems that capture the outcomes of interest for your program. If these communities or states have different programs and policies, they constitute a natural experiment insofar as the variations between or among them can be compared on some common outcome.

For example, when the U.S. tobacco industry settled with the states' attorneys general in an agreement to provide the states large sums in compensation for the Medicaid expenses that the states had incurred as a result of decades of tobacco promotion, the state legislators and public health officials scrambled to decide how best to spend this windfall of new funds for tobacco control. The CDC Office on Smoking and Health (OSH) compiled a "Best Practices" manual to guide the states on the optimal amounts and distribution of funds to different components of a comprehensive, statewide tobacco control program. But this manual departed from the usual best practices manual insofar as it went beyond the published, peer-reviewed evidence from controlled trials and based many of its budgetary allocation recommendations on the best experiences of two states. California and Massachusetts had far outpaced the other 48 states at this point in time (1999), both in tax revenues dedicated to tobacco control and in aggressive mass media, community, school, and work site programs and policy initiatives. The routine data collected by all of the states through the Behavioral Risk Factor Surveillance System and compiled by CDC, together with other state and national data, enabled OSH to recommend per capita expenditures for different components of comprehensive programs. Multiplied by the populations of different states, these recommendations could be made as specific dollar amounts for different states.[23]

Our term *best experiences* to express this range of alternatives to evidence-based best practices that are based on controlled trials is not meant to minimize the value of these alternatives, but rather to lay the emphasis on the experience rather than a prescribed practice. One should consider the experiences of others in your setting, or in other settings, as lending greater plausibility and credibility to what might become a best practice with more formal testing if the practice, intervention, or program component has met one or more of the following "plausibility criteria" suggested by Cameron and colleagues:

Evaluation attributes
- *Formative evaluation and pilot testing* were used to assess relevance, comprehension, and acceptability of activities, materials, methods, etcetera.
- *Process evaluation* was conducted in the previous experience to assess implementation, site response, practitioners' response, participants' response, and capacity of providers to deliver the intervention appropriately.

Content attributes
- *Objectives match those of your program,* for example, a specific desired behavioral change or environmental change that is sought in your program corresponds to one or more of the objectives in the previous experience.
- *Behavioral change principles incorporated* and operationalized in the prior experience, for example, active participation, skill building, self-monitoring, social support, and other reinforcement.[24]

Cameron and his associates also listed a series of "process attributes" as additional plausibility criteria that would increase the credibility of what we are calling best experiences, in the absence of controlled experimental data, but we place these under our third line of intervention mapping and patching, which we call "best processes."

"Best Processes."   One is still left with options, choices, and gaps in most instances where the controlled experimental research literature cannot unequivocally recommend specific evidence-based best practices for each of the targets of change in specific populations, and the best experiences from previous or concurrent programs leave some doubt about their fit. As this is usually the case, one must combine the two foregoing guidelines with a third set of processes for matching interventions or program components with objectives and their mediator variables. This third set we call "best processes" because it emphasizes the very processes of planning that we have been laying out in the foregoing chapters, with a highly participatory and theory-based invention of methods, messages, intervention channels, and combinations into programs. This stage of mapping and patching seeks (1) to retrace the program theory and logic model we constructed in the previous chapters; (2) to draw heavily on theory from the last phase (the educational and ecological diagnosis) to map theoretical assumptions to interventions relevant to each of the most important predisposing, enabling, and reinforcing factors; and (3) to patch any remaining gaps in the most important predisposing, enabling, and reinforcing factors with innovation and evaluation.

1. Retracing the logic model constructed in previous phases, we review the original impulse, concerns, demand, or aspiration from the community that provided the impetus for the program planning effort. This revisiting of the social or quality-of-life concerns usually suggests ways to frame the messages and communication appeals to link them to the ultimate goals and values for the changes sought. It also identifies the essential logic connecting the changes the program will ask of people to their own ultimate goals so that the messages can ensure that those changes and their connections to expected outcomes are made understandable and acceptable. A mainstay of the PATCH process is to package and present the local data on health and risk factors in a way that clearly communicates the connections and the importance of one to solving the other (see also the box below).

DEVELOPING INTERVENTIONS FOR THE IOWA STATE PATROL

Recognizing how important it was to play back to the overweight law enforcement officers (LEOs) the data collected from them, and to the state highway patrol officials who commissioned the planning, Ramey and her colleagues proposed from their application of PRECEDE-PROCEED the following list of interventions to reduce cardiovascular disease (CVD) and its risk factors in LEOs (in parentheses are our association of each with predisposing, enabling, and reinforcing factors for behavioral and environmental change objectives):

Behavioral

- Apprise officers of the findings of the cardiovascular risk survey (predisposing factor of awareness, belief in susceptibility)
- Calculate and communicate the actual, local 10-year risk of CVD in specific groups (same predisposing factors)
- Communicate the patterns of relationships of their common risk factors to CVD and diabetes (same predisposing factors)
- Strengthen the relationship and coordinate communication between Iowa State University and the state personnel services (enabling)
- Establish a physical fitness program within the department (with specific components identified for predisposing and enabling factors)
- Provide specific information on nutrition and stress at LEO meetings and inservice training sessions (enabling skills for self-care)
- Organize forums for LEOs to voice their concerns about health issues they perceive to be work related (reinforcing factors)
- Organize annual dialogues about issues arising from annual health screening (enabling and reinforcing factors)
- Perform risk assessment for each LEO, predicting the 10-year outcome (reinforcing factor)

Environmental

- Revisit the social diagnosis definition of health and examine its congruence with the department's mission statement (predisposing and reinforcing for management, framing the communications noted above with the departmental mission)
- Shift focus from fitness to health within the Iowa State Patrol (enabling an environmental change to reinforce LEO behavior change)
- Further analysis of historical fitness data over past 20 years to reinforce understanding of risk factor trend (reinforcing management's commitment to organizational-environmental change)
- Track medical disability numbers and associated morbidity to establish baseline and evaluate progress
- Provide access to web sites and training sessions on risk factors, leadership, et cetera (enabling organizational-environmental change)
- Implement longer periods of time for shift rotation, considering the stress of shift work (enabling environmental change)
- Implement the four-item perceived stress scale monthly for 6–12 months (enabling the organizational adjustments via monitoring)

The developers of this set of recommendations for program components in nine midwestern states were rewarded with the adoption of the program by the Iowa state highway patrol department, but disappointed that eight other states in which a similar diagnostic planning process was carried out did not adopt the recommendations. They believe that the mounting fiscal deficits in those states prevented adoption of new programs (and dismantling of some standing programs). These fiscal and other administrative, organizational, and policy issues will be addressed in the second part of this chapter.[25]

2. Returning to the theories reviewed in Chapter 4, the planner can map specific changes required in predisposing, enabling, and reinforcing factors for specific behavioral and environmental changes to the health beliefs, attitudes, intentions, stages of change, skills, social supports, and enabling or reinforcing policies suggested for each. Some of the theories and models are more explicit than others in suggesting specific interventions, methods, or messages, which leads us to the need to innovate and evaluate.[26]

3. At this third and deepest level of ambiguity and uncertainty about what might work, we are in the highly *important*, but low *changeability* quadrant of the fourfold table identified in our earlier graphic representations of priority setting on two dimensions. Because the remaining gaps are highly important to the change process sketched by our logic model, we cannot leave them without interventions, but the scant evidence of changeability leaves us no choice but to innovate and evaluate.

Innovate and Evaluate. The ultimate requirement for innovation and evaluation to fill the remaining intervention gaps in a new program plan calls for some special features of the approach to developing and evaluating this component of the program. It must be an approach that is sensitive to the reasons such interventions have not been formally evaluated with randomized controlled trials to an extent that would move them up to the best practices category of interventions. One reason is that such interventions will likely be unique to the local setting, population, and/or circumstances. Unique interventions have limited generalizability, so a large investment in their evaluation can only be justified if they are also very expensive, or are expected to be used for a long time. If they are not uniquely suited to the local setting, population, or circumstances, but might have generalizability to other programs in other settings, populations, and circumstances, then greater attention should be paid to the potential reach, adaptability, adoption potential, cost or resources required, and sustainability of the program or of the changes produced.[27]

What Is an Innovation? One can try to improve on previous efforts to change a particular predisposing, enabling, or reinforcing factor by increasing the quantity or improving the quality of the previous interventions. The evaluation research literature refers to the quantity approach as dose-response, increased exposure time, or increased intensity of the intervention.[28] The quality approach seeks to make an intervention or program more effective in changing a predisposing, enabling, or reinforcing factor, or a more distal outcome, than in previous efforts by changing some features of the intervention or the mix of interventions in a program. We define an **innovation** more in relation to the latter, that is, improving upon a previously tried method by improving its quality, ideally without increasing its cost. Since cost is a major limiting factor in dose or quantity, we do not gain much with qualitative improvements that cost more per unit of delivery or impact (per person reached, predisposing factor effected, behavioral or environmental factor changed, etc.). An innovation, then, is a qualitative change in the method or process of an intervention such that it

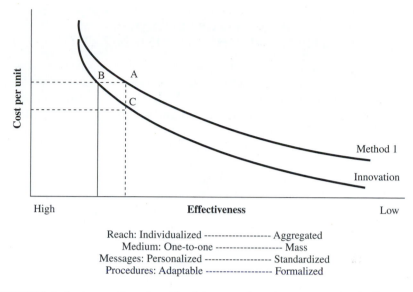

Reach: Individualized ------------------- Aggregated
Medium: One-to-one ------------------- Mass
Messages: Personalized ------------------ Standardized
Procedures: Adaptable ------------------ Formalized

FIGURE 5-6 An innovation should achieve a reduced cost per unit of effective delivery (A–C) or more effective delivery for a given cost per unit of delivery (A–B).
Source: Green, 1978; Green & Lewis, 1984, p. 260; adapted from Oettinger & Zapol, 1972.

increases effectiveness at a fixed cost per unit of delivery, or it achieves the same effectiveness at a lower cost per unit of delivery, as shown in Figure 5-6.

Comparing the two hypothetical method curves on the two dimensions of cost and effectiveness, we see that the innovation curve gains an advantage (reduction) in cost for a fixed level of effectiveness (the difference between points A and C as measured on the vertical "cost per unit" scale). Examples of innovations that have been demonstrated to achieve these cost or efficiency advantages are the use of indigenous workers in place of professionals where the former cost less and can compensate for the technical knowledge of the professional with greater sensitivity to the culture and attitudes of clients and greater identification with their needs.[29] Innovations in the use of personnel tend to produce notable cost savings because personnel costs are usually among the largest parts of program budgets.

Another major source of innovation is technology. Here the advantages are more likely to show up on the several dimensions of effectiveness displayed at the bottom of Figure 5-6. Of greatest interest in recent years have been the innovations in computer-based tailoring of health communications. These innovations capture some of the same advantages of mass media in their reach, but produce gains at the same time, almost ironically, in the features of more personalized communications. Thus, they are more effective than mass media, while having much greater reach and economies of scale than the personalized communications they mimic.[30]

Finally, the most cost-effective interventions of all are likely to be the policy changes that can achieve change uniformly across an entire population, or

TAILORED CALENDARS:
BOOSTING CHILDHOOD IMMUNIZATION

Matthew Kreuter and his colleagues at St. Louis University (SLU) sought to determine the effectiveness of tailored and personalized calendars as a means to increase the rate of immunization among babies. The calendars were computer generated and featured a color picture of the child. The information and messages in the calendar (including prompts for scheduled immunization dates) were tailored to the self-reported interests expressed by the parents.

The study was carried out at two federally funded neighborhood health centers in St. Louis, Missouri. Ninety-nine percent of the families involved in the study were African American and virtually all were enrolled in the WIC program.

At the end of the nine month enrollment period, 82 percent of the babies whose parents received a tailored immunization calendar were up to date with their recommended immunization schedule. Among babies from the same health center who were matched on age and sex but did not receive the calendars, only 65 percent were up to date. At age 24 months, 66 percent of babies whose families received calendars were up to date in their immunizations versus 47 percent of babies who did not receive calendars. During the decade prior to the study, immunization rates in the city of St. Louis ranged from 26 to 50 percent.

Qualitative analysis revealed that for the study population, the color photograph of the baby was one of the calendar's essential features. Many of the participants reported having no professional photographs of their baby and valued the ones provided at each appointment. Participants were given a new color photograph and additional calendar pages every time they visited and their child received an immunization.

Program costs were estimated in 2000 by combining the fixed costs (computer, printer, digital camera, lighting fixtures, etc.) and the variable costs (labor, paper, toner cartridges, tubes for transporting calendars, etc.) The tailored program was developed by the SLU research team and made available to the clinics (and all other users) at no cost. Based on those estimates, once the number of families exposed to the tailored calendar program reaches 1000, the per child cost per year is $10 or less.*

Source: Kreuter MW, Caburnay CA, Chen JJ, Donlin MJ. (2004). Effectiveness of individually tailored calendars in promoting childhood immunization in urban public health centers. *American Journal of Public Health,* 94, 1, (in press).

* personal communication with Dr. Matthew Kreuter (12/19/03)

change environmental conditions affecting the behavior or health of an entire population.

A Summary of the Developmental Process Steps to a Comprehensive Program.   To summarize the foregoing steps in crafting the interventions for a program is also to review their coverage of essential targets. It sets up the final step of blending these interventions into comprehensive programs that address the essential predisposing, enabling, and reinforcing factors identified in the previous chapter. The first step was the *matching* of major categories of interventions needed to address the various ecological levels for intervention, from individual or family to community or state. For this matching task, we refer the reader to the MATCH model as one example of a systematic approach to this first step, but we have addressed these different levels of determinants throughout the diagnostic chapters and will dig deeper into appropriate strategies for the different settings in the chapters that follow. The second step was *mapping* specific interventions to the specific predisposing, enabling, and reinforcing factors within each level or setting, using best practices where available from the research literature. The third step was the *pooling* of best experiences from previous and concurrent programs to address the most important predisposing, enabling, and reinforcing factors. The fourth was *patching* the remaining gaps and refining the proposed interventions by reviewing the social diagnosis, reviewing the theories used in the previous phase, and finally innovating and evaluating where gaps remain.

Fidelity to "Best Practices" Versus Adaptation to Population and Circumstances.   Most of this discussion has assumed that evidence-based best practices must be supplemented with experience-based and theory-based adaptations and innovations to address some of the predisposing, enabling, and reinforcing factors. Even when the literature offers evidence-based recommendations for a best practice, one is faced in a local situation with the question of whether to adhere strictly to every detail of the intervention or practice, or whether to innovate and adapt to certain local circumstances. A reasonable assumption is that an evidence-based best practice can only be expected to work in practice if it is implemented exactly as in the protocol employed in the study or studies in which it was experimentally tested. This assumption leads to efforts to provide rigorous training and strict supervision of practitioners who will be called upon to implement the best practice. Equally important, if not more important to the success of a program, however, might be the training of practitioners to make appropriate adaptations within the program mix of best practices, best experiences, and best processes. Making a better fit to the circumstances and characteristics of the people with whom they are practicing should be a matter of professional discretion by the practitioner "on the ground" by the "street-level bureaucrat."[31] Professional judgment and discretionary decision making in the face of newly presenting problems are hallmarks of professionalism and are what distinguish professionals from technicians. Training and supervision should support and encourage these in most complex practice situations, as well as understanding of and skill in implementing the specific features of an evidence-based best practice that are presumed to have made it successful in its experimental tests.

Alignment 3: From Formative Evaluation to Process Evaluation: Pretesting Components of Program for Feasibility, Acceptability, and Fit

Everything in the foregoing developmental steps can also be referred to as *formative evaluation.* One final step in this developmental or formative phase is the beginning of **process evaluation.** This is where we turn the corner from PRECEDE to PROCEED. **Pretesting** is a first step in process evaluation and an extension and further elaboration of formative evaluation insofar as it tests the ideas and candidates for intervention for their feasibility, acceptability and fit within the local situation in real time before making a commitment to include them in the program plan. It actually implements components of the program within samples of typical end-users or recipients of the interventions to see if the presumed feasibility and acceptability actually adhere in the population or program context. Pretesting, then, is a *pilot test* of **feasibility** in its trial of implementation, and of acceptability in its trial of reaction to the intervention by people representative of those who would be the ultimate purveyors and recipients. It is *not,* however, a test of efficacy or effectiveness of the intervention against outcomes specified in the objectives. That comes in later phases of *process evaluation* against organizational and implementation objectives, *impact evaluation* against educational, ecological, behavioral, and environmental objectives, and *outcome evaluation* against health and social objectives.

Burhansstipanov and her colleagues provide an example of pretesting in their work with Native Americans to develop a program that would enable the tribal communities to make informed choices about allowing selected clinical trials to be conducted. The pretesting provided valuable developmental information to the program planners on "allocating sufficient time and resources to tailor presentations for diverse tribal settings and workshop participants, addressing barriers to participation in clinical trials through culturally appropriate strategies, providing information to foster informed decision making related to participation, and writing as a team to increase cultural breadth of examples and interactive experiences."[32]

Because this step begins the process evaluation phase, it is also time to pretest the measurement instruments (surveys, questionnaires, observational tools, record-keeping systems) that would be used to evaluate processes of implementation, as well as any instruments that were not already developed during the gathering of diagnostic-baseline measures in previous phases.[33]

One further distinction that these types of evaluation raise is between evaluation of components of a program, which is most relevant to the formative and process stages of evaluation, versus evaluation of the whole program. All of the evaluation steps to this point have been concerned with assessing components of the developing program, or interventions, rather than with the program itself. The program probably does not yet exist; its component interventions are still taking shape and blending into the whole, and there remains yet another stage in development, to be described in the next section of this chapter, where we must test the capacity of the sponsoring organization or community partners to provide the necessary resources to implement the program. Thus, we come now to the moment of truth in "testing" the viability of the program that has taken form in these various steps.[34]

THE ADMINISTRATIVE ASSESSMENT AND PROCESS EVALUATION

Still pursuing the objectives formulated for change in educational and ecological determinants in Chapter 4, and the interventions needed to make a program likely to change those determinants in the foregoing parts of this chapter, we shall turn now to the process of assessing the resources required and available to mobilize and deploy those interventions. One begins at this stage budgeting the time and material resources to implement the methods and strategies chosen in the preceding steps. Additional considerations of selecting or developing and implementing the methods and strategies will be addressed in the setting-specific chapters, because it is the setting or channel through which one will reach the population that dictates which methods and strategies are most appropriate. A comprehensive program may involve several settings, possibly all of the settings analyzed in Chapters 6 through 8. Representatives of those settings would ideally have been included in the planning processes leading up to this point; however, at times it only becomes clear at this point that a setting not previously involved needs to be a channel for the program. Involvement in this phase of planning can ensure that developers will address the resource requirements of such a setting.

Step 1: Assessment of Resources Needed[35]

The first step in administrative assessment is to review the resources required to implement the proposed program methods and strategies. This entails an examination of the time frames for accomplishing the objectives and of the types and numbers of people needed to carry out the program.

Time. Because it is nonrenewable, the first and most critical resource is time. Once expended, time cannot be recovered. It is inflexible in its supply, and it affects the availability and cost of all other resources. Time required is estimated at several levels of PRECEDE with the formulation of realistic objectives. Each objective states the time (date) by which that objective needs to be accomplished in order for the next higher level objective to be accomplished. Thus, certain educational and organizational objectives must be accomplished before certain behavioral and environmental objectives can be expected to materialize, and these in turn must precede any palpable change in health or quality-of-life outcomes. For example, suppose you have established the following predisposing educational objectives:

> Within the first four months of a measles immunization program, parents in the target population will (1) show a 60% increase in their knowledge that a measles vaccine is available and (2) show a 50% increase in their belief that their children are susceptible to measles.

Your enabling objectives might include a 4-month target of dispatching 60 mobilized immunization stations, one in each school and shopping center in the community, and a 3-month target of obtaining commitments from 50 school principals and 10 shopping center managers. All these objectives must be accomplished within the time frames stated to achieve a behavioral objective of a 4% increase in schoolchildren receiving measles immunization (from 90% previously immunized to 94%) at the end of 6 months. (Because this is a one-time behavior, you need not bother with an objective for reinforcing factors.)

These objectives would clearly limit your time frame for implementing specific aspects of the program plan. A timetable or **Gantt chart** can be laid out as in Figure 5-7 to show graphically the start and finish dates for each activity. It also shows the sequence and overlap of activities in time, as well as the number of different activities that will be proceeding simultaneously during each period.[36]

From the Gantt chart in Figure 5-7, you could explicitly state the time requirements for each activity and compare them with those of every other activity. This allows an analysis not only of time requirements for each activity

FIGURE 5-7 Time requirements can be graphed in the form, of a Gantt chart to identify the specific periods when activities must be implemented, shown here for a school-entry immunization program.

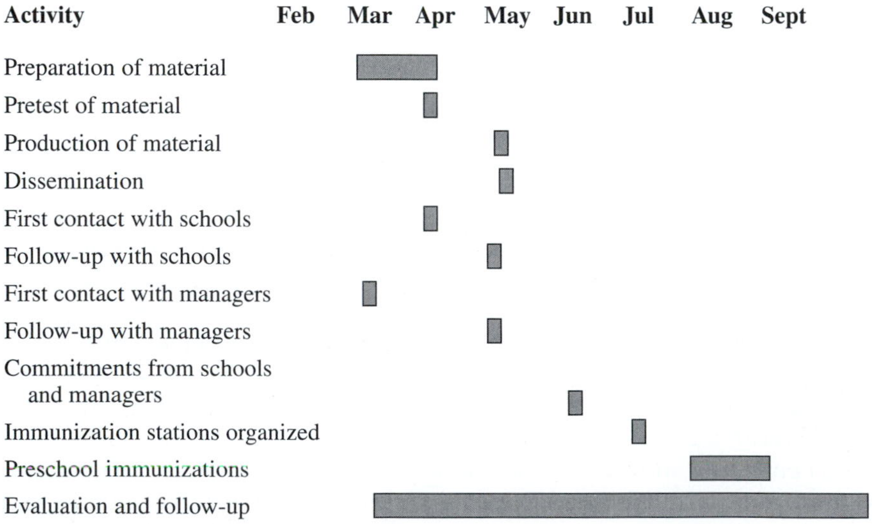
Activity
Feb
Mar
Apr
May
Jun
Jul
Aug
Sept
Preparation of material
Pretest of material
Production of material
Dissemination
First contact with schools
Follow-up with schools
First contact with managers
Follow-up with managers
Commitments from schools and managers
Immunization stations organized
Preschool immunizations
Evaluation and follow-up

but also, reading down a column, of activity requirements for each period. Some activities are discrete events or actions that span less than a month. Others, such as the first and the last two in Figure 5-7, span a period of two or more units of time (the chart may be drawn in units of days, weeks, months, quarters, or years). This takes the administrative assessment of resources required to the second resource, personnel.

Personnel.   Staffing requirements take precedence over other budgetary considerations in the resource analysis, because the personnel category generally constitutes the largest and most restricted line item in most budgets. People cost more than most resources and are more difficult to put in place than most equipment and material resources. Civil service and affirmative action hiring policies, union contracts, and due process in moving personnel all limit the flexibility and discretion with which you could mold this resource to your program needs. The personnel analysis is further complicated by the subtle considerations of talent, skills, personalities, and personal preferences and attitudes toward particular types of work to be done. The human resource frame for analysis of the interplay between an organization and its people emphasizes the skills, insights, ideas, energy, and commitment of people as the most important assets of an organization.[37]

A Gantt chart displaying your time analysis (Figure 5-7) can provide the basis for the first cut in analyzing personnel requirements. For example, the talents and skills of different personnel will quite likely be required at different times. You could define these in your situation by using the names of existing personnel; however, you would more properly define them by their function or the professional, technical, administrative, or clerical skills required. Here it is often useful to break the Gantt chart into smaller units of time, say weeks, days, or even hours, depending on the overall duration and scope of the program. The quantitative analysis of personnel requirements then might take the form shown in Table 5-1.

TABLE 5-1 Personnel loading can be charted for the example of the 6-month immunization program by attaching estimated hours for each category of worker to the tasks shown in Figure 5-7

| | WEEK | | | | | | | | | | Total |
Person	1	2	3	4	5	6	7	8	9 ... 24	Hours
Administrator	20	20	20	20	20	20	20	20	20	...	480
Health educator	40	40	40	40	40	40	40	40	40	...	960
Medical consultant	8	8	8	4	4					30	62
Graphic artist	8		8								16
Nurses										800	800
Secretary	20	20	20	20	20	20	20	20	20	...	480

Each activity in Figure 5-7 contains several subtasks, which are performed by different types of personnel. To move from a Gantt chart to a more specific understanding of the types of personnel and other costs required, you would consider the specific tasks or steps inherent in each activity.

For example, preparing material might require the following tasks or steps:

Research content of materials

Interview experts

Develop first draft

Review first draft

Prepare final draft

Pretesting—the next activity[38]—might require some different tasks, such as:

Arrange pretest logistics—space, schedule, sampling

Contact pretest participants

Document pretest reactions

Revise draft materials

Final production would require meeting with printers, proofing final copy, and ordering the print run.

The estimate of personnel hours required each week enables planners to make a cost analysis of personnel, as well as a time allocation (loading) analysis that permits the administrator at the next higher level to consider where and when existing personnel might be reassigned to support the program without hiring new personnel. The personnel loading chart documents two sets of assumptions critical to effective project administration: (1) What types of staff members are needed? (2) How many hours (or days) of each member's time are required to complete each task and activity successfully? In the example shown in Table 5-1, the personnel requirements include a half-time administrator and a full-time health education specialist throughout the program. The administrator might be a health education specialist with a master's degree and community experience. The other health educator, assigned to the communication and dissemination responsibilities, might hold a baccalaureate degree and have less experience. This kind of personnel analysis must be based on a matching of personnel with administrative, educational, technical, and organizational requirements dictated by the process objectives outlined in the previous chapter.

Budget.   You can easily convert the time and personnel requirements into cost estimates by multiplying each line in the personnel loading chart by an average hourly wage or salary estimate for each category of worker. You might hire these personnel, borrow them from another program within the same organization, or contract for their services as consultants (e.g., the medical consultant and graphic artist, during the developmental phase, the two full-time nurses during the final 10 weeks). Whatever the method of payment, the hourly costs should be recorded in the budget requirement at this stage because these are real requirements and therefore real costs to be anticipated. If they prove too much for the sponsoring organization, you can explore options for transfer of personnel, borrowing of personnel, recruitment of volunteers, donated services from other agencies, and other possibilities. If some of these can be contributed or volunteered hours in the final negotiation and allocation of responsibilities, they can be credited to the project as "in-kind" contributions mobilized by the organization or the community coalition. The more in-kind resources the proposed program can show it has raised, the more convincing the proposal will be as a community initiative to which organizations have a real commitment.

Other budgetary requirements will include personnel *benefits* for salaried workers (usually 20–25% of salaries for professional workers), plus materials or supplies, printing costs, postage, photocopying, telephone costs, equipment, data processing, and travel. In addition, most organizations have a fixed overhead or indirect cost rate such as 20% or 50%. This is an average maintenance rate they add to any direct cost estimate to provide for the administrative services of the front office, the rental and upkeep of the building and offices, utilities, and sometimes local telephone or other fixed costs of the offices in which special projects will be housed. For example, if the direct cost of a program is estimated at $10,000 in personnel time and materials, the budget might be $12,000 to cover the usual 20-percent overhead the agency has established as necessary from experience. See Table 5-2 for an example of a preliminary budget.

Attention to Detail.   Whether preparing a budget for their organization or for an external grant application to support their program, planners must pay close attention to the requirements of the funding organization. For example, some funders limit the indirect cost rate that can be charged. Some prefer to see personnel time expressed as a percentage of the individual's annual work hours (to help gauge the level of commitment to the project), instead of being expressed as a number of project hours (as in Table 5-2). Some funders may even request both versions of personnel time—percent of time and project hours by task.

One should always be prepared to back up every line item in the budget with a more detailed version and narrative justification, even if one does not submit the detailed budgets. For example, if travel costs are listed as a lump sum on a summary project budget, that sum should be derived from estimates for the component parts—such as air travel, meals, ground transportation, and hotel costs—not a "ballpark guesstimate" for the broader category. Always review a project budget from the perspective of the reader, as with any written work, and ask these questions: Do the items make sense? Are any unusual items explained? Is there back-up documentation for each estimate?

Spreadsheet software (such as Lotus 1-2-3 or Microsoft Excel) can help one create budget estimates and manipulate them ("what-if" analyses) to gauge the budgetary impact of different scenarios (e.g., another staff member, fewer

TABLE 5-2 Initial budget spreadsheets can be based on the foregoing analysis of requirements, estimated here based on 1998 costs or rates

Initial budget estimates based on analysis of resource requirements before assessment of resources available

Budget Items	Hours	Rate	Totals
Personnel			
Administrator	480	$35	$ 16,800
Health educator	960	28	26,880
Nurses	800	25	20,000
Secretary	480	17	8,160
Subtotal			$ 71,840
Personnel benefits (fringe) @ 20%			$ 14,368
Total personnel costs			**$ 86,208**
Supplies			
Printing brochure			$ 2,000
Postage (20,000 × .37)			7,400
Office supplies			500
Vaccination supplies (800 × $3)			2,400
Total supplies			**$ 12,300**
Services			
Telephone			$ 500
Photocopying			400
Consultants			
Data processing	25	$20	$ 500
Medical consultant	62	75	4,650
Graphic artist	16	25	400
Total services			**$ 6,450**
Travel			
Local (400 mi. @ .31)			$ 124
State conference ($650 air; $150 per diem)			800
Total travel			**$ 924**
Total Direct Costs			**$105,882**
Indirect Costs (20% of direct costs)			**$ 21,176**
Total Budget Estimate			**$127,058**

brochures, more travel). Spreadsheet programs are generally faster and more accurate than is repeatedly entering numbers by hand on a calculator, but they still require careful data entry and double-checking of each total and subtotal. As you gain project experience, compare your initial budget estimates to actual expenditures to understand which items consistently have been underestimated (or overestimated), and adjust future budgets accordingly.

Step 2: Assessment, Enhancement, and Process Evaluation of Available Resources

The previous section of this chapter presented ways to identify methods or materials, interventions, and program components appropriate to some of the educational and ecological objectives. Such materials and methods might need to be developed from scratch, as implied by the budget items in Table 5-2 for the development and printing of a brochure to blanket the community with information about measles and the need to immunize children before school starts. Sometimes the material has been developed in a previous program or by a national or state agency that can make the material available at little or no cost to one's agency. The costs saved by using centrally developed educational materials or materials developed previously for another program can sometimes reduce a budget considerably, but the materials might not be tailored well to the local situation or current circumstances. Such tradeoffs between costs and the ideal arrangements for your program will arise throughout the administrative and policy assessments.

Personnel.   In most health promotion programs, you may find a common assumption: Existing personnel will suffice throughout the implementation of the program. If the preceding assessments, however, have produced a program design that requires more personnel than the sponsoring organization has available at its disposal, then you may want to consider the following options:

1. Identify and seek part-time commitments from personnel from other departments or units within your organization. If they are not authorized to allocate their own time, you will need commitments from their supervisors as well. Temporary arrangements of this kind are common when separate departments share common goals, which is often the case if the other department has the kind of personnel you need.
2. Retrain personnel within your department to take on tasks outside their usual scope.
3. Explore the potential for recruitment of volunteers from the community. Short-term programs, in particular, can tap the underutilized pool of talent and energy available for volunteer effort for a worthy cause.[39] Evaluations of the use of lay health workers for outreach, follow-up, and communications tasks have shown them to be cost-effective substitutes for permanent professional staff, even when paid.[40]
4. Explore the potential for cooperative agreements with other agencies or organizations in the community to fill in the gaps in your personnel. Be sure your organization can reciprocate in the future.
5. Develop a grant proposal for funding, partial funding, or matched funding of your program by a government agency, philanthropic foundation, or corporate donor. The work you will have done in following the Precede planning process follows the logical format most granting agencies wish to see in an application. With the addition of your evaluation plan and final budget request, you will have a grant application in hand.

6. Appeal directly to the public for donations.
7. Price the service at a cost-recovery level of fees you will charge some or all users of the services. With options 6 and 7, you must be cautious that you stay within affordable limits, that you stay within range of market value for the services, and that you provide assurances that those in your priority target groups who might not be able to afford the services will still have access to them.
8. If none of the previous options seems appropriate, feasible, or sufficient, and if the program represents a permanent or long-term commitment of the organization, then you may justifiably pursue policy changes in the organization such that a more fundamental reorganization or redistribution of resources to your department or unit would be established before embarking on the program. This could necessitate the abandonment of services or programs previously considered core functions of the agency.

Other Budgetary Constraints.   The foregoing options for augmenting personnel might apply to some other resources available from other departments or organizations as financial or in-kind contributions to the program.[41] They represent the main courses of action you can pursue singly or in combination to close the gap between resources required and resources available within your organization to carry out the desired program.

When you cannot find resources, the fallback position, of course, is to trim the sails on your program plan and to propose more modest objectives and less powerful methods of intervention. Because this course represents a compromise of the plan, you should undertake it only with due consideration to the consequences for the integrity of the plan. Specific questions you should ask before giving up too many parts of the plan or levels of intervention with budget cuts include the following:

1. *The threshold level.* Will the reduced level of resources still allow enough intervention to reach a threshold of impact that will achieve subsequent objectives? The notion of a threshold level of resources suggests that there is a minimum level of investment below which the program will be too weak to achieve a useful result.[42] Although threshold level studies are common in drug trials to establish the minimal useful dose and in nutritional research to establish minimum daily requirements of vitamins and minerals, only a few documented examples of spending levels in health programs[43] support this theoretical notion.
2. *The point of diminishing return.* Is there a point of diminishing returns beyond which additional resources do not necessarily achieve commensurate gains in impact or outcome? If so, fewer resources might not hinder the achievement of at least some benefits. This, too, is a largely theoretical concept in health programs.[44] The same studies cited in the previous paragraph contain the limited data available on points of diminishing returns.
3. *Critical elements.* Does the program plan have a critical element without which the objectives cannot be achieved? If so, will the budget cut or shortage of resources preclude achieving that one objective or element? In a

work site program to reduce lower-back injuries in nurses, for example, one might determine that everything that can be done in the program depends on the nurses having release time from their duties to participate in the educational and exercise training program. If the hospital cannot provide such time for these nurses, the director of occupational health would be advised not to proceed with the program.

4. *Critical expectations.* Can the target levels of the objectives be lowered without jeopardizing the integrity of the program or the expectations of the constituents or sponsors of the program? If the behavioral change target of immunization can be reduced from 94% to 92% for schoolchildren without risking a major outbreak of measles, the savings in outreach resources could be considerable. This is because, as we have seen in the earlier discussions of diffusion theory, the **late adopters** are harder for a program to reach than the **late majority.** An equivalent reduction in the target levels during the early phases of a program, say from 14% to 10%, would not yield a commensurate cost savings because early adopters are easier to reach than late ones.

5. *Critical timing and cash flow.* Can the target dates for the objectives be set back to spread the program effort over a longer period? By itself, this will not save resources in the long run, but it will reduce costs in the initial year by shifting them to later periods. The initial costs or "front loading" could be the major budgetary barrier because of temporary fiscal circumstances. By slowing the pace of the program implementation, some outlays could be delayed in anticipation of better budgetary times. This amounts to an adjustment of cash flow.

6. *Critical population segments.* Can the types of people selected as priority target groups be reordered to give lower priority to the hard to reach? This is too often the most tempting adjustment in underfunded programs. Those who need the program the most are often the most expensive to reach and can least afford to subsidize the program with fees for service. This sometimes leads to a decision to make the underbudgeted program available on a first-come, first-served basis. This should be a last resort in accepting a reduced budget because the integrity of the longer-term objectives, including objectives to reduce disparities and increase equity, will likely be compromised. Although they cost more to reach per unit of service delivered, the poorer and more isolated segments of the target population will gain more in health improvement because they have more to gain if they are effectively reached.

Step 3: Assessment, Modification, and Process Evaluation of Factors Influencing Implementation

Besides the availability of resources, a host of other factors may enhance or hinder the smooth **implementation** of your program plan. We have elaborated the classically recognized obstacles to implementation to include facilitators to change in Table 5-3. The table groups several variables according to four general categories: policy, the implementing organization, the political milieu, and

TABLE 5-3 Effects of policy, organizational, and political factors on implementation are shown here as either facilitating or hindering implementation

Variables	Effects on Implementation	
	Positive or Facilitating	Negative or Hindering
Program plan or policy		
Theory and evidence	Widely tested	Limited evidence
Assumptions	Defined	Unclear
Goals	Stated explicitly	Vague or nonexistent
Change		
Amount	Small	Large
Rate	Incremental	Ambitious
Familiarity	Familiar	Unfamiliar
Centrality	Central	Peripheral
Complexity	Few transactions	Many transactions
Resources	Available	Nonexistent
Specification	Some	None
Flexibility	Alternative solutions	One right answer
Impact	Early stages	Later stages
Implementing organization		
Structure		
Goal	Relevant to policy	Irrelevant to policy
Task	Suitable	Unsuitable
Scale	Small	Large
Climate	Supportive	Unsupportive
Technical capacity		
Technology	Appropriate	Inappropriate
Resources	Available	Unavailable
Employee disposition		
Approach	Problem solving	Opportunistic
Motivation	Maintained	Declines
Values	Congruent	Incongruent
Attitudes	Favorable	Unfavorable
Beliefs	Faith in policy	No faith in policy
Employee behavior	Changeable	Resistant
Political milieu		
Power		
Strength	Strong	Weak
Support	Present	Absent
Environment		
Timing	"Right"	"Wrong"
Intended beneficiaries	Needs	No needs
Other organizations	Controllable	Uncontrollable

Source: Adapted from "Reconciling Concept and Context: Theory of Implementation," by J. M. Ottoson and L. W. Green, 1987, in W. B. Ward and M. H. Becker (Eds.), *Advances in Health Education and Promotion,* vol. 2, Greenwich, CT: JAI Press; used with permission of the publisher.

the environment. Notice that each variable, depending upon the circumstances, can be a positive, facilitating force or a negative, hindering one. We come to the policy diagnosis in the next section. Here we focus on the organizational and staffing issues, the features of the plan that make it more or less acceptable and absorbable by the organization, community circumstances, and considerations for ensuring the quality of the implementation. Most of these have been examined variously in case studies and process evaluations of the implementation of Precede-Proceed plans.[45] A thoughtful implementation plan is not complete without a careful assessment of those factors, including a provision that assets and barriers can be acknowledged publicly. Clearly, some barriers will be essentially attitudinal or political or reflect power relationships that you cannot politely make a matter of public record in your formal plan, but you ignore them at the peril of your program.

Staff Commitment, Values, and Attitudes.   Before a plan is complete, it needs to make the rounds of comment and suggestions from those who will have a role in implementing it, especially if they have not been directly involved in formulating the plan up to this point. Staff members of the implementing agencies will be in the best position to anticipate barriers in their various roles and will welcome the opportunity to point out some of the pitfalls in your plan *before* you ask them to implement it. Though they may not have participated earlier in the planning, their involvement at this stage is essential to their commitment to the objectives and methods of the program. It does not guarantee their commitment, but without their participation in planning, their commitment and their attitude toward the program are almost certain to be undependable. Staff commitment as a predisposition to implementing a program, however, has been found to be less reliable as a predictor of implementation than is the enabling factor of community or organizational capacity. As with individual health behavior, organizational and staff "predisposition is a necessary but not sufficient condition for implementation to occur; capacity-related factors appear to be the primary constraint."[46]

Program Goal(s).   Plans that require changes in standard operating procedures place the goals and objectives of the new plans into question. If these contradict previously accepted goals and objectives, you must resolve the conflict by clarifying priorities.[47] As Ross and Mico put it, "The goals must accord with the client system's existing policy,"[48] but this can be accomplished either by adjusting the goals or by changing the policy, as we will discuss in the next section. A third option is to place on the shoulders of the practitioners or local managers the burden of reconciling the goals of the implementing organization with those of the program, which also lays a particular importance on external sources of enabling and reinforcing support to maintain the motivation and capability of the workers to function within an environment that seems at times hostile to their efforts. Such a case is analyzed in a school-based drug abuse prevention program, where the prevention workers in the schools were hired and trained by the health agency to work in schools that did not share their purpose.[49]

Rate of Change.   Incremental change is easier to implement than radical, ambitious, nonincremental changes.[50] Break your program plan's implementation steps down into small, manageable pieces.

Familiarity.   Are the procedures and methods to be employed familiar to staff members who must implement them? Do they depart radically from standard operating procedures? Even if skills are not at issue, unfamiliar methods and procedures require careful introduction and orientation to avoid being rejected, ignored, or poorly implemented.[51]

Complexity.   A change requiring multiple transactions or complex relationships and coordination will be more difficult to implement than will single-action or single-person procedures.[52]

Space.   One of the most precious commodities in many organizations is office space. If your program plan proposes to use existing office space for another purpose or to move staff members from one space to another, you will likely step on someone's toes. Space should be treated as a resource to be allocated according to rules or procedures similar to those suggested earlier for personnel and other budgetary items.

Community Circumstances.   Beyond your own organization, the community will respond to your proposed program at several levels. The principle of participation, emphasized throughout the previous chapters, should alert one to the need to weigh the community's assets and barriers as one moves through the planning process. Inevitably, even among those who have participated in the planning process, some people will express misgivings about how the new program will affect them and their programs. Some of these misgivings will translate into passive resistance, some into subtle efforts to minimize, discredit, or even sabotage the program or its perpetrators. The best protection against these defensive maneuvers in the community, besides education and earlier involvement in the planning, is to invite those organizations most threatened by the program to be cosponsors or collaborators. If, for whatever reason, early engagement and involvement did not occur, it is never too late to invite others to share in the credit and the public visibility of the program in exchange for their support.

Even the most thoughtful strategic plan will probably not be able to take all assets, potential barriers, and sources of opposition into account. What then? The remaining barriers and sources of support to be assessed can be considered broader political and structural barriers. These must be addressed in the final diagnostic phase, and some of them can only be changed through external political processes because they lie beyond the direct control of one's agency or the program planners within a larger bureaucracy.

Quality Assurance, Training, and Supervision.   When you board a jetliner, you probably trust that the pilot and crew have the competence and skill to get you to your destination. Your confidence has been established because airlines have to adhere to tested standards and are committed to ongoing in-service training to ensure high-quality performance in those who operate and maintain the aircraft. In the same sense, the effective implementation of a health promotion program requires competence and skill on the part of those delivering the program. Findings from the School Health Curriculum Project revealed that the teachers implemented only 34% of the teaching and learning activities in the curriculum as they were intended to be implemented.[53] Ottoson has examined the ways in which short-term training fails to consider the context in which the newly acquired knowledge and skills are to be applied.[54] This suggests the need for monitoring the implementation process as the first step (following any pretesting and pilot testing of interventions) in process evaluation.[55] It also suggests that policies and programs must provide for professional discretion and options so that they can be adapted to local situations and changing circumstances. Training and supervision of personnel provide the best assurance of implementation. Each training program is an educational program in itself and deserves a similar planning process to that described by the behavioral, environmental, ecological, and educational assessments in the Precede framework. Supervision can also be approached as an educational process: Behavior change goals can be set mutually by the supervisor and supervisee. Factors predisposing, enabling, and reinforcing the intended behavior can be analyzed periodically; interventions can be planned to predispose, enable, and reinforce implementation through staff meetings, training, written materials, and rewards for high performance. Examples of PRECEDE applied to professional training and **quality assessment** in specific settings will be presented in Chapters 6 through 8.

POLICY ASSESSMENT AND ACCOUNTABILITY

In Chapter 4, we identified various enabling factors that influence high-priority health behaviors. We also examined how to assess resources for the selected educational methods that help develop skills required to enable the behavior and some community organization methods that make resources more accessible to people whose motivation to act is frustrated by the inaccessibility of such factors.[56] We presented still other enabling factors that direct educational efforts or appeals to the community cannot be expected to change because they involve legal, political, or environmental conditions more or less "locked in" by existing policies or regulations. These issues constitute the focus of the policy assessment.

Step 1: Assessment of the Organizational Mission, Policies, and Regulations

Before implementing a plan, one needs to know how it fits with the existing organizational mission, policies, and regulations. Some of the barriers identified in the preceding administrative assessment also may have revealed incompatibilities between organizational mandates and the plan. Be aware that most organizations operate under a blend of formal and informal mandates—most of which are not set in stone. Conflicts might arise also with the policies of a collaborating organization or group. In the face of such incompatibilities, one has three choices: (1) to adapt the proposed plan to be consistent with the organizational mission and policies, (2) to seek to change the policy or organizational mandate, or (3) some of both. We also presented in the previous section the untenable option of shifting the burden of incompatible goals or mandate between the program plan and the host agency to the shoulders of the practitioners or field managers who would be left to cope with the daily dilemmas. Ultimately they, and the program planners, must decide to which—the organization's policy mandate or the program's goals—they will be accountable. You haven't come this far in designing a program that meets the felt needs of a population only to fold in the face of organizational policies that are outdated or inconsistent with the real needs of its constituency. Hence, the choice among options in the remainder of this chapter is the second: seek ways to interpret, adapt, or change the policies to make them conducive to the changes needed.

Being Informed.   Before choosing a course of action, one must understand the mission and culture of the organization. If new to the organization, one would be wise to follow the tenets of primary prevention by taking advantage of the customary orientation sessions offered new employees. One should read the organization's annual report, examine its vision and mission statements, and take the time to visit with veteran employees who have an "institutional memory." If the plan is consistent with existing policy and organizational mandates, one can strengthen it by documenting and communicating more effectively the specific policies it serves and the ways the plan and policies can support each other. Many new program plans are announced with an opening line invoking the organizational policy that authorizes or justifies the proposed program. The preamble to most new government plans or regulations, for example, will cite the authorizing legislation or statute that makes the plan necessary or possible. This kind of preface or covering memo is often signed by the director or chief executive officer, giving the plan not only the force of legislation or policy but also the prestige or authority of the chief administrator.

Anticipating.   One's plan can be in alignment with the organization's mission but *inconsistent* or at odds with a policy or position held by stakeholders or an influential organization. Health practitioners concerned with violence prevention, comprehensive school health, HIV/AIDS education, and tobacco control have learned the value of anticipating the reactions of these groups early in the planning process. Failure to address the concerns of groups with conflicting policy perspectives can have serious negative consequences, such as budget cuts or conflicts with key decision makers or legislators. Addressing such a situation after the fact is inevitably an uphill battle. By anticipating a potential conflict, planners can rely on their negotiation and communication skills, their political acumen, and the scientific and theoretical soundness of their plan to achieve support for the proposed outcome.

For example, imagine an HIV/AIDS prevention effort that includes a school health education component, a planning effort in a region with some history of ultraconservative groups organizing campaigns to derail any school program pertaining to sexuality. Although small in number, these groups are well organized, vocal, and typically make unsubstantiated, and often false, accusations about the content and intentions of such programs. For example, they may claim that school-based HIV/AIDS prevention programs lead to an increase in sexual activity among participating students. By anticipating such claims, program planners can, early in the planning process, educate community residents by sharing with them a well-documented evaluation of a school-based program designed to reduce HIV infection among adolescents in New York and Chicago. Gutmacher and colleagues found that making condoms available does significantly increase the use of condoms among sexually active teens. Their data also showed that "making condoms available does not encourage students who have never had sex to become sexually active."[57] Armed with credible documentation, experienced planners can, through their continuous interaction with the community, warn residents to be on the alert for false claims by special interest groups and preempt or "immunize" them against false accusations that are likely to follow.

Flexibility.   The first question one can ask about any policy that appears to be inconsistent with a program plan is, How flexible is that policy? Most good policies are flexible because it is impossible to know in advance all the problems and opportunities an implementing organization or program will face.[58] The best test of flexibility is to find a previous program implemented under the policy and to examine its deviations, if any, from the policy. This will provide one with both an indicator of flexibility and a precedent to cite in defending one's request for an exception or waiver of policy. If the previous implementation experience was uniformly or mostly positive, one may have a reason to invoke the policy in support of the program, but flexibility might still be the reason other programs flourished under the policy.

Step 2: Assessing Political Forces

How do political forces influence the planning or implementation of a health promotion program? Any time finite resources have to be allocated among several programs but the decision makers do not agree on the distribution of those finite resources, politics will likely influence the ultimate decision. Specifically, decisions will be influenced by what the decision makers do or do not know about the goals and content of the competing programs and also by how their friends or constituents value the proposed program. Planners should consider the following principles as they assess the very real political forces that shape policies and, therefore, their programs.

Level of Analysis.   The political milieu can be analyzed at both the intraorganizational[59] and the interorganizational level.[60] Most of the suggestions for intraorganizational analysis and change that can be considered legitimate

ANTICIPATING AND OVERCOMING BARRIERS: A PRACTICAL EXAMPLE IN MANAGED CARE

Identifying barriers to program implementation is one thing, taking action to overcome them is another. Imagine that a handful of physicians and health workers at one of the largest HMOs in the United States wanted to develop and implement a program of health promotion services appropriate for the clinical setting. Suppose further that as they conceptualized their plan, they identified the following familiar barriers:

1. The health care system and its culture limit flexibility for physicians, and the intention to help alone is inadequate justification for change.
2. Time constraints and patient demand make the physician's job one of responding to complaints, not one of initiating preventive action.
3. Feedback from preventive care is negative or neutral (e.g., the physician does not receive feedback about whether late-stage breast cancer was averted by promoting mammography).

These are precisely the barriers identified by Thompson and his colleagues at the Group Health Cooperative (GHC) in Puget Sound, Washington. In 1995, two decades after implementing their initiative, the GHC team presented the findings from their 20 years of experience providing clinical preventive health promotion services, using the Precede-Proceed model as the conceptual basis for their interventions at the organizational and patient level. Thompson and his co-workers reported the following outcomes: late-stage breast cancer was reduced by 32%; 89% of 2-year-old children had complete immunizations; the

activities of the salaried insider have been presented in the foregoing sections of this chapter. If one attempts to bring about change in another organization as an outsider, one has a greater need and justification for employing political methods, because organizations resist change from without. In health promotion and environmental health, the interorganizational level of analysis is particularly important, because many of the programs and policies needed to alter lifestyles and environments are controlled by multiple organizations, some of them entirely outside the health sector.

Much of the community organization literature in health deals with the development of cooperation between organizations within the health sector.[61] In his durable definition of community organization, Ross emphasized the cooperative element. He defined it as "a process by which a community identifies its needs or objectives, ranks these needs or objectives, develops the confidence and will to work at these objectives, finds the resources (internal and external) to do so, and in so doing, extends and develops cooperative and collaborative attitudes and practices in the community."[62] The World Health Organization's *Health for All* strategy is a classic example of a global effort to encourage cooper-

proportion of adult smokers decreased from 25% to 17% (1985–1994); and bicycle safety helmet use among children increased from 4% to 48% (1987–1992).

According to Thompson, these outcomes were achieved only after they had assessed, and developed a strategy to overcome, the aforementioned organizational barriers. A key element in their strategy was to establish, early on in the planning process, a GHC-wide committee on prevention. One of the principal purposes of this committee, which comprised representatives from virtually every interest group within the organization, was to "foster dialogue on prevention issues and to develop guidelines and program recommendations." In the face of potential organizational barriers, the successful formulation and management of the committee seemed to accomplish two things. One was increased dedication within the organization through the active participation and involvement of representatives across the GHC. The second was a legitimization of the program through the development of guidelines and standards for disease prevention and health promotion. This example highlights the practical relevance of working through an administrative assessment. It also offers another important, subtle reminder. Even in the earliest stages of planning, experienced practitioners have their antennae out—sensitive to potential barriers and ever cognizant of resource needs.

Source: Based on personal accounts and Thompson, R. S., Taplin, S. H., McAfee, T. A., Mandelson, M. T., & Smith, A. E. (1995). Primary and secondary prevention services in clinical practice: Twenty years' experience in development, implementation, and evaluation. *Journal of the American Medical Association, 273,* 1130–5.

ation while placing a strong emphasis on "intersectoral" coordination in health policies.[63] Many of the case studies of how such intersectoral action has been developed in health promotion come from nutrition programs involving public and private sector cooperation in Australia[64] and the United States.[65]

The Zero-Sum Game.   Contrary to the cooperation model of community organization, the political conflict perspective assumes that multiple, *independent* actors are in conflict over goals, resources, and actions. Parochial priorities, goals, interests, stakes, and deadlines determine their perceptions.[66] The actors may see the stakes as a fixed pool of resources to be divided among the political sides. This means each transaction results in a gain for someone that is won at someone else's expense—a zero-sum game with a winner and a loser.

Systems Approach.   Blending a systems approach with a political perspective, the separate actors with their separate goals are seen not as independent but as *interdependent*.[67] This means that one's gain need not be another's loss, because both depend on each other's success to make the community or system function effectively. Indeed, anyone's loss is everyone's loss, with perhaps a few exceptions. One exception occurs where two or more individuals or organizations have identical goals and depend on the same limited resources to pursue them. If both seek to maximize their goal without consideration for the other and exhaust the finite resources on which both depend, then the other must suffer. Such is the purely competitive marketplace. Such is the circumstance of a fitness center in competition with another center in a neighborhood with a limited number of people who can afford to pay the membership or user fees. Their options are for one center to move to another neighborhood, for both to recruit from a wider service area beyond the neighborhood, or for both to compete more aggressively through cost cutting, price cutting, and recruitment within the neighborhood. When one loses its competitive edge, the other might buy the weaker one and be done with the competition.

True, the competitive market model helps produce innovation and efficiencies. It sometimes misses the mark, however, in social and health services because the "market" tends to be defined by those who can afford to pay for the services rather than those who need them the most. When the availability of resources for the service is limited and when the health of people may suffer for lack of the service, publicly supported (tax-based) services may be required to fill gaps in a private-sector–dominated, market-driven service economy. A systems approach, democratically planned and cooperatively negotiated *with* the government, helps guard against the depletion of finite resources by a few.[68] It seeks to allocate resources in the most equitable and efficient way, to expand the market or service area, to provide for specialization within the market or service area, and to minimize duplication.

Those who enter the political arena do so because they have a stake in policy and must engage conflict, or sometimes even create it, to pursue their policy agenda.[69] One's purpose in assessing the politics of policy is to anticipate the political sides, the political actors, and the power relationships that will line up for and against the policies one must promote to bring about the enabling support, regulation, and organizational or environmental changes required for a given program. With the sides, actors, and relationships identified, the remaining task is to propose a set of exchanges that will enable each of the sides or actors to gain something in a "win-win" rather than "win-lose" transaction. Failing this, you must hope, or strive, to have political power in the form of votes or support of key decision makers on your side, for truth and good program planning alone will not overcome such power if the opposition has it and you do not.

Exchange Theory.   One theory of organizational and political behavior is that people cooperate when the organization or policy allows each of them to pursue their individual goals and supports each of them in some way. Under those circumstances, they are willing to give up something in order to gain the stability and predictability of the organization or policy that serves them in some way. The key to a practical political analysis, following the systems and exchange approach, is to find the "something" that each can gain in exchange for organizational or policy change.[70]

Power Equalization Approach.   Unfortunately, the gains and sacrifices of exchange theory are not equally distributed in a complex community or system. Some have less to gain and more to sacrifice than others. Some have more to gain, but the gain seems trivial relative to the sacrifice they would make. At this point in political analysis, one must stand back from the attempt to make everyone happy and ask, "What is the common good?" This raises the utilitarian ideal of John Stuart Mill, who sought a political philosophy that would ensure "the most good for the most people." Because power is unequally distributed in the community, the majority of people sometimes must make sacrifices or at least forgo their potential gains in favor of a few. Garrett Hardin's classic "Tragedy of the Commons" illustrated this in relation to population and the environment.[71] Where those sacrifices are basic human needs such as health, communities have the obligation to consider curtailment of the freedoms of the few to exploit or harm others. This is done through legal and regulatory means when a protective law exists, or by political means when the political will is strong enough to equalize the distribution of power long enough to get a new law or policy passed.

Power-Educative Approach.   The preferred means of bringing about policy and organizational changes, under the circumstances just described, is to educate community or organizational leaders, including those whose behavior jeopardizes the health of others. This approach seeks to enlighten them to the harm that is being done and to appeal to their humanity and long-term interest in maintaining the community or system. Implicit in this approach is the possibility of confrontation with legal action, boycotts, or other political action if the situation is not corrected. Also implicit is the risk of bad publicity and sweeping legislative or regulatory reforms if their behavior does not change voluntarily.[72]

Conflict Approach.   Failing the educative approach, the only avenue sometimes left to equalize or tilt the balance of power on a political issue is organized confrontation and conflict in the form of strikes, petitions, consumer boycotts, pickets, referenda, or legal action to bring about policy, regulatory, or organizational change. Similar effects on policy can be initiated through lobbying, organization of public interest groups to promote social action or to elect sympathetic candidates, and demonstrations or publicity to arouse public awareness and sentiment on the issue. This can become a program in itself, with a separate plan, or a part of a broader health promotion strategy.

Advocacy and Educating the Electorate.   Recent years have seen the growth of health promotion literature on advocacy toward overcoming the lobbying power of industry or other special interest groups, especially regarding tobacco, alcohol, and environmental issues, and now increasingly in relation to the food industry in response to the obesity epidemic.[73] Further, much literature describes general strategies and approaches taken by health professionals in policy advocacy. Specific approaches, guidelines, resources, and strategies have been proposed for health professionals to use the media and to engage the political process more directly and more effectively on behalf of specific populations and health promotion issues. Examples include health policy initiatives for minorities,[74] the elderly,[75] and other special populations and issues.[76]

Empowerment Education and Community Development.   A specific variation on the advocacy and **education-of-the-electorate** approaches represents a convergence of the self-care movement and the traditional community development approach in which the community takes much more of the initiative. In the advocacy approach, a politically skilled organization takes on the advocacy tasks on behalf of the community or interest group. In the educated electorate approach, either the organization or a small group within it sets out to educate people to bring about political action to change the organization or its policies. The **empowerment education** approach encourages people *within* the community to assume control over the entire process of educating themselves, defining their own problems, setting their own priorities, developing their own self-help programs, and, if necessary, challenging the power structure to remove hazards or to make resources available.[77] The box on the next page presents a more recent case example.[78]

Participatory Research and Community Capacity Approaches.   The empowerment and community development approach have evolved more recently into community capacity (sustaining and institutionalizing empowerment) and participatory research approaches (sharing the power to organize and analyze evidence with those who would be affected by the findings), combined with social capital and coalition development concepts and methods. These will be a focus of the next chapter, so we leave this subject for now, with the caveat that there is no inherent correctness or wrongness in any of these approaches to assessing and mobilizing or redirecting political forces in support of a program plan. The most appropriate approach, or blend of approaches, will be dictated by a careful reading of the needs and circumstances at hand.

IMPLEMENTATION AND EVALUATION: ENSURING REACH, COVERAGE, QUALITY, IMPACT, AND OUTCOMES

Within the context of *implementing* a health program or its elements, we define **quality assurance** as the systematic application of audits, checks, and corrections to ensure that the strategies and methods applied, relative to program objectives, reflect the highest quality feasible. This definition makes several

AN URBAN CASE EXAMPLE

A case study analyzing the effectiveness of planning and policy making to counter the reemergence of tuberculosis in two urban settings provides an appropriate summary for the main points highlighted in the section on policy assessment. Anne Dievler studied the contrasting experiences in planning specifically as it facilitated effective policy making to support tuberculosis (TB) control in Washington, D.C., and New York City. Dievler's analysis suggested that significantly different declines in TB case rates from 1992 to 1996 favoring New York occurred at least in part because planners there acknowledged the political and bureaucratic aspects of planning. Based on the findings from her comparative case study, Dievler offered the following suggestions; note how they overlap with the key elements we have mentioned regarding policy assessment.

CONSENSUS BUILDING:

It is important to be able to identify and agree on the scope and magnitude of the problem. In the District, the problem seemed to break over whether there was an epidemic, a potential for one, or no problem at all. In contrast, in NYC, the government clearly defined and delineated the problem and achieved a greater internal and external consensus on the magnitude of the problem. (p. 180)

FORMULATE STRATEGIES:

Planning processes need to address the inevitable politics of strategy formulation. In the District, higher level government officials pursued strategies based on their own goals and interests and reacted to pressure from the outside. In NYC, the leadership, in conjunction with program managers and staff, took a more proactive role in promoting scientifically sound strategies, as well as more controversial strategies.

OVERCOMING IMPLEMENTATION OBSTACLES:

Dievler documented that the District plan was "widely criticized as having inappropriate issues, vague tasks, and no means of implementation" (p. 175). Further,

One might argue that the District's unique political status . . . contributed to some of the implementation failure observed. . . . However, since the bulk of the funding for TB control was coming from the federal government and not District coffers, and since most of the policy decisions concerning TB were not subject to review by Congress . . . the kinds and extent of political and bureaucratic obstacles in the District were similar to other large metropolitan areas. In the District, the planning process did little to address these obstacles, but in New York City, some of the most critical bureaucratic obstacles were overcome. Resulting plans were also very specific in NYC, with activities, responsibilities, and time schedules for implementation outlined. (pp. 181–182)

Souce: Dievler, A. 1997. Fighting tuberculosis in the 1990s: How effective is planning in policy making? *Journal of Public Health Policy,* 18, 167–87.

assumptions. First, it assumes that quality strategies, techniques, and methods for implementation exist. Based on a rich literature demonstrating effective applications in a variety of settings, planners can often identify strategies and practices demonstrated to be effective. A second assumption is that the protocols or procedures for performing these strategies, techniques, or methods have been established. Finally, a third assumption is that some process or system is in place to enable the assessment of quality implementation. The administrative and policy assessment phase of the Precede-Proceed Model represents such a process.

For example, as was demonstrated earlier in this chapter, the administrative and policy assessment inevitably prompts an important question related to human resources: "Do we have, or can we get, the personnel necessary to implement the program as planned?" But this question leads to another, equally important question: "Assuming we have or can obtain the people needed, will they have the competencies and skills necessary to effectively implement the program?" This latter question highlights a universal reality— that targeted, high-quality training and attentive supervision of personnel are essential to ensuring effective program implementation. Thus, the assessment of training needs is quite an important aspect of administrative and policy assessment. Such training needs include the specific in-service content or skill development as demanded by the role that staff would be expected to fulfill in the specific program plan. As planners work through the first four phases of the Precede-Proceed process, their assessments will uncover areas of content and/or skill likely to be good candidates for in-service training. The steps in doing the assessment of training needs, consistent with earlier assessment tasks, will be familiar: (1) to identify the discrepancies between the current skills among the staff and those required in the proposed program, (2) to come to some consensus about which gaps matter most, and (3) given time and resource constraints, to determine which gaps are most modifiable through training.

Because training programs are by definition educational programs, they deserve a similar planning process to that described by the behavioral, environmental, and educational assessments in the Precede framework. Supervision can also be approached as an educational process: behavioral change goals can be set mutually by the supervisor and employee. Factors predisposing, enabling, and reinforcing the intended behavior can be analyzed periodically. One can also plan interventions to predispose, enable, and reinforce implementation through staff meetings, training, written materials, and rewards for high performance. Examples of PRECEDE applied to professional training in the community, school, work site, or medical care settings will be presented in the remaining chapters. In the final analysis, textbooks can offer little on implementation that will improve on a well-thought-out plan, an adequate budget, solid organizational and policy support, constructive training and supervision of staff, and careful monitoring in the process evaluation stage (to be discussed in the remainder of this chapter). The keys to successful implementation beyond these five ingredients are experience, sensitivity to people's needs, flexibility in the face of changing circumstances, keeping an eye on long-term goals, and a sense of humor.

Most of these ingredients come with time and the opportunity to start small and build on success. The only shortcut to some of the required experience might come through a critical reading of the literature, focusing particularly on readings that feature explanations of program applications. For example, one can read about effective community organization projects, or issues encountered in developing health promotion coalitions and consortia (as in Chapter 6), specific guidelines and good examples from descriptions of health program case studies in specific settings (as in Chapters 7–8), and case stories to illustrate and animate the effective application of community-based health promotion strategies and **tactics.**[79]

With the Internet, access to the best and most recent information about all aspects of the health promotion planning process, including implementation, lies virtually within everyone's reach. Of the following organizations, most have web sites: government, philanthropic, and voluntary health agencies at the national, state/provincial, and local level; private-sector health and medical care organizations; almost all colleges and universities; and the majority of professional health organizations and societies. The resources available from these various sites include, among other things, health status databases, program descriptions, guidelines and criteria for grant applications, evaluation reports, and technical assistance sources. For example, when planners use the web site at http://www.lgreen.net, they will be able to access and search—by author, setting, population, or health problem—over 950 published applications of the Precede-Proceed Model, as well as download updated bibliographies and news keyed to this book and guidelines for participatory research.

ESTIMATING AND CALCULATING THE INPUTS AND OUTPUTS OF YOUR PROGRAM

Practical Realities

Is your program working? How much does it cost? Is our investment in the program worth it? Whether it is in the business, public, or voluntary sectors, these are the kinds of questions that boards of organizations ask the directors and those whom they supervise. Not all questions related to costs require the counsel of a skilled economist or certified public accountant; often matters of cost can be sufficiently resolved by applying the routine evaluations that we make in our day-to-day affairs.

Suppose you have an urgent need to haul some trash over a fair distance to a dump site. From among the following vehicles, you need to select one to haul the trash: a rental moving van, a small and sometimes unreliable pickup truck that belongs to your neighbor, a wheelbarrow, and your brother's 1955 Corvette.

You rule out the wheelbarrow—it is too small and the distance too far; assuming you want to maintain a good relationship with your brother, you rule out the use of the Corvette. This leaves the rental moving van and the small pickup truck. Although both will do the job, you note the van will be more efficient in that it can do the job in only one trip; you estimate three trips if you use the pickup. Although you have to pay for the rental van, you determine that the "cost" will be more than offset by the time and energy you save. Thus, the decision depends on factors such as time and the availability of resources, as well as accountability to others.

Throughout this book we have argued that evaluation is "built in" to the planning process and that the information generated by ongoing evaluation is the planners' primary source of feedback that enables them to: (1) make necessary midcourse corrections, and (2) apprise stakeholders of program progress. Most health programs are managed on very tight budgets, the largest portion of which is usually dedicated to items tied to program implementation; what is available to support evaluation is modest. Prior to selecting intervention strategies and launching their program, we urge program planners to seek answers to these questions:

1. What indicators of progress are acceptable to the funding agency?
2. Is the timeline realistic?
3. How soon will impact or outcomes be measurable, relative to how soon they are expected?
4. How accessible is the population for which the program is intended?
5. Will the population in question be represented in the evaluation?
6. Do we have a system in place that will enable us to assess progress and detect intermediate outcomes of interest? Or, will a system have to be developed?
7. Are the financial and staff resources adequate to carry out this evaluation as intended?
8. Can we model or test for any of these questions prior to selecting the intervention and launching the program?

In seeking answers to these questions, suppose you get responses you can live with for Questions 1 through 6 but for Question 7, uncertainty remains about costs. Your supervisor asks, "Is the approach you are considering worth the investment?" That leads us to Question 8. Can we test, or make a projection of cost? Currently, you are considering the merits of two possible approaches outlined in the box below.

> ### Two Possible Strategies
> 1. A smoking-cessation program targeting 1,000 classroom teachers
> 2. A smoking-cessation program targeting 100 school principals or head teachers

Table 5-4 summarizes 13 calculations that provide a comprehensive analysis of needs, inputs, and outputs of a health promotion program. The table summarizes the calculations for two separate hypothetical statewide health programs addressing the problem of smoking cessation.

TABLE 5-4 The comparative calculations for each of two programs show the trade-offs between population estimates of need, reach, coverage, impact, efficacy, and on through various measures of effectiveness, efficiency, and benefits

Type of Calculation	Program 1 (teachers)	Program 2 (principals)
A Need (estimated population eligible)	10,000	100
B Reach (attendance)	1,000	50
C Coverage [(B/A) × 100]	10%	50%
D Impact (immediate effects)	100	40
E Efficacy [(D/B)100]	10%	80%
F Effectiveness [(D/A) × 100]	1%	40%
G Program cost	$10,000	$200
H Efficiency (G/B)	$10/teacher	$4/principal
I Cost-effectiveness (G/D)	$100/effect	$5/effect
J Benefits (D × value)	$100,000	$4,000
K Cost-benefit (J/G as ratio)	10/1	20/1
L Income	$6,000	0
M Net gain (or loss) (L − G)	(−$4,000)	(−$200)
N Start-up costs	$1,000	$100
O Operating cost (G − L − N)	$3,000	$100
P Operating cost-effectiveness (O/D)	$30/effect	$2.50/effect
Q Operating cost-benefit (J/D)	$33/$1	$40/$1

Source: Measurement and Evaluation in Health Education and Health Promotion, by L. W. Green & F. Marcus Lewis, 1986, Palo Alto, CA: Mayfield; reprinted with permission of Mayfield Publishing Co.

This process is designed to give planners a stepwise process that will enable them to model several cost-related issues associated with their proposed program.

The calculations summarized in Table 5-4 relate to 17 concepts derived from the first 12: **need, reach, coverage, impact, efficacy, effectiveness, program cost, efficiency, cost-effectiveness, benefits, cost-benefit,** and **income**. We shall define each of these concepts in terms of its standard calculations. In the analyses, the evaluator wants answers to the following questions:

1. Which of the two programs will provide the best coverage of the 100 schools?
2. Which program will achieve a greater adoption of health behaviors associated with the intervention?
3. What are the relative costs and cost-effectiveness of the two programs?
4. What are the relative benefits and cost-benefit ratios of the two programs?

Population Concerns

Need. *Need* refers to the population in need or the population eligible for the program. In Table 5-4, these are the 10,000 classroom teachers affiliated with the 100 schools in Program 1 or the 100 school principals for these same 100 schools in Program 2. Ideally, we would like to define *need* in terms of the number of participants who might benefit from the smoking-prevention program, such as the students who might not take up smoking if they were influenced by non-smoking teachers as role models, but this quantity is unknown and potentially infinite. Therefore, we define *need* in terms of the population eligible to receive the alternative programs.

The population in need is usually estimated from census data or from previous estimates of the target population. Any of these estimates must often be qualified by screening or exclusion criteria. For example, in Table 5-4 the target teachers and the target principals may be only those who currently smoke two or more packs of cigarettes a day. Estimates of need are interpolated from local, regional, or national data. The estimate is then a synthesized estimate based on available data and screening criteria.

The need estimate becomes the denominator for subsequent calculations for the proportion of the population reached by the program and the overall effectiveness of the program.

Reach. The second number or statistic we need is the count of the eligible population who would be or were actually exposed to the program being evaluated: This is the program's *reach*. Sometimes this figure is estimated from previous experience with such programs, from the rules that might be invoked to get people into the program, or from market analysis. If the analysis is completed after the program is implemented, reach is merely a count of the number of individuals who participated in the program during a period such as a month or a year. If the program is a mass media program, reach is much more difficult to estimate.

In Table 5-4, the reach for Program 1 is expected or observed to be 1,000 classroom teachers. Program 2 reaches 50 school principals.

Coverage. *Coverage* is the percentage reached of the number in need. Program 1 has a 10% coverage (1,000/10,000) and Program 2 has a 50% coverage (50/100). Coverage standardizes the absolute numbers of reach and need and allows us to compare the coverage of Program 1 with that of Program 2. By standardizing the figures, we can also compare the coverage of programs in the current fiscal or academic period with those offered in the past.

Impact. *Impact* refers to the immediate, short-term, or intermediate effects of the health promotion program. The evaluator includes the impact variables because they are available within the time frame of most evaluations and, in the absence of data on expected final outcomes, they provide some evidence of progress. Often, these impact variables are measures of health behavior changes because they provide more convincing evidence of the effects of the program than do measures of enabling, predisposing, or reinforcing variables.

Table 5-4 shows the impact of the two proposed programs: In Program 1, 100 of the 1,000 school teachers were still not smoking 6 months after the program stopped. In contrast, 40 of the 50 school principals were still not smoking at 6 months after the program.

Efficacy.   *Efficacy* refers to the impact of the program for those people who actually attended it. To obtain an estimate of program efficacy, we merely divide the impact number by the number reached (D/B) and multiply that amount by 100 to convert the proportion to a percentage.

From Table 5-4, we see that Program 1 produced the intended impact on more teachers than Program 2 did on school principals, but the efficacy of Program 2 was 80% for 50 school principals reached, compared with only 10% for the schoolteachers reached by Program 1.

Efficacy considers the relative impact of the program only on those who received it. What about the people who did not participate in the program but who were part of the target population?

Effectiveness.   *Effectiveness* is the proportion of people intended to receive the program who successfully changed as intended. In public health programs, one is particularly interested in the level of change for those who were initially intended to receive the program, not just in the change for those who actually participated in it.

Seldom is the distinction between efficacy and effectiveness maintained in evaluation reports. People tend to evaluate the effects of programs on captive audiences. We hold that such reports are evaluations of the program's efficacy, not its effectiveness. The figures on effectiveness in Table 5-4 suggest that Program 2 is more effective (it successfully changed a higher proportion of people eligible to receive it) than Program 1. Program 1 had a 1% rate of effectiveness; Program 2, 40%.

Economic Measures

Eventually we shall want to assure ourselves and others that we achieved the impact and both efficacy and effectiveness at a reasonable cost. To do this, we next consider measures of cost, efficiency, cost-effectiveness, and cost relative to benefits.

Program Cost.   *Cost* is an estimate of the program expenditures outside of the evaluation cost. Cost estimates, therefore, should not include data collection or other evaluation functions. The availability of cost data is often sufficient to advise policy on the preferred program alternative, especially when two or more competing programs appear equally effective in the impact analyses.

Record-keeping practices should be counted as part of the cost estimates only if they are essential to the ongoing implementation and integrity of the program. If pre- and posttests are viewed as part of the total program experience and not just as evaluation strategies, their costs should be included. To obtain unbiased estimates of program cost, ledgers should be initiated at the beginning of the program to keep accurate track of actual expenditures. Staff salary, including support staff, should be prorated and included in the cost estimate. In Table 5-4, Program 1 costs $10,000 and Program 2 costs $200.

Efficiency.   *Efficiency* is the proportion of program cost to reach; or, the unit cost of each person who actually attended the program. From Table 5-4 we see that the efficiency of Program 1 was $10 for each teacher who attended ($10,000/1,000) compared with $4 for each school principal who attended in Program 2.

Efficiency calculations convert the numbers expressing the reach and the raw cost of the program into a relatively comparable single expression of the cost per person attending or reached by the program. Note that Program 1 at $10,000 was 50 times more expensive than Program 2, but the efficiency measure reveals that Program 1 was actually only 2.5 times more expensive per professional reached than was Program 2.

Cost-Effectiveness.   *Cost-effectiveness* is the cost per unit of observed impact or effect; the measure standardizes cost relative to a specific effect. Results are expressed as a ratio of dollar cost per unit of impact. From Table 5-4 we see a ratio of $10,000/100 or $100 for every schoolteacher in Program 1 who quit smoking and $200/40 or $5 for every school principal who quit smoking in Program 2. It appears that we can obtain the same effect 20 times cheaper with school principals than we can with schoolteachers. These estimates might run counter to the initial first impressions from lines A, B, and D in Table 5-4, which we could use to argue for Program 1 over Program 2.

Benefits.   *Benefits* are the ultimate gains to a society, organization, or sponsor from the program's effects. Not limited to efficiency and cost-effectiveness data, benefit calculations interest primarily taxpayers and others who fund social programs. Such people want to know the program's profound effects, basic to society's quality of life—not merely the efficient transfer of resources into programs or the transfer of programs into behavioral or environmental impact.

How can analyses go beyond the measures of efficiency and cost-effectiveness to capture adequately the ultimate value of health programs? Unfortunately, economists, legislators, the public, and health professionals tend not to agree on a common yardstick. We use an approach that bases benefits on one or on a few tangible outcomes that go beyond the strictly medical outcomes but not beyond the measurable and near-future outcomes for which actual dollars can be tracked. With regard to modeling healthful behavior for the students in the schools, we assume that each teacher in Program 1 who changes his or her smoking practice will have greater influence on the students' smoking prevention and smoking-cessation behavior than will the school principals in Program 2. We make this assumption on the basis of the schoolteacher's more frequent personal contact with the students both during school and at after-school events. In addition, the classroom teacher often tangibly can affect the classroom environment and educational milieu in ways that directly support nonsmoking behavior.

With any previous research or with a set of informed conservative estimates, we can translate these relative advantages into monetary values for the changes in the schoolteachers' and the principals' behavior. Applying the most conservative assumptions, which is advisable in cost-benefit analyses, we assume the following:

1. Each schoolteacher in Program 1 will directly affect smoking-cessation or smoking-prevention behavior in 10 students per year, at an average value of $100 per year of smoking averted, for a total of $1,000 gained in non-smoking students for every year of nonsmoking teacher.
2. Each principal in Program 2 will directly affect smoking-prevention or smoking-cessation behavior in 1 student per year. The annual value in smoking averted in students by preventing smoking in principals can be placed at $100, using this outcome as the value.

Multiplying the number of teachers (100) and principals (40) on whom the program had an impact (D) by the value attached to each teacher's effects on the students ($1,000) and each principal's effects on the students ($100), we obtain the benefits in Table 5-4.

Cost-Benefit.   *Cost-benefit* is the ratio of the benefits to the program cost. By convention, this is typically expressed in terms of the benefits expected for every unit of currency invested in the program. From Table 5-4 we see that the calculations for cost-benefit suggest that we must recommend in favor of Program 2 over Program 1; we can predict two times as much return in the program for the school principals as in the other. Qualifications are in order, however.

A comparison between programs may cause us to ask, Which of the two programs gives us the best benefit-to-cost ratio? But a choice between programs may not always be necessary. Rather, we may want to get the best combination of results by taking into account the political and administrative realities, including access to health education resources.

Based on a criterion rather than a normative reference perspective, evidence from Table 5-4 shows that Program 1 produces a substantial return on the dollar investment. A 10-to-1 benefit-to-cost ratio is analogous to a 1,000% return in interest on savings or a 10-fold increase on the value of stocks. Such returns are noteworthy and provide evidence of the importance of Program 1 independent of its comparison with Program 2.

Income.   *Income calculations* are estimates of the revenue-generating potential of a program. Such calculations are particularly important when one must consider whether one can sustain the program. It is one thing to know that a program is a sure winner; it is another to have the resources available to make the investment. Sources of revenue include grants, donations, recurring or zero-based budgets from a parent organization, and fees for services rendered; however, most of these sources of revenue are unstable. The agency must often ask if the program could support itself or generate revenue.

In Table 5-4, we posit that each schoolteacher will pay $6 to attend the smoking-cessation program. The school principals, on the other hand, will most likely decline to pay anything. This represents a $6,000 income for Program 1 with no equivalent for Program 2.

Net Gain.   *Net gain or loss* is the computed difference between the generated income and the program's cost. Note that net gain or loss does not include the speculative future gains implied by the cost-benefit ratios in line K. If those benefits are expected, one can add them to future income. For example, if the $100,000 benefit from Program 1 with the classroom teachers is expected to be actual savings to the agency, the agency's net gain at the end of one year would be $96,000 ($100,000−$4,000) rather than a loss of $4,000. Most likely, some part of the savings reflected in the cost-benefit analysis would accrue to the agency, not all of it.

SUMMARY

This chapter makes the loop from PRECEDE to PROCEED. It consists of some final steps in diagnostic planning and some beginning steps in implementation; from formative evaluation to process evaluation. The program plan that takes further shape in this chapter builds on the program theory or logic model that evolved from the earlier diagnostic steps, matches and maps interventions to points at the left-hand end of that program theory, and then examines the resource, organizational, and policy needs of the plan and their availabilities in the implementing environment. It also suggests various approaches to mobilizing resources, organizational changes, and policy support for the program.

The chapter began with some definitions and principles related to evidence-based and participation-based planning. It sought in that first section to make the link from the diagnostic-baseline data gathered for assessment of needs in previous phases to the interventions that would need to be selected or developed to meet those needs. A first step is to *match* the ecological levels of program focus with the types of interventions needed at those levels (e.g., mass media at the community-wide level, training at the organizational level, counseling or parental supervision at the individual level). A second step is to *map* more specific, tested interventions to the predisposing, enabling, and reinforcing factors that were identified as priorities. After mapping best practices from previously evaluated interventions to specific behavioral or environmental changes in the program theory or logic model, a series of steps in pooling and patching less thoroughly tested interventions are suggested to fill the inevitable gaps in the best practices literature, including ones where a well-tested intervention is simply a poor fit for the population or circumstances at hand.

After all the previously tried methods are considered, some gaps in addressing a few of the priority predisposing, enabling, and reinforcing factors likely remain, so we come to a final series of program development and formative evaluation steps culminating in the need to innovate and evaluate.

The administrative assessment entails the analysis of resources required by the now specified program, the resources available in the organization or community, and the barriers to implementation of the program. The policy assessment then asks what political, regulatory, and organizational supports and barriers one can change to facilitate the program and to enable the development of educational and environmental supports for community action. These steps take one from Precede planning to Proceed implementation. Evaluation, then, becomes part of both the plan and the implementation process.

Planning and policy in health programs can provide a clear purpose, resources, and protection for the programs they produce, but administrators cannot mark every step on the path of implementation without retarding the very growth and development of the people they intend to help. Plans and policies must leave room to adapt to changing local circumstances, personalities, opportunities, and feedback from evaluation.

PRECEDE ensures that a program will be *appropriate* to a person's or population's needs and circumstances. PROCEED ensures that the program will be *available, accessible, acceptable,* and *accountable.* Only an appropriate program is worth implementing, but even the most appropriate program will fail to reach those who need it if the program is unavailable, inaccessible, or unacceptable to them. PROCEED assesses the resources required to ensure a program's *availability,* the/organizational changes required to ensure its *accessibility,* and the political and regulatory changes required to ensure its *acceptability.* Finally, quality assurance through evaluation and training ensures that the program will be *accountable* to the policy makers, administrators, consumers, clients, and any other stakeholders who need to know whether the program met their standards of acceptability.

Training and supervision of personnel combined with evaluation are the keys to accountability and provide the best assurance of implementation. In this context, *training needs* refers to specific in-service content or skill development as demanded by the role that staff would be asked to fulfill in the specific program being planned. Each training program deserves a full planning process similar to that in the Precede framework. Supervision can also be approached as an educational process for both supervisor and supervisee. Factors predisposing, enabling, and reinforcing the intended behavior of staff and volunteers can be analyzed periodically; interventions can be planned to predispose, enable, and reinforce implementation.

Evaluation, which began in Phase 1 and continued through each phase to this point, has established baseline measures of the population needs. In this phase, late formative evaluation turned to early process evaluation as it assisted with the pretesting or pilot testing of materials, methods, interventions, and program components for their feasibility and acceptability, but not yet for their behavioral or environmental impact or their health and social outcomes. Presented at the end of this chapter is a series of measures and simple calculation formulas for projecting expected results to be replaced with actual data as implementation rolls out. Implementation relies on a well-thought-out plan, an adequate budget, solid organizational and policy support, constructive training and supervision of staff, and careful monitoring in the process evaluation stage. Beyond this, successful implementation depends on experience, sensitivity to people's needs, flexibility in the face of changing circumstances, the maintaining of a long-term perspective, and a sense of humor.

EXERCISES

1. Propose the essential features of a program with at least one intervention directed at each high priority predisposing, enabling, and reinforcing factor, and indicate the source of your selection or design of the proposed interventions.
2. Identify the resources required for your program with a specific budget and timetable or Gantt chart.
3. Analyze how your program would affect and be affected by other programs and units within the sponsoring or implementing organization, and propose the organizational and policy changes required to support your program.
4. Describe the interorganizational and intersectoral coordination that would be required to implement your program.
5. Describe the approaches your program might take to ensure its sustainability beyond the initial funding cycle.
6. Retrieve at least one each of your predisposing, enabling, and reinforcing objectives from Chapter 4, and then (using your professional judgment and any evidence available to you, with a column for each in Table 5-3):
   - estimate for each of the three objectives the need, reach, and coverage required to achieve the impact as the objective proposes; adjust the budget accordingly.
   - assuming that impact equals each of your three objectives, calculate the efficacy, effectiveness, cost (assuming proportion of the adjusted budget devoted to that objective), efficiency, and cost-effectiveness.

NOTES AND CITATIONS

1. *Best practices versus best processes:* Green, L. W., 2001b. For example, Kaplan, et al. 2000 demonstrate how methods previously shown in more controlled efficacy trials of getting women to return for follow-up when they have a positive pap smear are highly variable in their effectiveness across settings and subpopulations in which they are applied in a broader community trial. This illustrates the importance of adapting the "best practice" methods with "best processes" of diagnosing predisposing, enabling, and reinforcing factors when they are applied in settings, populations, or circumstances not well represented in the controlled studies from which they were derived. See also Jones & Donovan, 2004.
2. *Ecological matching—Multilevel Approach to Community Health (MATCH):* Developed by Simons-Morton, et al., 1988; described most thoroughly in Simons-Morton, Greene, & Gottlieb, 1995, pp. 152–184. See also Butler, 2001, pp. 279–283.
3. *The renaissance of ecological approaches in public health, community, and population health:* Best, Stokols, et al., 2004; Green, Poland, & Rootman, 2000, esp: pp. 10–12; Kickbusch, 1989; McLeroy, Bibeau, Steckler, & Glanz, 1988; Stokols, Allen, & Bellingham, 1996; Stokols, Grzywacz, J. G., et al., 2003.
4. *The use of city and statewide averages and trends to estimate health goals:* For your data, go to this endnote in http://www.lgreen.net/hpp/Endnotes/Chapter5Endnotes.htm for the addresses of web sites containing continuously updated statistics, for example, on data from (1) the CDC 122 Cities Mortality Reporting System as printed in Table III of the *MMWR* each week; (2) *state cancer profiles* with 25-year trends, and more detailed 5-year trends on mortality and incidence rates, for each of 11 cancer sites, by age, sex, and race or

ethnic group, and for all 50 states and the District of Columbia; and prevalence estimates (3) *fatal injury reports,* by year, type of injury, cause of injury, by age, race/ethnic group, sex, and age; and by years of life lost from injuries; (4) *asthma,* by state since 1999, adult reported lifetime and current rates; (5) *HIV/AIDS* statistics, state and international, by exposure categories, age, race, and ethnicity; (6) *oral health* indicators; (7) *nutritional* indicators; (8) *alcohol*-related health indicators; and others. Most states' health department web sites also carry within-state breakdowns of health data by age, sex, and county, region, and/or major cities.

5. *Higher ecological levels provide context that moderates individual behavior:* As stated by Wilcox, (2003), "community-level contextual effects can impact directly both group and individual-level behavior (e.g., main effects), and they can also condition the effects of individual-level factors on individual behaviors (e.g., moderating effects)." We will distinguish these two types of effects later as mediating and moderating variables.

6. *Environmental effects through, or independent of, behavioral effects on health outcomes:* For example, Acevedo-Garcia, Lochner, et al., 2003; Chan & Austin, 2003; Molnar, Buka, et al., 2003. We covered these relationships in the previous two chapters, but revisit them here from the standpoint of selecting levels for intervention. Although their causal arrows approach health through individual behavior, Simons-Morton, et al. (1995) recognize "the influence of environmental factors on health behavior and on health itself (e.g., air pollution) . . ." (p. 155).

7. *The weak link between science and its appropriate application* "has much to do with the variability of the targets—the populations and their circumstancesThese circumstances include the particular population's health needs and resources that biomedical scientists and epidemiologists would have us analyze. They also include their cultural traditions that anthropologists would have us understand, their socioeconomic conditions that sociologists and economists would have us appreciate, and the contingencies of their behavior that psychologists would have us consider" (Green, 2001a, Foreword, p. xiii).

8. *Early delineation of intervening variables in public service and social action program evaluation:* Suchman, 1967, p. 173.

9. *Pooling information about prior interventions:* D'Onofrio, 2001, p. 158. For a spirited and passionate plea and a compelling case for more reliance on replication of model programs and less dependence on the plodding pace of randomized trials to educe "best practices," see Schorr, 1997, esp. her "elements of successful replication" (pp. 60–64).

10. *Sources of information for pooling of prior interventions:* D'Onofrio, 2001, pp. 177–193.

11. *Existing community programs and policies matrix in PATCH:* CDC, 2001, Chaps. 4 & Chap. 5, Table 2 (full text downloadable from http://www.cdc.gov/nccdphp/patch/00binaries/PATCHCh5.pdf.

12. *Research-tested intervention programs guidelines for choosing and adapting from prior interventions:* For examples of model programs in nutrition, physical activity, tobacco control, sun exposure, and various cancer screening interventions, go to http://cancercontrol.cancer.gov/rtips/. For guidelines on adaptation of these or other prior interventions, go to http://cancercontrol.cancer.gov/rtips/adaptation_guidelines.pdf. The programs and interventions recommended for replication and adaptation are scored on their "dissemination capability" (replicability, adaptability), cultural appropriateness for each of several ethnic groups, age appropriateness for each broad age category, gender appropriateness, integrity, and utility. The program descriptions on the web site also indicate the appropriateness for each of several settings, the intended audience, and required resources. The published references on which the scoring and description of the programs are based are also listed. For example, the Commit to Quit program for smoking cessation by women, based on intensive physical activity, is now in a second generation of trials to evaluate the effectiveness of moderate physical activity (see Marcus, Lewis, et al., 2003).

13. *Sussman's Six-Step Program Development Chain Model:* Sussman, 2001.

14. *Mediators as causal, intermediate variables between interventions and behavior change:* Simons-Morton, Greene, & Gottlieb, 1995, p. 170.

15. *Mediator variable as conditioning the effect of a causal variable:* Sussman & Sussman, 2001, p. 81.

16. *Moderator variables as exogenous or independent variables that enhance or suppress the effect of other variables:* Sussman & Sussman, 2001, p. 81. For more examples of the simple relationships shown in Figure 5-4, see Donaldson, 2001, pp. 473–493.

17. *Systematic reviews and guidelines for "best practices" from the Task Force on Community Preventive Services:* For the continuously updated reviews, go to http://www.thecommunityguide.org. For the background and methods, see Task Force on Community Preventive Services, 2000; and specific reviews, For example, Norris & Isham, 2002; Ramsey & Brownson, 2002.

18. *Other sources of "best practices" based on systematic reviews of multiple studies:* Atkins, Best, & Shapiro, 2001; International Union for Health Promotion & Education, 1999.

19. *Sussman's step 2, pooling and creating plausible intervention activities:* Sussman, pp. 17–18, quotation from p. 13. See also for methods of pooling, Chapters 7: D'Onofrio, 2001; and for an example of a pooling and warehousing resource on sexuality programs and adolescence, Niego & Peterson, 2001.

20. *Screening pooled experiences to identify the ones with greatest perceived efficacy and appropriateness:* Sussman, pp. 18–19, quotation from p. 13; see also Chapter 9 for description and classification of methods, Ayala & Elder, 2001; and Chapters 10–12 for case examples: Sussman, Lichtman, & Dent, 2001; Nezami, Davison, & Hoffman, 2001; Dent, Lichtman, & Sussman, 2001.

21. *Concept evaluation and "product-market fit" approaches of communications research and social marketing:* Kotler & Roberto, 1989, pp. 28–30; see also pp. 285–294 for a case study of Project LEAN, a national nutrition program. For other health applications, see Brieger, Nwankwo, et al., 1996.

22. *Definition of perceived efficacy:* Ayala and Elder, 2001, p. 240, citing Hinkle, Fox-Cardamone, et al., 1996.

23. *Best experiences of states or communities based on comparisons of outcomes, as a basis of recommending components of a comprehensive program:* Pechacek, Starr, Judd, Selin, Fishman, et al., 1999. For the resulting (and largely disappointing) allocation of tobacco settlement funds by states to their tobacco control programs, see Albuquerque, Pechacek, & Kelly, 2001. For the annual payments to each state under the tobacco settlement, go to National Association of Attorneys General, Annual Payments to Each State, http://www.naag.org.

24. *"Plausibility criteria" to apply to "best experiences" from prior or concurrent programs that have not been formally tested with controlled experimental trials:* Cameron, Jolin, Walker, McDermott, & Gough, 2001. Plausible practices are also referred to elsewhere as "promising practices" (e.g., Lambert, Donahue, Mitchell, & Strauss, 2003; available online at http://www.samhsa.gov).

25. *Example of retracing the diagnostic data and logic model in framing interventions for a program:* Ramey, et al., 2003.

26. *Procedures for mapping theory to interventions required for coverage of gaps in the predisposing, enabling, and reinforcing factors* have been outlined in five detailed steps in a textbook by Bartholomew, Parcel, Kok, & Gottlieb, 2001.

27. *The RE-AIM evaluation framework:* See Glasgow, Vogt, & Boles, 1999 at http://www.re-aim.org/a99-gr-ajph.html) which addresses most of these factors. RE-AIM stands for consideration of five elements: *r*each into the target population, *e*fficacy or *e*ffectiveness of an intervention outcome, *a*doption of interventions by settings or communities, methods of *i*mplementing the intervention program, and *m*aintenance of behavior change or behavior change programs. See also http://www.pitt.edu/~super1/lecture/lec6851/index.htm.

28. *Quantitative approach to effecting outcomes:* For example, Resnicow et al. (1992) specifically altered the intensity and exposure time of students to the "Know Your Body" program, which was based on the Precede Model and Social Learning Theory. They showed that "program effects for several outcome variables were linearly related to level of student exposure to the curriculum, suggesting a dose-response effect" (p. 463). Similarly, programs that achieve a greater reach, such as self-help "cold-turkey" smoking cessation programs through the mass media, even if they are less effective than the more intensive alternative such as behavioral counseling, can achieve a much greater population effect (Shiffman, Mason, & Henningfield, 1998, p. 337; see also Table 7-1 in previous edition of this text, Green & Kreuter, 1999b, p. 223).

29. *Innovation gains in cost per unit of delivery without loss of effectiveness through use of indigenous personnel whose familiarity and identity with the clients compensate for their technical qualifications:* for example, Green, 1975; 1979. Among the classic studies in this vein, Cuskey & Premkuman (1973) demonstrated that a drug treatment center serving about 1,000 addicts could save up to $100,000 annually with ex-addict counselors in place of professional counselors with graduate-level training. Fisher (1974; 1975) took this logic a step further, experimentally demonstrating that unpaid patients of a family planning clinic, given postcards to distribute to their friends achieve recruitment rates at approximately one third the cost per new appointment in comparison with the next most cost-effective method. Fletcher (1973; Fletcher, Appel, & Bourgois, 1974) demonstrated the cost-effectiveness of a clerk in the emergency room assigned to call and remind patients of their return appointments, thereby reducing broken appointments. Whether this increased continuity of care improved long-term quality of care, however, depended on other interventions (Fletcher, Appel, & Bourgois, 1975). An example of recent work on the use of indigenous personnel to innovate in health interventions and programs is Struthers, Hodge, De Cora, & Geishirt-Cantrell, 2003.

30. *Tailoring as a way to achieve the effectiveness of personalized, culturally appropriate communications while also gaining the reach and economies of scale of mass media:* Caburnay, Kreuter, & Donlin, 2001; Kreuter, Lukwago, et al., 2003. A classic study that combined the use of an indigenous aide with a standardized tape-recorded message, believed to be the first truly randomized clinical trial in health education, was Roberts, Mico, & Clark, 1963. Kreuter, Oswald, et al. (2000) note the prospect that tailored interventions will gradually lose their edge in controlled trials comparing them with other approaches developed by methods outlined in this and the foregoing chapter: "if nontailored materials increasingly address important constructs from theories of health behavior change, there will be less and less of a difference between these materials and materials developed via behavioral construct tailoring" (p. 314).

31. *Necessity of professional discretion at the point of implementation:* Ottoson & Green, 1997.

32. *Example of pretesting interventions as final step in formative evaluation, first step in process evaluation:* Burhansstipanov, Krebs, et al., 2003; other examples within Precede-Proceed planning applications: Contento, Kell, et al., 1992; Dignan, Sharp, et al., 1995.

33. *Pretesting of measurement instruments:* for example, Beaman, Reyes-Frausto, & Garcia-Pena, 2003. Examples within the context of Precede-Proceed applications include Black, Stein, & Loveland-Cherry, 2001; Chang, Brown, et al., 2004. Grisé, Gauthier-Gagnon, & Martineau, 1993; Han, Baumann, & Cimprich, 1996; Hiddink, Hautvast, et al., 1999.

34. *The cart before the horse in considering resources last?* As co-authors, we have debated the relative merits of putting so much into the development work represented by this and the preceding chapters before giving formal attention to the resources that will pull this program cart of proposed interventions. One of us leaned toward putting the administrative and resource assessment first, the other toward sticking with the creation of the "best" (not to say ideal) program proposal, and letting it sell itself to those who might allocate resources to it. We come to no right or wrong answers, just a recognition of the trade-offs, the pros and cons of either approach. Such debate has begun to emerge within societal decisions on the allocation of medical care resources, and how much these should be guided by or even dictated by evidence-based "best practices" (e.g., Nunes, 2003). Mooney (2002) also emphasizes the ultimate need, in the inevitable absence of some certainty about the evidence-based practices, "to exercise value judgments . . . also a word of caution on the dangers of over-reliance on waiting for perfect evidence" (p. 65).

35. *For this and the following steps in administrative and policy diagnosis and analysis, see the module in the interactive "EMPOWER" (Expert Methods of Planning and Organizing Within Everyone's Reach) CD-ROM program and manual* for fill-in blanks and checklists, and a summary report of each, for assessing existing resources (p. 68), budget development (pp. 68–71), development of a Gantt Chart (pp. 71–72), assessment of staff commitment and attitudes (pp. 72–74), assessment of policy and organizational factors (pp. 74–75), and assessment of political factors (pp. 76–77). A sample "summary report" is shown on p. 78 of the manual (Gold, Green, & Kreuter, 1998).

36. *Software programs for computer construction of Gantt charts and other tools for planning the flow and cost of program activities are commercially available:* For specific applications of cost analyses in PRECEDE-PROCEED, see Bertera, E. M. & Bertera, 1981; Cantor, Morisky, et al., 1985; Cote, Gregoire, et al., 2003; Frauenknecht, Brylinsky, & Zimmer, 1998; Gold, Green, & Kreuter, 1998; Green, Wang, & Ephross, 1974; Hatcher, Green, Levine, & Flagle, 1986; Sayegh & Green, 1976.

37. *Personnel are usually the most expensive line item in health program budgets, but personnel costs are also sensitive to technological, organizational, and community capacity:* For example, Bolman & Deal, 1991; Boulton, Malouin, et al., 2003; Miller, Bedney, et al., 2003; Pelletier, 2001; Potter, Ley, et al., 2003; *and to new challenges:* For example, Fitch, Raber, & Imbro, 2003; Gewin, 2003.

38. *Preparing materials and pretesting them* might have been done as last step in the previous design and selection phase of interventions development, or might be the first step in the implementation phase. Much media evaluation in the selection phase tends to be done by checklists of qualities, rather than by formal pretesting or evaluation. Gilbert & Sawyer, 2000, p. 215, note "a paucity of meaningful evaluation . . . a sad commentary, particularly in the light of how frequently such materials are used today," so they caution planners to view them critically, using the various checklists (e.g., Martin & Stainbrook, 1986). In fairness to some of the producers and vendors of such audiovisual materials, they typically offer catalogues of multiple pamphlets, videotapes, etc., that provide variations on messages that have been tested, in which the variations are designed to appeal to different audiences by age and ethnicity, for example, based on well-grounded theories and previously evaluated generic models. Because such materials must be fresh and contemporary, it is probably impractical to expect each variation to have had a formal evaluation, but pretesting for a new setting and population for your program then becomes even more essential.

39. *Use of volunteer health workers:* Examples within Precede-Proceed applications include Adeyanju, 1987–88; Bertera, 1990b; DePue, Wells, et al., 1987; Hall & Best, 1997; Lasater, Abrams, et al., 1984; Seiden & Blonna, 1983; Watson, Horowitz, et al., 2001. Francisco, Paine, & Fawcett (1993) count "volunteers recruited" as one of eight key measures in their instrument to monitor and evaluate community coalitions. Stiell, Nichol, et al. (2003), found that "citizen CPR" produced good quality-of-life outcomes in out-of-hospital cardiac arrest survivors.

40. *Evaluations of lay health workers,* most with application of Precede-Proceed Model: Bird, Otero-Sabogal, et al., 1996; Dignan, Michielutte, Blinson, et al., 1996; Dignan, Michielutte, Wells, et al., 1998; Dignan, Sharp, et al., 1995; Earp, Eng, et al., 2002; Eng, 1993; Harrison, Li, et al., 2003; Kironde & Bajunirwe, 2002; Lam, McPhee, et al., 2003; Paskett, Tatum, et al., 1999; Sharp, Dignan, et al., 1999.

41. *Drawing on, or pooling, resources from other organizations:* We will delve more deeply into the issues of interorganizational exchange, and the forming, maintaining, and management of community coalitions in Chapter 6 on community applications of the Precede-Proceed Model. For purposes here, we refer the reader to a few key references on the transfer of resources among organizations: Berkowitz, 2001; Braitwaite, Taylor, & Austin, 2000; Butterfoss & Kegler, 2002; Chavis, 2001; Fawcett, Lewis, et al., 1997; Goodman & Wandersman, 1994; Kwait, Valente, & Celentano, 2001; Stachenko, 1996; and some caveats on coalitions as vehicles for community collaboration: Green, 2000; Green & Kreuter, 2002; Hallfors, Cho, et al., 2002.

42. *Threshold level of spending, below which one should not expect a palpable effect of the program:* Green, 1977.

43. *Few studies of the threshold level in health programs:* Bertera & Green, 1979; Chwalow, Green, et al., 1978; Connell, Turner, & Mason, 1985; Green, Wang, & Ephross, 1974; Holtgrave, 1998, especially Chapter 14 on "Threshold Analysis of AIDS Outreach and Intervention"; Risser, Hoffman, et al., 1985.

44. *Point of diminishing returns in program spending:* Fielding, 1982a; Green, 1977; Wang, Ephross, & Green, 1975.

45. *Factors influencing implementation:* Ottoson & Green, 1987. For specific case analyses of implementation issues within Precede-Proceed applications, some of which will be examined in Chapters 6–8, see for *arthritis self-care programs:* Brunk & Goeppinger, 1990; for *asthma:* Fisher, Strunk, et al., 1995; for *cystic fibrosis:* Bartholomew, Czyzewski, et al., 2000; for *environmental sustainability:* Boothroyd, Green, et al., 1994; for *cardiovascular risk prevention programs:* Bush, Downey, et al., 1987; Bush, Zuckerman, et al., 1989; Elliott, Taylor, et al., 1998; Morisky, Levine, et al., 1981; Paradis, O'Loughlin, et al., 1995; Taggart, Bush, et al., 1990; Taylor, Elliott, & Riley, 1998; Taylor, Elliott, Robinson, et al., 1998; Ward, Levine, et al., 1982; for *drug abuse prevention programs:* Lohrmann & Fors, 1986; MacDonald & Green, 2001; for *HIV prevention:* Cain, Schyulze, & Preston, 2001; for *staff adoption of planning tools (EMPOWER software; Information Technology):* Chiasson & Lovato, 2000; Kukafka, Johnson, et al., 2003; Lovato, Potvin, et al., 2003; Lehoux, Potvin, & Proulx, 1999; Lehoux, Proulx, et al., 1997; Roulx, Potvin, et al., 1999; for *injury prevention:* Cross, Hall, & Howatt, 2003; Wortel, de Vries, & de Geus, 1995; for *organizational and behavioral change of practitioners in support of clinical preventive services:* Curry, 1998; Eriksen, Green, & Fultz, 1988; Goodson, Gottlieb, & Radcliffe, 1999; Laitakari, Miilunpalo, & Vuori, 1997; Lomas, 1993; Mahlock, Taylor, et al., 1993; Mann & Putnam, 1989; Miilunpalo, Jukka, & Ilkka, 1995; Smith, Danis, & Helmick, 1998; Thompson, 1996, 1997; Thompson, Rivara, et al., 2000; Thompson, Taplin, et al., 1995; for *breast cancer mammography screening:* Dignan, Bahnson, et al., 1991; Dignan, Beal, et al., 1990; Dignan, Sharp, et al., 1995; Eng, 1993; Mahlock, Taylor, et al., 1993; for *cervical cancer screening:* Michielutte & Dignan, 1989; for *physical activity programs:* Hopman-Rock, 2000; for *work site programs:* Bertera, 1990b; Gottlieb, Lovato, et al., 1992; Parkinson and Associates, 1982; Pucci & Haglund, 1994; for *campus health promotion programs:* J. R. Weiss, Wallerstein, & MacLean, 1995; for *multifactor community health promotion:* Green & Kreuter, 1992; Green & McAlister, 1984; Hecker, 2000; Swannell, Steele, et al., 1992; Wickizer, Wagner, & Perrin, 1998; and for *various other applications:* Brink, Simons-Morton, et al., 1988; Ottoson, 1997.

46. *Staff attitudes as necessary but not sufficient predispositions for implementation:* See the application of PRECEDE in the survey and analysis of implementation experience in a Canadian heart health program: Elliott, Taylor, et al., 1998; Taylor, Elliott, & Riley, 1998; Taylor, Elliott, Robinson, & Taylor, 1998.

47. *Resolving conflicting goals within and between collaborating organizations:* The classic framework on this issue is that of Van Meter & Van Horn, 1975. See also Conway, Hu, & Harrington, 1997, for a community example. This problem has arisen most saliently in recent years with the dilemmas of physicians and other health care workers faced with conflicts between the economic, cost-containment goals of managed care organizations or federal guidelines and their professional guidelines or goals that seek to maximize health outcomes without a primary consideration of cost, e.g., Avorn, 2003; Oldroyd, Proudfoot, et al., 2003; Scheid, 2003.

48. *Change the program goals to fit policy, or change the policy to fit goals?* Ross & Mico, 1980, p. 222.

49. *Enabling and reinforcing staff who must implement programs where goals of the organization and goals of the program are inconsistent:* MacDonald & Green, 2001.

50. *Rate of change, incremental versus radical change, "trialability":* The classic study on the rate of change expected by program planners or policy makers and the implementation of change within organizations was T. Smith, 1973. But rate of change also relates to a characteristic of innovations, called "trialability," the feature of an innovation that allowed those responsible for its implementation to break it down into incremental steps, which was studied among other characteristics of agricultural innovations many years earlier in the classic diffusion research tradition of agricultural extension and rural sociology by Gross, 1942; Ryan, 1948; and Ryan & Gross, 1943. This tradition of research has been brought prominently to the study of public health innovations by Rogers, 1995 (first published in 1962); and to health care innovations and their adoption by physicians, by Coleman, Katz, & Menzel, 1957. Marshall Becker (1969, 1970) combined these two traditions with his study of the implementation of innovations by public health officials, as did Green (1970, 1975) in family planning and cardiovascular disease preventive innovations in the public. The recent developments in this line of research and application to health programs is reviewed by Oldenburg & Parcel, 2002.

Whereas rate of change translates in diffusion theory as "trialability," the previous considerations of both staff commitment and program goals are part of what diffusion theory calls "compatibility."

51. *Familiarity as a predictor of implementation:* For examples of the familiarity principle in health policy and planning applications of the Precede-Proceed Model, see N. H. Gottlieb, Lovato, Weinstein, Green, & Eriksen, 1992; MacDonald & Green, 2002.

52. *Complexity as a predictor of implementation:* The early work on this variable as applied within human service organizations was P. Berman & McLaughlin, 1976; Chase, 1979. In their analysis of the implementation of EMPOWER software as an innovation for using the Precede-Proceed Model in Montreal, Proulx, Potvin, et al. (1999) observed that the planning process guided by the model produced the necessary complexity of a robust plan, but also served to guide the planners through preparing for the implementation issues created by that complexity: "four functions of the model were identified: direction, coordination, articulation and transmission. Analysis of these functions demonstrated the structuring action of the model on planning" (p. 23). In another process evaluation of the implementation of EMPOWER, Chiasson & Lovato (2000, 2001) developed measures of each of the dimensions of compatibility, complexity, trialability, and other features of the innovation to assess their role in the implementation experience of users. They found that the software was complex, but at least it was simpler than the textbook (Green & Kreuter, then in its second edition)!

53. *Extent of implementation in school health:* Teachers implemented only 34% of the teaching and learning activities in the curriculum as they were intended to be implemented (Basch, Sliepcevich, et al., 1985). See also Hoelscher, Kelder, et al., 2001; MacDonald & Green, 2001; Renaud & Mannoni, 1997; Wickizer, Wagner, & Perrin, 1998; Wojtowicz, 1990. For an application of PRECEDE-PROCEED in assessing the parallel problems of implementation in a primary care setting, see P. H. Smith, Danis, & Helmick, 1998.

54. *Breakdown between training and implementation:* Ottoson, 1995, 1997; Ottoson & Patterson, 2000.

55. *Monitoring the implementation process to ensure quality:* Resnicow, Cohn, et al. (1992) experimentally varied the intensity of teacher interventions and monitored them to ensure adherence to the experimental protocol. Their result was an unequivocal difference in the measured behavioral and health outcomes for a program based originally on PRECEDE-PROCEED. See endnotes 28 and 45.

56. *Policy needs to be invoked or changed to mobilize or reallocate resources to support the program plan or to enable environmental change in support of the program objectives:* In a study of the enabling factor of access to a resource needed by women who were motivated to get Pap tests, for example, Bastani, Berman, et al. (2003) found that the addition of a mobile screening van produced a higher rate of Pap tests than a comparison program with communication alone.

57. *Example of evidence that counters a vocal minority opinion that might galvanize community resistance to a program or policy change:* Guttmacher, Lieberman, et al., 1997, p. 1433.

58. *Flexibility, first quality of a good policy:* The classic work on policy flexibility to accommodate implementation issues is that of Rein & Rabinovitz, 1997. For more recent examples of the examination of health policies for their responsiveness and flexibility, see Meyerson, Chu, & Mills, 2003; Rizack, Cunliffe, et at., 2003.

59. *Intraorganizational policy analysis:* A now classic work on this is Bolman & Deal, 1991. For examples of intraorganizational adaptations to facilitate the implementation of health-related innovations and policies, including "reinvention" of the innovation or policy, see Berwick, 2003; Dearing, Larson, Randall, & Pope, 1998; Dusenbury, Brannigan, et al., 2003; Everett Jones, Brener, & McManus, 2003. Grol, 2002, specifically invoked the Precede-Proceed Model in his analysis of individual, interpersonal, and organizational factors accounting for physician acceptance or rejection of new practices.

60. *Interorganizational policy analysis:* One of the classic works on this subject in the health field is Levine, White, & Scotch, 1963. For more recent examinations of interorganizational policies, governance, and exchange, see the growing literature on this aspect of coalitions, e.g.,

Braithwaite, Taylor, & Austin, 2000; Butterfoss & Kegler, 2002; Fawcett, Lewis, et al., 1997; Kwait, Valente, & Celentano, 2001; and see endnote 41 above.

61. *The recent community organization literature in health:* Bracht, 1998; Breckon, Harvey, & Lancaster, 1998; Levy, Baldyga, et al., 2003; Minkler, 1997; Minkler, Thompson, et al., 2002; Minkler & Wallerstein, 2002, 2003.

62. *Murry Ross's classical definition of community organizing:* M. Ross & Lappin, 1967, p. 14. The first edition of this influential book on community organization was 1955.

63. *World Health Organization's emphasis on intersectoral collaboration beyond the health sector:* World Health Organization, 1986.

64. *Australia's public-private sector collaboration on nutrition:* Chapman, 1990.

65. *U.S. examples of public-private cooperation on nutrition:* Samuels, 1990; Samuels, Green, & Tarlov, 1989.

66. *Conflict models of community organization:* Alinsky, 1972; Chapman & Lupton, 1995; Pertchuck, 2001.

67. *Systems approach to community encourages interdependence view of partnerships:* Best, Stokols, et al., 2003; Butterfoss & Kegler, 2002; Kreuter, & Lezin, 2002; Kreuter, Lezin, & Young, 2000.

68. *Cooperation between public and private sector partners can help fill gaps in services and prevent the depletion of scarce resources:* Levine, White, & Scotch, 1963.

69. *Engaging politics because you care, and because you may have little choice if you care a lot:* Freudenberg, 1984; Hinkle, Fox-Cardamone, et al., 1996; McKinlay, 1975; Paehlke, 1989; Patton, 1985; Spretnak & Capra, 1984; Studlar, 2002; Wallack, Woodruff, Dorfman, & Diaz, 1999.

70. *Exchange theory as an approach to collaboration, change, or compromise:* Best, Stokols, et al., 2003; Yukl, 1994; Zaric & Brandeau, 2001.

71. *The "tragedy of the commons" parable for self-interest over population good:* Hardin (1968) suggested an evolutionary principle of selfish consumption of common resources at the peril of the common good. For a recent example, see Corral-Verdugo, Frias-Armenta, et al., 2002. For a counter-argument with evidence that people can overcome the tragedy of the commons, see Feeny, Berkes, Mccay, & Acheson, 1990; and the use of indirect reciprocity, "give and you shall receive," in the exchange process, together with reputation or "image scoring" for giving reliably in return for support: Milinski, et al., 2002; Wedekind & Milinski, 2000. For an application to ethical issues in health communications, see Guttman & Ressler, 2001.

72. *The "power-educative" approach appeals to enlightened self-interest of those whose power needs to be redirected for the public good:* For example, Cataldo & Coates, 1986, esp. pp. 399–419; Lovato, Green, & Stainbrook, 1993.

73. *Media advocacy and education-of-the-electorate approach:* For example, Asbridge (2004) attempts to partition the effects of media, advocacy, legislative debate, and science in the passage of local clean air laws in Canada between 1970 and 1995. Biglan, Mrazek, et al., 2003, forsee increasing use of media advocacy to promote the application of research in practice. Puska (2002), speaking for the World Health Organization, sees a growing role for that agency in the interface with the food industry and advocacy with governments to improve the nutritional value of foods. For strategies, see American Public Health Association, 2000; Hoffman, 1989; Steckler, Dawson, et al., 1987; Wallack, 1997; Wallack, Dorfman, et al., 1993. See also Blum & Samuels, 1990; Farrant & Taft, 1988; Goldstein, 1992; and endnote 69 for applications to specific areas of public health.

74. *Engaging media, organizations, and policy on behalf of minority populations:* For example, Braithwaite, Taylor, & Austin, 2000; Fernandez-Esquer, Espinoza, et al., 2003; S. B. Thomas, 2001; some specifically within applications of PRECEDE-PROCEED, e.g., Earp, Eng, et al., 2002; Fleisher, Kornfeld, et al., 1998; Huff & Kline, 1999; Liburd & Bowie, 1989.

75. *Engaging media, organizations, and policy on behalf of aging populations:* For example, Minkler, 1985, 1997; and within applications of the Precede-Proceed Model, e.g., McGowan, & Green, 1995; Weinberger, Saunders, et al., 1992.

76. *Engaging media and organizations to educate the electorate on other issues:* For example, Freudenberg, 1984; Rundall & Phillips, 1990.

77. *Empowerment education approach:* For example, Cargo, Grams, et al., 2003; Green, 1983; Laverack & Wallerstein, 2001; Minkler, 1985; Shor & Freire, 1987.

78. *An urban case example of planning gone bad:* Dievler, 1997.

79. *Sources of case studies, examples of programs, and case stories:* Go to http://www.lgreen.net for links from specific endnotes aligned with this text to various resource centers, clearinghouses, and databases of bibliographies and case materials. For case stories, see Kreuter, Lezin, et al., 2003. Within the EMPOWER software, each screen has a drop-down menu called "Consult on Tap," under which one of the choices is "Case Example," in which a real or hypothetical case is described to illustrate the specific steps in the Precede-Proceed Model called for by that screen (Gold, Green, & Kreuter, 1998).

6

Applications in Communities

Precede asks and helps answer what, who, and why questions. What are the quality-of-life, health, behavioral, and environmental problems or aspirations? Who has those problems or aspirations? Why do they have them (what are their causes or determinants)? What assets can be built on? PROCEED asks: What resources, barriers, policies, regulations, and organizational factors need to be adjusted so one can make a program work and can set up an implementation and evaluation design? The overall process is ecological because, from the social assessment through to implementation and evaluation, the program's future context and circumstances directly influence planning decisions. The next four chapters discuss the application of the Precede-Proceed Model in specific settings or contexts: community, work site and school, and health care.

This chapter addresses key issues planners need to consider when applying the Precede-Proceed Model in the community setting. It is divided into three sections. The first begins with an expanded definition of the word *community* and follows with a description of the differences between *community interventions* and *interventions in communities*. It also discusses the realities and limitations of *participation*. The second section examines the complexities inherent in establishing, managing, and maintaining community coalitions. The third section illustrates how the application of Precede-Proceed principles in the community setting leads to multiple intervention tactics that constitute a comprehensive health program. Practical tools to help planners identify and apply multiple intervention tactics are reviewed, with special emphasis on mass media applications.

COMMUNITY: A MEDIUM FOR CHANGE AND A CHANGING MEDIUM

Defining Community

Village, barrio, neighborhood, and *town*—these words call to mind the notion of community because they connote those local places where individuals, families, and groups are, for better or worse, bound by common connections. Those

common connections range from geographic boundaries and physical characteristics to social norms, institutions, and values; collectively they provide the
context for the social, economic, and environmental determinants highlighted
in previous chapters.

This chapter uses the term *community* to refer to two characteristics—the
first structural, the second functional. Structurally, a community is an area with
geographic and often political boundaries demarcated as a district, county,
metropolitan area, city, township, or neighborhood.[1] Functionally, a community is a place where "members have a sense of identity and belonging, shared
values, norms, communication, and helping patterns."[2]

Effective planners understand the dynamic social characteristics and the
less dynamic cultural traditions of a community; their planning reflects their
sensitivity to those characteristics and traditions and the unique political
nuances that accompany them.

In some instances, *informal* political forces exert more influence on policy
formulation and program implementation than do the *formal* political structures usually associated with official boundaries.[3] For example, it would be
foolhardy to launch a health program in Harlem simply on the grounds that the
mayor of New York City endorsed it, just as it would be in London's Lewisham
area with merely the blessing of that city's lord mayor. On the other hand, proceeding without such political support could be equally foolhardy. For instance, attempts to organize Nigerian villagers to control malaria or guinea
worm disease outbreaks would be impossible without the overt approval and
support of the village chief.

Ultimately, the geopolitical scope of a program must be left to the prudent
judgment and sensitive action of those working with the program; the ideal
being a thoughtful balance between insights of local people who know the culture and traditions of the community and results from the analyses of the
resources available from the community and other levels (state, provincial, or
national) to support the program.[4] Even though the structural aspect of the definition limits activity to a local focus, attention to the larger national, provincial,
and state endeavors remains critical in the planning process.[5]

Grounded in the principles of participatory democracy and social justice,
community-based programs are often described with the kind of passion
implicit in Morone's concept of the *democratic wish*: "the image of a single
united people, bound together by a consciousness over the public good, which
is discerned through direct citizen participation in community settings."[6]
Community-based health programs hold considerable potential for making
population changes primarily as a result of reaching larger numbers of people
through mass media and multiple channels of communication, building widespread normative, economic, and political support for the changes, and possibly stimulating change in a community's social fabric. Furthermore, the
justification for community-based approaches is by no means limited to passionate rhetoric. Numerous studies support and justify the theoretical and
philosophical tenets underlying community-based approaches,[7] and research
findings from community interventions constitute some of public health's most
significant success stories.[8]

Community Interventions
and Interventions in Communities

The terms sound alike, but they are different. *Community interventions* seek small but pervasive changes that apply to the majority of the population; the approach is community-wide. *Interventions in a community* seek more intensive or profound change in a subpopulation, usually within or from a specific community site such as a workplace, hospital or clinic, nursing home, or school; this approach is targeted and setting specific.

The social arithmetic underlying the *community intervention* approach is that the net effect of influencing a small change in an entire population will yield more profound public health benefits than will those strategies aimed exclusively at a smaller percentage of the population deemed to be at highest risk.[9] Demonstration programs reported in the international literature, beginning with the large-scale family planning and immunization programs reported in the 1960s and early 1970s, have fueled enthusiasm for the community-based approach to health programs.[10] This trend gained ground through reports on a series of cardiovascular and cancer community-intervention trials initiated in the late 1970s and early 1980s,[11] and it continued with descriptions of a wide variety of community applications supported by government[12] and philanthropy[13] in the 1990s. The environmental movement has sought a similar level of community-wide activation around issues such as recycling, toxic waste disposal, water conservation, and carpooling.[14] The AIDS epidemic and HIV infections revived a parallel and converging interest in community approaches to infectious disease health programs.[15]

Numerous public health analysts[16] have offered epidemiological and sociological justifications for supporting these population approaches, but we alert planners to the reality that either-or thinking about the trade-offs between community-wide and high-risk subpopulations can be counterproductive. Both approaches aim at promoting health and reducing preventable health problems and disability, and both have independent and additive effects.[17] The benefits of creating a balance between community interventions and interventions in communities become especially compelling when their complementary merits are examined from different perspectives.

The Epidemiological Case for the Community Approach.   By the numbers alone, the community-wide approach appears irresistibly advantageous to the point that some would argue to transfer resources from high-risk approaches. In North Karelia, only 2% of the target population lost weight in the initial years, but this amounted to 60,000 persons, far more than could have been reached through doctors' offices.[18] The Australian "Quit. For Life" media campaign produced what might seem a measly 2.8% reduction in smoking prevalence,[19] which would be considered a failure by targeted smoking-cessation program standards,[20] but it amounted to 83,000 fewer smokers in Sydney. A television and community organization effort to support smokers' quitting in Canada yielded a 2.9% reduction in smoking prevalence, which translated to 8,800 fewer smokers than expected from extrapolated trends in Canada.[21]

The scattered but relentless antismoking efforts in the United States between 1964 and 1978 produced a net annual smoking prevalence reduction of only 1%. But this produced in turn an estimated 200,000 fewer premature smoking-related deaths, with many more expected to be avoided as former smokers aged through the 1980s and 1990s.[22] These epidemiological examples of the extensive, though proportionately small, benefits of community-wide or population interventions relative to the more effective but limited range of targeted, institutionally based interventions provide evidence for the benefits of health programs that take a well-planned community approach.

The Social-Psychological Case for the Community Approach.   From their review of the decades of work on sexually transmitted disease control, Solomon and DeJong conclude, "More than any other recommendation, we urge that AIDS risk-reduction strategies focus on establishing a social climate in which people feel that it is the norm and not the exception to adopt AIDS risk-reduction behavior."[23] The concept of a social climate where norms support behavioral and environmental actions conducive to health lies at the heart of the social psychological justification for community approaches to health programs.[24] Clearly the antismoking policy initiatives have succeeded in doing just that. The use of designated drivers as a means to counter drinking and driving appears to be making similar strides in becoming a norm. Low-fat and now low-carb eating have taken on the markings of social norms, at least in more affluent communities and their upscale restaurants.[25]

The social psychological case does not argue for a choice between community-wide and targeted approaches. It argues for a combination of them. As every social marketing and classroom experience demonstrates, targeting, or market segmentation, effectively produces tailored, relevant, and effective teaching and persuasive communications that reach and influence the actions of individuals.[26] At the same time, individual change can be powerfully *predisposed* by the individual's own perception that others have made the change successfully (role models) and with satisfaction (vicarious reinforcement). Furthermore, the individual process of making the change can be *enabled*, by imitation or modeling and by help from friends, and *reinforced*, by the approval of significant others. These processes of social support and influence are facilitated if enough social change is taking place around the individual—that is, if other people and environmental circumstances support the change in the same period. This is the fundamental thesis of reciprocal determinism in social cognitive theory.[27]

The combination of targeted and community approaches reconciles the debate between individualized and system approaches, which some have characterized as a debate between educational and environmental approaches.[28] Community approaches count on individual innovators and early adopters to blaze the trail for social change, but such approaches must reinforce their changes and increase their reach by building greater environmental and normative supports for the changes. Ordinances to control smoking in public places, for example, support those who have quit smoking and protect them from exposure to others' smoking while encouraging still others to quit.[29]

Community programs strive to provide the general environmental and social supports for change through policies and mass media; they also try to bring about the institutional interventions to strengthen psychological readiness through families, schools, work sites, and health care settings, where relatively individualized communications can be organized. In the long run, policies and mass media also help shape psychological readiness. Institutional settings provide ideal opportunities for social and environmental supports for change. By developing programs with a combination of interventions at multiple levels, planners are, in effect, creating community diffusion "systems." That is, they are increasing the number of places or channels (program or policy components) through which members of a given community are likely to find support for the health issues of interest. Such a system is essential in those circumstances where it is known that some portion of participants cannot be reached directly by the program.

The Economic Case for the Community Approach.   Consistent with virtually all policy declarations related to the enhancement of health and quality of life, we have repeatedly emphasized that the major determinants of health, for both populations and individuals, are directly linked to social, cultural, and economic factors.[30] As Frank has observed, "One's immediate social and economic environment and the way this environment interacts with one's psychological resources and coping skills, has much more to do with the determination of health status than was recognized in early epidemiological studies of chronic disease etiology."[31] For example, trends in market economies over the past two decades suggest that the initial demand for healthful food and fitness products tended to be driven by the consumer preferences of the more upscale and middle majority segments of the population and less so by the poorer, typically late-adopter segments. In this innovative stage, the consumption of healthful products was profitable to producers to the extent that prices, typically set for those in higher income brackets, were met. Those same prices were usually prohibitive to those with modest economic means. Over time, congruent with the principles of diffusion theory,[32] the interest in and demand for healthful products have spread beyond the middle majority segments of the population. This demand constitutes an economic incentive motivating producers and distributors to find ways to make these products accessible to larger portions of society. Such was the case when low-fat alternatives were introduced into the marketplace. Over time, healthful alternatives have gradually become more accessible, even though fast-food restaurants and convenience grocery stores prevail where the poorer segments obtain much of their food.[33]

The pricing of tobacco products represents a compelling flip side to this discussion—an example of a health benefit resulting from *higher* prices.

Figure 6-1 shows that increases in the tobacco tax from 1981 to 1992 in Canada were inversely related to decreases in tobacco consumption in those same years. Following the tax increase, as shown in Figure 6-2, the prevalence of smoking among teens, a lower income, hard-to-reach population, declined by over 50%. The Canadian experience with taxes on cigarettes as an effective means of controlling consumption among teenagers also needs to be seen in the

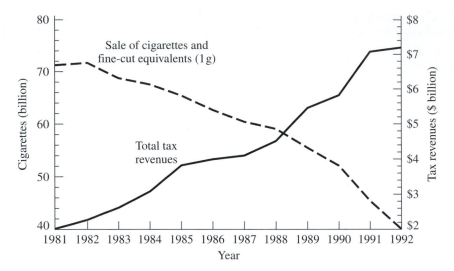

FIGURE 6-1 Domestic sales of cigarettes inversely mirrored domestic tobacco taxes in Canada between 1981 and 1992.
Source: Non-Smokers' Rights Association, Ottawa, Ontario, Canada.

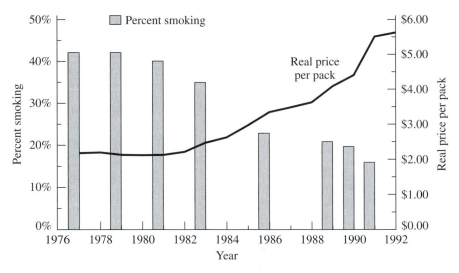

FIGURE 6-2 The percentage of Canadians 15 to 19 years old smoking daily between 1977 and 1992 followed the trend in real prices of cigarettes (adjusted for inflation).
Sources: National Clearinghouse on Tobacco and Health; Statistics Canada.

context of the controls on media exposure as a result of laws passed in Canada that restrict advertising more severely than those passed in the United States.

Globally, this same pattern of taxation stimulating a decline in tobacco consumption has continued. In reporting their business results for 2003, Japan

Tobacco Incorporated (JTI), Japan's largest seller of tobacco, made this announcement:

> Japan's aging population, growing health consciousness, the continuing down-
> turn in the domestic economy, and the aftereffects of the tobacco price hike due
> to the tax increase in July, has negatively affected cigarette demand nation-
> wide. JTI's domestic tobacco sales volume for the second fiscal quarter ending
> September 30, 2003 declined by 12.6 billion cigarettes or 21.1 percent, com-
> pared with the same quarter in the previous year.[34]

On October 1, 1997, the state of Alaska increased cigarette tax from $0.29 to $1.00 per package of 20 cigarettes. Since 1999, per capita consumption rates in Alaska (the number of taxable cigarettes sold per person each year) were de-clining at a rate of about 4.5% per year. In the first full year after the implemen-tation of tax increase, the per capita consumption rate dropped 14.8%. Similar declines in smoking rates among school-aged youth were also noted, reinforc-ing the Canadian experience noted above.[35]

It is estimated that for every 10% increase in cigarette prices, smoking rates among youth (aged 18 and younger) will decline by approximately 7.0%, adult rates by 2%, and total consumption by 4%.[36] While price does strongly influ-ence the consumption of tobacco, it is not the only force. During that same period of increasing taxes on tobacco, the tobacco industry in the United States carried out extensive advertising campaigns aimed at young smokers.

As in all other aspects of life, economic measures are powerful health pol-icy tools, with both positive and negative consequences for large segments of the population. Accordingly, those planning community-based health pro-grams should pay heed to the economic context of the population they plan to serve. Some jurisdictions have sought alternatives to taxation on products like alcohol and tobacco as a way of controlling consumption and paying for the damage of these products, viewing such taxes as regressive. British Columbia, for example, initiated legal action against the tobacco industry to collect a tax directly from them for health damages paid by the province; the terms specifically forbid the tobacco manufacturers from passing this tax on to the consumers.

The Political Case for the Community Approach.   The strength of numbers makes the epidemiological case, the strength of social norms makes the socio-logical case, and the strengths of purchasing power and taxes make the eco-nomic case for community-wide health programs; the combination of these creates the context for the political case. But how realistic is it for health pro-gram planners to be engaged in making the political case? Geoffrey Rose, the distinguished British epidemiologist offered us this insight:

> Political decisions are for the politicians. Their agenda is complex, and mostly
> hidden from public scrutiny. This is unfortunate, because often the public
> would give a higher priority to health than those who formulate political poli-
> cies. Anything that stimulates more public information and debate on health

issues is good, not just because it may lead to healthier choices among individuals but also because it earns a higher place for health issues on the political agenda.[37]

For elected officials, it goes without saying that the political power of social norms lies in voter sentiments and public opinion. Experienced health program planners, working hand-in-hand with indigenous community leaders and stakeholders, will seize every opportunity to heighten the awareness of political decision makers to the public's sentiments and opinion about the community's priority health needs.

Such advocacy should not stop with elected or appointed officials. Globally, it is becoming evident that the powerful actions and policies of corporations and businesses are subject to those same sentiments and norms. For example, the Corporate Citizenship Company is a firm in the United Kingdom whose mission is to assist international corporations in their efforts to become *good citizens*.[38] They use the results of social and health impact assessments as a means to motivate companies to take actions that result in tangible social, environmental, and economic contributions to local communities. In business parlance, this process is referred to as "social reporting." At the 2003 Business for Corporate Responsibility Conference in Los Angeles, the United Parcel Service (UPS) released its first-ever "Corporate Sustainability Report" in which it revealed its decision to spend $600 million to convert its domestic fleet of delivery trucks using new technology to gain higher fuel efficiency and lower emissions. The chairman and CEO of United Parcel Service, Michael Eskew, said:

> As a company with 360,000 employees and 88,000 vehicles and 2,850 facilities worldwide, we believe our stakeholders have a right to know where we stand on sustainability efforts, where we are headed and how we plan to get there. We place great value in the transparency of our business and the ways in which we hold ourselves accountable.[39]

In the development of community-wide health programs, we urge planners to engage stakeholders from the business sector with an attitude of seeking the "double-win": that is, advancing on the assumption that a program goal of health and environmental improvement is not, *ipso facto,* incompatible with the goals of business. This assumption underlies one of the core premises of Precede-Proceed: that health is an instrumental value, and such values will be acted upon by others to the extent that they perceive that those actions will enhance the ultimate values they hold and seek.

The Demonstration and "Multiplier" Value of Smaller Programs

With respect to intervention methods, the fundamental differences between community interventions and interventions in communities are primarily a matter of comparative magnitude and complexity: (1) the size of the group or population for whom the program is intended, and (2) the number of organizations, the multiple levels of organization needed to be involved, and the social and cultural complexity of the community or place in question.

Although they may focus on smaller, targeted populations interventions in a community offer planners many strategic opportunities. Interpersonal and small-group interventions are more common, more manageable, and probably better understood than are community-wide programs, as the next three chapters will show. Institution-based programs (e.g., school, work site, clinic) lend themselves better to systematic, controlled research, hence their stronger evidence base. Consistent with the ecological truism that "all things are connected," evidence suggests that site-specific interventions will have sustained effectiveness to the extent that they are able to establish important connections to the community at large. Cheryl Perry made that point in her critique of effective school-based health programs; she indicated that although a peer-led smoking prevention curriculum demonstrated substantial reductions in smoking onset among school-age youth, those same programs had diminished effects without community support.

> The careful links of behavioral curricula, parental involvement, community support, and peer participation and leadership, with messages that are consistent and coordinated, have demonstrated efficacy beyond the implementation of a single strategy.[40]

In addition, site- or area-specific interventions carried out within communities offer great potential for long-term, positive social change. When these smaller intervention efforts are sensitively carried out within the envelope of the community, they tend to become focal points for attention and candidates for expansion. At first these signs of expansion are likely to be modest. For example the AIDS Prevention Initiative in Nigeria (APIN), carried out in conjunction with Harvard University, uses a peer-education approach to AIDS prevention for known risk groups involving 85 secondary schools and the neighborhoods in the capital city of Ibadan. According to the project director, Lawrence Adeokin,

> the network of peer educators has nearly tripled as a result of the project implementation. This allows substantial increase in outreach activities on AIDS prevention. More importantly, the focus on Ibadan City made the multiplier effect of these peer educators higher than would have been the case in a statewide program.[41]

Over time, from modest beginnings like those in the Ibadan AIDS prevention example, programs can generate keen interest and imitation. As more people begin to sense that respectable individuals and organizations think the undertaking is good, more people agree to it.[42] As more organizations adopt or extend components of the program, they produce a multiplier effect.[43]

A classic example of this effect concerns three forces that accounted for health improvements in Mississippi from 1956 to 1981, especially among African Americans. The first was manifested by the passage of federal laws providing for new human service entitlement for food stamps, Head Start programs, Medicare and Medicaid, and housing improvements. From an ecological perspective, it may be hypothesized that these macro-level actions created a receptive environment that enabled the second and third forces to generate a multiplier effect.

A second force was the establishment of a variety of health services and health undertakings, originally by concerned external groups such as the Medical Commission on Human Rights and later by Mississippians themselves. These indigenous efforts were, in part, responses to innovations of outside origin, for example, in maternal and child care. Overall, while some health projects like the Tufts University's Mound Bayou Health Center were well funded, long lasting, and capable of providing a variety of services to a defined black population in the Delta, many projects were very small, ephemeral, and maintained on shoestrings. Nevertheless, the health projects of the 1960s and the early 1970s introduced new concerns for health standards, often improved methods, and involvements of communities in the improvement of health. The third force arose out of the first two. It was the growth of valid health information among both races. This led to an awareness of health needs, enhanced capacities for self-help, and greater demands for quality from health services providers.[44]

A contemporary extension of this multiplier effect is evident in the analysis reported by Schooler and her colleagues.[45] They document how technology and methods learned from the early cardiovascular disease prevention trials begun in the 1970s have been translated into specific applications worldwide. Table 6-1 presents a partial listing of these applications.

Community Participation

Early involvement of community members in the planning process is, in itself, a form of intervention. It provides the opportunity for ownership, empowerment and self-determination—those difficult-to-measure intangibles that can make the difference between long-term success and failure. As program planners take steps to create and nurture community participation, they must repeatedly ask themselves, Am I fostering participation that is real or symbolic? Consider just two of many factors that typically surface in community-based work. First, by definition, communities are made up of a variety of stakeholders who tend to hold very different views and expectations. Second, many community-based programs are driven or supported by outside funding, either in response to opportunities (in the form of grants from outside funders) or threats (which they must unite against to survive). Both of these factors— diversity in stakeholders and economic support—are certainly assets. Ironically however, these potential assets, if mismanaged, can become major sources of disruption to otherwise well-intended program efforts.

The Dilemma of Complex Problems and Multiple Stakeholders. H. L. Mencken said that for every human problem, there is a solution that is neat,

TABLE 6-1 Examples of community-based interventions shown here are modeled after the cardiovascular disease community prevention trials from the 1970s through the early 1990s

Description	Units and Population Size	Intervention Years	Intervention Activities	Population-Wide Risk Factor Results
The Martignacco Project (Italy)	2 towns: 1 treatment; 1 reference (N = 12,910)	1977–1983	Newpaper, other print, direct education, events	Cholesterol (men only), blood pressure, CHD risk, CVD events
North Coast Healthy Lifestyle Programme (Australia)	3 towns: 2 treatments; 1 reference (N = 61,560)	1978–1980	TV, radio, newspaper, other print, direct education, events	Smoking
Swiss National Research Programme	4 towns: 2 treatments; 2 references (N = 56,000)	1978–1980	TV, radio, newspaper, other print, direct education, events, environment	Smoking, blood pressure, obesity
Coronary Risk Factor Study (South Africa)	3 towns: 2 treatments; 1 reference (N = 17,750)	1979–1983	Other print, direct education, events	Smoking, blood pressure, composite CHD risk
German Cardiovascular Prevention Study	4 cities, 2 towns, 1 rural community; former West Germany reference (N = 1,228,400)	1985–1991	Newspaper, other print, direct education, events, environment	Blood pressure, smoking (men only), cholesterol
Norsjö study (Sweden)	3 areas: 1 municipality treatment; 2 counties reference (N = 5,300)	1985–1995	TV, radio, newspaper, direct education, events, environment	Cholesterol
Heart-to-Heart Project (South Carolina)	2 towns: 1 treatment; 1 reference (N = 107,254)	1987–1991	TV, radio, other print, direct education, events, environment	Smoking, cholesterol
Slangerup "Heart Area" Project (Denmark)	2 rural/small towns: 1 treatment; 1 reference (N = 8,000)	1989–1990	TV, radio, other print, direct education, events, environment	

Source: Adapted from "Synthesis and Issues from Community Prevention Trials," by C. Schooler, J. W. Farquhar, S. P. Fortmann, and J. A. Flora, 1997, *Annals of Epidemiology, 7* (Suppl.), S57, S59. With permission.

simple, and usually wrong![46] Those who grapple with difficult health problems complicated not only by varying interpretations of evidence by scientists, but also by conflicting political, cultural, and economic interests, can identify with Mencken's point. Clearly, not all problems and circumstances are the same!

As more and more health program planners have taken up the challenge of trying to solve complex health problems in communities, many have found their traditional orientation to problem solving incomplete. That is, the linear, causal-chain approach, which led to the eradication of small pox and the development of so many lifesaving vaccines, yields only part of the information needed to generate a fuller understanding of the problems that are embedded in highly complex social, economic, political, and cultural systems. Ironically, the scientifically sound methods we have used to control for confounding factors and employ experimental manipulation have had the effect of modifying, or excluding, the very conditions, forces, and factors that make the problem what it is. Consequently, planners charged with developing community programs face the difficult task of sustaining their traditional commitment to sound scientific analysis and assessment while simultaneously having to take into account the reality that the overall problem-solving process will be as much a social and political process as it will be scientific.

Elsewhere this has been described as the challenge of solving "wicked problems."[47] We hasten to point out that the term *wicked* is not meant to frame problems as (1) ethically deplorable, or (2) in any way a reflection of the character, ethics, or values of the community in which a problem surfaces. It is used to identify that a problem that is (1) illusive and difficult to pin down; (2) influenced by a wide range of complex social and political factors, some of which change during the problem-solving process; and (3) likely to be viewed differently depending upon the perspective and bias of those with a stake in the problem. All of these factors come into play in the planning of community-based health programs.

A juxtaposition of tame and wicked problems will help clarify the point. A viral infection, an engineering flaw, a fractured limb—these are tame problems. Although they can be very difficult and challenging, they can be solved by competent experts: laboratory scientists, engineers, or physicians. On the other hand, a problem is deemed wicked largely because there is no immediate agreement on the problem itself; it consists of an evolving set of circumstances and interconnected factors. Suppose a segment of a large metropolitan area had data revealing that the residents had disproportionately high rates of chronic diseases, violence, mental illness, and poor school performance. Does each one of those health areas constitute a separate problem? Or are they somehow connected perhaps by factors like the absence of, or deficiencies in, preventive services due to poverty? Could it be poor or undernutrition, or inadequate housing which place children at risk for lead poisoning? Or is it unemployment? To what extent are these factors exacerbated by discrimination? Have well-intended efforts aimed at economic development created environmental conditions that threaten health? Finally, who among the stakeholders will determine what the "real" problem is?

Thus, a problem may be deemed wicked to the extent that stakeholders, who often hold diverse perspectives, don't agree on the problem. Imagine a situation where residents of a community discover that they have been exposed to potentially harmful contaminants produced by an industry that has been a major source of employment and economic support in the community for decades. The residents express sentiments that range from gratitude for the opportunity for gainful employment over the years to fear, outrage, and mistrust for not being informed by the industry of the risk. During formal and informal meetings designed to determine how to address the problem, stakeholders representing businesses, the media, schools, public health, and political decision makers all bring different perspectives, and as a consequence, see "the problem" differently. This is precisely the kind of circumstance that calls for planning leadership that embraces the principle of participation. The experience and technical competence of scientific experts, while important, will inevitably be insufficient to rally the stakeholders to a common vision of what can and should be done.

Tackling Complex Community Problems.   As planners work through the Precede Model, they will uncover complex factors and forces, and for each, ascertain their comparative levels of importance and changeability and then choose or tailor intervention strategies to address each one. With stakeholder input and participation, this kind of planning process breaks wicked problems into more manageable components, many of which are likely to be amenable to traditional, tame, problem-solving strategies. From the outset planners must be transparent about the considerable time, patience, and understanding that will be required from all stakeholders including those responsible for the overall management and administration of the program. And, consistent with the theme of integrating evaluation throughout PRECEDE-PROCEED, process-evaluation and continuous quality-improvement strategies should be employed to determine the appropriate alignment and adaptation of best practices, and the extent to which the benefits of these investments, over time, are related to the costs.

It is not easy to facilitate the uncomfortable discussion of differences between individuals or groups, but planners will find it easier if they create a learning environment where mutual understanding is a priority. In *The Spirit Catches You and You Fall Down*, Anne Fadiman describes the conflict that arises when competent and caring medical practitioners try to treat a Hmong child with epilepsy only to have their efforts go awry because they didn't understand the beliefs and language of the Hmong culture.[48] Her message is not one that fixes blame on practitioners. Rather, it is a universal call for greater understanding as reflected in this rhetorical question: "if you cannot see that your own culture has its own set of interests, emotions, and biases, how can you expect to deal successfully with someone else's culture?" (p. 260)

Salk made a similar point in his classic book, *Survival of the Wisest*.[49] He argued that sustained improvements in health and quality of life will require resisting the separateness of the past and will embrace what he called "the characteristics of an *and* rather than an *or* philosophy—an "additive" philosophy rather than an "alternative" one" (p. 80). He characterized the "enemy" of effective problem solving not as those who hold alternative views or who come from different perspectives or disciplines, "but rather as those who are pathologically divisive or destructive of the unification and coalescence of healthy, contributing, constructive elements of the greater complexity, necessary to solve . . . problems" (p. 80). Planners who embrace balanced positions like those implied by Fadiman and Salk will find that it will help them minimize the contentiousness and mistrust that so often undermines well intended community-based health program efforts.[50]

The Dilemma of External Funding.   Ironically, successful efforts to secure federal or foundation resources to support large-scale community health demonstration programs can lead to problems around efforts to elicit broad-based community participation. These large-scale programs are most often conceived and, for the most part, planned by federal or state public health officials or technical advisory committees and by the professors who are instrumental in securing the grants. Too often, efforts to engage the community occur after the initial planning has started and after a formal external review process had approved the grant. In those instances, the active participation of the community came only after the grant was in hand. Asking communities and organizations to implement programs planned elsewhere and evaluated on someone else's terms might gain some followers, but often with commitments of only "as long as the money lasts." Whether through federal or philanthropic sources, these large community demonstration programs require research protocols designed by researchers.

Often, "participation" begins after key influencers in the target communities are informed of the institution's intent to apply for the grant and their agreement to cooperate is sought. If the community is invited to participate in the implementation but not the policy and planning stages, they may feel they are being used as free labor or a laboratory for university-initiated projects. This dilemma reflects an inability to design unbiased scientific tests of community interventions without damaging the variable (active community participation) that is most likely to account for successful community structural and cultural change, as well as behavioral change in individuals.[51] Early activation of the community in these instances may falsely raise community hopes and expectations should funding not be secured. Nevertheless, some communities take this aborted effort as a nudge to develop their own programs without external funding. Alternately, some of the communities that receive research grant funding fail to carry on the programs initiated under these or other grants.[52]

Public health practitioners at the state and community level face a similar dilemma with federally funded health programs. The majority of population health programs addressing specific chronic diseases, injuries, HIV-AIDS, and STDs are funded through federal categorical grants, most of which are made available through the Centers for Disease Control and Prevention. Furthermore, federal regulations restrict the way state recipients may use them. So, if a community- or state-level coalition wanted to combine resources from diabetes, cardiovascular disease, tobacco control, and nutrition and physical activity into a more robust, multifaceted program, they would likely face insurmountable administrative barriers. Thus, there is compelling evidence pointing to the benefits of community participation that demands a continuing search for funding mechanisms between levels of government and procedures of grant making that provide for greater community involvement. Recognizing this dilemma, the Institute of Medicine offered the specific recommendation

> that the federal government and states renew efforts to experiment with clustering or consolidation of categorical grants for the purpose of increasing local flexibility to address priority health concerns and enhance the efficient use of limited resources.[53] (p. 153)

Two Points of View.   A study of changes in the organization of local community services centers in Quebec provides a clear illustration of how differing perceptions of authority and, consequently power, can lead to problems and disagreements. The defenders of local autonomy opposed central government programming on the grounds that it would result in low-level adaptation to local needs, bureaucratization of services, and the discouragement of local participation. In response to these concerns, the Canadian health policy analyst, Bozzini, commented:

> This danger is real, but the analysis should be freed from ideological preconceptions. First, nobody should, *a priori* be scandalized because the state offers, over the whole Quebec territory, a homogeneous set of services addressing the most prevalent needs of the citizens. Furthermore, centralized programming does not mean a lack of local autonomy in the ways of doing things; against this anti-institutional rhetoric, the present situation shows that this autonomy is quite large including locally determined styles of community organization.[54]

All of this suggests the need for practitioners to be clear in their understanding of what community participation means. Having several influential community authorities on a steering committee is politically wise and undoubtedly will strengthen a program's chances for support, but it does not constitute "community participation." In reviewing the ethical issues inherent in fostering such participation, Minkler and Pies[55] pose this important question:

> When our agencies or funders propose what is really only symbolic or lip-service community participation, how do we formulate effective value based arguments to reinforce the importance of not only bringing community members to the table but also hearing their concerns and ensuring that their input is heavily reflected in the final product?

One way planners can begin to address this pithy question is to incorporate the principles of participatory research into both planning and evaluation. An essential feature of participatory research is that the people affected by an issue are involved in identifying the research questions about it and interpreting the results for the purposes of policy or other action in relation to it. Involving them early in the planning ensures that they have a say in the research assessment of needs and assets, which is part of the planning during PRECEDE. Maintaining their involvement through the evaluation phases of PROCEED will ensure that the results will be interpreted and translated into actions relevant to their further needs.

COALITIONS: COMPELLING, IMPORTANT, BUT NOT EASY AND NOT A PANACEA

Participation is a prominent, overarching principle for the development and implementation of community health programs; coalitions represent a form of participation. *Coalition* refers to a grouping of varied organizations in which the collective interests converge on a shared objective but whose member organizations have separate agendas and interests of their own. Thus, coalition members will bring their own organization's perspectives and resources to the table, but they also are expected to work toward achieving goals set by the coalition as a whole.

Depending on a given situation, a coalition can operate at different points on what Wandersman and Florin have described as a "continuum of decision making," ranging from an advisory role to full control over resources.[56] In the planning realm, they may be responsible for conducting needs assessments, setting priorities, and choosing interventions. At the financial end of the spectrum, coalitions and consortia may be responsible for disbursing and monitoring funds awarded to others in the community. In both cases, a coalition's capacity and skill in undertaking these managerial functions can drastically affect its survival.[57] As mentioned above in the discussion of "wicked problems," it is most notably in such complex situations that applications of the Precede-Proceed Model will help keep planners on track.[58]

Aphorisms like "none of us is as smart as all of us," "rich together, poor if separated," and countless others from cultures around the world sound a universal endorsement of the merits of alliances for the betterment of a social group. So, it is not surprising to realize that whether it is meeting basic needs in Nigeria,[59] trying to strengthen collaboration in a minority neighborhood,[60] establishing "healthy public policy" in an impoverished inner-city area of London,[61] or working to create health services for the rural homeless,[62] interorganizational partnerships, often with multiple partners called a coalition, emerge as a logical part of any community-based intervention program. Numerous studies have undertaken the task of trying to pinpoint the specific strategies and tactics that are most likely to predict positive program outcomes from a well-planned community-based approach.[63] We use the term *positive program outcomes* here to refer to evidence of effectiveness, rather than the term *efficacy,* because the latter implies a greater certainty of causal linkage to outcome than is often realistic for community-based interventions.[64] One example is a Mississippi-based group called Communities for a Clean Bill of Health. It is a broad-based coalition of community- and state-level groups who are committed to the

BOX 6-1 Communities for a Clean Bill of Health
Membership List

American Cancer Society • American Heart Association • American Lung Association • Mississippi Health Advocacy Program • Respiratory Care Society • American Academy of Pediatrics (MS Chapter) • Mississippi State Medical Association • Mississippi Alliance for School Health • Children's Defense Fund • Coastal Families Health Center • Mental Health Association of MS • South MS Home Care and Hospice • Delta Health Ventures • Mississippi Conference on Social Welfare • Mississippi Human Services Coalition • Diabetes Foundation of Mississippi • Catholic Charities • University of Southern Mississippi School of Nursing • Acute RTC Behavioral Health Institute for Disability Studies • Mid-Delta Health Systems, Inc. • Warren Yazoo Mental Health Services • Parkwood Behavioral Health Systems • Women First • Mississippi Immigrant Rights Association • Information and Quality Healthcare • Jackson Medical Mall Foundation • Surgery Associates, PA • Coordinating Council for the Children's Ministries of the MS United Methodist Church • Mississippi Low Income Child Care Initiative • Mississippi Forum on Children and Families • Mississippi Consumer Assistance Program • Kidney Care • Mississippi Family Physicians Association • Family Medical Center • Mississippi Academy of Family Physicians

proposition that by increasing the rate of excise tax on cigarettes, Mississippi will benefit by a reduction in the number of people, including children and pregnant mothers, who choose to smoke. This group provides an excellent example of a coalition strategy being a good fit for the task. First, its scope is statewide and unambiguously policy oriented: increasing the excise tax rate on cigarettes in Mississippi. Second, the breadth of coalition members is broad and impressively suited to the policy change agenda (Box 6-1). Box 6-2 provides a concrete, practical example of how the Communities for a Clean Bill of Health coalition used evidenced-based statements as the basis for a Web-based campaign to promote public awareness of, and advocacy for, their mission.[65]

Inevitably, one of the factors most often associated with positive program outcomes relates to forming and working with coalitions. In light of the powerful and compelling call for coalition development, planners need to be cognizant that the care and feeding of coalitions is a demanding task and that there may be instances where an alternative approach may be preferable, or at least where the number of organizational members of the coalition should be kept to a manageable few, or the scope of coalition responsibility contained.

In a systematic review of 68 published articles describing the use of coalitions or collaborative efforts designed to attain either health or system change effects, we found good news for coalitions and not so good news. While several studies demonstrated that coalition activities were clearly associated with strong, positive outcomes, the ratio of programs that attained that goal to those that did not was disappointing. Three conclusions emerged from the findings:

BOX 6-2 A Web-based "Questions and Answers" Campaign Used by the Mississippi Communities for a Clean Bill of Health

Q: Why is an increased tobacco tax in Mississippi a WIN, WIN, WIN situation?

A: Win #1: Fewer Kids Smoking
Win #2: Higher Revenue for States
Win #3: Public Support for Tobacco Taxes
http://tobaccofreekids.org/research/factsheets/pdf0167.pdf
http://tobaccofreekids.org/reports/prices/

Q: How much is Mississippi's current cigarette tax?

A: 18 cents per pack, allowing our state to rank 45th in the nation.

Q: What is the national average for cigarette tax?

A: 70.5 cents per pack.

Q: How much money did cigarette sales contribute to the state's economy last year? How much would they contribute if the tax were raised by 50 cents?

A: $44 million. If the tax were raised 50 cents, it would raise approximately $151 million.

Q: How much money does Mississippi stand to gain from a 50-cent increase in the tobacco tax?

A: On cigarettes sales alone, the increase would mean an additional $117.3 MILLION for health and education in Mississippi, ON TOP of the $363.8 MILLION in short-term health care savings. http://tobaccofreekids.org/research/factsheets/pdf/0148.pdf

Q: What are the health benefits of a 50-cent increase in Mississippi?

A: 15,000 fewer adult smokers and 20,000 fewer future children smokers! And more than $363 MILLION in health care dollars! http://tobaccofreekids.org/research/factsheets/pdf/0148.pdf

Q: Which states have significantly increased their tobacco tax and seen an increase in smoking?

A: NONE! Raising state cigarette taxes ALWAYS increases state revenue and ALWAYS decreases rates of smoking. http://tobaccofreekids.org/research/factsheets/pdf/0098.pdf

Q: Which states have significantly increased their tobacco tax and NOT seen an increase in state revenue?

A: NONE! Raising state cigarette taxes ALWAYS increases state revenue and ALWAYS decreases rates of smoking. http://tobaccofreekids.org/research/factsheets/pdf/0098.pdf

(1) planners, stakeholders, and funders tend to underestimate the complexity, resources, and time required to carry out an effective community-based collaborative initiative, (2) some stakeholders hold unrealistic expectations about what a collaboration can do, and (3) in the absence of a sound theoretical framework and logic model for evaluating community-based health promotion, program effects may be going undetected.[66]

Coalitions consist of collaborating organizations whose collective interests converge on a shared objective but whose member organizations each have

> **BOX 6-3** Experience-Based Caveats on Coalitions
>
> 1.   Most organizations will resist giving up autonomy, resources, credit, visibility, or autonomy.
>
> 2.   Not everyone insists on being the coordinator, but no one wishes to be the coordinatee.
>
> 3.   So much goes into maintaining the coalition that little remains for the program.
>
> 4.   Meeting attendance could easily be re-named "meeting attrition!" Regular attendees often lack authority to make commitments for the organization.
>
> 5.   Those who were good at organizing coalitions and securing broad agreement on goals are not necessarily best at implementing programs.

separate agendas and objectives of their own. Thus, coalition members will bring their own organization's perspectives and resources to the table, but they also are expected to work toward achieving goals set by the coalition as a whole.

We advocate a diagnostic planning process because we know that there are no "one size fits all" programs for the promotion of health and the prevention of population health problems. Assessments give planners important clues as to the directions and strategies that are most likely to yield the objectives they seek to achieve; as problems differ, so too do the solutions. In Box 6.3 we offer five caveats on coalitions. They are not meant to disparage coalition strategies; rather they are intended to serve as prompts to remind planners that coalitions can become too large or unnecessarily protracted to be of meaningful use. The more focused and specific the partnerships can be, the more likely they are to achieve a mutually satisfactory result; the more administratively cumbersome, time consuming, and micro-managing of program implementation coalitions become, and the more opaque and diffuse their vision and objectives, the more likely they are to buckle under their own weight.[67]

The Capacities of Communities to Support Health Programs

Another important feature of community-based health programs is the context of the community in which they are operating. For example, if a planner is trying to establish a health program coalition in an area where there is a legacy of mistrust or failed attempts, the coalition's formation may occur in an atmosphere of suspicion or hostility. No matter how well its members go about the tasks of forming and implementing collaborative activities, a history of strained relationships can only be overcome through the rebuilding of trust, and this

requires more time than some program planning and implementation schedules permit. Goodman noted that a community's readiness and capacity are
demonstrated through the ability to "mobilize, structure, initiate, refine, and
sustain an organized response," but that community development efforts are
often sacrificed in an effort to move quickly to interventions and results.[68] Ironically, lack of attention to these underlying factors may be what most jeopardizes the intervention.

Recent research findings related to the concepts of social cohesion[69] and
social capital[70] provide added weight to importance of social climate and supportive norms in community-based health improvement programs. Social capital is defined as those processes among people and organizations, working
collaboratively in an atmosphere of trust, that lead to accomplishing a goal of
mutual social benefit. Ecological studies have shown that there is a strong and
consistent association between high levels of social capital (manifested by evidence of trust, social support, reciprocity, and group membership) and a wide
range of positive health status indicators.[71] Social capital research has also
explored the extent to which a community's history and its underlying structures, beliefs, and levels of trust may mediate the success or failure of collaborative efforts. Focusing on the role social capital plays in influencing
community change, Tempkin and Rohe[72] found that indicators of social capital
were strongly associated with neighborhood stability. Their study employed a
model of neighborhood change that conceptualized two operational levels of
social capital: *sociocultural milieu* and *institutional infrastructure*. They defined
socio-cultural milieu as the manifestation of (1) residents' identity with the
neighborhood, and (2) the degree of social interaction neighbors have with one
another. *Institutional infrastructure* refers primarily to the presence of neighborhood organizations whose mission is to act on behalf of the residents. They also
indicated that an essential ingredient of the *institutional infrastructure* concept
was a strong commitment by those organizations to form alliances with influential sources *outside* the neighborhood.

> the neighborhood must be able to leverage a strong sense of place into a collec-
> tive movement that is able to form alliances with actors outside the community
> and influence decisions that affect the neighborhood's character over time.
> (p. 70)

The two operational levels of social capital cited by Tempkin and Rohe are
consistent with the distinction between *bonding* social capital and *bridging*
social capital described by Putnam.[73] *Bonding* social capital, similar to *sociocultural milieu*, is assumed to be a critical factor in creating and nurturing group
solidarity that one sees in close neighborhoods and ethnic enclaves. *Bridging*
social capital, analogous to *institutional infrastructure*, is detected at the organizational level where norms, values, and social structures facilitate linking
together different organizational entities within a community around a common purpose, and gaining resources and assets to aid the community from
sources outside the community.

From our research on social capital specifically as it relates to the matter of planning and developing community health programs, we would offer the following observations:[74]

- Principles and theories, supported by current evidence, suggest that collaboration and participation are essential and fundamental ingredients of community-based initiatives that seek to improve health.
- While there is research evidence demonstrating that community-based health initiatives using coalitions do yield positive benefits, overall findings tend to be equivocal.
- The absence of stronger evidence of success is in part due to researchers, practitioners, and funding agencies having underestimated the complexity, time, and cost of activating collaborative networks and holding unrealistic expectations about effects.
- Theory, combined with growing empirical evidence, indicates that key constructs of social capital strongly influence the way collaborative networks function.
- There appear to be valid macro-level (national, state, provincial) measures of the principal constructs of social capital, and there is evidence that progress is being made on assessing those constructs at the community level.
- The ability to assess *bridging* (organizational) social capital at the community level validly could enhance our understanding of the way community health program coalitions or networks function. Furthermore, the capacity to do such an assessment may help explain why research findings on the effects of community have been equivocal.

The capacity to assess levels of social capital in a community could have important methodological and policy implications for community health programs. Currently, in spite of the extensive literature pointing to the social, economic, and political determinants of contemporary health problems, very few government or philanthropic resources are earmarked for building or strengthening the community capacity needed to maintain coalitions or the complex community interventions those coalitions support. If valid measurement can show that social capital or some aspect of community capacity is clearly linked to the effective application of community-based public health programs, funders will have to reexamine their present policies. Specifically, funders will be able to make more informed decisions about the most productive ways to contribute infusions of health-related funding to a given community—either to bolster the capacity required for successful interventions or to move directly to the interventions themselves.

The Politics of Coalitions and Community Power

Experienced practitioners will find the following scenario quite familiar. Adminstrative decision makers receive several program initiatives for consideration in the budget for the coming year. All the options have merit, but the resources are finite. In spite of what seems to be compelling data and information to some, decision makers do not agree on how the resources should be disbursed. Under these circumstances, political factors enter the decision-making process. In this context, public perceptions, or the perceived needs of special-interest groups, tend to carry extraordinary weight. Political decision making is not inherently good or bad—it is just real. Communities are political. Over the years, academics[75] and political commentators[76] alike have used *game* as a metaphor to describe politics. Virtually all social systems have informal rules for the exchange of ideas and for negotiations. Those who want to initiate activities in a community need to be mindful of such rules. Here are some practical principles that will give you a feel for the game and its rules.

1. *There are never enough resources to cover all the demands for them.* A program is, figuratively speaking, in a competitive market. Thus, not only does a program have to meet the professional practice standards the planner sets for it, it must also have attributes that appeal to decision makers and a large segment of their constituents.
2. *Often, the ultimate decision as to what resources will be allocated to which demands are made by those who are not expert in the issues.* Therefore, special efforts need to be made to ensure that decision makers are informed by credible experts as to the value of a project and that the same information is reinforced through the decision makers' constituents or allies.
3. *Although decisions are sometimes influenced by the sheer weight of popular clamor, they are often influenced by the effective penetration of the decision makers' inner circle.* Therefore, program advocates need to know how to gain access to that inner circle.
4. *The conventional wisdom that people tend to support what they "own" is well supported in the literature.*[77] Therefore, because personal commitment follows ownership, one should make special efforts to help local leaders feel that the initiative or program in question is "theirs," including the community research that leads to the specification of the health issues and the diagnostic baseline survey data.

Even the entry-level practitioner quickly realizes that failure to pay attention to these and other political issues could prevent the best of programs from getting off the ground or, once initiated, from being sustained. Most health workers, however, especially those employed by official or government agencies, are discouraged, if not forbidden, from taking what might be construed as political action. Often they are informed that their program activities should remain independent of politics. Legally, this means that campaigning for a political candidate or lobbying for legislation is prohibited during work time or in the name of one's organization. Practically, it means avoiding any appearance of using public funds to influence legislative or electoral decisions. These important principles by no means prohibit government health workers from using one of their most powerful tools, education, to keep decision makers and the general public informed about the progress of health programs and the benefits they yield. Nor does it preclude nongovernmental organizations that are part of a coalition or alliance from being advocates and taking appropriate political action; recall our earlier reference to the Communities for a Clean Bill of Health coalition.

Coalitions: Some Basic Principles

In culling the literature in search of the indispensable rules that guide health program planners in the process of coalition building, one finds but a few.[78] More plentiful are examples of coalition efforts, each crafted to address the unique needs and sensitivities of a given community.[79]

To augment a review of the literature on the effectiveness of community coalitions for the Health Resources and Services Administration, Kreuter and Lezin[80] incorporated a telephone survey of health professionals[81] known to have extensive research or practical field experience with community health coalitions. The purpose of the survey was to elicit their expert views on what constitutes realistic expectations for community health coalitions. The results, summarized in Table 6-2, highlight the value of establishing a clear purpose, realistic expectations, and a reasonable time frame for a coalition.

Basic Steps to Keep in Mind

The concept of "bridging social capital" cited earlier reinforces what common sense tells us: that even though a community-based program may be built on a sound foundation of data and theory, and prepared to launch evidence-based strategies tailored to local needs and characteristics, the success and sustainability of that program will be compromised if the stakeholder agencies and organizations in that community had a poor history of cooperating with one another! In the parlance of social capital, the lack of cooperation is a manifestation of either a short supply or absence of trust, sense of mutual support, and reciprocity. So for planners, the practical question is, If I sense that bridging social capital is low, what are my options in the absence of evidence-based protocols?

Borrowing from the information in Table 6-2 and our own experiences, we offer the following practical steps. If followed, they will help create a context for planning that nurtures trust and establishes opportunities for open, reciprocal exchanges.

1. *Establish a common mission.* A small steering or planning committee, composed of colleagues dedicated to addressing the same health priority, is usually the first step in forming a coalition.

The steering committee can begin the work of the coalition by defining the purpose, proposing potential members, and organizing the first meeting. If the smaller group's deliberations lead to the formation of a broad-based coalition, the steering committee members may turn the leadership over to other members of the coalition or may retain a major management and support or staffing role.

TABLE 6-2 Expert panel opinions are shown here on realistic expectations for community coalitions

Goals judged to be realistic

- Exchange information among coalition members
- Achieve a common goal among coalition members
- Promote collaboration among coalition members
- Legitimize the issue or focus of coaltion

Goals judged to be realistic with reservations

- Program planning
- Influence policy
- Influence resource allocation for a given problem or issue

Goals judged to be generally unrealistic

- Program implementation
- Create organizational or systems change in a community
- Directly influence health outcomes

Key expectations for a coalition in the first year

- Get organized
- Establish a clear vision and mission—a common purpose
- Clarify mode of operations
- Formalize process, procedures; as necessary, establish subcommittees around agreed-on objectives
- Establish trust
- Develop an unambiguous plan of action
- Ascertain the group skills required to manage the coalition effectively

What factors predict the effectiveness of a coalition?

- Having a well-defined, specific issue on which to direct energies
- Having an agreed-on vision and goal
- Coalition members acknowledging that, given a problem or issue they are trying to address, they are more likely to succeed as part of an alliance rather than individually
- Having an adversary (e.g., health problem or an organizational or environmental threat to quality of life) that is clear and unambiguous
- A coalition taking a leadership, not a management, role—remaining focused on the vision, not getting bogged down in minute details

Source: "Are Consortia/Collaboratives Effective in Changing Health Status and Health Systems? A Critical Review of the Literature," by M. W. Kreuter and N. Lezin, prepared for the Office of Planning, Evaluation and Legislation (OPEL), Health Resources and Services Administration, June 19, 1998. With permission.

Because many of the people capable of making a difference at the community level are already committed to other community projects, the aim of the coalition and its agenda must be compelling and must appeal to the interests of these busy leaders. It must elicit in the prospective coalition member sentiments like "This is really important" or "This agenda ties in with our mission" or "I've heard Dr. Judith Francis, an influential community leader, challenge us to tackle this issue." In general, the more concrete and specific the coalition's goal, the better. Of course, if the goal is too specific, it discourages the formation of a broad constituency. Nevertheless, given the choice between a vague, motherhood-and-apple-pie goal and a precise, well-understood goal, one is better off negotiating the expansion of a specific goal than starting with a more general agenda that runs the risk of having universal but lukewarm appeal.[82]

2. *Seek appropriate representation.* Clarifying the key role(s) of the coalition will provide insight to the planners on the matter of recruiting the most effective coalition members. Nix's list of the types of leaders who typically influence community health programs offers a good point of departure:[83] (1) top-level community influentials who "legitimize" the program, (2) subarea (neighborhood) leaders if the program includes more than one area, (3) key health leaders, (4) leaders of the most influential organizations or companies, (5) leaders of factions and those who can act as "go-betweens" or links to several groups, (6) leaders of the target population (opinion leaders who represent the underserved, minority groups and those at high risk), (7) specialists with skills and knowledge relevant to the goals of the program, and (8) officials who control or support health programs (mayor, health director, commissioner, etc.).

We would add to this list two other influential groups: the media and the faith community. A formative evaluation of CDC's Planned Approach to Community Health (PATCH) program found that the most successful applications had media representation in the core group (coalition).[84] In addition to the obvious advantage of direct contact with a principal communication channel within the community and the political support that can bring, media representatives frequently bring invaluable skills in conducting market research. They also can articulate the health messages of the coalition to different audiences and reach out to other members of the media. Researchers have also demonstrated the influential role that the faith community can have on establishing community health programs.[85]

As coalition members are recruited, keep in mind that close collaboration and cooperation are not always the automatic byproducts of joining a coalition. Even with the shared goal of improving quality of life, public, private, and voluntary health organizations do compete with one another. For example, although the voluntary cancer, heart, lung, diabetes, and other health organizations may share prevention goals, they also compete with one another for donations from the community. If representatives of such competing organizations are a part of the same coalition, planners must maintain their sensitivity to the subtle, but very real differences among those groups. The key is to emphasize the common mission of the group and to reinforce the genuine importance of Salk's philosophy of the "double win."

One caveat for enthusiastic, early-career practitioners is this: Be wary of giving community members the impression that the effort they are undertaking is a brand-new idea that will be the answer to their prayers. The fact is that most communities are already organized and have probably been down this road before; some likely serve on other community groups that also have a health agenda. By demonstrating interest and respect for prior experience, the practitioner can capitalize on the experience of coalition members.

3. *Pay attention to details.* Establishing a strong, representative coalition with a common agenda is one thing; managing that coalition is another. When you enter a room full of the community's most influential people, will you be ready?

a. *Do your homework.* Generally, work goes better and faster when you know and understand the people you work with. Prior to your first meeting, find out about coalition members' interests and hobbies as well as their professional background and health concerns. If you have data describing the health issue(s) to be addressed, make certain that the coalition members have received it in advance and in a format and language they can easily understand.

b. *Be hospitable.* Because active community leaders usually have more requests for their participation than they can honor, they may sometimes look for a reason to say no. By creating a focused agenda and a hospitable environment for your coalition meetings, you increase the likelihood that people will participate. If at all possible, schedule meetings at the same location and a time most convenient for the majority of the group. The meeting room should be arranged to encourage discussion and the chairs comfortable. Be prepared for the meeting with easy-to-read name tags, plenty of typed agendas and handouts, and any audiovisual equipment that you think might be needed during the meeting. Depending on the norms of the group, provide refreshments or food as appropriate.

c. *Nurture people-to-people exchanges.* Knowing nurtures trust. Contentious relationships between organizations are often the extensions of historical conflicts, perpetuated even though they are no longer relevant. Face-to-face exchanges and familiarity can nurture new interests and break down old ghosts. Create meeting agendas that provide opportunities for informal exchanges and explore the use of meaningful e-mail exchanges among coalition members.

4. *The crucial first meeting.* The first meeting is the most important one. It sets the tone for the coalition and establishes a model for the meetings to follow. Consider the following steps for the first meeting.

First, frame the agenda by asking the question, What do we want the coalition members to leave the meeting with? At a minimum, participants should leave the first meeting (1) with an understanding of the key issues or problems the coalitions will be addressing, (2) aware of the potential to address those issues and problems, (3) believing that the work of the coalition could be a worthy priority for their organization and for the community at large, (4) knowing other members of the coalition and understanding what they and the organizations they represent can and cannot contribute to the work of the coalition, and (5) knowing that the coalition is well staffed and organized.

Second, begin the meeting with a round-robin of self-introductions limited to name, title, organization or group representation, and perhaps why they came. Keep it short—opportunities will arise for more detailed discussion at two points later in the meeting. Following the brief introductions, a presentation about the proposal should be given by a respected person in the community, one who is articulate and has been well briefed on the details of the program to-date. The presentation should include both a clear statement of the problem or goal the program will be addressing and local data to document its importance. An effective strategy is to describe the likely long-term health, social, and economic effects on the community if no action is taken on the problem. Even better, paint a vision of community well-being if action is taken. Keep this introductory presentation short, no more than 15 minutes. If visuals are used, make certain that they are clear, uncomplicated, and easy to grasp. Pretest all audiovisual equipment.

Third, provide time immediately following the presentation for questions and discussion. Have program staff ready to assist with the question and discussion period if necessary. Do not merely remain open for new ideas and criticism—ask for them.

Fourth, after the discussion, invite coalition members to share their responses to the following questions:

a. What is the primary mission of my agency, organization, or group?
b. What is it about this problem or program that is linked to our mission or interests?
c. With regard to the problem or the program envisioned, what kinds of activities would be appropriate for my agency or organization?
d. What *can't* my agency or organization do?
e. Do you know of others who ought to be part of this coalition?

Fifth, the final task will be defined in part by the extent to which the coalition reaches agreement on the overall coalition agenda or program goal. If the tone of the meeting reflects such a general consensus, the next step will be to begin a systematic process to delineate the major tasks that need attention and to identify coalition members willing to take on those tasks. If people still disagree on particular aspects of the coalition agenda, those disagreements will need to be clarified and resolved before moving on.

A crossroad will come when implementation responsibilities for the goals agreed upon must be allocated. The temptation to maintain the management of implementation at the coalition level is what leads to some of the problems identified in our "caveats on coalitions" box on p. 273. Coalitions are at their best in getting agreement on goals and advocating for policy changes; they may be at their worst trying to micromanage implementation. At this point, it is often advisable to assign implementation tasks to individual or pairs of partnering organizations.

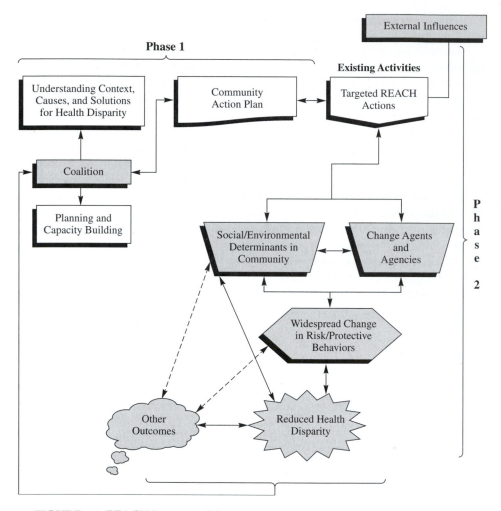

FIGURE 6-3 REACH Logic Model
Source: REACH Program Division of Adult and Community Health, National Centers for Disease Control and Prevention (NCCDPHP), National Centers for Disease Control and Prevention (CDC) 2002.

Creating an Organizational Framework

Although well worn, the aphorism "a picture is worth a thousand words" aptly describes the logic model that characterizes the U.S. national program entitled Racial and Ethnic Approaches to Community Health (REACH), which is presented in Figure 6-3. This logic model is consistent with planning principles of Precede-Proceed. Phase 1 begins with an effort to ensure collective understanding of the priority health disparities for a given community, the causes for those disparities, and the consideration of possible solutions. The best available quantitative and qualitative indicators of health and its collective determinants will be used in this process. The intention is that local residents will play a major role in coalition efforts at every stage including planning, implementation, and evaluation. Collectively, these actions will generate a community action plan.

The arrow leading from the community action plan to the box highlighting "targeted reach actions" surrounded by "existing activities" is strategically critical for planners. This element of the logic model takes into account the reality that when a new health program emerges in a community, inevitably there will be at least some activities occurring in the environment that might affect the level of health disparities. Accordingly, planners are alerted to the need to take these existing activities into account and make efforts to align with the proposed actions of the new program. This yields two benefits. First, it sets the stage and norm for a coordinated community initiative. Secondly, it acknowledges and values the work of others. It is through such gestures of inclusion that trust, respect, and collaboration are nurtured.

The two boxes below "targeted actions" urge planners to consider how intervention strategies might influence both the social and economic determinants of health in the community as well as the key agents and agencies of change. The logic then suggests that those forces will stimulate change in risk and protective factors which, in turn, will have a direct impact on the health disparity of interest. The arrow that goes directly from the "social/economic determinants" box to the outcome (bypassing the risk and protective behaviors) implies that robust actions, perhaps related to home ownership or employment and work, that dignify, can have a direct impact on health disparities.

"Other outcomes" refers to those goals consistent with the social diagnostic phase of PRECEDE; these might include measures related to quality of life or, for children, better school performance. All these arrows go in both directions. This allows for flexibility and inevitable self-correction as new knowledge is incorporated into a dynamic plan. Table 6-3 shows how each of the elements of the logical model, like PRECEDE-PROCEED, generates indicators (with examples) that enable planners to track and fully capture and assess the effects of REACH program activities. Table 6-4 offers an illustration of how the application of the REACH logic model could guide planners in the development of a creative program aimed at a challenging social determinant of health: home ownership.

APPLICATIONS IN COMMUNITIES

The diagnostic-assessment processes described in the previous chapters are designed to give planners insight into those multiple factors that influence health and quality of life for a given target population. These processes have been applied in community settings across numerous health problems, including, for example, domestic violence,[86] prevention of child pedestrian injuries,[87] cervical cancer screening and follow-up,[88] breast cancer screening

TABLE 6-3 Descriptions of REACH Logic Model Components

Stage	Effect	Brief Definition
1	**Capacity Building**	*Capacity building* refers to the readiness or ability of a coalition and its members to take action aimed at changing risk/protective behaviors and transforming community conditions and systems so that a supportive context exists to sustain behavior changes over time. This includes: • understanding context, causes, and solutions for health disparity • forming and maintaining an effective coalition • engaging in collaborative planning • accumulating resources needed to implement the action plan
2	**Targeted Action**	*Targeted action* refers to all the activities that compose the intervention believed to bring about desired effects. Action strategies include a broad range of tactics such as: • educational/interpersonal (e.g., peer educators) • political/legal (e.g., enforcing laws) • environmental (e.g., relocating toxic sites) • communication (e.g., media campaigns)
	Community and Systems Change	*Community and systems change* refers to changing "risk conditions" by altering the environmental context within which individuals and groups behave. This would include: • new or modified programs, policies, practices • changing physical or organizational infrastructure • changing overall rates of attitudes, beliefs or social norms
3	**Change Among Change Agents**	*Change among change agents* refers to documented changes in knowledge, attitudes, beliefs, or behavior among influential individuals or groups with the intent of diffusing similar changes to a broader community population. Change agents might include: • local opinion leaders or role models • business leaders or institutional gatekeepers • health or social service providers • specific community subgroups (e.g., HMO clients)
4	**Widespread Risk/Protective Behavior Change**	*Widespread risk/protective behavior change* refers to changing rates of behaviors that have been linked to health status, either as risk or protective factors, among a significant proportion of individuals in the identified community
5	**Health Disparity Reduction**	*Health disparity reduction* refers to narrowing gaps in health status relative to an appropriate referent, such as: • average rates for local, state, or national populations • relevent Healthy People 2010 objectives • other racial/ethnic groups at the local, state, or national level with rates that are the most favorable for health/quality of life

Source: Bobby Milstein MPH, Division of Adult and Community Health, National Centers For Disease Control and Prevention (NCCDPHP), National Centers for Disease Control and Prevention (CDC), 2002.

TABLE 6-4 REACH Logic Model Applied: Addressing Homeownership

Stage	Effect	Sample Case Example "Home Ownership Mobilization Effort (HOME)"
1	**Capacity Building**	• A team of neighborhood leaders and health experts produce a well-researched briefing report explaing the health and social benefits of home ownership • A community survey conducted in February 2002 reveals that Latinos and African Americans have disproportionately low rates of home ownership and high rates of excess disease and death, compared to either the state average or rates among local Caucasians • A coalition is formed among community residents, health professionals, area churches and faith groups, as well as public and private mortgage companies to address the issue of health and home ownership • A comprehensive community action plan is written to increase by 50% rates of minority home ownership by 2010 and to monitor changes in risk/protective behaviors as well as health status
2	**Targeted Action**	• 85 community education sessions (attended by 1,700 people) were conducted between October 2003 and May 2004 in area churches and faith groups explaining how to improve credit ratings • 5,000 self-study guides were distributed to community residents explaining how to improve credit rating and prepare for home ownership. • 10,000 calls to a toll-free home ownership hotline were answered between October 2002 and May 2003 • All staff members of area mortage companies were given in-service training on ways to improve social equity and prevent housing discrimination
	Community and Systems Change	• For the first time mortage companies, working with local leaders, established mortage services within area churches and faith groups • County health departments and hospitals collaborated with business leaders, banks, and financial services companies to create a combined "Financial, Physical, and Mental Health Improvement Campaign" • Average credit rating scores for members of the target community showed a statistically significant increase beginning in November 2003 • Rates of owner occupied housing in the target community began to increase in August 2005, and have steadily increased ever since • Activities of the neighborhood organization were revitalized due to the increasing number of new home owners; monthly meeting attendance increased by 300% between 2003 and 2005 • In 2005 the neighborhood organization negotiated with a local HMO to establish a satellite family health clinic, providing health education, risk assessment, screening, and immunization services
3	**Change Among Change Agents**	• Leaders from financial, health, faith, and business organizations publically rally around the HOME campaign • A front-page newspaper article is written profiling 5 families who purchased the homes that they've been renting for 6+ years • Attending housewarming parties of neighbors who purchased their own homes becomes a more frequent social event for adults and children

(continued)

TABLE 6-4 *(continued)*

Stage	Effect	Brief Definition "Home Ownership Mobilization Effort (HOME)"
4	Widespread Risk and Protective Behavior Change	• Average "readiness to change" scores began to increase among members of the target population for smoking cessation, physical activity, and five-a-day fruit and vegetable consumption by April 2006 • Rates of complete and on-time childhood immunization increased by 9.5% in the year after the satellite clinic opened • A random survey of neighborhood households conducted in October 2006 revealed that nearly 83% of women had received a mammogram and Pap smear within the past 2 years
5	Health Disparity Reduction	• Differences in health status indicators for Latinos and African Americans (compared to state averages) began to narrow in all six health priority areas.

Source: Bobby Milstein MPH, Division of Adult and Community Health, National Centers For Disease Control and Prevention (NCCDPHP), National Centers for Disease Control and Prevention (CDC), 2002.

among African American women,[89] and maternal nutrition, such as enhancing the consumption of food rich in vitamin A by women in Mali.[90] When carefully examined in the light of sound behavioral, social, and educational theory, information generated by these assessments will help uncover the most effective combination of educational, organizational, and policy approaches.

A Kentucky Case Study

A well-respected community intervention study illustrates how these principles of selection and rationale for multiple intervention strategies have been put into action with beneficial results. Kentucky is a rural state with high rates of mortality from cardiovascular disease and hypertension. As elsewhere, those with the lowest incomes and standards of living bear a disproportionate burden of those preventable deaths. In an attempt to address this public health problem, Kotchen and her colleagues[91] carried out a community-based study in two adjacent, sparsely populated, rural Kentucky counties. The combined population of the two intervention counties was approximately 32,000; many of those residents lived in relative isolation. The population was predominantly white, with adults having completed an average of 8 years of schooling. Coal mining was the major industry, but 20% of the men were unemployed, disabled, or retired.

Results.   After 5 years, comparisons of blood pressure outcomes of the intervention counties with those in a demographically similar control county revealed significant decreases in both systolic and diastolic blood pressure in both men and women in the two intervention counties. These decreases occurred despite 5-year increases in age; increased age tends to correlate with increased blood pressure. Results showed that the intervention influenced

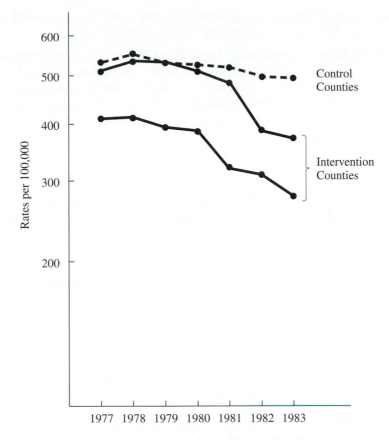

FIGURE 6-4   Three-year moving averages for cardiovascular disease death rates
by year for two intervention counties and one control county, shown here for the
Kentucky case study (1983 rates are based on 2-year moving averages). Control
county, • • • ; intervention counties, —. Significant decline in mortality is shown
for each of the intervention counties ($P < .0004$). Mortality trend coefficient for
the intervention counties is significantly different from that of the control county
($P < .04$).
*Source: "Impact of a Rural High Blood Pressure Control Program on Hypertension Control and Cardio-
vascular Disease Mortality," by J. M. Kotchen, H. E. McKean, S. Jackson-Thayer, et al., 1986, Journal of the
American Medical Association, 255, 2177–2182, with permission of the American Medical Association.*

improved medication compliance and, therefore, control over hypertensive disease. The most striking outcome was the evidence linking the intervention
effort to measurable declines in mortality. The 3-year moving averages for cardiovascular death rates, showing declines in the two intervention counties and
no change in the control county, are presented in Figure 6-4.

Strategy: Multiple Tactics.   What strategy did Kotchen and her co-workers
use to achieve such a dramatic public health success? First, they hired a full-
time coordinator who was enthusiastic and energetic and who knew the community and was respected in it. Then, using insights gained from a community

assessment, the implementers gradually began to implement a comprehensive strategy that included the following:

1. Establishing a "Community High Blood Pressure Control Program Council" with the charge to provide direction to community-wide activities aimed at controlling high blood pressure. Council membership included representatives from public schools, the Cooperative Agriculture Extension Service, local health departments, the local medical society, businesses, and interested citizens.
2. Using existing resources and organizations to play a major role in the delivery and promotion of the program.
3. Expanding an existing hypertension registry within the health department to include those people in the intervention counties identified as having high blood pressure. These individuals received periodic mailings of information on high blood pressure control and risk reduction, as well as descriptions of various community resources and activities of possible interest to them.
4. Using the local Cooperative Extension Service Nutrition Aide Program, already established in the community, as the channel to provide cardiovascular risk reduction assistance to those identified by their physicians as being in greatest need.
5. Developing a 4-H Club cardiovascular-risk-reduction program in which teenagers used peer-teaching techniques to present educational lessons to fifth graders.
6. Introducing a school blood pressure screening program into two high schools to identify adolescents with high blood pressure.
7. Creating a volunteer blood pressure screening and monitoring network in the smaller churches and in businesses in the area. This network provided outreach to individuals within these organizations and to the residents in close proximity.
8. Adding a work site high blood pressure screening program to an existing screening program provided by local health departments.
9. Securing the support of the local newspapers and radio stations as a means to reach the community as a whole with information about cardiovascular disease risk factors, benefits, and the feasibility of reducing those risks. While the project did purchase some air time, most of the media coverage was either aired as news or donated.
10. Implementing continuing education programs for nurses.
11. Providing health education programs to community clubs, homemaker groups, county fairs, health fairs, and large family reunions—a tradition in rural Kentucky.

The strategy taken in the Kentucky experience provides yet another reminder that the application of multiple intervention tactics is a hallmark of an effective community health program.

Implications for Practitioners.   The principal variable the program planners wanted to affect was the blood pressure level of those at highest risk. Yet, as evidenced by the list of activities, the program covered many other facets of the entire community, with special elements strategically aimed at those who were at high risk. How did they arrive at choosing that particular combination of strategies? The expansion and activation of the health department hypertension registry was an especially strategic method because it provided a channel through which direct contact could be made with those at highest risk.

One of the main reasons planners need to be thorough in the epidemiological, educational-ecological, and organizational assessment phases of PRE-CEDE is that such thoroughness increases the chances for detecting the critical targets for change. In the Kentucky case, the target behavior and its benefits are obvious; keeping blood pressure under control prevents strokes and saves lives. The predisposing, enabling, and reinforcing factors that influence behavior conducive to blood pressure control become the immediate targets that shape the program.

Recall from Chapter 3 the discussion of the broken-appointment cycle (Figure 3-5). The broken appointment ultimately resulted in a specific, problematic behavior: not taking medications. By retracing the loops in the cycle, we see a combination of affective, environmental, and behavioral barriers that would stop most of us in our tracks. The hypertension registry in the Kentucky program provided a means to make contact with, encourage, and reinforce people with known hypertension in using their medications and practicing risk-reduction behaviors, including coming into the health department or going to their physicians for blood pressure checks. Social support for their behavior came at three levels: (1) positive reinforcement from the nurses in the health department and from their physician; (2) the social norm endorsing risk reduction manifested by media, church activities, the cooperative extension service, school programs, community fairs, and family gatherings; and (3) messages in direct mail. Other community intervention projects have also found that mailings offer an inexpensive and effective follow-up method for high blood pressure screening programs.[92]

Implementation Lesson. Well-planned and grounded in sound theory, the Kentucky plan also gave thoughtful consideration to the practical implementation questions asked in PROCEED. This was not a program with "high-tech," expensive program components.[93] Although there were direct costs (materials, special training, travel) and indirect costs (volunteer time, participant time at screens), the costs for the intervention components were quite modest. This is not to suggest that they could be easily replicated—good planning and intervention are anything but easy—but cost should not be a prohibitive factor for replication of this kind of program in rural areas.

The Kentucky team also observed a change in the community physicians' perception that hypertension was indeed an important health problem. They also suspected that this change in physicians' perception was a precursor to the subsequent support of the program by the community physicians.[94] The project, and its multiple activities, apparently heightened physicians' attention to this modifiable public health problem. This, in turn, resulted in rather undramatic but critical changes in their interactions with patients regarding hypertension and cardiovascular disease risk factors.

COMMUNITY

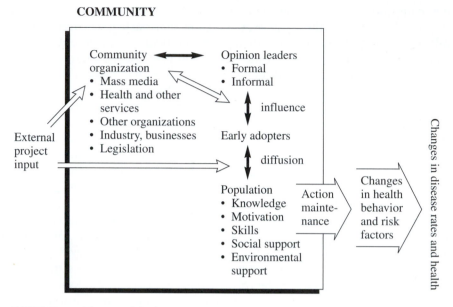

FIGURE 6-5 This model of community intervention in North Karelia reflects the
30 years of monitoring that have followed the initial program.
Source: "The Community-Based Strategy to Prevent Coronary Heart Disease: Conclusions From the 10
Years of the North Karelia Project," by P. Puska, A. Nissinen, J. Tuomilehto, et al., 1985, *Annual Reviews of
Public Health, 6,* 147–193. With permission, from the *Annual Reviews of Public Health,* Volume 6, © 1985, by
Annual Reviews.

The North Karelia Project

Those who plan comprehensive community health programs should find comfort in the fact that there were strong similarities between the Kentucky demonstration and one of the most thoroughly researched and well-documented
community-based intervention programs: the North Karelia, Finland Project.
The study was designed to determine whether important coronary heart disease risk factors (smoking, serum cholesterol, and elevated blood pressure)
could be reduced by multiple community-based interventions. The project
began in 1972 as an intervention trial comparing two provinces with populations over 200,000 each. North Karelia was the intervention community and
Kuopio was the reference or comparison.

The Design. Figure 6-5 presents a logic model or schema of the North Karelia
model that the investigators described as follows:

> The external input from the project affects the community both through mass
> media communication to the population at large (where its effect is mediated
> through interpersonal communication) and even more so through formal and
> informal opinion leaders acting as change agents to influence various aspects

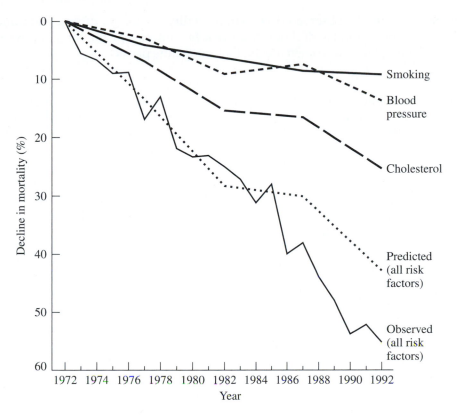

FIGURE 6-6 Observed and predicted decline in mortality from ischemic heart disease in men age 35–64 in Finland reflects the impact of the program.
Source: Reprinted from "Changes in Risk Factors Explain Changes in Mortality from Ischemic Heart Disease in Finland," by E. Vartiainen, et al., 1994, *British Medical Journal, 309*, p. 25. With permission of BMJ Publishing Group.

of community organization. This two-pronged approach is aimed at increasing knowledge, at persuasion, at teaching practical skills, and at providing the necessary social skills in the population. The acquisition and maintenance of new behaviors ultimately leads to a more favorable risk factor profile, reduced disease rates and improved health.[95]

The Impact.   Twenty-year results (1972–1992) revealed a decrease in coronary mortality of 52% in men and 68% in women for all of Finland.[96] The general trends in the risk factors between the intervention and comparison provinces over that same 20-year period are as follows. During the first 5 years, serum cholesterol and blood pressure levels fell more in North Karelia than in Kuopio; thereafter, both declined at a similar rate. Smoking declined more dramatically in North Karelia over the first decade. During the next 10 years, a small decline was noted in both areas. Figure 6-6 provides compelling evidence that the dramatic declines in risk factors among males from 1972 to 1992 were causally associated with the observed decline in mortality in Finland during that same 20-year period. Similar declines in all risk factors, except for smoking, were noted among Finnish women during that same time period.

Diffusion.   Initially undertaken as a community intervention research trial comparing two provinces within Finland, the intervention rapidly began to spread to the entire country. While we may never be able to account for all the forces that influence community change, the North Karelia experience offers health program planners some important lessons that we believe are generalizable. Early on in the project, research findings provided evidence that declines were occurring in risk factors within the North Karelia intervention population.[97] These findings generated a wide variety of national initiatives to promote heart health, including cholesterol guidelines endorsed by both the Finnish Cardiac Society and the Internists' Association. This was followed by national communication campaigns recommending screening and promoting public awareness of what constitutes a normal, healthy level of blood cholesterol. Interestingly, these health program efforts prompted a countercampaign by the dairy industry against the cholesterol hypothesis. The ensuing public debate elevated the national conversation about heart health and resulted in greater public awareness and interest in healthful nutrition. A marked decline in the consumption of milk fat and a corresponding increase in the consumption of vegetable oil followed this series of events.[98] Notice how these events follow the principles of diffusion theory discussed in Chapter 4.

When asked how he would explain the apparent success of the North Karelia Project, Pekka Puska, the project's director, said:

> Our philosophy was to get out into the community to meet and work with the people. We made special efforts to have meaningful discussions with representatives of businesses, the dairy industry, teachers, the media, and our colleagues in the health field. Our efforts went much deeper than television ads and posters. Although it was difficult work, everyone involved with the project followed this "boots deep in the mud" approach.[99]

Penetrate the Community.   Although on opposite sides of the world and working with markedly different cultures and political systems, the Kentucky and North Karelia projects used similar approaches to planning and organizing. Both actively engaged the community, used sound data assessment to frame their respective intervention strategies, and sought to strengthen environmental supports thorough organizational change and policies. These actions, inherent in PRECEDE-PROCEED, provided a sound foundation that led to dramatic public health benefits in both examples. In reviewing these two as well as other successful community projects documented in the literature, one finds that the capacity and ability to penetrate the community sufficiently to yield an outcome must accompany sound planning. In the Kentucky example, recall that they hired a full-time coordinator with energy and strong community ties. Recall as well Puska's description of working in the community "boots deep in the mud" with efforts that "went much deeper than television ads and posters."

One of the hallmarks of effective community health program interventions seems to be that they do more than scratch the surface of a community. The Bootheel Heart Health Project, a community-based cardiovascular risk-reduction project, targets a rural area in southeastern Missouri characterized by high rates of poverty and illiteracy, low education, high unemployment, and medical underservice. Five-year results indicate that the Bootheel intervention strategies have been responsible for favorable changes in levels of cholesterol, physical activity, and obesity.[100] Key to the success of the intervention was the formation and maintenance of countywide heart health coalitions. In a detailed account of how these coalitions sustained their functions over 5 years, Brownson and colleagues[101] provide added support for the view that undertakings are not only demanding but have to be taken slowly: "Each county had its own distinct character and infrastructure. Project staff found that our planned approach to development of these coalitions had to be tailored to the unique needs and interests of each group. Our 'plan' became more of an evolving process based on what we learned along the way." The level of effort and commitment implicit in these examples requires both skill and capacity: the technical, organizational, and interpersonal skills needed to communicate, listen, and negotiate with multiple stakeholders and interest groups and the capacity or resources to penetrate below the surface of the community and sustain the effort long enough to make an impact.

Never Promise Too Much Too Soon.   But how long is "long enough to make an impact?" In Kentucky, Missouri, and North Karelia, some results were detected within 5 years—some would say this is "quick" by health program standards. In North Karelia, however, the most dramatic effects accumulated over a 20-year period. These time frames suggest that in addition to skill and capacity, one needs patience to stay the course of a well-planned intervention. In our enthusiasm, we sometimes run the risk of promising too much, too soon. As PRECEDE-PROCEED illustrates, however, there are few direct, simple paths to lasting change—whether this change is to occur in individual behavior or in larger political and social systems.

Those reporting on the effectiveness of community-wide intervention approaches urge planners to make every effort to ensure that they establish achievable outcome goals within realistic time frames.[102] Figure 6-7 provides a graphic reminder of this counsel. It shows the conceptual planning framework for the Kaiser Family Foundation's Community Health Promotion Grant Program,[103] which was based partly on PRECEDE-PROCEED. First, note how examples of educational, organizational, and policy tactics are strategically matched to benchmarks positioned between the health goals identified in the far right box and the box to the left labeled "health promotion builds." Note

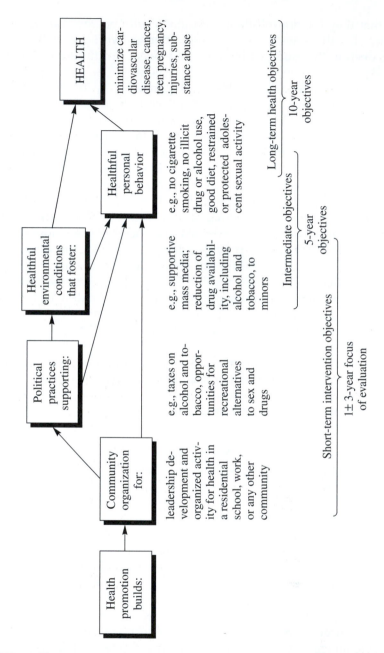

FIGURE 6-7 The sequence of relationships from community health promotion to health outcomes was reflected in the model for a national community health promotion grant program.

Source: Adapted from Kaiser Family Foundation, *Strategic Plan for Health Promotion Program* (Menlo Park, CA: Henry J. Kaiser Family Foundation, 1989) and from "The Future of Public Health: Prospects in the United States for the 1990s," by L. Breslow, 1990, *Annual Review of Public Health, 11,* 20. With permission, from the *Annual Review of Public Health,* Volume 11, © 1989, by Annual Reviews.

also how the multiple methods, expressed in terms of short-term, intermediate, and long-term objectives, have been bracketed into reasonable projected time frames. Encouraging results from many community studies offer a clear lesson: To achieve sustainable programs, we must be willing to get "boots deep in the mud" while keeping a realistic eye on the distant horizon, be that 5 or 25 years.

Selecting Multiple Strategies

For decades, many have tried to translate the intervention ideas developed in scientific, university-led community trials into practical, community-led applications in the field. Some of those highly controlled experiments would not translate easily into practice because of the artificial circumstances under which the experimental trials were conducted, or the unrepresentative populations in which they were tested.[104] Many of those translation efforts, however, have generated practical tools to help planners identify and apply multiple strategies for intervention. A few are reviewed here.

Ideas From PATCH. In 1983, the Centers for Disease Control (CDC) developed a program called the Planned Approach to Community Health (PATCH).[105] PATCH is grounded in the diagnostic-assessment planning principles of PRECEDE and is designed additionally to translate the complex methods of community health analysis and intervention to communities via the state health agency. All PATCH training goes on at the community level, in vivo, and involves the collaborative efforts of health program staff from the local and state health departments and CDC, as well as local community participants. Within this partnership context, methods in community mobilization, assessment, and intervention are covered in considerable detail. It takes about a year and a half for a PATCH community to move from the community mobilization and assessment process to the point of the first intervention.

Based on a 1992–1993 survey of local health departments in the United States conducted by the National Association of City and County Health Officers (NACCHO),[106] 239 local health agencies (12% of those responding) had used or applied the planning principles of the PATCH program. For example, the Adams County Health Department in Quincy, Illinois has a specific, standing PATCH program that was established in 1990 with a mission "to provide a process for community collaboration to reduce health disparities, disease, and increase the span of healthy life." The PATCH core committee consists of 20 leaders who represent all segments of the community including hospitals, schools, city government, social service agencies, churches, and many others.

There is a core committee consisting of a group of 25 residents who represent a cross section of public, private, and voluntary institutions and organizations with a stake in the health of the county; the core committee meets three times a year. There are also smaller "health issue specific" subcommittees that meet more frequently as needed. Since its inception in 1990, the Adams County PATCH program has undertaken successful, comprehensive programs to reduce community health disparities, improve access to mental health services,

BOX 6-4 Applications of PRECEDE by the Adams County PATCH Program

Social Assessment
- The Core Committee coordinates survey of parents regarding their needs for and view of services in the community.
- Focus Groups at Indian Hills—A subcommittee of PATCH conducted an assessment of the assets of people who live in a low-income housing complex.
- Wellness coalition completes two Adams County studies: (1) the perceived barriers, benefits, and motivating factors related to physical activity and sedentary lifestyle, (2) nutrition practices and attitudes in low-income families.
- Teen sexual behavior and pregnancy data study conducted.
- PATCH completed a study of the issues related to alcohol use, including use of a geographic information system to analyze local alcohol outlets and demographic information.
- Adams County United Way Survey—2001–2003 needs assessment of residents, key informant/leader survey, collection/assessment of key social community indicators, including an inventory of community assets.

Epidemiological Diagnosis
- PATCH engages in small-area analysis of local epidemiological data to determine priority health problems comparing Adams County indicators with those of state-wide Illinois and national *Healthy People 2010*.

Behavioral and Environmental Diagnosis
- PATCH has utilized a county-level analysis of Behavioral Risk Factor data for 12 years (see Leading Health Indicators in *Healthy People 2010*). PATCH has conducted three Behavior Risk Factor surveys. The first was in 1991 administered to 847 county residents, the second in 1997 with 401 county residents, and the third in 2001 with 407 county residents.

Educational and Organizational Assessment
- Needs assessment of oral health needs in the community. The assessment resulted in the opening of the Adams County Health Department Community Dental Clinic in 1995.
- When the largest local medical care provider stopped taking new Medicaid clients, PATCH organized a group to begin working on a federally qualified health center.
- Assessment conducted on access-to-care issues faced by the low-income population in Adams County.

reduce teen smoking, develop policy changes to create a smoke-free environment, and institute environmental changes to reduce underage drinking.[107] Box 6-4 presents specific examples of how the phases of PRECEDE covered in Chapters 2 through 4 guided the actions taken by the Adams County PATCH program and its subcommittees.

TABLE 6-5 The intervention planning matrix shown here was used in the community intervention handbooks and in the PATCH program sponsored by the U.S. Centers for Disease Control and Prevention

| | SETTING | | | |
Target	School	Work Site	Health-Care Institution	Community
Individuals	Students' health behaviors	Employees' health behaviors	Patients' behaviors	Community residents' health behaviors
Organizations	School policies, programs, practices, and facilities to foster healthful behaviors by students	Work site policies, programs, practices, and facilities to foster healthful behaviors by employees	Institution policies, programs, practices, and facilities to foster healthful behaviors by patients	Policies, programs, practices, and facilities of community-serving organizations, and institutions to foster healthful behaviors by community residents
Governments	Legislation, regulation, services, and resources affecting schools to foster healthful behaviors by students	Legislation, regulation, services, and resources affecting work sites to foster healthful behaviors by employees	Legislation, regulation, services, and resources affecting institutions to foster healthful behaviors by patients	Legislation, regulation, services, and resources affecting community sites to foster healthful behaviors by community residents

Source: "Community Intervention Handbooks for Comprehensive Health Promotion Programming," by S. G. Brink, D. Simons-Morton, G. Parcel, and K. Tiernan, 1988, *Family and Community Health, 11*, 28–35.

Intervention Matrix.   Table 6-5 provides a practical way to envision the strategic coordination of a multilevel intervention program. Schools, work sites, health care institutions, and the community appear as the general settings. Once these settings have been precisely identified (the specific schools, work sites, clinics, hospitals, etc.), planners might expand the variety of settings, depending on the problem in question. For example, in many areas, exercise facilities,[108] religious institutions,[109] health fairs,[110] bars and restaurants,[111] and grocery stores[112] can be useful settings for health program activity. In rural areas, outreach to the home may be necessary.[113] To see the relationships between the earlier planning principles of PRECEDE and PROCEED and the selection of intervention strategies, planners can work through an exercise that leads to an integrated summary chart similar to the one characterized in Table 6-5. In this example, the PATCH community chose the reduction of motor vehicle fatalities as the health problem and seat-belt nonuse and driving under the influence of alcohol or drugs as the primary behaviors; poorly marked and lighted streets and seat-belt laws that were unenforced were the primary environmental problems. Table 6-6 combines the intervention variables of site and actions for interventions with diagnostic information generated from the Precede process and from theory—in this case, the theory of stages of change described in detail in Chapter 4.[114]

Matrix techniques have several uses. They can help one to take an inventory of existing resources or to set priorities for new strategies or for fundraising where resources are lacking. They can serve as heuristic devices to expand the perspective of planners with limited experience in community work. Often, a talented practitioner hired to coordinate a community health program brings mostly experience gained in a given setting, perhaps in schools or working with clinic patients. Working through and understanding the rationale of intervention matrices can help call attention to the need for regulatory or media approaches that otherwise may not have come to mind.

Intervention Mapping.   In their conceptualization of intervention mapping, Bartholomew, Parcel, Kok, and Gottlieb have expanded on the matrix approach.[115] The process is designed to help fill a gap they had observed in health promotion practice: specific guidance in helping planners translate the findings from their social, epidemiological, educational, ecological, administrative, organizational, and policy assessments into theoretically sound and appropriate interventions. Intervention mapping is analogous to geographic mapping in that once planners locate where they are going (program objectives), they are guided by clear signposts in the form of instructive diagrams and matrices that incorporate the outputs of the assessment process with sound theory. Figure 6-8 illustrates how intervention mapping is integrated into the overall process that includes needs assessment, evaluation, and implementation. It begins in the upper right-hand corner of the figure with "needs assessment" steps consistent with the early phases of the Precede-Proceed Model. The five steps of intervention mapping are listed under "outcomes" and the tasks required to effectively carry out each step are listed next to bullets to the right.

The matrices used in the process provide planners with a specificity they will find most useful. For example, Table 6-7 provides a hypothetical example that focuses on the role of the parents who have children with asthma. This is the kind of matrix that would be created under the fourth bullet point for the first step in the mapping process in Figure 6-8.

Just as planners must take care not to establish unrealistic time and outcome expectations, neither should they view intervention mapping as a quick and easy way to identify interventions. As Bartholomew and her colleagues point out, unlike a road map, intervention mapping is an iterative process where the planner returns to early planning steps as insights are gained, and as the implications of early decisions on subsequent steps are realized.

TABLE 6-6 Summary matrix for planning community health promotion programs

Health Problem: To reduce motor vehicle fatalities

Behavioral Problems: Driving under the influence
                    Not using seat belts

Environmental Problems: Poorly marked and poorly lighted streets
                       Poorly enforced seat-belt law

	INTERVENTION FACTORS		DIAGNOSTIC FACTORS	
Strategies	Site	Action for Intervention	Contributing Factors	Adoption Stage
BEHAVIORAL PROBLEMS **Driving under the influence**				
Lobby concerning state liquor laws	C	LR	E	Sk
Substance-free high-school graduation party	S	En	P/E/R	Aw/Sk/R
Poster contest in middle schools	S	Ed	P/R	Aw/R
Bartender education	W	Ed	E	Sk
Substance-free events for teens	C/S	En	P/E/R	R/Mn
Education and community work assignments for those convicted of driving under the influence	H/C	Ed	E/R	Sk/Mn
News media events	C	Ed	P/E	Aw/Mn
Not using seat belts				
Poster contest in elementary school	S	Ed	P/R	Aw/R
Seat-belt use required in company car	W	LR	E	Sk
Buckle-up contest in high school	S	Ed	P/R	Mo/Mn
Buckle-up signs on major roads	C	Ed		Aw/R
Seat belts in school buses	C	En	E	Sk
Installation Saturday (to install seat belts on cars lacking them)	C	En	E	Sk
News media events	C	Ed	P/E	Aw/Mn
ENVIRONMENTAL PROBLEMS				
Conduct and publicize findings from study of hazards in areas of high fatality	C	En/Ed	E	Aw
Lobby local activities for improved markings and lighting	C	LR/Ed	E	Mn/Sk
Pressure local authorities to enforce seat belt law	C	LR/Ed	E	Mn/Sk

Note: Letters denote the following. *Site:* C = community, H = health care, W = work site, S = school.
Action for intervention: Ed = educational, En = environmental, LR = legislative/regulatory. *Contributing factors:* E = enabling, P = predisposing, R = reinforcing. *Adoption stage:* Aw = awareness, Mn = Maintenance, Mo = motivation, Sk = skills.

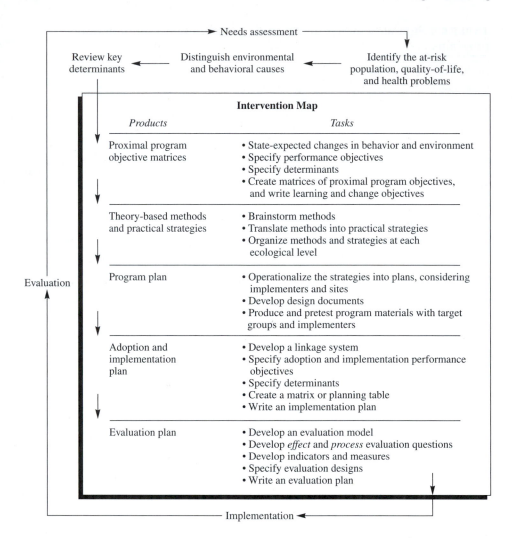

FIGURE 6-8 Steps, tasks, and products of the intervention mapping process.
Source: L. K. Bartholomew, G. S. Parcel, G. Kok, & N. Gottlieb, (2001). *Intervention Mapping.* Mountain View: Mayfield Publishing.

Reaching the Masses

It is almost impossible to find a community intervention program devoid of one or a combination of the following mass media strategies: Internet, television, radio, newspapers, magazines, outdoor advertising, transit advertising, direct mail, telemarketing, and special promotional events. The application of mass media techniques is second only to the activation of community participation through community organization and coalition building as a critical element in community intervention. The literature is abundant with detailed accounts of (1) large-scale national or regional public health applications,[116]

TABLE 6-7 This sample Matrix of Proximal Program Objectives at the Individual Level applies to parents of children with asthma

Parent Performance Objectives	Behavioral Capability	Self-Efficacy
	DETERMINANTS	
1. Monitors environment and circumstances to anticipate risk of asthma attack	Recognizes signs of impending attack, including environmental triggers	Feels confident in recognizing signs and environmental triggers that could trigger child's asthma
2. Effective communication with health care provider	Enters health care provider's office with a goal and technique to promote discourse and information gathering	Feels confident in developing goals for gathering information

Parent Performance Objectives	Outcome Expectancy	Rewards
	DETERMINANTS	
1. Monitors environment and circumstances to anticipate risk of asthma attack	Expects that recognizing signs and environmental triggers will lead to better asthma management	Parent sees that child is able to participate in wider range of activities due to better asthma management
2. Effective communication with health care provider	Expects that having a communication goal will increase effectiveness of interactions with health care provider	Health care provider comments on increased effectiveness of interactions. Parent feels they have better information about child's asthma

Source: Adapted from "Intervention Mapping: A Process for Developing Theory-Based Health Education Programs," by L. K. Bartholomew, G. S. Parcel, and G. Kok, 1998, *Health Education and Behavior* 25, 545–563. With permission.

(2) applications at the community level,[117] and (3) the theoretical rationale for planning and implementing mass media strategies.[118]

This explosion of interest in mass media techniques by health program planners is an international phenomenon that in part confirms Manoff's early insight about the power and utility of mass media in health programs. He identified seven beneficial aspects of mass media:[119]

1. *Mass media carry special authority.* That which is seen in the cinema or on television, heard on the radio, or read in the paper has special impact.
2. *Mass media ensure control over the message.* Since the content and tone of the health messages is critical, the most desirable means of communication is the one that guarantees that whatever it is, whenever it is communicated, and from whomever it comes, the message will stay the same.

3. *Media lend cumulative impact to the message.* The whole program is more than the arithmetic sum of the parts; mass media create a communications synergism.
4. *Mass media reach the masses.*
5. *Mass media telescope time.* They have maximum further/faster capacity.
6. *Mass media influence other major audiences in important ways while directing a message to the target audience.* Even though a seat-belt message may be targeted at middle-aged men, others exposed to the message (women, children, co-workers) can serve to reinforce the message or may themselves be influenced to consider action.
7. *The mass media campaign enhances all other methods employed in health education.* It provides an umbrella for attention to the issue.

Those characteristics were given a substantial credibility boost by the recommendations from the Community Guide to Preventive Services regarding effective strategies for increasing access to breast and cervical cancer screening in communities. In spite of the evidence showing the benefits of appropriate periodic exams for those site-specific cancers, utilization rates in the United States are below the recommended levels established by the *Healthy People 2010* objectives. Based on systematic reviews of scientific literature, a team of experts deemed "multi-channel educational interventions (including mass media) with increased access to screening for breast and cervical cancer to be effective." The community guide also cited strong evidence supporting the effectiveness of multicomponent mass media for increasing the cessation and reducing the initiation of smoking.[120]

Segmenting. Acknowledging the importance of coordinating multiple intervention strategies, Preston, Baranowski, and Higginbotham[121] have devised a practical scheme to aid practitioners in the selection of those strategies. Using diffusion and adoption of innovations as their primary theoretical base, they begin by identifying eight generic points of community intervention. Table 6-8 illustrates the eight points of intervention in the context of a dietary change example. These points move from methods employed primarily for heightening awareness, through those that can transmit messages about reasons for change, to potential early adopters and eventually to skills enhancement and changes in community standards.

The different points of intervention will have varying effects on persons at different stages of the community adoption process, based on diffusion theory categories, which align with needed emphasis on predisposing factors (for early adopters), reinforcing factors (for early majority), and enabling factors (for late majority).[122] Attention also must be paid to the sequencing and timing of those points of intervention. In the Proceed process highlighted in previous chapters, time was a critical element in assessing the barriers to and facilitators of program implementation. The multiple interventions of a program do not explode onto the scene at once. Based on a variety of factors, including the theoretical underpinnings of the program, the various intervention components need to be timed to address the strategic objectives of the program. In Table 6-9,

TABLE 6-8 Types of intervention and segments of the community likely to be reached

Types of Community Intervention	Early Adopters	Early Majority	Late Majority
1. Major media			
Newspaper	X	X	
Radio	X	X	
Cablevision and television	X	X	X
2. Minor media			
Church newsletters	X	X	X
Employer newsletters	X	X	
Customer bill inserts	X	X	
3. Institutional intervention (supermarkets, grocery stores, restaurants, fast-food stores)			
Point of purchase information	X	X	X
Making more food available	X	X	X
Grocery bag inserts	X	X	X
Taste testing	X	X	X
4. Special events			
Health screening events in churches, grocery stores	X	X	X
Cooking contests	X	X	
5. Existing formal social structures and networks			
Occupation-based programs	X	X	
Churches	X	X	
Community, fraternities, sororities			X
Medical care delivery	X		
Schools	X	X	X
6. Existing informal social networks			
Living room sessions (education and taste testing) with family-invited participants (Tupperware Party concept)		X	X
Events in service centers, beauty and barber shops, neighborhood action committees		X	X
Training community lay health advisors		X	X
7. Center-based programs			
Test kitchen taste testing of new versions of recipes	X	X	X
8. Created social networks			
Developing a ward or block system		X	X

Source: "Orchestrating the Points of Community Intervention," by M. A. Preston, T. Baranowski, and J. C. Higginbotham, 1988–1989, *International Quarterly of Community Health Education, 9,* 11–34. Reprinted with permission.

TABLE 6-9 Timeline for intervention strategy

Type of Intervention	Six Months Prior to Intervention						Six Months of Intervention					
	1	2	3	4	5	6	1	2	3	4	5	6
Center based												
Test kitchen	P	P	P	P	P	P						
Ongoing behavior, grocery stores												
Food purchasing		P	P	P	E	E	E	E	E	E	E	
Shelf labeling					P	P	I	I	I	I	I	I
Food tasting	P	P	P	P	P	P	I	I	I	I	I	I
Ongoing behavior, restaurants												
Additional menu selections	P	P	P	P	P	E	E	E	E	E	E	E
Menu labeling						I	I	I	I	I	I	I
Major media												
Newspaper						P	A	N	N	N	N	N
Radio						P	A	N	N	N	N	N
Television						P	A	N	N	N	N	N
Minor media												
Paycheck inserts						P	A	A	A			
Newsletter notices						P	A	N	N	N	N	N
Screening handouts						P	A	A				
Grocery bag stuffers						P	A	A	A	A	A	A
Special events												
Cooking contests						P	A	A				
Public health screenings						P	A	A				
Formal structures												
Group intervention	P	P	P	P	P	P	B	B	B	B		
Informal structures												
Group network intervention	P	P	P	P	P	P				B	B	B

Note: P = preparation, A = public awareness (media), N = notification (media), I = information dissemination, E = enabling behavior changes, B = behavior change (educational sessions).
Source: "Orchestrating the Points of Community Intervention," by M. A. Preston, T. Baranowski, and J. C. Higginbotham, 1988–1989, *International Quarterly of Community Health Education, 9,* 11–34. Reprinted with permission.

Preston and her colleagues project a timeline for the implementation of interventions, again using dietary change as the example.

The timing of the intervention strategy, therefore, takes into consideration four general purposes for the program: public awareness, the introduction of information and reasons for change into the established social system for earlier adopters, the enhancement of skills needed to make desired changes, and the modeling of new behaviors for later adopters.

Note how staging intervention components in terms of their timing for intervention addresses the central concern raised in DiClemente and Pro-

TABLE 6-10 Broad categories of the stages of change and the corresponding examples of media messages provided by role models on television in the *A Su Salud* project in southwest Texas

Three Stages of Smoking Cessation	Examples Provided by Role Models
I. Preparation	
Information about smoking: decisional balance	"I decided to quit because I was pregnant. It's OK to risk my own life, but not my unborn child."
Dissatisfaction with dependence on cigarettes	"I wanted to be here [living] to see my children grown."
II. Taking action	
Positive efficacy expectations	"My husband supported my decision and he joined me in the decision to stop smoking."
Social support and reinforcement for nonsmoking	"I physically feel better, less fatigued, less tense. I feel better."
Reevaluation of self	
III. Maintenance	
Increased efficacy expectations for specific situations	"In social situations, I would review the reasons why I quit smoking. . . ."
Avoiding stimuli associated with smoking	"When nervous due to not smoking, I would talk to someone or eat a piece of candy."
Acquisition of new coping responses	
General social support for stress-coping	

Source: "Mass Media Campaign: *A Su Salud,*" by A. G. Ramirez and A. L. McAlister, 1988, *Preventive Medicine, 17,* 608–621. Reprinted with permission.

chaska's stages of change model. Working with individuals in one-to-one counseling or teaching relationships makes such staging relatively easy, because the readiness of the learner can be readily detected or inferred. But in community health programs, generalizations must be made about where the population lies on the continuum or, more accurately, how the population distributes over the stages of change at a given time in the course of the program.

A Su Salud. *A Su Salud* ("To Your Health") was designed as a mass media health promotion program to reduce selected chronic disease risk factors among Mexican Americans in southwest Texas.[123] The smoking-cessation element of this program provides an excellent example of how one can use theory and data in the planning process. Data generated from formative evaluation methods, especially focus groups, were combined with two theories: (1) Bandura's conceptualization of social modeling and social support[124] and (2) the previously cited stages of change theory.

In developing the community organization components of the program, planners mobilized the community supports by actively involving community groups and institutions. Table 6-10 summarizes the three general stages of change applied specifically to smoking cessation; it also offers examples of role model messages for each stage as developed in the mass media component of

A Su Salud. Developers recruited Mexican Americans enrolled in smoking-cessation programs and had them present messages in their own words. Then, scripts were developed for narrators to highlight these messages.

Social Marketing: Square One for a Campaign.   Most definitions of *social marketing* characterize it as a system or process, using both qualitative and quantitative data and information about a given population, to bring about the adoption or acceptability of ideas or practices in that population. Lefebvre and Flora[125] add specificity to this general description when they describe the social marketing process in terms of eight specific components.

1. *Consumer orientation.* A focus on the needs and interests of the target population
2. *Voluntary exchanges.* The assumption that adoption of new ideas or practices involves the voluntary exchange of some resource (money, services, time) for a perceived benefit
3. *Audience analysis and segmentation.* The application of qualitative research methods to obtain information on the needs and special characteristics of the target population that has been segmented to permit a more specific message
4. *Formative research.* Message design and pretesting of materials to be used in the campaign
5. *Channel analysis.* The identification of the various channels of communication, including media outlets, community organizations, businesses, and "life path points"
6. *Marketing mix.* The process of identifying the product, price, place, and promotional characteristics of intervention planning and implementation
7. *Process tracking.* A system to track the delivery of the program and to assess trends in the use of services, resources, facilities, or information sources provided, promoted, or subsidized by the program; a critical evaluation tool
8. *Management.* A commitment to a coordinated management system to ensure quality of planning, implementation, and feedback

Quantitative health data, so essential in measuring the severity of a problem and in assessing the effects of a program, are rarely available to give the planner insights into why a target population resists the adoption of certain actions. It is the consumer-oriented aspect of the social marketing process that makes it so complementary to epidemiological data and, therefore, so relevant to planning an intervention.

Take It Outside.   A population-wide health promotion media campaign was carried out by the Kansas Health Foundation (KHF).[126] In 1997, the foundation's board approved a campaign taking a stand against secondhand smoke. In Sedgwick County, where the city of Wichita and the foundation headquarters are located, surveys showed that 40% of smokers had children living at home. These data, coupled with a desire to bring new information into the tobacco control debate, led the foundation, in cooperation with multiple local stakeholder groups, to focus the campaign on the dangers of secondhand smoke for children.

Focus-group data on smokers, combined with information gained through visiting Internet chat rooms, revealed that smokers had heard anti-smoking messages so often that the messages did not register. In response, the campaign specifically avoided asking smokers to quit, not to anger them. Instead, the specific call to action was "If you choose to smoke, *take it outside.*" This was a deliberate attempt to emphasize the smokers' choice and control over their behavior and to make the requested action easier to accept and implement. The campaign ran a gauntlet of both anticipated and unantici-pated difficulties before its launch date. The latter included negative reactions from focus groups, which led to the creation of new ads within a month of the launch date. Among the anticipated problems was a series of attacks from the tobacco industry, which targeted not only the foundation but many of its grantees.

To preempt controversy, the foundation reached out to key leaders in the community before the official launch date. The governor of Kansas not only joined a news conference with foundation staff but also participated by appear-ing in one of the later television spots. In a stroke of good fortune, a news con-ference to announce the campaign and emphasize children's health coincided with news of the impending tobacco settlements in states throughout the coun-try. Materials were also mailed to child care providers and a second news con-ference was held at a day care center.

The campaign included television and radio ads as well as billboards throughout Wichita. The goal was to reach 99% of the market with a frequency of 36 exposures in 6 months. In addition, nontraditional media—Internet ban-ners and the sides of buses—helped spread the message. Each ad featured a toll-free number; callers received packets with brochures and resources on smoking cessation. These calls averaged 40 per week, for a total of 1,492. After the pilot, surveys demonstrated that awareness of secondhand smoke as harm-ful had increased 14%, and 18% more smokers agreed that it was not too much trouble to "take it outside." In terms of smoking behaviors, surveys had consis-tently shown that 25% of Wichita's population were smokers. At the cam-paign's midpoint, 19% said they were smokers. To substantiate this drop, another survey with a larger sample was conducted—it showed the same per-centage. At the end of the campaign, 17% of respondents said they were smok-ers. Even if these respondents were not being truthful about their smoking behavior, the survey may at least have documented that the ads had helped create an environment in which people considered smoking unacceptable.

Examples From Developing Countries.   Considerable attention was paid to the creative use of social marketing methods in the major cardiovascular com-munity intervention trials. The effective application of social marketing to health programs is by no means limited to affluent "media markets," however. Brieger, Ramakrishna, and Adeniyi[127] applied social marketing research in an

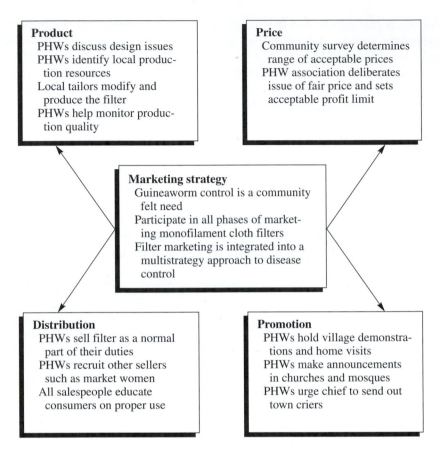

FIGURE 6-9 Community involvement in social marketing of monofilament nylon-cloth water filters for guineaworm control in Idere, Nigeria.
Source: "Community Involvement in Social Marketing: Guineaworm Control," by W. R. Brieger, J. Ramakrishna, and J. D. Adeniyi, 1987–1988, *International Quarterly of Community Health Education, 8,* 297–316. Reprinted with permission.

especially creative way. In their health program, aimed at controlling dracunculiasis (guinea worm) in Idere, Nigeria, they combined key principles of community participation with social marketing strategies to increase the use of filters as a means of protection against this infection. They took steps to include in the planning process people from the participating towns and hamlets. Based on results from qualitative research, including focus groups, a program was established wherein local tailors made the cloth used to filter the water, other community members helped debate the price, and public health workers (PHWs) and others became salespeople. Figure 6-9 illustrates their model of integrating community involvement with the application of social marketing principles.

We can also point to many other examples of social marketing strategies effectively applied in developing countries. A University of South Carolina team together with Ivory Coast collaborators[128] used focus groups as a cost-effective way to obtain rich and valid information that led to improvements in controlling childhood diarrhea and malaria in sub-Saharan Africa. Another group[129] used social marketing research to increase contraceptive use in Bangladesh. Gordon[130] showed that the coordination of a national media campaign with a well-planned community intervention effort effectively addressed the problem of dengue fever in the Dominican Republic.

So Much to Know and Do, So Little Time!

Wherever they are on the globe, program planners face the never-ending challenge of staying abreast of emerging methods of developing community-based programs using a wide range of strategies including those reviewed in this chapter. Developing a trusting contact with those whose culture, language, or beliefs differ from one's own is a complex task that takes resources: time, money, and skill. Planners must argue and budget for the first two; they must *possess* the third.

Unfortunately, gaps remain in our ability to reach individuals at high risk and in need of preventive services and education. In the past, even when we were able to reach populations in need, our methods of communications too often proved less than effective. For the most part, these gaps were not due to a lack of desire and effort to close them. They were the function of glaring deficiencies in communication and education training and the resources available to health organizations. Clearly, that is changing. Globally, research that produces methodological innovations that are evidence-based continues to accelerate. At the same time, there are signs that the long-standing rhetorical support for health promotion and disease prevention is gaining, albeit slowly, much needed fiscal support from public, philanthropic, and the business sectors. Ironically, this upsurge of innovation and support adds to the complexity facing planners of community programs because what is already an information-intensive process is becoming more intensive.

Fortunately, there is good evidence that technology can help turn the burden of that intensity into a practical and efficient asset to the planning process. The Community Tool Box (CTB) is an example of a technological innovation that is especially well suited to help with the task of community health planning. Developed by Fawcett and his colleagues in 1995,[131] the CTB is a well established, online source of very practical technical assistance offering users detailed, step-by-step guidelines on techniques and skills that are applicable to every phase of the Precede-Proceed Model, including evaluation. It provides over 6,000 pages of information that are maintained and regularly updated by the Work Group on Health Promotion and Community Development at the University of Kansas in Lawrence, Kansas (U.S.A). Users may guide their own searches for information and print information from the database within the CTB or use updated hyperlinks as gateways to a wide range of credible databases and networks, including those established by the Centers for Disease Control and Prevention.

SUMMARY

Practitioners who base their community intervention planning on the Precede-Proceed Model (1) build from a base of community ownership of the problems and the solutions; (2) base program decisions on sound theory, meaningful data, and local experience; (3) have an evaluation plan in place to monitor program progress and detect program effects; (4) know what types of interventions work best for specific populations and circumstances; and (5) have an organizational and advocacy plan to orchestrate multiple intervention strategies into a complementary, cohesive program. This chapter has emphasized community participation and has distinguished between interventions in communities and community interventions. Some guidelines were offered for engaging the realities of community politics, including practical suggestions for the formation, implementation, and maintenance of community coalitions. The importance of applying multiple strategies was highlighted in a review of well-documented, community-based health programs with a caveat: Don't underestimate the magnitude of the task and fall prey to setting unrealistic outcomes and time frames. Finally, practical guidelines for selecting multiple intervention tactics were offered, followed by examples of successful media and social marketing applications in communities.

EXERCISES

1. What is the difference between community intervention and interventions in a community? Why is it important to make that distinction?
2. Based on your interpretation of forces of change that occurred in Mississippi from 1965–1981, what should planners look for over the long term as a result of well-planned community-based interventions?
3. What is the paradox that major university-based community intervention trials have faced?
4. Consider any one of the following problems as the focus of a planned program effort: alcohol-related injuries and death, dracunculiasis, smoking, or AIDS. Name two political issues that planners might face if they were to try a community intervention in *your hometown*. Explain how you would keep those issues from becoming a problem.
5. Explain why the Kentucky program worked. Explain why it worked, using social cognitive theory as your explanation.
6. Apply the social marketing steps and the intervention matrix to your own program plan.
7. What is it about a planning process like the Precede-Proceed Model that would help planners in their efforts to address "wicked problems"?
8. Suppose someone said to you, "Marketing is Madison Avenue glitz, great for selling cars and beer, but there's no place for it in health science. Besides, it just focuses on the individual, which is victim blaming!" How would you respond?

NOTES AND CITATIONS

1. *Definition and meanings of community:* Green & Ottoson, 1999, pp. 40–41.

2. *Sense of community:* Israel, 1985, p. 72. *Sense of community* is defined and illustrated in J. Allen & Allen, 1990; Chavis & Wandersman, 1990; Kegler & Wyatt, 2003; McMillan & Chavis, 1986.

3. *Formal versus informal community political influence:* E. R. Brown, 1984. Brown's phases of development in community health care policy were later applied in the development of indicators of community action to promote "social health." See Rothman & Brown, 1989.

4. *Another dimension of* community *is the community of interest:* National advocacy organizations such as Public Voice for Food Policy, the Smoking Control Advocacy Resource Center, Americans for Nonsmokers' Rights, Mothers Against Drunk Driving, and others all relate to a constituency of concerned citizens scattered around a country. Voluntary health associations and professional associations, similarly, advocate and develop health promotion initiatives through their networks of members and chapters. Each of these represents a community in every sense except for the locality criterion applied in this chapter. Some can support local initiatives. Much of the discussion in this chapter, however, can be applied to organizing through these interest groups on a state, national, or international scale. For more on national advocacy groups and their methods, see Pertschuk & Erikson, 1987; Pertschuk, 2001; Wallack, Dorfman, Jernigan, & Themba, 1993.

5. *We have purposefully separated community-based from national, provincial, or state levels, but* the positive, complementary effect that national and regional policies and campaigns have on local efforts should not be minimized. In fact, where appropriate and feasible, community-based programs should try to time their interventions to coordinate with larger population campaigns to obtain the media benefits as well as other resources that support the campaign. See, for example, Ling & Glantz, 2002; Shoveller & Green 2002. Most of the principles and methods that apply to community health promotion can be applied with adaptation at the state-provincial or national level. See Arkin, 1990. For synthesis of PRECEDE-PROCEED with other models in guiding media campaigns, see Flynn, et al., 1992; Green & McAlister, 1984; Worden, Flynn, et al., 1988; Worden, Solomon, Flynn, et al., 1990.

6. *The ideal of community:* Morone, 1990, p. 7.

7. *Studies supporting the ideals and principles:* Berkman & Breslow, 1983; Berkowitz, 2001; Farquhar, 1978; Goodman, Wandersman, et al., 1996; Holder, Gruenwald, et al., 2000.

8. *Community health demonstration successes:* Farquhar, Fortmann, et al., 1990; Kottke, Puska, et al., 1985; Lastikainen, Delong, et al., 2002; Puska, 2000a.

9. *The trade-off of "most good for the most people" versus reduction of disparities by focus on high risk:* Kottke, Puska, et al., 1985; Rose, 1992 (see Chapter 2, What Needs to Be Prevented? pp. 6–14).

10. *Early community-wide trials in immunization and family planning:* Cuca & Pierce, 1977; Green & McAlister, 1984.

11. *Cardiovascular community trials:* For example, Carlaw, et al., 1984; Farquhar, Fortmann, Wood, & Haskell, 1983; Lasater, et al., 1984; Nutbeam & Catford, 1987; Puska & Uutela, 2000; Shea & Basch, 1990; Vartiainen, et al., 2000.

12. *Government-sponsored chronic disease community trials:* Elder, Schmid, et al., 1993; Michielutte, Dignan, et al., 1989, Plough & Olafson, 1994.

13. *Philanthropy-sponsored community trials:* Butler, et al., 1996; Green & Kreuter, 2002; Hallfors, Cho, et al., 2002; Kaiser Family Foundation, 1989; Schorr, 1997; Wickizer, Wagner, & Perrin, 1998; Williams, 1990.

14. *Environmental movement toward community-wide initiatives:* Freudenberg, 1984; Paehlke, 1989.

15. *HIV/AIDS epidemic revived community approaches to communicable disease control:* Becker & Joseph, 1988; Leviton & Valdiserri, 1990; Markland & Vincent, 1990; McKinney, 1993. Patton, 1985. For more specific applications of PRECEDE-PROCEED to community action on HIV/AIDS, see Freudenberg, 1989; Kroger, 1991; Mantell, DiVittis, & Auerbach, 1997, esp. pp.

199–203; Meredith, O'Reilly, & Schulz, 1989; Trussler & Marchand, 1997; U.S. Department of Health and Human Services, 1988a, esp. Section D.

16. *Public health arguments for community-wide approaches:* Integration of Risk Factor Interventions, 1986; Kottke, et al., 1985; Rose, 1992.

17. *Complementarity of the two approaches:* B. Lewis, Mann, & Mancini, 1986. For a case illustration of the systematic integration of community-wide and high-risk strategies using PRECEDE-PROCEED, see Daniel & Green, 1995. For further reflections on balancing these two perspectives in the context of health care and community, see Chapter 9 and Green, Costagliola, & Chwalow, 1991; Green, Lewis, & Levine, 1980.

18. *Initial reach times effectiveness = large number in Finland:* Puska, McAlister, et al., 1981.

19. *Australian "Quit for Life" campaign's reach:* Dwyer, Pierce, Hannam, & Burke, 1986; Pierce, Macaskill, & Hill, 1990.

20. *Focused intervention gets higher effectiveness, but lower reach:* Lando, Loken, Howard-Pitney, & Pechacek, 1990; Lando, McGovern, Barrios, & Etringer, 1990.

21. *Canadian example of reach versus effectiveness:* Millar & Naegele, 1987.

22. *U.S. 1% per year reduction in smoking produced 200,000 premature deaths over 14 years:* Warner & Murt, 1983.

23. *Denormalizing health risk behavior:* Solomon & DeJong, 1986, p. 314.

24. *Making community norms supportive of health behavior:* Dwore & Kreuter, 1980; Green, 1970a, 1970b; Green & McAlister, 1984. For applications of the concept of norms within Precede-Proceed planning or evaluation efforts, see Farley, 1997; N. H. Gottlieb, et al., 1990; Kristal, et al., 1995; Maxwell, Bastani, & Warda, 1998; Newman & Martin, 1982; M. W. Ross & Rosser, 1989; Schumann & Mosley, 1994; Secker-Walker, Flynn, & Solomon, 1996; B. G. Simons-Morton, Brink, & Simons-Morton, et al., 1989; Sleet, 1987; Sloane & Zimmer, 1992.

25. *Low-fat menus becoming more of a norm in restaurants:* Samuels, 1990.

26. *Relative efficacy of targeted interventions:* Campbell, et al., 1999; Kreuter, Vehige, & McGuire, 1996.

27. *Social cognitive theory:* Bandura, 1986, 2004; N. M. Clark, 1987.

28. *Educational versus environmental dichotomy counterproductive:* Kemm, 2003.

29. *Smoke-free environments as an environmental support for behavior change:* Crone, et al., 2003; Dijkstra & Borland, 2003.

30. *Health as instrumental value for social, cultural and economic ends:* Karanek, et al., 2000.

31. *Socioeconomic determinants of health:* J. W. Frank, 1995, p. 162.

32. *Diffusion theory* is described in Chapter 4 and later in this chapter.

33. *Distribution of low-fat and fast-food restaurants:* R. M. Goodman, Wheeler, & Lee, 1995; Green & Ottoson, 1999; Green & McAlister, 1984; Samuels, 1990. We are cognizant, however, of the limitations of this argument as it relates to the poorest segments, the unemployed and welfare-dependent; see W. J. Wilson, 1987.

34. *Japan Tobacco Inc's declining sales:* http://www.jti.co.jp/JTI_E/Release/03/031028_E.html (site accessed: 12/10/03)

35. *Alaska state tax and Canadian tobacco tax experiences:* Schumacher, 2000.

36. *Price elasticity rate for smoking and tax increases on tobacco:* Chaloupka, 1999; see also http://tigger.uci.edu/~fic; http://www.uci.edu/orgs/impacteen.

37. *Politics of health:* Rose, op cit., pp. 123–124.

38. *Helping corporations become good citizens:* The Corporate Citizenship Company, London, http://www.corporate-citizenship.co.uk.

39. *Corporate accountability on global health issues:* UPS Chairman Releases Corporate Sustainability Report, *Atlanta Business Chronicle,* Novermber 14, 2003—Full report called: Operating in Unision; http://www.sustainablity.ups.com.

40. *Value of support across sectors of community:* Perry, C., 2000, p. 122.

41. For a detailed account of the *AIDS Prevention Initiative in Nigeria* see http://www.apin.harvard.edu/program-arfh.html.

42. *Demonstration and diffusion effect of programs that are emulated:* Northridge, Vallone, et al., 2000.

43. *The multiplier effect of programs adopted by other organizations:* Carlaw, Mittlemark, Bracht, & Luepker, 1984; Green, Gottlieb, & Parcel, 1991.

44. *The multiplier effects of several mutually supportive programs:* Shimkin, 1986–1987, pp. 154–155.

45. *The multiplier effect of demonstration projects:* Schooler, Farquhar, Fortmann, & Flora, 1997.

46. *Complex problems require varied solutions:* Hoenig, 2000.

47. *Wicked problems:* Rittel and Webber, 1973.

48. *Understanding cultural differences:* Fadiman, 1998.

49. *Additive rather than alternative thinking:* Salk, 1973.

50. *Social capital:* Kreuter, & Lezin, 2002.

51. *Dilemmas of outside funding and community participation:* Green, 1977, 1986f; McGowan & Green, 1995; Green & Mercer, 2001.

52. *Grant funding for community research often fails to support programs:* Altman, 1995; R. M. Goodman & Steckler, 1989b.

53. *IOM recommends clustering grant categories:* Institute of Medicine, 2003.

54. *Centralized support versus local control:* Bozzini, 1988, p. 369; see also Green & Shoveller, 2000.

55. *Community participation:* Minkler & Pies, 1997, p. 134.

56. *Range of participatory options:* Wandersman & Florin, 2000.

57. *Coalition capacity:* Berkowitz, 2001; Braithwaite, Taylor, & Austin, 2000; Butterfoss & Kegler, 2002; Green & Ottoson, 1999.

58. *PRECEDE's help with "wicked problems":* Kass & Freudenberg, 1997.

59. *Nigerian examples:* Brieger, Onyido, & Ekanem, 1996. For Precede-Proceed applications with Nigerians, see Adenyanju, 1987–88; Gayle, 1987.

60. *Collaboration in minority communities:* E. B. Fisher, et al., 1992; R. M. Goodman & Steckler, 1989a, 1989b; Green, 1989; Shediac-Rizkallah & Bone, 1998.

61. *Healthy communities process and health policy:* Farrant & Taft, 1988. Cf. Wharf Higgins & Green, 1994.

62. *Health services access for rural homeless:* Dahl, Gustafson, & McCullagh, 1993.

63. *Examining the elements of effective community-based programs:* For example, Brownson, Smith, et al., 1996; Egan & Lackland, 1998; Shea, Basch, Lantiua, et al., 1992.

64. *From efficacy to effectiveness:* Fishbein, 1996; Flay, 1986; Green, 2001b.

65. *Communities for a Clean Bill of Health:* See http://www.mhap.org/communities/ccbh.

66. *Systematic review of coalitions:* Kreuter, Lezin, & Young, 2000.

67. *Caveats on coalitions; praise for partnerships:* Green, 2000.

68. *Developing community capacity:* R. M. Goodman, et al., 1996, p. 36.

69. *Social cohesion concept:* Berkman & Kawachi, 2000.

70. *Social capital concept:* Kreuter & Lezin, 2002.

71. *Ecological analyses of community social capital and health:* Edmondson, 2003; Kawachi, 1999.

72. *Social capital's influence on community change:* Tempkin & Rohe, 1998, p. 70.

73. *Bonding social capital versus bridging social capital:* Putnam, 2000.

74. *Social capital in planning and developing community health:* Adapted from Kreuter and Lezin, 2002.

75. *Gaming theory on politics:* J. M. Clark, 1939.

76. *Politician on gaming:* H. Smith, 1988.

77. *Community ownership of the initiative:* Flynn, 1995; Green & Mercer, 2001; Minkler & Wallerstein, 2003.

78. *Guidance on coalition building:* Braithwaite, Taylor & Austin, 2000; Butterfoss & Kegler, 2002.

79. *Accounts of coalition efforts:* Fisher, Strunk, et al., 1995; Freudenberg & Golub, 1987; Lefebvre, et al., 1986; McKinney, 1993.

80. *Survey of coalitions:* Kreuter & Lezin, 1997.

81. *The researchers and practitioners who participated in this survey* included David Altman, Bowman Gray School of Medicine, Wake Forest, NC; William Beery, Group Health Cooperative of Puget Sound, Seattle, WA; James Frankish, Institute of Health Promotion Research, University of British Columbia; Robert Goodman, School of Public Health, Tulane School of Public Health and Tropical Medicine, New Orleans, LA; Brick Lancaster, National Center for Chronic Disease Prevention and Health Promotion (NCCDPHP), Centers for Disease Control and Prevention (CDC), Atlanta, GA; Katherine Marconi, Bureau of Health Resources and Development, HRSA, Rockville, MD; Martha McKinney, Community Health Solutions, Inc.; Dearell Niemeyer, NCCDPHP, CDC; Randy Schwartz, Division of Health Promotion and Education, Maine Bureau of Health; and Nancy Watkins, NCCDPHP, CDC. The survey was conducted by telephone during April 1997.

82. *Specificity of objectives* has been addressed in previous chapters as an issue in planning and evaluation. The issue here is with specificity as a facilitator of interorganizational understanding, commitment and cooperation in implementing a policy or common objective. See Elmore, 1976; Van Meter & Van Horn, 1975.

83. *Leadership identification for coalition:* Nix, 1977, pp. 90–91. For software, see Gold, Green, & Kreuter, 1997.

84. *Media representation on coalition:* Steckler, Orville, Eng, & Dawson, 1989.

85. *Faith community on coalitions:* Vincent, Markland & Vincent, 1990; B. L. Wells, DePue, Lasater, & Carleton, 1988.

86. *Community applications in domestic violence:* Sanders-Phillips, 1996; P. H. Smith, Danis, & Helmick, 1998.

87. *Community applications child pedestrian injuries:* Stevenson, Jones, et al., 1996; Cross, Hall, et al., 2003.

88. *Community applications in cervical cancer:* Bastani, Berman, et al., 2002; Dignan, Michielutte, et al., 1994; Michielutte, Dignan, Wells, et al., 1989.

89. *Community applications in breast cancer screening:* Danigelis, et al., 1995; Earp, Eng, et al., 2002; Gold, Green, & Kreuter, 1998.

90. *Community applications in maternal nutrition:* Parvanta, Cottert, Anthony, & Parlato, 1997.

91. *Kentucky case study:* Kotchen, et al., 1986.

92. *Mailing and other screening follow-up reminders:* D. M. Murray, et al., 1988. For examples of direct mail strategies applied to other issues in health promotion, see also Kaplan, et al., 2000.

93. *Media considerations:* There was no need in rural Kentucky for more expensive communication efforts (such as a paid media campaign) given the efficiency of existing informal communications networks and the ready cooperation of the local radio and newspaper. We hasten to point out, however, that more expensive campaigns may be cost effective when indicated by geographic, demographic, and media characteristics.

94. *Perception of importance by professionals:* Personal communication, Jane Kotchen, August 25, 1989.

95. *The North Karelia project:* P. Puska, et al., 1985, pp. 162–163.

96. *Twenty-seven-year results of North Karelia community program:* Puska & Untela, 2000.

97. *Early tracking of results:* McAlister, Puska, Salonen, et al., 1982.

98. *Consumption data:* See discussion on p. 503 in Vartiainen, et al., 1994.

99. *"Boots deep in the mud":* Personal conversation between Marshall Kreuter and Pekka Puska in Budapest, May 31, 1996 [audiotaped].

100. *Bootheel project:* R. C. Brownson, Smith, et al., 1996.

101. *Go forth at community's pace:* C. A. Brownson, Dean, Dabney, & Brownson, 1998.

102. *Don't promise unachievable outcomes:* Hancock, Sanson-Fisher, et al., 1997.

103. *Community Health Promotion Grant Program of* Kaiser Family Foundation, 1989.

104. *Problem of translation of experimental trials to everyday practice settings:* Green, 2001 (full text online at http://www.ajhb.org/25-3.htm); Glasgow, et al., 2003. For Glasgow's RE-AIM online

course on planning for the translation of behavioral research to programs, http://www.pitt.edu/~super1/lecture/lec6851/index.htm.

105. *Community application tools and resources from PATCH:* Kreuter, 1992; Green & Kreuter, 1992; C. F. Nelson, Kreuter, & Watkins, 1986; C. F. Nelson, Kreuter, Watkins, & Stoddard, 1986, Chap. 47. For the fully downloadable PATCH manuals, including the guides for community coordinators and planners, meeting guides, visual aides, and other tools, go to http://www.cdc.gov/nccdphp/patch/.

106. *NACCHO survey of local health departments on PATCH:* National Association of County and City Health Officials and the Centers for Disease Control and Prevention, 1995, p. 60.

107. *Adams County application of PATCH:* Based on personal interview (12/10/03) with Julie Shepard, Director of Health Promotion, Adams County Health Department, Quincy, Illinois. http://www.co.adams.il.us/health/promotion/patch.htm (accessed Dec 16, 2003).

108. *Exercise facilities as a health program setting:* Sallis, et al., 1990.

109. *Religious sites and settings for health programs:* Campbell, Denmark, et al., 1999; DePue, Wells, Lasater, & Carleton, 1990; Markland & Vincent, 1990; Wells, DePue, et al., 1988.

110. *Health fairs as settings for health program activities:* Shepherd, Smart, & Marley, 2003.

111. *Bars and restaurants as settings for health program activities:* Mosher, 1990; Perry, Bishop, et al., 2004; Saltz, 1987.

112. *Grocery stores as settings for health program activities:* Cheadle, et al., 1990; Hunt, et al., 1990.

113. *Outreach to homes in rural areas:* A program that thoroughly applied the Precede Model to planning for the prevention of a veterinary health problem required direct outreach to individual dairy farmers: W. B. Brown, Williamson, & Carlaw, 1988. Results of the program are reported in N. B. Williamson, et al., 1988.

114. *Stages of change and diffusion theory:* Prochaska, Redding, & Evers, 2002; Rossi, Greene, et al., 2001; Rogers, 1995.

115. *Intervention mapping:* Bartholomew, Parcel, Kok, & Gottlieb, 2001.

116. *Mass media:* For example, Agha, 2003; R. Blum & Samuels, 1990; Green, Murphy, & McKenna, 2002; Stephenson, 2003. See examples of mass media spots developed by Health Canada for their national tobacco control program: http://www.hc-sc.gc.ca/hecs-sesc/tobacco/facts/mild/tvads.html (accessed March 21, 2004).

117. *Community-level mass media component of programs:* For example, Farquhar, et al., 1990; Lefebvre, et al., 1986. For examples of mass media applied within Precede-Proceed planning processes, see Ashley, 1993; Bakdash, 1983; Bakdash, Lange, & McMillan, 1983; Centers for Disease Control, 1987; Dignan, et al., 1991; Flynn, et al., 1992; Ramirez & McAlister, 1989; Secker-Walker, Worden, et al., 1997; Worden, et al., 1988; 1990, 1996.

118. *Planning mass media component:* General references include Glanz & Rimer, 1995; Tones & Tilford, 1994. For applications of PRECEDE, see also Bonaguro & Miaoulis, 1983; De Pietro, 1987; Kotler & Roberto, 1989, esp. pp. 285–294, which describes Project LEAN as a case study of planning a national social marketing program for dietary fat consumption; Miaoulis & Bonaguro, 1980–1981.

119. *Seven benefits of mass media:* Manoff, 1985, pp. 76–77.

120. *The Community Guide to Preventive Services:* See http://www.thecommunityguide.org (accessed March 21, 2004). Eng, Hopkins, Briss, et al., 2001; Ramsey & Brownson, 2002; Shults, Elder, et al., 2001.

121. *Types of intervention and segments of community they reach:* Preston, Baranowski, & Higginbotham, 1988–1989.

122. *Alignment of diffusion-adoption categories with predisposing, reinforcing, and enabling factors:* Green, 1976; Green, Gottlieb & Parcel, 1991.

123. *A Su Salud case:* Ramirez & McAlister, 1989.

124. *Model of social modeling:* Bandura, 1977, 2004. See also Parcel & Baranowski, 1981.

125. *Social marketing:* Lefebvre & Flora, 1988; Maibach, Rothschild, & Novelli, 2002.

126. *Kansas Health Foundation's Take It Outside program:* Telephone conversation with Tammi Bradley, Vice President for Communications, Kansas Health Foundation, Wichita, July 8, 1998; "Let's Take It Outside," 1998. See also Herreria, 1998.

127. *African social marketing application:* Brieger, Ramakrishna, & Adeniyi, 1986-1987.

128. *Ivory Coast use of focus groups in child diarrhea and malaria programs:* Glik, et al., 1987–1988.

129. *Bangladesh family planning application of social marketing:* Schellstede & Ciszewski, 1984.

130. *Dominican Republic application of media in dengue fever program:* A. J. Gordon, 1988.

131. *Community Toolbox:* Berkowitz, Fawcett, et al., 2003; Fawcett, Francisco, et al., 2000; Fawcett, Schultz, et al., 2003; Shultz, Fawcett, et al., 2003. Online at http://ctb.ku.edu (accessed March 21, 2004). See also: *Getting to Outcomes,* Wandersman, 2003; Wandersman & Chinman, 2004.

7

Applications
in Occupational Settings

Each setting in the community has its own peculiarities requiring contextual adaptations of plans that might have been developed previously at a national, state, provincial, or community-wide level. When the planning is undertaken initially *within* an organizational setting, the idiosyncrasies of occupational, educational, and health care settings call for different considerations for the planning process itself as well as for the contextual adaptations of the program content and strategies. This chapter and the following two will examine these contextual considerations for workplace, school, and medical care settings. PRECEDE-PROCEED is "robust" in its adaptability to and broad utility in various settings. Since the first publication of the Precede Model in 1974[1] the published literature has provided more than 900 examples of its application in planning and evaluating programs for various populations, most of them in specific settings within communities.[2]

This chapter examines some of the unique challenges of promoting and protecting health in the work site; it also explores how the application and adaptation of the Precede and Proceed phases can make that task more efficient and effective.[3] We might also refer to the model as a *minimalist* program theory (combining theory of the problem with theory of action), insofar as it offers the "simplest possible description or conceptualization of a field . . . [and] states some fundamental principles as part of or in addition to integrating the phenomena via new concepts."[4] The same Precede-Proceed principles stated in previous chapters—participation, assessing quality-of-life outcomes beyond health, and combining epidemiological, behavioral, and environmental perspectives in working back to the determinants of health—apply to the workplace. These all apply, whether the health program initiative comes from a federal agency, a community health agency, from the workers themselves, or from employers.

THE ECOLOGICAL CONTEXT
OF WORKPLACE HEALTH PROGRAMS

An educational and ecological approach to planning in any new setting calls first for an understanding of that setting's social history, purposes, and circumstances. Much of this understanding comes from the social diagnosis in the first part of the PRECEDE planning phase, but we did not discuss much in Chapter 2 of the historical and societal background that one assumes or should gather in approaching a new setting. We begin this chapter with such a review of those background considerations for occupational settings, also referred to as workplaces or work sites (and increasingly "worksites").

Since the 1980s, private and public sector employers and employees have fueled the rapid diffusion, expanding roles, and changing contexts of health-related work site programs and have increasingly sought alternatives to the escalating costs of health insurance. This initial review reconstructs the paths that health programs in the workplace have followed. It places experience from past programs in their historical, legislative, demographic, epidemiological, economic, technological, and scientific contexts. It also examines the changing ecological context of work site health programs as a convergence of developments in four related workplace contexts: economic and demographic changes, occupational health and safety, work site health promotion, and employee assistance programs. Though some of these changes have spurred developments in workplace health programs over the last two decades, others have threatened to undermine the development as the new century lurches forward. All of these contextual perspectives can be seen as background for the social diagnostic phase in applying the Precede-Proceed planning process to the workplace as a setting for health programs.

Historical Context of Health Programs in the Workplace

Without going back to the great labor union actions and government reforms of the late 19th and early 20th centuries, the more recent historical path is not marked so neatly by progressive milestones. Evidence from evaluations and reputations of occupational health and safety, ergonomics, employee assistance, and work site wellness and health promotion programs suggest overall progress, achieved by way of converging paths. The ecological context of today's workplace health programs can be seen in the historical evolution of these paths, as shown in Figure 7-1, out of the demographic, the economic, the regulatory or legislative, and the substance abuse contexts. This flowchart of the converging paths provides a map to the first part of this chapter.

These paths bring us to a crossroads at the millennium. The point of convergence in this first decade confronts workplace health programs with uncertainties about where they will lie in future organizational charts. Will the medical or engineering models of occupational health and safety and of ergonomics dominate? Or will the mental health models of employee assistance programs come forward? Will the behavioral science or the holistic health mod-

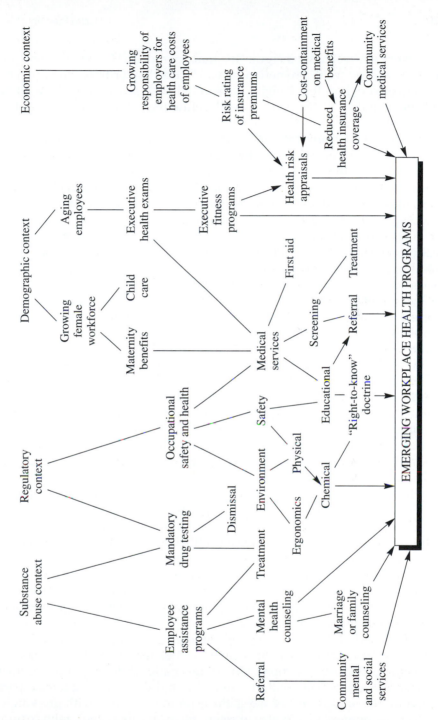

FIGURE 7-1 The ecological context of workplace health promotion can be understood in part from the historical convergence of pathways by which employers have adapted to earlier contexts of changing demography, economics, government regulation, and substance abuse by employees.

Source: Adapted from "The Changing Content of Health Promotion in the Workplace," adapted from L. W. Green and M. Cargo, 1994, in M. P. O'Donnell and J. S. Harris (Eds.), Albany, NY: Delmar. Reprinted with permission of Delmar Publishers, Inc.

els of work site wellness emerge as the main paradigm? Or will the new public health model of health promotion prevail? This chapter traces the converging paths to discern how the changing context of health programs in the workplace and the blending of these models will define the future of workplace health programs.

Several of the many paths in Figure 7-1 also reveal similar footprints in our tracings of the ecological context for health programs in the workplace. One set of footprints are those of academic research and government policies that have stimulated innovations in the workplace. Another set reflects the influence from innovative business and professional leaders whose vision and initiative in workplace health promotion have stimulated research and policy. The third set of footprints are from unions and worker initiatives in both stimulating health protection reforms in the workplace and resisting health promotion. To guard against bias and confusion of cause and effect in our presentation of issues and developments, we base this chapter on a combination of academic, business, and government sources from at least two countries—the United States and Canada. Though some differences exist between these sources, we find them generally consistent in their implications for the future of workplace health programs, at least in northern North America.

A new era concerned with employee health unfolded in response to several factors influencing standards for the workplace environment. **Occupational health services** developed originally to treat and later to prevent job-related injuries and illnesses. **Employee assistance programs** (EAPs) later grew out of the targeting of alcohol as a major determinant of industrial injuries, decreased productivity, and psychosocial problems. **Workplace health promotion** then emerged from myriad converging trends, the most influential of which, in the United States, where workplace health promotion has seen its greatest push, was the increased burden placed on employers by escalating health care costs for illnesses that were not necessarily or entirely job related. These three program areas have evolved independently, with the common (though seldom shared) goal of improving employee health. They also goaded and facilitated the development and implementation of occupational health and safety programs, employee assistance programs, and health promotion by business and industry. The social, economic, and scientific forces behind these three movements set the stage for their collective potential to facilitate change in employee health and emerging programs today.

We discuss below four societal phenomena, largely external to the workplace, that have influenced the growth and shape of work site health programs in postindustrial nations. One is the changing demographic profiles of the workforce, especially with the aging of, and the increased female participation in, the workforce. Second is the economic context, with growing concern for the burden on industry of rising medical care costs, health insurance premiums, and cost of lost productivity in unhealthy workers. Whether employers pay this cost directly, as in the United States, or indirectly through corporate and employer taxes, as in most countries, it represents a burden on industry that makes them less profitable than they might be. The third trend is the growing recognition of the influence of the behavioral and environmental determinants of health, absenteeism, and productivity, which has led to the political-regulatory and substance abuse context. The fourth is the mounting evidence that health education and health promotion strategies have been effective in altering some of the behavioral and environmental determinants of health, but other determinants require more attention to services and policies conducive to worker health and collaboration with other sectors in the community.

Demographic Context

"Because that's where the money is!" So answered Willie "The Actor" Sutton, the infamous American bankrobber when asked, "Why do you rob banks?" Population health programs for children tend to be organized around schools, and for adults around workplaces, because that's where the people are. Work sites are to many adults what schools are to children and youth—places where they spend most of their daylight hours, where they develop friendships, where they receive many of the rewards that make one feel worthy, and where they can be reinforced by peers and significant others. These settings are also places where one feels pressures to perform and deliver, to meet obligations, and worries of being judged and reprimanded, demoted, or even fired. Some of these personal functions of the workplace have become more compelling as the workforce has aged and feminized.

Figure 7-2 shows the rates of participation in the U.S. labor force for men and women. From 1970 to 1985, the increase in the female workforce participation rate, especially working mothers, reshaped the attitudes of employers toward employee benefits and working conditions.[5] The workplace has replaced the neighborhood as the community of reference and social identity for many urban and suburban North Americans and Europeans.[6] These demographic and social trends, combined with the pervasive influence of occupational environments on adult health, quality of life, behavior, and lifestyle, make them logical if not ideal settings for health programs.

Regulatory Context:
Occupational Health and Safety Legislation

Industrial hygiene and the occupational health and safety movement focused on protecting health through the control of potential hazards in the work environment. The field emerged from (1) the recognition that employees are strongly influenced by their work environment and (2) the realization that many illnesses related to the work environment could be controlled, some even eliminated.

Legislative Initiatives.   The passage in 1970 of the Occupational Safety and Health Act (OSHA) in the United States[7] and similar legislation in the United Kingdom (1974), Canada (1970s), Australia (1972, 1977, 1985), France (1946,

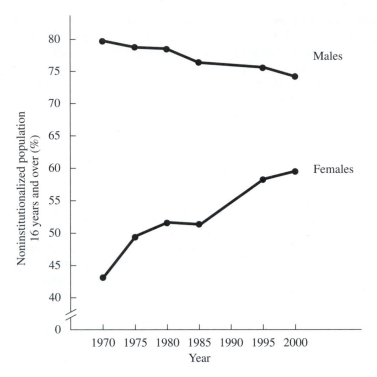

FIGURE 7-2 Civilian labor force participation rates for the U.S. population age
16 years and older, 1970–2000, show the striking increase in female employment.
Source: Monthly Labor Review, by U.S. Department of Labor, Bureau of Labor Statistics, 1998; *Statistical
Abstract of the United States, 1999,* by U.S. Bureau of the Census, 1998, Washington, DC: U.S. Government
Printing Office.

revised 1976, 1982), West Germany (1974), and Sweden (1978) led to the rise of
occupational health and safety activities. Standards were established to protect
the worker's health. These standards had the support of the international labor
movement and the advantage of the international codes that were developing
during this period.[8]

The Problem of Coordination.   The U.S. Occupational Safety and Health Act
of 1970 placed the responsibility for and enforcement of occupational health
and safety in one federal agency, the Occupational Health and Safety Administration, and its counterpart state agencies. Reactions to the act led to increasing
polarization between labor and management. The polarization and fragmenta-
tion does not end there. The legislation for employee assistance programs
(EAPs) and health promotion programs emerged from different congressional
committees and are governed by different federal and state agencies. The
National Institute of Alcoholism and Alcohol Abuse and the National Institute
of Drug Abuse in the Department of Health and Human Services (DHHS)
administer EAPs. The Department of Labor and the National Institute of Occu-

pational Safety and Health (NIOSH) administer OSHA provisions. NIOSH is located in the CDC, which is part of DHHS. The lack of horizontal integration among the various governing legislative committees and administrative agencies has constrained the development of a more comprehensive approach to program implementation in policies and regulations. The Office of Disease Prevention and Health Promotion under the Assistant Secretary of Health and its *Healthy People* objectives for the nation in disease prevention and health promotion, however, has provided a coordinating mechanism for these agencies and sectors to work together toward more comprehensive workplace health programs.

In Canada, labor legislation is under provincial jurisdiction, with each province and territory having its own occupational health and safety legislation. The federal government has laws for its own employees and for employees of industries under its jurisdiction. Occupational health and safety laws were passed in the 1970s for most provinces. In Britain, implementation of the Health and Safety Work Act is the responsibility of the Health and Safety Executive. As in most countries other than the United States, British employers have not experienced great economic pressures to prevent disease and promote health in their employees. This changed somewhat with the advent of the employer's responsibility for statutory sick pay under the 1986 Social Security Act. Britain's enlightened occupational health policies, though, had never been entirely motivated by either economic or health concerns. Rather, they originated from benevolent employers in the 18th and 19th centuries seeking to protect workers from occupational disease and injury.

Problems Requiring Regulatory Intervention.   Many people work in an environment containing a host of potential hazards such as harmful physical agents (e.g., heat, vibrations, noise), toxic chemicals, stressful routines, or dangerous equipment. These elements in the workplace take their toll in the form of employee illness, disability, and death. Increases in these exposure-related injuries occurred in the 1990s while injury deaths and work-related injury deaths were declining in general.[9] Some three-fourths of new cases of occupational illness in private industry occur in manufacturing. The service industry accounts for about one-eighth of the cases. Occupational illnesses associated with repeated trauma or conditions caused by repeated motion, pressure, or vibration constitute just over 50% of the reported cases, marking a significant increase in number and percentage of total illnesses reported. Industries with the highest accident frequency rates (disabling injuries per 100,000 work hours) also have the highest severity rates (days lost per 1 million work hours). By their very nature, certain industries such as agriculture, mining, marine transportation, quarrying, and construction tend to pose the greatest hazard. Motor vehicle injuries account for the greatest proportion of all work-related fatalities.[10]

Environmental Protections Versus Health Promotion.   The occupational health and safety acts in many countries resulted in strategies to protect employees from the biological, physical, chemical, and other environmental hazards of the workplace. The emphasis of employer responsibility for environmental protection began as early as 1912, with workmen's compensation laws. Many trade unions have consistently viewed worker health as the employer's responsibility. As a result, unions initially resisted the introduction of health promotion, which they viewed as a smokescreen to mask failed environmental reforms and to shift the blame for worker illness and injury onto the behavior of workers. This was of great concern for those workers exposed to potentially health-threatening working conditions such as chemicals. The work environment was the first target of employee health concerns and has persisted as the primary concern of labor unions and reform-minded health professionals. As health promotion moves closer to occupational health and safety, attention to the environment will increase in health promotion planning.

Protection of Women.   A decision by the U.S. Supreme Court in 1991 changed the occupational safety and health policy as it affects the working conditions of women. The court decision ruled against the Johnston Controls, which was originally legislated to protect women from exposure to potential reproductive hazards such as lead and which prevented women from being hired into positions that would place them at reproductive risk. The new legislation shifts the focus from hiring restrictions to environmental reforms, requiring hazard-free workplaces for high-risk employees to ensure their equal work opportunity.

Since World War II, women have moved increasingly into occupations previously designed for men, including heavy manual labor. The increase in the percentage of working mothers has reshaped the attitudes of employers toward working conditions and family matters such as day care, flexible working hours, job sharing, and childbirth leave for both parents.[11]

Educational Protections.   Legislative action introduced the "right to know" doctrine, ensuring workers information about workplace health hazards. Prior to OSHA, employers were not required to inform workers of chemical or other workplace hazards that could cause adverse health effects. Passage of the act was an attempt to remedy occupational injury and disease through primary prevention. This approach involved establishing safety standards and placing limits on exposures to hazardous substances. It then became the responsibility of the employers to comply with these standards or incur fines.

One could argue that educational methods directed at the behavior or the **informed consent** of workers, when combined with management and environmental reforms to improve the working conditions, gained greater participation and action because employers and employees were meeting each other halfway. Another advantage of the combined educational and environmental approach was that some of the work site hazards were synergistic in their effects with behavior, such as smoking and exposure to asbestos, solvents, and other air pollutants. Some had concomitant effects on the same health problems, such as alcohol and injury exposure. Some potentially affected worker productivity and health concomitantly but independently, such as stressful working conditions, being overweight, or being sedentary and lacking physical fitness. All of these interacting relationships called for intervention directed at (1) protecting the worker against hazardous and stressful working conditions and (2) promoting healthful practices such as exercise, nutritional eating, and self-examination for cancer signs and symptoms,[12] and some go a step further by intervening with the families of workers as well.[13]

The educational and right-to-know context of occupational health provided an additional wedge for health promotion approaches that informed workers more generally about health risks, among which lifestyle and behavioral risks could be shown to account for an even larger proportion of premature mortality and years of life lost than could the workplace environment.

Medical Surveillance and Risk Assessment.   Medical surveillance was first incorporated into the occupational health field as a weapon to prevent occupational disease and injury through preplacement examinations and periodic checkups. The pamphlet *Health Education in Industry*, published by the Metropolitan Life Insurance Company around 1963, characterized the typical workplace health program at that time as follows:

> Today, an employee health program generally starts with a pre-placement examination. This helps to determine a person's suitability for a specific job—his technical as well as his physical and emotional fitness. It follows through with regular check-ups, and concerns itself with the employee's general well-being as well as with the specific job hazards and work environment.

Medical surveillance now covers a range of services: medical screening, medical and biological monitoring, primary and secondary prevention strategies, and drug testing.[14] Medical surveillance activities systematically evaluate employees at risk for exposure to workplace hazards. When blood pressure screening was added to the battery of tests in occupational surveillance programs, issues began to arise about whether to attribute the cause of detected hypertension to the job or to other lifestyle risks.[15] The surveillance systems complemented the hazard control strategies, but they also raised ethical issues of privacy, confidentiality, and labeling, especially with the specter of HIV/AIDS testing and drug testing.[16] These have spilled into the health promotion arena with the advent of health risk appraisal questionnaires, some of which include medical screening items and questions of private behavior.[17] The possibility of genetic testing to identify risks makes the threat to privacy and the possibility of discrimination even more ominous, underscoring the urgent need for regulation.[18]

Workplace medical surveillance and risk assessment have evolved over the decades. Their primary role today is to enhance and assess the overall effect of the health examinations, drug-testing, and health promotion aspects of a comprehensive occupational health program. As we progress into the 21st century, we may expect to see a further blurring of the boundaries between work and private life, especially with increasing provisions for "telecommuting" work at home.

Psychosocial Factors. The occupational safety and health movement concerned itself with reducing work-related health problems resulting from exposure to hazards external to the control of employees.[19] Employers, however, tended to give greater consideration to the role of behavioral, motivational, and psychological factors in job health and safety, and did so increasingly as the union movement in the United States weakened and the global economy intensified.[20] Blending these environmental and psychosocial perspectives, a growing research focus has been on the psychosocial aspects of job demand such as pace, monotony, noise, and degree of controls as sources of stress to find additional ways to protect health and prevent safety risks to employees.[21] The attention given to individual psychosocial factors in job health and safety served as a stimulus for the appearance of the workplace mental health movement[22] and may represent a common historical linchpin of occupational health and safety, EAP, recent workplace health promotion, and emerging organizational reform promotion conducive to greater worker control of work stress.

Recent Trends. In reviewing the profile of occupational safety and health, one can observe significant progress in hazard control strategies, medical surveillance, and psychosocial factors in safety and health. Since the passage of the OSHA, considerable headway has been made in the prevention of occupational disease as recorded in U.S. and Canadian statistics. Some of the most serious workplace hazards have disappeared or declined in prevalence. Stringent regulatory controls and standards have replaced looser guidelines, requirements have replaced recommendations, and secrecy is less common.[23] The deregulatory emphases of recent federal policies in the United States and other nations, however, seeking to favor their industries in the intensified global competition, have loosened some of the controls on workplace hazards.[24]

Current Limitations. The preventability of work-related illness depends on the simultaneous control and further study of the interactions among environmental, behavioral, social, and economic factors that contribute to the persistence of, and emergence of new, occupational diseases and injuries. We still know relatively little about many synthetic chemicals, despite increases in public, regulatory, and scientific awareness and investigation. The capacity of physicians is limited to the extent that they are not diagnostically trained to infer work as a potential cause of disease. Most physicians receive little training in occupational medicine. Workers exposed to hazardous substances in many cases are not notified of exposure. Medical surveillance programs are probably underestimating the actual number of cases of occupational-related illnesses.

In addition to the regulatory roles of the Occupational Health and Safety Administration already discussed, it has mandated responsibilities for information dissemination on new legislation, regulations, and voluntary initiatives that are not being applied.[25] The National Institute for Occupational Safety and Health (NIOSH) is responsible for investigating the presence of hazardous working conditions. The budget of NIOSH was cut by over 50% during the 1980s and has not made up that deficit in the 1990s, limiting workplace inspections to a few high-risk industries. Advances in worker health and dramatic reductions in workplace diseases in the industrialized countries notwithstanding, much of the knowledge gained and methods of control of workplace hazards is "not being exported to developing countries along with the hazardous materials."[26] Globalization of trade has drawn attention to child labor abuses in the sweat shops of some countries, but a much wider range of worker protections need similar attention.

In summary, the environmental and medical orientation of occupational safety and health has made it compatible with and hospitable to some health promotion concepts emphasizing primary prevention. On the whole, however, the professionals and the workers (especially unions) invested in occupational health and safety have ranged from competitive to hostile in their attitude toward health promotion programs as they have been developed in many workplaces. The ascendancy of health promotion in U.S. government policy, at the same time that OSHA and NIOSH faced cutbacks in their budgets, their regulatory powers, and their influence in Washington, made many occupational safety and health workers unreceptive if not antagonistic toward the advancement of workplace health promotion. The convergence of interests around the organization of work as it affects health, and other supports for workers and their families such as child care, parental leave, flexible hours, and telecommuting, has opened new opportunities for collaboration within the workplace and between occupational and other community sectors concerned with health.

Economic Context

Another way to understand Willie Sutton's answer to why he robbed banks— "Because that's where the money is!"—would be to consider the costs and benefits of health promotion in the workplace. U.S. employers pay about a third of the some $1.3 trillion in medical care costs annually through employment-linked health insurance, workers' compensation, and other payment mechanisms. This continued the prior 25 years of increase in the business proportion of total health care expenditures since 1965, shown in Figure 7-3,[27] and accounts for the growing interest of employers to find new ways to keep their employees healthy. With the continuing decline in out-of-pocket personal expenditures, the total private to public share has decreased, but the absolute amounts shelled out by companies for their employees are "where the money is" that continues their search for alternatives in occupational settings.

Containing Health Care Costs.   U.S. business and industry took a fresh look at health promotion and disease prevention in the late 1970s as they faced alarming increases in the cost of medical care and insurance premiums for their employees. The increase in spending on health care fell more heavily on industry than on individuals (Figure 7-3), with business and government picking up a larger share of the continuing increase. Today, the division of the private insurance pie, as shown in Figure 7-4, has stabilized for employers, with employees

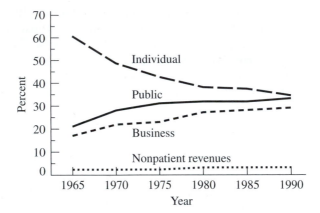

FIGURE 7-3 The business sector's and government's percentage of expenditures for health services in the United States has continued to increase since 1965, while personal expenditures decreased.

Source: Health Care Financing Administration and National Center for Health Statistics, *Healthy People Review, 1995–96,* by National Center for Health Statistics, 1996, Hyattsville, MD: Public Health Service, DHHS-PHS-96-1256.

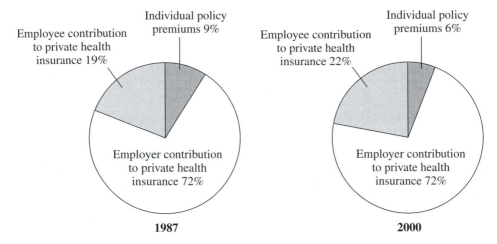

FIGURE 7-4 Sources of payment for private health insurance coverage, 1987–2000. Employees' share of health insurance premiums has grown, employers' share has stabilized, but amounts have increased sharply by the percentages shown in Figure 7-5.

Source: U.S. Department of Health and Human Services, Center for Medicare & Medicaid Services, Office of the Actuary, National Health Statistics Group, 2002. *Chartbook,* Chapter 4. Web site: http://cms.hhs .gov/charts/default.asp, accessed Dec 7, 2003.

picking up a slightly larger share of the premiums, but the rate of premium inflation has made the absolute dollar amounts paid out increase radically in relation to business profits and personal incomes (Figure 7-5).

Canada has not seen the same explosive growth of workplace health promotion programs or interest among employers in such programs, because its

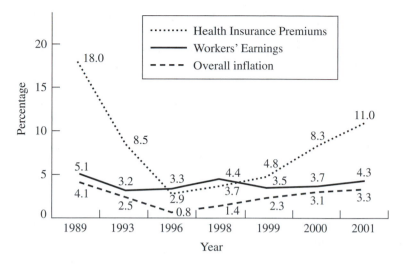

FIGURE 7-5 Changes (annual percentage increases) in employer health insurance premiums, overall inflation, and workers' earnings, 1989–2001. Employer health insurance premiums are rising rapidly again.

Source: Health Insurance Premiums from personal communication of data from KFF/HRET Employer Health Benefits Surveys from 1999, 2000, 2001: KPMG Survey of Employer-Sponsored Health Benefits: 1993, 1996; HIAA Employer-Sponsored Health Insurance Survey, 1989. Workers' Earnings from Bureau of Labor Statistics Current Employment Statistics Survey (April–April), 1988–2001. Overall inflation from Bureau of Labor Statistics, CPI estimates (April–April), 1988–2001, at www.bls.gov. Trends and indicators in the Changing Health Care Marketplace, 2002—Chartbook Center for Medicare and Medicaid Services, Chartbook 2002. Web site: http://cms.hhs.gov/charts/default.asp, accessed Dec 7, 2003.

companies do not shoulder as much of the direct cost for its sick and injured employees. Besides incurring a smaller proportion of their employee's health care costs, Canadian employers have seen a slower escalation of costs. The increased U.S. and Canadian interest in workplace health promotion was also influenced by changing demographic profiles, with older workers bringing more chronic conditions. Finally, both countries and others have recognized the influences of behavior and environment on health, as well as the converging evidence of the effectiveness and cost-benefit advantages of health education and health promotion strategies in altering the determinants of health.[28]

The imperative of OSHA legislation forced employers to implement environmental strategies to reduce the risk of disease, disability, and premature death among employees. Health promotion was enlisted as a strategy to contain health care costs, increase productivity, and provide personal benefit to employees, but it did not have the regulatory teeth that occupational hazard control and safety had in OSHA-type legislation. With the advent of smoke-free workplace legislation at the state, provincial, and local levels, a new era of regulatory support for health promotion was born.[29]

Econometric Evaluation.   Cost containment remains a primary motivating factor in the implementation of health promotion and related health programs. In the early 1980s, to address the lack of cost-effectiveness and cost-benefit data to support health promotion programs, researchers estimated the cost-effectiveness and cost-benefit of existing programs.[30] There was some concern that health promotion programs were subjected to greater economic scrutiny of their interventions and to more stringent criteria and requirements of acceptability, including evidence of effectiveness and cost savings, than was medical care intervention. Further, some worried that cost-benefit arguments might be oversold.[31] The continued growth of health promotion programs in the 1980s in the absence of evidence for cost-effectiveness suggests the importance of other factors, such as concern for employee health and well-being or quality of work life. The diverging views regarding the profitability of health promotion may reflect employers' various rationales for program adoption. Some employers place greater weight on cost-effectiveness or cost-benefit as measured by reduced absences or increased productivity, whereas other employers emphasize the health benefits derived by employees. There appears to be at least some consensus that the cost-benefit impact on the corporate bottom line by reducing health care costs, absenteeism, and other employment-related costs is probable, but it should not be the sole basis for program implementation.[32]

The concern for cost-effectiveness and cost-benefit data encouraged an increasing number of evaluations of single modality and comprehensive programs. Given the methodological limitations of the data, the combined evidence suggests that health promotion programs can support both health and cost-effectiveness. The majority of evaluations have focused on single modality programs such as smoking cessation, stress management, weight loss, and hypertension.[33]

Tobacco Control. Smoking-cessation and tobacco-control programs have taken varied forms in workplaces, ranging from clinical and self-help models to organizational, regulatory, and legal reforms of smoking policies. Meta-analyses and systematic reviews of long-term quit rates from controlled smoking cessation studies in workplaces reveal a modest but significant overall effect.[34] Generally, short-term quit rates are high and diminish over time, highlighting the problem of maintaining behavior change. Quit rates are increased if the company has a restrictive smoking policy and provides smoking-cessation programs; these policies depend in part on company size.[35] This clearly demonstrates the importance of the ecological context and the need for ecological interventions to support individual changes. Table 7-1 shows the 1998–99 baseline numbers of states that have smoke-free or clean-air policies banning or restricting smoking to ventilated areas in work sites and various public places.

The most compelling of the cost-benefit analyses of the health and economic implications of a work site smoking-cessation program is a simulation by Warner and his colleagues. They used long-term flow of costs and benefits, based on conservative estimates from previous studies. They also factored in employee turnover, which showed that approximately half of the considerable health and economic benefits generated by a work site smoking-cessation program accrue to the community rather than to the employer who sponsored the

TABLE 7-1 U.S. *Healthy People 2010* objectives and 1998 baselines for establishing laws on smoke-free indoor air that prohibit smoking or limit it to separately ventilated areas in public places and work sites.

Target and baseline:

Objective	Jurisdictions With Laws on Smoke-Free Air	1998 Baseline	2010 Target
		Number	
	States and the District of Columbia		
27-13a	Private Workplaces	1	51
27-13b	Public workplaces	13	51
27-13c	Restaurants	3	51
27-13d	Public transportation	16	51
27-13e	Day care centers	22	51
27-13f	Retail stores	4	51

Target setting method: Retain 2000 target.

Data source: State Tobacco Activities Tracking and Evaluation System (STATE System), CDC, National Center for Chronic Disease Prevention and Health Promotion, Office on Smoking and Health.

program. Nevertheless, the simulation shows that smoking cessation is a "very sound economic investment for the firm, and is particularly profitable when long-term benefits are included, with an eventual benefit-cost ratio of 8.75."[36] The analysis also highlights, however, that these benefits should not be overstated as to their solution to the smoking problem for the workplace and that the intervention successfully addresses only a small fraction of the costs that the firm incurs from smoking employees.

Stress Management, Nutrition, and Physical Activity.   The findings from stress management studies suggest that well-designed programs oriented toward individual behavior change lead to short-term changes in various physiological variables, the most important factor being lower blood pressure; but comprehensive or combined individual and environmental programs are more effective.[37] Stress management often accompanies smoking-cessation and weight control programs (nutrition and physical activity). Few studies have demonstrated the cost-effectiveness of workplace nutrition programs. Low participation rates have plagued the evaluation of stress and nutrition programs, as it has others.[38]

Compared with other approaches, work site competitions have been found to be highly cost-effective in recruiting participants without compromising outcome efficacy.[39] Because weight gain is such a major concern of some smokers in deciding whether to quit smoking, the linkage to smoking makes weight control and stress management a natural grouping of programs for an economically justified comprehensive set of programs. Table 7-2 shows the baseline

TABLE 7-2 Increase the proportion of work sites that offer employer-sponsored nutrition or weight management classes or counseling; and physical fitness programs. Source: *Healthy People 2010.*

Target: 85 percent for nutrition or weight management; 75 percent for physical activity and fitness programs.
Target setting method: 55 percent improvement.

Data source: National Worksite Health Promotion Survey, Association for Worksite Health Promotion (AWHP).

Work Sites, 1998–99	Offer Nutrition or Weight Management Classes or Counseling			Offer Physical Activity and Fitness Programs		
Work Site Size	Work Site or Health Plan	Work Site	Health Plan	Work Site or Health Plan	Work Site	Health Plan
	Percent					
Total (50 or more employees)	55	28	39	46	22	36
50 to 99 employees	48	21	39	38	21	24
100 to 249 employees	51	29	37	42	20	31
250 to 749 employees	59	44	42	56	25	44
750 or more employees	83	70	50	68	27	61

percentages of work sites of various sizes that provide nutrition classes or counseling and physical activity or fitness programs either onsite or subsidized through the employer-sponsored health plans. The table also shows the objectives for the year 2010 for these types of programs for work sites of varying sizes.

Hypertension.   Evidence suggests that by reducing absenteeism, hypertension control programs have a favorable cost-benefit ratio.[40] One study calculated the program cost at $150 per employee per year, which was considered a cost-saving investment in relation to the $10,000 incurred in medical costs at that time if an employee had a heart attack, and potentially more with a stroke.[41]

Comprehensive Programs.   As reviewed by Pelletier, there is sufficient evidence to support the cost-effectiveness of comprehensive programs.[42] Evaluation of the Johnson & Johnson Live for Life Program is an excellent example of a cost-effectiveness evaluation using existing data. Experimental groups had lower increases in inpatient costs, hospital days, and admissions than did control groups.[43] Besides methodological limitations, some have called into question how well even the "comprehensive corporate health promotion programs" meet the ecological demands of a systems model of health.[44]

Limitations of Evaluation.   Despite the growing body of evaluation literature supporting the cost-effectiveness of health promotion programs, researchers continue to identify the need for well-designed, methodologically sound studies. Yet, randomized, controlled designs and other rigorous methodological tools of evaluation are seen as barriers to implementation of programs in the workplace, and they have some limitations, even when carried out with rigor, in generalizing the results to other settings.[45] Work sites viewed as laboratories pose difficulties in incorporating and maintaining the integrity of a control group. With the difficulties in implementing randomized evaluation designs, researchers may need to settle on better analyses of quasi-experimental designs that statistically control for variables they cannot control by random assignment of large numbers of workers.

Employee Dependents.   Health promotion in the workplace is primarily concerned with supporting healthful lifestyle practices, but lifestyle has come to be seen as more than just behavior. The workplace has long been seen as a venue in which health promotion professionals could give greater attention to social factors influencing health.[46] This expanding focus is similar to EAP taking on family and emotional difficulties and financial problems associated with substance abuse or misuse. Some corporations have not limited health promotion to employees but have extended the efforts to family and retirees. Some employers recognize that these groups influence the firm's health care costs. An estimated 50% to 70% of health care costs accrue from the spouses and dependents of employees. In a 1993 survey of 20 companies, dependents and retirees accounted for more health care dollars than did employees in 18 of the 20 work sites.[47] Others saw the importance of family influence on the employee and the need to make health promotion a family endeavor.[48]

Large companies such as Du Pont (starting in 1994) and Johnson & Johnson have extended their health promotion efforts to dependents and retirees.[49] Programs directed at maternal health are a new addition to dependent care. One unhealthy baby can cost a company over $1 million, including impact on absenteeism and productivity.[50] The Baby Benefits Program and March of Dimes prenatal programs impart significant cost savings to employers. The former program is consumer oriented and encourages the mother to attend the prenatal program in the first trimester. Breast-feeding programs have been successful in assisting the mother in the transition back to work after maternity leave.[51] Pennsylvania Public Employees Health and Welfare concluded from an 18-month study that prevention programs for dependent children of employees provide effective protection of family health and reduce costs of medical care for preventable illnesses. The difficulty of changing the lifestyle of adults was given as another reason for the focus on children.[52]

Substance Abuse Context: Employee Assistance Programs

The U.S. Organizational Context.   In the United States, EAPs have no direct mandate from any federal legislation. Indirectly supported by the U.S. federal Drug-Free Work Act and the National Drug Control Strategy, EAPs leave private business and health professionals responsible for the development, implementation, and operation of EAPs. In the late 1970s, the Employee Assistance Program Association (EAPA), formerly known as ALMACA, released program standards that provided cursory rationalizations for the functions of EAPs.[53] As EAPs changed in scope during the 1980s, the standards were perceived as having conceptual and pragmatic deficiencies. A new set of standards released in 1990 addressed the design, implementation, and evaluation of EAPs. The new standards seek to clarify misconceptions among researchers and others about the elements of comprehensive EAPs. A managed-care monograph entitled "Maximizing Behavioral Health Benefit Value Through EAP Integration" was released along with the new standards. This document conveyed the message that management uses EAPs to save health care dollars with the added benefit of keeping employees healthy and on the job. In a pragmatic way, it assists businesses in applying EAP standards to the workplace, acknowledging the economic context, as in the preceding section of this chapter, but also seeking to adapt to the organizational culture.

The Canadian Organizational Context.   In Canada, EAPs function differently than in the United States. The Canadian federal and provincial governments provide a broader network of assessment and treatment services, with lesser emphasis on private facilities and private consultants. Companies therefore have less concern for cost barriers when they refer troubled employees to community resources. There is greater union involvement in and commitment to EAPs in Canada than in the United States. Some Canadian unions have successfully negotiated EAPs into the collective agreement, an issue of great contention in the United States. The Canadian Labor Congress (CLC) Employee Recovery Program assists union members in establishing EAPs in their workplace. EAPs appear to be developing in other countries, with the international interest and growth spurred by governments and multinational companies.

The Diffusion of EAPs.   The rise and proliferation of EAPs in the United States, Canada, and other countries underscore the role of alcohol as a major determinant in industrial injuries, psychosocial problems, and decreased productivity, the costs of which are borne largely by employers. Estimates from national surveys indicate that 10% of employees in North America experience serious alcohol problems.[54] Alcohol abuse is related to several serious problems that influence the health and welfare of employees, families, and employers. In addition, up to 57% of all industrial injuries are associated with alcohol, with as many as 75% of those involved in two or more industrial accidents having alcohol problems. Many non-work-related injuries are linked to alcohol, with approximately one-half of all motor vehicle injuries involving it. Alcohol is also implicated in the high costs of psychosocial disturbances and domestic violence that accrue to industry.[55] Decreased productivity is another result of alcohol abuse of particular interest to employers. Bertera estimated annual costs per employee at $389.[56]

From Medical Model to Constructive Confrontation.   Occupational alcoholism rehabilitation represents the forerunner of EAPs. Responsibility fell initially on occupational medicine departments to carry out these activities. These programs focused on tertiary care, or referral and treatment services to employees whose use of alcohol interfered with work performance.[57] Physicians treated the interference of alcohol with job performance as they would other diseases, by trying to eliminate the use of alcohol without addressing the underlying motivations for its use. It became evident that the medical model offered little help to the drinking employee. Alcohol consumption does not always manifest itself in physical illness, but rather represents behaviors requiring lifestyle modification rather than medical treatment.[58] The encounter between physician and patient was often antagonistic rather than cooperative, as patients did not voluntarily seek help for their problem but viewed it as forced on them. With federal support in the form of grant funds from the National Institute of Alcohol and Alcoholism, occupational alcoholism policies and programs incorporated a strategy referred to as constructive-confrontation.[59] This strategy, based on the identification by supervisors of workers experiencing alcohol-related problems, guided the formation and implementation of occupational alcoholism programs. Further development of this strategy—namely, the adoption of formal written policies by companies to guide the managerial actions, the training of supervisors to apply them, and the protection of employees' rights—led to the outgrowth of EAPs from occupational alcoholism programs. The ideological shift away from the disease orientation of alcoholism coincided with the expanded focus of EAPs to include other drug use and eventually other family or personal problems.

Evidence of program success and incentives provided by the National Institute of Alcoholism and Alcohol Abuse led to a dramatic increase of programs in the 1970s. Fewer than 100 programs were in operation in the 1960s. By 1980, an estimated 12% of the nation's workforce had access to occupational alcoholism programs.[60]

From Treatment to Secondary Prevention.   The limited focus on tertiary care inspired some EAP administrators to expand the program to include secondary prevention activities to identify and intervene with high-risk employees, including dependents and retirees. Among other consequences, the movement from tertiary to secondary prevention has increased employers' emphasis on personal responsibility for health and well-being. Based on the training of supervisors to detect deterioration in employee job performance and on the referral of troubled employees to counseling, the EAP model has shifted toward the promotion of employee self-awareness and voluntary self-referrals.[61]

Converging Interests of EAPs and Health Promotion.   EAP professionals felt some encroachment of workplace health promotion into their domain. The issue of territoriality or boundary maintenance was offset by the concomitant emphasis of health promotion programs on self-referrals, and the presence of "dual clients," employees who use both EAPs and health promotion services, suggested a "wellness-to-EAP-to-wellness" referral pattern. High blood pressure, for example, is a common condition among alcoholics. Physical fitness programs have been used as part of the prescription to rehabilitate employees from substance dependence or emotional problems.

Over the years there has been a gradual reorientation of substance abuse programs—from the referral and treatment of employees with identified alcohol or drug problems to a more basic focus on those factors that precipitate socioemotional problems. Comprehensive EAPs address the emotional and personal problems that interfere with work performance and can develop into more serious and costly psychiatric or physical health disorders. The evolution of EAPs has led most to extend their services to address family and emotional difficulties, financial crises, and problems with children and family.

Although EAPs remain at a secondary prevention level of intervention, their new comprehensive orientation was responsible for the increasing popularity of EAPs in the 1980s and 1990s. This broad focus reduced the stigma associated with an employee being labeled as an alcoholic. In addition, removal of this stigma helps reduce the denial often experienced by troubled employees in accepting referral and treatment. With the trend of increasing self-referrals, supervisors are now trained to assess employee job performance rather than diagnose potential problems related to alcohol or drug use.

One can view the substance abuse component of work site health promotion as the primary prevention arm of employee assistance programs. Herein, the boundaries of EAPs overlap with health promotion. The recognition of simultaneous unhealthful lifestyle behaviors and dual-client users will continue to generate even greater concern over the issue of territoriality and boundary maintenance. This particular crossroads is marked with signs reading "yield" and "proceed with caution."

The Blending of the Four Work Site Health Ecologies

A few remaining features of the workplace setting for health and its evolution illustrate how the approaches to health in the regulatory, medical, and psychological traditions of occupational health and safety, employee health services, EAPs, and health promotion have blended into the work of health and human resource professionals in the occupational setting.

Prevention Versus Health Promotion.   Early stages of occupational health emphasized the conservation of health status, while more recent efforts address the promotion of health to the optimal level, to improve quality of life and work performance. The definition of occupational disease and injury includes health problems that may be aggravated by work conditions, thus expanding the concept of occupational health to include conditions such as high blood pressure, cardiovascular disease, ulcers, and a variety of psychological problems.

Health Risk Appraisals.   The history of medical screening in occupational health, combined with the screening and self-referral traditions of EAPs, were expressed in work site health promotion with an early interest in the development of the Health Risk Appraisal (HRA). In the context of the work site, HRAs are used to assess the health risks and to motivate actions to reduce the lifestyle risks for chronic diseases and injury. The HRA provides a methodology for determining the probability of risk for illness and provides employers with a tool for planning, evaluation, and cost control.

Although HRAs are useful for identifying behaviors requiring modification at the individual level, programs based on this information alone tend not to attain much success. Program developers need to consider the role of the organizational environment and its resulting impact on health behavior and on health itself. This brings us to the most significant development in workplace health of recent years.

Work Organization, Control, and Health.   Karasek's pioneering work on stress in occupational health, beginning in the 1970s, helped establish the relationship between work organization and health.[62] A central theme that emerged from this line of inquiry is that a person's place and degree of control in the social and work environment affect health and well-being. Researchers emphasized the central role of the social environment in determining the health of individuals, and they stressed on-the-job environment as a factor in biological and social pathology. When workers have little control over their work pace and methods, higher levels of catecholamines, mental strain, coronary heart disease, and other health problems result.[63] Studies of civil servants in Britain[64] and bus drivers in San Francisco[65] showed similar effects of stress, work pace, isolation, and hierarchical position.

With the increase in office and service occupations, the relationship between work conditions and health is of great concern: millions of people work at video display terminals. This type of work encourages low control, social isolation, and repetition and monotony, which may have unduly influenced the increasing number of stress-related disability claims.[66]

Organizational Culture.   Many health programs struggle because they function in the absence of a supportive corporate culture. This could explain the problem of fit with prepackaged wellness programs: They would be ineffective when imposed on a corporate culture different from the one in which they were developed, especially when compounded by an initial mismatch between the program and employee needs. Successful implementation of health programs in part depends on the systematic change of norms that support unhealthful lifestyle practices.

Allen pioneered the Normative Systems Approach to Cultural Change.[67] *Norms* are the social group's expectations concerning appropriate behavior. In the work environment, employees establish certain standards of behavior that become the norms of that group. The systematic cultural change strategies outlined by Allen's approach serve to reinforce the norms for enhancing healthful behavior, empowering employees, and stimulating cooperation for change. In the 1970s and early 1980s, smoking in offices was the norm. Within a decade, support of restrictive smoking policies had changed the norm to nonsmoking.

Health programs that are designed and implemented in a way that fits the organizational culture tend to be more effective than those that do not. Program evaluations find that the implementation of identical programs in different work sites yield variable results, suggesting that work site characteristics have either a moderating or mediating effect on the desired outcome.[68] For example, the ecological effects of organizational characteristics on compliance with nonsmoking policies were studied in 710 work sites associated with the North American COMMIT study. Compliance of workers was highest in work sites where policies were more restrictive, communication of the policy was effective, cigarette vending machines were not present, smoking-cessation programs were offered, and labor-management relations were excellent.[69] The concept of fit of a given program with the organizational culture begets more sophisticated constructs for assessment and program development. It is important to design flexible programs that can be adapted to the employee group norms and organizational characteristics; alternatively, one could adapt selected organizational characteristics and policies to the proposed program.[70]

Individuals can easily change their own behavior when they have the necessary knowledge, skills, resources, and incentives; however, when the behaviors are deeply embedded in lifestyle, including conditions of work over which they have little or no control, change is difficult at best. Some behaviors have an addictive or compulsive component. While short-term behavior change occurs, often through exhaustive efforts, long-term change is even more difficult to achieve. Changes do occur with comprehensive programs addressing the necessary combination of predisposing, enabling, and reinforcing factors, including the organization of the worker's tasks, support, and environment.

In summary, health programs have been like tumbling snowballs in the workplace, accumulating layers of new ideas and old components from environmental programs. From a preoccupation with cost-effectiveness to growing interests in corporate culture and organization, and an array of outcomes from short-term to long-term intangibles, health promotion continues to evolve as it spreads to new firms and new work sites within large companies. The three spheres in Figure 7-6 illustrate the convergence at the turn of the century. We might anticipate a further merging of the three spheres as the 21st century proceeds, and this convergence might be expected to give greater consideration to the organization of work and human resources issues.

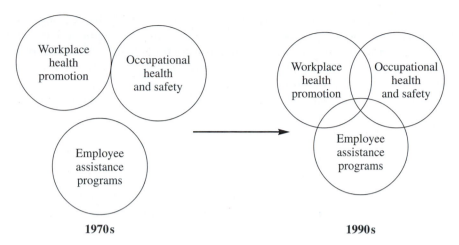

FIGURE 7-6 The three spheres of workplace health have separate histories, traditions, disciplinary attachments, ideological orientations, and legislative mandates, but they have taken on features of each other in the past decade to the point that they now overlap in their functions and activities.

CAVEATS

Attention to the assessment and formative evaluation steps of PRECEDE and the developmental and process evaluation steps of PROCEED can help practitioners avoid two traps that could sidetrack program efforts or undermine their credibility. The first is associated with potential ethical problems; the second, with the tendency to be too zealous with claims of cost containment.

Ethical Concerns

Problems may arise from (1) conflicting loyalties of health professionals, (2) an exclusive focusing attention on changing the behavior of victims of work site hazards rather than on the hazards themselves, (3) perceived paternalism of changing policies without adequate consultation (4) the labeling and coercion of individuals, and (5) unintended consequences such as the compromising of medical care benefits and discrimination in hiring practices.[71] These issues point to the need for sensitivity to issues of worker participation in planning programs, justice, and privacy in the implementation of health-related programs. Attention and commitment to the principle of participation highlighted in Chapter 2 is of paramount importance in helping the practitioner recognize and effectively address these critical issues.

The "Victim-Blaming" Versus Paternalism Problems.   Perhaps no work site health promotion issue is more sensitive than one that arises when attention to environmental and organizational problems in the workplace are ignored in favor of programs directed solely at individual responsibility for behavioral change among workers. One of the greatest concerns expressed by labor groups has been the issue of "blaming the victim," particularly for people working under potentially health-threatening conditions such as exposure to chemicals. The victim-blaming trap applies equally to the neglect of environmental factors constraining or compelling behavior. For example, some stress management programs have put the entire emphasis on personal coping strategies rather than on the management practices and environmental conditions that create stress.[72] The concern in both instances is that employers will use the concept of behavior change and worker responsibility for health as a smokescreen for hazards in the work environment. On the other side of the same problem is the apparent paternalism of management making policy changes in the professed interest of workers' health, but with ulterior motives or without adequate consultation.

The Divided Loyalties Problem.   The health professional negotiating a work site health program must struggle with issues of allegiance or neutrality with respect to the positions of management and workers.[73] The ideal resolution is one that combines behavioral and environmental approaches to health, with input from both management and workers.[74] Through the systematic application of the Precede assessment steps, the practitioner in the work site can guard against these ethical concerns in at least two ways: (1) The social assessment can promote greater collaboration between employers and employees, ensuring attention to the ultimate concerns of both. (2) The epidemiological, environmental, and behavioral assessments increase the likelihood that programs will include environmental reforms, balanced with appropriate behavioral strategies, to improve working conditions.

These assessments also help identify circumstances in which work site hazards interact with worker behavior. As we have seen, some are synergistic in their effects, some have concomitant and interacting effects, and others affect productivity and health concomitantly but independently.

Recognition of these interacting relationships between working conditions and health behavior will help health program planners justify the application of comprehensive approaches that provide for interventions that (1) help protect the worker against hazardous and stressful working conditions, (2) promote healthful practices such as physical activity, nutritional eating, or self-examination for cancer signs or symptoms, and (3) support self-referral and care for such symptoms and for signs of family emotional distress.

Employers and the white-collar workforce have responded well to the introduction and expansion of EAPs centered particularly on mental health, alcohol, and drug abuse and to health promotion programs emphasizing stress management, exercise facilities, and health education. Blue-collar workers have shown less interest in these programs and facilities except where their introduction has been through a process of collective bargaining with attention paid to perceived problems in the work environment and in the health service benefits provided by the employer.[75]

Caution: Do Not "Oversell" Economic Benefits.   Earlier, the case was made with caveats that health promotion programs in the work site had potential for containing the costs paid by employers for their employees' health care. While conventional wisdom may indicate that health promotion programs are good "investments" for employers, health economists and others caution practitioners to avoid exaggerating and thereby overselling the potential economic benefits to the employer's company or organization.[76]

The key to an appropriate and compelling social assessment, from the employer's perspective, is to calculate the cost per worker, or per 100 workers, of poor fitness or health outcomes and to relate these costs to the products or services central to the organization. Beyond that, however, the appeal should be as much to the inherent values of healthy workers, and of health to the workers and their families.

APPLICATION OF PRECEDE-PROCEED

Phase 1: Social Diagnosis and Participation

In the work setting, as in other organizational settings, the social diagnosis and assessment of quality-of-life concerns or potential benefits to be obtained from a health program produce quite different results when viewed from the distinct perspectives of different participants, in this case workers and management.

From the Perspective of Employers.   If quality of life is the bottom line for the public, then productivity or profit is the corresponding bottom line for the corporate world, where *bottom line* was coined. The term refers to the bottom of the accounting balance sheet or ledger where the assets and liabilities, or credits and debits, are totaled to get the net profit or loss, surplus or deficit. If you ask "Why?" after each reason a given employer offers for having a health program for his or her employees, eventually the answer will be profit if it is a for-profit company, productivity in some other terms if a nonprofit. Certainly, employers want to have happier, healthier workers. Even so, if an employer invests in a program the only outcome of which is employee "happiness," there's a good chance that the employer won't be happy very long. The day that happier, healthier workers start missing days of work or failing to produce because they are happier or healthier is the day that employers will begin to dismantle their work site health programs. That is the bottom line.

Employers can use various criteria to set bottom-line priorities among optional health programs. Some of the most commonly used criteria are listed in Table 7-3. These reflect the orientation of employers not to health as an end in itself but to other ultimate concerns as motives to provide health programs for their employees.

Companies have been most concerned in recent years about the increases in cost associated with their health care coverage of employees, as reflected in premium rates on group insurance, and in benefits paid on medical claims. As in most other settings, health is not an end in itself in the work site. Health is a

TABLE 7-3 Criteria used by employers in setting health promotion priorities

- Direct measures of productivity (cost-benefit analysis)
- Prior demonstration of benefits in comparable sites
- Time frame for the realization of benefits (discounting)
- Relevance of the program to health costs and risks in the company, taking the benefits package into consideration
- Employee interest in the program as an indication that having the program will help retain and recruit good employees
- Possible negative effects of the program, such as time away from work, injuries, and liability of the employer

resource that enables workers to perform more productively; it holds instrumental rather than terminal value. The social assessment, then, is something of a misnomer in the work setting as far as the employer is concerned. The social is largely financial in this case, where the Precede analysis would most fruitfully begin with an assessment of the "bottom-line" concerns of productivity and profitability such as absenteeism, medical claims, sick days, and worker's compensation claims that might relate to a wide range of health issues, plus injuries and property damage caused by smokers or security problems caused by alcohol- or drug-abusing employees. Other health-related financial concerns affecting productivity include health insurance premiums higher than average because of poor experience rating, turnover rates requiring more frequent hiring and training, and early retirement rates. Relatively direct productivity measures (output per worker) are compared or "benchmarked" with competing companies who may or may not have comparable health programs.

These would be analyzed in Phase 1 not as indicators of the health or morbidity of the organization but as meaningful consequences of employee morbidity. They are meaningful to the employer because they cost money, time, or productivity, any of which reduces the profit margin. They add to the cost of doing business or maintaining the workforce. These costs must be passed on to the consumer or be subtracted from the services rendered or the profit taken. The first makes the company's product or service uncompetitive; the second makes it unattractive to owners or stockholders. In the end, an unhealthy workforce can make an organization untenable.

From the Perspective of Employees.   The workers' perspective on quality-of-life concerns makes the social assessment for their purposes no different than for community programs. If the employers have the final say and they control the resources that will support a program in the work site, why would one bother with a social assessment of the workers? How do their social needs or their perspective matter? A community assessment carried out prior to the work site program could serve as the social assessment from the workers' perspective, making another assessment of their quality-of-life concerns within the work site redundant. It might suffice to concentrate the social assessment of the concerns of employers, previously outlined.

TABLE 7-4 The 10 leading work-related diseases and injuries identified by NIOSH for the United States

1. Occupational lung disorders
2. Musculoskeletal disorders
3. Occupational cancer
4. Fractures, amputations, traumatic deaths
5. Cardiovascular disease
6. Reproductive problems
7. Neurotoxic illness
8. Noise-induced hearing loss
9. Dermatological problems
10. Psychological disorders

A unionized shop or a highly participatory management structure in a given organization, however, makes an assessment of employee perspectives essential. Unions have opposed some behaviorally oriented health programs because they saw them either as smokescreens to divert attention from environmental or organizational problems in the work site or as substitutes for other benefits in the collective bargaining package. Knowing what matters most to the workers can help a health program adequately address environmental issues and appropriate other benefits. It can also serve to establish appropriate objectives and evaluation criteria for whatever programs are eventually offered. Finally, it can provide baseline data, against which later concerns can be compared, as a first step in program evaluation.

Phase 2: Epidemiological Assessment

Although the scope of occupational health and safety traditionally focused on those health conditions related to the physical and chemical hazards of the workplace, rather than on general health and mental health, the more recent movements described above toward integrating health promotion, employee health services, EAP, and occupational health have been directed toward the advancement of health to the optimal level to improve quality of life and performance. In the recent retrenchment and cutbacks, some of those commitments were undercut in many work sites, but the scope remains more inclusive than in the past.

Work-related diseases and injuries are those that the work environment entirely or partially causes. This definition includes health problems that may be aggravated by work conditions, thus expanding the concept of occupational health to include conditions such as high blood pressure, cardiovascular disease, ulcers, and a variety of psychological problems. Epidemiological assessment begins with the description and analysis of the distribution of health factors influencing the social-economic problem (descriptive epidemiology) and continues with the behavioral and environmental causes of the priority health problems (etiological epidemiology).

Table 7-4 lists the 10 leading work-related diseases identified by the National Institute of Occupational Safety and Health as the most frequent, the

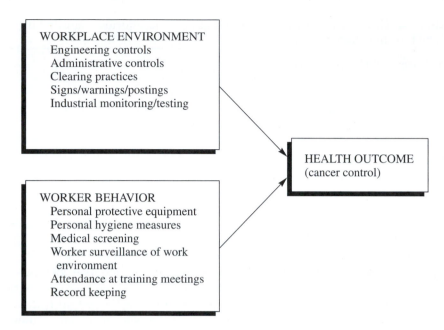

FIGURE 7-7 Behavioral and environmental assessments of cancer risks in five industries in collaboration with Painters Union representatives produced this set of relationships.
Source: Consultation report to Painters Union, by C. Y. Lovato and L. W. Green, 1986.

most severe, and of the highest priority on a national scale, reflecting the totals and averages across all work sites. For any given work site, the reality and priorities might be quite different, which is why a setting-specific descriptive epidemiological diagnosis is important. The local differences from national rankings and averages can also be instructive about what makes this work site different, a first step in the etiologic purpose of the epidemiological diagnosis.

Examples of worker behavior and workplace environmental factors influencing occupational cancer are shown in Figure 7-7. Program personnel representing five labor unions identified these factors. They participated in developing interventions designed to reduce the incidence of cancer for workers at high risk of cancer because of occupational exposure.[77]

Ideally, one will find surveillance data at the work site from which to obtain from the ongoing collection of data an updated snapshot of current prevalence or a recent year's incidence of the health problems of greatest importance (to employers and workers) and some of the determinants of those health problems. Additional data collection and analysis may be needed in this phase of the Precede planning process to further specify the distribution of health and injury problems in the particular work site and their behavioral and environmental determinants. A review of literature and experience will also be needed to assess their relative changeability. Among those found to be most important, some will be more amenable to change than others. Some will be related to each other, which will make change in one affect change in another.

One can use these ratings and relationships to set priorities on the behavioral and environmental factors deserving primary attention in the next phase.

The number of complex factors contributing to a given health indicator usually exceeds the program resources available. It is inevitable, therefore, that some behavioral or environmental factors will receive a low priority. By narrowing the focus of the program at this stage of analysis and assessment of needs, however, one saves considerable effort in each of the subsequent steps in planning. Failing to rule out less important objectives or targets of change at this phase will mean wasteful analysis of their determinants and appropriate interventions in the next two phases, only to discover in the final phase of planning that one has insufficient resources to provide for these low-priority needs.

Because environmental factors in the work site are usually more immediate and contained than in the larger community, they deserve special attention as candidates for change in work site health program planning. They also represent the factors most likely to convince workers that the commitment of the program to meaningful change is sincere. Some workers, especially those who perceive themselves at risk of environmental and organizational assaults on their health and well-being in the work site, are more likely to support and participate in the program if they see some significant attention to environmental-organizational concerns.

It seldom happens that a set of important health problems in the work site can be attributed singularly to environmental or behavioral causes. The choice is seldom between the two; rather, it usually lies among the numerous candidates competing for attention in both the behavioral and environmental categories. DeJoy has developed an adaptation of the Precede-Proceed Model that attempts to combine the occupational hygienic, ergonomic, and organizational factors and health promotion aspects of worker safety in a "comprehensive human factors model of workplace accident causation," more recently expanded to encompass "organizational health promotion."[78]

An epidemiological assessment of the problems of sick leave, absenteeism, and injury rates in San Francisco bus drivers found hypertension, musculoskeletal system problems, and gastrointestinal problems at excess levels in this population of workers. Conventional medical approaches to this assessment might have emphasized drug treatment for the hypertension, patient education on posture for the back pain, and diet for the gastrointestinal problems. By simultaneously examining the potential behavioral and environmental determinants, including the organization of work, planners found unreasonable work schedules for the bus drivers, in combination with long shifts and social isolation. A related coping behavior was the tendency for the drivers to remain at the bus yard for several hours after their shift to "wind down" before going home. This resulted in limited time with family and friends at home, which might account for some of the hostile and impatient behavior observed in the drivers. This narrowed the focus of the behavioral and environmental assessment of coping behavior of drivers and scheduling conditions of the work site. This example, as shown in Figure 7-8, illustrates the interactions of environmental and behavioral factors that need to be examined in this phase of

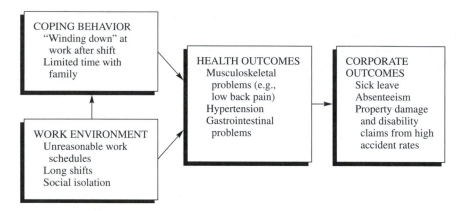

FIGURE 7-8 Behavioral and environmental assessment of work site conditions related to health outcomes and corporate outcomes in the Municipal Transit Authority of San Francisco.
Source: Based on "Strategies for Health Promotion," by L. W. Syme, 1986, *Prevention Medicine, 15,* 492–507. Reprinted with permission.

assessment, emphasizing the influence of the organization of work. Other examples of job conditions that may lead to health-compromising stress are shown in the box on page 347.[79]

The final step in these two phases of PRECEDE is to set objectives and the evaluation criteria for each of the outcomes found to be most important and changeable at the health problem and behavioral-environmental levels. These objectives might have to be long-range goals that will be unachievable within the first year or more of the program, but the data that led to their identification at this planning stage should also provide criteria and baselines for evaluation of the outcomes. For example, the objective of a cancer control program designed by the Workers Institute for Safety and Health specified the following goal: to reduce the mortality of workers exposed to the bladder carcinogens used in the manufacture of textile dyes. Impossible to measure directly in the short term, mortality reductions would be inferred (projected statistically, based on national averages) from the increase in lead time for treatment, resulting from the program's success in reducing delay in workers' seeking diagnosis after their symptoms first appeared, or from the program's early detection of cancer symptoms from screening offered onsite or through health insurance arrangements.[80]

Objectives should be stated in quantitative terms so that a clear vision of the program's contribution to the organization's "bottom line" can be brought out any time the program seems to be losing its way or its support. These objectives should state how much of what social, financial, health, behavioral, or environmental measure (e.g., a 20% reduction of medical claims for lower back pain) might be expected in which employees (e.g., in mail-room workers) by when (in the second year of the program).[81]

The objectives for each of the behavioral and environmental targets of change should state how much of what factors are expected to change by when.

JOB CONDITIONS THAT MAY LEAD TO STRESS

The Design of Tasks.   Heavy workload, infrequent rest breaks, long work hours and shiftwork; hectic and routine tasks that have little inherent meaning, do not utilize workers' skills, and provide little sense of control.

> *Example:* David works to the point of exhaustion. Theresa is tied to the computer, allowing little room for flexibility, self-initiative, or rest.

Management Style.   Lack of participation by workers in decision making, poor communication in the organization, lack of family-friendly policies.

> *Example:* Theresa needs to get the boss's approval for everything, and the company is insensitive to her family needs.

Interpersonal Relationships.   Poor social environment and lack of support or help from co-workers and supervisors.

> *Example:* Theresa's physical isolation reduces her opportunities to interact with other workers or receive help from them.

Work Rules.   Conflicting or uncertain job expectations, too much responsibility, too many "hats to wear."

> *Example:* Theresa is often caught in a difficult situation trying to satisfy both the customer's needs and the company's expectations.

Career Concerns.   Job insecurity and lack of opportunity for growth, advancement, or promotion; rapid changes for which workers are unprepared.

> *Example:* Since the reorganization at David's plant, everyone is worried about their future with the company and what will happen next.

Environmental Conditions.   Unpleasant or dangerous physical conditions such as crowding, noise, air pollution, or ergonomic problems.

> *Example:* David is exposed to constant noise at work.

The changes in behavior may be expressed in the behavioral objectives as percentages of employees in a given category of the workforce (e.g., an increase of 40% of mail-room workers) who will adopt a new behavior or abandon a negative health practice (e.g., practicing proper lifting techniques) by when (e.g., between the 1st week and the 12th week of the program).

The environmental objectives might be stated in terms of the actual installation of a new facility. For example, "Waist-high conveyor belts will be installed in the mail room next to each work station by the 12th week of the program." Environmental objectives would often reflect the removal of an environmental hazard: "All floor level bins for mail bags will be replaced with conveyor belts."

If the objective is to be used as the program's criterion of success, one might want to specify the measurement procedure as part of the objective or as an operational definition of the behavior. For the behavioral objective in the foregoing example, this might be "as measured by an observer during a randomly selected 1-hour work period each day for one week." For the environmental objectives, this might refer to a specific regulatory code or occupational health and safety standard (e.g., "in accordance with Section 1601 of the State Safety Code"), which often also provides for the inspection procedure. Alternately, it might refer to the terms of a contract or the contractor to be hired for the installation or removal of the facility or hazard (e.g., "as specified in contract number AB21" or "as specified in the standard contract of company XYZ"). In the absence of codes and standards or documented specifications, the objective might need to specify the size, shape, or type of materials to be installed or removed (e.g., "constructed with ball-bearing rollers").

With this level of specificity in the formulation of objectives, the evaluation is planned to a large degree even as the program plan is taking shape.

Phase 3: Educational and Ecological Assessment

The task in Phase 3 is to assess the relative importance and changeability of the factors predisposing, enabling, and reinforcing the selected behavioral and environmental targets for the work site program. These determinants of change in each of the behavioral and environmental objectives will become the immediate targets of the interventions. In a cancer-screening project for workers exposed to carcinogens, for example, the predisposing factors determining change were identified as knowledge and awareness of the risk of bladder cancer and the advantages of early detection. Enabling factors concentrated on the development of skill in detecting symptoms and on providing cancer screening. Reinforcing factors concentrated on building social support networks through the community, co-workers, and the family.

The educational and ecological assessment is where one brings to bear most cogently the appropriate behavioral science, social, or political science and economic studies and theories of change. Selecting which determinants might be influencing the behavioral or environmental targets is, once again, an exercise in narrowing the field from an enormous number of possible factors to a more manageable number of important and realistic targets for change.

For example, for a complex lifestyle objective such as increasing exercise or changing dietary practices to reduce fat intake, there would be dozens of component behaviors and, for each of those, dozens of possible predisposing, enabling, and reinforcing factors. The more complex the behavior or lifestyle, the more component parts or manifestations the behavior will have. Each component must be analyzed in Phase 3, so this phase will become too complex to be practicable unless Phase 2 has been rigorous in its priority-setting step. Critical professional judgment should eliminate the least important and least changeable behaviors from further analysis. Similarly, the environmental factors identified in Phase 2 can become too complex to analyze in Phase 3 if they have not been sufficiently delineated and reduced to the most important few deserving highest priority.

Here also, the time perspective of the previously developed objectives will dictate the pace at which change in the determinants must occur to meet the behavioral and environmental objectives. The degree of urgency, in turn, will dictate some of the selection of processes of change. To a population asked to make changes in its behavior, educational processes are slower but often more acceptable than are regulatory processes. Rules and regulations promulgated from management when the workers have not yet learned the need for the rules and have not been involved in the process of their formulation sometimes results in a backlash that offsets any gain in efficiency.[82] Our case study at the end of this chapter will illustrate this issue with smoke-free clear air policies initiated in work sites.

The point is that a balanced approach including both learning processes and environmental change processes is almost always advisable to ensure lasting results and changes that are both acceptable and efficient. Acceptability comes with learning and associating the proposed change with values; efficiency comes with structural or organizational facilitation and resources for change. In Phase 3, therefore, one needs to assess the predisposing *and* reinforcing *and* enabling factors determining *each* of the behavioral and environmental targets or objectives given high priority in Phase 2.

Predisposing Factors.   Assessing level of commitment, then, is the first order of business in Phase 4. This predisposing factor represents the base on which all other determinants may have their effect. If the employer and worker populations have a high level of awareness, commitment, or motivation for the behavioral or environmental changes identified in Phase 2, then less effort will be needed on enabling and reinforcing factors. If motivation is low, then little will happen with respect to behavioral change, no matter how much emphasis is placed on enabling and reinforcing factors. Motivation or level of commitment must be high enough to ensure participation in the program.

Studies of employee response and behavioral change in work site programs indicate that the predisposing factors with the highest correlations are (1) interest in health and (2) knowledge of the benefits of the recommended behavior.[83] Continued participation in weight control, smoking-cessation, alcohol abuse, physical activity, and other change programs also appears to be predicted by self-efficacy.[84] High levels of perceived job stress also predict participation in exercise, weight control, and stress management programs.[85] Work stress, however, may be negatively correlated with participation in a smoking-cessation program but positively correlated with assertiveness in asking smoking co-workers not to smoke. These effects of work stress may cancel each other out.[86]

"Loss of interest or motivation" is the most frequently cited reason for dropping out of a work site exercise program.[87] This suggests that the predisposing factors might need to be reassessed periodically to determine changes in attitudes, beliefs, or perceptions that need to be corrected to sustain the level of participation required to achieve the behavioral or environmental objectives. This brings one to the analysis of reinforcing factors, which might be thought of as boosters to reactivate fading predisposing factors.

Reinforcing Factors.   Motivation is a necessary but not sufficient determinant of participation. Some of the most highly motivated workers will not continue to participate in a work site health promotion program if they are bucking a supervisor who frowns on it or other workers who think it is silly or means more work for them. These social forces rewarding or punishing the proposed behavior are crucial determinants, assessed in Phase 3.

Research indicates that participant satisfaction plays a major role in continued employee participation. Satisfaction increases when employees are involved actively in planning the program.[88] Employees tend to be more satisfied with programs in which health care or health promotion personnel show warmth and personal concern in their interactions.[89] Amount of contact time and number of contacts with health care providers have been shown to relate to higher satisfaction and blood pressure control.[90]

Overall "organizational climate" has been cited frequently as a key factor in reinforcing worker participation and in ensuring supervisory support for worker participation as well.[91] Senior managers' attitudes and worker perception of their attitudes toward the program set up organizational norms encouraging participation and providing role models for behavioral change. But management-driven norms can also preclude the discussion among workers that leads to stronger self-enforcement of norms and a "subtle change in the frequency and nature of workplace interactions that may no longer discourage employee smoking," an example we will explore further in the case study at the end of this chapter.[92]

Confidentiality is an important reinforcing factor for some behavioral and environmental objectives. Participation in a screening program, for example, will be quickly discouraged if workers learn that information about their health condition or family history is shared with employers, supervisors, insurers, or others.[93] Recall the ethical issues of confidentiality, addressed earlier in this chapter.

Boredom with a repetitive routine discourages continued participation for some, though others may find a mindless routine comforting or liberating from work stress. Fun and variety, contests and competitions—in the health program, activities can reinforce participation and hold the interest of some, which might account in part for the popularity of group aerobic exercise classes and work site competitions in weight control, tobacco and other areas.[94] Caution must be exercised, however, not to substitute token rewards for the internalization of values and beliefs necessary to sustain real behavior change over time. Token reinforcements may only yield token behavior or deceptive claims of behavior change.[95]

Enabling Factors.   Accessibility and convenience are the key enabling factors to be assessed in Phase 3. Proximity of the program to workstations, convenience of scheduling, and cost determine program accessibility; lack of access usually represents the largest barrier to program participation. Enabling factors for environment change in the work site include cost of the environmental or organizational modifications, disruption of the flow or pace of work, and availability of space for new facilities or equipment.

An application of the Precede Model analyzing the injury prevention behavior of construction workers appears in Figure 7-9, illustrating the range of factors considered in Phase 3. In this era of the Precede Model, the environmental factors were encompassed in the enabling factors.

Phase 4: Administrative, Organizational, and Policy Assessment

Having now identified the key determinants of the behavioral and environmental objectives, one must assess the resources that could influence these determinants, as well as assess organizational or regulatory policies and practices that will facilitate or hinder the implementation of the program. The first resource of concern is time. Release time for worker participation in health programs of any kind can be a source of considerable controversy. The hours of work time lost for participants is added to the cost of the program. The usual solution is flexible schedules that allow workers to participate within their work shift but to make up the time during another shift.

Second among resource concerns for most work site health programs is space. The main purpose of the company or organization hosting the program is not employee health but rather some other product or service production; thus, devoting space to health programs cannot be done lightly. Use of space after hours, or dual use of otherwise underused space are the usual solutions. Sharing space with other companies or organizations is another solution.

Policies to support or protect employee health and health behavior have become the most hotly debated subject in the work site health program literature in recent years. Work site smoking policies have been tried and evaluated in several countries with varying success.[96] Employee assistance programs raise similar policy issues of cost-effectiveness, ethics, employee acceptance, and civil rights, as elaborated earlier in this chapter.

Policy, resources, and organizational support for health programs in the work site relate most directly to company profit or worker productivity issues. To understand managerial attitudes toward offering new policies, programs, or facilities, one must review a company's experiences with worker participation, satisfaction, and job performance in previous efforts to offer health programs. Management behavior is predisposed, enabled, and reinforced just as much as everyone else's behavior. This point should lead the health program planner to consider applying the Precede steps to an analysis of employer behavior or to the collective bargaining behavior of workers if the obstacle to starting a program for employees lies in the motivation of management.[97]

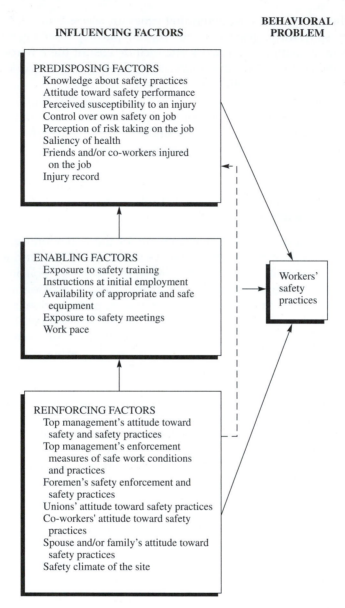

FIGURE 7-9 Predisposing, enabling, and reinforcing factors in the educational assessment of construction workers' safety practices.

Source: "Safety Practices in Construction Industry," by N. Dedobbeleer & P. German, 1987, *Journal of Occupational Medicine, 29,* 863–868. Reprinted with permission.

Implementation and Evaluation Phases

The circumstances and politics of each work site differ, and within each work site these will change over time. No amount of planning and policy development can anticipate each new employee's and each new day's special circumstances. Implementation must therefore adapt plans and policies to changing circumstances. The organization of advisory groups during the implementation phases should help the program stay on track regarding sensitivity to managers' and workers' concerns. The provision for continuous feedback through supervisory lines of communication and anonymous suggestion boxes and questionnaires can help.

The final phases of implementation-evaluation-modification-maintenance obviously represent a series of recursive steps. They essentially recycle through the previous steps, beginning at Phase 1 for the criteria, indicators, and baseline data for evaluation. If the changes required are so sweeping as to require renegotiation with management, one must revisit Phase 1 to reconsider the very justification for the program. Surveys and data collection would have been done at the earliest planning stages, for purposes of assessing employee and employer perceptions of needs, or at the stage of setting objectives, when survey data were needed to establish baselines for later evaluation. Data collection might not have been possible until the evaluation phase. Whenever they might be conducted, surveys of employees follow a series of steps that can be planned and phased as suggested by Figure 7-10.

The major challenge of resource allocation arises in the implementation phase when demand exceeds resources. Sometimes this is a problem of numbers, sometimes a problem of variable needs of different types of employees. One can consider three approaches for rationing and allocating scarce program resources during the implementation phase:

- Screening or wait-listing employees on the basis of a procedure or set of criteria agreed on in the planning
- Providing self-help materials and referrals to community resources, with or without subsidies or release time
- A systematic triage and stepped program of interventions based on individualized needs assessments and tailored interventions

Screening and Wait-Listing.   The most common method of rationing health resources in the work site is simply limiting the eligibility. Historically, work site health promotion programs were known as executive fitness programs, or executive health examination programs, with the obvious implication of their unavailability to many workers. Some programs screen at the other end of the hierarchy, restricting access to those with the highest risk, greatest exposure to workplace hazards, or greatest need for company subsidy or support. The use of health-risk appraisals and other screening tests to select the target groups for recruitment or admission to the program has a time-honored tradition in public health.[98]

Besides the usual screening on health and risk factor levels, one screening test particularly relevant to a program's effectiveness concerns level of motivation. Many workers will take up space in health programs without much commitment to follow through with the behavioral change recommendations. The requirement that applicants keep a diary of their behavior for a week before starting the program has served as an effective screen in some programs.[99]

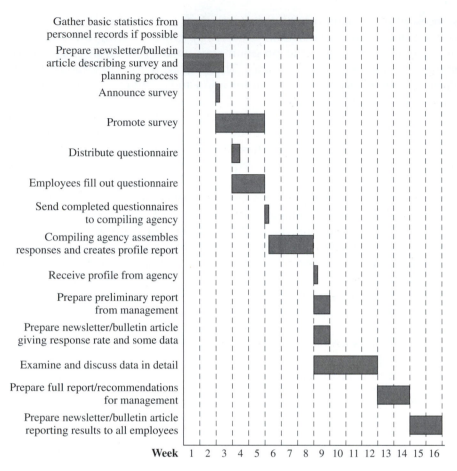

FIGURE 7-10 This sample Gantt chart from Health Canada suggests a series of overlapping steps in conducting a survey of employees for purposes of planning or evaluating a work site program.
Source: Workplace Health: Discovering the Needs, 1990, Ottawa: Health and Welfare Canada.

Self-Care and Community Referrals.   Much of what a company can offer through personnel and facilities provided at the work site could be obtained through other organizations in the community, either in the form of self-help materials or in classes and facilities. The advantages of access and convenience at the work site are obvious, and the advantages of group support among employees can be argued. But self-help materials have a good track record for the motivated.[100] Subsidy of worker participation in outside programs through direct contract with the vendor or agency, through payment to the worker, or at least through release time to participate can lend credence and effectiveness to the referral process.

Triage and Stepped Program of Interventions.   This third approach requires a more systematic process of assessing the needs of each employee, applicant,

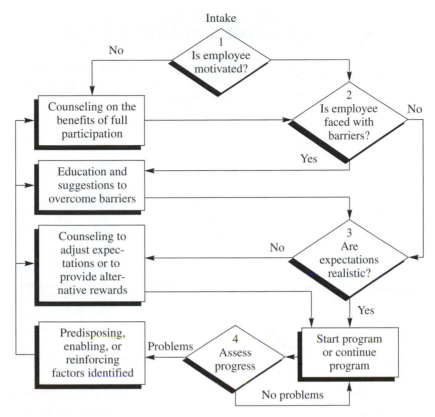

FIGURE 7-11 This algorithm follows the Precede Model for the purpose of assessing potential problems of employees in initiating and maintaining a behavioral change and allocating them to actions that conserve the resources of the program for those who need more tailored interventions.
Source: "Maintaining Employee Participation in Workplace Health Promotion Programs," by C. Y. Lovato and L. W. Green, 1990, *Health Education Quarterly, 17,* 73–88. Reprinted with permission of the publisher.

or participant in a program of interventions to determine which combination of interventions might be most needed and effective in achieving the program goals or that person's goals. The Precede Model can be applied in this process, especially in the educational assessment stage. Figure 7-11 offers an algorithm (flowchart) for the **triage** and **stepped approach** to assessing predisposing, enabling, and reinforcing factors in sequence and intervening to strengthen those needing more attention.[101]

Evaluation can be accomplished through program records to measure implementation and process variables, through self-tests, questionnaires, and self-monitoring reports to measure impact, and through company medical or insurance records to measure health outcomes. Absenteeism, productivity, and other company bottom-line concerns can be assessed as described in the evaluation literature cited earlier in this chapter.

A CASE STUDY:
AIR QUALITY CONTROL IN A STATE AGENCY

To illustrate issues concerning the planning process and the policy implementation and evaluation process in the work site, this case study reviews the experience of a well-documented intervention on tobacco control.[102]

Social and Epidemiological Assessment

A Texas state human services agency employs about 14,000 people and has its
headquarters in the state capital, with field offices organized into 10 regions.
Recently, in one of the regions, 1,500 employees moved into a newly constructed facility. Shortly thereafter, employees began to experience respiratory
problems and allergic reactions; they associated these reactions with the recent
move. They expressed their concern about these new events and the quality of
air in the environment to the building committee, who conducted an investigation of the building's ventilation system. The committee determined that, other
than systematic vigorous cleaning, little could be done to improve the turnover
rate of air, or the rate of replacing used air with fresh air. This finding, coupled
with the voice of employees who wished the new building to be smoke-free,
led to a concentrated approach to improve the air quality through reducing the
ambient smoke and other pollutants in the environment and encouraging
employees who smoked to stop.

   As seen from this description, movement from the social to the behavioral
and environmental assessment was as much a political process as one of professional planning. The agenda for the building committee was set by
employee concerns, and no systematic effort was made to set priorities among
quality-of-life concerns or health problems. The decision to change behavior
and the environment through a policy reform restricting smoking was a fore-
gone conclusion.

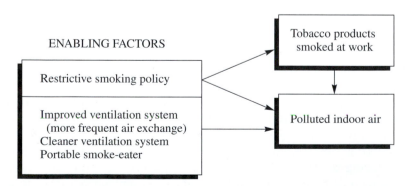

FIGURE 7-12 Enabling factors influencing air quality in an office building with
central heating and air conditioning.

Educational and Ecological Assessment

The building committee, which extended its membership to include both smokers and nonsmokers, did engage in an assessment process to determine its strategies for addressing the environmental issue. It forwarded responsibility for designing the smoking-cessation programs to the wellness committee, and it assessed the options for environmental and behavioral change as follows:

The Environment.   Figure 7-12 illustrates the determinants of environmental air quality. The importance and changeability of each of the enabling factors was considered as follows:

Enabling Factors	Importance	Changeability
• Ventilation system improvements to increase air exchange rate	+ +	− −
• Cleaning ventilation system	+	+ +
• Portable smoke-eaters	−	+ +
• Restrictive smoking policy	+ +	+ / −

Based on this organizational and engineering analysis, developers decided to make cleaning of the ventilation system a high priority and to reduce ambient smoke in the building by recommending that a restrictive smoking policy be established.

Behavior/Lifestyle.   The wellness committee decided to conduct smoking-cessation programs for smoking employees in the new headquarters building. These programs were also offered to employees in some of the regional offices as part of an evaluation research project. When the executive decision was made to adopt a restrictive smoking policy, the policy was applied statewide, so smoking-cessation programs were offered statewide.

An educational and organizational assessment was conducted to help design these programs. Table 7-5 displays predisposing, reinforcing, and enabling factors for stopping smoking. This analysis flows from a behavioral perspective.

The predisposing factors are drawn primarily from the perspective of social learning theory and the Health Belief Model. They include the individuals' expectations for the positive and negative results of smoking, their self-efficacy for quitting, their intentions to quit, and their health beliefs regarding their susceptibility to and the seriousness of smoking-related diseases. Measures of an individual's smoking history—smoking frequency and duration (habit strength) and number and duration of cessation attempts—are also predisposing factors shown to predict success in quitting. The predisposing factors vary across individuals and are useful (1) in designing interventions directed to getting persons to decide to quit smoking and (2) in tailoring cessation programs to the target population.

Although the cognitive factors include a motivational component of desired outcomes from quitting, social and material incentives provide an

TABLE 7-5 Educational and organizational assessment of predisposing, reinforcing, and enabling factors related to smoking cessation

Predisposing Factors

Attitudes, beliefs, and values concerning the positive aspects of smoking:
  Increases concentration
  Decreases tension
  Provides a high
  Controls my weight
  Helps me fit in

Attitudes, beliefs, and values concerning the negative aspects of smoking:
  Keeps me from fitting in
  Increases my health risk
  Increases the health risks of others
  Is not compatible with my value of health
  Costs a lot
  Makes my clothes and hair smell
  Is messy

Belief in self-efficacy for quitting

Habit strength: number of years smoked

Previous cessation attempts: experience with quitting

Reinforcing factors

Social encouragement to quit and remain abstinent
  Co-worker
  Family
  Cessation group "buddy"

Material incentives
  Financial rewards for quitting

Restrictive policy violations

Enabling factors

Skills for quitting

Restrictive smoking policy

---

important source of reinforcement for quitting. In addition, the restrictive policy brings negative reinforcement and punishment into play. Individuals will avoid penalties by not smoking in restricted areas, and smoking in these areas will lead to punishment. Expectation of these reinforcements is a strong source of motivation.

The possession of behavioral skills, including self-contracting, goal setting, monitoring of cigarettes, identification and management of environmental cues to smoke, self-reinforcement, and techniques for coping with urges to smoke are crucial to the individual's following through on the decision to quit. The work site setting makes it possible to move beyond individual management of environmental cues. To reduce triggering of the smoking impulse, cues for smoking are removed from areas in which policy restricts smoking. In this way, the policy restraint on one smoker becomes a support to another smoker trying to quit.

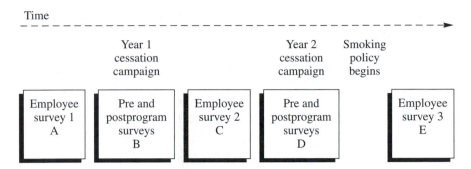

FIGURE 7-13 Quantitative data collection points in the assessment and evaluation phases of developing an educational and environmental approach to air quality in a state office building.

From Administrative and Policy Assessment to Implementation

In our example, a smoking cessation program was devised based on the educational and organizational assessment and the resources available in the budget and in the work site. *Freedom from Smoking in Twenty Days,* a low-cost self-help program, was chosen to provide information and exercises designed to influence the predisposing factors (e.g., those identified by questions such as "Why do you smoke?" and "Why do you want to quit?") and the specific skills listed earlier as enabling factors. The self-help manual includes forms for logging smoking patterns and analyzing cues or triggers for smoking, for making self-contracts, and for planning how one will cope with urges to smoke. With encouragement from the manual, smokers could select a "buddy" and find advice in the manual on how to make the most of this supportive relationship.

Additional reinforcement was mobilized at the organizational level, using two campaigns. The first was a competition between two work sites. The work site with the highest proportion of smokers recruited to the program and of nonsmokers becoming "supporters" won a cold-turkey buffet the day after the Great American Smoke-Out, which is sponsored by the American Cancer Society. This mobilized social reinforcement for recruitment. A second campaign conducted later, *Winning Choices,* provided chances to win savings bonds to smokers who joined the cessation programs.

The new policy restricting smoking served as an enabling factor for both the behavioral objective of smoking cessation and the environmental objective of cleaner air. As part of its work in advising the agency head on how to improve air quality, the building committee carried out a survey of employees to assess opinions on whether a more restrictive policy was needed. This survey (Box C in Figure 7-13) followed the employee surveys (A and B) that had provided assessments of predisposing, enabling, and reinforcing factors.

The committee also sponsored a roundtable on the smoking issue, a discussion open to all employees at the state headquarters. Based on its findings, the

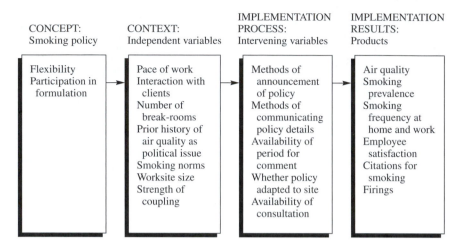

FIGURE 7-14 Smoking policy implementation in a large state agency must reconcile the concepts of the policy with the ecological context of the setting.

committee recommended that a restrictive smoking policy be adopted. The committee, however, played only an advisory role. There was concern that top administration would not act on the recommendation. A proposed Clean Air Act, which would have required smoking policies in all work sites across the state, did not pass in the state legislature that year.

At this point, an internal champion for the proposed policy emerged. A newly appointed high-level manager, who had successfully established a similar smoking policy at another agency, became an advocate for the recommended policy. The executive decision-making group developed a restrictive smoking policy for the entire agency, not just the state office.

Policy development and implementation always depend on context. Two of the few generalizable principles are (1) supervisors who must implement and employees who will be affected by policy should participate in the formulation of the policy and (2) the policy should be flexible enough to cover a variety of contingencies.[103]

A draft policy was published in the statewide employee newsletter, which invited comments. Experience in smoking policy development and implementation suggests that the mere opportunity to comment, even if employees do not avail themselves of the opportunity, goes a long way toward greater acceptance of a new policy. Sent to all employees 4 months before implementation, the final policy called for smoking to be restricted in each building, except in break rooms designated by the regional administrator. Employee meetings held at each site generated advice for the regional administrator on the preferred site of the designated break room. Had this state agency been unionized, representation of the union would have been crucial to the development and implementation of the policy.

Figure 7-14 provides an overview of key factors in policy development and implementation. The success of a smoking policy will depend on its concept or content and the process of its development (first box), on how it fits into the context of implementation (second box), and on its implementation process (third box). The careful planner will provide for employee ownership of the program through participation in its formulation and implementation. Anticipating variations in work sites helps build the necessary flexibility into the policy.

The more thorough cleaning of the ventilation system, the second environmental reform, was more easily implemented. A simple regulatory directive from the agency head to the maintenance supervisor accomplished this. Biweekly vacuuming of external vents and monthly inspections were incorporated into the job routine of maintenance personnel.

Implementation and Structural Evaluation

The implementation and structural evaluation of the new smoking regulations were planned using the flowchart in Figure 7-13 and the logic model or program theory in Figure 7-14. Both qualitative and quantitative methods were used. The process of policy development was documented using internal records such as newsletter articles, memoranda, minutes of committee meetings, and interviews. A survey of a random sample of employees following policy implementation ascertained their level of involvement in policy formulation and implementation (Figure 7-13, Box E). The new ventilation system maintenance was documented through memoranda and inspection reports.

An evaluation was also carried out for the implementation of the smoking-cessation program. Records were maintained of the numbers of nonsmokers volunteering as "supporters" and smokers signing up for the program, attending the orientation, and receiving the self-help manual. The percentages of smoking and nonsmoking employees in the program were calculated using prevalence estimates from an earlier baseline survey (Figure 7-13, Boxes A and C, respectively). This indicated the penetration of the program into the employee population.

These process evaluation reports were completed by each regional wellness coordinator and forwarded to the state coordinator. They served as the basis for making the awards in each region for the cold-turkey buffet and savings bonds drawings in the two campaigns. In addition, all media related to the campaigns were organized by date and submitted by each region to the state office. Based on this evidence, one could determine the extent of implementation of the program within each region.

Process Evaluation

Changes in predisposing factors among smokers were studied using pre- and posttest questionnaires (Figure 7-13, Boxes B and D) of the beliefs and attitudes outlined in Table 7-5. Program participants were also asked what behavioral skill components in the manual they had used and, for each they had used, how helpful it had been. Items related to co-workers and family encouraging and discouraging employees to quit documented the extent to which co-workers

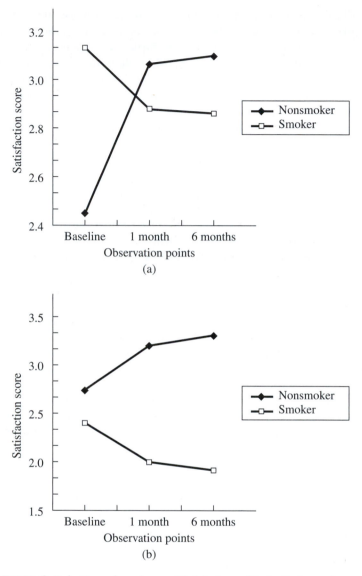

FIGURE 7-15 Satisfaction of workers with (a) air quality in their work area and (b) the smoking policy, at the time of implementation and 1 and 6 months following implementation, comparing smokers and nonsmokers.

Source: "Impact of a Restrictive Work Site Smoking Policy on Smoking Behavior, Attitudes, and Norms," by N. H. Gottlieb, M. P. Eriksen, C. Y. Lovato, et al., 1990, *Journal of Occupational Medicine, 32,* 16–23. Reprinted with permission.

and family had provided social reinforcement for the behavior change. The extent to which the new smoking policy was perceived as a factor in the processes of quitting and maintenance of cessation was also examined.

Satisfaction with the air quality in the work area and with the smoking policy was assessed. Figure 7-15 indicates the marked differences between satisfac-

TABLE 7-6 Smoking indicators versus time in regions with restricted smoking areas and in those with bans

	In Restricted Areas (%)			In Ban Areas (%)		
	Baseline	1 month	6 months	Baseline	1 month	6 months
	$n = 1432$	$n = 1111$	$n = 967$	$n = 279$	$n = 238$	$n = 169$
Current smokers	22.4%	21.4%	20.1%	25.1%	22.7%	16.6%
Former smokers	19.2	19.3	20.2	12.5	19.3	15.4
Never smoked	58.4	59.3	59.8	62.4	58.0	68.0
Smokers						
≥ 15 cigarettes at work	$n = 313$ 16.9	$n = 226$ 6.6	$n = 190$ 5.8	$n = 69$ 17.4	$n = 49$ 8.2	$n = 27$ 0.0
≥ 15 cigarettes daily total	$n = 314$ 48.7	$n = 232$ 40.9	$n = 194$ 52.1	$n = 69$ 63.8	$n = 51$ 53.8	$n = 28$ 60.7

Source: "Impact of a Restrictive Work Site Smoking Policy on Smoking Behavior, Attitudes, and Norms," by N. H. Gottlieb, M. P. Eriksen, C. Y. Lovato et al., 1990, *Journal of Occupational Medicine, 32,* 16–23. Reprinted with permission.

tion of smokers and nonsmokers. Most of the change occurred in the first month following implementation of the policy.

Several approaches provided for evaluation of changes in the two enabling factors related to air quality. For smoking policy, employees were surveyed regarding their satisfaction with the policy, whether employees abided by the policy, and the level of enforcement at their specific work site (Figure 7-13, Box E). The evaluation team analyzed whether these factors varied by work site context and by individuals' smoking status. Records were maintained by the state office of employee complaints about the policy, resignations related to the policy, and policy violations and associated personnel actions. The cleaning of the ventilation system was monitored through regular inspection reports of dust accumulation before and after the policy was implemented.

Impact Evaluation

Comparison of pre- and posttest patterns of smoking (Figure 7-13, Boxes B and D) indicated whether participants had reduced the number of cigarettes they smoked or quit smoking. These self-reports of quitting were validated using biochemical analysis on a sample of employees. Besides this study of program participants, a random sample of all employees was undertaken to see if the smoking prevalence had changed across the entire workforce, not just among the employees who were in the program (Figure 7-13, Boxes A, C, and E).

Comparisons were made also between smoking rates in work sites where smoking was allowed in restricted areas and those in which a complete ban was enforced within the buildings. Table 7-6 shows the results at 1 month and 6 months following implementation of the policies. Although the policies suc-ceeded in reducing smoking in the work sites, thereby achieving the program objective of improving air quality, smokers' daily total of cigarettes might have increased with more smoking at home for those working in restricted areas.

Air quality was measured using self-reports of employees on pre- and post-policy surveys (Figure 7-13, Boxes C and E). In addition, an environmental engineering firm conducted an analysis of air quality before and after the policy and program were implemented.

Outcome Evaluation

It is not feasible within program resources to measure long-term health consequences of smoking cessation and air quality improvement in a situation such as this. The time lag for health effects is too long, the employee turnover too great, and the cost of follow-up prohibitive for most organizations. Projections of outcome, however, can be made using risk-factor equations from studies such as the Framingham Heart Study. In this case, it was possible to examine changes in self-reported respiratory symptoms before and after the program and policy were implemented. Nonsmokers in smoke-free regions reported higher satisfaction with air quality and indicated they were bothered less frequently by co-workers' smoke than were their peers in regions with a restrictive smoking policy allowing smoking in break rooms.

SUMMARY

The common mission of occupational health and safety, EAPs, and workplace health promotion to improve employee health represents a point of convergence between the three philosophies. The emphasis of EAPs and health promotion on employee health and well-being rather than on work-related health problems displaced the locus of power—from determinants of health external to employees but internal to the work site to those determinants of health under greater control of employees and to those outside the work site. Although conspiratorial theories abound, it appears to us that the displacement of the foci of intervention was an unconscious result of a growing interest in behavioral risk factors rather than a conscious decision to "blame the victim."

Consequently, the ideologies that govern health promotion and EAPs led to an unconscious drift in responsibility for health from the environment to the individual. The tendency for many programs to emphasize behavior change at the individual level is inconsistent with our understanding of the primary determinants of health. As this chapter attempted to show, in an ecological context, employee health and behavior are first influenced by the broader economic, technological, cultural, and structural elements of the workplace and community. The additional influence of the proximal workplace social environment that predisposes, enables, and reinforces employee health behavior is not trivial. Placing the primary burden for health on the employee without provision for supportive "healthy policy" has limited the effectiveness of many health promotion programs. Barriers to behavior change include problems with participation, retention, and attrition, in addition to the maintenance of such change.

The work site presents an opportunity and a challenge for the development of health promotion. The growth of the labor force with the increased participation of women may be matched in future years with a corresponding growth in the employment of older people needing or choosing to work rather than retire. These demographic trends place new demands on employers to cope with issues of child care and employee health. Escalation of health care costs and the increasing proportion of the burden of medical costs borne by employees and an increased amount paid by them and by employers has brought about an explosion of alternative strategies to contain costs, with health programs being one among many.

Whether for cost-containment or other reasons, the planning, implementation, and evaluation of work site health promotion programs can follow the Precede and Proceed phases of the model with some adaptations. A first point of emphasis for workplace applications is in the social assessment phase, where the economic bottom-line of the employer must receive first consideration before one can expect to gain entry let alone attention to the health needs of employees. Particular attention in the epidemiological analyses of Phase 2 to balancing the emphasis on behavioral and environmental determinants of health can serve to ensure greater support from management and employees alike. Care in the implementation process to provide for continuous monitoring and feedback through advisory and communication structures will ensure the continuity and sustainability of the program.

EXERCISES

1. If the counterpart to social benefits for industry are the bottom-line issues of productivity and profit, how can you express your objectives for a work site program that will convince management to support the program?
2. Create an example in which a behavioral approach, though well-intentioned, may be construed as victim blaming. Then, using the appropriate steps in the Precede-Proceed Model, illustrate how the accountable practitioner can avoid that criticism.

NOTES AND CITATIONS

1. *First publications of PRECEDE-PROCEED:* Green, 1974; followed by formal tests in clinical and community settings, but the first test of the model on employee health in an occupational setting was R. L. Bertera, 1981; Bertera & Cuthie, 1984; Bertera, Levine, & Green, 1982.
2. *Subsequent publications of applications in occupational and other settings:* See continuously updated and searchable bibliography and links to abstracts at http://www.lgreen.net/bibliog

.htm. This website also updates the endnotes to this and the other chapters in this book and provides links to many of their abstracts and other resources.

3. *The most extensive application of the Precede-Proceed model in a series of work-site health programs,* with needs assessments and evaluation of efficiency and effectiveness at several levels, is that by Robert Bertera and his colleagues for the international employee health improvement programs of the Du Pont Corporation. For his most recent publications reporting and reflecting on the results of this series of programs, see R. L. Bertera, 1991, 1993, 1999. The article in which he describes how the Precede-Proceed model was applied is R. L. Bertera, 1990b.

4. *Precede-Proceed as a "minimalist theory" of program planning:* Scriven, 1998, p. 62. See also Glanz & Rimer, 1995.

5. *Changing workforce, aging and feminization:* O'Campo, Eaton, & Muntaner, 2003. The aging workforce might have been offset by the early retirement of many, except that the economy interfered with those plans for most, and those who took it did not fare well financially, so many of those returned to work; e.g., Haveman, Holden, et al., 2003.

6. *Workplace replacing neighborhood as community of identity and social support for many:* Dean & Hancock, 1992; Green, 1990. Lack of social support outside the workplace causes some, especially women, to forego early retirement possibilities; e.g., Elovainio, Kivimaki, et al., 2003.

7. *Occupational Safety and Health Act, 1970,* created the Occupational Safety and Health Agency within the U.S. Department of Labor. http://www.osha.gov, accessed Dec 6, 2003. Since the agency was created in 1971, workplace fatalities in the U.S. have been cut in half and occupational injury and illness rates have declined 40%, at the same time that U.S. employment has doubled from 56 million workers at 3.5 million worksites to 111 million workers at 7 million sites.

8. *History of work and workers' health protection:* Frank, 2002.

9. *Workplace hazard exposure injuries increased while other injuries and occupational deaths were decreasing in the 1990s and early 2000s:* U.S. Department of Labor, Bureau of Labor Statistics, http://data.bls.gov/cgi-bin/surveymost?cf, accessed March 21, 2004.

10. *Motor vehicle injuries account for largest proportion of work-related deaths:* http://www.bls.gov/iif/oshwc/cfoi/cfch0001.pdf, accessed March 21, 2004.

11. *Health issues arising with increases in working mothers:* For example, Anderson, Butcher, & Levine, 2003; Galambos, Barker, & Almeida, 2003; Lakati, Binns, & Stevenson, 2003.

12. *Combining interventions of work environment and employees' health behavior:* For example, DeJoy, & Wilson, 2003; Secker, & Membrey, 2003; Sorensen, Stoddard, et al, 2002.

13. *Combining interventions of work environment and employees' health behavior:* For example, Sorensen, Stoddard, et al., 1999, had a multilevel environmental and educational program on fruit and vegetable consumption at a work site, producing a 7% increase in consumption after statistical controls, whereas an added intervention with family members increased the rate of fruit and vegetable consumption by 19%. Sorensen, Emmons, et al., 2003, have extended this experience to a model for using the various social contexts in which a behavior occurs to structure interventions that address both the environment and the behavior.

14. *Range of worksite medical surveillance:* For example, Faucett & McCarthy, 2003, on *lower back and other chronic pain;* Office of the Secretary, Department of Transportation, 2001; Ozminkowski, Mark, et al., 2003, Wong, 2002, on *drug and alcohol testing.*

15. *Hypertension screening, elevated blood pressure caused by the job or other lifestyle risks?* R. L. Bertera, & Cuthie, 1984; Getliffe, Crouch, et al., 2000; Sheridan, Pignone, & Donahue, 2003.

16. *Privacy, confidentiality, and job discrimination issues arising from HIV and drug testing:* London, Benjamin, & Bass, 2002; E. Warner, Walker, & Friedmann, 2003.

17. *Health risk appraisal questionnaires:* Burton, Chen, et al., 2003; Sloan, Gruman, & Allegrante, 1987; Yen, McDonald, et al., 2003. For application with older adults, see Haber, 1994. Both Burton, et al. and Yen et al. found the health risk appraisal scores to be highly predictive of subsequent medical and pharmaceutical expenditures by the employees.

18. *Genetic testing at the worksite, ethical and legal complications:* Krumm, 2002; Makdisi, 2001; McCunney, 2002; Schill, 2000.

19. *Early occupational health and safety focused on hazards outside the control of employees:* DeJoy, 1990; Winett, King & Altman, 1989.

20. *Employers gave greater weight to individual behavioral and psychological determinants:* For example, Bellingham, 1994; Brailey, 1986; For critiques of this approach, see Bibeau, Mullen, et al., 1988; Eakin, 1992; Green, 1995; and Polanyi, Frank, et al., 2000, who characterize this as the "traditional worksite health promotion approach," (p. 141).

21. *Movement toward work organization and its influence on health:* Polanyi, Frank, et al., 2000. For applications of PRECEDE toward this approach, see Bailey, Rukholm, et al., 1994; Chiou, Huang, et al., 1998; Conrad, Campbell, et al., 1996; Daltroy et al., 1993; DeJoy & Wilson, 2003; Kaukiainen, 2000. In China, an application of PRECEDE concluded "that smoking is affected strongly by enabling factors and reinforcing factors . . . in the workplace" (Sun & Shun, 1995, p. 266), a step toward addressing work organization as a key point of intervention. In their implementation of smoking control policy in Sweden, Pucci & Haglund, 1994, observed that, ". . . on-the-job smoking may, in part, be associated with the structure and function of the work organization . . . tools developed and tested for assessing organizational climate and its link to worksite health promotion are required. Green & Kreuter propose an administrative diagnosis as part of their Precede model . . . Such a diagnosis might even facilitate adaptation of [our] implementation model to Swedish reality" (p. 66).

22. *Attention to psychosocial aspects of occupational health opened the door to the workplace mental health movement:* Lovato, Green, & Stainbrook, 1993; Vasse, Nijhuis, et al., 1997a; 1997b.

23. *Progress in occupational safety and health noted at the turn of the century:* Cullen, 1999.

24. *Recent deregulatory trends could reverse some gains:* for example, Chenet, & McKee, 1998; Rosner, 2000.

25. *Need for attention to the dissemination, translation, and application of legislative, regulatory, and voluntary initiative information:* for example, Schulte, Okun, et al., 2003.

26. *Globalization of trade requires more attention to equivalent worker protections in developing countries:* Frank, p. 854; Green & Frankish, 2001.

27. *Continuing growth of payout for health care of employees captures the attention of employers on health program innovations:* Data from Centers for Medicare and Medicaid Systems, 2002.

28. *Growing evidence of the workplace effectiveness and cost-containment potential of health education and health promotion strategies:* For example, Pelletier, 2001.

29. *Smoke-free workplace legislation gave worksite health promotion its first major regulatory support:* Eriksen, 1986; Fielding, 1990; Pucci & Haglund, 1994.

30. *Early attempts to estimate cost-benefit potential of health education and health promotion programs:* Warner, 1987. For applications of PRECEDE, see Bertera, 1990a, 1993; Eastaugh & Hatcher, 1982; Green, 1974; Windsor, Lowe, & Perkins, 1993. A recent review is Riedel, Lynch, et al., 2001.

31. *Concern that cost-benefit arguments for health promotion might be oversold:* Warner, 1987; Warner, Wickizer, et al., 1987; see also Warner's more recent reflections and analyses on some aspects of this issue as applied to smoking cessation and to tobacco control in developing countries, Warner, 2003; Warner, Hodgson, & Carroll, 1999.

32. *Cost impact on bottom line should not be sole basis for program implementation:* Warner, Smith, Smith, & Fries, 1996. Warner, 1998, also showed how the same problems of deferred benefits (10–25 years in the case of most economic benefits of smoking cessation), turnover (those who benefit might switch their employment or membership to a competitor, who then reaps the economic benefit) apply to managed care organizations' reluctance to invest more in prevention and health promotion counseling.

33. *Evaluations of cost-effectiveness of comprehensive, as distinct from categorical workplace programs:* Pelletier, 2003.

34. *Systematic reviews support effectiveness of workplace smoking cessation interventions:* Moher, Hey, & Lancaster, 2003.

35. *Factors enhancing or suppressing effectiveness of smoking cessation in workplace programs:* Brownson, Hopkins, & Wakefield, 2002; Burns, Shanks, et al., 2000; Hopkins, Briss, et al., 2001.

36. *Simulation of the stream of benefits accruing from workplace smoking-cessation program:* Warner et al., 1996, p. 981.

37. *Comprehensive behavioral-environmental stress management programs more effective than behavioral-only:* McLeroy, Green, et al., 1984; McVicar, 2003; Pelletier & Lutz, 1998. A problem that has plagued stress management programs has been the definition and measures used for stress. A book devoted to review and synthesis of the research on stress management and its measurement derives an approach from the cognitive ergonomics and brain research, Belik, 2003.

38. *Low participation rates in workplace health promotion programs limit generalizability of evaluation results:* Linnan, Emmons, et al., 2002, found that passive methods of recruitment produced a much greater reach and number enrolled, though lower rate of enrollment and a higher rate of attrition. The trade-off seems to favor the greater reach and enrollment, and the greater diversity and therefore representativeness of the passive method. See also, Linnan, Sorensen, et al., 2001; Lovato & Green, 1990. For evidence-based Guidelines to comprehensive programs to promote health eating and physical activity, see Gregory, 2002.

39. *Competitions help in recruiting participants:* Croghan, O'Hara, et al., 2001; Koffman, Lee, et al., 1998.

40. *Hypertension screening, benefits and absenteeism:* Sheridan, Pignone, & Donahue, 2003.

41. *Cost-benefit studies on hypertension:* Aldana, 2003. For cost-benefit applications of PRECEDE in hypertension, see Cote, Gregoire, et al., 2003; Eastaugh, & Hatcher, 1982; Hatcher, Green, et al., 1986.

42. *Cost-effectiveness of comprehensive workplace health promotion programs:* Pelletier, 2001. Recall the different meanings of comprehensive noted in endnote 37. The intended meaning in Pelletier's review is programs covering multiple risk factors, rather than programs necessarily addressing those risk factors at several ecological levels with multiple, coordinated interventions.

43. *Johnson & Johnson comprehensive "Live For Life" program:* Bly, Jones, & Richardson, 1986; Jones, Bly, & Richardson, 1990. Comprehensive has two meanings in the health program literature: Centers for Disease Control and Prevention, 1999a; Gregory, 2002; Pelletier, 2001.

44. *Comprehensive worksite health promotion programs are not necessarily ecological:* Best, Stokols, et al., 2003; Richard, Potvin, et al., 1996.

45. *Barriers to randomized controlled designs for program evaluation in the worksite; and limitations of their generalizability:* Green, 2001.

46. *Social support as a buffer for work stress:* The classic work on this subject is House, 1981. For PRECEDE applications: Daltroy et al., 1993; Hubball, 1996. Bailey, Richards, et al., 1987, noted in their PRECEDE-based study of education and social support for adults with asthma "the need to conduct research in diverse environments, rather than usually conducting research in the unusually favorable environment of a university medical center" (p. 345). This supports the point made in the previous section and endnote about the limitations of the highly research-controlled, socially artificial environment in which most randomized controlled trials are done. See also their later trial in which "usual care" control groups were now getting the interventions tested in their earlier trials (Bailey, Kohler, et al., 1999).

47. *Family of employees as major part of health care insurance expenditures.* Chenoweth, 1994.

48. *Family as secondary target of workplace health programs:* For example, Hunt, Lederman, et al., 2000; Schuster, Eastman, et al., 2001; Watts, Vernon, et al., 2003.

49. *Specific company programs:* For descriptions of these and 59 other U.S. company programs, some of which are international, see Office of Disease Prevention and Health Promotion, 1993. For Canada, a similar inventory provides descriptions of 62 company health promotion programs: Health and Welfare Canada, 1992. For the more recent status of workplace program statistics as used for 1998–2001 baselines for the U.S. *Healthy People 2010* objectives for the nation in disease prevention and health promotion, go to http://www.healthypeople.gov/hpscripts/SearchObjectives_FT.asp, accessed Dec 8, 2003.

50. *Cost of one unhealthy baby to an employer:* Howse, 1991.

51. *Prenatal and breastfeeding programs for working mothers:* Ibid. For PRECEDE analyses of breast-feeding and prenatal programs, Burglehaus, Smith, et al., 1997; Olson, 1994; Sword, 1999; Williams, Innis, et al., 1999.

52. *Programs directed at children of employees:* Vass & Walsh-Allis, 1990.

53. *Employee Assistance Program guidelines:* Employee Assistance Professionals Association, 1999.

54. *Prevalence of alcohol abuse by employees:* Marchand, Demers, et al. 2003.

55. *Alcohol and psychosocial disturbance, for example, domestic violence:* Stuart, Moore, et al., 2003.

56. *Alcohol costs to employers:* R. L. Bertera, 1991. See also Lipscomb, Demet, & Li, 2003.

57. *Early medical model of alcohol treatment and referral:* Glenn, 1994. Cf. Treno & Lee, 2002.

58. *Social-behavioral and ecological approaches to alcohol prevention, treatment and referral:* Polcin, 2003. For PRECEDE applications: Dedobbeleer, & Desjardins, 2001; Newman, Martin, & Weppner, 1982; Rice & Green, 1992.

59. *Constructive confrontation:* Trice & Beyer, 1984.

60. *NIAAA evidence of EAP effectiveness led to their expansion:* Kurtz, Googins, & Howard, 1984.

61. *From treatment to secondary prevention and self-referral:* Garrett, Landau-Stanton, 1997; Gossop, Stephens, et al., 2001. For a European example: Vasse, Nijhuis, Kok, & Kroodsma, 1997.

62. *Karasek's work on stress in work pace and worker control:* Karasek & Theorell, 1990. For a recent commentary on the significance of this work, see de Lange, Taris, et al., 2003.

63. *Physiological pathways for effects of the organization of work on health:* Ostry, Marion, et al., 2000; Schechter et al., 1997.

64. *Whitehall study of British civil servants:* One of the earliest and most frequently cited of the 57 or more publications from this study is Marmot, Rose, et al., 1978; see more recently, Ferrie, Shipley, et al., 2002; Steptoe, Feldman, et al., 2002.

65. *San Francisco bus drivers study:* Syme, 1986; 1987. See more recent secondary analyses: Vander-Voort, Ragland, & Syme, 2001.

66. *Disability claims for office work:* Schechter, Green, et al., 1997.

67. *Systems approach to workplace organizational culture change:* J. Allen & Allen, 1990.

68. *Same programs implemented in different sites have different outcomes:* Green & Cargo, 1994; Hubball, 1996. For our distinction between moderating and mediating, see Chapter 5.

69. *Characteristics of worksites that made a standardized smoking cessation program more effective:* Sorenson, Glasgow, et al., 1992.

70. *Adapting the organization to the intervention or the work:* Ottoson & Green, 1987. See also Hubbard & Ottoson, 1997. Polanyi, Frank, 2000, esp. pp. 147–55.

71. *The ethical and political traps:* Allegrante & Sloan, 1986; Eakin, 2000; Hollander & Hale, 1987; Warner, Walker, & Friedmann, 2003.

72. *Problem of stress management programs putting the entire emphasis on personal coping:* Karasek & Theorell, 1990; McLeroy, Green, Mullen, & Foshee, 1984.

73. *Health worker's divided allegiance and ethical dilemmas:* Botes, & Otto, 2003; Harvey, Fleming, & Patterson, 2002; Lutzen, Cronqvist, et al., 2003.

74. *Solution to the moral dilemmas usually lies in balance between individual-behavioral and environmental strategies, with input from both management and workers:* Vojtecky, 1986. PRECEDE example: Wong, Chan, Kok, & Wong, 1996; and see the case study at the end of this chapter.

75. *Blue collar response to workplace health programs:* For example, Elbel, Aldana, et al., 2003; Hart, Glover, et al., 2003.

76. *Caveats on the economic argument for work site health programs:* Warner, 1987, 2003; Warner, Hodgson, & Carroll, 1999.

77. *Sources of data for the epidemiological diagnosis in occupational settings.* For discussions of data sources for epidemiological surveillance of occupational illness and injury in the United States, see Dement, Pompeii, et al., 2003, on using a state cancer registry with workers' names;

Kim, Ridzon, et al., 2003, on designing a "no-name" surveillance system; Sauter, & the NORA Organization of Work Team Members, 2002, on surveillance of organization of work issues related to health and safety in an occupational setting.

78. *Adaptation of Precede-Proceed Model combining the several "ecologies" of work site health programs:* DeJoy, 1986a, b, 1990 (quotation from p. 11); DeJoy, Murphy, & Gershon, 1995; DeJoy & Southern, 1993; DeJoy & Wilson, 2003.

79. *Job conditions that may lead to stress defined and illustrated:* For additional examples and analytic approaches to these work conditions, see DeJoy & Wilson, 2003; Polanyi, Frank, et al., 2000.

80. *Use of national statistics to select criteria and indicators, and estimate targets for objectives:* For example, American Cancer Society (2003), *Statistics for 2003.* Online at http://www.cancer.org/docroot/STT/stt_0.asp, accessed Dec 9, 2003.

81. *Setting achievable objectives, with criteria, indicators, and targets:* Chomik & Frankish, 1999; Nutbeam, Wise, et al., 1995; Ratner, Green, et al., 1997. See also chapters 2–5 in this book.

82. *The trade-offs of expediency and durability of change:* Green, Wilson, & Lovato, 1986; Wong & Seet, 1998.

83. *Predisposing factors predicting employee behavior in response to work site health programs:* P. Conrad, 1987; Fielding, 1984. In *nutrition,* Kristal, Patterson, et al., 1995, specifically constructed a 5-item scale of predisposing factors, and a similar scale consisting of a combination of enabling and reinforcing factors. The predisposing factors were more predictive of adopting recommended dietary practices. In *sun protection,* outdoor workers maintain high levels of sun exposure without protective measures, even after having skin lesions removed, apparently because they get little support (enabling or reinforcing) from their employers to change their exposure behavior (Wooley, Buettner, & Lowe, 2002).

84. *Self-efficacy as predictor of employee continued participation in work site programs:* Hubball, 1996; King, Marcus, et al., 1996; Maurer, Weiss, & Barbeite, 2003. Lechner & De Vries, 1995, in the Netherlands, found the "The low-adherence group and the dropouts were least convinced of their ability to participate in a fitness program" (p. 429).

85. *Perceived job stress as a predictor of participation:* Keith, Cann, et al., 2001; Leo, 1996; Lovato & Green, 1990; McLeroy, Green, et al., 1984.

86. *Job stress as a motivator may work both for and against behavior conducive to health:* N. H. Gottlieb & Nelson, 1990.

87. *Loss of interest as reason most cited for dropping out of worksite programs:* Bellingham, 1994.

88. *Participation in planning predicts satisfaction with program:* Alderman, Green, & Flynn, 1982; Everly & Feldman, 1985; O'Donnell & Ainsworth, 1995.

89. *Employee satisfaction predicted by warmth and concern shown by health personnel:* P. H. Bailey, Rukholm, Vanderlee, & Hyland, 1994; Feldman, 1984.

90. *Contacts and contact time predict higher employee satisfaction and blood pressure control:* Alderman, Green, & Flynn, 1980.

91. *Organizational climate as a reinforcing factor:* Conrad, Campbell, et al., 1996. DeJoy, Searcy, et al., 2000, found in a study of nurses' compliance with universal safety standards that "All 3 categories of diagnostic factors (predisposing, enabling, and reinforcing) influenced general compliance, but . . . the greatest improvement in model fit occurred when the indirect effects of reinforcing factors were added" (p. 127). Another example was in Morisky, Pena, et al., 2002, on the impact of the work environment on condom use among female sex workers in bars in the Philippines. With management encouragement and regular meetings with employees, backed by a policy of 100% condom use, "female bar workers were 2.6 times more likely to consistently use condoms during sexual intercourse . . ." (p. 461).

92. *The paradox of senior management leadership and advocacy:* N. H. Gottlieb et al., 1990, p. 22.

93. *Confidentiality as a reinforcing factor:* Wong, Chan, Koh, & Wong, 1994–95; Wong, Chan, & Wee, 2000; Zuilhof & Mass, 1998.

94. *The value of games, contests, social activity to reinforce participation:* Blake, Caspersen, et al., 1996; Glasgow, Klesges, et al., 1985.

95. *Caveat: Token rewards may yield only token behavior:* Green, Wilson, Lovato, 1986.

96. *Worksite smoking policies:* Brownson, Hopkins, & Wakefield, 2002; Levy & Friend, 2003.

97. *For an application of PRECEDE to the activation of workers to bring pressure on management for a policy change regarding work-site hazards,* see Appendix C-1 in the first edition: Green, Kreuter, Deeds, & Partridge, 1980, pp. 212–224.

98. *Time-honored public health tradition of screening populations to identify and focus on high-risk sub-populations:* Haber, 1994; Robinson, 2002.

99. *Diary as a pre-participation screening on motivation:* P. D. Mullen & Culjat, 1980.

100. *Self-help materials most effective with the highly motivated:* Lancaster & Stead, 2002; Windsor, Cutter, et al., 1985.

101. *Algorithm for applying PRECEDE at the individual level to screen employees for focused intervention:* Lovato & Green, 1990.

102. *Source of the air quality case study:* This case description is based on work initiated at the University of Texas Center for Health Promotion Research and Development, with support from the Texas Affiliate of the American Heart Association and grant K07-CA01286 from the National Cancer Institute. See N. H. Gottlieb, Erikson, et al., 1990; N. H. Gottlieb & Nelson, 1990. Some variations on the actual history of the case have been introduced for illustrative purposes.

103. *Policy development and implementation ideally is context specific:* Ottoson & Green, 1987. Also, Hubbard & Ottoson, 1997. If not specific to a context, then policy must be highly flexible and adaptable.

8

Applications
in Educational Settings

In 2000, it was estimated that well over a billion students were enrolled in schools around the world.[1] In the United States, every school day sees nearly 53 million students attend elementary and secondary schools and about 5.7 million professional and nonprofessional workers staff those schools.[2] In the United States, schools constitute the specific place where 21% of the population gathers to learn and work.[3] From the relatively simple perspective of potential impact, these demographics clearly suggest that the school environment can be a powerful setting for local and global prevention strategies. The use of the word *powerful* in this context is by no means hyperbole. Evidence shows that school-based programs have been effective in reducing student tobacco use, unhealthful dietary patterns, physical inactivity, and rates of obesity, among other health problems.[4] Well-planned programs have also strengthened social dimensions known to contribute to healthy growth and development including family and community cohesion, resilience, self-determination, self efficacy, and the engagement in prosocial activities.[5] Furthermore, studies show that school health programs can also be cost effective for outcomes related to immunization,[6] tobacco use,[7] and the prevention of unintentional injuries.[8]

The purposes of this chapter are (1) to help program planners see how the application of the Precede-Proceed Model can assist them in their efforts to engage schools as a component of community-based health programs, and (2) to illustrate for school curriculum or school health planners, administrators, parents, teachers, and advocates for children how PRECEDE-PROCEED can assist them in their ongoing efforts to create health-protecting and health-promoting schools. First, we explain how the concept of a coordinated school health program, widely accepted internationally as a sound organizational framework for school health, is consistent with the key principles of the Precede-Proceed Model. Next, we offer examples of how findings from school health research continue to contribute to advances in school health. Then, starting with the social assessment process, we provide examples of how aspects of PRECEDE and PROCEED relate specifically to the school setting. Finally, we offer a hypothetical case applying the steps and principles to a specific school-community setting.

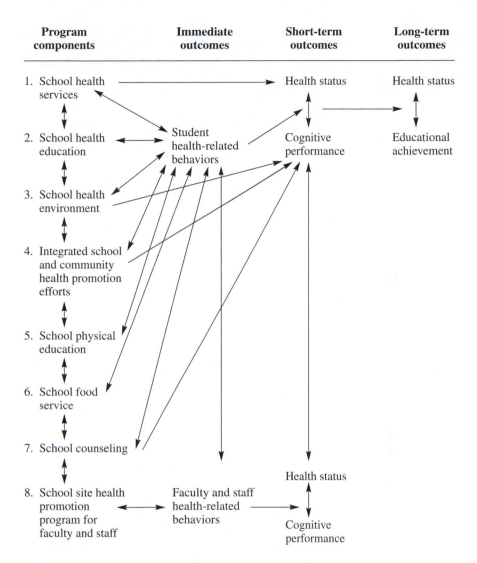

FIGURE 8-1 School health program components and outcomes.
Source: Kolbe, L. (1986). "Increasing the impact of school health promotion programs: Emerging research perspectives." *Health Education, 17*(5), 47–52.

WHAT IS A SCHOOL HEALTH PROGRAM?

In 1935, the American Physical Education Association declared that a school health program should consist of three interdependent components: (1) school health services, (2) school health education, and (3) healthful school environment.[9] That three-part structure stood as the foundation[10] for school health programs for half a century until Kolbe and Allensworth[11] offered an expanded conceptualization of school health, which is characterized in Figure 8-1. Five new components are added to the original configuration: (1) integrated school and community health promotion efforts, (2) school physical education, (3) school food service, (4) school counseling, and (5) school-site health promotion program for faculty and staff, as shown in Figure 8-1.

The vertical arrows between the eight program components connote the interdependence of the program activities. The remaining arrows suggest various ways in which intermediate, short-term, and long-term outcomes can be influenced. Definitions for the eight components are listed in the glossary. The added components of the expanded version give the school health program added depth, breadth, and visibility. They also create the added challenge that accompanies the demand for coordination among those from multiple disciplines: school nurses, physicians, health educators, counselors, psychologists, food service workers, physical educators, and those responsible for the school's physical and psychosocial environment. An important element in establishing and maintaining a coordinated effort is to stay focused on the aim of the program as it relates to the mission of the school.

> We must all maintain sensitivity to the unique educational mission of schools and the complex social and economic conditions that frequently surround them. The institutions of public health and education are complementary and, as such, they must work as partners, sharing their expertise, time, energy and resources if everyone is to realize the potential schools have in contributing to the goal of a healthier citizenry, whether that be 1990 or 2090.[12]

Key Concept: "Coordinated"

We urge health program planners to keep in mind that the eight-component, coordinated school health program represents an ideal conceptual approach. It provides a context and framework that will encourage planners to seek out relevant connection among the components. In *Health Is Academic: A Guide to Coordinated School Health Programs*,[13] care is taken to emphasize the word *coordinated* in reference to the school health *program.* The rationale is that since each of the organizational entities representing the eight components has independent identities and standards, they can contribute most effectively to the promotion of student health when their collective efforts are *coordinated.* For example, the component focusing on "family and community involvement in school health" directly reinforces the goal of public health professionals to engage the community, including parents, in active roles on behalf of the health of school-age children.[14]

While it reflects the comprehensive nature of the school health program, Figure 8-1 also reflects the complexity inherent in the task of coordinating the efforts of multiple entities that seek to achieve a common goal. The complexity inherent in the notion of a coordinated school health program makes a working knowledge of the Precede-Proceed Model especially useful at several levels. First, the tasks necessary to determine the long-term outcomes of educational achievement and health status parallel the tasks of social and health diagnosis. Understanding the ecological links between student health-related behaviors, cognitive performance, faculty and staff health-related behaviors, and the presence, absence, or quality of the multiple program components will be facilitated by applying the principles of behavioral, environmental, and educational diagnosis. Second, even though "health" constitutes a common denominator for all eight of the program components, each has its own unique aims, including many that are not primarily directed at health. There is a difference between ordering or preparing food and preparing lesson plans to teach soccer, just as there's a difference between counseling students under stress and coordinating a safe-walk-to-school program. Thus, the principles of participation and collaboration, so central to PRECEDE-PROCEED, are also directly applicable to the challenge of establishing and sustaining a coordinated school health program. Finally, the eight components of the coordinated school health program collectively address a wide range of factors that influence school performance, health, and health-related behaviors. Assessment for planning will inevitably require careful consideration of predisposing, enabling, and reinforcing factors as well as environmental and policy factors, both within the school setting and in the wider community.

PROGRESS IN SCHOOL HEALTH RESEARCH AND POLICY

Since the printing of the first edition of this book in 1980, research on health programs and health determinants in schools has grown exponentially, generating new evidence and insights about the effectiveness of comprehensive and coordinated approaches to school health. Among those advances, policy-related strategies are noteworthy.

Assessing the Effects of School Health Education

After decades of defending comprehensive school health on the basis of learning principles and research evidence borrowed from other fields, contemporary school health literature is now replete with evaluations of well-designed school health education and school health programs. The most sweeping evidence to arrive in the 1980s was the nationwide evaluation of the comprehensive School Health Curriculum Project. From a handful of small-scale studies conducted before 1980 with limited controls (usually pretest-posttest designs) and with little behavioral impact measured (usually knowledge and attitude changes only), the opportunity arose in 1981 to carry out a multisite randomized evaluation of this and several other health curricula with support from the U.S. Office of Disease Prevention and Health Promotion and the Centers for Disease Control.

The School Health Education Evaluation was a pioneering 3-year prospective study, involving 30,000 students in grades 4–7 from 20 states. It revealed that students who were exposed to comprehensive school health education not only showed significant positive changes in their health-related knowledge and attitudes, compared with students in matched schools without such exposure, they also were considerably less likely to take up smoking. Especially relevant were those findings clearly demonstrating that administrative support and teacher training were directly linked to the positive student outcomes detected, as were the cumulative hours of classroom time devoted to comprehensive school health education.[15]

The National Institutes of Health

Following the lead of other agencies in the Public Health Service, the National Institutes of Health began to lend their considerable scientific prestige to the study of school health. In 1988, an expert advisory group convened by the National Cancer Institute reviewed 20 years of research on school-based efforts to prevent tobacco use. The panel found nine areas with sufficient data or experience to reach preliminary conclusions and recommendations: program, impact, focus, context, length, ideal age for intervention, teacher training, program implementation, and need for peer and parental involvement.[16]

During the mid-1980s, the National Heart Lung and Blood Institute supported a variety of school-based research efforts, 10 of which are summarized in Table 8-1.[17] As the table indicates, these studies reflect diversity in the demographic characteristics of the populations studied, in the risk-factor focus, and in methods and channels of intervention. The importance of **family and community involvement** in the coordinated school health program is reinforced by the fact that 7 of the 10 studies used the strategy of linking home and school to create a mutually reinforcing setting for the behavior of children.[18] Several of the studies applied the Precede model and emphasized the importance of a planning model to complement and organize specific theoretical models.[19]

The success of this research effort, combined with growing interest in the concept of coordinated school health programs, prompted the National Heart Lung and Blood Institute to support for another multisite randomized intervention trial to assess the effectiveness of school-based efforts to promote cardiovascular health. The Child and Adolescent Trial for Cardiovascular Health (CATCH) was a 3-year trial (1991–1994) involving 5,000 students from 96 schools in four states. CATCH used a multicomponent, coordinated approach focused on the school organization and environment, classroom curricula, and the family.[20] Results from the CATCH trials showed significant positive change with respect to school environmental goals, including a reduction in fat in school lunches and an increase in moderate to vigorous activity in physical education classes. Results in other intervention categories were less pronounced but still showed significant changes in knowledge mediated through the family intervention component[21] and individual-level changes in dietary intention, food choice, knowledge, and perceived social support for healthful food choices.[22]

The Challenge of Parental Participation

Whether from India,[23] Finland,[24] or the United States,[25] findings confirm what seems obvious: Children tend to be physically, emotionally, and socially healthy when they are raised in an environment where they are cared for and nurtured by parents and adults. Getting such participation from parents, however, remains a formidable challenge for schools. A Metropolitan Life Foundation survey,[26] sampling over 4,000 students from 199 public schools and 500 randomly selected parents of schoolchildren, revealed that while the majority of both teachers and parents believe that parental involvement in children's health education would be of considerable help in encouraging good health habits for children, most parents (71%) report never getting involved in the process. This lack of parental involvement may in part explain why parents do not know the extent of drinking, smoking, or drug taking by their children. While 36% of the parents indicated that their child has had at least one alcoholic drink, 66% of the students reported that they had alcohol at least once or twice. Similarly, only 14% of the parents reported that their child had smoked a cigarette, while 41% of the students said they had smoked, and 5% of the parents said that their child had used drugs, whereas 17% of the students reported having used drugs.

Findings from the CATCH trial revealed, not surprisingly, that level of parental participation is influenced by both gender and ethnicity. This finding led to the assumption that the effectiveness of parental program components is likely to depend on how well those components are tailored to relevant cultural and ethnic factors.[27]

Policy Analysis and Advances

Progress in research has spurred progress in school health policy. A policy has three components: (1) the clear statement of a problem (or potential problem) that needs attention, (2) a goal to mitigate or prevent that problem, and (3) a set of strategic actions to accomplish that goal. This leaves tactics to the implementers of policy. Well-designed regional or national surveys provide the substance and clarity that make policy credible and influence it.

Policy Surveys.   The WHO cross-national survey of health behavior in schoolchildren,[28] the Behavioral Risk Factor Surveillance System,[29] and the Canadian national surveys on youth fitness and health[30] are just three examples of numerous large surveys that have begun to influence national and international policy with regard to the health of school-age youth.

In 1994, the School Health Policies and Programs Study (SHPPS) was the first national study undertaken to measure the status of policies and programs related to health education, physical education, health services, food services, and policies prohibiting the use of tobacco, alcohol, other drugs, and violence;

TABLE 8-1 A summary of NHLBI school-based health promotion studies

Investigator Institution Study	Ethnicity[a] SES Grade State	Schools[b] Classes Students	Channel: Curriculum, Food Service, Home	Provider	Target Areas	Outcomes
Perry, Cheryl, Ph.D. Univ of Minn "Healthy Heart" "The Home Team"	W, A SES (M) Grade 3 MN, ND	24T/7C — 1405T 422C	Curr Home	Teachers Mail	Eating	Changes in knowledge, total fat, saturated fat, complex carbohydrate intake
Parcel, Guy, Ph.D. Univ of Texas "Go for Health"	W, H, B SES (L, M) Grades 3–4 TX	2T/2C 40 1156	Curr Food Serv	Teachers Food workers	Eating Exercise	Changes in knowledge, self-efficacy, behavioral expectations, food service, PE classes, diet
Walter, Heather, M.D. American Health Fdn "Know Your Body"*	W, B, A, H SES (L, M, H) Grades 4–9 NY	22T/15C — 2075T 1313C	Curr Home	Teachers	Eating Exercise Smoking BP WT	Changes in knowledge, total fat, complex carbohydrate intake, chol, initiation of smoking
Bush, Patricia, Ph.D. Georgetown Univ "Know Your Body"*	B SES (L, M, H) Grades 4–9 DC	6T/3C — 707T 334C	Home	Teachers	Eating Exercise Smoking BP WT	Change in knowledge, smoking attitudes, BP, HDL chol, fitness, thiocyanate
Nader, Philip, M.D. Univ of CA/SD "Family Health Project"	H, W SES (L, M) Grades 5–6 CA	6T/6C — 163T/160C	Home	Inst	Eating Exercise	Changes in diet, chol, BP, knowledge

(continued)

* Based substantially on the Precede Model.

Investigator Institution Study	Ethnicity[a] SES Grade State	Schools[b] Classes Students	Channel: Curriculum, Food Service, Home	Provider	Target Areas	Outcomes
Cohen, Rita, Ph.D. Brownell, Kelly, Ph.D. Univ of Penn "CV Risk Reduction"	W SES (M) Grades 5–7 PA	— 1062T 992C	Curr Home	Teachers Peers	Eating BP Smoking	Changes in knowledge, initiation of smoking, peers were equally or more effective than teachers
Fors, Stuart, Ed.D. Univ of Georgia "3R's + HBP"*	W, B SES (L, M) Grade 6 GA	14T/7C 60 853T 351C	Curr Home	Teachers Students	BP	Changes in knowledge, taking BP
Ellison, R. Curtis, M.D. Univ of Mass "Food Service Project"	W, B, A SES (M, H) Grade 9 MA, NH	2 — 1100	Food Serv	Food workers	BP Eating	Changes in BP, chol, and food service
Weinberg, Armin, Ph.D. Baylor College of Med "CV Curr/Family Tree"	W, H, B SES (L, M) Grades 9–10 TX	7 40 5787	Curr Home	Teachers	Eating Exercise BP	Changes in knowledge, attitudes, self-report behavior, parents used smoking + wt + exercise
Killen, Joel, Ph.D. Farquhar, John, M.D. Stanford Univ "CV Risk Reduction"	W, H, A SES (M) Grade 10 CA	2T/2C 8 1447	Curr	Inst	Eating Exercise BP Smoking	Changes in knowledge, exercise, smoking, resting heart rate, BMI, skinfolds

* Based substantially on the Precede Model.

[a] Predominant ethnic or racial group: A = Asian, B = Black, H = Hispanic, W = White; SES = socioeconomic status

[b] T = treatment, C = control

Source: "Synthesis of Cardiovascular Behavioral Research for Youth Health Promotion," by E. J. Stone, C. L. Perry, and R. V. Luepker (1989), Health Education Quarterly, 16(2), 155–169.

TABLE 8-2 Percentage of schools in the United States that require physical education by grade

Grade	% of Schools
Kindergarten	39.7
1	50.6
2	50.5
3	51.3
4	51.5
5	50.4
6	32.2
7	26.2
8	25.1
9	13.3
10	9.5
11	5.8
12	5.4

Source: C. R. Burgeson, H. Wechsler, N. D. Drener, J. C. Young, and C. G. Spain, "Physical Education and Activity: Results for the School Health Policies and Programs Survey," *Journal of School Health,* Sept. 2001, Vol. 71, No. 7 p. 284.

it took measurements at the state, district, and local level. Supported and conceptualized by the U.S. Centers for Disease Control and Prevention (CDC), all 50 states and the District of Columbia were surveyed; personal interviews were used at the local school level.[31] The primary purpose of SHPPS was to fill national data gaps for measuring progress on 14 of the 111 national health objectives that address adolescents.[32]

In 2000, CDC carried out the second SHPPS which was broader in scope and constituted the first study to examine the eight components of a coordinated school health program described earlier.[33] Data were collected from all 50 states and the District of Columbia and included representative samples of public and private schools at the elementary, junior high, and high school levels. Table 8-2 provides a practical illustration of how data generated from a survey strategy like SHPPS 2000 can be used to shape policies at the national, state, or local level. In that table, SHPPS 2000 data are used to provide the baseline markers for selected *Healthy People 2010* objectives relevant to school health. The comparative size of the gaps between the baseline indicators and the goals gives policymakers tangible evidence that can inform their decision process. Given the global epidemic of obesity among children and the role that regular physical activity can play in countering that epidemic, what is the state of physical education in the United States?

Table 8-2 offers us an answer: "it's disappearing!" After grade 5, the percentage of schools requiring physical education shows a steady decline from approximately 50% to 5% by grade 12. This pattern moves in the opposite direction of what research is telling us. After a rigorous review of well-controlled demonstrations, the Task Force on Community Preventive Services deemed well-planned physical activity interventions (based on health benefits and effectiveness) worthy of a "strong recommendation" for implementation.[34] When taking into account the well-documented collateral physical and mental health benefits of regular physical activity, the trend reflected in Table 8-2 provides concerned parents, and practitioners in health, education, mental health services, and recreation with a substantial lever to advance policies that require regular physical education in schools.

Policy Analysis.   Data from such surveys require the additional effort of investigators, policy analysts, and practitioners to translate them into action or policy. For example, Mackie & Oickle describe how strategic planning and systematic analysis and dissemination of the results of national surveys in Canada can produce physician support for policies, resources, and programs targeted at improving the health of Canadian children and youth.[35]

Other policy analyses supporting or promoting school health have emerged from national commissions[36] and international study groups for the World Health Organization.[37] In addition, voluntary health organizations [38] and professional associations have also undertaken activities that have led to the publication of strong advocacy statements and policy analyses in support of school health programs. A notable example is the Center for Health Improvement (CHI), a national, nonpartisan, nonprofit health policy center based in Sacramento, California. Originally funded by The California Wellness Foundation, the goal of CHI is to advance policies and provide technical assistance services that improve population health and encourage healthy behavior. One of CHI's priorities is *Children's Health*—including enhancing school readiness, universal preschool, oral health, and access to care. A fundamental strategy employed by CHI is to conduct well-designed, scientifically valid public opinion polls on their priority health topics.

In November of 1997 CHI commissioned the Field Institute to conduct a survey to ascertain parents' and Californians' attitudes regarding the risks children face when transitioning from their early years into adolescence and on to adulthood.[39] Of the 1,168 California adults who were surveyed, 498 were parents and 854 were registered voters. Box 8-1 contains excerpts of the information from the survey. This information was used to heighten public awareness, craft briefs for state and local lawmakers, and develop op-ed articles in newspapers throughout the state.

From a planning perspective at the local level, policy development is primarily the act of joining forces in support of positive change; it entails tailoring a solution to address the unique health problems and resources in a community, school, or school system. An important aspect of policy action involves increasing public awareness, developing community partnerships to better understand the legislative process, and evaluating existing policies that affect health. A website called *Health Policy Coach*, supported by CHI, is a practical

BOX 8-1 Adolescent Risk Taking: A Summary of a CCI Policy Poll

SACRAMENTO—With an ever-present threat of substance abuse, juvenile delinquency, alcohol and tobacco use and sexual activity in today's society, California parents reported in a statewide survey that their community is playing a greater role to help children and youth grow up healthy today. A majority of California parents say community groups, coaches and recreation instructors, employers and churches are more important today in helping children and youth grow up healthy than a generation ago.

Greater than two in three Californians say they are very or somewhat worried about each of six different threats facing children and youth today:

- Substance abuse worries 87%;
- Juvenile delinquency worries 79%;
- Lack of parental support worries 78%;
- Domestic violence and child abuse worries 75%;
- Substance abuse in the family worries 67%; and
- Depression and other mental health worries 65%.

Parents whose annual household income is less than $20,000 express an even greater level of concern, with greater than six in ten very concerned about each problem.

Three teenage pregnancy prevention approaches garner support from two-thirds or more of California adults surveyed. More than nine in ten, 93%, agree strongly or somewhat with placing an emphasis on

technical assistance resource that will aid planners in walking through the fundamental steps of policy development and a variety of strategies to support policy implementation.[40]

Comprehensive School Health Education: A Response to the AIDS Epidemic

History is full of examples where breakthroughs for public good are borne out of tragedy; behind such clouds there is sometimes a silver lining. The tragic circumstances that define the global problem of AIDS have given rise to opportunities never before afforded to school health. The severity of the epidemic and the essential role of education in the world of prevention strategy, together with the public demand for action, have offered the perfect opportunity for a proactive response in the global fight against AIDS by strengthening coordinated school health.

BOX 8-1 *(continued)*

teen pregnancy prevention efforts that promote a greater sense of responsibility among adolescent and young male adults. A total of 89%, also agree strongly or somewhat that teen pregnancy prevention efforts should be directed toward helping adolescents make more informed personal decisions about sexuality to offset peer pressures. Finally, 69% said they agree strongly or somewhat that making contraceptives available to teens is an effective way to prevent unintended pregnancies. Support for pregnancy prevention programs that are limited to only discussions about sexual abstinence and ways teens can postpone becoming sexually active was more divided. 50% of adults said they agree strongly or somewhat with this approach, while 47% disagreed strongly or somewhat with the approach.

Parents surveyed said they would like more information from their healthcare providers about such issues as substance abuse, pregnancy prevention, and behavioral problems to help them keep their children well. More than eight in ten parents said they would find information in all of the following areas either somewhat or extremely useful:

- 86% of parents would benefit from more information about the challenges their teens may face regarding tobacco, alcohol or other drug use;
- 85% of parents would benefit from more information about how better to inform their children about sex education or teen pregnancy prevention; and
- 86% of parents said they would find more information about how to address their children's behavioral or discipline problems somewhat or very useful.

Source: Center for Health Improvement, Sacramento, CA, 1998.

"Guidelines for Effective School Health Education to Prevent the Spread of AIDS"[41] was an excellent example of the influence that strong, timely policy documents can have in focusing and implementing national and local school health programs.[42] At the time they were presented, these guidelines legitimized the school as a credible national focal point for an important aspect of AIDS prevention. They were developed by CDC staff in close collaboration with leaders representing 16 national school or health organizations. With the support of these broad-based and influential constituencies, the guidelines were crafted such that there could be no mistake in interpreting the strategy for implementation: close collaboration between the health and education sectors, active participation and review by and with parents, and programs carried out in the context of comprehensive school health education. In sum, AIDS education interventions will have the greatest chance for success when they are implemented within a coordinated school program. Such programs strive to create a context for understanding the relationships between personal behaviors, social circumstances, and health.

USING PRECEDE AND PROCEED
FOR PLANNING IN SCHOOLS

The school setting differs from other settings most significantly in the age range of the population, although the school setting is also a work site for teachers and staff. It also differs, however, in the social functions it serves, its mission, and its ways of accounting for its successes. These latter differences pertain most to the social assessment phase of Precede-Proceed planning and evaluation. For health program planners who are outside of the school milieu but who envision the participation of a school or school system as part of their overall program, we emphasize again the importance of being mindful of health as an instrumental, rather than ultimate, value.

Social Assessment

Schools have education, not health, as their mission and as their criterion of success or failure. They are accountable for improvements in the learning and preparedness of children and youth to take on a wider range of life challenges than just the preservation or enhancement of their health.

Health: An Instrumental Value for Schools.   In their background justification of the School Health Policies and Programs Study, Kann and her colleagues documented the following health status profile for youth in the United States:

- Among persons aged 5–24, three quarters of all mortality is due to motor vehicle crashes (30%), other unintentional injuries (12%), homicide (19%), and suicide (11%).
- Significant physical, mental, and social problems result from the 1 million pregnancies among adolescents annually and from the 10 million cases of sexually transmitted diseases that occur each year among those aged 15–29.
- As well as being associated with the early initiation of sexual intercourse and unintended pregnancy, alcohol is a key factor in half of the deaths attributed to motor vehicle crashes, homicide, and suicide.
- Six categories of behaviors make a major contribution to the leading causes of death and disability: (1) safety behaviors (use of seat belts, weapon carrying), (2) tobacco use, (3) alcohol and other drug use, (4) sexual behaviors that contribute to unintended pregnancy or STD or HIV infection, (5) unhealthy dietary behaviors, and (6) physical inactivity.[43]

Data like these, combined with the reality that school-aged children constitute a huge audience, reinforce the long-standing perceptions of public health professionals that schools constitute an opportunistic focal point for health promotion. But do those who administer and work in schools hold that same perspective? Recall that in Chapter 2, health was described as an *instrumental* value —a resource for everyday life, not the objective of living. Thus, to the question, What is your mission? the school administrator would respond, "To educate the students, to prepare them to be competent citizens capable of coping with the demands of daily living." A first response, "to improve the health status of students and faculty," would be highly unlikely. If asked to identify the indicators that would best reflect "success" for his or her school, the administrator would likely include the following:

1. Academic progress (literacy, cognitive development)
2. Low absenteeism (students and faculty)
3. Low rates of student dropouts
4. Competitive salary schedule
5. Minimal discipline problems
6. Parental and community support for school
7. Stable, supportive faculty and staff
8. Student pride in the school

Objective data usually available at the school level can provide insight into the kind of issues identified in items 1–5. For input on items 6–8, one could obtain valuable qualitative information through questionnaires or focus groups.[44] The latter information, often referred to as "soft data," should not be taken as lesser in value than more objective "hard data." Experiences around the world have taught planners, sometimes quite painfully, this lesson: Failure to acknowledge and address the perceptions and feelings held by administrators, teachers, and parents, however difficult those sentiments may be to quantify, can stop the best-designed, well-intended program dead in its tracks.

For health institutions, the mission is improved health; for schools, the mission is education. While these missions are not mutually exclusive, they reflect differences in institutional priorities. Health promotion planners need to be especially sensitive to such differences. Whether it involves curriculum, counseling, food services, or community participation, efforts to promote school health programs will be problematic if they are not framed as contributing to the educational mission of the school.[45]

Reciprocally, school health personnel and advocates need to seek more aggressively the cooperation and resources of community agencies and media to support the school's mission. True, students spend one third of workweek hours in school, but they spend more than two-thirds of their total hours— counting weekends, holidays, and summer vacations—outside school. Furthermore, some of the children and youth who most need health promotion have dropped out of school or have such high absenteeism and inattention that they will not be reached by school programs.

Education and Health: A Two-Way Relationship.   The capsule findings presented in Table 8-3 should remind planners that health and social circumstances are inextricably tied to the school performance of school-aged youth in the United States. This pattern is not unique to the United States; in the 1994 report, *Health of Young Australians,* child abuse, children living in poverty, and youth suicide are listed among the top five concerns related to improving the health status of youth in Australia.[46]

TABLE 8-3 Selected social factors that influence school performance among students within the United States

- One third of children entering kindergarten are unprepared to learn—that is, they lack physical health, confidence, maturity, and general knowledge.
- One child in four—fully 10 million—is at risk of failure in school because of social, emotional, and health handicaps.
- During the 1980s, poverty among children in the United States worsened by 22%.
- Between 12% and 22% of children experience mental, emotional, or behavioral disorders, yet few receive mental health services.
- Twenty-two percent of ninth graders report carrying a weapon in the previous month.
- Almost one fourth of high-school students report having seriously considered suicide in the previous year, and 8.6% made an attempt.
- One fourth of 10–16 year olds report being assaulted or abused in the previous year.
- Over 40% of children living below the poverty level have deficient intakes of iron.
- On any given night, more than 100,000 children are homeless.

Source: Reprinted by permission of the publisher from *Health Is Academic: A Guide to Coordinated School Health Problems,* (p. 6), edited by Eva Marx and Susan Frelick Wooley, with Daphne Northrop, 1998, New York: Teachers College Press. © 1998 by Educational Development Center, Inc. All rights reserved.

In addition to documenting subjective priorities and concerns, a social assessment of school health promotion illuminates an important public message: that the cause-effect relationship between education and health is reciprocal.[47] The National Commission on the Role of the School and the Community in Improving Adolescent Health has declared that education and health are inextricably intertwined, that "poor health is an important reason why a large percentage of young people today are unable or not motivated to learn."[48] Furthermore, epidemiological research has consistently shown that the number of years of schooling completed by adolescents is a consistent and strong correlate to health status at any subsequent age.

Developmental Assets. Because schools cannot solve society's health and social problems alone, a meaningful commitment to the kind of community participation and collaboration highlighted in the social assessment phase of PRECEDE-PROCEED should remain a priority for planners seeking to nurture health-promoting schools. Research on social factors that influence children's health offers considerable promise for activating broad community support for children's health in general and school health in particular. For example, Benson and his co-workers observed that 40 quantifiable factors appeared to have a strong influence on the behavior of youth.[49] These 40 factors are called "developmental assets" because they represent the *positive* experiences, opportunities, and personal qualities of a given population.

The 40 developmental assets are grouped into two general categories: external and internal assets, as shown in Table 8-4. *External assets* refer to those factors made available through existing social circumstances in the community; they emerge as children who come in contact with a community's interlocking

TABLE 8-4 The Search Institute's 40 developmental assets

Ｅxternal Assets

Support

1. Family support—Family life provides high levels of love and support.
2. Positive family communication—Young person and her or his parent(s) communicate positively, and young person is willing to seek advice and counsel from parent(s).
3. Other adult relationships—Young person receives support from three or more nonparent adults.
4. Caring neighborhood—Young person experiences caring neighbors.
5. Caring school climate—School provides a caring, encouraging environment.
6. Parent involvement in schooling—Parent(s) are actively involved in helping young person succeed in school.

Empowerment

7. Community values youth—Young person perceives that adults in the community value youth.
8. Youth as resources—Young people are given useful roles in the community.
9. Service to others—Young person serves in the community one hour or more per week.
10. Safety—Young person feels safe at home, at school, and in the neighborhood.

Boundaries & Expectations

11. Family boundaries—Family has clear rules and consequences and monitors the young person's whereabouts.
12. School boundaries—School provides clear rules and consequences.
13. Neighborhood boundaries—Neighbors take responsibility for monitoring young people's behavior.
14. Adult role models—Parent(s) and other adults model positive, responsible behavior.
15. Positive peer influence—Young person's best friends model responsible behavior.
16. High expectations—Both parent(s) and teachers encourage the young person to do well.

Constructive Use of Time

17. Creative activities—Young person spends three or more hours per week in lessons or practice in music, theater, or other arts.
18. Youth programs—Young person spends three or more hours per week in sports, clubs, or organizations at school and/or in the community.
19. Religious community—Young person spends one or more hours per week in activities in a religious institution.
20. Time at home—Young person is out with friends "with nothing special to do" two or fewer nights per week.

Internal Assets

Commitment to Learning

21. Achievement motivation—Young person is motivated to do well at school.
22. School engagement—Young person is actively engaged in learning.
23. Homework—Young person reports doing at least one hour of homework every school day.
24. Bonding to school—Young person cares about her or his school.
25. Reading for pleasure—Young person reads for pleasure three or more hours per week.

(continued)

TABLE 8-4 *(continued)*

Internal Assets

Positive Values

    26. Caring—Young person places high value on helping other people.

    27. Equality and social justice—Young person places high value on promoting equality and reducing hunger and poverty.

    28. Integrity—Young person acts on convictions and stands up for her or his beliefs.

    29. Honesty—Young person "tells the truth even when it is not easy."

    30. Responsibility—Young person accepts and takes personal responsibility.

    31. Restraint—Young person believes it is important not to be sexually active or to use alcohol or other drugs.

Social Competencies

    32. Planning and decision making—Young person knows how to plan ahead and make choices.

    33. Interpersonal competence—Young person has empathy, sensitivity, and friendship skills.

    34. Cultural competence—Young person has knowledge of and comfort with people of different cultural/racial/ethnic backgrounds.

    35. Resistance skills—Young person can resist negative peer pressure and dangerous situations.

    36. Peaceful conflict resolution—Young person seeks to resolve conflict nonviolently.

Positive Identity

    37. Person power—Young person feels he or she has control over "things that happen to me."

    38. Self-esteem—Young person reports having a high self-esteem.

    39. Sense of purpose—Young person reports that "my life has a purpose."

    40. Positive view of personal future—Young person is optimistic about her or his personal future.

Source: All Our Kids Are Our Kids (pp. 32–33), by Peter L. Benson, 1997, San Francisco: Jossey-Bass. Copyright © 1997 Jossey Bass Publishers Inc. Reprinted with permission from the publisher.

systems of support and with the expectations of community members. Such assets appear consistent with the theory of social capital discussed in Chapter 6. *Internal assets* refer to the personal qualities of a child or adolescent—her or his personal values, commitment to learning, social competencies, and self-identity.

Using the *Profiles of Student Life: Attitudes and Behaviors Survey*, the Search Institute studied over 254,000 children in 460 communities and found a strong association between the level of developmental assets and level of health risk behaviors within a given population. Specifically, Table 8-5 shows that high levels of developmental assets are associated with fewer high-risk behaviors among youth and adolescents in Albuquerque and Minneapolis.

These data are generally consistent with findings from surveys administered across the United States. Based on nearly 100,000 survey questionnaires from different parts of the country, Figure 8-2 shows that youth in grades 6–12 with more assets are less likely than youth with fewer assets to engage in four different categories of risk behavior. Using data from the same sample, Figure 8-3 shows that higher levels of developmental assets are associated with higher levels of key educational goals, including both success in school and valuing diversity.

TABLE 8-5 40 developmental assets and high-risk behavior patterns: Albuquerque and Minneapolis

	Patterns of High-Risk Behavior		Percentage of Youth Engaged in High-Risk Behavior Patterns			
Category	Definition	City	If 0–10 Assets	If 11–20 Assets	If 21–30 Assets	If 31–40 Assets
Alcohol	Has used alcohol three or more times in the past month or got drunk one or more times in the past two weeks	Albu. Minn.	53 63	35 52	16 24	4 12
Tobacco	Smokes one or more cigarettes every day or uses chewing tobacco frequently	Albu. Minn.	36 35	19 18	7 7	2 2
Sexual Intercourse	Has had sexual intercourse three or more times in lifetime	Albu. Minn.	38 44	28 32	17 17	5 4
Violence	Has engaged in three or more acts of fighting, hitting, injuring a person, carrying or using a weapon, or threatening physical harm in the past year	Albu. Minn.	65 69	41 49	21 31	7 10

Notes: Albuquerque sample is a census of public-school students, grades six to twelve ($N = 12,440$). Minneapolis sample is a census of public-school students, grades seven, eight, ten, and eleven ($N = 5,235$).
Source: All Our Kids Are Our Kids (p. 57), by Peter L. Benson, 1997, San Francisco: Jossey-Bass. Copyright © 1997 Jossey-Bass Publishers Inc. Reprinted with permission from the publisher.

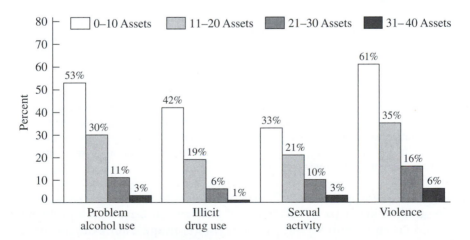

FIGURE 8-2 Developmental assets and high-risk behavior patterns: 100,000 U.S. public school students—1996–1997.
Source: Assets: The Magazine for Healthy Communities and Healthy Youth, 1997, 2(4), 10.

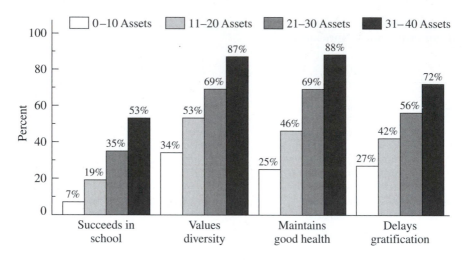

FIGURE 8-3 Developmental assets and positive attitudes/behaviors: 100,000 U.S. public school students—1996–1997.
Source: Assets: The Magazine for Healthy Communities and Healthy Youth, 1997, 2(4), 10.

While the use of developmental assets can add important quantitative insights for social assessment, health program planners working primarily with culturally diverse populations need to take the usual prudent step of carrying out pretests to confirm the validity of the questions for the population and/or culture in question.[50]

Epidemiological Assessment

Barbara Starfield and Peter Budetti, highly respected scholars in the field of child health, urged that efforts to gather health information about school-aged youth need to focus on multiple sources:

> No one method is sufficient to describe the frequency of health problems in childhood. Some problems are known only to parents or families, because they are not manifested outside the home and are not brought in for medical care. Some are noticed only by teachers, who observe children under different circumstances than do their parents. Some health conditions become known only upon special questioning by qualified personnel, and some require a physician's assessment for their diagnosis.[51]

Using Multiple Approaches.   Program planners can follow the same steps as those outlined in Chapter 3 to identify the current priority health problems of the children and youth served by the school(s) in question. Sources for such information might include health records from the school (school health nurse, school-based clinic), data from the local health department, social services agencies, the police department, the highway safety department, reports on pediatric health from local physicians or clinics, and special surveys covering the area or region. Information gathered through this triangulation procedure would enable planners to (1) increase the chances of detecting the incidence of extraordinary health events, (2) compare the prevalence of various health conditions within a given school population, (3) compare incidence or prevalence data of a given school population with those of the district, neighboring region, state, or perhaps nation, and (4) compare the prevalence of risk factors among students with those of adults within the same community.

Because demographic characteristics, environmental conditions, and social norms together shape the unique health status of a given community, it is ideal for planners to use local data. However, local data on the health of children and youth are sometimes limited; even when available, these data are sometimes difficult to obtain or may have dubious reliability. In such cases, planners can consider a second approach—estimating the epidemiological assessment by calling attention to the leading health problems for school-aged youth in the region, state, province, or nation. This approach has considerable merit, despite the obvious deficiency of not being able to detect problems unique to a given school or community.

Based on information presented in Chapter 3, it is fair to say that health problems and their determinants are a matter of degree and are relative. For example, the rate of alcohol-related motor vehicle fatalities among teens in Community X may be 35% lower than the national average, but motor vehicle crashes remain the leading cause of death and injury for youth aged 15–24 throughout the nation. A school need not await "higher than" status to address a nation's leading cause of death for youth. The same sentiment can be expressed for other problems, including teen pregnancy, sexually transmitted diseases (STDs), alcohol and drug use, smoking, obesity, and physical inactivity. There is merit in promoting a global view of the priority problems of any country. "Think globally, act locally," as the environmental movement's slogan says. "Peace starts at home," as child abuse prevention advocates say. Such a perspective emphasizes that the individual efforts of schools and communities are a part of a larger overall nationwide response to those health problems that threaten the health of all school-aged youth.

Health Problems and Health Behaviors.   Virtually all reports listing health problems among school-aged youth will mix health and health behaviors (as used within the context of the Precede-Proceed Model). Such lists will include discrete health events such as motor vehicle–related deaths, suicide, asthma, and sexually transmitted disease, but also will include behaviors such as alcohol consumption, sexual activities, eating patterns, and levels of physical activity.

The temporal relationship between the behavior, such as not taking hypertensive medicine, and the health problem, such as stroke, is likely to be quite immediate for the 60-year-old hypertensive man. For the teenager, however, the relationship is more distal, as in the behavior smoking and the health problem lung cancer. Nevertheless, school health planners can justifiably consider smoking or chewing tobacco as health problems. Although the deleterious health effects of smoking and chewing, alcohol and drug abuse, high dietary fat intake, and lack of exercise may not be immediate, their effects on learning and school performance may be. Furthermore, the more traditional application of linking a behavioral problem to a health problem remains useful because not all behavioral problems manifested by school-aged youth are distant from health outcomes. For example, the time between drinking alcohol or taking drugs and an automobile fatality is tragically and dramatically short.

Emphasize Flexibility.   The Precede Model was never intended to be a rigid process. Rather, it was designed as an organizing framework to enable planners to sort through the complexities inherent in addressing the multiple behavioral, social, economic, and environmental factors that influence health and quality of life. The results of that sorting process should provide focus and insights for developing or selecting effective health promotion strategies. The intermingling of health and behavioral problems for school-aged youth puts both planners and PRECEDE to the test of flexibility. As the studies cited earlier in this chapter indicate, schools do not operate in a vacuum. They are part of a larger community, and their programs and activities have traditionally reflected the values, interests, and expectations of that community. Accordingly, social and epidemiological assessments will be richer if they include information about, and input from, the community as well as the school. Although amplifying the assessment in this way will demand more time and effort, the benefits are worth it.

The School Health Index: A Practical Example of Epidemiological Assessment.   The School Health Index (SHI) is a self-assessment tool designed by the CDC to help those responsible for planning coordinated school health programs in their efforts to: (1) identify the strengths and weaknesses of the school or school system's current health promotion programs and policies, (2) develop an action plan to improve student health, and (3) involve teachers, parents, students, and the community in efforts to improve school policies and programs.[52]

The SHI has been applied in states and communities throughout the United States. Maine provides a practical example of how officials at the state and local level have used SHI to create systematic and sustained change in schools that promotes health and school success. This is done through a coordinated approach to school health programs and through a statewide initiative called Healthy Maine Partnerships (HMP).[53] The HMP, a collaborative effort involving several health-related programs in the Maine Bureau of Health and the Maine Department of Education, leverages resources from multiple sources to assist advancing health promotion and disease prevention activities across a wide range of programmatic areas including school health. Critical to the HMP are 31 local-partners that cover virtually the entire state. These 31 local-level partnerships are alliances connecting community-wide health interests with local school districts. Establishing and sustaining coordinated school health programs is a clear priority across all 31 local partnerships.

MHP, including the 31 local partnerships, used the School Health Index as the core to developing a Coordinated School Health Program Survey (CSHP) adapted from the SHI and tailored to the specific needs of Maine.[54] At the local level, the CSHP is administered to three groups: school staff, school administrators, and parents. A simplified version of the survey is also administered to middle and/or high school students. Data are analyzed to ascertain the perceived existence and importance of a variety of CSHP characteristics and the extent to which the perceptions reported by the three cohorts are in alignment. Each school system leadership team uses the findings from its site specific CSHP to come to consensus on the "strengths," "challenges," and "recommendations," of their school health program. They use this information to guide their efforts to strengthen their local coordinated school health programs as a means to attain measurable gains in student health and school performance. Table 8-6 presents a summary of results for two categories of questions in the CSHP ("characteristics of the health programs in our schools" and "physical education") by participants from the town of Kittery, which is in the partnership region serving the southernmost part of Maine.

Anyone with even modest practical experience will recognize that organizing and administering these kinds of assessments are tedious and, at times, frustrating tasks. Do they yield results? Following are some of the achievements documented by the Maine Bureau of Health during the first two and one-half years after the Health Maine Partnerships had been established:

- Among the 31 partnership schools and communities, 163 behavioral and environmental policy changes have been enacted—these include specific school policy actions related to tobacco and nutrition (especially vending machines) and environmental changes related to availability of and accessibility to physical activity.
- All HMP school districts have implemented the evidence-based Life Skills Program, and three-fourths of all schools are implementing the CATCH curriculum (both cited in Table 8-1 earlier in this chapter).
- School health coordinators have attained over $1 million for physical education/physical activity equipment and training.
- During 2002–03, over 8,000 students received services from school-based health centers.

Behavioral, Environmental, and Educational Assessment

What Is the Goal?   Behavioral, environmental, and educational assessments in the school setting follow the same process described in Chapters 3 and 4. School health research consistently confirms the long-standing assumption that qualified teachers can greatly influence the health knowledge, attitudes, and practices of their students. Should teachers, then, be held accountable for manifest changes in students' behavior?

Because schools serve communities, teachers and the curricula and programs they implement are clearly accountable to community members, especially parents. Parents should be able reasonably to expect their children to learn enough to matriculate each year. If fifth-grade pupils are supposed to be able to read at a certain rate and comprehend at a certain level, valid tests

TABLE 8-6 Examples of Strengths/Challenges/Recommendations Based on CSHP Among Schools in Kittery, Maine

Characteristics of the Health Programs in our Schools	
Strengths	• Student health is a priority in our schools
Challenges	• There is no written policy and no procedure calling for health programs to be coordinated
	• There is no formal coordination between schools and the health department
	• School health staff does not communicate to other staff, administration, superintendent, or school board on a regular basis about the status and progress of school health programs
Recommendations	• Develop a mission that aligns with Kittery School Department's strategic vision
	• Develop a multiyear action plan and decide how the team will organize itself to accomplish the plan
	• Provide ongoing communication/advocacy/training about coordinated school health programs
	• Assess student health needs
	• Develop formal Coordinated School Health Program policy.

Physical Education and Activity	
Strengths	• Certified PE teachers
	• Students in PE classes are active half of the time in class
	• An emphasis on lifelong fitness
	• Wide variety of PE/fitness activities available
Challenges	• All students don't participate in PE
	• Students receive less PE than national and state recommendations
	• Parents not provided with information about benefits of PE and how to encourage family activity
Recommendations	• Implement mandated PE K–12 Implement "Feeling Good Mileage Club" at all schools
	• Increase PE options in selected schools
	• Model fitness (increasing fitness levels of faculty and staff)
	• Provide students and staff with better access to exercise/fitness equipment and facilities

Source: Based on communication (Dec. 12–20, 2003) with Jacqueline Ellis (director of the Coordinated School Health Programs, Maine Bureau of Health, Maine Department of Human Services) and Paul Primmerman (director of the Coordinated School Health Programs, Maine Department of Education).

should be devised to ascertain those competencies. In health education, such tests would provide both a short-range evaluation of impact and evidence that progress has been made toward enabling future behavior conducive to health.

One should not expect measurable and convincing success in school health programs that do not use epidemiological analysis to find and focus on specific problematic behaviors and environmental risk conditions. Further, programs will be more successful if efforts are made to assess whether these behaviors and environmental conditions, or suitable surrogates, increase, decrease, or remain the same over time.

Skills: A Legitimate Focus.   School health educators are faced with the unique problem of linking health education activities to future behaviors, a problem confounded by the potential multitude of variables intervening over time. The Precede framework can be useful in attacking this problem, with the addition of skills as an intermediary between the behavioral construct and the educational constructs (predisposing, reinforcing, and enabling factors).

School health researchers, whose work has demonstrated positive outcomes, are unanimous in their conclusion that development of relevant cognitive skills, resistance to peer pressure, and social competence skills, in some combination, facilitate change or resistance to change.[55] Environmental changes through regulatory and policy actions further enhance the results achieved through educational processes. Figure 8-4 shows the Precede framework as it was adapted and applied by Bush and her colleagues in a 5-year study to determine the impact of the Know Your Body Program on selected cardiovascular risk factors among students in grades 4–6 in the District of Columbia. Note that the predisposing, enabling, and reinforcing factors center on the skills linked to the target behaviors of smoking, drinking, weight management, and exercise. Note also that the program derived from the educational assessment required the participation of representative advisory boards and multiple actors, including parents.

Many investigators and program planners have applied PRECEDE in the school setting to a wide range of topics, from cardiovascular disease,[56] cancer,[57] and the attending risk factors, to human sexuality,[58] infectious disease control,[59] general health promotion and wellness,[60] nutritional policy,[61] seat-belt and helmet use,[62] and drinking.[63] Others have given particular attention to enabling and reinforcing factors contributing to a given behavior or range of behaviors.[64]

Using Theory.   Working knowledge of social, behavioral, and educational theories is essential for the expeditious identification of the predisposing, enabling, and reinforcing factors most likely to influence the skills or behaviors in question. One practical benefit from a command of theory is that it enables planners to be selective in which questions to include in a survey, thus saving precious teacher time and minimizing the chance of using questionnaires that are overly burdensome. In this regard, practitioners will find reviews of the major theories relevant to school health and school health education especially useful.[65]

In 1985, the smoking prevalence among adult male smokers (aged 30–50) in China was nearly 75%.[66] Zhang and her colleagues[67] applied the steps of the Precede-Proceed Model in developing a school-based approach to address the long-range prevention of health problems associated with similar rates of smoking in Hangzhou, Zhejiang Province, People's Republic of China. The project

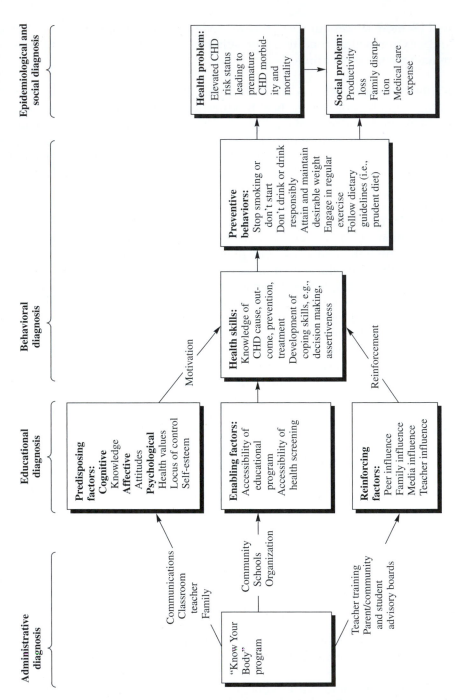

FIGURE 8-4 Application of the Precede Model to the Know Your Body research project.

Source: Bush, P. J., et al. (1989)."Cardiovascular risk factor prevention in black school children: Two-year results of the 'Know Your Body' Program." *American Journal of Epidemiology, 129*(3), 466–482.

was directed at students in primary grades 2–6; there were approximately 10,000 children in the intervention group and 10,000 in the reference group. Students in the former group received a special curriculum designed to enhance their knowledge about tobacco. Survey questions from stages of change theory had revealed that a substantial proportion of smokers were in the "precontemplative stage." This assessment led to the creation of a parental component for the intervention: Students brought home a personal letter which was written to reinforce the Chinese cultural tradition that parents and grandparents are not viewed by their children and grandchildren as "old" in the sense of age, rather they are "venerable" and their wisdom is respected for guidance. Specifically, the letters expressed the child's hope that the father would consider quitting, enhancing the likelihood that the father would live a long life and provide wisdom and guidance as the child grew older. A community-wide campaign was also designed to heighten public awareness and public support for the program. Among the 6,843 fathers in the intervention group who were smokers, 90% reported quitting for at least 10 days; 64% were still not smoking at 20 days; 30% were not smoking by 60 days; and at 210 days, 11% were still not smoking. In the reference group, only 2% had quit after 10 days, and the quit rate was .02% after 210 days.

PRECEDE-PROCEED AND SCHOOLS:
A HYPOTHETICAL CASE

The Greenfield School District provides administrative support for 10 elementary schools, 4 junior high schools, and 2 high schools. Greenfield is in a state that takes great pride in its system of public education. The state ranks in the top 15 in the nation in expenditures of state and local government resources for education expressed as percentage of personal income; the national percentage of adults 25 years of age and over who graduated from high school is 65%, the average in the state in which Greenfield lies is 71%. Within the state, however, Greenfield ranks below the mean on all of these indicators.

Where Are We?

The recently appointed superintendent of the Greenfield school district established a school health committee consisting of two students and representatives from the eight components that constitute a coordinated school health program. The committee was charged with the mission of developing a proposal to promote and maintain health in the district. The superintendent committed to support their recommendations "within reason." As a first step, the committee elected to conduct districtwide social and epidemiological assessments.[68] Their data were derived from (1) school records organized by school year and grade; (2) surveys and focus groups with school administrators, teachers, parents, students, and community gatekeepers; and (3) health statistics from school nurses, the local health department, and selected clinics and

TABLE 8-7 Hypothetical student social assessment information from school records and survey

Problem	Greenfield	Heights
Time missed last year (per student)		
Grades K–6 (mean days)	4.8	7.2
Grades 7–12 (mean days)	5.3	8.4
10th-graders who are 1 or more years below expected grade level (%)	17	32
Dropouts by grade (%)	5	29
Students who "don't eat breakfast"		
Grades K–6 (%)	5	15
Grades 7–12 (%)	25	34

community health centers. The information obtained from the assessment was voluminous, far more than the committee imagined they would get and far more than they could handle.

What Matters?

During the course of trying to sort the information into manageable chunks, a committee member who was a pediatrician in a health center in the Greenfield neighborhood known as the Heights asked if the information collected in her service area could be compared with data on the community in general. The Heights population is primarily low-income and about 60% Hispanic. The committee agreed that such a comparative approach made sense and would be a good way to focus their analysis. Table 8-7 compares information obtained from school records and some recent surveys. Table 8-8 provides a summary of the comparative concern expressed by school personnel and parents from both the Greenfield and the Heights areas. Comparative data from the epidemiological assessment for the students are displayed in Table 8-9 and student perceptions are summarized in Table 8-10.

The committee gathered additional information from various sources. For example, a health department report indicated that in the Greenfield area last year, there were 1,220 births to women under 20, 102 of which were out-of-wedlock births. This represented a 19% increase in out-of-wedlock births in the last 5 years. The rates were only slightly higher in the Heights. Also, a nutritionist on the committee presented preliminary data gathered by Greenfield's Cooperative Extension Agency, showing that the intake of total fat, saturated fat, and sodium among teenagers throughout Greenfield exceeded recommended levels. She said the Extension staff expressed their concern over poor nutritional habits, especially among younger students in the Heights area. They wondered if the general trend (both areas) of declining performance on aerobic fitness scores by students was related to low activity, poor nutrition, or both. Statistics from the State Department of Public Safety indicated that there were 34 automobile fatalities among youth aged 14–19 in the Greenfield area. Although the data did not allow for comparison between the

TABLE 8-8 School personnel and parent response to the question "What concerns you most about your school?"

Greenfield

Availability of drugs

Low SAT scores

Lack of parental and community support

Mass media reporting only the problems

Questionable competence of some school personnel

Some of the building in disrepair

Need equipment (e.g., computers, afterschool recreational facilities)

Alcohol-related events (vandalism, auto crashes)

Heights

Violence and fighting

Increase in teen pregnancy

Absenteeism, truancy

Some students coming to school hungry

Student apathy

Low teacher morale

Poor facilities and very limited resources

TABLE 8-9 Epidemiological assessment: Comparative health problems in Greenfield and the Heights

Self-Reported Use	Greenfield (%)	Heights (%)
Smoking (grades 6–9)	17	22
Smoking (grades 10–12)	26	35
Alcohol (grades 6–9)	58	60
Alcohol (grades 10–12)	90	97
Drugs (grades 6–9)	29	24
Drugs (grades 10–12)	57	52
Regular seat-belt use (grades 10–12)	14	22

TABLE 8-10 Students' concerns in hypothetical case

Greenfield	Heights
Nothing to do	Nothing to do
Not enough parking spaces	Prejudice in some teachers
Cafeteria food not good	School no good
Too much drinking	Drinking and drugs
	Boring weekends

Heights and the rest of Greenfield, 70% of the fatalities occurred among white male youth.

It may be impossible or inappropriate in some communities to compare data in this way, but the example serves to illustrate what the data-collection aspect of social and epidemiological assessment is supposed to do: get planners in a position to set priorities for programmatic action based on the best information available, including input from those for whom the program is intended.

Put yourself in the place of one of the Greenfield school health committee members. What do the data tell you? They certainly confirm what we suspect the pediatrician in the Heights already knew: The population she served bore a disproportionate burden of both social and health problems. Regardless of the setting, questions of inequities and justice must be foremost in setting priorities.

The high rates of teen pregnancy are troubling because they trigger so many other problems: more low-birth-weight babies who are vulnerable to a host of immediate and future complications, and mothers dropping out of school, severely compromising their future and significantly increasing their need for income maintenance and public assistance. Beyond the effects of the pregnancy, teen pregnancy implies a pattern of early unprotected sexual activity that indicates a risk of contracting STDs, including AIDS.

The tobacco, alcohol, and drug use rates are equally troubling for some of the same reasons. The short- and long-term health effects of these addictive substances are compounded by their devastating secondary effects: absenteeism; poor academic performance; loss of part-time employment; severe mood changes that can lead to depression, suicide, or violence; arrests; fines; detention; and auto crashes. Frequently, these secondary outcomes hurt others. Less spectacular in the attention they get, but problematic nonetheless, are the recurring issues of inadequate nutrition and concurrent declines in levels of physical activity.

Sorting Out the Complexity

The committee has no shortage of problems to tackle, and it is quite likely that they have more questions than they had at the outset. But, having completed this phase of PRECEDE, their questions will be qualitatively different. Questions like What should we do as a committee to address our mission? will be replaced by insightful questions generated by thoughtful planning, like Here are five documented health problems affecting the children in our schools, and they need attention. Which ones are the most important, and in which ones can we make a difference? As the committee digs into these questions and the issues associated with them, other confounding issues will surface, such as the need for more resources, the lack of community and parent involvement and support, and attitudes that school is boring and is no good. When planners come face to face with the interplay of these very real social, behavioral, institutional, economic, and emotional factors, the complexity of it all can be overwhelming and, therefore, crippling. Yet, it is the complexity of this challenge that calls on the ultimate strength of the Precede Model: its demonstrated ability to analyze those complexities and then use the results of that analysis to develop robust programs specifying multiple strategies from multiple sectors. One might say that attention to PRECEDE is good prevention, in that it can help save the school health planner from the illusion of expecting great out-comes after making changes in only one component area.

Can the Literature and Other "Outside" Sources Help Us?

We can imagine planners on the Greenfield school health committee being encouraged by the findings in the literature that even the most complicated prob-lems can be effectively addressed through a well-planned, school-based effort. Vincent and his co-workers[69] have demonstrated how a program with school, community, and church support reduced teen pregnancy in a predominantly black, low-income, South Carolina county. Over a 4-year period, teen pregnancy declined over 50% in the intervention county; the study also demonstrates diffu-sion beyond the school. There were four comparison sites: one in the same county and three in separate counties. Pregnancy rates in the comparison site in the same county declined approximately 22% while the pregnancy rates increased in all three comparison counties. The researchers could not identify what element or combinations of elements accounted for the changes, including perhaps increased use of contraceptives. Nevertheless, the Greenfield planners' review of the Vincent study might call attention to a subtle but important point common in most successful programs: Credible sources *outside* the school act as a major force for change. Perhaps success is driven by the resources these outside interests bring to the problem, their credibility, or some combination of the two. As a result, the Greenfield school health committee might seek consultation from both the state education agency and faculty with school health expertise from a nearby university. The Greenville school health committee can also go to the Internet. If they search for insight on the issue of reducing sexual risk-taking behaviors, they are likely to find RECAPP: Resource Center for Adolescent Pregnancy Prevention managed by ETR, a private, nonprofit health education promotion organization in Santa Cruz, California.[70] The RECAPP web site provides users with credible resources ranging from references to evidenced-based school curricula and com-munity programs to online programs that offer learning activities and skills train-ing for teachers and youth. ETR also offers an online course called the BDI (Behavior, Determinants, Intervention) Logic Model. Because the BDI Logic Model is consistent with the principles and intent of the Precede Model, planners may find it a helpful resource. Online resources like RECAPP, the BDI Logic Model and the Community Tool Box mentioned in Chapter 6, constitute a grow-ing source of credible, timely, and affordable technical support for health pro-gram planners whether they are situated in Paris, France, or Paris, Texas; Melbourne, Australia, or Melbourne, Florida; Rome, Italy, or Rome, Georgia!

Time and Resources

Have you ever heard the following rationale as the reason for a new idea or program floundering or not getting off the ground? "It was just too far ahead of its time!" The implication is that the idea or program in question was too inno-vative. The timing was off or resources were limited; whatever the reason, the decision makers in authority were not ready to take action. The Proceed process reviewed in Chapter 5, however, assumes that the health program or health promotion program planned in the Precede process is indeed an innovation. Furthermore, PROCEED acknowledges the reality that matters of timing, resources, or other organizational or administrative factors, including policies, must be carefully assessed as a part of the strategic planning process; failure to take these institutional and environmental forces into account could lead to implementation delays or failure. In other words, failure stems not from innovation per se but from unrealistic expectations that are most often related to matters of time, resource needs, or both. All the elements of PROCEED apply to the school setting. Time constraints can be a limiting factor for all aspects of a comprehensive school health program. The school day is finite. Curricula for math, science, language, history, health, physical education, art, music, and countless other meritorious subjects or activities must compete for a part of that time. Furthermore, school or district policies or even state codes may require that certain subjects receive a specific portion of the school day. Organizational policies can also influence program implementation. For example, while the allocation of professional and support staff obviously depends on the school budget, it is sometimes influenced by regulations or policies that govern the personnel ceiling. In some instances, such ceilings or hiring freezes may prohibit new personnel even if economic resources can be obtained.

Whether a program is new or just a logical extension of an ongoing effort, the question of budget is inescapable. Nothing is free. All aspects of a proposed program—personnel needs, space, educational materials, health services resources and equipment, teacher and staff training—are inextricably tied to budget considerations. Although health planners should not be paralyzed by budget constraints, they must be practical about costs when designing an intervention.

The planner's Proceed task then is to make a careful assessment of time, personnel, materials, and other resources needed for the proposed program, and then juxtapose those needs with two things: (1) the administrative and organizational realities of current operations in the school and (2) an assessment of the potential for making changes in those administrative and organizational elements that may bar program implementation. The identification of program needs should be a natural outgrowth of the Precede planning process. Further, while the assessment of current administrative, organizational, and policy factors can by no means be taken for granted, the steps outlined in Chapter 5 can be readily applied by members of the planning group. The question of assessing the potential for influencing change in selected administrative, organizational, or policy elements merits further consideration here.

"Within Reason."   Let us return to the Greenfield scenario. Recall that the recently appointed superintendent of schools called for the formation of the school health committee, charged them with a health promotion mission, and promised support "within reason." Did "within reason" refer to resources? To public opinion? Both? The expression of support is a signal that health is high on the superintendent's agenda, and the committee would be well advised to take prudent steps not only to keep it there but to elevate it. This is where the principles of community participation, highlighted throughout this book and incorporated in the formation of the Greenfield school health committee, are so critical.

Public Opinion

Many things influence the decisions school officials make. One of the most important is community opinion. The most obvious example is the loud and persistent opposition to sex education. Yet, in most cases, it is not the loud outcry that influences a decision on an innovative program, it is quiescence. Regardless of how good a program may be, decision makers can easily withhold support if they believe that constituents do not care one way or another about it. An uninformed, quiescent community is a barrier to change. The committee should make a concerted effort to apprise parents and local leaders and involve them in planning and implementing the proposed program.[71] This process can ensure that the community committee members understand the important problems the program is designed to mitigate. Creating a groundswell of interest and eventual support will legitimize the exploration of creative ways to obtain the resources for the program and will help implementers overcome administrative problems. One sure way to squelch an administrator's enthusiasm for school health activities is to propose programs that require large budgetary increases for personnel and materials without an accompanying plan outlining a realistic means to meet those increases.

Using Policy

As was pointed out in our earlier discussion citing the policy actions of the Center for Health Improvement, policy issues merit special attention. A new health education curriculum, however creative and well-conceived, would by itself be no match for the problems in Greenfield. Lohrmann and Fors[72] are among many investigators whose work addresses this reality. In an analysis of recommendations for school-based education to prevent drug abuse, they conclude that many of the factors influencing adolescent drug use cannot be affected by exposure to a preventive curriculum. They call for greater attention to policy changes, teacher training, and special programs for high-risk children, as well as greater participation from social institutions outside the school.

Parcel and his colleagues[73] carried out a 3-year study directed at influencing the dietary habits and exercise behaviors of third- and fourth-grade children. The program, "Go for Health," incorporated classroom instruction, school food services, and physical education as intervention components and was consistent with the expanded concept of school health programs cited earlier in this chapter.

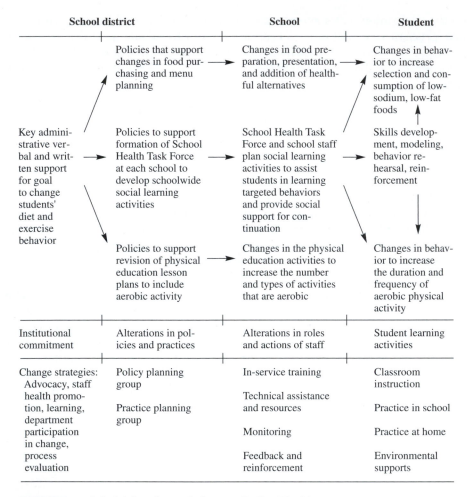

FIGURE 8-5 Model for planned change: Go For Health
Source: Parcel, B. Simons-Morton, & Kolbe (1988). "Health promotion: Integrating organizational change and student outcomes and self-reported behavior," *Health Education Quarterly, 15,* 435–450.

The unique aspect of this study, however, was not the comprehensive nature of components for intervention. Rather, it was the detailed attention paid to salient issues in the Proceed process—that is, those organizational factors and dynamics that either facilitate or hinder implementation. Parcel's group made the assumption, based on prior work done by Charter and Jones,[74] that program changes in schools generally occur sequentially in four steps: first, with institutional commitment, followed by changes in policies, then alterations in the roles of staff, and finally changes in the students' learning activities. These four phases of change are illustrated in Figure 8-5. Note how looking at the change process from this organizational and policy perspective creates a natural inventory of change strategies to addresses personnel and resource needs.

SUMMARY

This chapter tests the applicability of the Precede framework to school health. A review of the current status of school health and school health education reveals a vigorous field in which the traditional innovation and diversity in the classroom has been strengthened by greater involvement with the community. Policy innovations together with remarkable research advances are beginning to give school health the national and international attention it deserves.

In developing school health programs, one must focus on the needs of the school and community when using PRECEDE and PROCEED. One must also establish a clear relationship between the quality of both community and school life. The innovative application of developmental assets is a positive means to activate community participation and support for roles the school can play in promoting community health. The analytic strength of the Precede process is maximized when applied within the context of the expanded concept of a coordinated approach to school health promotion. It is also important to address the administrative, organizational, and policy factors inherent in schools that can lead to severe problems or can facilitate program implementation.

For the most part, outcome evaluation research in school health has been and continues to be the job of academic researchers. School health personnel and teachers, as a part of their planning, instruction, and leadership, should incorporate the critically important tasks of (1) monitoring the quality of their programs, curricula, and instructional practices, and (2) systematically measuring the effects of their programs on students' knowledge, attitudes, intentions, and self-reported health practices. However, the act of evaluation will be seen as just a task or exercise unless the products of evaluation are used. At minimum, those productions should be used as markers to inform teachers, administrators, students, parents, and community members of the gaps that need to be addressed or the progress that is being made. This level of "use" is precisely what localities in Maine did with the information generated by the Coordinated School Health Survey.

EXERCISES

1. What is the ultimate goal of schools, and how does that goal influence the school health planning process?
2. Traditionally, the school health program has been described as consisting of three complementary components: instruction, services, and the school environment. Recently, an expanded concept of the school health program has emerged. Even though the two share commonalities, describe the advantages of the expanded model.
3. The productivity of school health researchers in the 1980s was substantial both in quality and quantity; as a result, we can now say with confidence that well-planned school health and school health education, carried out by qualified staff, make a difference. Using the summary information in Table

8-1, interpret the nature of the intervention strategies used in the NHLBI studies in light of the components and rationale of the expanded concept of school health promotion.

4. You are urged to use the Developmental Assets Survey as a means to assess social supports and local community norms. What preliminary steps would you take, if any, before using that survey? Use the discussion of the application of the School Health Index in Maine to explain how national- and state-level school health policy can be beneficial in promoting programs at the local level.

5. Review the strategy employed by CDC in the development of the national guidelines *School Health to Prevent the Spread of AIDS*. What lessons learned from that effort can be directly applied by school health planners at the local level?

6. Using the data collected by the school health committee in Greenfield:

a. Give an example of how a program or activity, generated by *each component* in the expanded model, could be targeted to address one or more of the problems identified.

b. Use PROCEED to identify potential administrative, organizational, or policy barriers and give an example of how each might be addressed.

c. List two process outcomes and two impact outcomes that could be assessed for each component program example you gave in (a).

NOTES AND CITATIONS

1. *Where the kids are:* In 2003, the world's population was estimated at 6,355,543,400 (http://www .worldgazetteer.com/st/stata.htm). Nearly one fifth of them (1.2 billion) are in educational settings. College, university, and vocational educational settings beyond high school enroll some 100 million of those, and this sector is growing faster (in annual percentage increases) than primary and secondary (http://nces.ed.gov/programs/digest/d02/tables/dt395.asp). Remember to go to http://www.lgreen.net for links to the abstracts or other web sites cited or relevant to these endnotes.

2. *The numbers and proportion of school-based people is larger if one includes colleges, universities, and the rapidly growing number of preschool and day care centers:* The principles discussed in this chapter apply similarly to college and to preschool health programs. For applications of PRECEDE-PROCEED in college and university settings, see Bonaguro, 1981; Calabrio, Weltge, et al., 1998; Hofford & Spelman, 1996; Hunnicutt, Perry-Hunnicutt, Newman, Davis, & Crawford, 1993; Kraft, 1988; Melby, 1985–86; Neef, Scutchfield, et al., 1991; Ostwald & Rothenberger, 1985; Shine, Silva, & Weed, 1983; B. G. Simons-Morton, Brink, Parcel, et al., 1989; B. G. Simons-Morton, Brink, Simons-Morton, et al., 1989; Sloane & Zimmer, 1992; Squyres, et al., 1985, part 2; J. R. Weiss, Wallerstein, & MacLean, 1992; Zapka & Averill, 1979; Zapka & Dorfman, 1982; Zapka & Mamon, 1982; Zapka & Mamon, 1986. Applications of PRECEDE-PROCEED in preschool settings can be found in Huang, Green, & Darling, 1997; Keintz, Fleisher, & Rimer, 1994; Lafontaine & Bedard, 1997; Mesters, Meertens, Crebolder, & Parcel, 1993; D. B. Reed, 1996; Wortel, de Geus, et al., 1994; Wortel, de Vries, & de Geus, 1995; Wouters, Stadlander, et al., 1986.

3. *U.S. school students plus staff:* U.S. Department of Education, National Center for Education Statistics, 2002.

4. *Evidence of effective school-based health programs:* For example, in *drug abuse prevention:* Botvin, Baker, et al., 1995; *increasing physical activity:* Centers for Disease Control and Prevention, 2001;

reducing obesity: Gortmaker, Peterson, et al., 1999; *improving nutrition:* Leupker, Perry, et al., 1996; *increasing bicycle safety:* Nagel, Hankenhof, et al., 2003; *telehealth pediatric acute care service as a cost-effective alternative for improving access to primary and psychiatric health care for underserved children:* Young & Ireson, 2003; and *tobacco control:* Valente, Hoffman, et al., 2003.

5. *Schools as an effective point of intervention on social determinants:* For example, Cargo, Grams, et al., 2003; Kear, 2002.

6. *Schools as cost-effective site for delivery of immunizations:* Deuson, Hoekstra, et al., 1999; Jacobs, Saab, & Meyerhoff, 2003; Trotter & Edmunds, 2002; Wilson, 2001.

7. *Schools as cost-effective setting for tobacco control:* Orleans & Cummings, 1999; Wang, Crossett, et al., 2001.

8. *Schools as cost-effective setting for injury control:* For example, Azeredo, & Stephens-Stidham, 2003; Miller & Spicer, 1998. For an application of PRECEDE in *school violence prevention,* see Chaney, Hunt, & Schulze, 2000. For one directed at protecting children as *pedestrians,* see Cross, Hall, & Howat, 2003; Cross, Stevenson, et al., 2000; Howat, Cross, et al., Howat, Jones, et al., 1997. For applications with better use of *bicycle helmets,* see Farley, 1997; Farley, Haddad, & Brown, 1996; Farley, Laflamme, & Vaez, 2003; Starker, 2000; and for *athletic safety equipment:* Fraukenknecht, Brylinsky, & Zimmer, 1998.

9. *Early delineation of three components of school health program:* American Physical Education Association, 1935.

10. *Foundation of school health for half century:* Cornacchia, Olsen, & Nickerson, 2004; Creswell & Newman, 1997; Pollock & Middleton, 1994.

11. *The expansion from three program components to eight (see Fig. 8-1):* Kolbe, 1986; Allensworth & Kolbe, 1987.

12. *Partnership of health and educational sectors:* Mason, & McGinnis, 1985; Kolbe, Kann, et al., 2004.

13. *The scientific and theoretical rationale for the eight components of a coordinated school health program:* Marx & Wooley, 1998. Although the individual chapters were written by recognized scholars and practitioners, the overall framework and organization of the book was grounded on input from those representing over 50 national organizations in the United States whose constituencies have a stake in at least one of the eight components.

14. *Each component represents a different constituency in school-community health:* For example, American Dietetic Association, Society of Nutrition Education, American School Food Service Association, 2003; Weist, Gold, et al., 2003.

15. *Summary of main findings of the breakthrough School Health Education Evaluation:* Connell, Turner, & Mason, 1985. In this reference, the whole issue of the journal is devoted to the School Health Education Evaluation.

16. *Main findings of the NCI school-based smoking prevention studies:* T. J. Glynn, 1989. This article describes the 15 school-based smoking prevention studies supported by the National Cancer Institute (NCI). In the same issue, eight studies of smokeless tobacco prevention trials supported by NCI are described by G. M. Boyd & Glover, 1989 and the American Cancer Society's and NCI's application of the Precede Model to a school nutrition and cancer education curriculum is described in Light & Contento, 1989; Contento, Kell, et al., 1992.

17. *Summarizing NHLBI-supported school health program studies:* Stone, Perry, & Luepker, 1989. All work cited in Table 8-1 appears in separate articles in this theme issue of *Health Education Quarterly.* Two other studies supported by the National Heart, Lung and Blood Institute, under a separate program of grants was Heart Smart, an extension of the Bogalusa Heart Study in Louisiana that applied the Precede Model in its design (Arbeit, Johnson, et al., 1992; Berenson, Harsha, et al., 1998; Bush, Downey, et al., 1987; Downey, Butcher, et al., 1987; Downey, Cresanta, & Berenson, 1989; Downey, Frank, et al., 1987; Downey, Virgilio, et al., 1988; Johnson, Powers, et al., 1994); and the "Know Your Body" program, which was widely evaluated, also based on PRECEDE (Bush, Zuckerman, Taggart, et al., 1989; Bush, Zuckerman, Theiss, et al., 1989; Taggart, Bush, et al., 1990; Walter, 1989; Walter & Connelly, 1985; Walter, Hofman, Barrett, et al., 1987; Walter, Hofman, Connelly, et al., 1985; 1986; Walter & Vaughan, 1993; Walter & Wynder, 1989; Zuckerman, Olevsky-Peleg, et al., 1989).

18. *Family and community in support of school's role:* In the Nader study, the family is the primary locus of change rather than the school and its environment, which serve a supportive role. See Nader, et al., 1989; Perry, Leupker, et al., 1988; Saelens, Sallis, Nader, et al., 2003.

19. *Table 8-1 studies that used PRECEDE in developing their interventions:* See Bush, et al. and Walter, et al. in endnote 17; and Fors, Owen, et al., 1989. For commentary on these studies, see Best, 1989.

20. *Description of the CATCH program of school-based cardiovascular interventions:* Stone, et al., 1996.

21. *Student health knowledge mediated through the family program component:* P. R. Nader, et al., 1996.

22. *Other changes observed in the CATCH trial:* Resnicow, Robinson, & Frank, 1996.

23. *The effects of supportive home environments in India:* Gupta, Mehortra, Arora, & Saran, 1991.

24. *Supportive home environments in Finland:* Vartiainen & Puska, 1987.

25. *Supportive home environments in the United States:* Parcel, Kelder, & Basen-Enquist, 2000.

26. *Survey of parental involvement:* Metropolitan Life Foundation, 1988.

27. *Cultural and ethnic sensitivity of programs:* See p. 463 in Nader, et al., 1996; Huff & Kline, 1999.

28. *International surveys of adolescent health behavior:* For example, Haugland & Wold, 2001; Haugland, Wold, et al., 2001; Torsheim, Aaro, & Wold, 2001.

29. *The Youth Media Campaign Longitudinal Survey (YMCLS),* a U.S. nationally representative survey of children aged 9–13 years and their parents. CDC, 2003.

30. *Canadian surveys:* Nationally representative data from the 1981 Canada Fitness Survey, the 1988 Campbell's Survey on the Well-Being of Canadians and the 1996 National Longitudinal Survey of Children and Youth, analyzed by Tremblay & Willms, 2000.

31. *The first national School Health Policies and Programs Study (SHPPS):* Kann, Collins, et al., 1995; Lowry, Kann, & Kolbe, 1996; Pateman, Grunbaum, & Kann, 1999.

32. *Objectives for the nation in adolescent health: Healthy people 2000,* 1991; Green, 1996.

33. *School Health Policies and Programs Study* (SHPPS) 2000: Brener, Everett Jones, et al., 2003; Grunbaum, Rutman, & Sathrum, 2001. (Entire issue dedicated to findings from SHPPS 2000.)

34. *U.S. Community Preventive Services Task Force recommendation on physical activity:* Kahn, Ramsey, et al., 2002.

35. *Canadian trends and policy actions:* Mackie & Oickle, 1997; Tremblay & Willms, 2000.

36. *National U.S. and European commissions on school health:* For example, Carnegie Council on Adolescent Development, 1989; Deutch, 1998; National Commission on the Role of the School and the Community, 1990; Williams & Jones, 1993.

37. *International collaboration on school health:* Konu & Rimpela, 2000; World Health Organization, 1997; World Health Organization and United Nations Children's Fund, 1986.

38. *Voluntary health organizations supporting school health:* The American Cancer Society, for example, has developed programs based on the Precede Model. Contento, Kell, et al., 1992; Corcoran & Portnoy, 1989; Light & Contento, 1989; Pateman, Irvin, et al., 2000.

39. *CHI's policy activities related to health and children* and other prevention issues, see http://www.chipolicy.org.

40. *CHI's technical assistance website:* http://www.healthpolicycoach.org.

41. *Federal report legitimates schools as locus for prevention of HIV/AIDS:* Centers for Disease Control, 1988. The President's Commission on the HIV Epidemic, in its 1988 report, also concluded that the school's contribution to AIDS education should take place in the context of comprehensive school health education: *Report of the Presidential Commission on the Human Immunodeficiency Virus Epidemic,* 1988.

42. *An account of the HIV/AIDS policy to school programs experience:* Kolbe, Jones, et al., 1988.

43. *Justifications for the survey of school health policies and programs:* Kann, Collins, et al., 1995, p. 291.

44. *For school indicators of these and other criteria for social, epidemiological, behavioral, environmental, organizational, and educational indicators,* see Kolbe, 1989.

45. *Necessity of framing health objectives within the educational mission of schools:* Green, 1988a; MacDonald & Green, 1994, 1995, 2001.

46. *Australian report on health of youth gave highest priority to social problems:* Australian Health Ministers Advisory Council, 1994.

47. *Reciprocal relationship between health and education:* Green & Potvin, 2002; Wilkenson & Marmot, 1998.

48. *National Commission on the Role of the School and the Community:* 1990, p. 3.

49. *Identification of 40 factors contributing to health of youth:* See pp. 54–76 in Benson, 1997. The Profiles of Student Life: Attitudes and Behaviors Survey yields measures of the 40 developmental assets and self-reported behavioral risk factors. The survey instrument is proprietary and can be obtained from the Search Institute, 700 South Third Street, Suite 210, Minneapolis, MN 55415; http://www.search.org; (612) 376–8955.

50. *Need for pretesting surveys in culturally different populations:* Price, Kake, & Kucharewski, 2002.

51. *Need to use multiple sources of data:* Starfield & Budetti, 1985, p. 833.

52. *The School Index:* http://www.cdc.gov/Health Youth/SHI/.

53. *Source of details on the application of the School Health Index in Maine:* Communication with Jacqueline Ellis and Paul Primmerman, Directors of the Coordinated School Health Programs, respectively, for the Maine Bureau of Health, Department of Human Services; and the Maine Department of Education, December 12–20, 2003.

54. *"Imitation is the sincerest form of flattery":* Maine's incorporation of the CDC School Health Index is a clear illustration of how competent practitioners "tailor" generalized products to fit their specific needs, interests, and organizational cultures.

55. *Skills facilitating change or prevention:* Flay, 1987; Hanewinkel & Asshauer, 2004; Midford, Munroe, et al., 2002.

56. *Applications of PRECEDE in school cardiovascular prevention:* For example, Arbiet, et al., 1992; Bush, Zuckerman, et al., 1987; 1989; Downey, Butcher, et al., 1987; Downey, Cressanta, & Berensen, 1989; Downey, Frank, et al., 1987; Fors, et al., 1989; C. C. Johnson, Powers, et al., 1994; Meagher & Mann, 1990; Parcel, Simons-Morton, et al., 1989; Walter, 1989; Walter & Connelly, 1985; Walter, et al., 1985; 1987; Walter & Wynder, 1989; Zuckerman, et al., 1989.

57. *Applications of PRECEDE in school cancer prevention:* For example, C. Boyd, 1993; Contento, Kell, Keiley, & Corcoran, 1992; Iverson & Scheer, 1982; Light & Contento, 1989.

58. *Applications of PRECEDE in school sexuality risk and harm reduction programs:* For example, Alteneder, 1994; Alteneder, Price, et al., 1992; de Haes, 1990; Edet, 1991; Jensen, 1997; Mathews, Everett, et al., 1995; Nozu, Iwai, & Watanabe, 1995; Palti, et al., 1997; Rubinson & Baillie, 1981; Schaalma, et al., 1996; Walter & Vaughan, 1993.

59. *Applications of PRECEDE in school infectious disease control programs:* For example, Calabro, Keltge, Parness, Kouzekanani, & Ramirez, 1998; Ekeh & Adeniyi, 1989; Lafontaine & Bedard, 1997; Zapka & Averill, 1979.

60. *PRECEDE applications in general school health and wellness programs:* For example, Bonaguro, 1981; R. R. Cottrell, Capwell, & Brannan, 1995a, 1995b; Simpson & Pruitt, 1989; Sutherland, Pittman-Sisco, Lacher, & Watkins, 1987; J. R. Weiss, Wallerstein, & MacLean, 1995.

61. *PRECEDE applications in school nutrition policy analysis and development:* For example, G. C. Frank, Vaden, & Martin, 1987.

62. *PRECEDE applications in school-based seat-belt and bicycle helmet-use programs:* For example, Farley, 1997; Farley, Haddad, & Brown, 1996; Jones & Macrina, 1993.

63. *PRECEDE applications in alcohol consumption reduction programs in schools:* For example, Fawcett, Lewis et al., 1997; Higgins & McDonald, 1992; Hofford & Spelman, 1996; Hunnicutt, Perry-Hunnicutt, Newman, Davis, & Crawford, 1993; Kraft, 1988; Lipnickey, 1986; Newman, Martin, & Weppner, 1982; B. G. Simons-Morton, Brink, et al., 1989; 1991; Stivers, 1994; Vertinsky & Mangham, 1991; Villas, Cardenas, & Jameson, 1994.

64. *PRECEDE applications in other specific types of behavior or environmental changes:* For example, P. J. Bush, Zuckerman, Theiss, et al., 1989.

65. *PRECEDE applications in use of theories related to school-based services and programs:* Bartholomew, Parcel, et al., 2001; Grunbaum, Gingiss, & Parcel, 1995; Parcel, 1984; Parcel, Eriksen, et al., 1989;

Parcel, Green, & Bettes, 1989; Parcel, O'Hara-Tompksin, et al., 1995; Parcel, Rose, et al., 1991; Parcel, Simons-Morton, & Kolbe, 1988.

66. *China's smoking rates in the mid-1980s:* Xin-Zhi, Zhao-guang, & Dan-yang, 1987.

67. *Methods and preliminary results from China study* were provided during a World Bank consultation with the Chinese Ministry of Health in Hangzhou, Zhejiang Province. Information is presented here with the permission of the principal investigator, Zhang De-Xiu, M.D., Center for Health Education, Zhejiang Hygiene and Epidemic Prevention Center. See subsequent report, Zhang & Qiu, 1993.

68. *Combining social and epidemiological diagnoses:* The strategy of conducting the social and epidemiological assessment together is often practical because it encourages those planners who typically have a strong health bias to be mindful of linking health problems to salient social problems.

69. *South Carolina teenage pregnancy reduction:* Vincent, Clearie, & Schluchter, 1987. This and subsequent works on teenage pregnancy (e.g., Kirby, 1997) have led to a Program Plan Index for adolescent pregnancy prevention (Parra-Medina, Tayln, et al., 2003) similar to the more generic Plan Quality Index by Butterfoss, Goodman, et al., 1996.

70. *The RECAPP web site on sexual risk-taking behavior and programs:* See http://www.etr.org/recapp/.

71. *A method for identifying community leadership to participate in planning* and guiding the implementation of specific health programs has been developed in the context of a Precede application in North Carolina: Michielutte & Beal, 1990. For software to guide the process of identifying community leadership and participants in planning, see Gold, Green, & Kreuter, 1997.

72. *Limitations of school curriculum without policy support and support of other sectors:* For example, Lohrmann & Fors, 1986. See, however, Griffin, Botvin, et al., 2003; and Sussman, Dent, & Stacy, 2002.

73. *Implementation issues in school health programs:* Parcel, Simons-Morton, & Kolbe, 1988.

74. *Earlier work on implementation issues in schools:* Charter & Jones, 1973. Other works, in the context of PRECEDE-PROCEED, include Bartholomew, Parcel, & Kok, 1998; Bush, 1984; Basch, Sliepcevich, et al., 1985; Bush, Zuckerman, et al., 1989; Bush, Downey, et al., 1987; Contento, Kell, et al., 1992; Downey, Frank, et al., 1987; MacDonald & Green, 2001; Ottoson & Green, 1987; Resnicow, Cohn, et al., 1992; Simpson & Pruitt, 1989; Taggart, Bush, et al., 1990; Walter & Wynder, 1989; Weiss, Wallerstein, & MacLean, 1995; Worden, Flynn, et al., 1988; 1996.

9

Applications
in Health Care Settings

Nowhere is the evidence stronger for the efficacy of disease prevention and health promotion than in the health care setting.[1] As in schools, work sites, and other community settings, health program planning in hospitals, clinics, physicians' and other practitioners' offices, pharmacies, and other health care settings can be strengthened by the combined educational and ecological approach of PRECEDE and PROCEED, linking clinical and other community or population-based programs. This calls for several departures from the medical model that dominates health care planning in these settings. Each departure will constitute a section of this chapter.

The first departure for clinical practitioners is to recognize the need, the missed opportunities, and the effectiveness they can have in improving the lives of their patients. The first section of this chapter will examine these considerations from the perspective of clinical practice, with the understanding that acute care will always take precedence in one's practice insofar as acute cases are urgent and call directly on the practitioner's skills and resources.

A second departure called for is a break from the traditional medical approach of concentrating health care diagnosis and planning on the individual patient. The Precede-Proceed Model works at the individual level, but adds better value in health care settings when applied to a population of patients or potential patients. This population-based or epidemiological approach will be outlined in the second section of the chapter.

The educational and environmental approach requires a third departure from the traditional medical model as practiced in most health care settings. It calls for a greater emphasis on self-care and patient-centered authority and responsibility for planning and controlling the health care regimen. This break from medical tradition is not a break from nursing tradition. The earliest philosophies of nursing from Florence Nightingale to the present have emphasized self-care.[2] Health care providers need to emphasize the active and informed engagement of patient decision and control from the earliest stages of seeking diagnosis to the postmedical or postsurgical self-monitoring and maintenance of lifestyle and environmental changes. The second part of this chapter

411

offers a protocol for applying the Precede-Proceed Model to this style of health care. The third section examines how the same principles of behavioral and educational assessment apply to health care professionals and other personnel as they relate to populations of patients.

   The fourth section of this chapter addresses the health care system itself, recognizing that the culture, environment, and professional behavior of health care settings must change if they are to support disease prevention, health promotion and self-care objectives. In this section, we apply the Precede-Proceed Model to the assessment of behavioral and environmental factors in the health care setting that can be changed through the education of health care providers and through environmental and organizational reforms of the system itself. Empowerment and patients' rights are important considerations for managed-care firms seeking more satisfied and effective consumer partners and for government-sponsored care that seeks a population less dependent on the medical system. This idea does not appeal to potential consumers, however, when it is presented by the government, health insurance companies, or HMOs as a matter of patient or consumer responsibility for appropriate use of health services. The question the taxpayer or consumer reasonably asks is, Responsible to whom? One study revealed that subjects' perceived control over their health, rather than their sense of responsibility, had greater impact on health-related behaviors like breast self-examination, exercise, and membership in a health promotion program.[3]

   Finally, we seek to pull the strands of the last several chapters together by examining the combination of environmental factors in the community that can support the objectives of the health care system in preventing and controlling illness and promoting health.

DISEASE PREVENTION, HEALTH PROMOTION, AND SELF-CARE AS PRIORITIES OF CLINICAL CARE[4]

When one considers the range and pervasiveness of influences beyond the biomedical on lifestyle, behavioral, and health-related environments, one must wonder whether clinical and office-based practice is a reasonable place to invest public health, disease prevention, and health promotion resources. Lifestyle and behavior are influenced daily by psychological, social, cultural, occupational, recreational, economic, and political factors. Exposure of people to these influences shapes the attitudes, beliefs, and values that consciously drive their personal choices of **health-directed behavior,** such as seeking an immunization, a physical examination, a low-fat food, or a condom. These purposeful actions are usually time limited and reasonably responsive to clinical or office-based intervention. Even so, one's history of exposure to the social and other environmental conditions also shapes one's lifestyle, associated with enduring patterns of unconsciously **health-related behavior** such as food consumption, physical activity, ways of coping with stress, aggression, risk taking, and using alcohol and other drugs. Because such patterns of living are often deeply rooted in one's upbringing and social relationships, they resist intervention in such time-limited environments as medical care encounters.

Definitions

We return, then, to the distinction between behavior and lifestyle developed in Chapter 1. There we defined *behavior* as a discrete act or series of acts. When a person acts consciously for health improvement or health maintenance, we may refer to such behavior as *health directed*. *Lifestyle* is a pattern of behavior developed over time as a result of cultural, social, and economic conditions, usually without a specific purpose but with health consequences. Changing a lifestyle means calling on a much wider range of resources and influences than the average health care provider has at his or her disposal in relation to an individual patient. Indeed, many individuals themselves may be willing and able to make significant lifestyle changes only once or twice in a lifetime.

To avoid a false dichotomy, we should view these distinctions between behavior and lifestyle as a continuum. At the extreme of simplistic behavior is the discrete, singular act that an individual performs to satisfy a specific need or drive. A patient's **"compliance"** with each step in a set of instructions for taking a urine sample, for example, illustrates how a complex behavior can be broken down into discrete actions. The specificity of instructions for properly taking some medications or for following a low-sodium diet reflects the ways health care workers often disassemble complex behavior into discrete acts. The complex behavior with a specific purpose (e.g., reducing fat in the diet to lose weight) lies somewhere in the middle of the continuum. The combination of several of these complex behaviors as expressed in everyday living represents lifestyle, at the other end of the continuum. For example, daily consumption of high-fat foods from vending machines at work is part of a lifestyle related to work stress and coping. The working circumstances may preclude time for a more nutritious lunch. This, in turn, results in fatigue at the end of the day and a preference to sit in front of the television set with a beer, a cigarette, or some potato chips rather than going out to exercise.

The Opportunity

Health care workers can serve as powerful instigators and reinforcers of many specific behavioral changes. If sustained and integrated into an individual's pattern of living, these changes may in turn cause a change in lifestyle. The literature suggests that health care workers may reasonably expect to play a major role in strengthening the motivation and capabilities of their patients to change specific health-related behaviors; however, they should expect to play only a supporting role in the more complex, durable, and deep-seated lifestyle issues related to health. This supporting role should not be regarded as trivial or unnecessary; without support and encouragement from health care personnel, many patients will fail to start or to continue the process of change, and some of the critical community efforts to influence the broader determinants of lifestyles will falter.[5]

Clinical Credibility.   The opportunity for health care workers to play a part in the change process relates first to their credibility as authoritative sources of health information. In response to surveys asking people what was the most important source of information in their decision to change a particular health-directed behavior, they usually single out their personal physician and would respond to physician recommendations for health-related behavioral change. This tendency shows signs of increasing differentiation, however, among types of behavior and dimensions of lifestyle, as well as between sources of information and sources of help, especially as the Internet becomes a source of first recourse for many people.

Access to Teachable Moments.   Health care workers can also influence change through access to "teachable moments" or times when patients are particularly receptive to health care advice. Over 78% of the population in the United States, and a similar proportion in Canada, visits a physician at least once a year; the average North American has contact with a physician more than five times per year. About 58% of visits to doctors' offices are return visits. Of course, this is far less than the time children spend in schools, adults spend in the workplace, and both spend in front of television sets, so the physician's office cannot compete with school health programs, workplace health programs, or mass media programs for exposure time. The credibility and authority factor makes up for some of this. What matters more is that patients seek out health care workers at a time of heightened concern about their susceptibility and the potential severity of their condition. Probably half of patients seeing their physicians are basically well, but worried, providing enormous potential for prevention efforts by physicians. According to the Health Belief Model,[6] this concern about susceptibility and severity of consequences should make them more attentive, receptive, and responsive to change than they might be in the school, workplace, or home. Because of the large numbers of people who make at least one physician visit per year, a small proportion of patients responding to recommendations from health care workers translates to a large number at the population level. For example, 8% of physicians in 1991 considered themselves successful in changing the smoking habits 75% or more of the time,[7] and that was before most were prescribing nicotine replacement therapy. At a practice level, this would be interpreted by most physicians as failure, but at the population level, even this pessimistic estimate of $.08 \times .75 = 6\%$ quit rate is twice as good as the 3% unaided, "cold turkey" quit rate of most people (see Table 5-4), and far more significant in reducing smoking-related morbidity than most of the more purely medical interventions the physician might apply at later stages in relation to the same morbidities.

Public Interest.   The recent wave of health consciousness in the general population has enlarged the inherent interest of patients in seeking the counsel of health care workers to help them change health-directed behavior or to cope with lifestyle issues threatening their health. Today, adults who consult physicians demand more preventive medicine and health education than in the past.

Some studies show that patients seek and are more satisfied when they find greater physician participation in health promotion activities, and even more when coordinated with nurse interventions, even if some of it is not face-to-face counseling (e.g., telephone or e-mail follow-up).[8] Even so, such interest appears not to have penetrated lower socioeconomic populations, where lifestyle conspires most against health.[9]

Readiness of Clinical Practitioners.   The fourth opportunity for physicians to contribute to lifestyle change is the apparent readiness of the medical profession to take on this role. Surveys have shown physicians generally receptive to a larger role in health promotion and support its value to patients of all ages.[10] Regarding health promotion as challenging and enjoyable, they agree they should actively support legislation. Many believe medical schools should devote greater attention to preventive medicine. These indicators of support probably mirror broader societal trends to which physicians generally subscribe and respond. The increased interest of health care workers in health promotion is consistent with patient attitudes toward health care workers as the primary source of health information and as effective agents of behavioral change.[11]

The Missed Opportunity

Whether health care workers seize or miss these prevention and health promotion opportunities depends on several factors, including their preparation, practice environment, personal health beliefs and habits, and an understanding of effective prevention and health promotion interventions.

Health care workers are trained to diagnose and triage medical, not educational, problems. Medical and surgical specialties dominate the culture and curriculum of medical school, leaving little room for preventive medicine and health promotion.[12] As a result, physicians and other clinical or office-based practitioners under their direction may miss opportunities for intervention, underestimate patient interest or overestimate patient knowledge and skill, lack the confidence to intervene, hold unrealistic expectations about the results of interventions, or question the social and legal implications of educational interventions. For example, physicians perceive patients as unusually "noncompliant" in response to advice for health-related behavior change. Whether correct or not, this perception, combined with the lack of skill to change patients' behavior, may discourage physicians from implementing prevention in practice.

Furthermore, physicians and other health care workers practice in environments unconducive to health promotion. Tight clinic schedules, limited space, weak links to supporting resources, limited tracking capabilities, and economic disincentives preclude or at best discourage effective physician involvement in health promotion, even in maintaining their own health.

How physicians resolve these issues depends in part on their age, location of practice, type of practice, office management practices, and willingness to accept "outsider" (nonphysician) recommendations on health promotion practice. The routine use of computer-generated preventive reminders and reminders from office staff for special follow-up appointments are effective management practices in the clinical setting.[13] Physician attitudes, beliefs, and values, of course, are as important as determinants of physician practice patterns as they are of patient behavior. Mirand and her colleagues, for example, presented the predisposing, enabling, and reinforcing factors found in their study as shown in Table 9-1,[14] summarized in Figure 9-1.[15]

Even those health care workers inclined to offer primary prevention and health promotion might find, however, that patients expect more than advice. One body of literature suggests that modern medicine has cultivated a society in which patients have both high expectations for the receipt of a prescription drug and a low tolerance of discomfort.[16] The act of giving and receiving a prescription holds symbolic meaning for doctor and patient in that it represents a concrete expression of concern, inspires confidence, and legitimizes the doctor-patient relationship. Thus, physicians' readiness to change is tempered by the dominant role that pharmaceuticals convey to patients and the message it sends to the public. This accounts for much of the overprescribing of antibiotics.[17]

Until recently, scientific evidence of the potential effectiveness of patient education and counseling was not readily available in the medical literature. Recommendations to physicians about counseling too often fail to specify situations of practice and type of patient. Physicians feel uncertain of the empirical basis for implementing preventive services, especially when they perceive disagreement, for example, between recommendations from the U.S. Preventive Services Task Force, the Canadian Task Force on Preventive Health Care, the American Cancer Society, the Cochran Collaboration, the Community Preventive Services Task Force, and the specialty societies such as the American College of Physicians.[18] Information overload from professional societies, consensus conferences, and task forces has resulted in avoidance by some physicians.[19] Part of the problem lies also in the credibility of the guidelines for practitioners who may see them as having come from highly controlled, well-funded, artificially constructed research projects in university-based clinical settings unrepresentative of their own practice population or circumstances.[20] One solution to this is to engage practitioners (and even patients) more actively in the research, starting the research within more representative practice settings and with a more participatory research process.[21]

The Rationale

With biomedical science as the prevailing paradigm in clinical or office-based practice, health care workers interpret *technology, diagnosis,* and *prescription* as medical terms. Though these terms have more generic dictionary definitions, they have become synonymous with biomedical material and procedures that have acquired their credibility from clinical research. Clinical or office-based technologies are best known in the forms of drugs, instruments, and to a lesser

TABLE 9-1 Emerging themes from focus group study using PRECEDE with primary-care physicians, reflecting on the priority they do or don't give to primary prevention in their practice.

Physicians' Perspectives About Primary Prevention

Three distinct conceptions of prevention:

Traditional model of prevention: primary (avoid disease), secondary (modify disease), and tertiary (ameliorate disease).

Public health model: epidemiological-based prevention practiced largely outside of the clinic realm (e.g., sanitation, vaccination programs).

Wellness model: state of high functioning of mind, body, and spirit across the health/disease spectrum.

Summary: Physicians acknowledge and strongly endorse the benefits of primary prevention. However, medical training emphasis on secondary prevention (treatment) resulted in physicians feeling unskilled to deal with issues of primary prevention and health promotion, regardless of their conceptualization of prevention.

Physicians' View of Patients' Perspectives of Preventive Care

Patients typically entered the clinical arena seeking secondary prevention.

The lay media (i.e., television, advertisement, print, Internet) often influenced and distorted patients' perceptions of their risks and health care needs and wants.

Patients were predominantly interested in quick fixes to their health care needs.

Patients expressed "ignorant bliss" (i.e., if they weren't experiencing or knowledgeable about disease symptoms, then their health was not in jeopardy).

Summary: Physicians had to overcome the barriers associated with patients' mindsets and notions of risk in order to provide preventive care.

Focusing on Behavioral Change

Physicians wanted patients to accept more personal responsibility for their own health.

Unwilling patients were difficult to motivate and unlikely to change, regardless of suggested change method.

Physicians' lack of behavioral change training was a significant impediment to promoting patient behavioral change.

Summary: Behavioral change was perceived as an important base to the promotion of primary prevention and wellness. However, physician delivery of health behavioral counseling was hampered by physicians' lack of training in behavioral change concepts and techniques and perceived low self-efficacy.

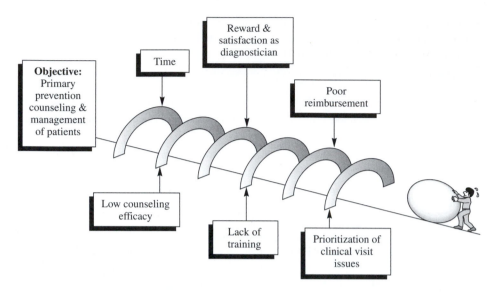

FIGURE 9-1 Physician-Reported Barriers to the Delivery of Primary Prevention
Source: BMC Public Health. 2003; 3(1): 15. Copyright © 2003, Mirand, et al.; licensee BioMed Central Ltd.
This is an Open Access article: verbatim copying and redistribution of this article are permitted in all
media for any purpose, provided this notice is preserved along with the article's original URL. Web site:
http://www.pubmedcentral.nih.gov/articlerender.fcgi?tool=pubmed&pubmedid=12729463

extent medical and surgical procedures codified in the form of protocols and
algorithms. As we shall show, behavioral and social science also offers diagnostic and prescriptive procedures, tested in clinical trials with protocols and
algorithms.

Clinical or office-based technology and scientific developments in medical
research have had limited effects in the primary prevention of the behavioral
and environmental risk factors in chronic disease. The modest successes with
smoking cessation, reductions in fat in the diet, and control of selected risk factors such as high blood pressure have begun to give grudgingly increased consideration to the role of social and behavioral determinants in the initiation and
maintenance of health-directed and health-related behaviors. The "compliance" problem in medicine has been addressed as much with pharmacological
solutions such as larger doses per tablet for lapses, and surgical solutions such
as implants and patches to avoid the pill-taking problem altogether, as it has
with behavioral change.

The successful implementation of patient education strategies requires
more secularization of and less medicalization of health in both philosophy and
practice. Health care workers are somewhat reluctant to provide preventive
care services when the patient is asymptomatic. In doing so, they ignore the
established 20-year latency in the development and manifestation of some
chronic diseases. Reflecting the greater value placed on treatment rather than
prevention, doctors are more likely to treat those smokers with a smoking-
related disease rather than treat asymptomatic smokers. Primary care practi-

tioners provide preventive services in less than a third of patient visits.[22] Physicians in practice do agree on the importance of counseling on smoking, alcohol, and other drug use. They assign less importance, however, to counseling on exercise, nutrition, and stress, though this is changing with the growing awareness of the obesity epidemic and its role in the growing number of diabetes and heart disease patients. Since 1989 when the first USTFPS *Guide to Clinical Preventive Services* identified patient education and counseling as one of the most important activities of clinicians, even more promising than screening for disease, these components of clinical practice have gained more mainstream attention in clinical research and in guidelines, if not in practice. Of all recommendations proposed by the USTFPS in that first edition, 54% were for patient education and counseling activities. The USTFPS report covered a wider range of preventive interventions than considered by previous groups. Its interdisciplinary committee of health experts adapted the Canadian Task Force's rigorous process for evaluating the quality of research on important conditions that were clearly preventable and evaluated the strength of evidence that supported the use of various preventive interventions in clinical practice. General approaches for patient education and counseling were recommended to enhance clinicians' effectiveness in achieving patient behavioral change. The guidelines demonstrated movement away from the simple classification of patients by age and gender for preventive services toward a stratification that considers additional risk factors and toward the development of prevention strategies tailored to risk profiles.[23]

AN ECOLOGICAL AND COMMUNITY APPROACH TO HEALTH CARE[24]

The changing epidemiology of diseases calls for a shift in clinical or office-based interventions within the epidemiological triad of host-agent-environment, from a primary emphasis on the agent to a greater emphasis on the **host** (patient) and the environment. Most efforts to maximize the benefits and to minimize the risks of medical interventions have concentrated on the regulation or control of the **agent**—the invading organism or pathology. Most clinical or office-based therapies employed have emphasized technological remedies such as drugs and surgical procedures. With the decline in acute communicable diseases and the increasing frequency of chronic conditions in the population, single causes in the form of a controllable pathological agent have been replaced with multiple, contributing agents, many of which are pervasively embedded in normal living conditions and lifestyle. Patients must often manage their own complex, long-term regimens of drugs and lifestyle modifications. This requires a refocusing of health care attention to environments and to more autonomous patients outside hospitals and other clinical settings.

Most studies of patient "compliance"[25] begin with the medical care setting as the locus of patient identification and intervention. A community approach to the problems of patient adherence to medical recommendations begins with a population in which many of the potential benefactors of medical advice have varying degrees of contact with clinical or office-based practitioners and some have no contact. PRECEDE-PROCEED provides a rationale and a framework for an analysis of health care issues that consider the total population at risk, including those who should be but are not receiving clinical or office-based care, as well as those who are misusing their prescribed medicines or recommended preventive or self-care practices. It also allows for targeting health care personnel and others in the community whose behavior may need to change if they are to influence the factors predisposing, enabling, and reinforcing patient behavior or environmental change in the right direction (see Figure 9-1 and 9-2). Several reviews of the continuing medical education literature have recommended a typology of interventions based on the Precede framework to improve physicians' practices in patient counseling or prevention.[26]

The following four questions will be addressed in presenting the framework:

1. What groups of people in the population have illnesses, conditions, or risk factors that would benefit from medical, dental, nursing, or related interventions not yet received?
2. What types of patients have illnesses or conditions that would benefit from more appropriate use of the medications or self-care procedures prescribed for them?
3. What types of patients, conditions, medical settings, drugs, and self-care regimens most likely would result in error and would benefit from improved education and monitoring?
4. What means of intervention for each group of patients and type of regimen appear most effective when (a) a condition is either diagnosed or undiagnosed, (b) a regimen is either prescribed or not prescribed, (c) it is either dispensed or not dispensed, and (d) it is either followed or not followed?

Epidemiology of Health Care Errors

In health care, one may make errors of commission or omission. For instance, a patient's error of commission occurs when he or she misuses a prescribed therapeutic or preventive regimen or uses a drug prescribed for another patient. A provider's error of commission could be the prescription of the wrong drug or therapy. An error of omission occurs when a patient fails to receive or to apply a clinically important medication or procedure as needed. One can characterize both types of error as failures of health care professionals, failures of patients, or both. The purpose of this epidemiological approach to assessing the errors is not to affix blame but to pinpoint the most strategic points for intervention.

Figure 9-3 identifies the several points in the flow of circumstances under which patients or would-be patients might benefit from health education or counseling. At Point A, an intervention to inform them about treatable signs and conditions would predispose and enable them to find care. At Point B, informing them about the risks and benefits of a preventive intervention, a drug, or alternative nonpharmacological therapies or self-care procedures would predispose them to seek the benefits or avoid the risks. At Point C,

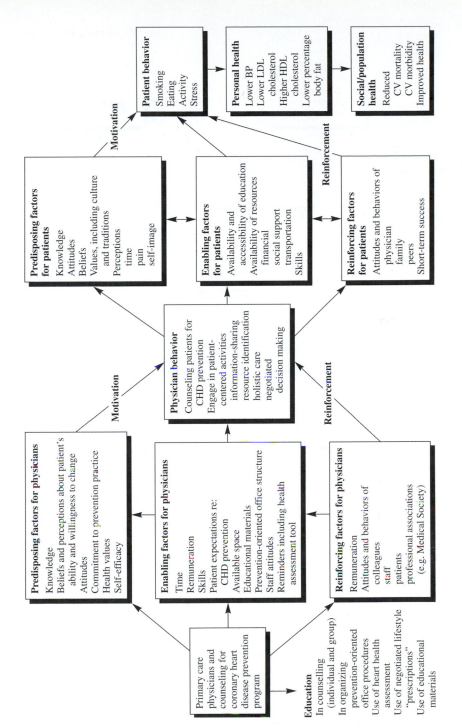

FIGURE 9-2 Primary care physicians were the initial target group in this study of physician counseling for coronary heart disease prevention, based on the Precede-Proceed Model.

Source: "Primary Care Physicians and Coronary Heart Disease Prevention," by L. Makrides, P. L. Veinot, J. Richard, and M. J. Allen, 1997, *Patient Education and Counseling, 32,* 207–217. Reprinted with permission.

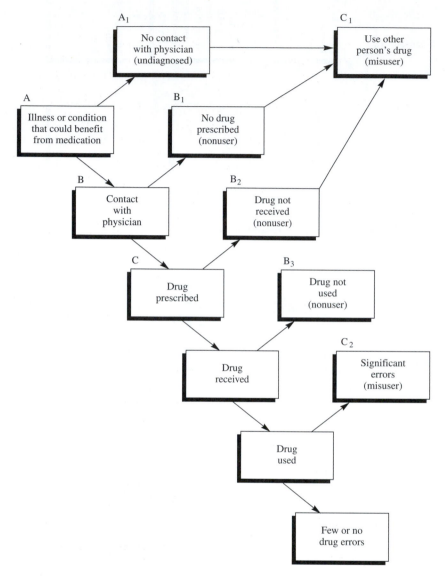

FIGURE 9-3 The flow of patients into categories of health care and health care errors can pinpoint stages in the process at which educational interventions can be strategically targeted.

Source: "An Epidemiological Approach to Targeting Drug Information," by L. W. Green, P. D. Mullen, and R. B. Friedman, 1986; and Chap. 29 in Cramer & Spilker, eds., 1991, *Patient Compliance in Medical Practice and Clinical Trials*. New York: Raven. Reprinted with permission from Elsevier.

efforts to inform them about the proper use of a medication or procedure should enable them to follow the regimen appropriately. The figure identifies needs for patient education and broader public-health education both to prevent errors of omission (in A and B) and to prevent errors of commission (in C_1 or C_2).

Health Care Errors of Omission

Potential patients can be classified into two groups, each of which could be the target of different health education programs to reduce health care errors of omission:

- Those who are not currently seeking or receiving medical care for their illness or condition (the undiagnosed), or a symptom or risk factor that could warrant examination and health counseling (the unscreened)
- Those who received a medical diagnosis but did not receive, fill, or use a prescription or recommendation for a procedure or medicine that could benefit them (the nonusers)

The Undiagnosed.   The purpose of health education for people with undiagnosed conditions is to predispose and enable them to obtain screening, or medical diagnosis and treatment, assuming that one or more tests, medications, or procedures would help prevent or treat their condition and would be prescribed for them. General communications targeted to these people would advise them that if they have certain high-risk characteristics or were experiencing specified symptoms, they should obtain periodic screening tests or consult a physician or other health care provider because medical or dental advice or treatment may be needed.

Health education of this kind has long been part of public health programs to induce high-risk populations to seek prenatal care, immunizations, contraceptives, blood pressure screening, and a variety of other preventive measures.[27] Such efforts have been effective in primary prevention and communicable disease control, accounting for the dramatic reductions in infant mortality and congenital defects, as well as the near eradication of some childhood diseases. It has been the mainstay of high blood pressure control programs and campaigns, accounting for dramatic reductions in the incidence of strokes and cerebrovascular death rates.[28] It has also proven pivotal to the successes of family planning, cancer control, mental health care, and other areas of secondary prevention and early diagnosis. Both those suffering overt symptoms and the "worried well" will be most responsive to media messages that encourage them to seek medical care to alleviate their symptoms or worries. Those with financial constraints and those with risk factors considered normal in their family, culture, or experience will require more intensive case-finding, outreach, and screening programs.

Nonusers.   The first class of nonusers (B_1 in Figure 9-3) consists of patients with preventable or treatable conditions who do not receive self-care education or medical recommendations from their physicians or who receive a prescription or recommendation for the wrong therapy or self-care regimen. Such patients might benefit from information normally directed to the undiagnosed. A more appropriate remedy, however, is improved quality assurance from prescribers, or from pharmacists or dispensers, who could head off the incorrectly prescribed products.[29]

In another category of nonusers are those patients who do not obtain recommended self-care devices (e.g., a blood pressure cuff) or medications or who fail to fill their prescriptions (B_2). This tends to occur when patients cannot get to pharmacies, when they are exceptionally fearful of side effects, and when the price of devices or drugs is unaffordable or perceived to exceed the value of the therapy.[30]

Where the medical conditions are not life threatening, educational communications would serve to increase awareness that the patient's condition may lead to complications, spread, or recur if untreated. Education for patients with symptoms that cannot consistently be seen or felt, such as high blood pressure, would attempt to strengthen the belief that the conditions may nevertheless be serious. For those who cannot afford drugs, information about less-expensive medicines and sources of financial aid would be most useful. In particular, the degree of benefit from palliative regimens should be clarified so that the user can weigh potential benefits against financial and other costs, including possible side effects.

Health Care Errors of Commission

Errors of commission include those made by physicians, pharmacists, or others recommending or prescribing medications or self-care procedures and those made by patients.

Professional Errors.   The first type of error of commission can occur when

- A diagnosis is applied without adequate confirmation
- Drugs are sometimes prescribed in lieu of more appropriate nonpharmacological therapies
- A new drug's potential interaction with other regimens has not been evaluated
- The proper drug is prescribed in the wrong dosage

Arguably, such errors can be reduced through professional media communication and continuing education or quality assurance for physicians and others who care for patients,[31] although general messages to high-risk subpopulations of the public may be helpful in shaping patients' expectations.[32] The benefits of effectively curtailing these errors have been documented, particularly among patients with chronic diseases. We shall consider physicians' errors of commission in greater detail further in the chapter.

Patient Errors.   Patients may also misunderstand instructions and make errors in their use of procedures or drugs.[33] The amount of information provided about a particular product to prevent such mistakes does not always correspond to the amount needed by the patient or, indeed, to what the patient can understand. In the debate over patient packaging inserts, some proponents argue that full disclosure in a consistently available written format can at least give patients access to all the information they need. In fact, however, as with any mass medium, some patients receive a great deal of unnecessary information, as with patient package inserts, while others may receive it but fail to notice, comprehend, or recall the specific information they need.

Uniformly distributed communications, such as brochures or videos in waiting rooms, are to medical care what mass media are to community programs. They are, by definition, cost effective as channels for reaching the largest numbers of people, especially those already motivated and eager to learn. However, they do not sufficiently ensure the education and support of those most in need of behavioral or environmental changes. They tend to be designed with the average patient in mind, and this "average" misses people at one or both ends of the normal curve on any particular characteristic such as reading ability, acculturation, motivation, socioeconomic status, or age. The health care providers who use mass-produced patient educational materials also must guard against the tendency to allow them to substitute for spending personal time with the patients who have questions or concerns and for being responsive to patients' cues.

A necessarily more complicated alternative to this universal informational strategy involves systematic surveying the behavioral and educational needs of each demographic or epidemiological grouping of patients. Certainly, this should be less a complicated and burdensome procedure for practitioners than attempting to do a systematic educational diagnosis on each patient. A simplification of this approach is to estimate the probabilities of errors in each group or subpopulation of patients and the severity of consequences associated with each potential error. A specific group's relative need for drug education or counseling may be defined mathematically and estimated from a combination of national survey data and local census data. Such formulas for estimating drug information needs in local populations have been proposed.[34] This approach has been made more practicable with computer-generated communications that take selected characteristics of individuals into account in producing tailored messages.[35]

Special Groups.   Two groups present special problems of patient errors of commission—pregnant women and people who use prescription drugs obtained for another illness or by another person. For women who are or intend to become pregnant or those who are breast-feeding, health education campaigns and outreach efforts need to be launched through the mass media, public health nurses, and fertility clinics.[36] The campaigns must urge them to report fully their use of prescription and nonprescription drugs, tobacco, and alcohol to their physician or to a drug information service for evaluation, even before other needs for prenatal care arise.

People who use medicines obtained for previous illnesses, or from other persons, risk making a variety of mistakes, including use of an inappropriate drug, the wrong dosage of the right drug, or the right drug at the wrong time. Only education through nonmedical channels can reach most of these consumers to warn them about these potential hazards.

PATIENT CONSIDERATIONS
IN TARGETING INTERVENTIONS

The preceding analysis leads to two conclusions:

- Broad-scale patient educational programs must reach beyond the clinical setting, but they can be contained and targeted to demographic groups in which the prevalence of risk factors, undiagnosed conditions, or untreated illnesses are high.
- The remaining patient education and counseling resources can be concentrated on clinical, home-visit, and self-help group settings.

Based on estimates of a 50% prevalence of "compliance" in patients,[37] the probability of preventing a potentially harmful error per patient per encounter could be as high as .50 if methods of patient education and counseling were 100% effective. To maximize their effectiveness, educational and counseling resources must be conserved and concentrated on those encounters with patients that represent the greatest need and opportunity to improve or protect health. The first task, then, is to determine which patients comprise these target groups and what kinds of "compliance" errors educating and counseling them effectively could prevent.

The Undiagnosed

Who are the undiagnosed? National statistics can help one identify groups or types of would-be patients who are most likely not to seek help or to receive drugs for various conditions. The prevalence of those types in a local area or population can then be estimated from census data. National statistics indicate, for instance, that women experience (or acknowledge) more symptoms than do men within most broad classifications of illness, and women also more frequently seek diagnosis, medical care, and prescription therapy for the same symptoms than do men, who are more likely to "tough it out" or prefer home remedies.[38]

When they do seek care, men account for 40% of the total number of patient visits to office-based physicians and 40% of drug "mentions." The same underrepresentation of men can be found in preventive care visits.[39]

Lower socioeconomic and nonwhite groups have higher incidence rates for most illnesses and lower medical and preventive care utilization rates relative to their greater need, as discussed in detail in previous chapters as related to the "socioeconomic gradient" in health.[40] White patients tend to receive more information from physicians than do African Americans, Hispanics, and other ethnic groups in the United States.[41] Low-income patients receive less than do affluent patients.[42]

Patients over 65 years of age are more often ill and require more visits and drugs than do those in younger age groups. Patients 65 years and older purchase almost 25% of all prescription and nonprescription drugs. The elderly require more medication than do younger patients for the management of acute disease, and they have a higher incidence of chronic disease.[43]

Although the elderly may not make more drug compliance errors than do younger patients with the same prescriptions, the deleterious consequences may be more serious, less easily detected, and less easily resolved than for younger patients. In addition, their complex medical regimens place the elderly at greater risk of combination drug and dietary errors.[44] The best indicators, then, for targeting broad patient education and counseling programs to reduce errors of omission in health care are male gender, lower socioeconomic status, and older age. The following are the most prevalent illnesses and conditions of older men in lower socioeconomic groups (listed from highest to lowest): high blood pressure, respiratory, mental, nervous, digestive, skin, urinary, eye and ear, arthritis, and pain in bones and joints.

Diagnosed Nonusers Who Received Inappropriate Medical Recommendations

Those patients who received no prescription or the wrong medical advice cannot be considered noncompliant, in the strictest sense, especially if they followed the wrong advice. Nevertheless, their medical care error puts them at risk, so this class of adherence errors must be prevented or corrected. Some professionals expect the current tradition of continuing medical education of physicians and other health care providers to prevent diagnostic and prescribing errors in individual practitioners and to build a level of knowledge and skill in the medical community that might detect and correct many of the individual errors that continue. Only weak and inconsistent evidence, however, supports this expectation.[45] Innovative modalities of continuing education involving patients, as well as more comprehensive quality assurance and participatory methods combining educational with behavioral, economic, and environmental approaches closer to physicians' and other professionals' practices, show greater promise but still mixed results.[46]

The evidence that mass media can influence prescribing also seems conflicted. Media events such as news of a shortage of influenza vaccine tend to result in exaggerated increases in the demand for selected medical or screening procedures such as vaccinations or mammography. Thus, it appears that certain mass communications can influence clinical behavior, prescribing patterns, and public demand for certain procedures, but the appropriateness and extent of the responses are more difficult to manage or contain when using mass media.[47]

Nonusers Who Did Not Obtain a Recommended Drug or Device

For nonusers who have failed to fill prescriptions, to purchase nonprescription drugs or devices, or to adopt recommended procedures, two further strategies of targeting health education and communications can be considered. One is direct-to-public advertising of the price advantage of one product or phar-macy over another. The second is patient education directed at patients in medical-care settings including pharmacies, especially for illnesses where the cost of drugs most frequently discourages the filling or refilling of prescriptions. Such discouragement most often occurs when the illness or condition is not life threatening, the symptoms are not very painful or noticeable, the patient is averse to taking drugs generally, or the patient simply cannot afford the drug.

Policy Changes

As with all the other categories of nonusers in which financial barriers to adequate health care restrict behavior, health promotion can play a role in educating the electorate and policy makers about the need for new provisions under health insurance, Medicare, Medicaid, managed care, or health care reform proposals. Direct political organizing with influential groups such as the Association of Retired Persons, national medical or nursing associations, and the Cancer Society or Foundation can influence legislation and regulatory changes in support of patients, providing important **advocacy** on their behalf.

Misusers.   Misusers (C_2 in Figure 9-3) provide a more efficient target for "compliance"-improving strategies than do nonusers for several reasons. They can be reached more readily—through providers of medical care—than can nonpatients and nonusers (B_3). Patient education also can be tailored more closely to their information needs and learning capacities. Misusers can be assumed to be more highly motivated, on average, to respond to drug information than can nonpatients and nonusers, because they have made the effort to obtain medical care and to fill their prescription or to purchase recommended nonprescription medications or devices. The cumulative evidence from 102 published evaluations of patient education directed at drug misuse indicates that patient education reduces drug errors by an average of 40–72% and improves clinical outcomes by 23–47%.[48]

The same meta-analysis of the 72 studies of patient education directed at drug "compliance" in chronic disease treatment showed that the medium, channel, or technique of communication mattered less than did the appropriate application of learning principles such as individualization, relevance, facilitation, feedback, and reinforcement.[49] These principles can be applied more efficiently, systematically, and strategically with an algorithm that sorts or triages patients into educational groupings according to their educational needs. Such an algorithm was presented in the occupational settings chapter, and one for patient education will be presented in the next section of this chapter. What these findings support is the founding principle on which the Precede-Proceed Model is based, namely that there is nothing inherently superior or inferior about any method of intervention; it always depends on the population and circumstances in which it is applied. That is what makes a diagnostic, ecological approach to planning indispensable.

Allocation Decisions

The foregoing demonstrates some efficiency and cost-*effectiveness* of interventions directed at patients classified as misusers or potential misusers of medical advice and prescriptions. Yet, the cost-*benefit* potential of providing preventive services to the healthy population, screening programs to the undiagnosed people with risk factors or incipient illness, and outreach to the dropouts from treatment could be much greater in the long run. These nonusers represent new or lost markets for the pharmaceutical companies, who should find it beneficial to support medical and public health agencies in their efforts to reach these would-be patients and to reduce the extent of untreated illness in the poorest populations. Pharmaceutical companies, the Food and Drug Administration (FDA), consumer groups, and advertising firms are now bringing medication information directly to the general public. Several companies have attempted to educate consumers about the signs of certain diseases—hypertension, diabetes, and depression—without mentioning products by name. Referred to as *institutional advertising*, these ads have been applauded by both consumers and the FDA. Institutional advertising could be an efficient and profitable method of reaching the undiagnosed and nonuser groups. More recent initiatives by the drug companies advertise brand names of drugs only available by prescription, encouraging potential users to consult with their physicians and to ask whether the drug would be appropriate. Viagra is a notable recent example of this "direct-to-consumer" drug advertising.

Efforts to bring more of the nonusers—the undiagnosed, the dropouts, the uninsured—into the medical care system will be frustrated if the burden on the system only makes the problems of compliance worse because of overworked staff spending too little time with patients. More widespread and more effective patient education and professional education related to the adherence problems, combined with organizational, economic, and environmental reforms of the system itself, will make the efforts to recruit the nonusers worthwhile and productive.

This has been the philosophy and developing strategy of a movement within the health services professions called Community-Oriented Primary Care (COPC). It has developed methods and procedures for practicing "denominator medicine" through community analysis of the population served by the health care institution or practice. COPC seeks to apply the Precede and Proceed assessments of community perceptions and epidemiological distributions of health problems and risk factors described in this chapter. COPC has been adopted variously within the community health centers and migrant health centers funded by the Health Services and Resources Administration, the Indian Health Service, and various foundations.[50]

APPLICATION OF EDUCATIONAL AND ECOLOGICAL
ASSESSMENT TO INDIVIDUAL PATIENTS

Although particularly suited to program planning for populations of patients, workers, students, or community residents, the Precede-Proceed concepts and methods have been widely applied to the individual level of clinical decision making in health care or counseling settings, including patient education, nutrition counseling, smoking-cessation, and self-care, self-management, or self-help programs. The model lends itself to a protocol for the triage and stepped care of patients and the continuing education of health care workers where complex behavioral changes and environmental influences must be taken into consideration.

All too often, physicians arrive at a correct medical diagnosis and nurses or dieticians devise appropriate management plans, only to be frustrated by unsatisfactory outcomes resulting from the patient's not understanding instructions or, in many instances, choosing to ignore them. What sustains an outpatient's adherence to a prescribed medical or dietary regimen between visits? The answer, apparently, is that not enough sustains their behavior. Patient adherence failure, or "noncompliance," is reflected most clearly in relapse rates ranging from 20% to 80%, not only in nonadherence to medications but even more in ignoring advice on lifestyle modifications.[51] Time and time again, patients make decisions affecting their health based on nonmedical aspects of their experience and other pushes and pulls in their environment, such as social influence networks, disposable income, or beliefs about their condition's origins and causes.

Reviews of patient education studies and epidemiological models suggest that more effective interaction between health care providers and patients could reduce drug errors by as much as 72%, improve behavioral outcomes by 38%-44%, and improve clinical outcomes by as much as 40% over conventional treatment.[52]

Improved interaction through systematic, evidence-based, PRECEDE-guided planning corrects not only many patient errors but also those errors attributable to the health care providers, who with better interactions become more conscious of the patient's specific needs and the related needs of other similar patients. Allegrante and his colleagues tested several components of a program to increase walking for patients with arthritis of the knee. Based on their application of the Precede-Proceed process, they developed a comprehensive intervention strategy that addressed factors both within and beyond the control of health care providers. Examples of the former included behavioral contracting, commitment strategies, and cognitive strategies—frameworks that the provider can compose with the patient's collaboration. In the larger community context, they addressed reinforcement measures and stimulus control.[53] A key to their success in extending these intervention experiences to prevention of osteoarthritis and hip fractures has been the recognition of the wide range of nonmedical, environmental forces over which patients and their support networks must exercise some control, as illustrated by Figure 9-4.

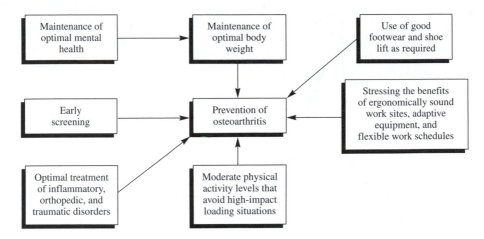

FIGURE 9-4 Each of the potential behavioral and environmental influences on the health problems of osteoarthritis could become an intervention for an individual patient, or a *program* of interventions based on an educational and ecological diagnosis of the specific behavior or environmental determinant in the patient population.
Source: Marks, R., & Allegrante, J. P. (2001). "Nonoperative management of osteoarthritis." *Critical Reviews in Physical and Rehabilitative Medicine, 13,* 131–158.

These various potential influences on prevention of osteoarthritis operate differently for each patient, requiring some tailoring of the interventions at an individual level; but each could be the subject of an educational and ecological diagnosis and component of a program plan for a population of patients.

The typical relapse pattern in a variety of practices recommended to patients, especially those practices relating to addiction, compulsive behavior, pleasures, comforts, unpleasant side effects, inconveniences, costs, or even simple habits, is shown in Figure 9-5. Assuming that nearly 100% of the patients who leave a medical care encounter are committed to adopting the prescribed practice, studies have uncovered a characteristic drop of 40% to 80% in actual maintenance behavior during the first 6 weeks.[54]

Though the shape of the curve is highly predictable, the drop in percentage before it levels off is not. More effective intervention for selected self-care practices can alter the curve's slope and plateau levels.[55] For example, physicians can reduce a patient's daily consumption of cigarettes by simply giving advice and referring a patient to one of the community smoking cessation programs offered by various health organizations, as shown in Figure 9-6, where three different smoking-cessation clinics achieved identical relapse curves in terms of their shape but different levels of plateau, depending on their effectiveness in applying educational and behavioral principles.

PRECEDE had its earliest controlled trials as a systematic planning and evaluation model to design interventions for doctors and nurses treating patients with asthma or hypertension, for the patients themselves, and for significant others who could support them in adjusting their medical and dietary

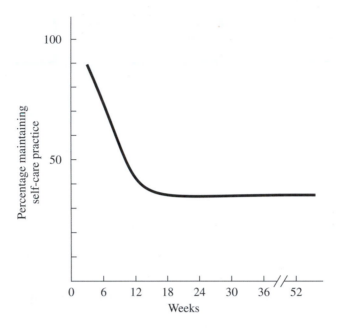

FIGURE 9-5 The typical shape of the relapse curve applies to a variety of self-care practices, especially those involving an addictive element such as smoking cessation or the addition of a complex lifestyle behavior such as physical activity.
Source: "How Physicians Can Improve Patients' Participation and Maintenance in Self-Care," by L. W. Green, 1987, *Western Journal of Medicine, 147,* 346–349. Reprinted with permission.

regimens to their living circumstances.[56] In randomized controlled trials in the Johns Hopkins outpatient clinics, significant improvements in emergency room visits for asthma were obtained over an 18-week period,[57] and significant improvements in blood pressure control were obtained over an 18-month period in the hypertension trial.[58] These and related improvements correlated significantly with the extent of patient, staff, and family exposure to the planned interventions to predispose, enable, and reinforce the patients in adhering to the prescribed regimens for controlling their blood pressure.[59] A long-term follow-up of the patients found lower relapse rates, greater sustained improvement in blood pressure control, and more than 50% fewer deaths in those who had received any combination of three patient education methods than in those who received the usual medical care.[60]

In another early series of applications of PRECEDE in smoking cessation, women in a family-planning clinic smoked less after they were exposed to a combination of a physician's counseling and waiting room media than when they were exposed only to waiting room media.[61] In a series of related smoking-cessation studies applying the Precede-Proceed Model in rural public health clinics with pregnant women, significant reductions in smoking were obtained. The quit rate was more than twice as high (14% versus 6%) for the women exposed to the Precede-planned intervention than for those given a self-help

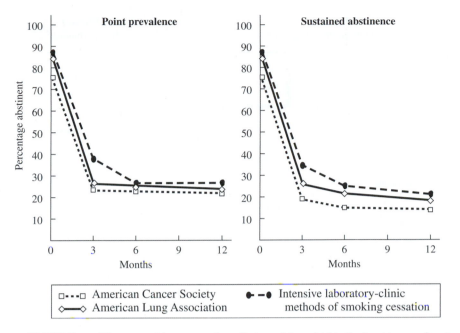

FIGURE 9-6 Three smoking-cessation clinics achieved identical patterns of quitting or relapse but slightly different levels of effectiveness depending on their populations and success in applying education and behavior principles.
Source: "Comparative Evaluation of American Cancer Society and American Lung Association Smoking Cessation Clinics," by H. A. Lando, P. G. McGovern, F. X. Barrios, and B. D. Etringer, 1990. *American Journal of Public Health, 80,* 554–559. Reprinted with permission.

manual developed by the American Lung Association. The rates were seven times greater for the Precede-planned program participants than for the control group receiving usual clinical care.[62] A simplified rendering of their application of the Precede Model is shown in Figures 9-7 (social and epidemiological diagnosis) and 9-8 (educational-ecological diagnosis and administrative-policy diagnosis). Since then, literally hundreds of other studies have shown the effectiveness of well-designed patient education and self-care education programs in reducing relapse of patients in adherence to medical advice, including lifestyle and home environmental modifications for primary prevention and health promotion. Clearly, a common theme among these reviews is the need to address some combination of predisposing factors, enabling factors, and reinforcing factors, both within the health care encounter and outside the setting through arrangements with other agencies, family, employers, or others, to deal with environmental factors enabling and reinforcing the behavior.

A more positive way of interpreting the relapse curve is to note that as much as 40% to 60% of the population does maintain its self-care practices. This fact indicates that any global intervention program designed to prevent relapse may be unnecessary and probably wasteful for a large portion of patients entering health care programs. Furthermore, the interventions designed to prevent

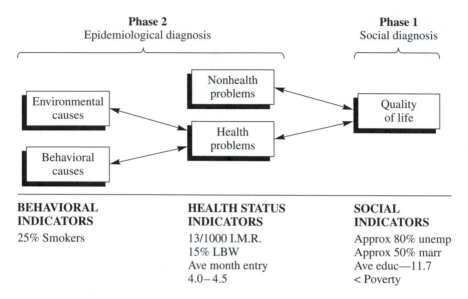

BEHAVIORAL INDICATORS	HEALTH STATUS INDICATORS	SOCIAL INDICATORS
25% Smokers	13/1000 I.M.R.	Approx 80% unemp
	15% LBW	Approx 50% marr
	Ave month entry	Ave educ—11.7
	4.0–4.5	< Poverty

FIGURE 9-7 An early application of the Precede Model in planning a program for pregnant women in rural public health clinics produced significant reductions in smoking rates.

Source: "An Application of the PRECEDE Model for Planning and Evaluating Educational Methods for Pregnant Smokers," by R. A. Windsor, 1986, *Hygie, 5,* 38–43. Reprinted with permission of the International Union for Health Promotion and Education.

relapse range from simplistic, inexpensive methods effective for only a few patients to complex, obtrusive, and costly methods effective for most but needed by few. Morisky and his colleagues demonstrated in the Los Angeles Tuberculosis Control Program that the rate of dropouts or relapse in adherence to antituberculosis medical regimens can be reduced from 73% to 36% in preventive therapy patients when one applies the Precede-Proceed Model in designing a targeted educational counseling and incentives program.[63] Figure 9-9 shows the relapse curves for the two groups of patients, indicating similar dropout patterns for the two groups during the first 3 months and higher rates for the usual-care group. Then, the special intervention group leveled off in its relapse rate, while the usual-care group continued to lose patients to follow-up for the next 2 years.

A HIERARCHY OF FACTORS AFFECTING SELF-CARE BEHAVIOR

The characteristics of patients or participants in medical care and health programs who typically drop out or fail to sustain their recommended behavioral or environmental changes, tend to cluster in four sets of correlates that predict adherence or relapse: (1) demographic and socioeconomic characteristics;

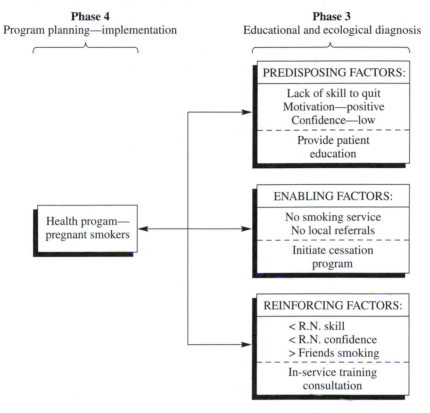

FIGURE 9-8 In Phase 3, the key predisposing, enabling, and reinforcing factors influencing smoking cessation were identified.

Source: "An Application of the PRECEDE Model for Planning and Evaluating Educational Methods for Pregnant Smokers," by R. A. Windsor, 1986, *Hygie, 5,* 38–43. Reprinted with permission of the International Union for Health Promotion and Education.

(2) motivational characteristics; (3) physical, manual, or economic facilitators and barriers; and (4) circumstantial rewards and penalties associated with the behavior, especially in the social environment.

One can view the first of the four sets of factors as predisposing or enabling factors, but they cannot be easily changed, especially in the clinical setting. The other three sets of factors can. These modifiable factors are the predisposing, enabling, and reinforcing factors of the Precede-Proceed Model. Predisposing factors need to change before enabling factors can be expected to change or to have much effect if they do change. A patient will not devote much effort to learning skills or pursuing resources if he or she has little motivation or commitment to the goal of the behavior. Enabling factors need to change before the reinforcing factors can be expected to make much difference. Efforts to reward a behavior that has not yet been enabled would be largely wasted. This hierarchy of factors influencing adherence and relapse suggests a logical order of intervention at the individual level that should maximize the support to ⌐

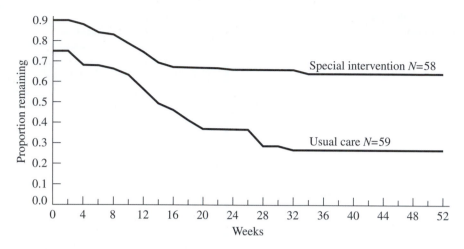

FIGURE 9-9 Here are the cumulative proportions of people receiving Precede-planned interventions or usual care who were lost to follow-up, presumably having lapsed in their antituberculosis preventive treatment.

Source: "A Patient Education Program to Improve Adherence Rates with Antituberculosis Drug Regimens," by D. E. Morisky, et al., 1990, *Health Education Quarterly, 17,* 253–267. Reprinted with permission of the Society for Public Health Education.

patient (or to a worker in an occupational setting, as shown in Chapter 7, Figure 7-11) while conserving the energy and time of health care staff. Logic would dictate the concentration of educational resources on patients according to which of the three changeable characteristics they possess. It would further dictate that if a patient possesses more than one of the changeable characteristics predicting relapse, a combination of interventions designed to change the characteristics should be applied.

The three sets of changeable characteristics predicting adherence or relapse reflect a natural hierarchy of action from wanting to do, being able to do, and being rewarded for doing. This hierarchy produces a logical flow of intervention from strengthening motivation to enabling to reinforcing the self-care behavior. A need to conserve resources, however, dictates skipping those interventions not required if a patient is already motivated, enabled, or reinforced. The skip pattern can be guided by a minimum of questions designed to detect the patient's motivational state, barriers, the potential rewards, and the likely side effects. The skip pattern can also include assessments, decision nodes, and recursive loops in an algorithm for patient education, diagnosis, and intervention as suggested in Figure 9-10.

The recommended procedure entails assessing a patient's educational needs by asking a sequence of "diagnostic" questions to ensure the relevance of the intervention to the patient's motivation, skill, and resources and to reinforce adherence to the prescribed medical regimen or lifestyle modifications. The sequence of questions and interventions minimizes the time required of staff and patients and maximizes the probability of medical benefit to the

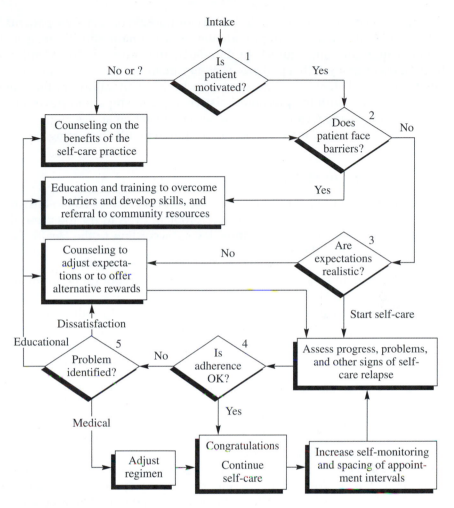

FIGURE 9-10 An algorithm for assessing predisposing, enabling, and reinforcing factors in patient education for self-care or lifestyle and environmental modification leads to a triage and stepped-care approach to patient education and counseling. This can save clinical staff time and other resources, resulting in more effective intervention.

Source: How Physicians Can Improve Patients' Participation and Maintenance in Self-Care," by L. W. Green, 1987, *Western Journal of Medicine, 147,* 346–349. Reprinted with permission.

patient. Physicians, nurses, dieticians, pharmacists, counselors, and others who work with patients on a one-to-one basis can apply the protocol. It can also be adapted to work with self-help groups and counseling for behavior change in healthy individuals. The interventions in response to the diagnostic questions apply the principles of relevance (predisposing factors), facilitation (enabling factors), and feedback combined with social support (reinforcing factors).

A more refined model of patient decisions in accepting influenza vaccination has been derived from patient questionnaires and tested prospectively with correct prediction of vaccination behavior for 82% of high-risk patients.[64] This model questionnaire could provide the source of more specific answers to the initial questions in Figure 9-10. Similarly, the protocols for identifying which "stage of change" that patients or others are in, relative to specific health-related behavioral changes, could be drawn from the literature on the Transtheoretical Model, with the precontemplative and contemplation stages aligning with predisposing factors, the preparation and action stages aligning with enabling factors, and the maintenance stage aligning with reinforcing factors.[65]

Triage According to Motivation

The first question a physician, nurse, or other clinical staff needs to answer is whether a patient cares enough about the problem even to try the prescribed regimen. This can be answered on three levels, according to the Health Belief Model (as described in detail in Chapter 4):

1. Does the patient believe he or she is susceptible to continuing problems if the recommended behavior is not adopted?
2. Does the patient believe the problems associated with failure to comply with the recommended behavior are severe?
3. Does the patient perceive the benefits of adopting the recommended behavior to be greater than the perceived risks, costs, side effects, and barriers?

If the answer to all three questions is yes, the patient is likely to be willing to try the recommended behavior. The clinical staff need not strive to convince the patient of the importance of following the prescribed regimen. The patient has sufficient motivation and is likely beyond the precontemplation stage and at least contemplating some action.

With a willing patient, considerable time and energy otherwise spent on persuasion can be conserved for training or support. If a patient is not motivated according to these three criteria, however, then it would be premature to train the patient in skills or to counsel the patient to overcome barriers in the home environment. The time and resources of the health care worker should be spent first on educating the patient on the importance and benefits of the recommended practice. The purpose of this initial education is to strengthen the three beliefs in the patient.

In this situation, written materials are no substitute for face-to-face, two-way communication. In the meta-analysis of 102 controlled studies of patient education related to prescription drugs, the factors that predicted the magnitude of change in patient knowledge or beliefs, as well as in drug errors and clinical effects, were not the media or channels of communication. The most influential factors were individual attention, relevance, and feedback provided in the communication.[66] These findings held up in subsequent meta-analyses of clinical health promotion and counseling for lifestyle modifications.[67]

If a patient's level of prior motivation cannot be assessed after a few direct questions, the best predictor of the need for patient education and counseling at this first level is the years of school completed by the patient. Less formal education means a greater need for patient education. This might seem too obvious to warrant mention, but an irony of medical practice is that physicians tend to talk more to patients who ask more questions—typically those of higher educational achievement—than to those who ask fewer questions but probably need more answers.[68] In addition, age and gender of physician and patient can play a significant role. Older patients may ask fewer questions (though the assumption that physicians spend less time with them is not upheld), and patients ask more questions and get more time with female physicians in primary care, with the possible exception of obstetricians and gynecologists.[69] Cultural and language barriers similarly impede effective interaction between health care providers and patients, with racial and ethnic concordance between doctor and patient showing significantly longer and more affectively positive visits than those interactions between doctors and patients of different race or ethnicity.[70] Regardless of the patient's level of education or the provider's level of cultural sensitivity, a health care provider can easily probe for a patient's level of understanding by asking the patient to repeat the instructions he or she is to follow.

Triage According to Enabling Factors

Once the interaction between staff and patient establishes that a patient is motivated, the next diagnostic step is to ensure that the patient can carry out the prescribed behavior. Staff members need to investigate the skills, resources, and barriers in the home or work environment that the patient needs help to develop or overcome. If the patient is highly motivated and willing to try the regimen prescribed by the physician but faces inability, lack of needed resources, or barriers that cannot be overcome alone, the patient will become frustrated and ultimately discouraged. Skill deficiencies are most common in young children; arthritic patients who cannot open certain containers; illiterate, low-literate, or non-English-speaking patients who cannot read or understand directions; old patients whose eyesight or mobility makes adherence to certain regimens impossible; and other disabled or poor patients without the necessary resources to follow the recommended practices.

If patients lack any of these enabling factors, the professionals recommending the unattainable regimen have some obligation to help the patient find ways to overcome the deficiency. Minimal interventions expected of the physician include some training of the patient in the necessary skills or modification of the regimen to fit the patient's circumstances. At the very least, the health care worker owes it to the patient to provide systematic referral to other agencies or resources in the community to help deal with such problems.

Assessing Reinforcing Factors Necessary for Patients' Adherence

Even with the predisposing and enabling factors in place, there remains one more level of possible breakdown in a patient's "compliance" with a prescribed regimen. If the recommended behavior is met with side effects, inconvenience, derision by family or friends, criticism by employers or teachers, or other sources of discouragement, the patient will likely discontinue the practice prescribed or recommended. The opposite of these discouraging factors are reinforcing factors. The health care staff can help build reinforcement of patient "compliance" in two ways.

First, health care personnel can provide reinforcement by ensuring that the patient's expectations are realistic, so that when something happens during the course of the treatment the patient expects it rather than sees it as a rude shock. Side effects should be anticipated. Counseling can help prevent the relapse typically associated with the first signs of side effects.[71] Difficulties in following a diet or in stopping smoking should be described in advance, coupled with encouragement for the patient to expect and cope with them rather than to give up at the first discouraging experience or event. If a patient has unrealistic expectations about the smooth course of recovery, weight loss, abstention, or adoption of a new health practice, the caregiver needs to correct these misperceptions before they become an excuse for giving up.

The second way the health care professional can help reinforce the adoption of a complex regimen requiring behavioral change at home or at work is to communicate directly or indirectly with family members or others in a patient's immediate circle of daily contacts. The importance of family support and ways to mobilize it on behalf of patients have been widely documented.[72] Family members can be invited to accompany the patient in discussing the prescribed regimen with the physician. Often, family members are left sitting in the waiting room when they could be participating in the discussion of home strategies to support the patient in adapting the prescribed regimen to daily routines. Cancer patients have reported that two factors influenced their decision to seek information during a physician consultation: the behavior and attitude of the physicians and the presence and disposition of a companion.[73] If the important parties cannot be influenced in the physician's office, a written message to them from the physician, carried by the patient or mailed or phoned to them with the patient's permission, could carry as much weight.

Balancing the Three Sets of Determinants.   The power of involving family members in reinforcing support of patients has been well established, but it is not as crucial, at least in the short term, as the predisposing and enabling factors. A Chicago study demonstrated that failure to find the needed family support can be overcome with sufficient concentration on overcoming predisposing and enabling barriers: African American women with type 2 diabetes residing in difficult living environments (i.e., poverty, high crime, and lack of family support) can achieve good compliance and health outcomes with a structured health promotion program provided that barriers to participation (e.g., transportation, cost, and commitment) are removed prior to and during the intervention.[74]

We can think of the order of priority of predisposing, enabling, and reinforcing factors as cumulative, in the sense that a strong enough desire or commitment, based on abiding beliefs and perceived importance to one's own values and needs, can produce a sufficiently high level of predisposition that this motivation can overcome most barriers to action. Using a hydraulic analogy, think of the enabling factors as a dam and the predisposing factors as the level of water coming down the motivational stream behind the dam. If the motivation is strong enough, it will rise to overflow the dam, that is, highly motivated behavior can overcome most barriers. Secondly, the barriers can be lowered slightly, as in opening chutes in the dam at the water level, to enable people with a modicum of motivation to proceed.

It is usually in the longer term that reinforcing factors become so important, and that applies particularly when the behavior has to be maintained over a prolonged regimen or a regimen must continue after symptom relief (as with antibiotics), or in the case of lifestyle modifications, potentially for a lifetime. But even in these instances, external or "extrinsic" reinforcement through other people need not be the deciding factor. As in the hydraulic analogy, a sufficient level of "intrinsic" motivation or commitment, based on beliefs, values, perceived needs, and understanding, can overcome the absence of family or other social support (as in the Chicago example), or even the unpopularity of the action among one's friends.

Making Reinforcement Intrinsic Rather Than Extrinsic.   The key to making motivation or predisposing factors work in the absence of extrinsic reinforcement or reward is to make the rewards intrinsic. That must be done through a more thorough educational process, depending less on support from the social environment (because it can't be depended on), and depending more on the person valuing the behavior and perceiving it to be important enough to make sacrifices or to put out more effort for it. The ecological approaches to building a supportive social climate for the behavior and making the behavior easier through enabling factors are more efficient when they can be implemented by the patient. They may be impossible in the short term and difficult to achieve for some in the longer term, as in the circumstances of the African American diabetes patients in Chicago. An educational approach that helps people in such circumstances gain greater control of their own micro-environments and develop a stronger commitment to make effort and even sacrifices for the medically prescribed actions is not only an ethical imperative for the practitioner, but advantageous for all patients in becoming more autonomous in self-management of their conditions. As we have argued elsewhere, the educational approach trades off some efficiency and expediency of behavioral change for greater durability and autonomy of the behavior.[75] Within the approach, the possibility of building **vicarious reinforcement,** in lieu of a supportive social environment, presents itself through modeling and audio-visual materials that present positive and valued role models for the behavior.[76]

Self-Monitoring

Once the patient is motivated and the provider has addressed the enabling and reinforcing factors as well as the counseling, referrals, and support necessary to make the patient's self-care possible, return appointments can be spaced with increasing intervals. With each subsequent visit, some of what the provider examines as signs, symptoms, risk factors, or problems can be made the responsibility of the patient in self-monitoring. Transferring increasing responsibility for self-care to the patient should be accompanied by an increase in the patient's self-monitoring skills.

Health care providers miss a powerful educational tool when they hoard patients' data and the methods of observation that would make patients capable of obtaining their own feedback on progress and achieving success in self-management. By transferring these skills and tools—such as self-monitoring blood pressure devices—to patients, providers enable them to obtain more immediate feedback on health adjustments. Over time, feedback from self-monitoring can become the most powerful source of reinforcement for positive behavior, far more dependable than extrinsic social reinforcement.

It can also help garner social reinforcement if the scores or measures derived from the self-monitoring (e.g., blood pressure or blood sugar reading, weight, calorie counts, etc.), are important to someone else in the environment, such as a family member or a health care practitioner, who expresses praise and admiration for the accomplishment represented by the measures. If a patient continues to depend on the health care professional for this reinforcement, the patient can fail to make the conversion to self-reliance that is so essential to long-term maintenance for control of chronic or compulsive disorders. A recently developed model, which uses the Precede-Proceed components as a guiding framework, identifies tools that can change both physician and patient behavior.[77] Mapping the motivational and reinforcing components of physicians *and* patients in a collinear model [see Figure 9-2] clarifies the interdependence of the two agents. This illustration also enumerates the pressures that make the triage model presented in Figure 9-10 necessary and effective.

In their qualitative assessment of physician practices, Makrides and associates have identified obstacles to *both* physician and patient success. Physicians' obstacles include personal, organizational, and structural factors, while those of patients involved individual and socioenvironmental components. The authors encourage physicians to acknowledge and address the socioenvironmental influences their patients face and to operationalize processes in a way similar to the process described in Figure 9-10. Another model for the physician-organizational-patient triad, also based on PRECEDE, has been proposed by Walsh and McPhee with an emphasis on change in each of the three levels.[78]

CHANGING THE BEHAVIOR OF HEALTH CARE STAFF

What makes physicians, nurses, and other health care workers behave as they do with respect to prevention and health promotion? Although medical education and training have emphasized neither prevention nor health promotion, physicians and allied health professionals show growing interest in enhancing their prevention practices.

Nursing education and the professional preparation of dieticians, pharmacists, and other health care workers have given greater emphasis to patient counseling, but working circumstances often conspire against enabling and reinforcing their engagement in preventive practices. In addition, applications of the Precede-Proceed Model, including its integration with health belief, preventive, stages of change, and adaptation principles, indicate that barriers to change exist for *both* patient and practitioner.[79]

In the concluding sections of this chapter, we present some principles of behavioral change that apply to the continuing education and support of health care workers to become more effective in counseling their patients to change lifestyles and environments.

EDUCATIONAL AND ECOLOGICAL ASSESSMENT OF PRACTITIONERS' BEHAVIOR

The following discussion could apply to any of the health care professions, but let us take the physician as the example. Other health care professionals may wish to contemplate how the Precede and Proceed concepts might be applied to behavioral changes of decision makers and policy changes in the health care system. Until recently, most people assumed that physicians routinely carried out preventive measures and patient counseling as part of their practice. They probably did until specialization and technology, along with rapidly expanding medical information and new economic circumstances, began to crowd these elements out of medical care. Now, even primary care physicians have difficulty devoting much time, attention, or effort to the education of their patients about behavioral and environmental risk factors and ways to modify them.[80] Many studies have found large discrepancies among physicians' preventive initiatives, patients' expectations, and published guidelines.[81]

To understand the practices of physicians, nurses, and other health care personnel, the three categories of behavioral and organizational influence (predisposing, enabling, and reinforcing factors) provide a convenient classification. They represent a practical grouping of the more specific influences—such as knowledge, attitudes and beliefs, skills, incentives, and rewards—under broader rubrics according to the strategies that might be used to change behavior.

Predisposing Factors

The problem is partly attitudinal. Physicians and others trained in the biomedical tradition appear to doubt the importance of some behavioral risk factors. Primary care physicians have tended to underrate the importance of moderating or eliminating alcohol use, decreasing salt consumption, avoiding saturated fats, engaging in regular exercise, avoiding cholesterol, and minimizing sugar intake, relative to more medical screening procedures such as colorectal, breast, cervical, and blood lipid or blood sugar tests.[82] Most physicians, however, increasingly agree that their interventions to reduce cigarette smoking and now obesity and osteoporosis are important, This suggests that physicians' attitudes are determined in part by the strength and general acceptance of scientific evidence and epidemiological trends.[83]

Some studies indicate large differences among medical specialties in their rates of applying recommended prevention procedures and patient counseling.[84] Pediatricians have tended to be more prevention and counseling oriented, but even they miss most of the opportunities and many of the needs for parental counseling and testing that arise in their practice. For example, "pediatricians said that they discussed a newborn or maternal HIV screening test with only 10.4% of the mothers whose HIV infection status was unknown."[85]

Health care personnel are becoming more interested in the health behavior of their patients. This probably reflects demographic and epidemiological trends and societal interests, to which health professionals generally subscribe and respond. Studies on obesity and nutrition counseling report that physicians believe it is important to educate their patients about health risks, but they devote little time to it because they do not think patients want or would follow their advice.[86]

The predisposing attitudinal factors, then, seem to be shifting toward a greater appreciation of the importance of behavioral risk factors and the importance of intervening to modify those factors. The problem now appears to center on the physician's diffidence in carrying out the intervention. This, in turn, relates to a justifiable lack of self-confidence in knowing how to intervene effectively and a perception that the patients are not receptive to advice or willing to change. On the other side of the same coin, patients often perceive their physicians to be uninterested in their efforts to change, such as attempts to quit smoking or lose weight, sometimes because they perceive the physician to be a smoker or obese.[87]

These cognitive, attitudinal, and perceptual problems can be classified as the predisposing factors influencing professional behavior. Depending on a health care provider's degree of self-confidence and his or her perception of the patient's willingness and ability to change, he or she will be more or less predisposed to take action to support the patient in making behavioral changes. Predisposing factors include the professional's values, beliefs, attitudes, and perceptions. Values include basic orientations, such as the role of the professional, patient autonomy, and issues of privacy of patient behavior or lifestyle outside the immediate medical realm. Though important, these have not been well studied. They can potentially predispose health care workers to pursue or avoid counseling that would encourage patients to pursue healthful lifestyles.

Beliefs include the more immediate and changeable viewpoints of the professional on matters such as patients' willingness to change their lifestyles or their ability to change their health practices. Related to the professional's beliefs about the patient's ability is the professional's belief in his or her own ability. This is referred to in social learning theory as a **self-efficacy** belief. Many physicians apparently feel unprepared to counsel patients about their lifestyles and consequently tend to avoid doing do. Nurses and allied health professionals face some of the same barriers to their use of health promotion that physicians face and have similar reservations about training or self-efficacy that can limit their attempts to educate patients.[88] The need for attention at the undergraduate and graduate levels of medical, nursing, and allied health professional education to these matters should be apparent.

Enabling Factors

The foregoing predisposing factors account for the health care professional's motivation and confidence, but even with motivation, professionals sometimes fail to take the appropriate action because they lack the necessary skills or resources to do so. The combination of low self-efficacy and a lack of fiscal and other resources to offer smoking-cessation services may account for most of the missed counseling opportunities reported by physicians and patients. When preventive services are not reimbursed, a physician may be discouraged from both learning new skills and applying them.[89] Predisposing factors must be quite strong to offset the disincentives of cost and time. In addition, while many practices might determine that preventive services could best be provided by someone other than the physician, there may not be another person, or space for such a person, available. These obstacles represent a second class of factors influencing behavior—those that enable behaviors.

The paucity of tested educational materials is also a barrier to preventive services.[90] Computerized health maintenance prompting systems are generally accepted by physicians and seem to improve their efforts toward health promotion.[91] Actual skills in the practice of patient counseling represent another set of enabling factors. A lack of skills, usually because of education, differs from a poor "perceived self-efficacy" in that it represents a real deficit, not just a lack of confidence. Perceptions of skill predispose; competence enables.

Enabling factors, then, can be as simple as available space, materials, or reminders. They often take a more substantial form in the minds of professionals. Adequate reimbursement functions as an enabling factor by promising that the health care professionals' investment of time and effort in patient education and preventive medicine will not be wasted. Attention to the necessary combination of these enabling factors is probably the key to success. As stated by a Cochrane Systematic Review of the research on improving preventive practices by physicians, "tailoring interventions to address specific barriers to change in a particular setting is probably important. Multifaceted interventions may be more effective than single interventions, because more barriers to change can be addressed."[92]

Reinforcing Factors

Actual reimbursement functions later as a reinforcing factor. Because it rewards behavior, it increases the probability that the behavior will recur at the next opportunity. Reinforcing factors also include visible results, support from colleagues, and shared decision making with and feedback from patients.[93] Colleague behavior both reinforces and eventually predisposes.

Curative treatment yields visible, usually short-term results that are satisfying to the patient and therefore rewarding to the health care professional. Because preventive measures often yield no palpable results, at least in the short term, they provide little or no positive feedback and reinforcement. "Treatment failures," or the absence of visible results, are more common in preventive care and lifestyle modification than in acute care. Since much illness is self-limited, the efficacy of treatment and the natural history of the illness combine to create the perception of efficacy. Preventive care has a longer time frame, and its effect—a change in prospective health status—is delayed or may never be evident or attributable to the patient or the provider.

Examinations of preventive care pressures within the managed-care environment reveal opportunities to apply Precede-Proceed planning and evaluations to the expanded population of patients insured by these systems. Several critically important challenges within the sector also emerge. These must be overcome for significant change to occur.

Managed Care

Individual managed-care organizations or health maintenance organizations (HMOs) possess the structural tools to incorporate health promotion activities and preventive care into the practices of physicians' and other health care personnel.[94] They can effectively disseminate educational materials and practice guidelines, follow up by monitoring practice patterns through medical chart review and claims data, and generate a wide variety of data-generated tools (reminders, tracking tools, etc.) for preventive interventions. Efficiencies in this area often significantly exceed those available to government entities interested in attaining similar goals. A single HMO's tracking system, after providing physician feedback and individual patient reminders regarding immunizations for young children, based on PRECEDE-PROCEED, showed an improvement in full compliance from 62% to a sustained rate of 90% within 2 years.[95]

An HMO can be particularly effective when its contractual relationship with physicians involves *capitation,* a payment mechanism that obligates a physician or medical group to provide comprehensive care in exchange for an agreed-on monthly payment. The providers of care are then motivated to prevent costly conditions rather than waiting to treat them once they emerge. Otherwise, physicians often have no financial incentive to spend the time to counsel for, perform, or interpret the results of screening procedures such as mammography.[96]

In addition, some see the impact of market forces on HMOs as advantageous to health promotion and disease and injury prevention. Trends in the managed-care industry indicate that competition for members will increasingly depend on demonstrated quality-of-care measures—which often include screening rates and other preventive care activities. Individual U.S. plans report data on a wide variety of preventive, administrative, and clinical activities to the National Committee for Quality Assurance (NCQA). This reporting process can occur either through the Health Plan Employer Data and Information Set

(HEDIS) or accreditation procedures, both of which are becoming increasingly critical to effective competition in the marketplace and are sometimes required by state legislation.

HMO "wellness" programs, highlighted by some in the 1980s as a beacon of hope for health promotion advocates, incorporate need and risk assessments, which in turn often generate the delivery of educational materials; but delivery of educational materials alone, though they take advantage of the reach of the HMO membership, does not necessarily produce improved outcomes.[97] Some multifactor patient education and organizational programs, difficult or impossible to implement in a fee-for-service environment, have generated encouraging results in the managed-care setting.

Complications and Barriers

Just as individual managed-care organizations can build effective structures to promote health among their own members, the larger system of managed care can make interventions more complicated for practitioners. Often, physicians and their staffs receive guidelines, tracking forms, and requests for data from a variety of managed-care organizations. This can cause uncertainty and confusion regarding preferred practice patterns, which has been shown to influence negatively physician adherence to recommendations for preventive services. It can also create serious impediments to implementing comprehensive tracking or reminder systems within an office setting.

Health care providers who are directly employed by an HMO or other managed-care organization, rather than operating under a contractual relationship with one or several, can avoid some of these complications and build on cooperation with other community organizations that relate to the HMO. A collaborative relationship between HMOs, physicians, and other community organizations remains crucial to the success of programs such as patient education, workman's compensation plans, Medicaid, school health services, and other programs sensitive to the social and economic ecology of a community.[98] However, many providers throughout the U.S. system continue to lack any automated data systems used in managing clinical care or coordinating screening programs. This impedes the creation of enabling factors for providers and patients alike.

Challenges for these two groups also arise from two structural components of the managed-care system. One of these challenges is the general pressure to provide care to more patients at lower cost. Concerns have emerged regarding attention to quality of care and efficacy of one-step patient education and self-management programs. A second challenge is the push to apply self-care skills to a wider array of illnesses as coverage for inpatient care continues to shrink. Research assessing the impact of this pressure on patient health remains incomplete.

In the wake of intense reevaluations in both the United States and Canada, various components of the health care systems have been undergoing change, expansion, and in some cases elimination. Health promotion, disease and injury prevention, and community-based care are now receiving more attention

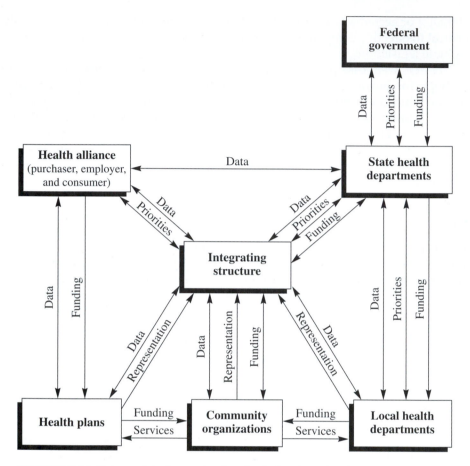

FIGURE 9-11 This model of organizational relationships for disease prevention and health promotion among public, private, and voluntary organizations suggests greater collaboration than has been characteristic of health sector organizations in medical care. An integrating structure will be needed.

Source: Schauffler, H. H., Faer, M., Faulkner, L., & Shore, K. Contract report to the California Wellness Foundation, University of California School of Public Health, October 1993.

from Canadian officials looking to deliver more long-term health for less money. For example, recognition of Precede-Proceed interactions has shaped the redesigning of patient care at a large integrated teaching and health care system located in the southeastern United States. The designers acknowledged that, traditionally, "decision making and goal setting have been the functions of the health care provider."[99] Their redesign instead uses principles of collaboration to bring patients into a position of equal stature. The principles of collaboration, capacity building, and coalitions apply reciprocally to health plans, other community organizations concerned with health, and state or provincial and federal government agencies, as suggested by Figure 9-11.

SUMMARY

Determinants or factors predisposing, enabling, and reinforcing patients and the health care professionals who provide preventive care and education to their patients about health care, lifestyle changes, and self-management of chronic conditions have been identified in various recent studies. The organization of these findings within a framework for planning educational, organizational, and behavioral change interventions suggests a series of principles that can be applied within health care settings. Essentially the same Precede-Proceed steps and principles that apply to change in patients, communities, and populations apply to change in health care professionals and health care organizations.

The opportunities and needs for patient education and counseling exceed the current supply, not as much in quantity as in quality, willingness, and distribution. Much of the available energy devoted to patient education and counseling fails to reach the patients who need it most, when they need it, and in ways that would be most helpful to them. This chapter describes "compliance" problems in terms of errors of omission and errors of commission. An epidemiological assessment of needs for intervention on the various categories of such errors would segment the potential patient population into five high-risk groups:

1. Nonusers who are not under medical care but who would benefit from the use of a prescription or other medical or lifestyle regimen
2. Nonusers whose medical care provider has not recommended or prescribed a needed drug, device, or lifestyle regimen
3. Nonusers who did not purchase a recommended drug or device or adopt a recommended lifestyle modification
4. Misusers who are using someone else's drug or a medication or procedure previously recommended or prescribed for another problem
5. Misusers who are not following the schedule or dosage recommended

The environments, channels, and methods for communicating effectively with each of these groups vary systematically in ways that recommend new strategies for the support of professional, public health, and patient education.

Pharmaceutical companies and third-party payers could play a more active role in direct mass communications to the public about the risk factors, signs, and symptoms of diseases and conditions for which medical or self-care measures are available. Encouraging and enabling affected patients to seek screening or medical advice would improve the public health more in the long run than would increased efforts to eliminate "noncompliance" for those already under care. On the other hand, burdening the medical system with more patients when providers have too little time to spend understanding and interacting with patients will only make the problems worse.

The efficiency of patient education and counseling for those under care could be improved by systematic analyses of compliance error rates in various

subpopulations of patients. This would lead in most settings to a greater allocation of patient education and counseling effort for older men lower on the
socioeconomic scale than for younger women with high incomes. A similar epidemiological analysis of the relative rates of compliance error for specific
pathologies or symptomatologies could segment the patient population for
effective educational triage within demographic groups.

Medical schools and other continuing education and quality assurance
resources could be targeted more sharply to those physicians who are prescribing drugs incorrectly or who remain unconvinced that underused drugs or
procedures are a problem. Physicians, for example, do not have as much conviction and belief in their ability to modify dietary practices in their patients as
in their ability to control blood pressure. Similarly, these educational resources
could give greater emphasis to those patient education and counseling skills
required by physicians in educating and strengthening the motivation of their
patients to fill prescriptions and to adhere to the prescribed regimens. According to the net results of 102 published evaluations of patient education related
to errors with drug regimens, such an investment would reduce drug errors by
40–72% and improve clinical outcomes such as blood pressure control and
reduced emergency room visits by 23–47%.

Sufficient knowledge has now accumulated to enable health care professionals to approach the problem of patient "compliance" with greater confidence, effectiveness, and efficiency than before. Greater confidence should
come from the accumulated evidence offered by studies of teaching and counseling patients on self-medication and more complex lifestyle changes. Greater
effectiveness should come from the increased awareness among health professionals that basic principles of learning have been instrumental in transferring
knowledge, skills, and responsibility to patients. Greater efficiency should
come from the stepped-care approach to patient education and counseling. By
focusing their time and effort at the level of help needed by each patient, health
professionals can bypass needless motivational appeals and skill development
for some patients and use the same effectively for others.

A final maneuver in consigning greater responsibility to patients for their
own care and health maintenance is to transfer self-monitoring skills and tools
to them. These become both enabling and reinforcing factors in patients' long-
term maintenance of behaviors conducive to health. In the final analysis, they
enable people to take ownership and control of their own lives—the determinants of their own health and quality of life. The systems of care, as represented
by managed-care organizations, public health agencies, employers, and schools
will need to collaborate more effectively to make the community more conducive to such integrated care.

EXERCISES

1. For a given clinical setting, describe the distribution of health problems presented by patients and justify the selection of a particular problem as the
   first priority for health education planning.

2. For the priority health problem, show the epidemiological procedures you would follow and write a behavioral objective for the highest priority behavior you identify in this population of patients.

3. For the chosen behavior, develop an inventory of predisposing, enabling, and reinforcing factors, set priorities on one or two of each, and write educational objectives, methods of intervention, and evaluation measures for these.

4. Develop a parallel set of objectives and interventions to address the provider behavior and organizational changes necessary to support the necessary patient changes.

NOTES AND CITATIONS

1. *The health care literature and our citations here:* Because the literature is so prolific for this setting, we refer the reader to the 233 endnotes for this chapter in our previous edition (Green & Kreuter, 1999, pp. 461–469), and to our endnotes Web page for updates to the current citations (http://www.lgreen.net/hpp/endnotes/Chapter9endnotes.htm). We will focus here on those citations that represent recent contributions since the 1999 edition, a few of the classic or most representative earlier contributions, and those earlier contributions that were specific applications of the Precede-Proceed Model. A few meta-analyses of the earlier literature include Mullen & Green, 1985; Mullen, Green, & Persinger, 1985; Mullen, Mains, & Velez, 1992; Mullen, Ramirez, & Groff, 1994; Mullen, Simons-Morton, et al., 1997. Other meta-analyses and systematic reviews of the continuing and professional education literature in medical care settings have applied PRECEDE in examining the factors influencing behavioral and organizational change in practitioners and health care settings, revealing the necessity of including attention to enabling and reinforcing factors, in addition to the usual emphasis on predisposing factors: Davis, Thomson, et al., 1992, 1995; Oxman, Thomson, et al., 1995; Tamblyn & Battista, 1993.

2. *The evolution of the self-care concept:* can be traced from Nightingale's "helping the helpless" and her distinction between "sick nursing and health nursing," through Shaw and Harmer's textbooks of nursing at the turn of the century, to current nursing concepts of self-care such as those of Orem (Taylor, Geden, et al., 2000). For a broader history of the concept of self-care and well-care in contrast to the medical model, as well as relationships to parallel movements such as consumer participation and community health nursing, see Green, Werlin, Schauffler, & Avery, 1977; Rafael, 2000.

3. Ziff, Conrad, & Lachman, 1995. For applications of PRECEDE in examining the issues of perceived control and empowerment in relating patient or community needs and capacities to those of health professionals, see Allison, 1991; Garvin, 1995; Hill, 1996; Jenny, 1993; O'Brien, Smith, et al., 1990; Sanders-Phillips, 1991; and the control typology of Padilla & Bulcavage, 1991, including processual, contingency, cognitive, behavioral, and existential controls.

4. *Disease prevention, health promotion, and self-care as priorities of clinical care:* This section is adapted from Green, 1993, 2003; Green, Cargo, & Ottoson, 1994.

5. *The opportunity to initiate, support, or reinforce complex lifestyle changes from within clinical settings:* For example, Glanz, 1999; Pellmar, Brandt, & Baird, 2002; Williams, Chinnis, & Gutman, 2000.

6. *Health Belief Model suggests that a health care visit is a motivated or "teachable" moment for change:* See Chapter 4, including references to studies using the Health Belief Model within the context of health care encounters.

7. *Physician reach × effectiveness could translates to large population effect:* Moser, McCance, & Smith, 1991.

8. *Patients seek and are more satisfied with physician and nurse initiative in prevention and health promotion:* Hughes, 2003; Kottke, Brekke, & Marquez, 1997; Litaker, Mion, et al., 2003.

9. *Exception of lower SES patients:* Green & Potvin, 2002.

10. *Growing interest in prevention and health promotion by physicians and other health professionals:* For example, compare Mann & Putnam, 1990 with Mann, Lindsay, et al., 1997. Most of what we review here concerning physicians, who control or at least influence the professional practices of most other health care workers in clinical settings, applies also to those other professions. *For applications of PRECEDE-PROCEED in assessing or influencing the health promotion practices of other clinical health workers,* see *for: nurses:* Berland, Whyte, & Maxwell, 1995; Cretain, 1989; DeJoy, Murphy, & Gershon, 1995; Han, Baumann, & Cimprich, 1996; Laitakari, Miilunpalo, & Vuori, 1997; Macrina, Macrina, et al., 1996; Shamian & Edgar, 1987; Whyte & Berland, 1993; and see Chapter 1, endnote 29; *for dentists:* Canto, Drury, & Horowitz, 2001; Frazier & Horowitz, 1990; Mann, Viscount, et al., 1996; *for dietitians:* McKell, 1994; McKell, Chase, & Balram, 1996; Miilunpalo, Laitakari, & Vuolo, 1995; P. H. Smith, Danis, & Helmick, 1998; *for health educators:* Candeias, 1991; Chiason & Lovato, 2000; Glanz & Oldenburg, 1997; *for pharmacists:* Paluck, Green, et al., 2003; and others in Chapter 1, endnote 30; for *physical therapists and rehabilitation professionals:* Furst, Gerber, & Smith, 1985; Laitakari, Miilunpalo, & Vuori, 1997; and for other *allied health professionals:* Bennett, 1977; Goldenhar, et al., 2001.

11. *Studies applying PRECEDE-PROCEED to assessment of physician attitudes, barriers, and practices in clinical health promotion:* Battista, Williams, & MacFarlane, 1990; Burglehaus, Smith, et al., 1997; Costanza, 1992; Donovan, 1991; Downey, Cresanta, & Berenson, 1989; Duke, McGraw, et al., 2000; Green, 1987; Green, Cargo, & Ottoson, 1994; Green, Eriksen, & Shor, 1988; Herbert, 1999; Heywood, Firman, Sanson-Fisher, & Mudge, 1996; Hiddink, Hautvast, et al., 1995, 1997a, b, c, d, 1999 (and others by this group, see Chapter 1 endnote 31); Langille, Mann, & Gailiunas, 1997; Love, et al., 1993; Makridee, et al., 1997; Mann & Putnam, 1989, 1990; Singer, Lindsay, & Wilson, 1991; D. H. Solomon, Hashimoto, et al., 1998; V. M. Taylor, Taplin, et al., 1994; Thamer, et al., 1998; J. M. E. Walsh & McPhee, 1992; Weinberger, et al., 1992; Wiggers & Sanson-Fisher, 1994. See Chapter 1, endnote 32 for others.

12. *Medical education leaves little time for prevention and health promotion:* Abrams Weintraub, Saitz, & Samet, 2003; Hymowitz, Schwab, & Eckholdt, 2001. See also Chapter 1, endnote 32.

13. *Use of chart reminders, personnel, or computer-generated reminders to cue preventive actions by physicians:* For example, Gary, Bone, et al., 2003 in the context of a Precede application; O'Malley, Gonzalez, et al., 2003.

14. *Physician predisposing, enabling, and reinforcing factors predict their practice much as such factors predict patient behavior:* Green, Eriksen, & Schor, 1988; Mirand, et al., 2002, 2003.

15. *The characterization of barriers to physicians practicing primary prevention:* based on Precede analysis of focus groups themes, using grounded theory analysis of findings: Mirand, Beehler, et al., 2003. See also Thompson, Rivara, et al., 2000.

16. *Patients' demand for prescription drug and low tolerance for discomfort:* Vanden Eng, Marcus, et al., 2003; Walley, 2002.

17. *Reasons for overprescribing of antibiotics:* Haltiwanger, Hayden, et al., 2001; Turnidge, 2001; Vanden Eng, Marcus, et al., 2003.

18. *Discrepancies in practice guidelines from different sources of research synthesis and review:* For example, Assendelft, Morton, et al., 2003, on discrepancies among guidelines on management of low back pain; Costanza, 1992, re American Cancer Society guidelines on mammography versus USPSTF and NCI; J. Mann, 2002, on the alternatives to randomized controlled trials for long-lagged nutrition interventions, e.g., in cancer treatment.

19. *Information overload for the practitioner makes guidelines less likely to be applied:* Dodek & Ottoson, 1996. For example, "more than 40 clinical practice guidelines pertaining to chronic obstructive pulmonary disease have been published since 1985" (Heffner & Ellis, 2003, p. 1257). Nurses are increasingly faced with a similar overload and additional "tension between standardization of service, client choice and the use of clinical expertise in decision making" (Hewitt-Taylor, 2003, p. 41).

20. *Guidelines often seen by practitioners as derived from artificially constructed research in populations and circumstances unrepresentative of their own:* Garfield, et al., 2003; Glasgow, et al., 2003; Green, 2001b.

21. *Making the research more relevant to practitioners and their patients through participatory research:* For example, Green & Mercer, 2001, 2004; Macaulay, Commanda, et al., 1999.

22. *Primary care practitioners provide preventive services in less than one third of patients seen:* U.S. Preventive Services Task Force, 1996.

23. *Contributions of the U.S. Preventive Services Task Force to putting patient education and counseling interventions into the mainstream of clinical prevention:* U.S. Preventive Services Task Force, 1989.

24. *The ecological focus of this section,* based on adaptations and updates of Green, 1994, and of Green, Mullen, & Friedman, 1986, and Ibid as Chapter 29 in Cramer & Spilker, 1991, *is on the environments of patients, including the home, school, workplace, and the health care setting itself. For consideration of the role of hospitals and health care workers in community health promotion, school health, or work site health promotion, see the respective previous chapters. For applications of PRECEDE in hospital settings:* see Bartholmew, Koenning, et al., 1994; Bartholomew, Seilheimer, et al., 1988. This project received the Award of Program Excellence from the Society for Public Health Education, 1994. Berland, Whyte, & Maxwell, 1995; Burglehaus, Smith, et al., 1997; Calabro, Weltge, et al., 1998; Han, Baumann, & Cimprich, 1996; Fulmer, et al., 1992; Kovar, et al., 1992; Larson, et al., 1991, 1997; Macrina, Macrina, Horvath, Gallaspy, & Fine, 1996; McGovern, Kochevar, et al., 1997; Macarthur, Macarthur, & Weeks, 1995; Mamon, Green, et al., 1979; Malo & Leviton, 1987; Michalsen, et al., 1997; Parcel, et al., 1994; van Veenendal, Grinspun, & Adriaanse, 1996; Taggart, Zuckerman, et al., 1991.

25. *The terms* compliance *and* patient are used here for convenience and convention, even though several of the types of errors discussed here are not patient errors of failing to follow physicians' directions, and when they are errors of the recipients of medical instructions, the errors are not strictly within the role of patient. Many are errors sometimes of physicians, nurses, or pharmacists themselves, or of patients who have not yet received appropriate directions from a physician or other health care provider. We shall introduce the phrase "health care error" to encompass the wider range of behavioral and environmental sources of medical or health care problems that PRECEDE-PROCEED attempts to address. The issue of practitioner compliance with best practices guidelines has become one of the focal points for many applications of PRECEDE-PROCEED. See, e.g., Makrides, Veinot, Richard, & Allen, 1997; Mann & Putnam, 1989, 1990; Mann, Putnam, Lindsay, & Davis, 1996; and endnotes 18–20 above. For more on the concept and language of compliance, see P. D. Mullen, 1997.

26. *Reviews of continuing medical education and dissemination of best practices based on Precede framework:* Burr & Johanson, 1998; D. A. Davis, Thomson, Oxman, & Haynes, 1992, 1995; Lomas, 1993; Lomas & Haynes, 1988; Mann, 1994; Oxman, Thomson, Davis, & Haynes, 1995; Tamblyn & Battista, 1993. See also endnotes 10 and 11 above.

27. *Applications of PRECEDE in assessing or planning for screening behavior and programs:* K. D. Allen, 1992; Bird, Otero-Sabogal, 1996; Black, Stein, & Loveland-Cherry, 2001; Buller, Modiano, et al., 1998; Chie & Chang, 1994; Cockburn, Tompson, et al., 1997; Coleman, Lord, et al., 2003; Curry & Emmons, 1994; Danigelis & Roberson, 1995; Desnick, Taplin, et al., 1999; Dignan, Michielutte, et al., 1994, 1998; Engelstad, Bedeian, et al., 1996; Mercer, et al., 1997; Rimer, 1993; Rimer, et al., 1983, 1988, 1989; Zapka, et al., 1989; Zapka, et al., 1993.

28. *For specific applications of PRECEDE for increased use of health services for high blood pressure control:* see R. L. Bertera & Cuthie, 1984; Fors, Owen, et al., 1989; Grueninger, Duffy, & Goldstein, 1995; Haber, 1994; D. M. Levine, et al., 1982; Livingston, 1985; Mamon, et al., 1987; Mann, 1989; Modeste, Abbey, & Hopp, 1984–1985; Morisky, Levine, Wood, et al., 1981; Salazar, 1985; Wallenius, et al., 1995; Ward, et al., 1982.

29. *Pharmacists' interventions to clarify or correct drug errors:* Herbert & Paluck, 1997; Paluck, 1998; Paluck, Green, et al., 2003.

30. *When drug prices are too high:* Cockburn, et al., 1997; Danzon & Towse, 2003.

31. *For reviews of the continuing medical education literature applying PRECEDE:* see Bertram & Brooks-Bertram, 1977, and the more recent reviews cited in endnote 26. For other approaches based on quality control, see Canadian Council of Cardiovascular Nurses, 1993, which uses the Precede Model to set clinical health promotion standards of practice and quality assurance

guidelines for cardiovascular nurses; see also Eriksen, Green, & Fultz, 1988; Goldrick & Larson, 1992; Grol, 2002; Mann, Putman, et al., 1990; Mann, Viscount, et al., 1996; Ottoson, 1995; Tamblyn & Battista, 1993.

32. *Applications of PRECEDE in accomplishing patient education through mass media:* Bakdash, 1983; Centers for Disease Control, 1987; Kroger, 1994; Meredith, O'Reilly, & Schulz, 1989.

33. *PRECEDE applied in assessing understanding and perceptions of patients with osteoarthritis* who had been prescribed nonsteroidal anti-inflammatory drugs: Yeo, 1998.

34. *Baysean formulas proposed to estimate drug error propensities in populations of patients:* Green, Mullen, & Friedman, 1986.

35. *Tailoring of patient information to needs based on estimates of medical error now possible with computer:* Casebeer, Strasser, et al., 2003; Flottorp & Oxman, 2003; Kreuter, Oswald, et al., 2000; Kukafka, Lussier, et al., 2002.

36. *Applications of PRECEDE in prenatal assessment or clinical preventive care:* Covington, Peoples-Sheps, et al., 1998; Donovan, 1991; V. C. Li, et al., 1984; Olson, 1994; Sword, 1999; Williams, Innis, et al., 1999; Windsor, 1984, 1986; Windsor, et al., 1985.

37. *Some applications of PRECEDE in assessing patient "compliance," "adherence," or "concordance" problems in selected care issues and settings:* Allegrante, Kovar, et al., 1993; W. C. Bailey, et al., 1987; Barnhoorn & Andriannse, 1992; Bowler & Morisky, 1983; Bowler, Morisky, & Deeds, 1980; Chwalow, Green, et al., 1978; Cramer, 1994; Cramer & Spilker, 1991; Eastaugh & Hatcher, 1982; Estey, Tan, & Mann, 1990; Fedder, 1982; Fireman, Friday, et al., 1981; Green, Levine, et al., 1979; Green & Simons-Morton, 1988; Kelly, 1990; Leppik, 1990; Levine, Green, et al., 1979; Mann & Putnam, 1989; Morisky, 1986; Morisky, DeMuth, et al., 1985; Opdycke, Ascione, et al., 1992; Parcel, Swank, et al., 1994; Rimer, Davis, et al., 1988; Rimer, Keintz, et al., 1989; Roter, 1977; Tamez & Vacalis, 1989; Zapka et al., 1993.

38. *Women acknowledge more symptoms and seek more care for them than do men:* For example, some assessments of health care utilization patterns applying PRECEDE include W. C. Bailey, et al., 1987; Barner, Mason, & Murray, 1999; Coleman, Lord, et al., 2003; Covington, Peoples-Sheps, et al., 1998; Knazan, 1986; Maxwell, Bastani, & Warda, 1998; Mercer, et al., 1997; Muus & Ahmed, 1991; Rimer, 1993; Zapka, Harris, et al., 1993; Zapka, Stoddard, et al., 1989.

39. *Underrepresentation of men in health care visits:* Bertakis, Azari, et al., 2000. By convention, the National Disease and Therapeutic Index employs the term *mentions* (including refills and renewal of prescriptions) to reflect drug usage. The term should not be interpreted as equivalent to number of patients, visits, or prescriptions.

40. *Some applications of PRECEDE in addressing the socioeconomic gradient in health care utilization:* Barnhoorn & Andriaanse, 1992; Dignan, Michielutte, et al., 1994; Hiatt, Pasick, et al., 1996; C. B. McCoy, Nielsen, et al., 1991.

41. *Applications of PRECEDE that have addressed health issues in racial or ethnic populations:* Airhihenbuwa, 1995; Daniel & Green, 1995; Daniel, Green, et al., 1999; Dedobbeleer & Desjardins, 2001; Dignan, Michielutte, Wells, & Bahnson, 1995; Doyle, Beatty, & Shaw, 1999; Earp, Eng, et al., 2000; Englestad, Bedeian, et al., 1996; Glanz, Carbone, & Song, 1999; Gottlieb & Green, 1987; Hiatt, Pasick, et al., 1996; Keith & Doyle, 1998; McGowan & Green, 1995; Modeste, Abbey, & Hopp, 1984–1985; Neef, Scutchfield, et al., 1991; O'Brien, Smith, et al., 1990; Pasick, D'Onofrio, & Otero-Sabogal, 1996; Sanders-Phillips, 1991; 1996; Satia-Abouta, J., Patterson, et al., 2002; Sutherland, Pittman-Sisco, et al., 1989; Walter & Vaughan, 1993.

42. *Affluent and white patients receive more information from health practitioners:* Edwards, Burns, et al., 2003; Reed, 1996; Sanders-Phillips, 1996.

43. *Older patients have more chronic illnesses, medical visits, and drug prescriptions:* Noble, 2003; Yeo, 1998.

44. *Complications of errors in following prescribed regimens are greater for older patients:* Green, Mullen, & Stainbrook, 1986; Noble, 2003. *Applications of PRECEDE in planning and evaluating programs for the elderly:* include Keintz, Rimer, et al., 1988; Kemper, 1986; Knazan, 1986; Lian, Gan, et al., 1999; McGowan & Green, 1995; Morisky, Levine, Green, & Smith, 1982; Oliver-Vazquez, Sanchez-Ayendez, et al., 1999; 2002; Opdycke, Ascione, et al., 1992; Pichora-Fuller, 1997;

Rainey, Mayo, et al., 2000; Rainey & Cason, 2001; Rimer, Jones, et al., 1983; A. Ryan, 1998; Weinberger, et al., 1992; Yeo, 1998; Zapka, Costanza, et al., 1993; Zapka, Harris, et al., 1993; Zapka, Hosmer, et al., 1992.

45. *Limited evidence that continuing medical education will result in changed practice:* See endnotes 1, 11, 19, 26, and 31 above.

46. *Mixed results still of more recent innovations in continuing education:* Haber, 1994; Han, Baumann, & Cimprich, 1996; K. V. Mann, 1994; Rootman, 1997; Speller, Evans, & Head, 1997; *but promising developments in more practice-based and participatory research approaches:* Cervero, 2003; Green & Mercer, 2001; Moore & Pennington, 2003.

47. *Mass media influence on medical prescribing and patient demands for drugs:* For example, hormone replacement therapy (HT) was called into question as to its safety by the Women's Health Initiative, with much media coverage in 2002; "during the 6–8 months after publication of Women's Health Initiative trial findings, most regular postmenopausal HT users tried to stop using HT, despite not being well informed about the Women's Health Initiative findings" (Ettinger, Grandy, et al., 2003, p. 1225).

48. *Patient education improves patient adherence and clinical outcomes:* P. D. Mullen & Green, 1985. More recent systematic reviews confirm the benefits in *Type 1 diabetes:* Loveman, Cave, et al., 2003; in 63 studies of patient education interventions to control *Type 2 diabetes* showing improved blood sugar control and weight loss (Gary, Genkinger, et al., 2003; in 32 studies of educational interventions on *asthma control in children and adolescents* showing improved lung function and feelings of self control, reduced absenteeism from school, number of days with restricted activity, number of visits to an emergency department, and possibly number of disturbed nights: Guevara, Wolf, et al., 2003; in 15 trials of optimum self-management education for *adult asthma:* that produced reduced hospitalization, ER visits, unscheduled doctor visits and nocturnal asthma: Powell & Gibson, 2003; in 31 studies (randomized controlled trials) of patient education with *rheumatoid arthritis* showing "small short-term effects on disability, joint counts, patient global assessment, psychological status and depression": Riemsma, Kirwan, et al., 2003; in 37 published, controlled studies that investigated the effectiveness of psychosocial interventions on *quality of life in adult cancer patients:* Rehse & Pukrop, 2003; in 95 cohorts receiving behavioral, educational or combined interventions in 61 studies *to improve medication adherence,* revealing an increase in adherence of 4–11%; Peterson, Takiya, & Finley, 2003. Results of two meta-analyses on *smoking cessation* self-help materials and counseling were not so conclusive as to effectiveness: Lancaster & Stead, 2002; Wiggers, Smets, et al., 2003.

49. *Meta-analyses show positive effects of educational and counseling interventions, but usually no significant differences between the average effect sizes of different interventions:* P. D. Mullen, Green, & Persinger, 1985; Peterson, Takiya, & Finley, 2003.

50. *Community-oriented primary care:* Cashman & Stenger, 2003; Geiger, 2002; Glasser, Holt, et al., 2003; Iliffe & Lenihan, 2003.

51. *Estimated "noncompliance" or relapse rates ranging from 20% to 80%:* first documented in a systematic review by Haynes, Taylor, & Sackett, 1979; but the increasing prescription of complex lifestyle modifications (such as weight loss) as the regimen would make the higher end (80%) closer to the average today than the 20%–50% when the prescribed regimens were more frequently drugs. The increasing cost of drugs could also push the nonadherence rate upward.

52. *Estimated improvements in outcomes from systematic educational-behavioral-environmental interventions derive from systematic reviews of controlled trials:* Green, Mullen, & Friedman, 1986; Mullen, Green, & Persinger, 1985; Mullen, Simons-Morton, et al., 1997; and the continuing rates of change found in the more recent reviews cited in endnote 50.

53. *Osteoarthritis program of interventions to reduce pain and increase functioning:* Allegrante, Kovar, et al., 1993; Blake, Allegrante, et al., 2002; Kovar, Allegrante, et al., 1992; Marks & Allegrante, 2001; Ruchlin, Allegrante, et al., 1997; Sullivan, Allegrante, et al., 1998; extended to *prevention strategies for younger women:* Kasper, Peterson, & Allegrante, 2001, *prevention of hip fractures and other comorbidities in older patients:* Marks & Allegrante, 2002; Marks, Allegrante, et al., 2003, and *patient education with high-intensity strength training to improve rehabilitation after hip fracture, yielding cost-benefit ratios exceeding 4.5:* Ruchlin, Elkin, & Allegrante, 2001.

54. *Typical relapse curve for complex behavioral changes:* Marlatt & Gordon, 1985. See also Allen, Lowman, & Miller, 1996; and *weight control examples:* Birketvedt, Thom, et al., 2000; Skender, Goodrick, et al., 1996.

55. *Relapse prevention strategies can change the level at which the curve bottoms out:* Green, Cargo, & Ottoson, 1994. See further examples and applications of relapse prevention strategies in Conn, Minor, et al., 2003; Lowe, Windsor, & Woodby, 1997.

56. *The first randomized trials testing the Precede Model were in patient care settings for asthma and hypertension:* Green, 1974; Green, Levine, & Deeds, 1975.

57. *First randomized trial of Precede application showed 50% reduction in emergency room visits for asthma in 18-week follow-up:* Green, Werlin, et al., 1977. This trial achieved a 1:7 cost-benefit ratio (Green, 1974).

58. *Hopkins hypertension trial results showed significantly better blood pressure control after 18-month follow-up compared with controls:* D. M. Levine, Green, Deeds, et al., 1979; D. M. Levine, Green, Russell, et al., 1979.

59. *Outcomes correlated with exposure to interventions and mediating or moderating variables:* Green, Levine, & Deeds, 1977; Green, Levine, Wolle, & Deeds, 1979.

60. *Long-term results showed 50% reduction in mortality in the hypertension patients:* Morisky, Levine, et al., 1983.

61. *First trial of PRECEDE with smoking cessation:* V. C. Li, Coates, et al., 1984.

62. *Further trials of PRECEDE on smoking cessation in pregnant women multiplied the quit rate by 2 against self-help manuals, by 7 against usual care in the public health clinic:* Windsor, 1984, 1986; Windsor & Cutter, 1983; Windsor, et al., 1985. See also recent adaptations and extensions of this work by Lowe, et al., 1997; Windsor, 2003; with interventions that evolved into the SCRIPT protocol for smoking cessation in pregnancy: Windsor, 2000, and combined with other recommendations from the Agency for Healthcare Research and Quality guidelines, an intervention that doubled the rate of smoking cessation in Medicaid maternity clinics: Windsor, Woodby, et al., 2000.

63. *Tuberculosis medication dropouts reduced from 73% to 36%:* Morisky, Malotte, et al., 1990. For continuing work of Morisky and his colleagues on this issue, see Morisky, Ebin, et al., 2003; Morisky, Malotte, et al., 2001.

64. *Example of predictive questionnaires for triaging and staging patients on readiness for change:* for example, Carter, et al., 1986, for *immunization:* Nielson, Jensen, & Kerns, 2003, for readiness to adopt specific *pain management:* skills training; and *others developed specifically for analysis of predictors of behavior using the Precede framework:* for example, for *bulimic tendencies:* Benson & Taub, 1993; for *breast self-examination:* Morrison, 1996; for *mammography screening:* Black, Stein, & Loveland-Cherry, 2001; for *cervical cancer screening:* Buller, Modiano, et al., 1998; Michielutte, Dignan, et al., 1999; for *compliance with use of protective equipment:* DeJoy, Searcy, et al., 2000; for *HIV-risk behaviors among injection drug users:* Deren, Kang, et al., 2003. Polcyn, Price, et al., 1991 specifically validated a questionnaire and the Precede Model for predicting users of *smokeless tobacco.*

65. *Adapting "stages of change" questionnaires by aligning stages with predisposing, enabling, and reinforcing factors:* for example, for *domestic violence:* Anderson, 2003; for *fitness and physical activity:* Cox, Gorely, et al., 2003; Proper, Van der Beek, et al., 2003.

66. *Individual attention, relevance, and feedback provided in the communication are better predictors of effective intervention to change prescriptive drug adherence than are the specific modes or channels of communication:* P. D. Mullen, Green, & Persinger, 1985. See also Green & Frankish, 1994.

67. *Same three principles held up as best predictors of effective intervention to change lifestyle health practices in patients:* Kok, van den Borne, & Mullen, 1997; P. D. Mullen, Simons-Morton, et al., 1997.

68. *Physicians talk more, with more qualifications, and on more psychosocial rather than strictly biomedical topics with higher socioeconomic patients:* Gordon, Joos, & Byrne, 2000; Roter, Stewart, et al., 1997. Roter's (1977) original work on measuring the qualities of doctor-patient interactions was an adaptation of Bale's Interaction Analysis in a Precede-based study of factors in the activation

of patients to ask more questions of their physician. Her methodology has been validated independently in comparison with other methods of measuring doctor-patient interactions (Inui, Carter, et al., 1982; Roter, 2003) and applied extensively in studies of the quality of physician-patient communications and patient education (e.g., Bensing, Roter, & Hulsman, 2003; and see the other citations in this and the next two endnotes).

69. *Age and gender characteristics of physicians and patients that may influence the quality of communication and the interaction time in primary care visits:* Hall & Roter, 2002; Mann, Sripathy, et al., 2001; Roter, Hall, & Aoki, 2003.

70. *Racial and ethnic differences between doctors and their patients produce less time per visit and less interaction at socioemotional levels:* Cooper & Roter, 2003; Cooper, Roter, et al., 2003.

71. *Anticipatory counseling on side-effects can be framed to reduce quitting of the regimen at the first sign of the side-effects:* Albright, Binns, & Katz, 2002; Donovan & Jalleh, 2000.

72. *Family support for patients' adherence to medical regimens or advice:* For example, Friese & Wamboldt, 2003; MacIntyre, Goebel, et al., 2003; and within Precede constructs, Bartholomew, Seilheimer, et al., 1989; Glanz, Grove, et al., 1999; Lian, Gan, et al., 1999; Morisky, DeMuth, et al., 1980.

73. *Presence of a companion during physician consultations influenced patients to ask more questions:* Borgers, Mullen, et al., 1993. See also the importance of conferring with significant others about symptoms as a factor in the delay in seeking medical diagnosis, de Nooijer, Lechner, & de Vries, 2001, 2003; Plowden & Miller, 2000.

74. *Overcoming deficiencies of extrinsic reinforcing factors by strengthening predisposing (intrinsic reinforcement) and enabling factors:* For example, Rimmer, Silverman, et al., 2002; quotation from p. 571, *or making the reinforcement more vicarious:* Dye, Haley-Zitlin, & Willoughby, 2003.

75. *Educational approach to make reinforcing factors more intrinsic as predisposing factors in the absence of social or tangible rewards:* Green, 1988b, 2004.

76. *Vicarious reinforcement through educational materials and modeling, presenting positive and valued role models:* Curry & Cole, 2001; Siela, 2003.

77. *Model for changing physician and patient behavior in a two-phased Precede application:* Makrides, Veinot, et al., 1997; Mirand, Beehler, et al., 2002 from the same group at Roswell Park (see endnotes 14 and 15 above).

78. *Another model emphasizing the physician-organization-patient triad in prevention, based on PRECEDE:* Walsh & McPhee, 1992; and their more recent reflections on continuing challenges in primary care: Walsh & McPhee, 2002.

79. *Other applications of PRECEDE relating change in professional practitioners to prevention in patients:* Mahloch, et al., 1993; K. V. Mann, et al., 1996; and see endnotes 10 and 11 above.

80. *Constraints on practice of prevention in primary care:* Bullock, 1999; Easton, Husten, et al., 2001; Friedmann, McCullough, & Saitz, 2001; N. H. Gottlieb, Mullen, & McAlister, 1987; Haley, Maheux, et al., 2000; Mann & Putnam, 1990; Mullen & Holcomb, 1990.

81. *Discrepancies among practitioners' preventive practices, patients' expectations, and best practices guidelines:* Beaulieu, Hudon, et al., 1999; Larson, 2003; Okene & Zapka, 2000.

82. *Physicians tend to give less credence to the importance of counseling on behavioral risk factors for primary prevention than to their need to provide medical screening procedures for secondary prevention:* for example, Marcell, Halpern-Felsher, et al., 2002. *But even with secondary prevention, they miss on average more than half the opportunities to screen high-risk patients, for example for colorectal cancer:* V. Taylor, Lessler, et al., 2003, *skin cancer:* Geller, Emmons, et al., 2003, *mothers and newborn of unknown HIV risk:* Kline & O'Conner, 2003; and *cardiovascular disease:* McDermott, Hahn, et al., 2002. See also endnotes 12–15 above.

83. *Improved recognition of need to intervene on tobacco, obesity, and osteoporosis:* For example, McIlvain, Backer, et al., 2002; Ogden, Bandara, et al., 2001; Taylor, Sterkel, et al., 2001.

84. *Differences by medical specialty:* Heywood, Firman, et al., 1996; Kline & O'Conner, 2003; McDermot, Hahn, et al., 2002; Yarzebski, Bujor, et al., 2002.

85. *Even pediatricians miss prevention and counseling opportunities and needs:* For example, Kline & O'Conner, 2003, p. e367.

86. *Attitudes and practices of physicians on obesity:* Hamilton, James, & Bazargan, 2003.

87. *Practitioners' and patients' beliefs regarding determinants of health behavior and their own efficacy in changing them:* Hash, Munna, et al., 2003; Love, Davoli, & Thurman, 1996; Ogden, Bandara, et al., 2001.

88. *Nurses and allied health professionals face many of the same opportunities and limitations in approaching complex lifestyle changes in patients:* Brehm, Rourke, & Cassell, 1999; Han, Bauman, & Cimprich, 1996; Jenny, 1993; Whittemore, Bak, et al., 2003.

89. *Reimbursement policies for preventive services limit effort by practitioners:* Fitzner, Caputo, et al., 2003; Pickering, Clemow, et al., 2003; Tamblyn & Battista, 1993.

90. *Inadequate patient educational materials in clinical settings:* For example, Davis, Fredrickson, et al., 2001; McIntosh & Shaw, 2003.

91. *Provider prompting systems to enable preventive actions:* Bookaloo, Bobbin, et al., 2003; Secker-Walker, Solomon, et al., 1998.

92. *Need for tailoring and multiple interventions to enable preventive actions in order to address the specific and multiple barriers in a given clinical setting:* Cochran systematic review, Hulscher, Wensing, et al., 2001.

93. *Feedback from colleagues and patients as reinforcing factors:* For example, Keefe, Thompson, & Noel, 2002; *but not necessarily when the feedback is more punitive and less collaborative:* for example, Sandbaek & Kragstrup, 1999.

94. *Managed care organizations have greater potential to make prevention systematically and organizationally supported:* Brugge, Bagley, & Hyde, 2003; Marcy, Thabault, et al., 2003; esp. R. S. Thompson, 1996, 1997, accounts of the Group Health Cooperative successes built on an adaptation of PRECEDE; *but the potential is not always realized:* For example, Gunter, Beaton, et al., 2003; Schauffler, & McMenamin, et al., 2001.

95. *An HMO's success in increasing immunizations:* R. S. Thompson, 1997. Also Thompson, Taplin, McAfee, Mandelson, & Smith, 1995. See, however, O'Malley & Mandelblatt, 2003, who found that community public health clinics performed as well on several preventive measures as private physicians' offices and HMOs.

96. *Capitation makes HMOs more cost-containment oriented, and thus more prevention oriented:* For example, Catalano, Libby, et al., 2000; Cheadle, Wickizer, et al., 1999.

97. *HMO advantages in reach with educational materials, counseling, and organizational arrangements:* Golaszewski, 2000; Hickman, Stebbins, et al., 2003; Lawrence, Watkins, et al., 2003; Parnes, Main, et al., 2002.

98. *Mutual value of collaborative relationships among health plans, employers, schools, other community organizations, and physician providers:* Armbruster, 2002; Fielding, Luck, & Tye, 2003; Galvin, 2000; Klein, Sesselberg, et al., 2003; Mays, Halverson, & Stevens, 2001.

99. *Collaborative approaches at the system and patient levels, applying PRECEDE:* Yingling & Trocino, 1997, quote from p. 246. See also Makrides, Veinot, et al., 1997; R. S. Thompson, 1996; Walsh & McPhee, 1992, 2002.

GLOSSARY

administrative assessment   An analysis of the policies, resources, and circumstances prevailing in an organizational situation to facilitate or hinder the development of the health program.

advocacy   Working for political, regulatory, or organizational change on behalf of a particular interest group or population.

age-adjusted rate   The total rate for a population, adjusted to ignore the age distribution of the specific population by multiplying each of its age-specific rates by the proportion of a standard population (usually national) in that age group, and then adding up the products.

agent   An epidemiological term referring to the organism or object that transmits a disease from the environment to the host.

attitude   A relatively constant feeling, predisposition, or set of beliefs directed toward an object, person, or situation.

behavioral diagnosis   Delineation of the specific health-related actions that most likely effect, or could effect, a health outcome.

behavioral intention   A mental state in which the individual expects to take a specified action at some time in the future.

behavioral objective   A statement of desired outcome that indicates who is to demonstrate how much of what action by when.

belief   A statement or proposition, declared or implied, that is emotionally and/or intellectually accepted as true by a person or group.

benefits   Valued health outcomes or improvements in quality of life or social conditions having some known relationship to health promotion or health care interventions.

best practice   Recommendations for an intervention, based on a critical review of multiple research and evaluation studies that substantiate the efficacy of the intervention in the populations and circumstances in which the studies were done, if not its effectiveness in other populations and situations where it might be implemented.

best processes   An alternative, or complement, to best practices, emphasizing the diagnosis of needs for change in a specific population, by methods such as PRECEDE, before prescribing and adapting a particular intervention or program tested in other populations.

causal theory   The set of testable explanations for the relationship between an independent variable or input and the dependent variable or outcome. See *program theory*.

central location intercept   A survey procedure that seeks interviews with an unsystematic sample of people on the street or in a shopping center to represent the opinions of those likely to be the target of a program.

coalition   A group of organizations or representatives of groups within a community joined to pursue a common objective.

coercive strategies   Preventive methods that bypass the motivation and decisions of people by dictating or precluding choices.

community   A collective of people identified by common values and mutual concern for the development and well-being of their group or geographical area.

community capacity   Combined assets that influence a community's commitment, resources, and skills used to solve problems and strengthen the quality of life for its citizens (Gold, Miner, Fiori, et al., 2001).

community organization   The set of procedures and processes by which a population and its institutions mobilize and coordinate resources to solve a mutual problem or to pursue mutual goals.

compliance   Adherence to a prescribed therapeutic or preventive regimen.

conditions of living   The combination of behavioral and environmental circumstances that make up one's lifestyle and health-related social situation.

construct   The representation of concepts within a causal explanation or theoretical framework. For example, predisposing, enabling, and reinforcing factors are constructs for the representation of more specific concepts or variables such as health beliefs, attitudes, skills, and rewards.

cost-benefit   A measure of the cost of an intervention relative to the benefits it yields, usually expressed as a ratio of dollars saved or gained for every dollar spent on the program.

cost-effectiveness   A measure of the cost of an intervention relative to its impact, usually expressed in dollars per unit of effect.

coverage   A ratio (C) of the number of people reached (B) relative to the number in need or eligible (A) for the service or program, also C = B/A can be participants or attendees (B) as a ratio of the target population (A); (see Table 5-7).

delphi method   A method of sampling the opinions or preferences of a small number of experts, opinion leaders, or informants, whereby successive questionnaires are sent by mail and the results (rankings or value estimates) are summarized for further refinement on subsequent mailings.

determinants of health   The forces predisposing, enabling, and reinforcing lifestyles, or shaping environmental conditions of living, in ways that affect the health of populations.

diagnosis   Health or behavioral information that designates the "problem" or need; its status, distribution, or frequency in the person or population; and the probable causes or risk factors associated with the problem or need.

disability   The inability to perform specific functions resulting from disease, injury, or birth defects.

dose-response relationship   A term borrowed from clinical trials of drugs; when applied in epidemiology, it refers to a gradient of risk ratios corresponding to degrees of exposure; in health programs it refers to the increases in outcome measures associated with proportionate increases in the program resources expended or intervention exposure.

early adopters   Those in the population who accept a new idea or practice soon after the innovators (but before the middle majority), and who tend to be opinion leaders for the middle majority.

ecology   Study of the web of relationships among behaviors of individuals and populations and their environments, social and physical.

ecological diagnosis   A systematic assessment of factors in the social and physical environment that interact with behavior to produce health effects or quality-of-life outcomes. Also referred to as ecological assessment.

economy of scale   The point in the growth of a program or service at which each additional element of service costs less to produce.

education of the electorate   A process of political change in which those affected by policies are educated so that they will be more likely to vote for candidates or referenda that are in their best interests.

educational assessment   The delineation of factors that predispose, enable, and reinforce a specific behavior, or through behavior, environmental changes.

effectiveness   The extent to which the intended effect or benefits that could be achieved under optimal conditions are also achieved in practice.

efficacy   The extent to which an intervention can be shown to be beneficial under optimal conditions.

efficiency   The proportion of total costs (e.g., money, resources, time) that can be related to the number of people served or reached, or sometimes to benefits achieved in practice.

employee assistance programs   A confidential, voluntary set of procedures and arrangements to provide information, referral, counseling, and support to workers and sometimes their family members to help them deal with personal problems that might interfere with their work.

empowerment education   A process of encouraging a community to take control of its own education, assess its own needs, set its own priorities, develop its own self-help programs, and, if necessary, challenge the power structure to provide resources.

enabling factor   Any characteristic of the environment that facilitates action and any skill or resource required to attain a specific behavior. (Absence of the resource blocks the behavior; barriers to the behavior are included in lists of enabling factors to be developed. Skills are sometimes listed separately as predisposing factors or intermediate outcomes of education.)

environment   The totality of social, biological, and physical circumstances surrounding a defined quality-of-life, health, or behavioral goal or problem.

environmental factor   One of the specific elements or components of the social, biological, or physical environment determined during the ecological diagnosis to be causally linked to health or quality-of-life goals or problems identified in the social or epidemiological diagnosis.

epidemiological diagnosis   The delineation of the extent, distribution, and causes of a health problem in a defined population.

epidemiology   The study of the distribution and causes of health problems in populations.

etiology   The origins or causes of a disease or condition under study; the first steps in the natural history of a disease.

evaluation   The comparison of an object of interest against a standard of acceptability.

evidence   Data on the population, the problem, or the proposed solutions that inform planning decisions.

evidence-based practice   Program decisions or intervention selections made on the strength of data from the community concerning needs and data from previously tested interventions or programs concerning their effectiveness, sometimes using theory in the absence of data on the specific alignment of interventions and population needs.

fear   A mental state that motivates problem-solving behavior if an action (fight or flight) is immediately available; if not, it motivates other defense mechanisms such as denial or suppression.

focus group method   Used in testing the perception and receptivity of a target population to an idea or method by recording the reactions of a sample of eight to ten people discussing it with each other.

formative evaluation   Any combination of measurements obtained and judgments made before or during the implementation of materials, methods, activities, or programs to discover, predict, control, ensure, or improve the quality of performance or delivery. (Measurements during implementation are sometimes called process evaluation.)

Gantt chart   A timetable showing each activity in a program plan as a horizontal line that extends from the start to the finish date so that at any given time a program manager can see what activities should be underway, about to begin, or due to be completed.

Health Belief Model   A paradigm used to predict and explain health behavior, based on value-expectancy theory.

health care system   That subsystem of the broader health system that is financed and organized to respond mainly to needs for treatment or continuing care of illnesses and chronic conditions that compromise health.

health-directed behavior   The conscious pursuit of actions for the purpose of protecting or improving health.

health education   Any planned combination of learning experiences designed to predispose, enable, and reinforce voluntary behavior conducive to health in individuals, groups, or communities.

health outcome   Any medically or epidemiologically defined characteristic of a patient or health problem in a population that results from health promotion or care provided or required as measured at one point in time.

health promotion   Any planned combination of educational, political, regulatory, and organizational supports for actions and conditions of living conducive to the health of individuals, groups, or communities.

health protection   A strategy parallel to health promotion in some national policies; the focus is on environmental rather than behavioral determinants of health, and the methods are more like those of engineers and regulatory agencies than those of educational and social or health service agencies.

health-related behavior   Those actions undertaken for reasons other than the protection or improvement of health, but which have health effects.

health system   The totality and relationships of individuals, groups, organizations, and sectors of public and private activity that respond to threats to health and opportunities to promote, protect, and repair or palliate health.

host   A concept from epidemiology referring to an individual who harbors or is at risk of harboring a disease or condition.

immediacy   A criterion for judging the importance of a factor, based on how urgent or imminent the factor is in its influence on the outcome desired.

impact (evaluation)   The assessment of program effects on intermediate objectives including changes in predisposing, enabling, and reinforcing factors, behavioral and environmental changes, and possibly health and social outcomes.

implementation   The act of converting program objectives into actions through policy changes, regulation, and organization.

incidence   A measure of the frequency of occurrence of a disease or health problem in a population based on the number of new cases over a given period of time (usually one year).   An incidence *rate* is obtained by dividing this number by the midyear population and multiplying the quotient by 1,000 or 100,000.

informed consent   A medical-legal doctrine that holds providers responsible for ensuring that consumers or patients understand the risks and benefits of a procedure or medicine before it is administered.

innovators   Those in a population who are first to adopt a new idea or practice, usually based on information from sources outside the community.

internal validity   Assurance that the results of an evaluation can be attributed to the object (method or program) evaluated.

intervention   The part of a strategy, incorporating method and technique, that actually reaches a person or population.

late majority   The segment of the population most difficult to reach through mass communication channels or to convince of the need to adopt a new idea or practice, either because they cannot afford it or cannot get to the source or because of cultural and language differences or other difficulty.

leverage   The use of initial investments in a program to draw larger investments.

lifestyle   The culturally, socially, economically, and environmentally conditioned complex of actions characteristic of an individual, group, or community as a pattern of habituated behavior over time that is health related but not necessarily health directed.

market testing   The placement of a message or product in a commercial context to determine how it influences consumer behavior.

mediators   Causal or intermediate variables between interventions and intended effects that can directly affect outcomes.

middle majority   The segment of the population who adopts a new idea or practice after the innovators and early adopters but before the late adopters, usually influenced by a combination of mass media, interpersonal communication, and endorsements by famous personalities or organizations of which they are members.

moderators   Characteristics of individuals, settings, channels, and circumstances that can ameliorate or enhance the effect of program variables on mediator variables, or the latter on outcome variables.

morbidity   The existence or rate of disease or infirmity.

mortality   The event or rate of death.

necessity   A criterion for judging the importance of a factor, based on whether the outcome can occur without this factor.

need   (1) Whatever is required for health or comfort, or (2) an estimation of the interventions required based on a diagnosis of the problem and, in populations, the number of people eligible to benefit from the intervention(s).

nominal group process   An interactive group method for assessing community needs by having opinions listed without critique from the group and then rated by secret ballot, thereby minimizing the influence of interpersonal dynamics and status on the ratings.

norms   Perceived social patterns of and expectations for behavior.

objective   A defined result of specific activity to be achieved in a finite period of time by a specified person or number of people. Objectives state *who* will experience *what* change or benefit by *how* much and by *when*.

organization   The act of marshaling and coordinating the resources necessary to implement a program.

outcome evaluation   Assessment of the effects of a program on the ultimate objectives, including changes in health and social benefits or quality of life.

planning   The process of defining needs, establishing priorities, diagnosing causes of problems, assessing resources and barriers, and allocating resources to achieve objectives.

policy   The set of objectives and rules guiding the activities of an organization or an administration, and providing authority for allocation of resources.

positional leader   A person whose influence is based, or perceived to be based, on his or her official standing or office such as an elected or appointed official, executive of a firm, or head of a voluntary organization.

PRECEDE   Acronym for the diagnostic planning and evaluation model outlined in this book, emphasizing *p*redisposing, *r*einforcing, and *e*nabling *c*onstructs in *e*cological *d*iagnosis and *e*valuation.

predisposing factor   Any characteristic of a person or population that motivates behavior prior to the occurrence of the behavior.

prevalence   A measure of the extent of a disease or health problem in a population based on the number of cases (old and new) existing in the population at a given time. See also *incidence*.

principle of intervention specificity   The necessity of aligning interventions with specific characteristics of the individual or population, and with the environment and circumstances in which the program is to be delivered and change is expected to occur.

principle of multiplicity and comprehensiveness   The necessity for successful programs to combine interventions that address at least the three major determinants of change: those that predispose, those that enable, and those that reinforce the necessary changes in behavior or the environment.

PROCEED   Acronym for *p*olicy, *r*egulatory, and *o*rganizational *c*onstructs in *e*ducational and *e*nvironmental *d*evelopment, the phases of resource mobilization, implementation, and evaluation following the diagnostic planning phases of PRECEDE.

process evaluation   The assessment of policies, materials, personnel, performance, quality of practice or services, and other inputs and implementation experiences.

program   A set of planned activities over time designed to achieve specified objectives.

program theory   The testable assumptions linking the combination of interventions or inputs with the expected outcomes or objectives for their implementation.

quality assessment   Measurement of professional or technical practice or service for comparison with accepted standards to determine the degree of excellence.

quality assurance   Formal process of implementing quality assessment and quality improvement in programs to ensure stakeholders that professional activities have been performed appropriately.

quality of life   The perception of individuals or groups that their needs are being satisfied and that they are not being denied opportunities to achieve happiness and fulfillment.

reach   The number of people attending or exposed to an intervention or program.

regulation   The act of enforcing policies, rules, or laws.

reinforcing factor   Any reward or punishment following or anticipated as a consequence of a behavior, serving to strengthen the motivation for the behavior after it occurs.

relative risk   The ratio of mortality or incidence of a disease or condition in those exposed to a given risk factor (e.g., smokers) to the mortality or incidence in those not exposed (e.g., nonsmokers). A relative risk (RR) ratio of 1.0 indicates no greater risk in those exposed than in those not exposed.

reputational leader   One whose leadership power is based on perceived performance as an influential person, but not necessarily on his or her position.

risk conditions   Those determinants of health that are more distal in time, place, or scope from the control of individuals than the more proximal and malleable "risk factors," such as current behavior.

risk factors   Characteristics of individuals (genetic, behavioral, environmental exposures, and sociocultural living conditions) that increase the probability that they will experience a disease or specific cause of death as measured by population relative risk ratios.

risk ratio   The mortality or incidence of a disease or condition in those exposed to a given risk factor divided by the mortality or incidence in those not exposed. See also *relative risk*.

segmentation   The division of a population into segments according to characteristics (demographic, socioeconomic, or localities) that predict their likelihood to respond to one form or another of interventions such as communication messages. See *tailoring*.

self-efficacy   A construct from social cognitive theory referring to the belief an individual holds that he or she is capable of performing a specific behavior.

settings   Organizational or institutional places in which health programs are carried out. More generally, setting is a mileu in which people gather for schooling, work, cohabitation, or other mutually supportive activity, governed by rules and norms specific to the place.

settings approach   The use of place as a primary consideration in assessing, planning, and organizing health programs, because of the ecological and social exchange and reciprocal relationships that govern the behavior of people in the place, and the potential to restructure those relationships or systems to change behavior and make them more conducive to health.

situation analysis   The combination of social and epidemiological assessments of conditions, trends, and priorities with a preliminary scan of determinants, relevant policies, resources, organizational support, and regulations that might anticipate or permit action in advance of a more complete assessment of behavioral, environmental, educational, ecological, and administrative factors.

social assessment   The assessment in both objective and subjective terms of high-priority problems or aspirations for the common good, defined for a population by economic and social indicators and by individuals in terms of their quality of life.

social capital   The processes and conditions among people and organizations that lead to accomplishing a goal of mutual social benefit, usually characterized by four interrelated constructs: trust, cooperation, civic engagement, and reciprocity.

social determinants of health   The cumulative effects of a lifetime of exposure to conditions of living that combine to strengthen or compromise optimum health, and many of which are beyond the control of the individual. See also *risk conditions*.

social diagnosis   The focus within a *social assessment* or *social reconnaissance* on the social problems and quality-of-life issues that might be related to health.

social indicator   A quality having a numerical value whose change is expected to reflect a change in the quality of life for a population.

social problem   A situation that a significant number of people believe to be a source of difficulty or unhappiness. A social problem consists of objective circumstances as well as a social interpretation of its unacceptability.

social reconnaissance   Assessment procedures applied to a large geographic area with the active participation of people having various levels of authority and resources, including government officials and professionals in health and other sectors, and potential recipients of new programs or services.

stakeholders   People who have an investment or a stake in the outcome of a program and therefore have reasons to be interested in the evaluation of the program.

stepped approach   A method of intervention following triage, in which minimal resources or effort is expended on the first group or level, more intensive effort on the second level, and most intensive on the third.

subsystems   The components of a system, each a system unto itself with possible subsystems of its own, overlapping in the network connections with other systems and subsystems.

summative evaluation   The application of design, measurement and analysis methods to the assessment of outcomes of a program or specific interventions within a program.

system   A set of interlocking relationships such that change in one part results in changes in other parts, with feedback and a resulting further change to the part that first changed to establish equilibrium.

tactic   A method or approach employed as part of a strategy.

tailoring   The use of information about individuals to shape the message or other qualities of a communication or other intervention so that it has the best possible fit with the factors predisposing, enabling, and reinforcing that person's behavior. See *segmentation.*

triage   A method of sorting people into (usually three) groups for purposes of setting priorities on allocation of resources.

triangulation   Using data from three sources so that if two are inconsistent, a third provides a tie break between the other two. More generally, it refers to the use of multiple sources, observers, and methods of data collection to ensure that the problem is seen through more than the sometimes biased single lens.

value   A preference shared and transmitted within a community.

vicarious reinforcement   The response to a behavior that strengthens its probability of continuing or being repeated based on the perception of the person that such behavior is similar to that valued by other people who are role models.

BIBLIOGRAPHY

References marked with an asterisk are applications of at least parts of the Precede or Precede-Proceed model. For links to abstracts of these, go to www .lgreen.net/precede apps/preapps.htm, or for these and other references, go to the endnote links at www.lgreen.net/hpp/Endnotes/Endnotes.html.

Abelson, R. P., Aronson, E., McGuire, W. J., et al. (1968). *Theories of cognitive consistency: A sourcebook*. Chicago, IL: Rand McNally College.

Abrams Weintraub, T., Saitz, R., & Samet, J. H.. (2003). Education of preventive medicine residents: alcohol, tobacco, and other drug abuse. *American Journal of Preventive Medicine, 24,* 101–5.

Acevedo-Garcia, D., Lochner, K. A., Osypuk, T. L., & Subramanian, S. V. (2003). Future directions in residential segregation and health research: a multilevel approach. *American Journal of Public Health, 93,* 215–21.

Ackerknecht, E. (1953). *Rudolph Virchow: Doctor, statesman, anthropologist*. Madison, Wis: University of Wisconsin Press.

*Ackerman, A., & Kalmer, H. (1977). Health education and a baccalaureate nursing curriculum—Myth or reality (paper presented at the 105th annual meeting of the American Public Health Association, Washington, DC, 1 Nov).

Aday, L. A. (2001). *At risk in America: The health and health care needs of vulnerable populations in the United States*. 2nd ed. San Francisco: Jossey-Bass.

*Adeyanju, O. M. (1987–88). A community-based health education analysis of an infectious disease control program in Nigeria. *International Quarterly of Community Health Education, 8,* 263–79.

Agency for Healthcare Research and Quality. (2000.) *Efficacy of interventions to modify dietary behavior related to cancer risk*. Summary, Evidence Report/Technology Assessment: Number 25. Rockville, MD: Agency for Healthcare Research and Quality, AHRQ Publication No. 01–E028.

Agha, S. (2003). The impact of a mass media campaign on personal risk perception, perceived self-efficacy and on other behavioural predictors. AIDS Care, 15, 742–62.

Aguirre-Molina, M., Molina, C. W., & Zambrana, R. E. (Eds.). (2001). *Health issues in the Latino community*. San Francisco: Jossey-Bass.

*Airhihenbuwa, C. (1995). *Health and culture: Beyond the Western paradigm*. Thousand Oaks: Sage Publications, Inc.

Airhihenbuwa, C., Kumanyika, S., & Lowe, A. (1995). Perceptions and beliefs about exercise, rest and health among African-Americans. *American Journal of Health Promotion, 9,* 426–29.

Airhihenbuwa, C., Kumanyika, S., Agurs, T. D., et al. (1996). Cultural aspects of African American eating patterns. *Ethnicity & Health, 1*, 245–60.

Ajzen, I., & Madden, J. T. (1986). Prediction of goal-directed behavior: Attitudes, intentions, and perceived behavioral control. *Journal of Experimental Social Psychology, 22*, 453–74.

Albarracin, D., Johnson, B. T., Fishbein, M., & Muellerleile, P. A. (2001). Theories of reasoned action and planned behavior as models of condom use: A meta-analysis. *Psychological Bulletin, 127*, 142–61.

Albright, T. A., Binns, H. J., & Katz, B. Z. (2002). Side effects of and compliance with malaria prophylaxis in children. *Journal of Travel Medicine, 9*, 289–92.

Albuquerque, M., Pechacek, T. F., & Kelly, A. (2001). *Investment in tobacco control: State highlights—2001.* Atlanta: U.S. Department of Health and Human Services, Centers for Disease Control and Prevention, National Center for Chronic Disease Prevention and Health Promotion, Office on Smoking and Health.

Aldana, S. G. (2003). Financial impact of health promotion programs: A comprehensive review of the literature. *American Journal of Health Promotion, 15*, 296–320.

Alderman, M., Green, L. W., & Flynn, B. S. (1980). Hypertension control programs in occupational settings. *Public Health Reports, 90.* Also in R. S. Parkinson & Associates (Eds.), *Managing health promotion in the workplace: Guidelines for implementation and evaluation* (pp. 162–72). Palo Alto, CA: Mayfield.

Ali, N. S. (2002). Prediction of coronary heart disease preventive behaviors in women: A test of the Health Belief Model. *Women and Health, 35*, 83–96.

Alinsky, S. D. (1972). *Rules for radicals: A pragmatic primer for realistic radicals.* New York: Vintage Books.

*Allegrante, J. P., Kovar, P. A., MacKenzie, C. R., Peterson, M. G., & Gutin, B. (1993). A walking education program for patients with osteoarthritis of the knee: Theory and intervention strategies. *Health Education Quarterly, 20*, 63–81.

Allegrante, J. P., & Sloan, R. P. (1986). Ethical dilemmas in workplace health promotion. *Preventive Medicine* 15: 313–20.

Allen, B., Jr., Bastani, R., Bazargan, S., et al. (2002). Assessing screening mammography utilization in an urban area. *Journal of the National Medical Association, 94*, 5–14.

Allen, J., & Allen, R. F. (1990). A sense of community, a shared vision and a positive culture: Core enabling factors in successful culture-based change. In R. D. Patton & W. B. Cissel (Eds.), *Community organization: Traditional principles and modern applications* (pp. 5–18). Johnson City, TN: Latchpins Press.

Allen, J., Lowman, C., & Miller, W. R. (1996). Introduction: Perspectives on preciptitants of relapse. *Addiction, 91* (Suppl.), S3–S5.

*Allen, K. D. (1992). Predisposing, enabling and reinforcing factors associated with women's reported Pap smear screening behaviour (Master's thesis). Toronto, ON: University of Toronto, Graduate Department of Nursing Science.

Allensworth, D., & Kolbe, L. J. (Eds.). (1987). The comprehensive school health program: Exploring an expanded concept. *Journal of School Health, 57*, 409–73 (whole issue).

Allison, K. R. (1991) Theoretical issues concerning the relationship between perceived control and preventive health behaviour. *Health Education Research, 6,*141–51.

Allott, R., Paxton, R., & Leonard, R. (1999). Drug education: a review of British government policy and evidence on effectiveness. *Health Education Research, 14*, 491–505.

*Alteneder, R. R. (1994). Use of an educational program on HIV/AIDS with junior high students. *International Conference on AIDS, 10(2)*, 355 (abstract no. PD0601).

*Alteneder, R. R., Price, J. H., Telljohann, S. K., Didion, J., & Locher, A. (1992). Using the PRECEDE model to determine junior high school students' knowledge, attitudes, and beliefs about AIDS. *Journal of School Health, 62*, 464–70.

Altman, D. G. (1995). Sustaining interventions in community systems: On the relationship between researchers and communities. *Health Psychology, 14*, 526–36.

Altman, D. G., & Green, L. W. (1988). Area review: Education and training in behavioral medicine. *Annals of Behavioral Medicine, 10,* 4–7.

Altpeter, M., Earp, J., Bishop, C., & Eng, E. (1999). Lay health advisor activity levels: Definitions from the field. *Health Education & Behavior, 26,* 495–512.

Amaro, F., Frazao, C., Pereira, M. E., & da Cunha Teles, L. (2004). HIV/AIDS risk perception, attitudes and sexual behaviour in Portugal. *International Journal of STD and AIDS, 15,* 56–60.

American Dietetic Association, Society for Nutrition Education, American School Food Service Association. (2003). Position of the American Dietetic Association, Society for Nutrition Education, and American School Food Service Association: Nutrition services: an essential component of comprehensive school health programs. *Journal of Nutrition Education & Behavior, 35,* 57–67.

American Physical Education Association. (1935). Health education section, committee report, American Physical Education Association. *Journal of Health and Physical Education, 6,* 204–9.

American Public Health Association. (2000). *APHA advocate's handbook: A guide for effective public health advocacy.* Washington, D.C.: American Public Health Association.

Andersen, R. M. (1968). *A behavioral model of families' use of health services.* Chicago: University of Chicago, Center for Health Administration Studies, Research Series No. 25, University of Chicago Press.

Andersen, S., Keller, C., & McGowan, N. (1999). Smoking cessation: The state of the science. *Online Journal of Knowledge Synthesis in Nursing, 22,* 6–9.

Anderson, C. (2003). Evolving out of violence: an application of the transtheoretical model of behavioral change. *Research & Theory for Nursing Practice, 17,* 225–40.

Anderson, P. M., Butcher, K. F., & Levine, P. B. (2003). Maternal employment and overweight children. *Journal of Health Economics, 22,* 477–504.

Andersson, C. M., Bjaras, G. E. M., & Ostenson, C.-G. (2002). A stage model for assessing a community-based diabetes prevention program in Sweden. *Health Promotion International, 17,* 317–27.

*Antoniadis, A., & Lubker, B. B. (1997). Epidemiology as an essential tool for establishing prevention programs and evaluating their impact and outcome. *Journal of Communication Disorders, 30,* 269–83; quiz 283–84; review.

*Arbeit, M. L., Johnson, C. C., Mott, D. S., et al. (1992). The heart smart cardiovascular school health promotion: Behavior correlates of risk factor change. *Preventive Medicine, 21,* 18–21.

Arkin, E. B. (1989). *Making health communication programs work: A planner's guide.* Bethesda, MD: Office of Cancer Communications, National Cancer Institute, NIH–89–1493.

Arkin, E. B. (1990). Opportunities for improving the nation's health through collaboration with the mass media. *Public Health Reports, 105,* 219–23.

Armbruster, P. (2002). The administration of school-based mental health services. *Child & Adolescent Psychiatric Clinics of North America, 11,* 23–41; review.

Armitage, C. J., & Conner, M. (2001). Efficacy of the theory of planned behaviour: A meta-analytic review. *British Journal of Social Psychology, 40* (Pt. 4), 471–99.

Asbridge, M. (2004). Public place restrictions on smoking in Canada: Assessing the role of the state, media, science and public health advocacy. *Social Science & Medicine, 58,* 13–24.

*Ashley, N. (1993). *King county regional domestic violence public education campaign.* Seattle: Human Services Roundtable.

Assendelft, W. J., Morton, S. C., Yu, E. I., Suttorp, M. J., & Shekelle, P. G. (2003). Spinal manipulative therapy for low back pain. A meta-analysis of effectiveness relative to other therapies. *Annals of Internal Medicine, 138,* 871–81.

Atkins, D., Best, D., & Shapiro, E. N. (Eds.). (2001). The third U.S. preventive services task force: Background, methods, and first recommendations. *American Journal of Preventive Medicine, 20* (Suppl. 3S), 1 108

Atkins, L. A., Oman, R. F., Vesely, S. K., Aspy, C. B., & McLeroy, K. (2002). Adolescent tobacco use: The protective effects of developmental assets. *American Journal of Health Promotion, 16*, 198–205.

Ausems, M., Mesters, I., van Breukelen, G., & De Vries, H. (2003). Do Dutch 11–12 years olds who never smoke, smoke experimentally or smoke regularly have different demographic backgrounds and perceptions of smoking? *European Journal of Public Health, 13*, 160–7.

Austin, L. T., Ahmad, F., McNally, M. J., & Stewart, D. E. (2002). Breast and cervical cancer screening in Hispanic women: A literature review using the Health Belief Model. *Women's Health Issues, 12*, 122–28.

Australian Health Ministers' Advisory Council. (1994). *The health of young Ausralians.* Canberra: Australian government Printing Service.

Avorn, J. (2003). Balancing the cost and value of medications: The dilemma facing clinicians. *Pharmacoeconomics, 20* (Suppl. 3), 67–72.

Ayala, G. X., & Elder, J. P. (2001). Verbal methods in perceived efficacy work. In S. Sussman (Ed.), *Handbook of program development for health behavior research and practice.* Thousand Oaks, CA: Sage.

Azeredo, R., & Stephens-Stidham, S. (2003). Design and implementation of injury prevention curricula for elementary schools: Lessons learned. *Injury Prevention, 9*, 274–78.

*Bailey, P. H., Rukholm, E. E., Vanderlee, R., & Hyland, J. (1994). A heart health survey at the worksite: The first step to effective programming. *AAOHN Journal, 42*, 9–14.

*Bailey, W. C., Kohler, C. L., Richards, J. M., Jr., et al. (1999). Asthma self-management: Do patient education programs always have an impact? *Archives of Internal Medicine, 159*, 2422–28.

*Bailey, W. C., Richards J. M., Jr., Manzella, B. A., et al. (1987). Promoting self-management in adults with asthma: An overview of the UAB program. *Health Education Quarterly, 14*, 345–55.

*Bakdash, M. B. (1983). The use of mass media in community periodontal education. *Journal of Public Health Dentistry, 43*, 128–31.

*Bakdash, M. B., Lange, A. L., & McMillan, D. G. (1983). The effect of a televised periodontal campaign on public periodontal awareness. *Journal of Periodontology, 54*, 666–70.

*Balch, G. I., Loughrey, K. A., Weinberg, L., Lurie, D., & Eisner, E. (1997). Probing consumer benefits and barriers for the national 5 A Day Campaign: Focus group findings. *Journal of Nutrition Education, 29*, 178–83.

Bandura, A. (1977). *Social Learning Theory.* Englewood Cliffs, NJ: Prentice Hall.

Bandura, A. (1982). Self-efficacy mechanisms in human agency. *American Psychologist, 37*, 122–47.

Bandura, A. (1986). *Social foundations of thought and action: A social cognitive theory.* Englewood Cliffs, NJ: Prentice-Hall.

Bandura, A. (2001). Social cognitive theory: An agentic perspective. *Annual Review of Psychology, 52*, 1–26.

Bandura, A. (2002). Social cognitive theory. In L. Breslow, et al., *Encyclopedia of public health,* Vol. 4 (pp. 1121–22). New York: Macmillan Reference USA.

Bandura, A. (2004). Health promotion by social cognitive means. *Health Education and Behavior, 31*, 143–64.

Baranowski, T., Perry, C. L., & Parcel, G. S. (2002). How individuals, environments, and health behavior interact: Social Cognitive Theory. In K. Glanz, F. M. Lewis, & B. K. Rimer (Eds.), *Health behavior and health education: Theory, research, and practice* (pp. 165–84). 3rd ed. San Francisco: Jossey-Bass.

Barkin, S. L., Balkrishnan, R., Manuel, J., Andersen, R. M., & Gelberg, L. (2003). Health care utilization among homeless adolescents and young adults. *Journal of Adolescent Health 32*, 253–56.

*Barner, J. C., Mason, H. L., & Murray, M. D. (1999). Assessment of asthma patients' willingness to pay for and give time to an asthma self-management program. *Clinical Therapeutics, 21*, 878–94.

*Barnhoorn, F., & Adriaanse, H. (1992). In search of factors responsible for noncompliance among tuberculosis patients in Wardha District, India. *Social Science & Medicine, 34*, 291–306.

Baranowski, T., Perry, C. L., & Parcel , G. S. (2002). How individuals, environments, and health behavior interact: Social Cognitive Theory. In K. Glanz, F. M. Lewis, and B. K. Rimer (Eds.). *Health behavior and health education: Theory, research, and practice.* 3rd edition (pp. 165–84). San Francisco: Jossey-Bass.

*Bartholomew, L. K., Czyzewski, D. I., Parcel, G. S., et al. (1997). Self-management of cystic fibrosis: Short-term outcomes of the cystic fibrosis family education program. *Health Education and Behavior, 24*, 652–66.

*Bartholomew, L. K., Czyzewski, D. I., Swank, P. R., McCormick, L., & Parcel, G. S. (2000). Maximizing the impact of the cystic fibrosis family education program: Factors related to program diffusion. *Family and Community Health, 22*, 27–47.

*Bartholomew, L. K., Koenning, G., Dahlquist, L., & Barron, K. (1994). An educational needs assessment of children with juvenile rheumatoid arthritis. *Arthritis Care and Research, 7*, 136–43.

*Bartholomew, L. K , Parcel, G. S., & Kok, G. (1998). Intervention mapping: A process for developing theory- and evidence-based health education programs. *Health Education and Behavior, 25*, 545–63.

*Bartholomew, L. K, Parcel, G. S., Kok, G., & Gottlieb, N. H. (2001). *Intervention mapping: Designing theory- and evidence-based health promotion programs.* Mountain View, CA: Mayfield (now McGraw-Hill).

*Bartholomew, L. K., Seilheimer, D. K., Parcel, G. S., Spinelli, S. H., & Pumariega, A. J. (1989). Planning patient education for cystic fibrosis: Application of a diagnostic framework. *Patient Education and Counseling, 13*, 57–68.

*Bartlett, E. E. (1982). Behavioral diagnosis: A practical approach to patient education. *Patient Counseling and Health Education, 4*, 29–35.

Basch, C. E. (1984). Research on disseminating and implementing health education programs in schools. *Journal of School Health, 54*, 57–66.

Basch, C. E. (1987). Focus group interview: An underutilized research technique for improving theory and practice in health education. *Health Education Quarterly, 14*, 411–48.

Basch, C. E., Sliepcevich, E. M., Gold, R. S., et al. (1985). Avoiding type III errors in health education program evaluations: A case study. *Health Education Quarterly, 12*, 315–31.

Bashford, K. (2003). Going green more easily. *Health Estate, 57*(6), 27–30.

Bastani, R., Berman, B. A., Belin, T. R., et al. (2002). Increasing cervical cancer screening among underserved women in a large urban county health system: Can it be done? What does it take? *Medical Care, 40*, 891–907.

*Battista, R. N., Williams, J. L., & MacFarlane, L. A. (1986). Determinants of primary medical practice in adult cancer prevention. *Medical Care, 24*, 216–24.

Bauman, A., Smith, B., Stoker, L., et al. (1999). Geographical influences upon physical activity participation: Evidence of a "coastal effect." *Australia and New Zealand Journal of Public Health, 23*, 322–24.

Beaglehole, R. (2002). Overview and framework (for section on "Determinants of health and disease"). In R. Detels, J. McEwen, R. Beaglehole, & H. Tanaka (Eds.), *Oxford Textbook of public health:* Vol. 1: *The scope of public health* (pp. 83–87). 4th ed. New York: Oxford University Press.

Beaman, P. E., Reyes-Frausto, S., & Garcia-Pena, C. (2003). Validation of the health perceptions questionnaire for an older Mexican population. *Psychological Reports, 92* (3 Pt. 1), 723–34.

Beaulieu, M. D., Hudon, E., Roberge, D., et al. (1999). Practice guidelines for clinical prevention: Do patients, physicians and experts share common ground? *Canadian Medical Association Journal, 161,* 519–23.

Becker, H., Hendrickson, S. L., & Shaver, L. (1998). Nonurban parental beliefs about childhood injury and bicycle safety. *American Journal of Health Behavior, 22,* 218–27.

Becker, M. H. (1969). Predictors of innovative behavior among local health officers. *Public Health Reports, 84,* 1063–68.

Becker, M. H. (1970). Factors affecting diffusion of innovations among health professionals. *American Journal of Public Health, 60,* 294–304.

Becker, M. H., & Joseph, J. (1988). AIDS and behavioral change to reduce risk: A review. *American Journal of Public Health, 78,* 394–410.

Belik, K. (2003). *The occupational stress index: An approach derived from cognitive ergonomics and brain research for clinical practice.* Cambridge, UK: Cambridge International Science Publishing.

Bellingham, R. (1994). *Critical issues in worksite health promotion.* New York: Macmillan Publishing Co.

Belloc, N. B. (1973). Relationship of health practices and mortality. *Preventive Medicine, 3,* 125–35.

Belloc, N. B., & Breslow, L. (1972). Relationship of physical health status and health practices. *Preventive Medicine, 1,* 409–21.

Bengel, J., Belz-merk, M., & Farin, E.(1996). The role of risk perception and efficacy cognitions in the prediction of HIV-related preventive behavior and condom use. *Psychology and Health, 11,* 505–25.

*Bennett, B. I. (1977). A model for teaching health education skills to primary care practitioners. *International Journal of Health Education, 20,* 232–39.

Bensberg, M., & Kennedy, M. (2002). A framework for health promoting emergency departments. *Health Promotion International, 17,* 179–88.

Bensing, J. M., Roter, D. L., & Hulsman, R. L. (2003). Communication patterns of primary care physicians in the United States and the Netherlands. *Journal of General Internal Medicine, 18,* 335–42.

Benson, P. L. (1997). *All kids are our kids.* San Francisco: Jossey-Bass.

*Benson, R., & Taub, D. E. (1993). Using the PRECEDE model for causal analysis of bulimic tendencies among elite women swimmers: Predisposing, reinforcing, and enabling causes in educational diagnosis. *Journal of Health Education, 24,* 360–68.

*Berenson, G. S., Harsha, D. W., Hunter, S. M., et al. (1998). *Introduction of comprehensive health promotion for elementary schools: The Health Ahead/Heart Smart Program* (esp. Chapters 3 and 6). New York: Vantage Press.

Berkman, L. F., & Breslow, L. (1983). *Health and ways of living: The Alameda County study.* New York: Oxford University Press.

Berkman, L. F., & Kawachi, I. (2000). *Social epidemiology.* New York: Oxford University Press.

Berkowitz, B. (2001). Studying the outcomes of community-based coalitions, *American Journal of Community Psychology, 29,* 213–27.

Berkowitz, B., Fawcett, S. B., Francisco, V. T., et al. (2003). *An Internet-based textbook for promoting community health development.* Lawrence, KS: University of Kansas.

*Berland, A., Whyte, N. B., & Maxwell, L. (1995). Hospital nurses and health promotion. *Canadian Journal of Nursing Research, 27,* 13–31.

Berlin, X., Barnett, W., Mischke, G., & Ocasio, W. (2000). The evolution of collective strategies among organizations. *Organization Studies, 21,* 325–54.

Berman, P., & McLaughlin, M. (1976). Implementation of educational innovation. *The Educational Forum, 40,* 347–70.

Bertakis, K. D., Azari, R., Helms, L. J., Callahan, E. J., & Robbins, J. A. (2000). Gender differences in the utilization of health care services. *Journal of Family Practice, 49,* 147–52.

*Bertera, E. M., & Bertera, R. L. (1981). The cost-effectiveness of telephone vs. clinic counseling for hypertensive patients: A pilot study. *American Journal of Public Health, 71,* 626–29.

*Bertera, R. L. (1981). *The effects of blood pressure self-monitoring in the workplace using automated blood pressure measurement.* Unpublished doctoral dissertation. Baltimore: Johns Hopkins University, School of Hygiene and Public Health.

*Bertera, R. L. (1990a). The effects of workplace health promotion on absenteeism and employment costs in a large industrial population. *American Journal of Public Health, 80,* 1101–105.

*Bertera, R. L. (1990b). Planning and implementing health promotion in the workplace: A case study of the Du Pont Company experience, *Health Education Quarterly, 17,* 307–27.

*Bertera, R. L. (1991). The effects of behavioral risks on absenteeism and health-care costs in the workplace. *Journal of Occupational Medicine 33,* 1119–24.

*Bertera, R. L. (1993). Behavioral isk factor and illness day changes with workplace health promotion: Two-year results. *American Journal of Health Promotion, 7,* 365–73.

Bertera, R. L. (1999). Worksite health promotion. In B. Poland, L. W. Green, & I. Rootman (Eds.), *Settings approaches to health promotion.* Thousand Oaks, CA: Sage.

*Bertera, R. L., & Cuthie, J. C. (1984). Blood pressure self-monitoring in the workplace. *Journal of Occupational Medicine, 26,* 183–88.

Bertera, R. L., & Green, L. W. (1979). Cost-effectiveness of a home visiting triage program for family planning in Turkey. *American Journal of Public Health, 69,* 950–53.

*Bertera, R. L., Levine, D. M., & Green, L. W. (1982). Behavioral effects of blood pressure self-monitoring in the workplace using automated measurements. *Preventive Medicine, 11,* 158–63.

*Bertera, R. L., Oehl, L. K., & Telepchak, J. M. (1990). Self-help versus group approaches to smoking cessation in the workplace: eighteen-month follow-up and cost analysis. *American Journal of Health Promotion, 4,* 187–92.

*Bertram, D. A., & Brooks-Bertram, P. A. (1977). The evaluation of continuing medical education: A literature review. *Health Education Monographs, 5,* 330–62.

Berwick, D. M. (2003). Disseminating innovations in health care. *Journal of the American Medical Association, 289,* 1969–75.

Best, J. A. (1989). Intervention perspectives on school health promotion research. *Health Education Quarterly, 16,* 299–306.

*Best, J. A., Stokols, D., Green, L. W., et al. (2003). An integrative framework for community partnering to translate theory into effective health promotion strategy. *American Journal of Health Promotion, 18,* 168–76.

Bibeau, D. L., Mullen, K. D., McLeroy, K. R., et al. (1988). Evaluations of workplace smoking cessation programs: A critique. *American Journal of Preventive Medicine, 4,* 87–95.

Biglan, A., Ary, D. V., Smolkowski, K., Duncan, T., & Black, C. (2000). A randomised controlled trial of a community intervention to prevent adolescent tobacco use. *Tobacco Control, 9,* 24–32.

Biglan, A., Mrazek, P. J., Carnine, D., & Flay, B. R. (2003). The integration of research and practice in the prevention of youth problem behaviors. *American Psychology, 58,* 433–40.

*Bird, J. A., Otero-Sabogal, R., Ha, N.-T., & McPhee, S. J. (1996). Tailoring lay health worker interventions for diverse cultures: lessons learned from Vietnamese and Latina communities. *Health Education and Behavior, 23* (Suppl.), S105–S122.

Birketvedt, G. S., Thom, E., Bernersen, B., & Florholmen, J. (2000). Combination of diet, exercise and intermittent treatment of cimetidine on body weight and maintenance of weight loss: A 42 month follow-up study. *Medical Science Monitor, 6,* 699–703.

Bjaras, G., Haglund, B., & Rifkin, S. (1991). A new approach to community participation assessment. *Health Promotion International, 6,* 199–206.

Black, D. R., Tobler, N., & Sciacca, J. P. (1998). Peer helping/involvement: An efficacious way of meeting the challenge of reducing illicit drug use? *Journal of School Health, 68,* 87–93.

*Black, M. E. A., Stein, K. F., & Loveland-Cherry, C. J. (2001). Older women and mammography screening behavior: Do possible selves contribute? *Health Education and Behavior, 28,* 200–16.

Blake, S. M., Caspersen, C. J., Finnegan, J., et al. (1996). The shape up challenge: A community-based worksite exercise competition. *American Journal of Health Promotion, 11,* 23–34.

Blake, V. A., Allegrante, J. P., Robbins, L., et al. (2002). Racial differences in social network experience and perceptions of benefit of arthritis treatments among New York City Medicare beneficiaries with self-reported hip and knee pain. *Arthritis & Rheumatism, 47,* 366–71.

Blankertz, L., & Hazem, D. (2002). Assessing consumer program needs: Advantages of a brief unstructured format. *Community Mental Health Journal, 38,* 277–86.

Blum, R., & Samuels, S. E. (Eds.). (1990). Television and teens: Health implications. *Journal of Adolescent Health Care, 11,* 1–92 (whole issue no. 1).

Bly, J. L., Jones, R. C., & Richardson, J. E. (1986). Impact of worksite health promotion on health care costs and utilization. *Journal of the American Medical Association, 256,* 3235–40.

Boekeloo, B. O., Bobbin, M. P., Lee, W. I., et al. (2003). Effect of patient priming and primary care provider prompting on adolescent-provider communication about alcohol. *Archives of Pediatric & Adolescent Medicine, 157,* 433–39.

Bolman, L., & Deal, T. (1991). *Reframing organizations: Artistry, choice, and leadership.* San Francisco: Jossey-Bass, Inc.

*Bonaguro, J. A. (1981). PRECEDE for wellness. *Journal of School Health, 51,* 501–6.

*Bonaguro, J. A., & Miaoulis, G. (1983). Marketing: A tool for health education planning. *Health Education, 14* (Jan/Feb), 6–11.

Boothroyd, P., Green, L. W., Hertzman, C., et al. (1994). Tools for sustainability: Iteration and implementation. In C. Chu & R. Simpson (Eds.), *Ecological public health: From vision to practice* (chap. 10, pp. 111–21). Toronto: Centre for Health Promotion, University of Toronto.

Borgers, R., Mullen, P. D., Meertens, R., et al. (1993). The information-seeking behavior of cancer outpatients: A description of the situation. *Patient Education and Counselling, 22,* 35–46.

Boston, P., MacNamara, S. J. E., Karne, K., et al. (1997). Using participatory action research to understand the meanings Aboriginal Canadians attribute to the rising incidence of diabetes. *Chronic Diseases in Canada, 18,* 5–12.

Botes, A., & Otto, M. (2003). Ethical dilemmas related to the HIV-positive person in the workplace. *Nursing Ethics, 10,* 281–94.

Botvin, G. J., Baker, E., Dusenbary, L., Botvin, E., & Diaz, T. (1995). Long-term follow-up results of a randomized drug abuse prevention trial in a white middle-class population. *Journal of the American Medical Association, 273,* 1106–12.

*Boulet, L-P., Chapman, K. R., Green, L. W., & FitzGerald, J. M. (1994). Asthma education. *Chest, 106* (Suppl. 4), 184–96.

Boulton, M. L., Malouin, R. A., Hodge, K., & Robinson, L. (2003). Assessment of the epidemiologic capacity in state and territorial health departments—United States, 2001. *MMWR Morbidity & Mortality Weekly Reports, 52,* 1049–51.

Bowler, M. H., & Morisky, D. E. (1983). Small group strategy for improving compliance behavior and blood pressure control. *Health Education Quarterly, 10,* 57–69.

*Bowler, M. H., Morisky, D. E., & Deeds, S. G. (1980). Needs assessment strategies in working with compliance issues and blood pressure control. *Patient Counselling and Health Education, 2,* 22–27.

*Boyd, C. (1993). Up in smoke: Teens 'n' tobacco. Tobacco-Free Canada: First National Conference on tobacco or Health, Toronto. Ottawa: Health Promotion Directorate, Health Canada.

Boyd, G. M., & Glover, E. D. (1989). Smokeless tobacco use by youth in the U.S. *Journal of School Health, 59,* 189–94.

Boykin, A., Schoenhofer, S. O., Smith, N., St. Jean, J., & Aleman, D. (2003). Transforming practice using a caring-based nursing model. *Nursing Administration Quarterly, 27,* 223–30.

Bozzini, L. (1988). Local community services centers (LCSC) in Quebec: Description, evaluation, perspectives. *Journal of Public Health Policy, 9,* 346–75.

Bracht, N. F. (Ed.). (1998). *Health promotion at the community level: New advances.* 2nd ed. New York: Sage.

Brailey, L. J. (1986). Effects of health teaching in the workplace on women's knowledge, beliefs, and practices regarding breast self-examination. *Research in Nursing and Health, 9,* 223–31.

Braithwaite, R. L., Taylor, S., & Austin, J. (2000). *Building health coalitions in the Black community.* Thousand Oaks, CA: Sage.

Braun, S. (2003). The history of breast cancer advocacy. *Breast Journal, 9* (Suppl. 2), S101–3.

Breckon, D. J., Harvey, J. R., & Lancaster, R. B. (1994). *Community health education: Settings, roles, and skills for the 21st Century.* 4th ed. Rockville, MD: Aspen.

Brehm, B. J., Rourke, K. M., & Cassell, C. (1999). Training health professionals: A multidisciplinary team approach in a university-based weight-loss program. *Journal of Allied Health, 28,* 226–29.

Brener, N. D., Everett Jones, S., Kann, L., & McManus, T. (2003). Variation in school health policies and programs by demographic characteristics of U.S. schools. *Journal of School Health, 73,* 143–49.

Breslow, L. (2003). An interview with Dr. Lester Breslow [interview by JoAna Stallworth and Jeffery L. Lennon]. *American Journal of Public Health, 93,* 1803–5.

Breslow, L., & Engstrom, J. D. (1980). Persistence of health habits and their relationship to mortality. *Preventive Medicine, 9,* 469–83.

*Brieger, W. R., Nwankwo, E., Ezike, V. I., et al. (1996). Social and behavioral baseline for guiding implementation of an efficacy trial of insecticide impregnated bed nets for malaria control at Nsukka, Nigeria. *International Quarterly of Community Health Education, 16,* 47–61.

Brieger, W. R., Onyido, A. E., & Ekanem, O. J. (1996). Monitoring community response to malaria control using insecticide-impregnated bed nets, curtains and residual spray at Nsukka, Nigeria. *Health Education Research, 11,* 133–46.

Brieger, W. R., Ramakrishna, J., & Adeniyi, J. D. (1986–87). Community involvement in social marketing: Guineaworm control. *International Quarterly of Community Health Education, 7,* 19–31.

*Brink, S. G., Simons-Morton, D., Parcel, G., Parcel, G., & Tiernan, K. (1988). Community intervention handbooks for comprehensive health promotion programming. *Family and Community Health, 11,* 28–35.

British Columbia Ministry of Health, Community Health Division. (1994). *School-based prevention model handbook.* Victoria: BC Ministry of Health.

*Brosseau, L. M., Parker, D. L., Lazovich, D., Milton, T., & Dugan, S. (2002). Designing intervention effectiveness studies for occupational health and safety: The Minnesota Wood Dust Study. *American Journal of Industrial Medicine, 41,* 54–61.

Brown, E. R. (1984). Community organization influence on local public health care policy: A general research model and comparative case study. *Health Education Quarterly, 10,* 205–34.

Brown, T. M., & Fee, E. (2002). "Palliatives will no longer do": The deep roots and continuing dynamic of community-oriented primary care. *American Journal of Public Health, 92,* 1711–12.

Brown, W. B., Williamson, N. B., & Carlaw, R. A. (1988). A diagnostic approach to educating Minnesota dairy farmers in the prevention and control of bovine mastitis. *Preventive Veterinary Medicine, 5,* 197–211.

Brown, W. J., Basil, M. D., & Bocarnea, M. C. (2003). The influence of famous athletes on health beliefs and practices: Mark McGwire, child abuse prevention, and Androstenedione. *Journal of Health Communication, 8,* 41–57.

Brownson, C. A., Dean, C., Dabney, S., Brownson, R. C. (1998). Cardiovascular risk reduction in rural minority communities: The Bootheel Heart Health Project. *Journal of Health Education, 29,* 158–65.

Brownson, R. C., Hopkins, D. P., & Wakefield, M. A. (2002). Effects of smoking restrictions in the workplace. *Annual Review of Public Health, 23,* 333–48.

Brownson, R. C., Smith, C. A., Pratt, M., et al. (1996). Preventing cardiovascular disease through community-based risk reduction: The Bootheel Project. *American Journal of Public Health, 86,* 206–12.

*Bruce, S., & Grove, S. K. (1994). The effect of a coronary artery risk evaluation program on serum lipid values and cardiovascular risk levels. *Applied Nursing Research, 7,* 67–74.

*Bruerd, B., Kinney, M. B., & Bothwell, E. (1989). Preventing baby bottle tooth decay in American Indian and Alaska Native communities: A model for planning. *Public Health Reports, 104,* 631–40.

Brugge, D., Bagley, J., & Hyde, J. (2003). Environmental management of asthma at top-ranked U.S. managed care organizations. *Journal of Asthma, 40,* 605–14.

*Brunk, S. E., & Goeppinger, J. (1990). Process evaluation: Assessing re-invention of community-based interventions. *Evaluation and the Health Professions, 13,* 186–203.

Bryant, C. A., Forthofer, M. S., McCormack Brown, K. R., Landis, D. C., & McDermott, R. J. (2000). Community-based prevention marketing: The next steps in disseminating behavior change. *American Journal of Health Behavior, 24,* 61–68.

Buchanan, D. R. (2000). *An ethic for health promotion: Rethinking the sources of human well-being.* New York: Oxford University Press.

*Buller, D., Modiano, M. R., Guernsey de Zapien, J., et al. (1998). Predictors of cervical cancer screening in Mexican American women of reproductive age. *Journal of Health Care for the Poor and Underserved, 9,* 76–95.

Bullock, K. (1999). Dental care of patients with substance abuse. *Dental Clinics of North America, 43,* 513–26.

Bunker, J. P. (2001). The role of medical care in contributing to health improvements within societies. *International Journal of Epidemiology, 30,* 1260–63.

Burdine, J. N., Felix, M. R., Abel, A. L., Wiltraut, C. J., & Musselman, Y. J. (2000). The SF-12 as a population health measure: An exploratory examination of potential for application. *Health Services Research 35,* 885–904.

Burdine, J. N., Felix, M. R., Wallerstein, N., et al. (1999). Measurement of social capital. *Annals of the New York Academy of Science, 896,* 393–95.

*Burglehaus, M. J., Smith, L. A., Sheps, S. B., & Green, L. W. (1997). Physicians and breast-feeding: Beliefs, knowledge, self-efficacy and counselling practices. *Canadian Journal of Public Health, 88,* 383–87.

Burhansstipanov, L., Krebs, L. U., Bradley, A., et al. (2003). Lessons learned while developing "Clinical Trials Education for Native Americans" curriculum. *Cancer Control, 10* (5 Suppl.), 29–36.

Burke, V., Mori, T., A., Giangiulio, N., et al. (2002). An innovative program for changing health behaviours. *Asia Pacific Journal of Clinical Nutrition, 11* (Suppl. 3), S586–97.

Burnet, D., Plaut, A., Courtney, R., & Chin, M. H. (2002). Practical model for preventing type 2 diabetes in minority youth. *Diabetes Educator, 28,* 779–95.

Burns, D. M., Shanks, T. G., Major, J. M., Gower, K. B., & Shopland, D. R. (2000). Restrictions on smoking in the workplace. In *Population based smoking cessation: Proceedings of a conference on what works to influence cessation in the general population.* Smoking and Tobacco Control Monograph No. 12. Bethesda, MD: U.S. Department of Health and Human Services, National Institutes of Health, National Cancer Institute, NIH Pub. No. 00–4892.

*Burr, R., & Johanson, R. (1998). Continuing medical education: An opportunity for bringing about change in clinical practice. *British Journal of Obstetrics & Gynecology, 105,* 940–45.

Burton, W. N., Chen, C. Y., Conti, D. J., Schultz, A. B., & Edington, D.W. (2003). Measuring the relationship between employees' health risk factors and corporate pharmaceutical expenditures. *Journal of Occupational Environmental Medicine, 8,* 793–802.

*Bush, P. J., Downey, A. M., Frank, L. S., & Webber, L. S. (1987). Implementation of "Heart Smart": Cardiovascular school health promotion program. *Journal of School Health, 57,* 98–104.

*Bush, P. J., Zuckerman, A. E., Taggart, V. S., et al. (1989). Cardiovascular risk factor prevention in black school children: The 'Know Your Body' evaluation project. *Health Education Quarterly, 16,* 215–27.

*Bush, P. J., Zuckerman, A. E., Theiss, P. K., Peleg, E. O., & Smith, S.A. (1989). Cardiovascular risk factor prevention in black school children—2–year results of the Know Your Body Program. *American Journal of Epidemiology, 129,* 466–82.

Butler, J. T. (2001). *Principles of health education and health promotion.* 3rd ed. Belmont, CA: Wadsworth/Thomson Learning.

Butler, M. O., Abed, J., Goodman, K., et al. (1996). *A case-study evaluation of the Henry J. Kaiser Family Foundation's community health promotion grants program in the southern states: Phase 2 final report.* Arlington, VA, Menlo Park, CA, and Atlanta, GA: Battelle Centers for Public Health Research and Evaluation, Henry J. Kaiser Family Foundation, and Centers for Disease Control.

Butterfoss, F. R., Goodman, R. M., Wandersman, A., Valois, R. F., & Chinman, M. (1996). The Plan Quality Index: An empowerment evaluation tool for measuring and improving the quality of plans. In D. Fetterman, S. Kaftarian, & A. Wandersman (Eds.), *Empowerment evaluation: Knowledge and tools for self-assessment and accountability* (pp.304–31). 2nd ed. Thousand Oaks, CA: Sage.

Butterfoss, F. R., & Kegler, M. C. (2002). Toward a comprehensive understanding of community coalitions: Moving from practice to theory. In R. J. DiClementi, R. A. Crosby, & M. C. Kegler (Eds.), *Emerging theories in health promotion practice and research: Strategies for improving public health* (pp. 157–93). San Francisco: Jossey-Bass.

Caburnay, C. A., Kreuter, M. W., & Donlin, M. J. (2001). Disseminating effective health promotion programs from prevention research to community organizations. *Journal of Public Health Management & Practice, 7,* 81–89.

*Cadman, R. (1996). *Ski injury prevention: An epidemiological investigation of the social, behavioural, and environmental determinants of injury.* Unpublished doctoral dissertation, University of British Columbia, Vancouver.

*Cain, R. E., Schyulze, R. W., & Preston, D. B. (2001). Developing a partnership for HIV primary prevention for men at high risk for HIV infection in rural communities. *Promotion and Education: International Journal of Health Promotion and Education, 8,* 75–78.

*Calabro, K., Weltge, A., Parnell, S., Kouzekanani, K., & Ramirez, E. (1998). Intervention for medical students: Effective infection control. *American Journal of Infection Control,* 26: 431–36.

Cameron, R., Jolin, M. A., Walker, R., McDermott, N., & Gough, M. (2001). Linking science and practice: Toward a system for enabling communities to adopt best practices for chronic disease prevention. *Health Promotion Practice, 2,* 35–42.

Campbell, M. K., Demark-Wahnefried, W., Symons, M., et al. (1999). Fruit and vegetable consumption and prevention of cancer: The Black Churches United for Better Health Project. *American Journal of Public Health, 89,* 1390–96.

*Canadian Council of Cardiovascular Nurses. (1993). *Standards for cardiovascular health education.* Ottawa: Heart and Stroke Foundation of Canada.

Canadian Task Force on the Periodic Health Examination. (1979). The periodic health examination. *Canadian Medical Association Journal, 121,* 1193–254.

*Candeias, N. M. F. (1991). Evaluating the quality of health education programmes: Some comments on methods and implementation. *Hygie: International Journal of Health Education, 10*(2), 40–44.

Candel, M. (2001). Consumers' convenience orientation towards meal preparation: Conceptualization and measurement. *Appetite, 36,* 15–28.

Cannuscio, C., Block, J., & Kawachi, I. (2003). Social capital and successful aging: The role of senior housing. *Annals of Internal Medicine, 139* (5 Pt. 2), 395–99.

*Canto, M. T., Drury, T. F., & Horowitz, A. M. (2001). Maryland dentists' knowledge of oral cancer risk factors and diagnostic procedures. *Health Promotion Practice, 2*(3), 255–62.

*Canto, M. T., Goodman, H. S., Horowitz, A. M., Watson, M. R., & Duran-Medina C. (1998). Latino youths' knowledge of oral cancer and use of tobacco and alcohol. *American Journal of Health Behavior, 22,* 411–20.

*Cantor, J. C., Morisky, D. E., Green, L. W., et al. (1985). Cost-effectiveness of educational interventions to improve patient outcomes in blood pressure control. *Preventive Medicine, 14,* 782–800.

Cargo, M., Grams, G. D., Ottoson, J. M., Ward, P., & Green, L. W. (2003). Empowerment as fostering positive youth development and citizenship. *American Journal of Health Behavior, 27* (Suppl. 1), S66–79.

*Carlaw, R. W., Mittlemark, M., Bracht, N., & Luepker, R. (1984). Organization for a community cardiovascular health program: Experiences from the Minnesota Heart Health Program. *Health Education Quarterly, 11,* 243–52.

Carnegie Council on Adolescent Development, Task Force on Education of Young Adolescents. (1989). *Turning points: Preparing American youth for the 21st century.* Washington, DC: Carnegie Council on Adolescent Development, Carnegie Corporation of New York.

Carolina, M. S. & Gustavo, L. F. (2003). Epidemiological transition: Model or illusion? A look at the problem of health in Mexico. *Social Science and Medicine, 57,* 539–50.

Carpenter, C. (2003). Seasonal variation in self-reports of recent alcohol consumption: Racial and ethnic differences. *Journal of Studies in Alcoholism, 64,* 415–18.

Carr, M. (2000). Social capital, civil society, and social transformation. In R. F. Woollard & A. S. Ostry (Eds.). *Fatal consumption: Rethinking sustainable development* (pp. 69–97). Vancouver, BC: UBC Press.

Carter, W. B., Beach, L. R., Inui, T. S., et al. (1986). Developing and testing a decision model for predicting influenza vaccination compliance. *Health Service Research, 20,* 897–932.

Casebeer, L. L., Strasser, S. M., Spettell, C. M., et al. (2003). Designing tailored web-based instruction to improve practicing physicians' preventive practices. *Journal of Medical Internet Research, 5,* e20.

Cashman, S. B., & Stenger, J. (2003). Healthy communities: A natural ally for community-oriented primary care. *American Journal of Public Health, 93,* 1379–80.

*Castilla y Leon, Junta de (1993). *Plan sectorial de educacion para la salud.* Madrid: Graficas Don Bosco, Arganda del Rey.

*Castro, F. G., Cota, M. K., & Vega, S. C. (1999). Health promotion in Latino populations: A sociocultural model for program planning, development, and evaluation. In R. M. Huff & M. V. Kline (Eds.), *Promoting Health in Multicultural Populations: A Handbook for Practitioners* (pp. 137–68). Thousand Oaks, CA: Sage.

Catalano, R., Libby, A., Snowden. L., & Cuellar, A. E. (2000). The effect of capitated financing on mental health services for children and youth: The Colorado experience. *American Journal of Public Health, 90,* 1861–65.

Cataldo, M. F., & Coates, T. J. (Eds.). (1986). *Health and industry: A behavioral medicine perspective.* New York: Wiley.

Center for Health Promotion and Education (1987). *Smoking control among women: A CDC community intervention handbook* (145 pp.). Atlanta, GA: Centers for Disease Control and Prevention, Department of Health and Human Services.1987.

*Centers for Disease Control. (1987). *Information/education plan to prevent and control AIDS in the United States.* Washington, DC: U.S. Public Health Service, Department of Health and Human Service.

Centers for Disease Control. (1988). Guidelines for effective school health education to prevent the spread of AIDS. *Morbidity and Mortality Weekly Report, 37* (suppl. No. S–2.), 1–14. Also in *Health Education, 19*(3), 6–13.

Centers for Disease Control and Prevention. (1999a). *Best practices for comprehensive tobacco control programs*—August 1999. Atlanta, GA: U.S. Department of Health and Human Services, Centers for Disease Control and Prevention, National Center for Chronic Disease Prevention and Health Promotion, Office on Smoking and Health.

Centers for Disease Control and Prevention. (1999b). *CDCynergy content and framework workbook.* Atlanta, GA: Office of Communication, Centers for Disease Control and Prevention, U.S. Department of Health and Human Services.

Centers for Disease Control and Prevention. (1999c). Neighborhood safety and the prevalence of physical inactivity—selected states. *Morbidity and Mortality Weekly Report, 48,* 143–6.

Centers for Disease Control and Prevention. (2000). *Measuring healthy days: Population assessment of health-related quality of life.* Atlanta, GA: Health Care and Aging Studies Branch, Division of Adult and Community Health, National Center for Chronic Disease Prevention and Health Promotion, CDC.

Centers for Disease Control and Prevention. (2001). Increasing physical activity: A report on recommendations of the Task Force on Community Preventive Services. *Morbidity and Mortality Weekly Reports, 50, RR18,* 1–16. Atlanta, GA: U.S. Government Printing Office.

Centers for Disease Control and Prevention. (2002). *Smoking-attributable mortality, morbidity, and economic costs (SAMMEC): Adult SAMMEC and maternal and child health (MCH) SAMMEC software.* Atlanta: Office on Smoking and Health, National Center from Chronic Disease Prevention and Health Promotion, Centers for Disease Control and Prevention.

Centers for Disease Control and Prevention. (2003). *Guidance for comprehensive cancer control planning: Guidelines,* Vol. 1. CDC:
http://www.cdc.gov/cancer/ncccp/guidelines/index.htm.

Centers for Disease Control and Prevention. (2003). Physical activity levels among children aged 9–13 years: United States, 2002. *MMWR Morbidity and Mortality Weekly Reports, 52,* 785–88.

Centers for Disease Control and Prevention. (2004). Declining prevalence of no known major risk factors for heart disease and stroke among adults—United States, 1991–2001. *Morbidity and Mortality Weekly Reports, 53,* 4–7.

Centers for Medicare and Medicaid Systems. (2002). *U.S. health care system.* Chapter 1 slides at http://cms.hhs.gov/charts/default.asp, accessed December 7, 2003.

Center for Substance Abuse Prevention. (2002). *A practitioner's guide to science-based interventions: A handbook of promising, effective, and model programs.* Washington, DC: CSAP, Substance Abuse and Mental Health Services Administration, U. S. Department of Health and Human Services.

Cervero, R. M. (2003). Place matters in physician practice and learning. *Journal of Continuing Education and the Health Professions, 23* (Suppl 1), S10–8.

Chaloupka, F. J. (1999). Macro-social influences: The effects of prices and tobacco-control policies on the demand for tobacco products. *Nicotine Tobacco Research, 1* (Suppl. 1), S105–9.

Champion, V. L., & Skinner, C. S. (2003). Differences in perceptions of risk, benefits, and barriers by stage of mammography adoption. *Journal of Women's Health, 12,* 277–86.

Chan, B. T., & Austin, P. C. (2003). Patient, physician, and community factors affecting referrals to specialists in Ontario, Canada: A population-based, multi-level modelling approach. *Medical Care, 41,* 500–11.

*Chaney, J. D., Hunt, B. P., & Schulz, J. W. (2000). An examination using the precede model framework to establish a comprehensive program to prevent school violence. *American Journal of Health Studies, 16,* 199–204.

Chang, L., McAlister, A. L., Taylor, W. C., & Chan, W. (2003). Behavioral change for blood pressure control among urban and rural adults in Taiwan. *Health Promotion International, 18,* 219–28.

*Chang M. W., Brown, R. L., Nitzke, S., & Baumann, L. C. (2004). Development of an instrument to assess predisposing, enabling, and reinforcing constructs associated with fat intake behaviors of low-income mothers. *Journal of Nutrition Education and Behavior, 36,* 27–34.

Chapman, S. (1990). Intersectoral action to improve nutrition: The roles of the state and the private sector. A case study from Australia. *Health Promotion International, 5,* 35–44.

Chapman, S., & Dominello, A. (2001). A strategy for increasing news media coverage of tobacco and health in Australia. *Health Promotion International, 16,* 137–43.

Chapman, S., & Lupton, D. (1995). *The fight for public health: Principles and practice of media advocacy.* London: BMJ Publishing Group.

Chapman, S., & Wakefield, M. (2001). Tobacco control advocacy in Australia: Reflections on 30 years of progress. *Health Education and Behavior, 28,* 274–89.

Charter, W., & Jones, J. (1973). On the risk of appraising non-events in program evaluation. *Educational Research, 2*(11), 5–7.

Chase, G. (1979). Implementing a human services program: How hard can it be? *Public Policy, 27,* 385–435.

Chaskin, R. J., Brown, P., Venkatesh, S., & Vidal, A. (2001). *Building community capacity.* New York: Aldine de Gruyter.

Chavis, D. M. (2001). The paradoxes and promise of community coalitions. *American Journal of Community Psychology, 29,* 309–20.

Chavis, D. M., & Wandersman, A. (1990). Sense of community in the urban environment: A catalyst for participation and community development. *American Journal of Community Psychology, 18,* 55–81.

Cheadle, A., Psaty, B., Wagner, E., et al. (1990). Evaluating community-based nutrition programs: Assessing the reliability of a survey of grocery store product displays. *American Journal of Public Health, 80,* 709–11.

Cheadle, A., Wickizer, T. M., Franklin, G., et al. (1999). Evaluation of the Washington State Workers' Compensation Managed Care Pilot Project II: Medical and disability costs. *Medical Care, 37,* 982–93.

Checkland, P. (1999). *Systems thinking, systems practice: A 30–year retrospect.* Chichester: John Wiley & Sons.

Chenet, L., & McKee, M. (1998). Down the road to deregulation. *Alcohol and Alcoholism, 33,* 337–40.

Cheng, T. L., DeWitt, T. G., Savageau, J. A., & O'Connor, K. G. (1999). Determinants of counseling in primary care pediatric practice. *Archives of Pediatrics and Adolescent Medicine, 153,* 629–35.

Chenoweth, D. (1994). Positioning health promotion to make an economic impact. In J. P. Opatz (Ed.), *Economic impact of worksite health promotion*, Chap. 2 (pp. 33–49). Champaign, IL: Human Kinetics.

Chew, F., Palmer, S., Slonska, Z., & Subbiah, K. (2002). Enhancing health knowledge, health beliefs, and health behavior in Poland through a health promoting television program series. *Journal of Health Communication, 7*, 179–96.

*Chiang, L., Huang, J., & Lu, C. (2003). Educational diagnosis of self-management behaviors of parents with asthmatic children by triagulation based on PRECEDE-PROCEED model in Taiwan. *Patient Education and Counseling, 49*, 19–25.

*Chiasson, M. W., & Lovato, C. Y. (2000). The health planning context and its effect on a user's perceptions of software usefulness. *Canadian Journal of Public Health, 91*, 225–28.

*Chiasson, M. W., & Lovato, C. Y. (2001). Contextual factors influencing the formation of a user's perceptions of a software innovation. *Database for Advances in Information Sciences, 32*(3), 16–35.

Chie, W. C., & Chang, K. J. (1994). Factors related to tumor size of breast cancer at treatment in Taiwan. *Preventive Medicine, 23*, 91–97.

*Chiou, C. J., Huang, Y. H., Ka, J. K., Chun, F. J., & Huang, H. Y. (1998). Related factors contributing to the healthy lifestyle of urban employees through the PRECEDE model. (Chinese). *Kaohsiung Journal of Medical Sciences (Kao-Hsiung i Hsueh Ko Hsueh Tsa Chih), 14*, 339–47.

Cho, H. (2003). Communicating risk without creating unintended effects. *American Journal of Health Studies, 18*, 104–10.

Christoffersen, M. N., & Soothill, K. (2003). The long-term consequences of parental alcohol abuse: A cohort study of children in Denmark. *Journal of Substance Abuse Treatment, 25*, 107–16.

Chu, C., & Simpson, R, (Eds.). (1994). *Ecological public health: From vision to practice*. Toronto: Centre for Health Promotion, University of Toronto.

Church, J., Saunders, D., Wanke, M., et al. (2002). Citizen participation in health decision-making: Past experience and future prospects. *Journal of Public Health Policy, 23*, 12–32. www.hc-sc.gc.ca/hppb/healthcare/Building.htm.

*Chwalow, A. J., Green, L. W., Levine, D. M., & Deeds, S. G. (1978). Effects of the multiplicity of interventions on the compliance of hypertensive patients with medical regimens in an inner-city population. *Preventive Medicine, 7*, 51.

Clark, J. M. (1939). *The social control of business*. New York: McGraw-Hill.

Clark, N. M. (1987). Social learning theory in current health education practice. In W. B. Ward, S. K. Simonds, P. D. Mullen, & M. H. Becker (Eds.), *Advances in Health Education and Promotion*, Vol. 2 (pp. 251–75). Greenwich, CT: JAI Press.

*Clarke, V., Frankish, C. J., & Green, L. W. (1997). Understanding suicide among indigenous adolescents: A review using the PRECEDE model. *Injury Prevention, 3*, 126–34.

Clarke-Tasker, V. A., & Wade, R. (2002). What we thought we knew: African American males' perceptions of prostate cancer and screening methods. *ABNF Journal, 13*, 56–60.

Clayton, R. R., Cattarello, A. M., & Johnstone, B. M. (1996). The effectiveness of Drug Abuse Resistance Education (project DARE): 5–year follow-up results. *Preventive Medicine, 25*, 307–18.

*Clearie, A. F., Blair, S. N., & Ward, W. B. (1982). The role of the physician in health promotion: Findings from a community telephone survey. *The Journal of the South Carolina Medical Association, 78*, 503–5.

*Cockburn, J., Hennrikus, D., Scott, R., & Sanson-Fisher, R. (1989). Adolescent use of sun-protection measures. *Medical Journal of Australia, 151*, 136–40.

*Cockburn, J., Tompson, S. C., Marks, R., Jolley, D., Schofield, P., & Hill, D. (1997). Behavioural dynamics of a clinical trial of sunscreens for reducing solar keratoses in Victoria, Australia. *Journal of Epidemiology and Community Health, 51*, 716–21.

Cohen, H., Harris, C., & Green, L. W. (1979). Cost-benefit analysis of asthma self-management educational programs in children. *Journal of Allergy and Clinical Immunology, 64*, 155–56.

Cohen, J. E., de Guia, N. A., Ashley, M. J., et al. (2001). Predictors of Canadian legislators' support for public health policy interventions. *Canadian Journal of Public Health, 92*, 188–89.

Cohen, J. E., de Guia, N. A., Ashley, M. J., et al. (2002). Predictors of Canadian legislators' support for tobacco control policies. *Social Science and Medicine, 55*, 1069–76.

Cokkinides, V. E., Johnston-Davis, K., Weinstock, M., et al. (2001). Sun exposure and sun-protection behaviors and attitudes among U.S. youth, 11 to 18 years of age. *Preventive Medicine, 33*, 141–51.

Coleman, E. A., Lord, J., Heard, J., et al. (2003). The Delta Project: Increasing breast cancer screening among rural minority and older women by targeting rural healthcare providers. *Oncology Nursing Forum, 30*, 669–77.

Coleman, J. S., Katz, E., & Menzel, H. (1957). The diffusion of an innovation among physicians. *Sociometry, 20*, 253–70.

Collings, G. H., Jr. (1982). Perspectives of industry regarding health promotion. In R. S. Parkinson and Associates, *Managing health promotion in the workplace: Guidelines for implementation and evaluation* (pp. 119–26). Palo Alto, CA: Mayfield.

Collins, R. L., Schell, T., Ellickson, P. L., & McCaffrey, D. (2003). Predictors of beer advertising awareness among eighth graders. *Addiction, 98*, 1297–306.

Commission on Risk Assessment and Risk Management. (1996). *Risk assessment and risk management in regulatory decision-making.* Washington, DC: Author.

Conn, V. S., Minor, M. A., Burks, K. J., Rantz, M. J., & Pomeroy, S. H. (2003). Integrative review of physical activity intervention research with aging adults. *Journal of the American Geriatric Society, 51*, 1159–68.

Connell, D. B., Turner, R. R., & Mason, E. F. (1985). Summary of findings of the School Health Education Evaluation: Health promotion effectiveness, implementation, and costs. *Journal of School Health, 55*, 316–21.

*Conrad, K. M., Campbell, R. T., Edington, D. W., Faust, H. S., & Vilnius, D. (1996). The worksite environment as a cue to smoking reduction. *Research in Nursing and Health, 19*, 21–31.

*Contento, I. R., Kell, D. G., Keiley, M. K., & Corcoran, R. D. (1992). A formative evaluation of the American Cancer Society *Changing the Course* nutrition education curriculum. *Journal of School Health, 62*, 411–16.

Conway, T., Hu, T.-C., & Harrington, T. (1997). Setting health priorities: Community boards accurately reflect the preferences of the community residents. *Journal of Community Health, 22*, 57–68.

Cooke, B. E. M. (1995). Health promotion, health protection, and preventive services. *Primary Care, 22*, 555–64.

Cooke, B., & Kothari, U. (Eds.). (2001). *Participation: The new tyranny?* London, New York: Zed Books.

Cooper, L. A., & Roter, D. L. (2003). Patient-provider communication: The effect of race and ethnicity on process and outcomes of health care. In B. D. Smedley, A. Y. Stith, & A. R. Nelson (Eds.), *Unequal treatment: Confronting racial and ethnic disparities in health care* (pp. 552–93). Committee on Understanding and Eliminating Racial and Ethnic Disparities in Health Care. Washington, DC: National Academies Press.

Cooper, L. A., Roter, D. L., Johnson, R. L., et al. (2003). Patient-centered communication, ratings of care, and concordance of patient and physician race. *Annals of Internal Medicine1, 39*, 907–15.

*Corcoran, R. D., & Portnoy, B. (1989). Risk reduction through comprehensive cancer educa-
tion: The American Cancer Society Plan for Youth Education. *Journal of School Health, 59,*
199–204.

Cornacchia, H. J., Olsen, L. K., & Nickerson, C. J. (1988). *Health in elementary schools.* 7th ed.
St. Louis: Times Mirror/Mosby College Publishing.

Corral-Verdugo, V., Frias-Armenta, M., Perez-Urias, F., Orduna-Cabrera, V., & Espinoza-
Gallego, N. (2002). Residential water consumption, motivation for conserving water
and the continuing tragedy of the commons. *Environmental Management, 30,* 527–35.

*Costanza, M. E. (1992). Physician compliance with mammography guidelines: Barriers and
enhancers. *Journal of the American Board of Family Practice, 5*(2), x1–x10.

Cote, I., Gregoire, J. P., Moisan, J., Chabot, I., & Lacroix, G. (2003). A pharmacy-based health
promotion programme in hypertension: Cost-benefit analysis. *Pharmacoeconomic, 21,*
415–28.

Cottrell, L. S. (1976). The competent community. In B. H. Kaplan, R. N. Wilson, & A. H.
Leighton (Eds.), *Further exploration in social psychiatry* (pp. 195–209). New York: Basic
Books.

*Cottrell, R. R., Capwell, E., & Brannan, J. (1995). A follow-up evaluation of non-returning
teams to the Ohio Comprehensive School Health Conference. *Journal of Wellness Perspectives, 12*(1), 1–6.

*Covington, D. L., Peoples-Sheps, M. D., Buescher, P. A., Bennett, T. A. & Paul, M.V. (1998).
An evaluation of an adolescent prenatal education program. *American Journal of Health
Behavior, 22,* 323–33.

Cowling, D. W., Kwong, S. L., Schlag, R., Lloyd, J. C., & Bal, D. G. (2000). Decline in lung
cancer rates—California, 1988–1997. *Morbidity and Mortality Weekly Reports, 49,* 1066–99.

Cox, K. L., Gorely, T. J., Puddey, I. B., Burke, V., & Beilin, L. J. (2003). Exercise behaviour
change in 40– to 65–year-old women: The SWEAT Study (Sedentary Women Exercise
Adherence Trial). *British Journal of Health Psychology, 8,* 477–95.

Craig, C. L., Brownson, R. C., Craig, S. E., & Dunn, A. L. (2002). Exploring the effect of the
environment on physical activity: A study examining walking to work. *American Journal
of Preventive Medicine, 23* (Suppl. 2), 36–43.

*Cramer, J. A. (1994). Quality of life and compliance. In M. R. Trimble and W. E. Dodson
(Eds.), *Epilepsy and quality of life,* Chap. 4 (pp. 49–63). New York: Raven Press.

*Cramer, J. A., & Spilker, B. (Eds.). (1991). *Patient compliance in medical practice and clinical tri-
als.* New York: Raven Press.

Crenson, M. A., & Ginsberg, B. (2002). *Downsizing democracy: How America sidelined its citizens
and privatized it public.* Baltimore: Johns Hopkins University Press.

Creswell, W., Jr., & Newman, I. M. (1997). *School health practice.* 10th Ed. St. Louis: Times
Mirror/Mosby.

*Cretain, G. K. (1989). Motivational factors in breast self-examination: Implications for
nurses. *Cancer Nursing, 12,* 250–56.

Crisp, B. R., Swerissen, H., & Duckett, S. J. (2000). Four approaches to capacity building in
health: Consequences for measurement and accountability. *Health Promotion International, 15,* 99–107.

Croghan, I. T., O'Hara, M. R., Schroeder, D. R., et al. (2001). A community-wide smoking cessation program: Quit and win 1998 in Olmsted county. *Preventive Medicine, 33,* 229–38.

Crone, M. R., Reijneveld, S. A., Willemsen, M. C., et al. (2003). Prevention of smoking in adolescents with lower education: A school based intervention study. *Journal of Epidemiology and Community Health, 57,* 675–80.

Crosby, R.A., Kegler, M.C., & DiClemente, R. J. (2002). Understanding and applying theory
in health promotion practice and research. In R. J. DiClemente, R. A. Crosby, & M. C.

Kegler (Eds.), *Emerging theories in health promotion practice and research: Strategies for improving public health* (pp. 1–15). San Francisco: Jossey-Bass.

*Cross, D., Hall, M., & Howat, P. (2003). Using theory to guide practice in children's pedestrian safety education. *American Journal of Health Education, 34* (5 Suppl.), S42–S47.

*Cross, D., Stevenson, M., Hall, M., et al. (2000). Child pedestrian injury prevention project: Student results. *Preventive Medicine, 30,* 179–87.

Crow, R., Blackburn, H., Jacobs, D., et al. (1986). Population strategies to enhance physical activity: The Minnesota Heart Health Program. *Acta Medica Scandinavica, 711* (Suppl.), 93–112.

Cuca, R., & Pierce, C. S. (1977). *Experiments in family planning: Lessons from the developing world.* Baltimore: The Johns Hopkins University Press, for the World Bank.

Cullen, M. R. (1999). Personal reflections on occupational health in the twentieth century: Spiraling to the future. *Annual Review of Public Health, 20,* 1–13.

Cummings, K. M., Hellmann, R., & Emont, S. L. (1988). Correlates of participation in a worksite stop-smoking contest. *Journal of Behavioral Medicine, 11,* 267–77.

*Curry, S. J. (1998). Building effective strategies to decrease tobacco use in a health maintenance organisation: Group Health Cooperative of Puget Sound. *Tobacco Control, 7* (Suppl.), S21–3; discussion S24–5.

Curry, S. J., & Emmons, K. M. (1994). Theoretical models for predicting and improving compliance with breast cancer screening. *Annals of Behavioral Medicine, 16,* 302–16.

Curry, V. J., & Cole, M. (2001). Applying social and behavioral theory as a template in containing and confining VRE. *Critical Care Nursing Quarterly, 24,* 13–9; review.

Cuskey, W. R., & Premkumar, T. (1973). A differential counselor role model for the treatment of drug addicts. *Health Services Reports, 88,* 663–68.

*Dabbagh, L., Green, L. W., & Walker, G. M. (1991–92). Case study: Application of PRECEDE and PROCEED as a framework for designing culturally sensitive diarrhea prevention programs and policy in Arab countries. *International Quarterly of Community Health Education, 12,* 293–315.

Dahl, S., Gustafson, C., & McCullagh, M. (1993). Collaborating to develop a community-based health service for rural homeless persons. *Journal of Nursing Administration, 23,* 41–45.

*Daltroy, L. H., Iversen, M. D., Larson, M. G., et al. (1993). Teaching and social support: Effects on knowledge, attitudes, and behaviors to prevent low back injuries in industry. *Health Education Quarterly, 20,* 43–62.

*Danforth, N., & Swaboda, B. (1978). *Agency for International Development Health Education Study.* Washington, DC: Westinghouse Health Systems, March 17.

*Daniel, M. (1997). Effectiveness of community-directed diabetes prevention and control in a rural Aboriginal population. Vancouver, BC: University of British Columbia, Faculty of Medicine and Faculty of Graduate Studies.

*Daniel, M., & Green, L. W. (1995). Application of the Precede-Proceed model in prevention and control of diabetes: A case illustration from an Aboriginal community. *Diabetes Spectrum, 8,* 80–123.

*Daniel, M., Green, L. W., Marion, S. A., et al. (1999). Effectiveness of community-directed diabetes prevention and control in a rural Aboriginal population in British Columbia, Canada. *Social Science & Medicine, 48,* 815–832.

Daniels, N., Kennedy, B., & Kawachi, I. (2000). Justice is good for our health. *Boston Review,* February/March.

*Danigelis, N. L., Roberson, N. L., Worden, J. K., et al. (1995). Breast screening by African-American women: Insights from a household survey and focus groups. *American Journal of Preventive Medicine, 11,* 311–17.

Dannenberg, A. L., Jackson, R. J., Frumkin, H., et al. (2003). The impact of community design and land-use choices on public health: A scientific research agenda. *American Journal of Public Health, 93,* 1500–8.

Danzon, P. M., & Towse, A. (2003). Differential pricing for pharmaceuticals: Reconciling access, R&D and patents. *International Journal of Health Care, Finance & Economics, 3,*183–205.

*Davis, D. A., Thomson, M. A., Oxman, A. D., & Haynes, R. B. (1992). Evidence for the effectiveness of CME: A review of 50 randomized controlled trials. *Journal of the American Medical Association, 268,*1111–17.

*Davis, D. A., Thomson, M. A., Oxman, A. D., & Haynes, R. B. (1995). Changing physician performance: A systematic review of the effect of continuing medical education strategies. *Journal of the American Medical Association, 274,* 700–5.

Davis, T. C., Fredrickson, D. D., Arnold, C. L., et al. (2001). Childhood vaccine risk/benefit communication in private practice office settings: A national survey. *Pediatrics, 107*(2), E17.

de Almeida, I. M., Binder, M. C., & Fischer, F. M. (2000). Blaming the victim: Aspects of the Brazilian case. *International Journal of Health Services, 30,* 71–85.

Dean, K., & Hancock, T. (1992). *Supportive environments for health: Major policy and research issues involved in creating health promoting environments.* Copenhagen: World Health Organization, Regional Office for Europe.

Dearing, J. W., Larson, R. S., Randall, L. M., & Pope, R. S. (1998). Local reinvention of the CDC HIV prevention community planning initiative. *Journal of Community Health, 23,* 113–26.

*Dedobbeleer, N., & Desjardins, S. (2001). Outcomes of an ecological and participatory approach to prevent alcohol and other drug abuse among multiethnic adolescents. *Substance Use and Misuse, 36,* 1959–91.

*Dedobbeleer, N., & German, P. (1987). Safety practices in construction industry. *Journal of Occupational Medicine, 29,* 863–68.

*Deeds, S. G., Apson, J. R., & Bertera, R. (1979). *Steps to lung health education programming.* Baltimore: Johns Hopkins Health Services Research and Development Center and School of Public Health, Division of Health Education, for American Lung Association.

*Deeds, S. G., & Gunatilake, S. (1989). Behavioural change strategies to enhance child survival. *Hygie* (now *Promotion & Education*), *8,* 19–22.

DeFrancesco, S., Bowie, J. V., Frattaroli, S., et al. (2002). From the schools of public health. The Community Research, Education, and Practice Consortium: Building institutional capacity for community-based public health. *Public Health Reports, 117,* 414–20.

*de Haes, W. (1990). Can prevention be achieved through health education? [La prévention par l'éducation sanitaire est-elle possible?] In N. Job-Spira, B. Spencer, J. P. Maalti, & E. Bouvel (Eds.), *Santé Publique et Maladies à Transmission Sexuelle* (pp. 217–33). Paris: John Libby Eurotext.

DeJoy, D. M. (1986a). Behavioral-diagnostic model for self-protective behavior in the workplace. *Professional Safety, 31,* 26–30.

DeJoy, D. M. (1986b). Behavioral-diagnostic analysis of compliance with hearing protectors. *Proceedings of the 30th meeting of the Human Factors Society,* Vol. II (pp. 1433–37). Santa Monica, CA: Human Factors Society.

DeJoy, D. M. (1986c). A behavioral-diagnostic model for fostering self-protective behavior in the workplace. In Karwowski (Ed.), *Trends in Ergonomics and Human Factors III.* Amsterdam: Elsevier Science Publishers.

DeJoy, D. M. (1990) Toward a comprehensive human factors model of workplace accident causation. *Professional Safety, 35,* 11–16.

DeJoy, D. M. (1996). Theoretical models of health behavior and workplace self-protective behavior. *Journal of Safety Research*, *27*(2), 61–72.

*DeJoy, D. M., Murphy, L. R., & Gershon, R. M. (1995). The influence of employee, job/task, and organizational factors on adherence to universal precautions among nurses. *International Journal of Industrial Ergonomics, 16,* 43–55.

DeJoy, D. M., Searcy, C. A., Murphy, L. R., & Gershon, R. R. (2000). Behavioral-diagnostic analysis of compliance with universal precautions among nurses. *Journal of Occupational Health Psychology, 5,* 127–41.

*DeJoy, D. M., & Southern, D. J. (1993). An integrative perspective on work-site health promotion. *Journal of Occupational Medicine, 35,* 1221–30.

*DeJoy, D. M., & Wilson, M. G. (2003). Organizational health promotion: Broadening the horizon of workplace health promotion. *American Journal of Health Promotion, 17,* 337–41.

de Lange, A. H., Taris, T. W., Kompier, M. A., Houtman, I. L., & Bongers, P. M. (2003). The very best of the "millennium": Longitudinal research and the demand-control-(support) model. *Journal of Occupational Health Psychology, 8,* 282–305.

Delbecq, A. L. (1983). The Nominal Group as a technique for understanding the qualitative dimensions of client needs. In R. A. Bell, et al. (Eds.), *Assessing health and human service needs* (pp. 191–209). New York: Human Sciences Press.

Dement, J., Pompeii, L., Lipkus, I. M., & Samsa, G. P. (2003). Cancer incidence among union carpenters in New Jersey. *Journal of Occupational & Environmental Medicine, 45,* 1059–67.

De Moura S. L., Harpham, T., & Lyons, M. (2003). The social distribution of explanations of health and illness among adolescents in Sao Paulo, Brazil. *Journal of Adolescence, 26,* 459–73.

de Nooijer, J., Lechner, L., & de Vries, H. (2001). A qualitative study on detecting cancer symptoms and seeking medical help: An application of Andersen's model of total patient delay. *Patient Education and Counseling, 42,* 145–57.

de Nooijer, J., Lechner, L., & de Vries, H. (2003). Social psychological correlates of paying attention to cancer symptoms and seeking medical help. *Social Science and Medicine, 56,* 915–20.

De Pietro, R. (1987). A marketing research approach to health education planning. In W. B. Ward & S. K. Simonds (Eds.), *Advances in Health Education and Promotion,* Vol. 2 (pp. 93–118). Greenwich, CT: JAI Press Inc.

DePue, J. D., Wells, B. L., Lasater, T. M., & Carleton, R. A. (1987). Training volunteers to conduct heart health programs in churches. *American Journal of Preventive Medicine, 3,* 51–57.

DePue, J. D., Wells, B. L., Lasater, T. M., & Carleton, R. A. (1990). Volunteers as providers of heart health programs in churches: A report on implementation. *American Journal of Health Promotion, 4,* 361–66.

*Deren, S., Kang, S.-Y., Rapkin, B., Robles, R. R., Andia, J. F., & Colon, H. M. (2003). The utility of the PRECEDE Model in predicting HIV risk behaviors among Puerto Rican injection drug users. *AIDS and Behavior, 7,* 405–12.

*Desnick, L., Taplin, S., Taylor, V., Coole, D., & Urban, N. (1999). Clinical breast examination in primary care: Perceptions and predictors among three specialties. *Journal of Women's Health, 8,* 389–97.

Deuson, R. R., Hoekstra, E., Sedjo, R., et al. (1999). The Denver school-based adolescent hepatitis B vaccination program: A cost analysis with risk simulation. *American Journal of Public Health, 89,* 1722–27.

Deutsch, C. (1998). The university and the health of children. *Promotion and Education, 5,* 5–8.

Devine, E. C., & Cook, T. D. (1983). A meta-analytic analysis of effects of psycho-educational interventions on length of postsurgical hospital stay. *Nursing Research, 32,* 267–74.

*DeVries, H., Dijkstra, M., & Kok, G. (1992). A Dutch smoking prevention project: An overview. *Hygie, 11,* 14–18.

*DeVries, H., Dijkstra, M., & Kuhlman, P. (1988). Self-efficacy: The third factor besides attitude and subjective norm as a predictor of behavioral intentions. *Health Education Research, 3,* 273–82.

*DeVries, H., & Kok, G. J. (1986). From determinants of smoking behaviour to the implications for a prevention programme. *Health Education Research, 1,* 85–94.

Dewar, A., White, M., Toros, P. S., & Dillon, W. (2003). Using nominal group technique to assess chronic pain patients' perceived challenges and needs to enhance better targeted services in a community health region. *Health Expectations, 6,* 44–52.

DiClemente, C. C., & Prochaska, J. O. (1982). Self-change and therapy change of smoking behavior: A comparison of process of change in cessation and maintenance. *Addictive Behaviors, 7,* 133–42.

Dievler, A. (1997). Fighting tuberculosis in the 1990s: How effective is planning in policy making? *Journal of Public Health Policy, 18,* 167–87.

*Dignan, M., Bahnson, J., Sharp, P., et al. (1991). Implementation of mass media community health education: The Forsyth County Cervical Cancer Prevention Project. *Health Education Research, 6,* 259–66.

*Dignan, M., Beal, P. E., Michielutte, R., Sharp, P. C., et al. (1990). Development of a direct education workshop for cervical cancer prevention in high risk women: The Forsyth County project. *Journal of Cancer Education, 5,* 217–23.

*Dignan, M., Sharp, P., Blinson, K., et al. (1995). Development of a cervical cancer education program for native American women in North Carolina. *Journal of Cancer Education, 9,* 235–42.

*Dignan, M., Michielutte, R., Blinson, K., et al. (1996). Effectiveness of health education to increase screening for cervical cancer among eastern-band Cherokee Indian women in North Carolina. *Journal of the National Cancer Institute, 88,* 1670–76.

*Dignan, M., Michielutte, R., Wells, H. B., & Bahnson, J. (1994). The Forsyth County Cervical Cancer Prevention Project—I. Cervical cancer screening for black women. *Health Education Research, 9,* 411–20.

*Dignan, M., Michielutte, R., Wells, H. B., et al. (1998). Health education to increase screening for cervical cancer among Lumbee Indian women in North Carolina. *Health Education Research, 13,* 545–56.

Dijkstra, A., & Borland, R. (2003). Residual outcome expectations and relapse in ex-smokers. *Health Psychology, 22,* 340–6.

*Division of Health Education, Center for Health Promotion and Education, Centers for Disease Control. (1988). *Reference manuals: Planned approach to community health.* Atlanta: Centers for Disease Control.

Dobalian, A., Andersen, R. M., Stein, J. A., et al. (2003). The impact of HIV on oral health and subsequent use of dental services. *Journal of Public Health Dentistry, 63,* 78–85.

Docherty, B. (2001). Education campaigns in coronary heart disease. *Professional Nurse, 16,* 1048–51.

Dodek, P., & Ottoson, J. M. (1996). The implementation link between clinical practice guidelines and continuing medical education. *Journal of Continuing Education in the Health Professions, 16,* 82–93.

Doll, L., Bartenfeld, T., & Binder, S. (2003). Evaluation of interventions designed to prevent and control injuries. *Epidemiological Reviews, 25,* 51–59.

Donaldson, S. I. (2001). Mediator and moderator analysis in program development. In S. Sussman (Ed.), *Handbook of program development for health behavior research and practice* (pp. 470–96). Thousand Oaks, CA: Sage Publications, Inc.

Donaldson, S. I., Graham, J. W., Piccinin, A. M., et al. (1995). Resistance-skills training and onset of alcohol use: Evidence for beneficial and potentially harmful effects in public schools and in private Catholic schools. *Health Psychology, 14,* 291–300.

D'Onofrio, C. N. (2001). Pooling information about prior interventions: A new program planning tool. In S. Sussman (Ed.), *Handbook of program development for health behavior research and practice* (pp. 158–203). Thousand Oaks, CA: Sage Publications, Inc.

*Donovan, C. L. (1991). Factors predisposing, enabling and reinforcing routine screening of patients for preventing fetal alcohol syndrome: A survey of New Jersey physicians. *Journal of Drug Education, 21*, 35–42.

Donovan, R. J., & Jalleh, G. (2000). Positive versus negative framing of a hypothetical infant immunization: The influence of involvement. *Health Education and Behavior, 27*, 82–95.

*Dovell, R. (2001). *Cigarette smoking by adolescents: Exploring a hypothesis of social marginalization*. Vancouver, BC: University of British Columbia, Institute of Health Promotion Research, unpublished doctoral dissertation.

*Downey, A. M., Butcher, A. H., Frank, G. C., Webber, L. S., Miner, M. H., & Berenson, G. S. (1987). Development and implementation of a school health promotion program for reduction of cardiovascular risk factors in children and prevention of adult coronary heart disease: "Heart Smart." In B. Hetzel & G. S. Berenson (Eds.), *Cardiovascular risk factors in childhood: Epidemiology and prevention* (pp. 103–121). Amsterdam, NY & Oxford: Elsevier Science Publishers B.V.

*Downey, A. M., Cresanta, J. L., & Berenson, G. S. (1989). Cardiovascular health promotion in "Heart Smart" and the changing role of physicians. *American Journal of Preventive Medicine, 5*, 279–95.

*Downey, A. M., Frank, G. C., Webber, L. S., et al. (1987). Implementation of "Heart Smart": A cardiovascular school health promotion program. *Journal of School Health, 57*, 98–104.

*Downey, A. M., Virgilio, S. J., Serpas, D. C., et al. (1988). Heart Smart—A staff development model for a school-based cardiovascular health intervention. *Health Education, 19*(5), 64–71.

*Doyle, E. I., Beatty, C. F., & Shaw, M. W. (1999). Using cooperative learning groups to develop health-related cultural awareness. *Journal of School Health, 69*, 73–6.

*Doyle, E. I., & Feldman, R. H. L. (1997). Factors affecting nutrition behavior among middle-class adolescents in urban area of northern region of Brazil. *Revista de Saude Publica, 31*, 342–50.

Doyle, E., Smith, C. A., & Hosokawa, M. C. (1989). A process evaluation of a community-based health promotion program for a minority target population. *Health Education, 20*(5), 61–64.

Dubos, R. (1958, 1987). *Mirage of health: Utopias, progress, and bological health.* Garden City, NY: Doubleday, Inc.

Duhl, L. (1986). The healthy city: Its function and its future. *Health Promotion, 1*, 55–60.

*Duke, S. S., McGraw, S. A., Avis, N. E., & Sherman, A. (2000). A focus group study of DES daughters: Implications for health care providers. *Psychooncology, 9*, 439–44.

Durrant, R., Wakefield, M., McLeod, K., Clegg-Smith, K., & Chapman, S. (2003). Tobacco in the news: An analysis of newspaper coverage of tobacco issues in Australia, 2001. *Tobacco Control, 12* (Suppl. 2), II75–II81.

Dusenbury, L., Brannigan, R., Falco, M., & Hansen, W. B. (2003). A review of research on fidelity of implementation: Implications for drug abuse prevention in school settings. *Health Education Research, 18*, 237–56.

Dwore, R. B., & Kreuter, M. W. (1980). Update: Reinforcing the case for health promotion. *Family and Community Health, 2*, 103–19.

Dwyer, T., Pierce, J. P., Hannam, C. D., & Burke, N. (1986). Evaluation of the Sydney "Quit For Life" anti-smoking campaign (Part II: Changes in smoking prevalence). *Medical Journal of Australia, 144*, 344–47.

Dye, C. J., Haley-Zitlin, V., & Willoughby, D. (2003). Insights from older adults with type 2 diabetes: Making dietary and exercise changes. *Diabetes Educator, 29*, 116–27.

Eades, S. J., Read, A. W., & the Bibbulung Gnarneep Team. (1999). The Bibbulung Gnarneep Project: Practical implementation of guidelines on ethics in indigenous health research. *Medical Journal of Australia, 170*, 433–36.

Eakin, J. M. (2000). Commentary. In B. D. Poland, L. W. Green, & I. Rootman (Eds.), *Settings for health promotion: Linking theory and practice* (pp. 166–74). Thousand Oaks, CA: Sage Publications.

*Earp, J. A., Eng, E., O'Malley, M. S., et al. (2002). Increasing use of mammography among older, rural African American women: Results from a community trial. *American Journal of Public Health, 92*, 646–54.

*Earp, J. A., Ory, M. G., & Strogatz, D. S. (1982). The effects of family involvement and practitioners home visits on the control of hypertension. *American Journal of Public Health, 72*, 1146–54.

*Eastaugh, S. R., & Hatcher, M. E. (1982). Improving compliance among hypertensives: A triage criterion with cost-benefit implications. *Medical Care, 20*, 1001–17.

Easton, A., Husten, C., Malarcher, A., et al. (2001). Smoking cessation counseling by primary care women physicians: Women Physicians' Health Study. *Women's Health, 32*, 77–91.

*Edet, E. E. (1991). The role of sex education in adolescent pregnancy. *Journal of the Royal Society of Health, 111*(1), 17–18.

Edmondson, R. (2003). Social capital: A strategy for enhancing health? *Social Science and Medicine, 57*, 1723–33.

Edwards, R., Burns, J. A., McElduff, P., Young, R. J., & New, J. P. (2003). Variations in process and outcomes of diabetes care by socio-economic status in Salford, UK. *Diabetologia, 46*, 750–59. Epub 2003 May 23.

Egan, B. M., & Lackland, D. T. (1998). Strategies for cardiovascular disease prevention: The importance of public and community health programs. *Cardiovascular Disease Prevention, 8*, 228–39.

Ekeh, H. E., & Adeniyi, J. D. (1989). Health education strategies for tropical disease control in school children. *Journal of Tropical Medicine and Hygiene, 92*(2), 55–59.

Elbel, R., Aldana, S., Bloswick, D., & Lyon, J. L. (2003). A pilot study evaluating a peer led and professional led physical activity intervention with blue-collar employees. *Work, 21*, 199–210.

Elder, J. P., Schmid, T. L., Dower, P., & Hedlund, S. (1993). Community heart health programs: Components, rationale, and strategies for effective interventions. *Journal of Public Health Policy, 14*, 263–79.

Elder, J. P., Talavera, G. A., Gorbach, P. M., & Ayala, G. X. (2003). Theories and structures of public health behavior. In F. D. Scutchfield & C. W. Keck (Eds.), *Principles of public health practice* (pp. 253–72). 2nd ed. Clifton Park, NY: Delmar Learning.

Elder, R. W., & Shults, R. A. (2002). Involvement by young drivers in fatal alcohol-related motor-vehicle crashes—United States, 1982–2001. *Morbidity and Mortality Weekly Report, 651*(48), 1089–91.

*Elliott, S. J., Taylor, S. M., Cameron, R., & Schabas, R. (1998). Assessing public health capacity to support community-based heart health promotion: The Canadian Heart Health Initiative, Ontario Project (CHHIOP). *Health Education Research, 13*, 607–22.

Elmore, R. (1976). Follow through planned variation. In W. Williams & R. Elmore (Eds.), *Social program implementation.* New York: Academic Press.

Elnicki, D. M., Kolarik, R., & Bardella, I. (2003). Third-year medical students' perceptions of effective teaching behaviors in a multidisciplinary ambulatory clerkship. *Academic Medicine, 78*, 815–19.

Elovainio, M., Kivimaki, M., Vahtera, J., et al. (2003). Social support, early retirement, and a retirement preference: A study of 10,489 Finnish adults. *Journal of Occupational and Environmental Medicine, 45*, 433–39.

Emery, J., Crump, C., & Bors, P. (2003). Reliability and validity of two instruments designed to assess the walking and bicycling suitability of sidewalks and roads. *American Journal of Health Promotion, 18,* 38–46.

Employee Assistance Professionals Association. (1999). *EAPA standards and professional guidelines—1999.* Arlington, VA: Employee Assistance Professionals Association. http://www.eapassn.org/store/, accessed December 8, 2003.

*Eng, E. (1993). The save our sisters project: A social network strategy for reaching rural black women. *Cancer, 72* (3, Suppl.), 1071–77.

Eng, E., Parker, E. A., & Harlan, C. (Eds.). (1997). Lay health advisors: A critical link to community capacity building (Special issue). *Health Education and Behavior, 24,* 407–510.

*Engelstad, L., Bedeian, K., Schorr, K., & Stewart, S. (1996). Pathways to early detection of cervical cancer for a multiethnic, indigent, emergency department population. *Health Education and Behavior, 23* (Suppl.), S89–S104.

Entman, R. M. (1993). Framing: Toward clarification of a fractured paradigm. *Journal of Communication, 43,* 41–58.

Eriksen, M. P. (1986). Workplace smoking control: Rationale and approaches. *Advances in Health Education and Promotion,* Vol. 1, Pt. A (pp. 65–103). Greenwich, CT: JAI Press.

Eriksen, M. P., & Gielen, A. C. (1983). The application of health education principles to automobile child restraint programs. *Health Education Quarterly, 10,* 30–55.

*Eriksen, M. P., Green, L. W., & Fultz, F. G. (1988). Principles of changing health behavior. *Cancer, 62,* 1768–75.

Espy, K. A., & Senn, T. E. (2003). Incidence and correlates of breast milk feeding in hospitalized preterm infants. *Social Science and Medicine, 57,* 1421–28.

*Estey, A. L., Tan, M. H., & Mann, K. (1990). Follow-up intervention: Its effect on compliance behavior to a diabetes regimen. *Diabetes Education, 16,* 291–95.

Ettinger, B., Grady, D., Tosteson, A. N., Pressman, A., & Macer, J. L. (2003). Effect of the Women's Health Initiative on women's decisions to discontinue postmenopausal hormone therapy. *Obstetrics and Gynecology, 102,* 1225–32.

Evans, R. G., Barer, M. L., & Marmor, T. L. (Eds.). (1994). *Why are some people healthy and others not?* Hawthorne, NY: Aldine De Guyter.

Everett Jones, S., Brener, N. D., & McManus, T. (2003). Prevalence of school policies, programs, and facilities that promote a healthy physical school environment. *American Journal of Public Health, 93,* 1570–75.

Everly, G. S., & Feldman, R. H. (Eds.). (1985). *Occupational health promotion: Health behavior in the workplace.* New York: Wiley.

Ewing, R., Schmid, T., Killingsworth, R., Zlot, A., & Raudenbush, S. (2003). Relationship between urban sprawl and physical activity, obesity, and morbidity. *American Journal of Health Promotion, 18,* 47–57.

Eyler, A. A., Matson-Koffman, D., & Macera, C. (Eds.). (2003). Physical activity in women from diverse racial/ethnic groups: Environmental, policy, and cultural factors. *American Journal of Preventive Medicine, 25* (Whole issue 3, Suppl. 1), 1–105.

Fadiman, A. (1998). *The spirit catches you and you fall down.* New York: Farrar, Straus, & Giroux.

Fan, D. P. (1996). News media framing sets public opinion that drugs is the country's most important problem. *Substance Use and Misuse, 31,* 1413–21.

*Farley, C. (1997). Evaluation of a four-year bicycle helmet promotion campaign in Quebec aimed at children ages 8 to 12: Impact on attitudes, norms and behaviours. *Canadian Journal of Public Health, 88,* 62–66.

*Farley, C., Haddad, S., & Brown, B. (1996). The effects of a 4–year program promoting bicycle helmet use among children in Quebec. *American Journal of Public Health, 86,* 46–51.

*Farley, C., Laflamme, L., & Vaez, M. (2003). Bicycle helmet campaigns and head injuries among children. Does poverty matter? *Journal of Epidemiology and Community Health, 57*(9), 668–72.

Farquhar, J. W. (1978). The community-based model of life style intervention trials. *American Journal of Epidemiology, 108,* 103–11.

Farquhar, J. W., Fortmann, S. P., Flora, J. A., et al. (1990). Effects of community-wide education on cardiovascular disease risk factors—the Stanford 5-city Project. *Journal of the American Medical Association, 264,* 359–65.

Farquhar, J. W., Fortman, S. P., Wood, P. D., & Haskell, W. L. (1983). Community studies of cardiovascular disease prevention. In N. M Kaplan & J. Stamler (Eds.), *Prevention of coronary heart disease: Practical management of risk factors.* Philadelphia: W.B. Saunders.

*Farr, L. J., & Fisher, L. J. (1991). "Bring your body back to life": The 1990 Western Australian Quit Campaign. *Health Promotion Journal of Australia, 1,* 6–10.

Farrant, W., & Taft, A. (1988). Building healthy public policy in an unhealthy political climate: A case study from Paddington and North Kensington. *Health Promotion International, 3,* 287–92.

Farrar, S., Ryan, M., Ross, D., & Ludbrook, A. (2000). Using discrete choice modelling in priority setting: An application to clinical service developments. *Social Science and Medicine 50,* 63–75.

*Farthing, M. (1994). Health education needs of a Hutterite colony. *The Canadian Nurse/ L'Infirmiere Canadienne, 90,* 20–26.

Faucett, J., & McCarthy, D. (2003). Chronic pain in the workplace. *Nurses' Clinic of North America, 38*(3), 509–23.

Fawcett, S. B., Francisco, V. T., Schultz, J. A., et al. (2000). The community tool box: An Internet-based resource for building healthier communities. *Public Health Reports, 115,* 274–78.

*Fawcett, S. B., Lewis, R. K., Paine-Andrews, A., et al. (1997). Evaluating community coalitions for prevention of substance abuse: The case of project freedom. *Health Education and Behavior, 24,* 812–28.

Fawcett, S. B., Schultz, J. A., Carson, V. L., Renault, V. A., & Francisco, V. T. (2003). Using Internet based tools to build capacity for community based participatory research and other efforts to promote community health and development. In M. Minkler & N. Wallerstein (Eds.), *Community-based participatory research for health* (pp. 155–78). San Francisco: Jossey-Bass.

*Fedder, D. O. (1982). Managing medication and compliance: Physician-pharmacist-patient interactions. *Journal American Geriatric Society, 11* (Suppl.), 113–17.

*Fedder, D. O., & Beardsley, R. (1979). Preparing pharmacy patient educators. *American Journal of Pharmacy Education, 43,* 127–29.

Feeny, D., Berkes, F., Mccay, B. J., & Acheson, J. M. (1990). The tragedy of the commons: Twenty-two years later. *Human Ecology, 18,* 1–19.

Feldman, R. H. (1984). Increasing compliance in worksite health promotion: Organizational, educational, and psychological strategies. *Corporate Commentary, 1*(2), 45–50.

Fellows, J. L., Trosclair, A., Adams, E. K., & Rivera, C. C. (2002). Annual smoking-attributable mortality, years of potential life lost, and economic costs—United States, 1995–1999. *Morbidity and Mortality Weekly Report, 51,* 300–3.

Fernandez-Esquer, M. E., Espinoza, P., Torres, I., Ramirez, A. G., & McAlister, A. L. (2003). A su salud: A quasi-experimental study among Mexican American women. *American Journal of Health Behavior, 27,* 536–45.

Fernando, D., Schilling, R. F., Fontdevila, J., & El-Bassel, N. (2003). Predictors of sharing drugs among injection drug users in the South Bronx: Implications for HIV transmission. *Journal of Psychoactive Drugs, 35,* 227–36.

Ferrans, C. E. (1996). Development of a conceptual model of quality of life. *Scholarly Inquiry for Nursing Practice,10,* 293–304.

Ferrie, J. E., Shipley, M. J., Stansfeld, S. A., & Marmot, M. G. (2002). Effects of chronic job insecurity and change in job security on self reported health, minor psychiatric morbidity, physiological measures, and health related behaviours in British civil servants: The Whitehall II study. *Journal of Epidemiology and Community Health, 56,* 450–54.

Festinger, L. (1957). *A theory of cognitive dissonance.* Stanford, CA: Stanford University Press.

Fetterman, D. M. (2000). Foundations of empowerment evaluation: Step by step. Thousand Oaks, CA: Sage.

Fichtenberg, C. M., & Glantz, S. A. (2000). Association of the California Tobacco Control Program with declines in cigarette consumption and mortality from heart disease. *New England Journal of Medicine, 343,* 1772–77.

Fielding, J. E. (1982). Effectiveness of employee health improvement programs. *Journal of Occupational Medicine, 24,* 907–16.

Fielding, J. E. (1990). Worksite health promotion programs in the United States: Progress, lessons, and challenges. *Health Promotion International, 5,* 75–84.

Fielding, J. E., Luck, J., & Tye, G. (2003). Reinvigorating public health core functions: Restructuring Los Angeles county's public health system. *Journal of Public Health Management & Practice, 9,* 7–15.

Fiese, B. H., & Wamboldt, F. S. (2003). Tales of pediatric asthma management: Family-based strategies related to medical adherence and health care utilization. *Journal of Pediatrics, 143,* 457–62.

Fink, A. (Ed.). (2002). *The survey kit: Ten volume set.* 2nd ed. Thousand Oaks, CA: Sage.

Fiore, M. C., Bailey, W. C., Cohen, S. J., et. al. (2000). *Treating tobacco use and dependence: Quick reference guide for clinicians.* Rockville, MD: U.S. Department of Health and Human Services. Public Health Service.

Fiorentine, R., & Hillhouse, M. P. (2003). Replicating the addicted-self model of recovery. *Addictive Behavior, 28,* 1063–80.

*Fireman, P., Friday, G. A., Gira, C., Vierthaler, W. A., & Michaels, L. (1981). Teaching self-management skills to asthmatic children and their parents in an ambulatory care setting. *Pediatrics, 68,* 341–48.

First International Conference on Health Promotion. (1986). The Ottawa Charter for Health Promotion. *Health Promotion* (now *Health Promotion International*), 1(4), iii–v.

Fiscella, K., Franks, P., Gold, M. R., & Clancy, C. M. (2000). Inequality in quality: Addressing socioeconomic, racial, and ethnic disparities in health care. *Journal of the American Medical Association, 283,* 2579–84.

Fishbein, M. (Ed.). (1967). *Readings in attitude theory and measurement.* New York: Wiley.

Fishbein, M. (1996). Great expectations, or do we ask too much from community level interventions? *American Journal of Public Health, 86,* 1075–76.

Fishbein, M., & Ajzen, I. (1975). *Belief, attitude, intention, and behavior: An introduction to theory and research.* Reading, MA: Addison-Wesley.

Fisher, A. A. (1974). *The characteristics of family planning opinion leaders and their influence on the contraceptive behavior of others.* Doctor of Science dissertation. Baltimore: Johns Hopkins University School of Public Health.

Fisher, A. A. (1975). The measurement and utility of the opinion leadership concept for family planning programs. *Health Education Monographs, 3,* 168–80.

Fisher, A., Green, L. W., McCrae, A., & Cochran, C. (1976). Training teachers in population education institutes in Baltimore. *Journal of School Health, 46,* 357–60.

*Fisher, E. B., Strunk, R. C., Sussman, L. K., et al. (1995). Acceptability and feasibility of a community approach to asthma management: The Neighborhood Asthma Coalition (NAC). *Journal of Asthma, 33,* 367–83.

Fitch, J. P., Raber, E., & Imbro, D. R. (2003). Technology challenges in responding to biological or chemical attacks in the civilian sector. *Science, 302*, 1350–54.

Fitzner, K., Caputo, N., Trendell, W., et al. (2003). Recent tax changes may assist treatment of obesity. *Managed Care Interface, 16*, 47–51, 55.

Flay, B. R. (1986). Efficacy and effectiveness trials in the development of health promotion programs. *Preventive Medicine, 15*, 451–74.

Flay, B. R. (1987). Social psychological approaches to smoking prevention: Review and recommendations. In W. B. Ward & P. D. Mullen (Eds.), *Advances in health education and promotion*, Vol. 2 (pp. 121–80). Greenwich, CT: JAI Press.

*Fleisher, L., Kornfeld, J., Ter Maat, J., et al. (1998). Building effective partnerships: A national evaluation of the Cancer Information Service Outreach Program. *Journal of Health Communication, 3* (Suppl.), 21–35.

Fletcher, S. W. (1973). *A study of effectiveness of a follow-up clerk in an emergency room*. Master of Science thesis. Baltimore: Johns Hopkins University, School of Public Health.

Fletcher, S. W., Appel, F. A., & Bourgois, M. (1974). Improving emergency-room patient follow-up in a metropolitan teaching hospital. Effect of a follow-up check. *New England Journal of Medicine, 291*, 385–88.

Fletcher, S. W., Appel, F. A., & Bourgois, M. (1975). Management of hypertension. Effect of improving patient compliance for follow-up care. *Journal of the American Medical Association, 233*, 242–44.

Flood, R. L. (2001). The relationship of "systems thinking" to action research. In P. Reason & H. Bradbury (Eds.), *Handbook of action research: Participative inquiry and practice* (pp. 133–44). Thousand Oaks, CA: Sage.

Flottorp, S., & Oxman, A. D. (2003). Identifying barriers and tailoring interventions to improve the management of urinary tract infections and sore throat: A pragmatic study using qualitative methods. *BMC Health Services Research, 3*, 3.

Flynn, B. (1995). Measuring community leaders' perceived ownership of health education programs: Initial tests of reliability and validity. *Health Education Research, 10*, 27–36.

Flynn, B. S., Worden, J. K., Secker-Walker, R. H., et al. (1992). Prevention of cigarette smoking through mass media intervention and school programs. *American Journal of Public Health, 82*, 827–34.

Fors, S. W., Owen, S., Hall, W. D., et al. (1989). Evaluation of a diffusion strategy for school-based hypertension education. *Health Education Quarterly, 16*, 255–61.

Foshee, V. A., Linder, F., MacDougall, J. E., & Bangdiwala, S. (2001). Gender differences in the longitudinal predictors of adolescent dating violence. *Preventive Medicine, 32*, 128–41.

Foster-Fishman, P., Berkowitz, S., Lounsbury, D., Jacobson, S., & Allen, N. (2001). Building collaborative capacity in community coalitions: A review and integrative framework. *American Journal of Community Psychology, 29*, 241–57.

Fowler, F. J., Jr. (2001). *Survey research methods*. 3rd ed. Thousand Oaks, CA: Sage.

*Francisco, V. T., Paine, A. L., & Fawcett, S. B. (1993). A methodology for monitoring and evaluating community health coalitions. *Health Education Research, 8*, 403–16.

Frank, A. L. (2002). Occupational safety and health. In L. Breslow, B. Goldstein, L. W. Green, C. W. Keck, J. M. Last, & M. McGinnis (Eds.), *Encyclopedia of public health* (pp. 849–55). New York: Macmillan Reference USA.

*Frank, G. C., Vaden, A., & Martin, J. (1987). School health promotion: Child nutrition. *Journal of School Health, 57*, 451–60.

Frank, J. W. (1995). Why "population health"? *Canadian Journal of Public Health, 86*, 162–64.

*Frankish, C. J., Lovato, C. Y., & Shannon, W. J. (1999). Models, theories, and principles of health promotion with multicultural populations. In R. M. Huff & M. V. Kline (Eds.), *Promoting health in multicultural populations: A handbook for practitioners* (pp. 41–72). Thousand Oaks, CA: Sage.

Franks, M. M., Pienta, A. M., & Wray, L. A. (2002). It takes two: Marriage and smoking cessation in the middle years. *Journal of Aging and Health, 14*, 336–54.

Franzini, L., Ribble, J. C., & Keddie, A. M. (2002). Understanding the Hispanic paradox. In T. A. LaVeist (Ed.), *Race, ethnicity, and health: A public health reader* (pp. 280–310). San Francisco: Jossey-Bass.

Fraser, W., Maunsell, E., Hodnett, E., & Moutquin, J-M. (1997). Childbirth alternatives post-Cesarean study group: Randomized controlled trial of a prenatal vaginal birth after cesarean section education and support program. *American Journal of Obstetrics and Gynecology, 176*, 419–25.

Frauenknecht, M., & Black, D. R. (2003). *Social problem-solving inventory for adolescents (SPSI-A): A manual for application, interpretation and psychometric evaluation.* Morgantown, WV: PNG Publications.

*Frauenknecht, M., Brylinsky, J. A., & Zimmer, C. G. (1998). "Healthy Athlete 2000": Planning a health education initiative using the PRECEDE model. *Journal of Health Education, 29*, 312–18.

*Frazier, P. J., & Horowitz, A. M. (1990). Oral health education and promotion in maternal and child health—A position paper. *Journal of Public Health Dentistry, 50* (NSI), 390–95.

*Freed, G. L., Bordley, W. C., & Defriese, G. H. (1993). Childhood immunization programs: An analysis of policy issues. *The Milbank Quarterly, 71*(1), 65–96.

Freire, P. (1970). *Pedagogy of the oppressed.* New York: The Seabury Press.

French, S. A., Story, M., & Jeffrey, R. W. (2001). Environmental influences on eating and physical activity. *Annual Review of Public Health, 22*, 309–35.

Freudenberg, N. (1984). *Not in our backyards! Community action for health and the environment.* New York: Monthly Review Press.

*Freudenberg, N. (1989). *Preventing AIDS: A guide to effective education for the prevention of HIV infection.* Washington, DC: American Public Health Association.

Freudenberg, N., & Golub, M. (1987). Health education, public policy and disease prevention: A case history of the New York City Coalition to End Lead Poisoning. *Health Education Quarterly, 14*, 387–401.

Friedmann, P. D., McCullough, D., Saitz, R. (2001). Screening and intervention for illicit drug abuse: A national survey of primary care physicians and psychiatrists. *Archives of Internal Medicine, 161*, 248–51.

Fries, J. F., & Crapo, L. M. (1981). *Vitality and aging.* San Francisco: W. H. Freeman.

Froguel, P., & Boutin, P. (2001). Genetics of pathways regulating body weight in the development of obesity in humans. *Experimental Biology and Medicine, 226*, 991–96.

*Fulmer, H. S., Cashman, S., Hattis, P., Schlaff, A., & Horgan, D. M. (1992). Bridging the gap between medicine, public health and the community: PATCH and the Carney Hospital experience. *Journal of Health Education, 23*, 167–70.

*Furst, G. P., Gerber, L. H., & Smith, C. B. (1985). *Rehabilitation through learning: Energy conservation and joint protection—A workbook for persons with rheumatoid arthritis.* Washington, D.C.: U.S. Govt. Printing Office, GPO Stock No. 017–045–00107–4, NIH Publ. No. 85–2743, and *Rehabilitation through learning . . . : Instructor's guide.* Washington, DC: GPO Stock No. 017–045–00103–9, NIH Publication No. 85–2743.

*Furst, G. P., Gerber, L. H, Smith, C. C., Fisher, S., & Shulman, B. (1987). A program for improving energy conservation behaviors in adults with rheumatoid arthritis. *American Journal of Occupational Therapy, 41*, 102–11.

Galambos, N. L., Barker, E. T., & Almeida, D. M. (2003). Parents do matter: Trajectories of change in externalizing and internalizing problems in early adolescence. *Child Development, 74*, 578–94.

Galvin, D. M. (2000). Workplace managed care: Collaboration for substance abuse prevention. *The Journal of Behavioral Health Services & Research, 27*, 125–30.

Garfield, S. A., Malozowski, S., Chin, M. H., et al. (2003). Considerations for diabetes translational research in real-world settings. *Diabetes Care, 26,* 2670–74.

Garrett, J., Landau-Stanton, J., Stanton, M. D., Stellato-Kabat, J., & Stellato-Kabat, D. (1997). ARISE: A method for engaging reluctant alcohol- and drug-dependent individuals in treatment. Albany-Rochester Interventional Sequence for Engagement. *Journal of Substance Abuse Treatment, 14,* 235–48.

*Garvin, T. (1995). "We're strong women": Building a community-university research partnership. *Geoforum, 26,* 273–86.

*Gary, T. L., Bone, L. R., Hill, M. N., et al. (2003). Randomized controlled trial of the effects of nurse case manager and community health worker interventions on risk factors for diabetes-related complications in urban African Americans. *Preventive Medicine, 37,* 23–32.

Gary, T. L., Genkinger, J. M., Guallar, E., Peyrot, M., & Brancati, F. L. (2003). Meta-analysis of randomized educational and behavioral interventions in type 2 diabetes. *Diabetes Education, 29,* 488–501.

*Gauthier-Gagnon, C., Grise, M.-C., & Potvin, D. (1998). Predisposing factors related to prosthetic use by people with a transtibial and transfemoral amputation. *Journal of Prosthetics and Orthotics, 10,* 99–109.

*Gayle, J. A. (1987). Health as the universal language: International students as teaching resources. *Health Education, 18*(2), 29.

Geiger, H. J. (2002). Community-oriented primary care: A path to community development. *American Journal of Public Health, 92,* 1713–16.

Geller, A. C., Emmons, K., Brooks, D. R., et al. (2003). Skin cancer prevention and detection practices among siblings of patients with melanoma. *Journal of the American Academy of Dermatology, 49,* 631–38.

George, M. A., Daniel, M., & Green, L. W. (1998–99). Appraising and funding participatory research in health promotion. *International Quarterly of Community Health Education, 18,* 181–97.

Gerstein, D., & Green, L. W. (Eds.). (1993). *Preventing drug abuse: What do we know?* Washington, DC: National Academy Press.

Getliffe, K. A., Crouch, R., Gage, H., Lake, F., & Wilson, S. L. (2000). Hypertension awareness, detection and treatment in a university community: Results of a worksite screening. *Public Health, 114*(5), 361–66.

Gewin V. (2003). With the United States on high alert over the possibility of bioterror attacks, epidemiologists are in huge demand. *Nature, 423,* 784–85.

*Gielen, A. C. (1992). Health education and injury control: Integrating approaches. *Health Education Quarterly, 19,* 203–18.

*Gielen, A. C., & McDonald, E. M. (2002). Using PRECEDE/PROCEED to apply health behavior theories in health promotion program planning. In K. Glanz, B. K. Rimer, & F. M. Lewis (Eds.), *Health behavior and health education: Theory, research and practice.* 3rd ed. San Francisco: Jossey-Bass.

*Gielen, A. C. & Radius, S. (1984). Project KISS (Kids in Safety Belts): Educational approaches and evaluation measures. *Health Education, 15,* 43–47.

*Gielen, A. C., & Sleet, D. (2003). Application of behavior-change theories and methods to injury prevention. *Epidemiologic Reviews, 25,* 65–76.

*Gilbert, G., & Sawyer, R. (2000). *Health education: Creating strategies for school and community health.* 2nd ed. Boston: Jones and Bartlett Publishers.

*Gilmore, G. D., & Campbell, M. D. (2003). *Needs assessment strategies for health education and health promotion.* 2nd ed. Sudbury, MA: Jones & Bartlett.

Glanz, K. (1999). Progress in dietary behavior change. *American Journal of Health Promotion, 14,* 112–17.

Glanz, K. (2000). Health promotion planning: An educational and ecological approach. 3rd ed. *American Journal of Preventive Medicine, 18,* 104–5 (book review).

*Glanz, K., Carbone, E., & Song, V. (1999). Formative research for developing targeted skin cancer prevention programs for children in multiethnic Hawaii. *Health Education Research, 14,* 155–66.

Glanz, K., Grove, J., Lerman, C., Gotay, C., & Le Marchand, L. (1999). Correlates of intentions to obtain genetic counseling and colorectal cancer gene testing among at-risk relatives from three ethnic groups. *Cancer Epidemiology Biomarkers & Prevention, 8,* 329–36.

Glanz, K., & Oldenburg, B. (1997). Relevance of health behavior research to health promotion and health education. In D. S. Gochman (Ed.), *Handbook of health behavior research IV: Relevance for professionals and issues for the future*, Chap. 8 (pp. 143–61). New York: Plenum Press.

*Glanz, K., & Rimer, B. (1995). *Theory at a glance: A guide for health promotion practice.* Bethesda, MD: National Cancer Institute, NIH Pub. No. 95–3896, Public Health Service, U.S. Dept. of Health and Human Services, July.

Glanz, K., Rimer, B. K., & Lewis, F. M. (Eds.). (2002). *Health behavior and health education: Theory, research, and practice.* 3rd ed. San Francisco: Jossey-Bass.

Glasgow, R. E., Klesges, R., Mizes, J., & Pechacek, T. (1985). Quitting smoking: Strategies used and variables associated with success in a stop-smoking contest. *Journal of Consulting and Clinical Psychology, 53,* 905–12.

Glasgow, R. E., Lichtenstein, E., & Marcus, A. C. (2003). Why don't we see more translation of health promotion research to practice? Rethinking the efficacy-to-effectiveness transition. *American Journal of Public Health, 93,* 1261–67.

Glasgow, R. E., Schafer, L., & O'Neill, H. K. (1981). Self-help books and amount of therapist contact in smoking cessation programs. *Journal of Consulting and Clinical Psychology, 49,* 659–67.

Glasgow, R. E., Vogt, T. M., & Boles, S. M. (1999). Evaluating the public health impact of health promotion interventions: The RE-AIM framework. *American Journal of Public Health, 89,* 1323–27.

Glasser, M., Holt, N., Hall, K., et al. (2003). Meeting the needs of rural populations through interdisciplinary partnerships. *Family and Community Health, 26,* 230–45.

*Glenn, M. K. (1994). Preparing rehabilitation specialists to address the prevention of substance abuse problems. *Rehabilitation Couseling, 38,* 164–79.

Glik, D., Gordon, A., Ward, W., et al. (1987–88). Focus group methods for formative research in child survival: An ivoirian example. *International Quarterly of Community Health Education, 8,* 297–316.

Glynn, T. J. (1989). Essential elements of school-based smoking prevention programs. *Journal of School Health, 59,* 181–88.

Godin, G., & Kok, G. (1996). The theory of planned behavior: A review of its applications to health-related behaviors. *American Journal of Health Promotion, 10,* 467–68.

Goksen, F. (2002). Normative vs. attitudinal considerations in breastfeeding behavior: Multi-faceted social influences in a developing country context. *Social Science and Medicine, 54,* 1743–53.

Golaszewski, T. (2000). The limitations and promise of health education in managed care. *Health Education and Behavior, 27,* 402–16.

*Gold, R. S., Green, L. W., & Kreuter, M. W. (1998). *EMPOWER: Enabling methods of planning and organizing within everyone's reach.* Sudbury, MA: Jones and Bartlett Publishing Co. [CD–ROM disk and manual, International Ver 2.25].

Gold, R. S., Miner, K. R., Fiori, F., et al. (2001). Report of the 2000 Joint Committee on Health Education and Health Promotion Terminology. *American Journal of Health Education, 32,* 89–104.

Goldenhar, L. M., LaMontagne, A. D., Katz, T., Heaney, C., & Landsbergis, P. (2001). The intervention research process in occupational safety and health: An overview from the national occupational research agenda intervention effectiveness research team. *Journal of Occupational and Environmental Medicine, 43,* 616–22.

*Goldrick, B. A., & Larson, E. (1992). Assessing the need for infection control programs: A diagnostic approach. *Journal of Long Term Care Administration, 20,* 20–23.

Goldsmith, J. R. (1969). Air pollution epidemiology. A wicked problem, an informational maze, and a professional responsibility. *Archives of Environmental Health, 18,* 516–22.

Goldstein, M. S. (1992). *The health movement: Promoting fitness in America.* New York: Twayne Publishers.

Goodman, R. M. (2001). Community-based participatory research: Questions and challenges to an essential approach. *Journal of Public Health Management and Practice 7*(5), v–vi.

*Goodman, R. M., Spears, M. A., McLeroy, K. L., et al. (1998). An attempt to identify and define the dimensions of community capacity to provide a basis for measurement. *Health Education and Behavior, 25,* 258–78.

Goodman, R. M., & Steckler, A. B. (1989a). A framework for assessing program institutionalization. *Knowledge in Society, 2,* 57–71.

Goodman, R. M., & Steckler, A. B. (1989b). A model for the institutionalization of health promotion programs. *Family and Community Health, 11*(4), 63–78.

*Goodman, R. M., Steckler, A. B., Hoover, S., & Schwartz, R. (1993). A critique of contemporary community health promotion approaches: Based on qualitative review of xsx programs in Maine. *American Journal of Health Promotion, 7,* 208–20.

Goodman, R. M., & Wandersman, A. (1994). FORCAST: A formative approach to evaluating community coalitions and community-based initiatives. *Journal of Community Psychology, 6*–25 (special issue).

Goodman, R. M., Wandersman, A., Chinman, M., Imm, P., & Morrisey, E. (1996). An ecological assessment of community-based interventions for prevention and health promotion: Approaches to measuring community coalitions. *American Journal of Community Psychology, 24,* 33–61.

*Goodson, P., Gottlieb, N. H., & Radcliffe, M. (1999). Put prevention into practice: Evaluation of program initiation in nine Texas clinical sites. *American Journal of Preventive Medicine, 17,* 73–78.

Goodwin, R., & Andersen, R. M. (2002). Use of the behavioral model of health care use to identify correlates of use of treatment for panic attacks in the community. *Social Psychiatry and Psychiatric Epidemiology, 37,* 212–19.

Gordon, A. J. (1988). Mixed strategies in health education and community participation: An evaluation of dengue control in the Dominican Republic. *Health Education Research, Theory and Practice, 3,* 399–419.

Gordon, G. H., Joos, S. K., Byrne, J. (2000). Physician expressions of uncertainty during patient encounters. *Patient Education and Counseling, 40*(1), 59–65.

Gordon-Larsen, P., Mullan Harris, K., Ward, D. S., & Popkin, B. M. (2003). Acculturation and overweight-related behaviors among Hispanic immigrants to the US: The National Longitudinal Study of Adolescent Health. *Social Science and Medicine, 57,* 2023–34.

Gortmaker, S. L., Peterson, K., Wiecha, J., et al. (1999). Reducing obesity via a school-based interdisciplinary intervention among youth. *Archives of Pediatric and Adolescent Medicine, 153,* 409–18.

Gossop, M., Stephens, S., Stewart, D., et al. (2001). Health care professionals referred for treatment of alcohol and drug problems. *Alcohol and Alcoholism, 36,* 160–64.

*Gottlieb, N. H., Eriksen, M. P., Lovato, C. Y., et al. (1990). Impact of a restrictive work site smoking policy on smoking behavior, attitudes, and norms. *Journal of Occupational Medicine, 32,* 20–23.

*Gottlieb, N. H., & Green, L. W. (1984). Life events, social network, life-style, and health: An analysis of the 1979 National Survey of Personal Health Practices and Consequences. *Health Education Quarterly, 11,* 91–105.

Gottlieb, N. H., & Green, L. W. (1987). Ethnicity and lifestyle health risk: Some possible mechanisms. *American Journal of Health Promotion, 2,* 37–45.

*Gottlieb, N. H., Lovato, C. Y., Weinstein, R., Green, L.W., & Eriksen, M. P. (1992). The implementation of a restrictive worksite smoking policy in a large decentralized organization. *Health Education Quarterly, 19,* 77–100.

Gottlieb, N. H., Mullen, P. D., & McAlister, A. L. (1987). Patients' substance abuse and the primary care physician: Patterns of practice. *Addictive Behavior,* 1223–32.

*Gottlieb, N. H., & Nelson, A. (1990). A systematic effort to reduce smoking at the worksite. *Health Education Quarterly, 17,* 99–118.

Gray, B., Morgan, G. T., & Shirer, R. (2001). Condom use and partner characteristics among young adult males in urban Ghana, aged 15–24. *Social Biology, 48,* 234–55.

Green, L. W. (1970a). Identifying and overcoming barriers to the diffusion of knowledge about family planning. *Advances in Fertility Control, 5,* 21–29.

Green, L. W. (1970b). Should health education abandon attitude-change strategies? Perspectives from recent research. *Health Education Monographs* 1(30), 25–48.

Green, L. W. (1970c). *Status identity and preventive health behavior.* Berkeley: Pacific Health Education Reports No. 1, University of California School of Public Health.

*Green, L. W. (1974). Toward cost-benefit evaluations of health education: Some concepts, methods, and examples. *Health Education Monographs, 2* (Suppl. 1), 34–64.

*Green, L. W. (1975). Diffusion and adoption of innovations related to cardiovascular risk behavior in the public. In A. Enelow & J. B. Henderson (Eds.), *Applying behavioral sciences to cardiovascular risk.* New York: American Heart Association.

*Green, L. W. (1976a). Change process models in health education. *Public Health Reviews, 5,* 5–33.

*Green, L. W. (1976b). Site- and symptom-related factors in secondary prevention of cancer. In J. Cullen, B. Fox, & R. Isom (Eds.), *Cancer: The behavioral dimensions* (pp. 45–61). New York: Raven Press.

Green, L. W. (1977). Evaluation and measurement: Some dilemmas for health education. *American Journal of Public Health, 67,* 155–61.

*Green, L. W. (1978a). Determining the impact and effectiveness of health education as it relates to federal policy. *Health Education Monographs, 6,* 28–66.

Green, L. W. (1978b). The oversimplification of policy issues in prevention. *American Journal of Public Health, 68,* 953–54.

Green, L. W. (1979). Health promotion policy and the placement of responsibility for personal health care. *Family and Community Health, 2,* 51–64.

*Green, L. W. (1980). Healthy people: The Surgeon General's report and the prospects. In W. J. McNerney (Ed.), *Working for a healthier America* (pp. 95–110). Cambridge, MA: Ballinger.

Green, L. W. (1981). The objectives for the nation in disease prevention and health promotion: A challenge to health education training. Keynote address for *National Conference for Institutions Preparing Health Educators: Proceedings* (pp. 61–73). Washington, DC: US Office of Health Information and Health Promotion, DHHS Publication No. 81–50171.

*Green, L. W. (1983). New policies in education for health. *World Health* (April–May), 13–17.

*Green, L. W. (1984a). Health education models. In J. D. Matarazzo, S. M. Weiss, et al. (Eds.), *Behavioral health: A handbook of health enhancement and disease prevention* (pp. 181–98). New York: Wiley.

*Green, L. W. (1984b). Modifying and developing health behavior. *Annual Review of Public Health, 5,* 215–36.

Green, L. W. (1985a). Behavior is an inescapable product, whether we call it an objective or not. *The Eta Sigma Gamma Monograph Series, 4,* 37–39.

Green, L. W. (1985b). Some challenges to health services research on children and elderly. *Health Service Research, 19,* 793–815.

Green, L. W. (1986a). Evaluation model: A framework for the design of rigorous evaluation of efforts in health promotion. *American Journal of Health Promotion, 1*(1), 77–9.

Green, L. W. (1986b). The theory of participation: A qualitative analysis of its expression in national and international health policies. In W. B. Ward (Ed.), *Advances in health education and promotion,* Vol. 1, Pt. A (pp. 211–36). Greenwich, CT: JAI Press Inc. Reprinted in Patton, R. D. & Cissell, W. B. (Eds.). (1989). *Community organization: Traditional principles and modern application.* Johnson City, TN: Latchpins Press.

Green, L. W. (1987a). How physicians can improve patients' participation and maintenance in self-care. *Western Journal of Medicine, 147,* 346–49.

*Green, L. W. (1987b). *Program planning and evaluation guide for lung associations.* New York: American Lung Association.

Green, L. W. (1988a). Bridging the gap between community health and school health. *American Journal of Public Health, 78,* 1149.

Green, L. W. (1988b). The trade-offs between the expediency of health promotion and the durability of health education. In S. Maes, C. D. Spielberger, P. B. Defares, & I. G. Sarason (Eds.), *Topics in health psychology* (pp. 301–12). New York: Wiley.

Green, L. W. (1989). Comment: Is institutionalization the proper goal of grantmaking? *American Journal of Health Promotion, 3,* 44.

Green, L. W. (1990). The revival of community and the obligation of academic health centers to the public. In R. J. Bulger, S. J. Reiser, & R. E. Bulger (Eds.), *Institutional values and human environments for teaching, inquiry and healing* (pp. 148–164). Des Moines: University of Iowa Press.

Green, L. W. (1991). Preface. In *Healthy People 2000: National health promotion and disease prevention objectives* (pp. vii–xi). Sudbury, MA: Jones and Bartlett Publishing, Inc.

*Green, L. W. (1992). The health promotion research agenda revisited. *American Journal of Health Promotion, 6,* 411–13.

*Green, L. W. (1993). Modifying lifestyle to improve health. In W. D. Skelton & M. Osterweis (Eds.). *Promoting community health: The role of the academic health center* (pp. 54–69). Washington, DC: The Association of Academic Health Centers..

Green, L. W. (1994). Refocusing health care systems to address both individual care and population health. *Clinical and Investigative Medicine, 17,* 133–41.

*Green, L. W. (1995). Health promotion in the worksite: Theory and practice. *Japan Health and Culture Promotion Center newsletter, 3,* 2–13 (in Japanese).

Green, L. W. (1996). Commentary. In *Healthy People 2000 mid-decade review and revised objectives.* Boston: Jones and Bartlett Publishers.

*Green, L. W. (1998). Prevention and health education in clinical, school, and community settings. In R. B. Wallace (Ed.), *Maxcy-Rosenau-Last preventive medicine and public health* (pp. 889–904). 14th ed. Stamford, CT: Appleton & Lange.

Green, L. W. (1999a). Health education's contributions to public health in the twentieth century: A glimpse through health promotion's rear-view mirror. *Annual Review of Public Health, 20,* 67–88.

*Green, L. W. (1999b). What can we generalize from research on patient education and clinical health promotion to physician counseling on diet? *European Journal of Clinical Nutrition, 53* (Suppl. 2), S9–S18.

Green, L. W. (2000). In praise of partnerships: Caveats on coalitions. *Health Promotion Practice, 1,* 64–65.

Green, L. W. (2001a). Foreword. In S. Sussman (Ed.), *Handbook of program development for health behavior research and practice* (pp. xiii–xiv). Thousand Oaks, CA: Sage.

Green, L. W. (2001b). From research to "best practices" in other settings and populations (American Academy of Health Behavior Research Laureate address). *American Journal of Health Behavior, 25,* 165–78.

Green, L. W. (2003). Tracing federal support for participatory research in public health. In M. Minkler & N. Wallerstein (Eds.), *Community-based participatory research.* San Francisco: Jossey-Bass.

Green, L. W. (2004). Introduction of Albert Bandura for the Healthtrac Foundation Prize in Health Education. *Health Education and Behavior, 31,* 141–142.

Green, L. W., & Cargo, M. (1994). The changing context of health promotion in the workplace. In M. P. O'Donnell & J. S. Harris (Eds.), *Health promotion in the workplace* (pp. 497–524). 2nd ed. Albany, NY: Delmar Publishers.

*Green, L. W., Cargo, M., & Ottoson, J. M. (1994). The role of physicians in supporting lifestyle changes. *Medicine, Exercise, Nutrition and Health, 3,* 119–30. Also in *Proceedings of the twenty-ninth annual meeting of the Society of Prospective Medicine* (pp. 89–129). St. Louis, Missouri, Indianapolis, IN: Society of Prospective Medicine, Publishers.

*Green, L. W., Costagliola, D., & Chwalow, A. J. (1991). Diagnostic éducatif et évaluation de stratégies éducatives (modèle PRECEDE): Méthodology pratique pour induire des changements de comportements et d'état de santé. *Journées Annuelles de Diabétologie de l'Hotel Dieu* (pp. 227–40). Paris: Flammarion Médecine-Sciences.

Green, L. W., Daniel, M., & Novick, L. (2001). Partnerships and coalitions for community based research. *Public Health Reports, 116,* 15–26.

*Green, L. W., Eriksen, M. P., & Schor, E. L. (1988). Preventive practices by physicians: Behavioral determinants and potential interventions. *American Journal of Preventive Medicine, 4* (Suppl. 4), 101–7. Reprinted in R. N. Battista & R. S. Lawrence (Eds.), *Implementing preventive services* (pp. 101–7). New York: Oxford University Press.

*Green, L. W., Fisher, A., Amin, R., & Shafiullah, A. B. M. (1975). Paths to the adoption of family planning: A time-lagged correlation analysis of the Dacca Experiment in Bangladesh. *International Journal of Health Education, 18,* 85–96.

*Green, L. W., & Frankish, C. J. (1994). Theories and principles of health education applied to asthma. *Chest, 106* (Suppl.), 195–205.

Green, L. W., & Frankish, C. J. (1996). Implementing nutritional science for population health: Decentralized and centralized planning for health promotion and disease prevention. In *Beyond nutritional recommendations: Implementing science for healthier populations.* Ithaca, NY: Cornell University.

Green, L. W., & Frankish, C. J. (2001). Health promotion, health education, and disease prevention. In C. E. Koop, C. E. Pearson, & M. R. Schwarz (Eds.), *Critical issues in global health* (pp. 321–30). San Francisco: Jossey-Bass.

Green, L. W., George, A., Daniel, M., et al. (2003). Guidelines for participatory research, reproduced from *Study of participatory research in health promotion in Canada.* Ottawa, Royal Society of Canada, 1996. In M. Minkler & N. Wallerstein (Eds.), *Community-based participatory research for health* (pp. 135–54). San Francisco: Jossey-Bass.

Green, L. W., Glanz, K., Hochbaum, G. M., et al. (1994). Can we build on, or must we replace, the theories and models in health education? *Health Education Research, 9,* 397–404.

Green, L. W., Gottlieb, N. H., & Parcel, G. S. (1991). Diffusion theory extended and applied. In W. Ward & F. M. Lewis (Eds.), *Advances in health education and promotion,* Vol. 3. London: Jessica Kingsley Publishers.

Green, L. W., & Jan, Y. (1964). Family planning knowledge and attitude surveys in Pakistan. *Pakistan Development Review, 4,* 332–55.

Green, L. W., & Johnson, J. L. (1996). Dissemination and utilization of health promotion and disease prevention knowledge: Theory, research and experience. *Canadian Journal of Public Health, 87* (Suppl. 1), S17–S23.

*Green, L. W., & Kreuter, M. W. (1990). Health promotion as a public health strategy for the 1990s. *Annual Review of Public Health, 11*, 319–34.

*Green, L. W., & Kreuter, M. W. (1991). *Health promotion planning: An educational and environmental approach.* 2nd ed. Mountain View, CA: Mayfield.

*Green, L. W., & Kreuter, M. W. (1992). CDC's Planned Approach to Community Health as an application of PRECEDE and an inspiration for PROCEED. *Journal of Health Education, 23*, 140–47.

Green, L. W., & Kreuter, M. W. (1999a). Health education's contributions to public health in the 20th century: A glimpse through health promotion's rear-view mirror. *Annual Review of Public Health*, Vol. 20 (pp. 67–88). Palo Alto, CA: Annual Reviews Inc.

*Green, L. W., & Kreuter, M. W. (1999b). *Health promotion planning: An educational and ecological approach.* 3rd ed. Mountain View, CA: Mayfield.

Green, L. W., & Kreuter, M. W. (2002). Fighting back, or fighting themselves? Community coalitions against substance abuse and their use of best practices. *American Journal of Preventive Medicine, 23*, 303–6.

*Green, L. W., Kreuter, M. W., Deeds, S. G., & Partridge, K. B. (1980). *Health education planning: A diagnostic approach.* Palo Alto, CA: Mayfield.

Green, L. W., & Krotki, K. J. (1968). Class and parity biases in family planning programs: The case of Karachi. *Social Biology, 15*, 235–51.

*Green, L. W., Levine, D. M., & Deeds, S. G. (1975). Clinical trials of health education for hypertensive outpatients: Design and baseline data. *Preventive Medicine, 4*, 417–25.

*Green, L. W., Levine, D. M., Wolle, J., & Deeds, S. G. (1979). Development of randomized patient education experiments with urban poor hypertensives. *Patient Counseling and Health Education, 1*, 106–11.

*Green, L. W., & Lewis, F. M. (1986). *Measurement and evaluation in health education and health promotion.* Palo Alto, CA: Mayfield.

Green, L. W., Lewis, F. M., & Levine, D. M. (1980). Balancing statistical data and clinician judgments in the diagnosis of patient educational needs. *Journal of Community Health, 6*, 79–91.

*Green, L. W., & McAlister, A. L. (1984). Macro-intervention to support health behavior: Some theoretical perspectives and practical reflections. *Health Education Quarterly 11*, 323–39.

Green, L. W., & Mercer, S. L. (2001). Participatory research: Can public health researchers and agencies reconcile the push from funding bodies and the pull from communities? *American Journal of Public Health, 91*, 1926–29.

Green, L. W., & Mercer, S. L. (2004). Participatory research. In N. Anderson (Ed.), *Encyclopedia of health and behavior* (pp. 650–653). Vol 2. Thousand Oaks, CA: Sage Publications.

Green, L. W., Mullen, P. D., & Friedman, R. (1986). An epidemiological approach to targeting drug information. *Patient Education & Counseling, 8*, 255–68.

Green, L. W., Mullen, P. D., & Stainbrook, G. L. (1986). Programs to reduce drug errors in the elderly: Direct and indirect evidence from patient education. *Journal of Geriatric Drug Therapy, 1*, 3–16.

Green, L. W., Murphy, R. L., & McKenna, J. W. (2002). New insights into how mass media works for and against tobacco. *Journal of Health Communications, 7*, 245–48.

Green, L. W., & Ottoson, J. M. (1999). *Community and population health.* 8th ed. New York and Toronto: WCB/McGraw-Hill.

Green, L. W., Poland, B. D., & Rootman, I. (2000). The settings approach to health promotion. In B. D. Poland, L. W. Green, & I. Rootman (Eds.), *Settings in health promotion: Linking theory and practice* (pp. 1–43). Thousand Oaks, CA: Sage.

Green, L. W., & Potvin, L. (2002). Education, health promotion, and social and lifestyle determinants of health and disease. In R. Detels, J. McEwen, R. Beaglehole, & H. Tanaka

(Eds.), *Oxford textbook of public health: The scope of public health,* Vol. 1. (pp. 113–30). 4th ed. New York: Oxford University Press.

Green, L. W., & Raeburn, J. (1990). Contemporary developments in health promotion: Definitions and challenges. In N. Bracht (Ed.), *Health promotion at the community level* (pp. 29–44). Newbury Park, CA: Sage.

Green, L. W., Richard, L., & Potvin, L. (1996). Ecological foundations of health promotion. *American Journal of Health Promotion, 10,* 270–81.

Green, L. W., & Shoveller, J. A. (2000). Local versus central influences in planning for community health. In R. F. Woollard & A. S. Ostry (Eds.), *Fatal consumption: Rethinking sustainable development* (pp. 166–96). Vancouver, BC: UBC Press.

Green, L. W., & Simons-Morton, D. (1988). Denial, delay and disappointment: Discovering and overcoming the causes of drug errors and missed appointments. In D. Schmidt & I. E. Leppik (Eds.), *Compliance in epilepsy* (Epilepsy Research, Suppl. 1, pp. 7–21). Amsterdam: Elsevier Science Publishers B.V.

*Green, L. W., Wang, V. L., Deeds, S. G., et al. (1978). Guidelines for health education in maternal and child health programs. *International Journal of Health Education, 21* (Suppl.), 1–33.

Green, L. W., Wang, V. L., & Ephross, P. (1974). A three-year longitudinal study of the effectiveness of nutrition aides on rural poor homemakers. *American Journal of Public Health, 64,* 722–24.

*Green, L. W., Werlin, S. H., Shauffler, H. H., & Avery, C. H. (1977). Research and demonstration issues in self-care: Measuring the decline of medicocentrism. *Health Education Monographs, 5,* 161–89; also in J. G. Zapka (Ed.), *The SOPHE heritage collection of Health Education Monographs,* Vol. 3 (pp. 40–69). Oakland, CA: Third Party Publishing.

Green, L. W., Wilson, A. L., & Lovato, C. Y. (1986). What changes can health promotion achieve and how long do these changes last? The tradeoffs between expediency and durability. *Preventive Medicine, 15,* 508–21.

*Green, L. W., Wilson, R. W., & Bauer, K. G. (1983). Data required to measure progress on the Objectives for the Nation in Disease Prevention and Health Promotion. *American Journal of Public Health, 73,* 18–24.

Gregory, S. (2002). *Guidelines for comprehensive programs to promote healthy eating and physcial activity.* Champaign, IL: Human Kenetics.

Griffin, K. W., Botvin, G. J., Nichols, T. R., & Doyle, M. M. (2003). Effectiveness of a universal drug abuse prevention approach for youth at high risk for substance use initiation. *Preventive Medicine, 36,* 1–7.

*Grisé, M-C. L., Gauthier-Gagnon, C., & Martineau, G. G. (1993). Prosthetic profile of people with lower extremity amputation: Conception and design of a follow-up questionnaire. *Archives of Physical Medicine and Rehabilitation, 74,* 862–70.

*Grol, R. (2002). Changing physicians' competence and performance: Finding the balance between the individual and the organization. *Journal of Continuing Education in the Health Professions, 22,* 244–51.

Gross, N. C. (1942). *The diffusion of a culture trait in two Iowa townships.* Master of Science thesis. Ames: Iowa State College.

Grubbs, L. M., & Tabano, M. (2000). Use of sunscreen in health care professionals: The Health Belief Model. *Cancer Nursing, 23,* 164–67.

*Grueninger, U. J. (1995). Arterial hypertension: Lessons from patient education. *Patient Education and Counseling, 26,* 37–55.

*Grueninger, U. J., Duffy, F. D., & Goldstein, M. G. (1995). Patient education in the medical encounter: How to facilitate learning, behavior change, and coping. In M. Lipkin, Jr., S. M. Putnam, & A. Lazare (Eds.), *The medical interview: Clinical care, education, and research* (pp. 122–33). Bern: Mack Lipkin, Jr., MD.

*Grunbaum, J. A., Gingiss, P., Orpinas, P., Batey, L. S., & Parcel, G. S. (1995). A comprehensive approach to school health program needs assessments. *Journal of School Health. 65,* 54–59.

Grunbaum, J. A., Rutman, S. J., & Sathrum, P. R.. (2001). Faculty and staff health promotion: results from the School Health Policies and Programs Study 2000. *Journal of School Health, 71,* 335–39.

Guevara, J.,Wolf, F. M., Grum, C. M., & Clark, N. M. (2003). Effects of educational interventions for self management of asthma in children and adolescents: Systematic review and meta-analysis. *British Medical Journal, 326,* 1308–9.

Gullette, D. L., & Turner, J. G. (2003). Pros and cons of condom use among gay and bisexual men as explored via the internet. *Journal of Community Health Nursing, 20,* 161–77.

Gunter, M. J., Beaton, S. J., Brenneman, S. K., et al. (2003). Management of osteoporosis in women aged 50 and older with osteoporosis-related fractures in a managed care population. *Disease Management, 6,* 83–91.

Gupta, M. C., Mehrotra, M., Arora, S., & Saran, M. (1991). Relation of childhood malnutrition to parental education and mother's nutrition related KAP. *Indian Journal of Pediatrics, 58,* 269–74.

*Gutierrez English, J., & Le, A. (1999). Assessing needs and planning, implementing, and evaluating health promotion and disease prevention programs among Asian American population groups. In R. M. Huff & M. V. Kline (Eds.), *Promoting health in multicultural populations: A handbook for practitioners* (pp. 357–73). Thousand Oaks, CA: Sage.

Guttmacher, S., Lieberman, L., Ward, D., Freudenberg, N., Radosh, A., & Des Jarlais, D. (1997). Condom availability in New York City public high schools: Relationships to condom use and sexual behavior. *American Journal of Public Health, 87,* 1427–33.

Guttman, N., & Ressler, W. H. (2001). On being responsible: Ethical issues in appeals to personal responsibility in health campaigns. *Journal of Health Communications, 6,* 117–36.

*Haber, D. (1994). Medical screenings and health assessments. In D. Haber (Ed.), *Health promotion and aging* (pp. 41–76). New York: Springer Publishing Company.

Habib, S., Morrissey, S. A., & Helmes, E. (2003). Readiness to adopt a self-management approach to pain: Evaluation of the pain stages of change model in a non-pain-clinic sample. *Pain, 104,* 283–90.

Hackam, D. G., & Anand, S. S. (2003). Commentary: Cardiovascular implications of the epidemiological transition for the developing world: Thailand as a case in point. *International Journal of Epidemiology, 32,* 468–69.

Hackbarth, D. P., Schnopp-Wyatt, D., Katz, D., et al. (2001). Collaborative research and action to control the geographic placement of outdoor advertising of alcohol and tobacco products in Chicago. *Public Health Reports, 116,* 558–67.

Haley, N., Maheux, B., Rivard, M., & Gervais, A. (2000). Lifestyle health risk assessment. Do recently trained family physicians do it better? *Canadian Family Physician, 46,* 1609–16.

Haley, S. M., Jette, A. M., Coster, W. J., et al. (2002). Late life function and disability instrument: II. Development and evaluation of the function component. *Journal of Gerontology: A, Biological Science & Medical Science, 57,* M217–22.

Halfon, N., & Hochstein, M. (2002). Life course health development: An integrated framework for developing health, policy, and research. *The Milbank Quarterly, 80,* 433–79.

Hall, J. A., & Roter, D. L. (2002). Do patients talk differently to male and female physicians? A meta-analytic review. *Patient Education & Counseling, 48,* 217–24.

*Hall, N., & Best, J. A. (1997). Health promotion practice and public health: Challenge for the 1990s. *Canadian Journal of Public Health, 88,* 409–15.

Hallfors, D., Cho, H., Livert, D., & Kadushin, C. (2002). How are community coalitions "Fighting Back" against substance abuse, and are they winning? *American Journal of Preventive Medicine, 23,* 237–45.

Halperin, A. C., & Rigotti, N. A. (2003). U.S. public universities' compliance with recommended tobacco-control policies. *Journal of American College Health, 51,* 181–88.

Haltiwanger, K. A., Hayden, G. F., Weber, T., Evans, B. A., & Possner, A. B. (2001). Antibiotic-seeking behavior in college students: What do they really expect? *Journal of American College Health, 50,* 9–13.

Halverson, P., & Mays, G. P. (2001). Public health assessment. In L. F. Novick & G. P. Mays (Eds.), *Public health administration: Principles for population-based management* (pp. 266–99). Gaithersburg, MD: Aspen Publishers, Inc.

Hamilton, J. L., James, F. W., & Bazargan, M. (2003). Provider practice, overweight and associated risk variables among children from a multi-ethnic underserved community. *Journal of the National Medical Association, 95,* 441–48.

*Han, Y., Baumann, L. C., & Cimprich, B. (1996). Factors influencing registered nurses teaching breast self-examination to female clients. *Cancer Nursing, 19,* 197–203.

Hancock, L., Sanson-Fisher, R. W., Redman, S., et al. (1997). Community action for health promotion: A review of methods and outcomes 1900–1995. *American Journal of Preventive Medicine, 13,* 229–39.

Hanewinkel, R., & Asshauer, M. (2004). Fifteen-month follow-up results of a school-based life-skills approach to smoking prevention. *Health Education Research, 19,* 125–37.

*Hanson, P. (1988–89). Citizen involvement in community health promotion: A rural application of CDC's PATCH Model. *International Quarterly of Health Education, 9,* 177–86.

Hardin, G. (1968). The tragedy of the commons. *Science, 143,* 1243–46.

Harrison, J. A., Mullen, P. D., & Green, L. W. (1992). A meta-analysis of studies of the Health Belief Model. *Health Education Research, 7,* 107–16.

*Harrison, R. L., Li, J., Pearce, K., & Wyman, T. (2003). The community dental facilitator project: Reducing barriers to dental care. *Journal of Public Health Dentistry, 63,* 126–28.

Hart, A. R., Glover, N., Howick-Baker, J., & Mayberry, J. F. (2003). An industry based approach to colorectal cancer screening in an asymptomatic population. *Postgraduate Medical Journal, 79,* 646–49.

Hart, N. (2002). Social, economic, and cultural environment and human health. In R. Detels, J. McEwen, R. Beaglehole, & H. Tanaka (Eds.), *Oxford textbook of public health: Vol. 1: The scope of public health* (p. 89). 4th ed. New York: Oxford University Press.

Harvey, H. D., Fleming, P., & Patterson, M. (2002). Ethical dilemmas and human rights considerations arising from the evaluation of a smoking policy in a health promoting setting. *International Journal of Environmental Health Research, 12,* 269–75.

Hash, R. B., Munna, R. K., Vogel, R. L., & Bason, J. J. (2003). Does physician weight affect perception of health advice? *Preventive Medicine, 36,* 41–44.

*Hatcher, M. E., Green, L. W., Levine, D. M., & Flagle, C. E. (1986). Validation of a decision model for triaging hypertensive patients to alternate health education interventions. *Social Science and Medicine, 22,* 813–19.

Haugland, S., & Wold, B. (2001). Subjective health complaints in adolescence—reliability and validity of survey methods. *Journal of Adolescence, 24,* 611–24.

Haugland, S., Wold, B., Stevenson, J., Aaro, L. E., & Woynarowska, B. (2001). Subjective health complaints in adolescence: A cross-national comparison of prevalence and dimensionality. *European Journal of Public Health, 11,* 4–10.

Haveman, R., Holden, K., Wilson, K., & Wolfe, B. (2003). Social security, age of retirement, and economic well-being: Intertemporal and demographic patterns among retired-worker beneficiaries. *Demography, 40*(2), 369–94.

Hawe, P. (1996). Needs assessment must become more needs focused. *Australian and New Zealand Journal of Public Health, 20,* 473–78.

Hawe, P., Noort, M., King, L., & Jordens, C. (1997). Multiplying health gains: The critical role of capacity-building within health promotion programs. *Health Policy, 39,* 29–42.

Hawe, P., & Shiell, A. (2000). Social capital and health promotion: A review. *Social Science and Medicine, 51*, 871–85.

Haynes, R. B., Taylor, D. W., & Sackett, D. L. (Eds.). (1979). *Compliance in health care*. Baltimore: Johns Hopkins University Press.

Health and Welfare Canada. (1992). *Health promotion in the workplace: A sampling of company programs and initiatives*. Ottawa: Minister of Supply and Services.

*Health Education Center. (1977). *Strategies for health education in local health departments*. Baltimore: Maryland State Department of Health and Mental Hygiene.

Healthy People 2000: National health promotion and disease prevention objectives. (1991). Washington, DC: Public Health Service, U.S. Department of Health and Human Services; and reprinted in Sudbury, MA: Jones and Bartlett Publishers.

*Hecker, E. J. (2000). Feria de Salud: Implementation and evaluation of a communitywide health fair. *Public Health Nursing, 17*, 247–56.

Heffner, J. E., & Ellis, R. (2003). The guideline approach to chronic obstructive pulmonary disease: How effective? *Respiratory Care, 48*, 1257–68.

Heller, R. G., & Page, J. (2002). A population perspective to evidence based medicine: "Evidence for population health." *Journal of Epidemiology and Community Health, 56*, 45–47.

Helmes, A. W. (2002). Application of the protection motivation theory to genetic testing for breast cancer risk. *Preventive Medicine, 35*, 453–62.

*Hendrickson, S. G., & Becker, H. (1998). Impact of a theory-based intervention to increase bicycle helmet use in low income children. *Injury Prevention, 4*, 126–31.

*Herbert, C. P. (1999). Editorial: Should physicians assess lifestyle risk factors routinely? *Canadian Medical Association Journal, 160*, 1849–50.

Herbert, C. P., & Paluck, E. (1997). Can primary care physicians be a resource to their patients in decisions regarding alternative and complementary therapies for cancer? *Patient Education and Counseling, 31*, 179–80.

*Herbert, R., & White, R. (1996). Healthy hearts at work: Prince Edward Island Heart Health Program CSC Worksite Pilot Project. *Canadian Journal of Cardiovascular Nursing 7*(2), 12–18.

Herreria, J. (1998). "Let's Take It Outside" campaign raises awareness, changes attitudes. Kansas Health Foundation. *Profiles in Healthcare Marketing, 14*(5), 19–24.

Hertzman, C., Power, C., Matthews, C., & Manor, O. (2001). Using an interactive framework of society and lifecourse to explain self-rated health in early adulthood. *Social Science and Medicine, 53*, 1575–85.

Heslin, K. C., Andersen, R. M., & Gelberg, L. (2003a). Case management and access to services for homeless women. *Journal of Health Care for the Poor and Underserved, 14*, 34–51.

Heslin, K. C., Andersen, R. M., & Gelberg, L. (2003b). Use of faith-based social service providers in a representative sample of urban homeless women. *Journal of Urban Health, 80*, 371–82.

Hewitt-Taylor, J. (2003). Developing and using clinical guidelines. *Nursing Standards, 18*, 41–44.

*Heywood, A., Firman, D., Sanson-Fisher, R., & Mudge, P. (1996). Correlates of physician counseling associated with obesity and smoking. *Preventive Medicine, 25*, 268–76.

*Hiatt, R. A., Pasick, R. J., Perez-Stable, E. J., et al. (1996). Pathways to early cancer detection in the multiethnic population of the San Francisco Bay area. *Health Education Quarterly, 23* (Suppl.), S10–S27.

Hickman, D. E., Stebbins, M. R., Hanak, J. R., & Guglielmo, B. J. (2003). Pharmacy-based intervention to reduce antibiotic use for acute bronchitis. *The Annals of Pharmacotherapy, 37*, 187–91.

*Hiddink, G. J., Hautvast, J. G. A. J., van Woerkum, C. M. J., Fieren, C. J., & van't Hof, M. A. (1995). Nutrition guidance by primary-care physicians: Perceived barriers and low involvement. *European Journal of Clinical Nutrition, 49*, 842–51.

*Hiddink, G. J., Hautvast, J. G. A. J., van Woerkum, C. M. J., Fieren, C. J. & van't Hof, M. A. (1997a). Consumers' expectations about nutrition guidance: The importance of primary care physicians. *American Journal of Clinical Nutrition, 65* (Suppl.), 1974S–1995S.

*Hiddink, G. J., Hautvast, J. G. A. J., van Woerkum, C. M. J., Fieren, C. J., & van't Hof, M. A. (1997b). Driving forces for and barriers to nutrition guidance practices of Dutch primary care physicians. *Journal of Nutrition Education, 29*(1), 36–41.

*Hiddink, G. J. , Hautvast, J. G. A. J., van Woerkum, C. M. J., Fieren, C. J., & van't Hof, M. A. (1997c). Information sources and strategies of nutrition guidance used by primary care physicians. *American Journal of Clinical Nutrition, 65* (Suppl.), 1996S–2003S.

*Hiddink, G. J., Hautvast, J. G. A. J., van Woerkum, C. E. J., Fieren, C. J. & van't Hof, M. A. (1997d). Nutrition guidance by primary-care physicians: LISREL analysis improves understanding. *Preventive Medicine, 26*, 29–36.

*Hiddink, G. J., Hautvast, J. G. A. J., van Woerkum, C. M. J., van't Hof, M. A., & Fieren, C. J. (1999). Cross-sectional and longitudinal analyses of nutrition guidance by primary care physicians. *European Journal of Clinical Nutrition, 53* (Suppl. 2), S35–S43.

*Higgins, J. W., & MacDonald, M. (1992). *The school-based prevention model: A training handbook*. Victoria, BC: Alcohol and Drug Programs, British Columbia Ministry of Health.

*Hill, A. J. (1996). Predictors of regular physical activity in participants of a Canadian health promotion program. *Canadian Journal of Nursing Research, 28*, 119–41.

Hill, J. (1990). Patient education: What to teach patients with rheumatic disease. *Journal of the Royal Society of Health, 110*, 204–7.

*Hindi-Alexander, M., & Cropp, G. J. (1981). Community and family programs for children with asthma. *Annals of Allergy, 46*, 143–48.

Hinkle, S., Fox-Cardamone, L., Haseleu, J. A., Brown, R., & Irwin, L. M. (1996). Grass roots political action as an intergroup phenomenon. *Journal of Social Issues, 52*, 39–51.

Hochbaum, G. M. (1956). Why people seek diagnostic X-Rays. *Public Health Reports, 71*, 377–80.

Hochbaum, G. M. (1959). *Public participation in medical screening programs: A social-psychological study*. Washington, DC: Public Health Service, PHS–572.

Hoehner, C. M., Brennan, L. K., Brownson, R. C., Handy, S. L., & Killingsworth, R. (2003). Opportunities for integrating public health and urban planning approaches to promote active community environments. *American Journal of Health Promotion, 18*, 14–20.

Hoelscher, D. M., Kelder, S. H., Murray, N., Cribb, P. W., Conroy, J., & Parcel, G. S. (2001). Dissemination and adoption of the child and adolescent trial for cardiovascular health (CATCH): A case study in Texas. *Journal of Public Health Management and Practice, 7*, 90–100.

Hoenig, C. (2000). *The problem solving journey*, Cambridge, MA: Perseus Publishing.

Hoffman, L. M. (1989). The politics of knowledge: Activist movements in medicine and planning. Albany: State University of New York Press.

*Hofford, C. W., & Spelman, K. A. (1996). The community action plan: Incorporating health promotion and wellness into alcohol, tobacco and other drug abuse prevention efforts on the college campus. *Journal of Wellness Perspectives, 12*, 70–79.

Holden, C. (2003). Ecology: "Tragedy of the commons" author dies. *Science, 302*, 32.

Holder, H. D., Gruenewald, P. J., Ponicki, W. R., et al. (2000). Effect of community-based interventions on high-risk drinking and alcohol-related injuries. *Journal of the American Medical Association, 284*, 2341–7.

Holder, H. D., & Treno, A. J. (1997). Media advocacy in community prevention: News as a means to advance policy change. *Addiction, 92*, S189–99.

Hollander, R. B., & Hale, J. G. (1987). Worksite health promotion programs: Ethical issues. *American Journal of Health Promotion, 2*(2), 37–43.

Holley, H. (Ed.). (1998). Quality of life measurement in mental health. *Canadian Journal of Community Mental Health* (Special Suppl. No. 3), Ottawa, Health Canada.

Holm, K., Kremers, S. P., & de Vries, H. (2003). Why do Danish adolescents take up smoking? *European Journal of Public Health, 13*, 67–74.

Holtgrave, D. (1998). *Handbook of economic evaluation of HIV prevention programs.* New York: Plenum Publishing Corp.

Holtzman, D. (2003). Analysis and interpretation of data from the U.S. Behavioral Risk Factor Surveillance System (BRFSS). In D. V. McQueen & P. Puska (Eds.), *Global behavioral risk factor surveillance* (pp. 35–46). New York: Kluwer Academic/Plenum Publishers.

Hopkins, D. P., Briss, P. A., Ricard, C. J., et al. (2001). Task force on community preventive services: Reviews of evidence regarding interventions to reduce tobacco use and exposure to environmental tobacco smoke. *American Journal of Preventive Medicine, 20* (2 Suppl.), 16–66.

Hopkins, D. P., & Fielding, J. E. (Eds.). (2001). The guide to community preventive services: Tobacco use prevention and control, reviews, recommendations, and expert commentary. *American Journal of Preventive Medicine, 20* (Suppl. 2S), 1–88.

*Hopman-Rock, M. (2000). Towards implementing physical activity programmes: The health promotion approach. *Science and Sports, 15*, 180–86.

Horey, D., Weaver, J., & Russell, H. (2004). Information for pregnant women about Caesarean birth. *Cochrane Database Syst Rev, (1)*, CD003858.

*Horowitz, A. M. (1998). Response to Weinstein: Public health issues in early childhood caries. *Community Dentistry and Oral Epidemiology, 26* (Suppl. 1), 91–95.

House, J. S. (1981). *Work stress and social support.* Reading MA: Addison-Wesley.

House, J. S., & Williams, D. R. E. (2000). Understanding and reducing socioeconomic and racial/ethnic disparities in health. In Committee on Capitalizing on Social Science and Behavioral Health to Improve the Public's Health, Institute of Medicine, *Promoting health: Intervention strategies from social and behavioral research.* Washington, DC: National Academy Press.

*Howat, P., Cross, D., Hall, M., et al. (2001). Community participation in road safety: Barriers and enablers. *Journal of Community Health, 26*, 257–69.

*Howat, P., Jones, S., Hall, M., Cross, D., & Stevenson, M. (1997). The PRECEDE-PROCEED model: Application to planning a child pedestrian injury prevention program. *Injury Prevention, 3*, 282–87.

Howse, J. D. (1991). *Lessons learned from the Babies and You Program.* White Plains, NY: March of Dimes Birth Defects Foundation.

Huang, G. H., Palta, M., Allen, C., LeCaire, T., & D'Alessio, D. (2004). Self-rated health among young people with type 1 diabetes in relation to risk factors in a longitudinal study. *American Journal of Epidemiology, 159*, 364–72.

*Huang, Y. W., Green, L. W., & Darling, L. F. (1997). Moral education and health education for elementary school and preschool children in Canada. *Journal of the National School Health Association* (Taiwan), *30*, 23–35.

*Hubball, H. (1996). *Development and evaluation of a worksite health promotion program: Application of critical self-directed learning for exercise behaviour change.* Unpublished doctoral dissertation. Vancouver, BC: University of British Columbia, Faculty of Graduate Studies, Institute of Health Promotion Research.

Hubbard, L., & Ottoson, J. M. (1997). When a bottom-up innovation meets itself as a top-down policy: The AVID untracking program. *Science Communication, 19*, 41–55.

*Huff, R. M., & Kline, M. V. (1999). The cultural assessment framework. In R. M. Huff & M. V. Kline (Eds.), *Promoting health in multicultural populations: A handbook for practitioners.* Thousand Oaks, CA: Sage.

Hughes, L. C., Hodgson, N. A., Muller, P., Robinson, L. A., & McCorkle, R. (2000). Information needs of elderly postsurgical cancer patients during the transition from hospital to home. *Journal of Nursing Scholarship, 32*, 25–30.

Hughes, S. (2003). The use of non face-to-face communication to enhance preventive strategies. *Journal of Cardiovascular Nursing, 18*, 267–73.

Hulscher, M. E., Wensing, M., van Der Weijden, T., & Grol, R. (2001). Interventions to implement prevention in primary care. *Cochrane Database of Systematic Reviews, 1,* CD000362.

Hunnicutt, D. M., Perry-Hunnicutt, C., Newman, I. M., Davis, J. M., & Crawford, J. (1993). Use of the Delphi Technique to support a comprehensive campus alcohol abuse initiative. *Journal of Health Education, 24,* 88–96.

Hunt, M. K., Lederman, R., Stoddard, A., et al. (2000). Process tracking results from the Treatwell 5–a-Day Worksite Study. *American Journal of Health Promotion, 14,* 179–87.

Hunt, M. K., Lefebvre, C., Hixson, M. L., et al. (1990). Pawtucket Heart Health Program point-of-purchase nutrition education program in supermarkets. *American Journal of Public Health, 80,* 730–31.

Hutubessy, R. C., Baltussen, R. M., Torres-Edejer, T. T., & Evans, D. B. (2002). Generalised cost-effectiveness analysis: An aid to decision making in health. *Applied Health Economics and Health Policy, 1,* 89–95.

Hyman, I., & Guruge, S. (2002). Review of theory and health promotion strategies for new immigrant women. *Canadian Journal of Public Health, 93,* 183–87.

Hymowitz, N., Schwab, J., & Eckholdt, H. (2001). Pediatric residency training on tobacco: Training director tobacco survey. *Preventive Medicine, 33,* 688–98.

Ikeda, R., & Dodge, K. A. (Eds.). (2001). Youth violence prevention: The science of moving research to practice. *American Journal of Preventive Medicine, 20* (Suppl. 1S), 1–71.

Iliffe, S., & Lenihan, P. (2003). Integrating primary care and public health: Learning from the community-oriented primary care model. *International Journal of Health Services, 33,* 85–98.

Institute of Medicine. (1997). *Improving health in the community: A role for performance monitoring.* Washington, DC: National Academy Press.

Institute of Medicine. (2001). *Health and behavior: The interplay of biological behavioral, and societal influences.* Washington, DC: National Academy Press.

Institute of Medicine. (2002). *Unequal treatment: Confronting racial and ethnic disparities in health care.* Washington, DC: National Academies Press.

Institute of Medicine. (2003a). *The future of public health in the 21st century.* Washington, DC: The National Academies Press.

Institute of Medicine. (2003b). *Who will keep the public healthy?* Washington, DC: The National Academies Press.

Integration of Risk Factor Interventions. (1986). Washington, DC: ODPHP Monograph Series, U.S. Department of Health and Human Services.

Inui, T. S., Carter, W. B., Kukull, W. A., & Haigh, V. H. (1982). Outcome-based doctor-patient interaction anaylsis: I. Comparison of techniques. *Medical Care, 20,* 535–49.

Iscoe, I. (1974). Community psychology and the competent community. *American Psychologist, August,* 607–13.

Israel, B. A. (1985). Social networks and social support: Implications for natural helper and community level interventions. *Health Education Quarterly, 12,* 65–80.

*Iverson, D. C., & Scheer, J. K. (1982). School-based cancer education programs: An opportunity to affect the national cancer problem. *Health Values: Achieving High Level Wellness, 6*(3), 27–35.

Jacobs, L.A. (2002). Health beliefs of first-degree relatives of individuals with colorectal cancer and participation in health maintenance visits: A population-based survey. *Cancer Nursing, 25,* 251–65.

Jacobs, R. J., Saab, S., & Meyerhoff, A. S. (2003). The cost effectiveness of hepatitis immunization for US college students. *Journal of American College Health, 51,* 227–36.

Jacobsen, P. D., Lantz, P. M., Warner, K. E., Wasserman, J., Pollack, H. A., & Ahlstrom, A. A. (2001). *Combating teen smoking: Research and policy strategies.* Ann Arbor: The University of Michigan Press.

Jamner, M., & Stokols, D. (Eds.). (2000). *Promoting human wellness: New frontiers for research, practice, and policy.* Berkeley, CA: University of California Press.

Janz, N. K., Champion, V. L., & Strecher, V. J. (2002). The health belief model. In K. Glanz, B. K. Rimer, & F. M. Lewis (Eds.), *Health behavior and health education: Theory, research, and practice* (pp. 45–66). 3rd ed. San Francisco: Jossey-Bass.

Jardine, C. G. (2003). Development of a public participation and communication protocol for establishing fish consumption advisories. *Risk Analysis, 23,* 461–71.

*Jenny, J. (1993). A future perspective on patient/health education in Canada. *Journal of Advanced Nursing, 18,* 1408–14.

*Jensen, K. L. (1999). *Lesbian and bisexual epiphanies: Identity deconstruction and reconstruction.* PhD dissertation, Union Institute Graduate School, Cincinnati, Ohio, September 1997, published as *Lesbian Epiphanies: Women Coming Out Later in Life.* Binghamton, NY: Haworth Press, 1999.

Jette, A. M. (1993). Using health related quality of life measures in physical therapy outcomes research, *Physical Therapy 73*: 528–537.

Jette, A. M., & Keysor, J. J. (2002). Uses of evidence in disability outcomes and effectiveness research. *Milbank Quarterly, 80,* 325–45.

*Johnson, C. C., Powers, C. R , Bao, W., Harsha, D. W., & Berenson, G. S. (1994). Cardiovascular risk factors of elementary school teachers in a low socio-economic area of a metropolitan city: The Heart Smart Program. *Health Education Research, 9,* 183–91.

Johnson, L. M., Mullick, R., & Mulford, C. L. (2002). General versus specific victim blaming. *Journal of Social Psychology, 142,* 249–63.

*Jones, C. S., & Macrina, D. (1993). Using the PRECEDE Model to design and implement a bicycle helmet campaign. *Wellness Perspectives: Research, Theory and Practice, 9,* 68–95.

Jones, R. C., Bly, J. L., & Richardson, J. E. (1990). A study of a work site health promotion program and absenteeism. *Journal of Occupational Medicine, 32,* 95–99.

*Jones, S. C., & Donovan, R. J. (2004). Does theory inform practice in health promotion in Australia? *Health Education Research, 19,* 1–14.

Jungers, E. A., Guenthner, S. T., Farmer, E. R., & Perkins, S. M. (2003). A skin cancer education initiative at a professional baseball game and results of a skin cancer survey. *International Journal of Dermatology, 42,* 524–29.

Kahan, B., & Goodstadt, M. (2001). The interactive domain model of best practices in health promotion: Developing and implementing a best practices approach to health promotion. *Health Promotion Practice, 2,* 43–67.

Kahn, E. B., Ramsey, L. T., Brownson, R. C., et al.. (2002). The effectiveness of interventions to increase physical activity: A systematic review. *American Journal of Preventive Medicine, 22* (4S), 73–107.

Kahn, J. A., Goodman, E., Slap, G. B., Huang, B., & Emans, S. J. (2001). Intention to return for Papanicolaou smears in adolescent girls and young women. *Pediatrics, 108* (2, Pt. 1), 333–41.

*Kaiser Family Foundation. (1989). *Strategic plan for the health promotion program, 1989–1991.* Menlo Park, CA: The Henry J. Kaiser Family Foundation.

Kalnins, I., Hart, C., Ballantyne, P., Quartaro, G., Love, R., Sturis, G., & Pollack, P. (2002). Children's perceptions of strategies for resolving community health problems. *Health Promotion International, 17,* 223–33.

Kann, L. K., Collins, J. L., Pateman, B. C., et al. (1995). The School Health Policies and Programs Study (SHPPS): Rationale for a nationwide status report on school health programs. *Journal of School Health, 65,* 291–94.

Kannel, W. B., et al. (1984). Report of the inter-society commission for heart disease resources: Optimal resources for primary prevention of atherosclerotic diseases. *Circulation, 70,* 155A–205A.

Kaplan, C. P., Bastani, R., Belin, T. R., er al. (2000). Improving follow-up after an abnormal pap smear: Results from a quasi-experimental intervention study. *Journal of Women's Health & Gender Based Medicine, 9,* 779–90.

Karanek, N., Sockwell, D., Jia, H., & CDC. (2000). Community indicators of health-related quality of life—United States, 1993–1997. *Morbidity and Mortality Weekly Report, 49,* 281–85.

Karasek, R., & Theorell, T. (1990). *Healthy work: Stress, productivity, and the reconstruction of working life.* New York: Basic Books.

Karpati, A., Galea, S., Awerbuch, T., & Levins, R. (2002). Variability and vulnerability at the ecological level: Implications for understanding the social determinants of health. *American Journal of Public Health, 92,* 1768–72.

Kasper, M. J., Peterson, M. G., & Allegrante, J. P. (2001). The need for comprehensive educational osteoporosis prevention programs for young women: Results from a second osteoporosis prevention survey. *Arthritis & Rheumatism, 45,* 28–34.

Kass, D., & Freudenberg, N. (1997). Coalition building to prevent childhood lead poisoning: A case study from New York City. In M. Minkler (Ed.), *Community organizing and community building for health.* New Brunswick, NJ: Rutgers University Press.

Kass, L. R. (1980). Medical care and the pursuit of health. In C. Lindsay (Ed.), *New directions in public health care* (pp. 16–17). 3rd ed. San Francisco: Institute for Contemporary Studies.

*Kaukiainen, A. (2000). *Promotion of the health of construction workers.* Tampere, Finland: Finnish Institute of Occupational Health, Research Reports 35. (Esp. pp. 24–38, 60–62.)

Kawachi, I. (1999). Social capital and community effects on population and individual health. *Annals of the New York Academy of Sciences, 896,* 120–30.

Kawachi, I., Kennedy, B. P., Lochner, K., & Prothro-Stith, D. (1997). Social capital, income inequality, and mortality. *American Journal of Public Health, 87,* 1491–98.

Kawachi, I., Subramanian, S. V., & Almeida-Fillio, N. (2002). A glossary for health inequalities. *Journal of Epidemiology and Community Health, 56,* 647–52.

Kear, M. E.. (2002). Psychosocial determinants of cigarette smoking among college students. *Journal of Community Health Nursing, 19,* 245–57.

Keating, D. P., & Hertzman, C. (Eds.). (1999). *Developmental health and the wealth of nations: Social, biological and educational dynamics.* New York: Guilford Press.

Keefe, C. W., Thompson, M. E., & Noel, M. M. (2002). Medical students, clinical preventive services, and shared decision-making. *Academic Medicine, 77,* 1160–61.

Kegler, M. C., Crosby, R. A., & DiClemente, R. J. (2002). Reflections on emerging theories in health promotion practice. In R. J. DiClemente, R. A. Crosby, & M. C. Kegler (Eds.), *Emerging theories in health promotion practice and research* (pp. 386–95). San Francisco: Jossey-Bass.

Kegler, M. C., & Wyatt, V. H. (2003). A multiple case study of neighborhood partnerships for positive youth development. *American Journal of Health Behavior, 27,* 156–69.

*Keintz, M. K., Fleisher, L., & Rimer, B. K. (1994). Reaching mothers of preschool-aged children with a targeted quit smoking intervention. *Journal of Community Health, 19,* 25–40.

*Keintz, M. K., Rimer, B. K., Fleisher, L., & Engstrom, P. (1988). Educating older adults about their increased cancer risk. *Gerontologist, 28,* 487–90.

*Keintz, M. K., Rimer, B. K., Fleisher, L., Fox, L., & Engstrom, P. F. (1988). Use of multiple data sources in planning a smoking cessation program for a defined population. In P. F. Engstrom, P. N. Anderson, & L. E. Mortenson (Eds.), *Advances in cancer control: Cancer control research and the emergence of the oncology product line* (pp. 31–42). New York: Alan R. Liss, Inc.

Keith, M. M., Cann, B., Brophy, J. T., Hellyer, D., Day, M., Egan, S., Mayville, K., & Watterson, A. (2001). Identifying and prioritizing gaming workers' health and safety concerns using mapping for data collection. *American Journal of Industrial Medicine, 39,* 42–51.

*Keith, S. E., & Doyle, E. I. (1998). Using PRECEDE/PROCEED to address diabetes within the Choctaw Nation of Oklahoma. *American Journal of Health Behavior, 22,* 358–67.

*Kelly, G. R. (1990). Medication compliance and health education among outpatients with chronic mental disorders. *Medical Care, 28,* 1181–97.

Kemm, J. (2003). Health education: A case for resuscitation. *Public Health, 117,* 106–11.

*Kemper, D. (1986). The healthwise program: Growing younger. In K. Dychtwald (Ed.), *Wellness and health promotion for the elderly* (pp. 263–73). Rockville, MD: Aspen.

Kerlinger, F. N. (1986). *Foundations of behavioral research.* 3rd ed. New York: Holt, Rinehart & Winston.

*Kern, D. E., Thomas, P. A., Howard, D. M., & Bass, E. B. (1998). *Curriculum development for medical education: A six-step approach.* Baltimore: Johns Hopkins University Press.

Kernaghan S. G., & Giloth, B. E. (1988). *Tracking the impact of health promotion on organizations: A key to program survival.* Chicago, IL: American Hospital Association.

Key, M., & Kilian, D. (1983). Counseling and cancer prevention programs in industry. In G. R. Newell (Ed.), *Cancer prevention in clinical medicine.* New York: Raven Press.

Kickbusch, I. (1989). Approaches to an ecological base for public health. *Health Promotion, 4,* 265–68.

Killingsworth, R., Earp, J., & Moore, R. (2003). Supporting health through design: Challenges and opportunities. *American Journal of Health Promotion, 18,* 1–2.

Kim, D. Y., Ridzon, R., Giles, B., et al. (2003). A no-name tuberculosis tracking system. *American Journal of Public Health, 93,* 1637–39.

King, A. C., Stokols, D., Talen, E., Brassington, G. S., & Killingsworth, R. (2002). Theoretical approaches to the promotion of physical activity: Forging a transdisciplinary paradigm. *American Journal of Preventive Medicine, 23* (2 Suppl.), 15–25.

King, T. K., Marcus, B. H., Pinto, B. M., Emmons, K. M., & Abrams, D. B. (1996). Cognitive-behavioral mediators of changing multiple behaviors: Smoking and a sedentary lifestyle. *Preventive Medicine, 25,* 684–91.

Kirby, D. (1997). *No easy answers: Research findings on programs to reduce teen pregnancy.* Washington, DC: The National Campaign to Prevent Teen Pregnancy.

Kironde, S., & Bajunirwe, F. (2002). Lay workers in directly observed treatment (DOT) programmes for tuberculosis in high burden settings: Should they be paid? A review of behavioural perspectives. *African Health Sciences, 2,* 73–78.

Kirscht, J. P. (1974). The health belief model and illness behavior. *Health Education Monographs, 2,* 387–408.

Klein, J. D., Sesselberg, T. S., Gawronski, B., et al. (2003). Improving adolescent preventive services through state, managed care, and community partnerships. *Journal of Adolescent Health, 32* (6 Suppl.), 9–97.

Kline, M. W., & O'Connor, K. G. (2003). Disparity between pediatricians' knowledge and practices regarding perinatal human immunodeficiency virus counseling and testing. *Pediatrics, 112,* e367.

*Knazan, Y. L. (1986). Application of PRECEDE to dental health promotion for a Canadian well-elderly population. *Gerodontics, 2,* 180–85.

Kobus, K. (2003). Peers and adolescent smoking. *Addiction, 98* (Suppl. 1), 37–55.

Koffman, D. M., Lee, J. W., Hopp, J. W., & Emont, S. L. (1998). The impact of including incentives and competition in a workplace smoking cessation program on quit rates. *American Journal Health Promotion, 13,* 105–11.

*Koivula, M., & Paunonen, M. (1998). Smoking habits among Finnish middle-aged men: Experiences and attitudes. *Journal of Advanced Nursing, 27,* 327–34.

*Kok, F. J., Matroos, A. W., van den Ban, A. W., & Hautvast, J. G. A. J. (1982). Characteristics of individuals with multiple behavioral risk factors for coronary heart disease: The Netherlands. *American Journal of Public Health, 72,* 986–91.

Kok, G., van den Borne, B., & Mullen, P. D. (1997). Effectiveness of health education and health promotion: Meta-anayses of effect studies and determinants of effectiveness. *Patient Education and Counseling, 30,* 19–27.

Kolbe, L. J. (1989). Indicators for planning and monitoring school health programs. In S. B. Kar (Ed.), *Health promotion indicators and actions* (pp. 221–48). New York: Springer.

Kolbe, L., Jones, J., Nelson, G., et al. (1988). School health education to prevent the spread of AIDS: Overview of a national programme. *Hygie, 7,* 10–13.

Kolbe, L., Kann, L., Patterson, B., et al. (2004). Enabling the nation's schools to help prevent heart disease, stroke, cancer, COPD, diabetes, and other serious health problems. *Public Health Reports, 119,* 286–302.

Konu, A., & Rimpela, M. (2002). Well-being in schools: A conceptual model. *Health Promotion International, 17,* 79–87.

Korenbrot, C. C., & Moss, N. E. (2000). Preconception, prenatal, perinatal and postnatal influences on health. In *Promoting health: Intervention strategies from social and behavioral research* (pp. 125–69). Washington, DC: National Academy Press.

Kosinski, M., Kujawski, S. C., Martin, R., et al. (2002). Health-related quality of life in early rheumatoid arthritis: Impact of disease and treatment response. *American Journal of Managed Care, 8*(3), 231–40.

Kotchen, J. M., McKean, H. E., Jackson-Thayer, S., et al. (1986). Impact of a rural high blood pressure control program on hypertension control and cardiovascular mortality. *Journal of the American Medical Association, 255,* 2177–82.

*Kotler, P., & Roberto, E. L (1989). *Social marketing: Strategies for changing public behavior.* New York: The Free Press.

Kottke, T. E., Brekke, M. L., & Marquez, M. (1997). Will patient satisfaction set the preventive services implementation agenda? *American Journal of Preventive Medicine, 13,* 309–16.

Kottke, T. E., Puska, P., Solonen, J. T., et.al. (1985). Projected effects of high-risk versus population-based prevention strategies in coronary heart disease. *American Journal of Epidemiology, 121,* 697–704.

*Kovar, P. A., Allegrante, J. P. MacKenzie, R., et al. (1992). Supervised fitness walking in patients with osteoarthritis of the knee: A randomized, controlled trial. *Annals of Internal Medicine, 116,* 529–34.

*Kraft, D. P. (1988). The prevention and treatment of alcohol problems on a college campus. *Journal of Alcohol and Drug Education, 34,* 37–51.

Kreuter, M. W. (1984). Health promotion: The public health role in the community of free exchange. *Health promotion monographs,* no. 4. New York: Teachers College, Columbia University.

Kreuter, M. W. (1989). Activity, health, and the public. In *Academy Papers,* Chap. 15. Reston, VA: Academy of Physical Education, Alliance for Health, Physical Education, Recreation and Dance.

*Kreuter, M. W. (1992). PATCH: Its origin, basic concepts, and links to contemporary public health policy. *Journal of Health Education, 23*(3), 135–39.

Kreuter, M. W., Christenson, G. M., & DiVincenzo, A. (1982). The multiplier effect of the Health Education-Risk Reduction Grants Program in 28 states and 1 territory. *Public Health Reports, 97,* 510–15.

Kreuter, M. W., Christianson, G. M., Freston, M., & Nelson, G. (1981). In search of a baseline: The need for risk prevalence surveys. In *Proceedings of the annual National Risk Reduction Conference.* Atlanta, GA: Centers for Disease Control.

Kreuter, M. W., DeRosa, C. R., Howze, E., & Baldwin, G. (2004). Understanding wicked problems: A key to environmental health promotion. *Health Education and Behavior, 31,* (in press).

Kreuter, M. W., & Lezin, N. S. (2002). Social capital theory: Implications for community-based health promotion. In R. J. DiClementi, R. A. Crosby, & M. C. Kegler (Eds.), *Emerg-*

ing theories in health promotion practice and research: Strategies for improving public health (pp. 228–54). San Francisco: Jossey-Bass.

Kreuter, M. W., Lezin, N., & Young, L. (2000). Evaluating community-based collaborative mechanisms: Implications for practitioners. *Health Promotion Practice, 1*, 49–63.

*Kreuter, M. W., Lezin, N., Kreuter, Matt. W., & Green, L. W. (2003). *Community health promotion ideas that work: A field-book for practitioners.* 2nd ed. Sudbury, MA: Jones and Bartlett.

Kreuter, M. W., Lezin, N., Young, L., & Koplan, A. N. (2001). Social capital: Evaluation implications for community health promotion. *WHO Registered Publication of European Service, 92*, 439–62.

Kreuter, Matt. W., Caburnay, C. A., Chen, J. J., & Donlin, M. J. (2004). Effectiveness of individually tailored calendars in promoting childhood immunization in urban public health centers. *American Journal of Public Health, 94*, 122–27.

Kreuter, Matt. W., Oswald, D. L., Bull, F. C., & Clark, E. M. (2000). Are tailored health education materials always more effective than non-tailored materials? *Health Education Research, 15*, 305–15.

Kreuter, Matt. W., Vehige, E., & McGuire, A. G. (1996). Using computer-tailored calendars to promote childhood immunization. *Public Health Reports, III*, 176–78.

Krieger, J. W., Cheadle, A. C., Higgins, D., Schier, J., Senturia, K., & Sullivan, M. (2002). Using community-based participatory research to address social determinants of health: Lessons learned from Seattle Partners for Healthy Communities. *Health Education and Behavior, 29*, 361–82.

Krieger, N. (1994). Epidemiology and the web of causation: Has anyone seen the spider? *Social Science and Medicine, 39*, 887–903.

*Kristal, A. R., Patterson, R. E., Glanz, K., Heimendinger, J., Herbert, J. R., Feng, Z., & Probart, C. (1995). Psychosocial correlates of healthful diets: Baseline results from the Working Well study. *Preventive Medicine, 24*, 221–28.

*Kroger, F. (1994). Toward a healthy public. *American Behavioral Scientist, 38*, 215–23.

Krueger, R. A., & Casey, M. A. (2000). *Focus groups: A practical guide for applied research.* 3rd ed. Newbury Park, CA: Sage.

Krumm, J. (2002). Genetic discrimination. Why Congress must ban genetic testing in the workplace. *Journal of Legislative Medicine, 23*(4), 491–521.

*Kukafka, R., Johnson, S. B., Linfante, A., & Allegrante, J. P. (2003). Grounding a new information technology implementation framework in behavioral science: A systematic analysis of the literature on IT use. *Journal of Biomedical Information, 36*, 218–27.

Kukafka, R., Lussier, Y. A., Eng, P., Patel, V. L., & Cimino, J. J. (2002). Web-based tailoring and its effect on self-efficacy: Results from the MI-HEART randomized controlled trial. *Proceedings of the AMIA Symposium*, 410–14.

Kurtz, N. Rk., Googins, B., & Howard, W. C. (1984). Measuring the success of occupational alcoholism programs. *Journal of Studies on Alcohol, 45*, 35–45.

Kwait, J., Valente, T. W., & Celentano, D. D. (2001). Interorganizational relationships among HIV/AIDS service organizations in Baltimore: A network analysis. *Journal of Urban Health, 78*, 468–87.

Kwon, E. H. (1971). Use of the agent system in Seoul. *Studies in Family Planning, 2*, 237–340.

Laatikainen, T., Delong, L., Pokusajeva, S., et al. (2002). Changes in cardiovascular risk factors and health behaviours from 1992 to 1997 in the Republic of Karelia, Russia. *European Journal of Public Health, 1*, 37–43.

*Lafontaine, G., & Bedard, L. (1997). La prevention des infections dans les services de garde a l'enfance: Les facteurs potentials d'influence (Prevention of infections in daycare centers: Potential factors to monitor). *Canadian Journal of Public Health, 88*, 250–54.

*Laitakari, J., Miilunpalo, S., & Vuori, I. (1997). The process and methods of health counseling by primary health care personnel in Finland: A national survey. *Patient Education and Counseling, 30*, 61–70.

Lakati, A., Binns, C., & Stevenson, M. (2003). Breast-feeding and the working mother in Nairobi. *Public Health Nutrition, 5,* 715–18.

LaLonde, M. A. (1974). *A new perspective on the health of Canadians.* Ottawa, Canada: Ministry of National Health and Welfare.

*Lam, T. K., McPhee, S. J., Mock, J., et al. (2003). Encouraging Vietnamese-American women to obtain Pap tests through lay health worker outreach and media education. *Journal of General Internal Medicine, 18,* 516–24.

Lambert, D., Donahue, A., Mitchell, M., & Strauss, R. (2003). *Rural mental health outreach: Promising practices in rural areas.* Rockville, MD: Substance Abuse and Mental Health Services Administration, U.S. Department of Health and Human Services.

Lancaster, T., & Stead, L. F. (2002). Self-help interventions for smoking cessation. *Cochrane Database of Systematic Reviews, 3,* CD001118.

Lando, H. A., Loken, B., Howard-Pitney, B., & Pechacek, T. (1990). Community impact of a localized smoking cessation contest. *American Journal of Public Health, 80,* 601–3.

Lando, H. A., McGovern, P. G., Barrios, F. X., & Etringer, B. D. (1990). Comparative evaluation of American Cancer Society and American Lung Association smoking cessation clinics. *American Journal of Public Health, 80,* 554–59.

*Langille, D. B., Mann, K. V., & Gailiunas, P. N. (1997). Primary care physicians' perceptions of adolescent pregnancy and STD prevention practices in a Nova Scotia county. *American Journal of Preventive Medicine, 13,* 324–30.

Larson, E. L. (2003). Status of practice guidelines in the United States: CDC guidelines as an example. *Preventive Medicine, 36,* 519–24.

*Larson, E. L., Bryan, J. L., Adler, L. M., & Blane, C. (1997). A multifaceted approach to changing handwashing behavior. *American Journal of Infection Control, 25,* 3–10.

*Larson, E. L., McGeer, A., Quraishi, Z. A., et al. (1991). Effect of an automated sink on handwashing practices and attitudes in high-risk units. *Infection Control and Hospital Epidemiology, 12,* 422–27.

*Lasater, T., Abrams, D., Artz, L., et al. (1984). Lay volunteer delivery of a community-based cardiovascular risk factor change program: The Pawtucket experiment. In J. D. Matarazzo, S. M. Weiss, J. A. Herd, et al., (Eds.), *Behavioral health: A handbook of health enhancement and disease prevention.* New York: Wiley.

Lasker, R., Weiss, E., & Miller, R. (2001). Parnership synergy: A practical framework for studying and strengthening the collaborative advantage. *Milbank Quarterly, 79,* 179–205.

Last, J. (2000). *Dictionary of epidemiology.* 4th ed. New York: Oxford University Press.

Last, J. (2002). Health. In L. Breslow, B. D. Goldstein, L. W. Green, et al. (Eds.), *Encyclopedia of public health,* Vol. 2 (pp. 519–26). New York: Macmillan Reference USA, Gale Group.

Last, J., & McGinnis, J. M. (2003). The determinants of health. In F. D. Scutchfield & C. W. Keck (Eds.), *Principles of public health practice* (pp. 45–58). 2nd ed. Clifton Park, NY: Delmar Learning.

Laverack, G., & Wallerstein, N. (2001). Measuring community empowerment: A fresh look at organizational domains. *Health Promotion International, 16,* 179–85.

Lawrence, J. M., Watkins, M. L., Ershoff, D., et al. (2003). Design and evaluation of interventions promoting periconceptional multivitamin use. *American Journal of Preventive Medicine, 25,* 17–24.

Lawverc, S., Mahoney, M. C., Englert, J. J., et al. (2003). Nurse practitioners' knowledge, practice and attitudes about tobacco cessation and lung cancer screening. *Journal of the American Academy of Nurse Practitioners, 15,* 376–81.

*Lazovich, D. A., Parker, D. L., Brosseau, L. M., Milton, T., & Dugan, S. (2002). Effectiveness of a worksite intervention to reduce occupational exposure: The Minnesota Wood Dust Study. *American Journal of Public Health, 92,* 1498–1505.

Lechner, L., & De Vries, H. (1995). Participation in an employee fitness program: Determinants of high adherence, low adherence, and dropout. *Journal of Occupational and Environmental Medicine, 37,* 429–36.

Lee, M. C. (2000). Knowledge, barriers, and motivators related to cervical cancer screening among Korean-American women: A focus group approach. *Cancer Nursing, 23,* 168–75.

*Lee, M., Lee, F., & Stewart, S. (1996). Pathways to early breast and cervical detection for Chinese American women. *Health Education and Behavior, 23* (Suppl.), S76–S88.

Lee, V. P. (2001). Public health data acquisition. In L. F. Novick & G. P. Mays (Eds.), *Public health administration: Principles for population-based management* (pp. 171–201). Gaithersburg, MD: Aspen Publishers.

*Lefebvre, C. R., Doner, C. L., Johnston, C., et al. (1995). Use of database marketing and consumer-based health communication in message design: An example from the Office of Cancer Communications' "5 a Day for Better Health" Program. In E. Maibach & R. L. Parrott (Eds.), *Designing health messages: Approaches from communication theory and public health practice* (pp. 217–46). Thousand Oaks, CA: Sage.

Lefebvre, C. R., & Flora, J. A. (1988). Social marketing and public health intervention. *Health Education Quarterly, 15,* 299–315.

Lefebvre, R. C., Peterson, G. S., McGraw, S. A., et al. (1986). Community intervention to lower blood cholesterol: The "Know Your Cholesterol" campaign in Pawtucket, Rhode Island. *Health Education Quarterly, 13,* 117–29.

*Lehoux, P., Potvin, L., & Proulx, M. (1999). Linking users' views with utilization processes in the evaluation of interactive software. *The Canadian Journal of Program Evaluation, 14,* 117–40.

*Lehoux, P., Proulx, M., Potvin, L., & Green, L. (1997). An evaluation in Montreal of interactive software to support decisions in planning screening mammography programs [abstract]. *Annual Meeting of International Society of Technology Assessment in Health Care, 13,* 94.

*Lelong, N., Kaminski, M., Chwalow, J., Bean, K., & Subtil, D. (1995). Attitudes and behavior of pregnant women and health professionals towards alcohol and tobacco consumption. *Patient Education and Counseling, 25,* 39–49.

Leo, R. (1996). Research note. Managing workplace stress: A Canadian study among resource managers. *Work and Stress, 10,* 183–91.

*Leppik, I. E. (1990). How to get patients with epilepsy to take their medication: The problem of noncompliance. *Postgraduate Medicine, 88,* 253–56.

*Levin, S., Martin, M. W., McKenzie, T. L., & DeLouise, A. C. (2002). Assessment of a pilot video's effect on physical activity and heart health for young children. *Family and Community Health, 25,* 10–17.

*Levine, D. M., Fedder, D. O., Green, L. W., et al. (National High Blood Pressure Education Program Working Group on Health Education in High Blood Pressure Control). (1987). *The physician's guide: Improving adherence among hypertensive patients.* Bethesda, MD: National Heart, Lung, and Blood Institute, National Institutes of Health.

*Levine, D. M., & Green, L. W. (1981). Cardiovascular risk reduction: An interdisciplinary approach to research training. *International Journal of Health Education, 24,* 20–25.

*Levine, D. M., Green, L. W., Deeds, S. G., et al. (1979). Health education for hypertensive patients. *Journal of the American Medical Association, 241,* 1700–3.

*Levine, D. M., Green, L. W., Russell, R. P., Morisky, D., Chwalow, A. J., & Benson, P. (1979). Compliance in hypertension management: What the physician can do. *Practical Cardiology, 5,* 151–60.

*Levine, D. M., Morisky, D. E., Bone, L. R., Lewis, C., Ward, W. B., & Green, L. W. (1982). Data-based planning for educational interventions through hypertension control programs for urban and rural populations in Maryland. *Public Health Reports, 97,* 107–12.

Levine, S., White, P., & Scotch, N. (1963). Community interorganizational problems in providing medical care and social services. *American Journal of Public Health, 53,* 1183–95.

Levit, K. R., Freeland, M. S., & Waldo, D. R. (1989). Health spending and ability to pay: Business, individuals, and government. *Health Care Financing Review, 10*(2), 1–11.

Leviton, L. C., & Valdiserri, R. O. (1990). Evaluating AIDS prevention: Outcome, implementation, and mediating variables. *Evaluation and Program Planning, 13,* 55–66.

Levy, D. T., & Friend, K. B. (2003). The effects of clean indoor air laws: What do we know and what do we need to know? *Health Education Research, 18,* 592–609.

Levy, S. R., Baldyga, W., & Jurkowski, J. M. (2003). Developing community health promotion interventions: Selecting partners and fostering collaboration. *Health Promotion Practice, 4,* 314–22.

Lewis, B., Mann, J. I., & Mancini, M. (1986). Reducing the risks of coronary heart disease in individuals and in the population. *Lancet, 14,* 956–59.

*Li, V. C., Coates, T. J., Spielberg, L. A., et al. (1984). Smoking cessation with young women in public family planning clinics: The impact of physician messages and waiting room media. *Preventive Medicine, 13,* 477–89.

*Lian, W. M., Gan, L., Pin, C. H., Wee, S., & Ye, H. C. (1999). Determinants of leisure-time physical activity in an elderly population in Singapore. *American Journal of Public Health, 89,* 1578–80.

*Liburd, L. C., & Bowie, J. V. (1989). Intentional teenage pregnancy: A community diagnosis and action plan. *Health Education, 20,* 33–38.

*Light, L., & Contento, I. R. (1989). Changing the course: A school nutrition and cancer education program by the American Cancer Society and the National Cancer Institute. *Journal of School Health, 59,* 205–9.

Ling, P. M., & Glantz, S. A. (2002). Using tobacco-industry marketing research to design more effective tobacco-control campaigns. *Journal of the American Medical Association, 287,* 2983–89.

Linnan, L. A., Emmons, K. M., Klar, N., et al. (2002). Challenges to improving the impact of worksite cancer prevention programs: Comparing reach, enrollment, and attrition using active versus passive recruitment strategies. *Annals of Behavioral Medicine, 24,* 157–66.

Linnan, L. A., Sorensen, G., Colditz, G., Klar, D. N., & Emmons, K. M. (2001). Using theory to understand the multiple determinants of low participation in worksite health promotion programs. *Health Education Behavior, 28,* 591–607.

Linstone, H. A., & Turoff, M. (1975). *The Delphi Method: Techniques and applications.* Reading, MA: Addison-Wesley.

*Lipnickey, S. C. (1986). Application of the PRECEDE Model to a school-based program of drug, alcohol and tobacco education. [microform] ERIC database ED281126 Government Publications / Microforms Div. 12pp. Paper presented at the Annual Meeting of the American Public Health Association (114th, Las Vegas, NV, Sept. 28–Oct. 2, 1986).

Lipscomb, H. J., Dement, J. M., & Li, L. (2003). Health care utilization of carpenters with substance abuse-related diagnoses. *American Journal of Industrial Medicine, 43,* 120–31.

Litaker, D., Mion, L., Planavsky, L., et al. (2003). Physician–nurse practitioner teams in chronic disease management: The impact on costs, clinical effectiveness, and patients' perception of care. *Journal of Interprofessional Care, 17,* 223–37.

*Liu, C., & Feekery, C. (2001). Can asthma education improve clinical outcomes? An evaluation of a pediatric asthma education program. *Journal of Asthma, 38,* 269–78.

*Livingston, I. L. (1985). Hypertension and health education intervention in the Caribbean: A public health appraisal. *Journal of the National Medical Association, 77,* 273–80.

Lochner, K. A., Kawachi, I., Brennan, R. T., & Buka, S. L. (2003). Social capital and neighborhood mortality rates in Chicago. *Social Science & Medicine, 56,* 1797–805.

*Lohrmann, D. K., & Fors, S. W. (1986). Can school-based educational programs really be expected to solve the adolescent drug abuse problem? *Journal of Drug Education, 16,* 327–39.

*Lomas, J. (1993). Diffusion, dissemination, and implementation: Who should do what? In K. S. Warren & F. Mosteller (Eds.), *Doing more good than harm: The evaluation of health care interventions,* Vol. 703 (pp. 226–37). New York: Annals of the New York Academy of Sciences.

*Lomas, J., & Haynes, R. B. (1988). A taxonomy and critical review of tested strategies for the application of clinical practice recommendations: From "official" to "individual" clinical policy. *American Journal of Preventive Medicine, 4* (Suppl.), 77–94.

London, L., Benjamin, P., & Bass, D. H. (2002). HIV testing and the Employment Equity Act: Putting an end to the confusion. *South African Medical Journal, 92*(3), 199–201.

Lopez-Escobar, E., Llamas, J. P., & McCombs, M. (1998). Agenda setting and community consensus: First and second level effects. *International Journal of Public Opinion Research, 10,* 335–45.

Lorence, D. P., & Richards, M. C. (2003). Adoption of regulatory compliance programmes across United States healthcare organizations: A view of institutional disobedience. *Health Services Management Research, 16,* 167–78.

Lorig, K. R., & Holman, H. (2003). Self-management education: History, definition, outcomes, and mechanisms. *Annals of Behavioral Medicine, 26,* 1–7.

Lorig, K. R., Laurent, D. D., Deyo, R. A., et al. (2002). Can a back pain e-mail discussion group improve health status and lower health care costs? A randomized study. *Archives of Internal Medicine, 162,* 792–96.

*Lorig, K. R., & Laurin, J. (1985). Some notions about assumptions underlying health education. *Health Education Quarterly, 12,* 231–43.

Lorig, K. R., Ritter, P. L., Stewart, A. L., et al. (2001). Chronic disease self-management program: 2–year health status and health care utilization outcomes. *Medical Care, 39,* 1217–23.

Lorig, K. R., Stewart, A., Ritter, P., et al. (1996). *Outcome measures for health education and other health care interventions.* Thousand Oaks, CA: Sage.

*Lovato, C. Y., & Green, L. W. (1990). Maintaining employee participation in workplace health promotion programs. *Health Education Quarterly, 17,* 73–88.

Lovato, C. Y., Green, L. W., & Stainbrook, G. (1993). The benefits perceived by industry in supporting health promotion programs in the worksite. In J. P. Opatz (Ed.), *Economic impact of worksite health promotion* (pp. 3–31). Champaign, IL: Human Kinetics Press.

*Lovato, C., Potvin, L., Lehoux, P., et al. (2003). Implementation and use of software designed for program planning: A case study. *Promotion & Education: International Journal of Health Promotion & Education, 10,* 120–26.

Love, M. B., Davoli, G. W., & Thurman, Q. C. (1996). Normative beliefs of health behavior professionals regarding the psychosocial and environmental factors that influence health behavior change related to smoking cessation, regular exercise, and weight loss. *American Journal of Health Promotion, 10,* 371–79.

Loveman, E., Cave, C., Green, C., et al. (2003). The clinical and cost-effectiveness of patient education models for diabetes: A systematic review and economic evaluation. *Health Technology Assessment, 7*(iii), 1–190.

Lowe, J. B., Windsor, R., & Woodby, L. (1997). Smoking relapse prevention methods for pregnant women: A formative evaluation. *American Journal of Health Promtion, 11,* 244–46.

Lowry, R., Kann, L., & Kolbe, L. J. (1996). The effect of socioeconomic status on chronic disease risk behaviors among US adolescents. *Journal of the American Medical Association, 276,* 792–97.

Luepker, R., Perry, C., McKinlay, S., et al. (1996). Outcomes of a field trial to improve children's dietary patterns and physical activity: The child and adolescent trial for cardiovascular health. *Journal of the American Medical Association, 275*, 768–76.

Lutzen, K., Cronqvist, A., Magnusson, A., & Andersson, L. (2003). Moral stress: Synthesis of a concept. *Nursing Ethics, 10*, 312–22.

*Lux, K. M., & Petosa, R. (1994). Preventing HIV infection among juvenile delinquents: Educational diagnosis using the health belief model. *International Quarterly of Community Health Education, 15*, 145–64.

*Macarthur, A., Macarthur, C., & Weeks, S. (1995). Epidural anaesthesia and low back pain after delivery: A prospective cohort study. *British Medical Journal, 311*, 1336–39.

Macaulay, A. C., Commanda, L. E., Freeman, W. L., et al. (1999). Participatory research maximises community and lay involvement. North American Primary Care Research Group. *British Medical Journal, 319*, 774–78.

*Macaulay, A. C., Paradis, G., Potvin, L., et al. (1997). The Kahnawake schools diabetes prevention project: Intervention, evaluation, and baseline results of a diabetes primary prevention program with a native community in Canada. *Preventive Medicine, 26*, 779–90.

*MacDonald, M., & Green, L.W. (1994). Health promotion and adolescent health. In R. Tonkin (Ed.), *Current issues of the adolescent patient* (pp. 227–45). London: Baillier's Clinical Paediatrics.

*MacDonald, M., & Green, L. W. (1994). Health education. In A. Lewy (Ed.), *International encyclopedia of education*. London: Pergamon Press.

*MacDonald, M. A., & Green, L. W. (2001). Reconciling concept and context: The dilemma of implementation in school-based health promotion. *Health Education & Behavior, 28*, 749–68.

MacIntyre, C. R., Goebel, K., Brown, G. V., et al. (2003). A randomised controlled clinical trial of the efficacy of family-based direct observation of anti-tuberculosis treatment in an urban, developed-country setting. *International Journal of Tuberculosis & Lung Disease, 7*, 848–54.

Mackie, J. W., & Oickle, P. (1997). School-based health promotion: The physician as advocate. *Canadian Medical Association Journal, 156*, 1301–5.

MacQueen, K. M., McLellan, E., Metzger, D. S., et al. (2001). What is community? An evidence-based definiition for participatory research. *American Journal of Public Health, 91*, 1929–38.

*Macrina, D., Macrina, N., Horvath, C., Gallaspy, J., & Fine, P. R. (1996). An educational intervention to increase use of the Glasgow Coma Scale by emergency department personnel. *International Journal of Trauma Nursing, 2*, 7–12.

Macrina, D. M., & O'Rourke, T. W. (1986–87). Citizen participation in health planning in the U.S. and the U.K.: Implications for health education strategies. *International Quarterly of Community Health Education, 7*, 225–39.

Maes, S., Spielberger, C. D., Defares, P. B., & Sarason, I. G. (Eds.). (1988). *Topics in health psychology*. New York: Wiley.

*Mahloch, J., Taylor, V., Taplin, S., & Urban, N. (1993). A breast cancer screening educational intervention targeting medical office staff. *Health Education Research, 8*, 567–79.

Maibach, E. W., Rothschild, M. L., & Novelli, W. D. (2002). Social marketing. In K. Glanz, B. K. Rimer, & F. M. Lewis, *Health behavior and health education: Theory, research, and practice* (pp. 437–61). 3rd ed. San Francisco: Jossey-Bass.

*Maiburg, H. J. S., Hiddink, G. J., van't Hof, M. A., Rethans, J. J., & van Ree, J. W. (1999). The NECTAR-Study: Development of nutrition modules for general practice vocational training; determinants of nutrition guidance practices of GP-trainees. *European Journal of Clinical Nutrition, 53* (Suppl. 2), S83–S88.

*Maiman, L. A., Green, L. W., Gibson, G., & MacKenzie, E. J. (1979). Education for self-treatment by adult asthmatics. *Journal of the American Medical Association, 241*, 1919–22.

Makdisi, J. M. (2001). Genetic privacy: New intrusion a new tort? *Creighton Law Review, 34*(4), 965–1026.

*Makrides, L., Veinot, P. L., Richard, J., & Allen, M. J. (1997). Primary care physicians and coronary heart disease prevention: A practice model. *Patient Education & Counseling, 32,* 207–17.

Malo, E., & Leviton, L. C. (1987). Decision points for hospital-based health promotion. *Hospital and Health Services Administration, 32,* 49–61.

*Mamon, J., Green, L. W., Gibson, G., Gurley, H. T., & Levine, D. M. (1987). Using the emergency department as a screening site for high blood pressure control: Development of a methodology to improve hypertension detection and appropriate referral. *Medical Care, 25,* 770–80.

*Mamon, J. A., & Zapka, J. G. (1986). Breast self-examination by young women. I. Characteristics associated with frequency. *American Journal of Preventive Medicine, 2,* 61–69.

Mann, J. (2002). Discrepancies in nutritional recommendations: The need for evidence based nutrition. *Asia Pacific Journal of Clinical Nutrition, 11* (Suppl 3), S510–15.

*Mann, K. V. (1989). Promoting adherence in hypertension: A framework for patient education. *Canadian Journal of Cardiovascular Nursing, 1,* 8–14.

*Mann, K. V. (1994). Educating medical students: Lessons from research in continuing education. *Academic Medicine, 69,* 41–47.

*Mann, K. V., Lindsay, E. A., Putnam, R. W., & Davis, D. A. (1996). Increasing physician involvement in cholesterol-lowering practices. *Journal of Continuing Education in the Health Professions, 16,* 225–40.

*Mann, K. V., & Putnam, R.W. (1989). Physicians' perceptions of their role in cardiovascular risk reduction. *Preventive Medicine, 18,* 45–58.

*Mann, K. V., & Putnam, R. W. (1990). Barriers to prevention: Physician perceptions of ideal versus actual practices in reducing cardiovascular risk. *Canadian Family Physician, 36,* 665–70.

*Mann, K. V., Putman, R. W., Lindsay, E. A., & Davis, D. A. (1990). Cholesterol: Decreasing the risk. An educational program for physicians. *Journal of Continuing Education in the Health Professions, 10,* 211–22.

*Mann, K. V., & Sullivan, P. L. (1987). Effect of task-centered instructional programs on hypertensives' ability to achieve and maintain reduced dietary sodium intake. *Patient Education and Counseling, 10,* 53–72.

*Mann, K. V., Viscount, P. W., Cogdon, A., et al. (1996). Multidisciplinary learning in continuing professional education: The heart health Nova Scotia experience. *Journal of Continuing Education in the Health Professions, 16,* 50–60.

Mann, S., Sripathy, K., Siegler, E. L., et al. (2001). The medical interview: Differences between adult and geriatric outpatients. *Journal of the American Geriatric Society, 49,* 65–71.

Manne, S., Markowitz, A., Winawer, S., et al. (2002). Correlates of colorectal cancer screening compliance and stage of adoption among siblings of individuals with early onset colorectal cancer. *Health Psychology, 21,* 3–15.

Manne, S., Markowitz, A., Winawer, S., et al. (2003). Understanding intention to undergo colonoscopy among intermediate-risk siblings of colorectal cancer patients: A test of a mediational model. *Preventive Medicine, 36,* 71–84.

Manocchia, M., Keller, S., & Ware, J. E. (2001). Sleep problems, health-related quality of life, work functioning and health care utilization among the chronically ill. *Quality of Life Research, 10,* 331–45.

Manoff, R. K. (1985). *Social marketing: New imperative for public health.* New York: Praeger.

*Mantell, J. E., DiVittis, A. T., & Auerbach, M. I. (1997). *Evaluating HIV Prevention Interventions.* New York: Plenum Press (Medical & Health Research Association of New York City and HIV Center for Clinical & Behavioral Studies, New York State Psychiatric Institute, NY; especially pp 199–203).

Marcell, A. V., Halpern-Felsher, B., Coriell, M., & Millstein, S. G. (2002). Physicians' attitudes and beliefs concerning alcohol abuse prevention in adolescents. *American Journal of Preventive Medicine, 22,* 49–55.

Marchand, A., Demers, A., Durand, P., & Simard, M. (2003). The moderating effect of alcohol intake on the relationship between work strains and psychological distress. *Journal of Studies on Alcohol, 64,* 419–27.

Marcus, B. H., Lewis, B. A., King, T. K., et al. (2003). Rationale, design, and baseline data for Commit to Quit II: An evaluation of the efficacy of moderate-intensity physical activity as an aid to smoking cessation in women. *Preventive Medicine, 36,* 479–92.

Marcy, T. W., Thabault, P., Olson, J., et al. (2003). Smoking status identification: Two managed care organizations' experiences with a pilot project to implement identification systems in independent practice associations. *American Journal of Managed Care, 9,* 672–76.

Markland, R. E., & Vincent, M. L. (1990). Improving resource allocation in a teenage sexual risk reduction program. *Socio-Economic Planning Science, 24,* 35–48.

Marks, R., & Allegrante, J. P. (2001). Nonoperative management of osteoarthritis. *Critical Reviews in Physical and Rehabilitative Medicine, 13,* 131–58.

Marks, R., & Allegrante, J. P. (2002). Comorbid disease profiles of adults with end-stage hip osteoarthritis. *Medical Science Monitor, 8*(4), CR305–9.

Marks, R., Allegrante, J. P., Ronald MacKenzie, C., & Lane, J. M. (2003). Hip fractures among the elderly: Causes, consequences and control. *Ageing Research Reviews, 2,* 57–93.

Marlatt, G. A., & Gordon, J. R. (Eds.). (1985). *Relapse prevention: Maintenance strategies in the treatment of addictive behaviors.* New York: Guilford Press.

Marmot, M. (2000). Social determinants of health: From observation to policy. *Medical Journal of Australia, 17,* 541–44.

Marmot, M. G., Rose, G., Shipley, M., & Hamilton, P. J. (1978). Employment grade and coronary heart disease in British civil servants. *Journal of Epidemioliology & Community Health, 32,* 244–49.

Marmot, M., & Wilkenson, R. G. (Eds.). (1999). *Social determinants of health.* New York: Oxford University Press.

*Marsick, V. J. (1987). Designing health education programs. In P. M. Lazes, L. H. Kaplan, & K. A. Gordon (Eds.). *Handbook of health education,* Chap. 1 (pp. 3–30). 2nd ed. Rockville, MD: Aspen.

Martin, C., & Stainbrook, G. L. (1986). An analysis checklist for audiovisuals when used as educational resources. *Health Education, 17*(4), 31–33.

Marx, E., Wooley, S. G., & Northrop, D. (1998). *Health is academic: A guide to coordinated school health programs.* New York: Teachers College Press.

Mason, J. O., & McGinnis, J. M. (1985). The role of school health. *Journal of School Health, 55,* 299.

*Mathews, C., Everett, K., Binedell, J., & Steinberg, M. (1995). Learning to listen: Formative research in the development of AIDS education for secondary school students. *Social Science and Medicine, 41,* 1715–24.

Maurer, T. J., Weiss, E. M., & Barbeite, F. G. (2003). A model of involvement in work-related learning and development activity: The effects of individual, situational, motivational, and age variables. *Journal of Applied Psychology, 88,* 707–24.

Max, W. (2001). The financial impact of smoking on health-related costs: A review of the literature. *American Journal of Health Promotion, 15,* 321–31.

*Maxwell, A. E., Bastani, R., & Warda, U. S. (1998). Mammography utilization and related attitudes among Korean-American women. *Women and Health, 27,* 89–107.

Mays, G. P., Halverson, P. K., & Stevens, R. (2001). The contributions of managed care plans to public health practice: Evidence from the nation's largest local health departments. *Public Health Reports, 116* (Suppl. 1), 50–67.

Mazmanian, D., & Sabatier, P. (1983). *Implementation and public policy* (preface). Glenview, IL: Scott, Foresman.

McAlister, A., Mullen, P. D., Nixon, S. A., et al. (1985). Health promotion among primary care physicians in Texas. *Texas Medicine, 81,* 55–58.

*McAlister, A., Puska, P., Salonen, J. T., et al. (1982). Theory and action for health promotion: Illustrations from the North Karelia Project. *American Journal of Public Health, 72,* 43–50.

McAuley, E., Jerome, G. J., Elavsky, S., Marquez, D. X., & Ramsey, S. N. (2003). Predicting long-term maintenance of physical activity in older adults. *Preventive Medicine, 37,* 110–18.

McCombs, M. E., Shaw, D. L., & Weaver, D. (Eds.). (1997). *Communication and democracy: Exploring the intellectual frontiers of agenda-setting theory.* Mahwah, NJ: Lawrence Erlbaum Associates.

McCormick, L. K., Steckler, A. B., & McLeroy, K. R. (1995). Diffusion of innovations in schools: A study of adoption and implementation of school-based tobacco prevention curricula. *American Journal of Health Promotion, 9,* 210–19.

*McCoy, C. B., Nielsen, B. B., Chitwood, D. D., Zavertnik, J. J., & Khoury, E. L. (1991). Increasing the cancer screening of the medically underserved in South Florida. *Cancer, 67,* 1808–13.

McCunney, R. J. (2002). Genetic testing: Ethical implications in the workplace. *Occupational Medicine, 17*(4), 665–72.

McDermott, M. M., Hahn, E. A., Greenland, P., et al. (2002). Atherosclerotic risk factor reduction in peripheral arterial diseasea: Results of a national physician survey. *Journal of General Internal Medicine, 17,* 895–904.

*McDermott, R. J., & Sarvela, P. D. (1999). *Health education evaluation and measurement: A practitioner's perspective.* 2nd ed. St. Louis: McGraw-Hill Higher Education.

McDowell, I. (2002). Social determinants. In L. Breslow, B. D. Goldstein, L. W. Green, et al. (Eds.), *Encyclopedia of public health,* Vol. 4 (pp. 1122–23). New York: Macmillan Reference USA.

McDowell, I. (2002). Social health. In L. Breslow, B. D. Goldstein, L. W. Green, et al. (Eds.), *Encyclopedia of public health,* Vol. 4 (pp. 1123–24). New York: Macmillan Reference USA.

McGahee, T. W., Kemp, V., & Tingen M. (2000). A theoretical model for smoking prevention studies in preteen children. *Pediatric Nursing, 26,* 135–38, 141.

McGinnis, J. M. (1982). Targeting progress in health. *Public Health Reports, 97,* 295–307.

McGinnis, J. M. (1990). Setting objectives for public health in the 1990s: Experience and prospects. *Annual Review of Public Health, 11,* 231–49.

McGinnis, J. M., Williams-Russo, P., & Knickman, J. R. (2002). The case for more active policy attention to health promotion. *Health Affairs, 21,* 78–93.

*McGovern, P. M., Kochevar, L. K., Vesley, D., & Gershon, R. R. M. (1997). Laboratory professionals' compliance with universal precautions. *Laboratory Medicine, 28,* 725–30.

*McGowan, P., & Green, L. W. (1995). Arthritis self-management in native populations of British Columbia: An application of health promotion and participatory research principles in chronic disease control. *Canadian Journal of Aging, 14,* 201–12.

McIlvain, H. E., Backer, E. L., Crabtree, B. F., & Lacy, N. (2002). Physician attitudes and the use of office-based activities for tobacco control. *Family Medicine, 34,* 114–19.

McIntosh, A., & Shaw, C. F. (2003). Barriers to patient information provision in primary care: Patients'and general practitioners' experiences and expectations of information for low back pain. *Health Expectations, 6,* 19–29.

*McKell, C. J. (1994). *A profile of the New Brunswick Association of Dietitions: Results of the Educational Needs Assessment Survey, 1993.* Fredericton, NB: New Brunswick Health and Community Services and Health Canada.

*McKell, C. J., Chase, C., & Balram, C. (1996). Establishing partnerships to enhance the preventive practices of dietitians. *Journal of the Canadian Dietetic Association, 57,* 12–17.

*McKenzie, T. L., Alcaraz, J. E., & Sallis, J. F. (1994). Assessing children's liking for activity units in an elementary school physical education curriculum. *Journal of Teaching in Physical Education, 13,* 206–15.

McKinlay, J. B. (1975). A case for refocusing upstream: The political economy of illness. In A. J. Enelow & J. B. Henderson (Eds.), *Applying behavioral science to cardiovascular risk* (pp. 7–17). New York: American Heart Association.

McKinney, M. M. (1993). Consortium approaches to the delivery of HIV services under the Ryan White CARE Act. *AIDS and Public Policy Journal, 8,* 115–25.

McKnight, J. L., & Kretzmann, J. P (1997). Mapping community capacity. In M. Minkler (Ed.), *Community organizing and community building for health,* Chap. 10. New Brunswick, NJ: Rutgers University Press.

McLean, W., Gillis, J., & Waller R. (2003). The BC Community Pharmacy Asthma Study: A study of clinical, economic and holistic outcomes influenced by an asthma care protocol provided by specially trained community pharmacists in British Columbia. *Canadian Respiratory Journal, 10,* 195–202.

McLeod, D., Pullon, S., & Cookson, T. (2003). Factors that influence changes in smoking behaviour during pregnancy. *New Zealand Medical Journal, 116,* U418.

McLeroy, K. R., Bibeau, D., Steckler, A., & Glanz, K. (1988). An ecological perspective on health promotion programs. *Health Education Quarterly, 15,* 351–77.

McLeroy, K. R., Green, L. W., Mullen, K., & Foshee, V. (1984). Assessing the effects of health promotion in worksites: A review of the stress program evaluations. *Health Education Quarterly, 11,* 379–401.

McLoughlin, E., & Fennell, J. (2000). The power of survivor advocacy: Making car trunks escapable. *Injury Prevention, 6,* 167–70.

McMillan, D. W., & Chavis, D. M. (1986). Sense of community: A definition and theory. *Journal of Community Psychology, 14,* 6–23.

*McMurry, M. P., Hopkins, P. N., Gould, R., et al. (1991). Family-oriented nutrition intervention for a lipid clinic population. *Journal of the American Dietetic Association, 91,* 57–65.

*McPhee, S. J., Bird, J. A., Ha, N.-T., et al. (1996). Pathways to early cancer detection for Vietnamese women: Suc Khoe La Vang! (Health is gold!). *Health Education Quarterly, 23* (Suppl.), S60–S75.

McQueen, D. V., & Puska, P. (Eds.). (2003). *Global behavioral risk factor surveillance.* New York: Kluwer Academic/Plenum Publishers.

McVicar A. (2003). Workplace stress in nursing: A literature review. *Journal of Advances in Nursing, 44,* 633–42.

*Meagher, D., & Mann, K. V. (1990). The effect of an educational program on knowledge and attitudes about blood pressure by junior high school students: A pilot project. *Canadian Journal of Cardiovascular Nursing, 1*(5): 15–22.

*Melby, C. L. (1985–86). The personal laboratory for health behavior change. *Health Education, 16*(6): 29–31, December 1985–January 1986.

Melnick, A. L. (2001). Geographic information systems for public health. In L. F. Novick & G. P. Mays (Eds.), *Public health administration: Principles for population-based management* (pp. 248–65). Gaithersberg, MD: Aspen Publishers, Inc.

*Mercer, S. L., Goel, V., Levy, I. G., et al. (1997). Prostrate cancer screening in the midst of controversy: Canadian men's knowledge, beliefs, utilization, and future intentions. *Canadian Journal of Public Health, 88,* 327–32.

*Mercer, S. L., Green, L. W., Rosenthal, A. C., et al. (2003). Possible lessons from the tobacco experience for obesity control. *American Journal of Clinical Nutrition, 77*(4), 1073S–82S.

*Meredith, K., O'Reilly, K., & Schulz, S. L. (1989). Education for HIV risk reduction in the hemophilia community: Report of the meeting, Convening a Panel of Expert Consultants, Atlanta, GA, November 28–30.

Mermelstein, R., Hedeker, D., & Wong, S. C. (2003). Extended telephone counseling for smoking cessation: Does content matter? *Journal of Consulting and Clinical Psychology, 71,* 565–74.

*Mesters, I., Meertens, R., Crebolder, H., & Parcel, G. (1993). Development of a health education program for parents of preschool children with asthma. *Health Education Research, 8,* 53–68.

Meszaros, A., Orosz, M., Magyar, P., Mesko, A., & Vincze, Z. (2003). Evaluation of asthma knowledge and quality of life in Hungarian asthmatics. *Allergy, 58,* 624–28.

Metropolitan Life Foundation. (1988). *An evaluation of comprehensive health education in American public schools.* New York: Louis Harris and Associates, for the Metropolitan Life Foundation.

Meyerson, B., Chu, B. C., & Mills, M. V. (2003). State agency policy and program coordination in response to the co-occurrence of HIV, chemical dependency, and mental illness. *Public Health Reports, 118,* 408–14.

*Miaoulis, G., & Bonaguro, J. (1980–81). Marketing strategies in health education. *Journal of Health Care Marketing, 1,* 35–44.

*Michalsen, A., Delclos, G. L., Felknor, S. A., et al. (1997). Compliance with universal precautions among physicians. *Journal of Occupational and Environmental Medicine, 39,* 130–37.

*Michielutte, R., & Beal, P. (1990). Identification of community leadership in the development of public health education programs. *Journal of Community Health, 15,* 59–68.

*Michielutte, R., Cunningham, L. E., Sharp, P. C., Dignan, M. B., & Burnette, V. D. (2001). Effectiveness of a cancer education program for women attending rural public health departments in North Carolina. *Journal of Prevention and Intervention in the Community, 22,* 23–42.

*Michielutte, R., Dignan, M. B., Sharp, P. C., Blinson, K., & Wells, B. (1999). Psychological factors related to cervical screening among Lumbee women. *American Journal of Health Behavior, 23,* 115–27.

*Michielutte, R., Dignan, M. B., Wells, H. B., et al. (1989). Development of a community cancer education program: The Forsyth County, NC, Cervical Cancer Prevention Project. *Public Health Reports, 104,* 542–51.

Midford, R., Munro, G., McBride, N., Snow, P., & Ladzinski, U. (2002). Principles that underpin effective school-based drug education. *Journal of Drug Education, 32,* 363–86.

Midgley, G. (2000). *Systemic intervention: Philosophy, methodology, and practice.* New York: Kluwer Academic/Plenum Publishers.

*Miilunpalo, S., Laitakari, J., & Vuori, I. (1995). Strengths and weaknesses in health counseling in Finnish primary health care. *Patient Education and Counseling, 25,* 317–28.

Milinski, M., Semmann, D., & Krambeck, H. J. (2002). Reputation helps solve the "tragedy of the commons." *Nature, 415,* 424–26.

Milio, N. (1983). *Promoting health through public policy.* Philadelphia: F. A. Davis (reprinted by the Canadian Public Health Association, 1987).

Millar, W. J., & Naegele, B. E. (1987). Time to quit program. *Canadian Journal of Public Health, 78,* 109–14.

*Miller, D. R., Geller, A. C., Wood, M. C., Lew, R. A., & Koh, H. K. (1999). The Falmouth Safe Skin Project: Evaluation of a community program to promote sun protection in youth. *Health Education & Behavior, 26,* 369–84.

Miller, R. L., Bedney, B. J., Guenther-Grey, C., & CITY Project Study Team. (2003). Assessing organizational capacity to deliver HIV prevention services collaboratively: Tales from the field. *Health Education & Behavior, 30,* 582–600.

Miller, T. R., & Spicer, R. S. (1998). How safe are our schools? *American Journal of Public Health, 88,* 413–18.

Mindell, J. (2001). Lessons from tobacco control for advocates of healthy transport. *Journal of Public Health Medicine, 23,* 91–97.

Minkler, M. (1985). Building supportive ties and sense of community among the inner-city elderly: The Tenderloin Senior Outreach Project. *Health Education Quarterly, 12,* 303–14

Minkler, M. (Ed.). (1997). *Community organizing and community building for health.* New Brunswick, NJ: Rutgers University Press.

Minkler, M. (2000) Using participatory action research to build healthy communities. *Public Health Reports, 11,* 191–97.

Minkler, M., & Hancock, T. (2003). Community-driven asset identification and issue selection. In M. Minkler & N. Wallerstein (Eds.), *Community-based participatory research for health* (pp. 135–54). San Francisco: Jossey-Bass.

Minkler, M., & Pies, C. (1997). Ethical issues in community organization and community participation. In M. Minkler (Ed.), *Community organizing and community building for health.* Piscataway, NJ: Rutgers University Press.

Minkler, M., Thompson, M., Bell, J., Rose, K., & Redman, D. (2002). Using community involvement strategies in the fight against infant mortality: Lessons from a multisite study of the national Healthy Start experience. *Health Promotion Practice, 3,* 176–87.

Minkler, M., & Wallerstein, N. B. (2002). Improving health through community organization and community building. In K. Glanz, B. K. Rimer, & F. M. Lewis (Eds.), *Health behavior and health education: Theory, research, and practice* (pp. 279–311). 3rd ed. San Francisco: Jossey-Bass.

Minkler, M., & Wallerstein, N. (2003). *Community-based participatory research for health.* San Francisco: Jossey-Bass.

Minnesota Department of Health. (1982). Workplace health promotion survey. Minneapolis: Minnesota Department of Health.

*Mirand, A. L., Beehler, G. P., Kuo, C. L., & Mahoney, M. C. (2002). Physician perceptions of primary prevention: Qualitative base for the conceptual shaping of a practice intervention tool. *BioMed Central Public Health, 2*(1), 16.

*Mirand, A. L., Beehler, G. P., Kuo, C. L., & Mahoney, M. C. (2003). Explaining the de-prioritization of primary prevention: Physicians' perceptions of their role in the delivery of primary care. *BioMed Central Public Health, 3*(1), 15.

Missouri Foundation for Health. (2001). *A report to the Board.* Missouri State Department of Health. Missouri Foundation.

Mittelmark, M. B. (1999). The psychology of social influence and healthy public policy. *Preventive Medicine, 29* (6 Pt. 2), S24–9.

*Modeste, N. N., Abbey, D. E., & Hopp, J. W. (1984–85). Hypertension in a Caribbean population. *International Quarterly of Community Health Education, 5,* 203–11.

Moher, M., Hey, K., & Lancaster, T. (2003). Workplace interventions for smoking cessation. *Cochrane Database of Systematic Reviews* (2), CD003440.

Molnar, B. E., Buka, S. L., Brennan, R. T., Holton, J. K., & Earls, F. (2003). A multilevel study of neighborhoods and parent-to-child physical aggression: Results from the project on human development in Chicago neighborhoods. *Child Maltreatment, 8,* 84–97.

Monsó, E., Campbell, J., Tønnesen, P., G Gustavsson, G., & Morera, J. (2001). Sociodemographic predictors of success in smoking intervention. *Tobacco Control, 10,* 165–69.

Mooney, G. (2002). Priority setting in mental health services. *Applied Health Economics & Health Policy, 1,* 65–74.

Moore, D. E., Jr., & Pennington, F. C. (2003). Practice-based learning and improvement. *Journal of Continuing Education in the Health Professions, 23* (Suppl 1), S73–80.

Morgan, L. S., & Horning, B. G. (1940). The community health education program. *American Journal of Public Health, 30,* 1323–30.

*Morisky, D. E. (1986). Nonadherence to medical recommendations for hypertensive patients: Problems and potential solutions. *Journal of Compliance in Health Care, 1,* 5–20.

*Morisky, D. E., DeMuth, N. M., Field-Fass, M., Green, L. W., & Levine, D. M. (1985). Evaluation of family health education to build social support for long-term control of high blood pressure. *Health Education Quarterly, 12,* 35–50.

Morisky, D. E., Ebin, V. J., Malotte, C. K., Coly, A., & Kominski, G. (2003). Assessment of tuberculosis treatment completion in an ethnically diverse population using two data sources: Implications for treatment interventions. *Evaluation & the Health Professions, 26,* 43–58.

*Morisky, D. E., Levine, D. M., Green, L. W., et al. (1980). The relative impact of health education for low- and high-risk patients with hypertension. *Preventive Medicine, 9,* 550–58.

*Morisky, D. E., Levine, D. M., Green, L. W., et al. (1983). Five-year blood-pressure control and mortality following health education for hypertensive patients. *American Journal of Public Health, 73,* 153–62.

*Morisky, D. E., Levine, D. M., Green, L. W., & Smith, C. (1982). Health education program effects on the management of hypertension in the elderly. *Archives of Internal Medicine, 142,* 1935–38.

*Morisky, D. E., Levine, D. M., Wood, J. C., et al. (1981). Systems approach for the planning, diagnosis, implementation and evaluation of community health education approaches in the control of high blood pressure. *Journal of Operations Research, 50,* 625–34.

*Morisky, D. E., Malotte, C. K., Choi, P., et al. (1990). A patient education program to improve adherence rates with antituberculosis drug regimens. *Health Education Quarterly, 17,* 253–67.

Morisky, D. E., Malotte, C. K., Ebin, V., et al. (2001). Behavioral interventions for the control of tuberculosis among adolescents. *Public Health Reports, 116,* 568–74.

Morisky, D. E., Pena, M., Tiglao, T. V., & Liu, K. Y. (2002). The impact of the work environment on condom use among female bar workers in the Philippines. *Health Education and Behavior, 29,* 461–72.

Morone, J. A. (1990). *The democratic wish: Popular participation and the limits of American government.* New York: Basic Books.

*Morrison, C. (1995). Breast cancer detection behaviors in low income women over forty: Characteristics associated with frequency and proficiency of breast self examination. *Dissertation Abstracts International [A], 55*(10), 3101.

*Morrison, C. (1996). Using PRECEDE to predict breast self-examination in older, lower-income women. *American Journal of Health Behavior, 20,* 3–14.

Morrison, D. M., Golder, S., Keller, T. E., & Gillmore, M. R. (2002). The theory of reasoned action as a model of marijuana use: Tests of implicit assumptions and applicability to high-risk young women. *Psychology and Addictive Behavior, 16,* 212–24.

Moser, R., McCance, K. L., & Smithy, K. R. (1991). Results of a national survey of physicians' knowledge and application of prevention capabilities. *American Journal of Preventive Medicine, 7,* 384–90.

Mosher, J. F. (1990). *Community responsible beverage service programs: An implementation handbook.* Palo Alto, CA: The Health Promotion Resource Center, Stanford Center for Research in Disease Prevention.

Moudon, A. M., & Lee, C. (2003). Walking and bicycling: An evaluation of environmental audit instruments. *American Journal of Health Promotion, 18,* 21–37.

Mowatt, C., Isaly, J., & Thayer, M. (1985). Project Graduation—Maine. *Morbidity and Mortality Weekly Report, 34,* 233–35.

Mucchielli, R. (1970). *Introduction to structural psychology.* New York: Funk & Wagnalls.

Mullen, P. D., Evans, D., Forster, J., et al. (1995). Settings as an important dimension in health education/promotion policy, programs, and research. *Health Education Quarterly, 22,* 329–45.

Mullen, P. D., & Green, L. W. (1985). Meta-analysis points way toward more effective medication teaching. *Promoting Health, 6*(6), 6–8.

*Mullen, P. D., Green, L. W., & Persinger, G. (1985). Clinical trials of patient education for chronic conditions: A comparative meta-analysis of intervention types. *Preventive Medicine, 14*, 753–81.

*Mullen, P. D., Hersey, J., & Iverson, D. C. (1987). Health behavior models compared. *Social Science and Medicine, 24*, 973–81.

Mullen, P. D., & Holcomb, J. D. (1990). Selected predictors of health promotion counseling by three groups of allied health professionals. *American Journal of Preventive Medicine, 6*, 153–60.

Mullen, P. D., Mains, D. A., & Velez, R. (1992). A meta-analysis of controlled trials of cardiac patient education. *Patient Education and Counseling, 19*, 143–62.

Mullen, P. D., Ramirez, G., & Groff, J. Y. (1994). A meta-analysis of randomized trials of prenatal smoking cessation interventions. *American Journal of Obstetrics and Gynecology, 171*, 1328–34.

*Mullen, P. D., Simons-Morton, D. G., Ramirez, G., et al. (1997). A meta-analysis of trials evaluating patient education and counseling for three groups of preventive health behaviors. *Patient Education and Counseling, 32*, 157–73.

*Mummery, W. K., Spence, J. C., & Hudec, J. C. (2000). Understanding physical activity intention in Canadian school children and youth: An application of the theory of planned behavior. *Research Quarterly of Exercise and Sport, 71*, 116–24.

Muntaner, C., Lynch, J., & Smith, G. D. (2001). Social capital, disorganized communities, and the third way: Understanding the retreat from structural inequalities in epidemiology and public health. *International Journal of Health Service, 31*, 213–37.

Murimi, M. (2001). Short-term nutrition intervention increases calcium intake among 45–54 year old women. *Journal of Nutrition for the Elderly, 20*(3), 1–12.

Murray, D. M., Kurth, C. L., Finnegan, J. R., Jr., et al. (1988). Direct mail as a prompt for follow-up care among persons at risk for hypertension. *American Journal of Preventive Medicine, 4*, 331–35.

Musher-Eizenman, D. R., Holub, S. C., & Arnett, M. (2003). Attitude and peer influences on adolescent substance use: The moderating effect of age, sex, and substance. *Journal of Drug Education, 33*, 1–23.

Nader, P. R., Sallis, J. G., Patterson, T. L., et al. (1989). A family approach to cardiovascular risk reduction: Results from the San Diego Family Health Project. *Health Education Quarterly, 16*, 229–44.

Nader, P. R., Sellers, D. E., Johnson, C. C., et al. (1996). The effect of adult participation in a school-based family intervention to improve children's diet and physical activity: The child and adolescent trial for cardiovascular health. *Preventive Medicine, 25*, 455–64.

Nagel, R. W., Hankenhof, B. J., Kimmel, S. R., & Saxe, J. M. (2003). Educating grade school children using a structured bicycle safety program. *Journal of Trauma, 55*, 920–23.

Nansel, T. R., Weaver, N., Donlin, M., et al. (2002). Baby, be safe: The effect of tailored communications for pediatric injury prevention provided in a primary care setting. *Patient Education and Counseling, 46*, 175–90.

National Alliance of State and Territorial AIDS Directors. (2000). *HIV prevention and community planning.* Washington, DC: National Alliance of State and Territorial AIDS Directors. http://www.nastad.org.

National Association of County and City Health Officials. (1995). *1992–1993 national profile of local health departments.* Washington, DC: National Association of County and City Health Officials. Atlanta, GA: Public Health Practice Program Office, Centers for Disease Control and Prevention.

National Association of County and City Health Officials. (1998). *APEXPH '98 interactive software.* Washington, DC: Public Health Practice Program Office of CDC and National Association of County and City Health Officials.

National Association of County and City Health Officials. (2000). *Health departments take action: A compendium of state and local models addressing racial and ethnic disparities in health.* Washington, DC: National Association of County and City Health Officials.

National Center for Health Statistics. (2003). *Health, United States, 2003.* Hyattsville, MD: Centers for Disease Control and Prevention, U.S. Department of Health and Human Services, DHHS Pub No. 2003–1232.

National Civic League. (1999). *The civic index: Measuring your community's civic health.* Denver, CO: National Civic League.

National Civic League and Staff of the St. Louis County Department of Health. (2000). *A guide to a community-oriented approach to core public health functions.* Denver, CO: National Civic League.

National Commission on the Role of the School and the Community in Improving Adolescent Health. (1990). *Code blue: Uniting for healthier youth.* Washington, DC: National Association of State Boards of Education and the American Medical Association.

National Committee for Injury Prevention and Control. (1989). *Injury prevention: Meeting the challenge.* New York: Oxford University Press. Printed as a supplement to the *American Journal of Preventive Medicine, 5*(3).

National Committee on Vital and Health Statistics. (2002). *Shaping a vision of health statistics for the 21st century.* Washington: National Center for Health Statistics, Centers for Disease Control and Prevention, U.S. Department of Health and Human Services.

*Neef, N., Scutchfield, F. D., Elder, J., & Bender, S. J. (1991). Testicular self examination by young men: An analysis of characteristics associated with practice. *Journal of American College Health, 39,* 187–90.

Neiger, B. L., Thackeray, R., Barnes, M. D., & McKenzie, J. F. (2003). Positioning social marketing as a planning process for health education. *American Journal of Health Studies, 18,* 75–80.

Nelson, C. F., Kreuter, M. W., Watkins, N. B., & Saxe, J. M. (1986). A partnership between the community, state, and federal government: Rhetoric or reality. *Hygie* (Paris), *5*(3), 27–31.

*Nelson, C. F., Kreuter, M. W., Watkins, N. B., & Stoddard, R. R. (1987). Planned approach to community health: The PATCH Program. In P. A. Nutting (Ed.), *Community-oriented primary care: From principle to practice,* Chap. 47. Washington, DC: Government Printing Office, U.S. Department of Health and Human Services, HRS-A-PE 86–1.

Neufeld, V. R., & Norman, G. R. (Eds.). (1985). *Assessing clinical competence.* New York: Springer.

*Neumark-Sztainer, D., & Story, M. (1996). The use of health behavior theory in nutrition counseling. *Topics in Clinical Nutrition, 11,* 60–73.

*Newman, I. M., & Martin, G. L. (1982). Attitudinal and normative factors associated with adolescent cigarette smoking in Australia and the USA: A methodology to assist health education planning. *Community Health Studies, 6,* 47–56.

*Newman, I. M., Martin, G. L., & Weppner, R. (1982). A conceptual model for developing prevention programs. *International Journal of the Addictions, 17,* 493–504.

*Ngtuyen, T. T., McPhee, S. J., Nguyen, T., Lam, T., & Mock, J. (2002). Predictors of cervical pap smear screening awareness, intervention, and receipt among Vietnamese-American women. *American Journal of Preventive Medicine, 23,* 207–14.

*Nguyen, M. N., Grignon, R., Tremblay, M., & Delisle, L. (1995). Behavioral diagnosis of 30 to 60 year-old men in the Fabreville Heart Health Program. *Journal of Community Health, 20,* 257–69.

Niego, S., & Peterson, J. (2001). The program archive on sexuality, health, and adolescence (PASHA): A study of activity warehousing. In S. Sussman (Ed.), *Handbook of program development for health behavior research and practice* (pp. 210–36). Thousand Oaks, CA: Sage Publications.

Nielson, W. R., Jensen, M. P., & Kerns, R. D. (2003). Initial development and validation of a multidimensional pain readiness to change questionnaire. *The Journal of Pain, 4,* 148–58.

Nies, M. A., Hepworth, J. T., Wallston, K. A., & Kershaw, T. C. (2001). Evaluation of an instrument for assessing behavioral change in sedentary women. *Journal of Nursing Scholarship, 33,* 349–54.

Nies, M. A., & Kershaw, T. C. (2002). Psychosocial and environmental influences on physical activity and health outcomes in sedentary women. *Journal of Nursing Scholarship, 34,* 243–49.

Nix, H. L. (1969). Concepts of community and community leadership, *Sociology and Social Research, 53,* 500–10.

Nix, H. L. (1970). *Identification of leaders and their involvement in the planning process.* Washington, DC: U.S. Public Health Service, Pub. No. 1998.

Nix, H. L., & Seerly, N. R. (1971). Community reconnaissance method: A synthesis of functions. *Journal of Community Development Society, 11* (Fall), 62–69.

Nix, H. L., & Seerly, N. R. (1973). Comparative views and actions of community leaders and nonleaders. *Rural Sociology, 38,* 427–28.

Noble, R. E. (2003). Drug therapy in the elderly. *Metabolism, 52*(10 Suppl 2), 27–30.

Norman, P., Searle, A., Harrad, R., & Vedhara, K. (2003). Predicting adherence to eye patching in children with amblyopia: An application of protection motivation theory. *British Journal of Health Psychology, 8* (Pt. 1), 67–82.

Norris, S. L., & Isham, G. J. (Eds.). (2002). The guide to community preventive services: Reducing the burden of diabetes. *American Journal of Preventive Medicine, 22* (Suppl. 4S), 1–66.

Northridge, M. E., Vallone, D., Merzel, C., et al. (2000). The adolescent years: An academic-community partnership in Harlem comes of age. *Journal of Public Health Management and Practice, 6,* 53–60.

Norton, B. L., McLeroy, K. R., Burdine, J. N., Felix, M. R. J., & Dorsey, A. M. (2002). Community capacity: Concept, theory, and methods. In R. J. DiClementi, R. A. Crosby, & M. C. Kegler (Eds.), *Emerging theories in health promotion practice and research: Strategies for improving public health,* Chap. 8 (pp. 194–227). San Francisco: Jossey-Bass.

Nose, M., Barbui, C., Gray, R., & Tansella, M. (2003). Clinical interventions for treatment non-adherence in psychosis: Meta-analysis. *British Journal of Psychiatry, 183,*197–206.

*Nozu, Y., Iwai, K., & Watanabe, M. (1995). AIDS-related knowledge, attitudes, beliefs and skills among high school students in Akita: Results from Akita AIDS education for Adolescent Survey (AAAS). Abstract No. 234. *Proceedings.* Makuhari, Japan: XVth World Conference of the International Union for Health Promotion and Education, August.

Nunes, R. (2003). Evidence-based medicine: A new tool for resource allocation? *Medical and Health Care Philosophy, 6,* 297–301.

Nutbeam, D., & Catford, J. (1987). The Welsh heart programme evaluation strategy: Progress, plans and possibilities. *Health Promotion, 2,* 5–18.

Nutbeam, D., Wise, M., Bauman, A., Harris, E., &. Leeder, S. (1993). *Goals and targets for Australia's health in the year 2000 and beyond.* Portland, OR: International Specialized Books Services. Also published by Canberra: Australian Government Publishing Service.

Nutting, P. A. (1990). Community-oriented primary care: A critical area of research for primary care. *Primary care research: An agenda for the 90s.* Washington, DC: U.S. Department of Health and Human Services, Agency for Health Care Policy and Research.

Nyswander, D. (1942). *Solving school health problems.* New York: Oxford University Press.

*O'Brien, R. W., Smith, S. S., Bush, P. J., & Peleg, E. (1990). Obesity, self-esteem, and health locus of control in black youths during transition to adolescence. *American Journal of Health Promotion, 5,* 133–39.

O'Campo, P., Eaton, W. W., & Muntaner, C. (2004). Labor market experience, work organization, gender inequalities and health status: Results from a prospective analysis of U.S. employed women. *Society for Science and Medicine, 58*(3), 585–94.

Ockene, J. K., & Zapka, J. G. (2000). Provider education to promote implementation of clinical practice guidelines. *Chest, 118* (2 Suppl), 33S–39S.

O'Donnell, M. P (Ed.). (2002). *Health promotion in the workplace.* 3rd ed. New York: Wiley.

O'Fallon, L. R., & Dearry, A. (2002). Community-based participatory research as a tool to advance environmental health sciences. *Environmental Health Perspectives, 110* (Suppl. 2), 161–71.

Office of Disease Prevention and Health Promotion. (1993). *Health promotion goes to work: Programs with an impact.* Washington, DC: U.S. Department of Health and Human Services.

Office of the Secretary, DOT. (2001). Procedures for transportation workplace drug and alcohol testing programs; technical amendments. Final rule. *Federal Registry, 66*(154), 41944–55.

Offir, J. T., Fisher, J. D., Williams, S. S., et al. (1993). Reasons for inconsistent AIDS-preventive behaviors among gay men. *Jounral of Sex Research, 30,* 62–69.

Ogden, J. (2003). Some problems with social cognition models: A pragmatic and conceptual analysis. *Health Psychology, 22,* 424–28.

Ogden, J., Bandara, I., Cohen, H., et al. (2001). General practitioners' and patients' models of obesity: Whose problem is it? *Patient Education and Counselling, 44,* 227–33.

*Oh, H., & Kim, Y. (1993). Planning process of health promotion programs for individuals with arthritis (in Korean). *Kanhohak Tamgu, 2,* 79–99, 100–101.

Oldenburg, B., & Parcel, G. S. (2002). Diffusion of innovations. In K. Glanz, B. K. Rimer, & F. M. Lewis (Eds.), *Health behavior and health education: Theory, research, and practice* (pp. 312–34). San Francisco: Jossey-Bass.

Oldroyd, J., Proudfoot, J., Infante, F. A., et al. (2003). Providing healthcare for people with chronic illness: The views of Australian GPs. *Medical Journal of Australia, 179,* 30–33.

Olds, R. S., & Thombs, D. L. (2001). The relationship of adolescent perceptions of peer norms and parent involvement to cigarette and alcohol use. *Journal of School Health, 71,* 223–28.

*Oliver-Vazquez, M., Sanchez-Ayendez, M., Suarez-Perez, E., & Velez-Almodovar, H. (1999). Planning a breast cancer health promotion: Qualitative and quantitative data on Puerto Rican elderly women. *Promotion and Education, 5,* 16–19.

*Oliver-Vazquez, M., Sanchez-Ayendez, M., Suarez-Perez, E., Velez-Almodovar, H., & Arroyo-Calderon, Y. (2002). Breast cancer health promotion model for older Puerto Rican women: Results of a pilot programme. *Health Promotion International, 17,* 3–11.

*O'Loughlin, J., Paradis, G., Kishchuk, N., et al. (1995). Coeur en Santé St-Henri: A heart health promotion programme in Montreal, Canada: Design and methods for evaluation. *Journal of Epidemiology and Community Health, 49,* 495–502.

*Olson, C. M. (1994). Promoting positive nutritional practices during pregnancy and lactation. *American Journal of Clinical Nutrition, 59* (Suppl.), 525S–31S.

O'Malley, A. S., Gonzalez, R. M., Sheppard, V. B., Huerta, E., & Mandelblatt, J. (2003). Primary care cancer control interventions including Latinos: A review. *American Journal of Preventive Medicine, 25,* 264–71.

O'Malley, A. S., & Mandelblatt, J. (2003). Delivery of preventive services for low-income persons over age 50: A comparison of community health clinics to private doctors' offices. *Journal of Community Health, 28,* 185–97.

Oman, R. F., Vesely, S. K., Kegler, M., McLeroy, K., & Aspy, C. B. (2003). A youth development approach to profiling sexual abstinence. *American Journal of Health Behavior, 27,* (Suppl. 1), S80–93.

Oman, R. F., Vesely, S. K., McLeroy, K. R., et al. (2002). Reliability and validity of the youth asset survey (YAS). *Journal of Adolescent Health, 31,* 247–55.

*O'Meara, C. (1993). An evaluation of consumer perspectives of childbirth and parenting education. *Midwifery, 9,* 210–19.

*Opdycke, R. A. C., Ascione, F. J., Shimp, L. A., & Rosen, R. I. (1992). A systematic approach to educating elderly patients about their medications. *Patient Education and Counselling, 19,* 43–60.

Orleans, C. T., & Cummings, K. M. (1999). Population-based tobacco control: Progress and prospects. *American Journal of Health Promotion, 14,* 83–91.

Ory, M. G., Jordan, P. J., & Bazzarre, T. (2002). The behavior change consortium: Setting the stage for a new century of health behavior-change research. *Health Education Research, 17,* 500–11.

Osgood, G. E., Cuci, G. J., & Tannenbaum, P. H. (1961). *The measurement of meaning.* Urbana: University of Illinois Press.

O'Shea E. (2003). Social gradients in years of potential life lost in Ireland. *European Journal of Public Health, 13,* 327–33.

Ostry, A., Marion, S., Green, L. W., et al. (2000). Downsizing and industrial restructuring in related to changes in psychosocial conditions of work in British Columbia sawmills. *Scandanavian Journal of Work and Environmental Health, 26,* 273–78.

*Ostwald, S. K., & Rothenberger, J. (1985). Development of a testicular self-examination program for college men. *Journal of the American College Health, 33,* 234–39.

*Ottoson, J. M. (1995). Use of a conceptual framework to explore multiple influences on the application of learning following a continuing education program. *Canadian Journal of Adult Education, 9*(2), 1–18.

*Ottoson, J. M. (1997). After the applause: Exploring multiple influences on application following adult education programs. *Adult Education Quarterly, 47,* 92–107.

Ottoson, J. M. (1998). The role of contextual variables in the application of community training in substance abuse prevention. *XVI World Conference on Health Promotion and Health Education. San Juan, Puerto Rico, June 21–26, 1998. Abstracts Book* (pp. 26–27). San Juan: Graduate School of Public Health, Medical Sciences Campus, University of Puerto Rico.

*Ottoson J. M., & Green, L. W. (1987). Reconciling concept and context: Theory of implementation. In W. B. Ward & M. H. Becker (Eds.), *Advances in health education and promotion,* Vol. 2 (pp. 353–82). Greenwich, CT: JAI Press.

*Ottoson, J. M., & Green, L. W. (2001). Public health education and health promotion. In L. F. Novick & G. P. Mays (Eds.), *Public health administration: Principles for population-based management* (pp. 300–23). Gaithersburg, MD: Aspen.

Ottoson, J. M., & Patterson, I. (2000). Contextual influences on learning application in practice. An extended role for process evaluation. *Evaluation and the Health Professions, 23,* 194–211.

Ottoson, J. M., & Wilson, D. H. (2003). Did they use it? Beyond the collection of surveillance information. In D. V. McQueen & P. Puska (Eds.), *Global behavioral risk factor surveillance* (pp. 119–32). New York: Kluwer Academic/Plenum Publishers.

Ounpuu, S., Kreuger, P., Vermeulen, M., & Chambers, L. (2000). Using the U.S. behavior[al] risk factor surveillance system's health related quality of life survey tool in a Canadian city. *Canadian Journal of Public Health, 91,* 67–72.

*Oxman, A. D., Thomson, M. A., Davis, D. A., & Haynes, R. B. (1995). No magic bullets: A systematic review of 102 trials of interventions to improve professional practice. *Canadian Medical Association Journal, 153,* 1423–31.

Ozminkowski, R. J., Mark, T. L., Goetzel, R. Z., Blank, D., Walsh, J. M., & Cangianelli, L. (2003). Relationships between urinalysis testing for substance use, medical expenditures, and the occurrence of injuries at a large manufacturing firm. *American Journal of Drug and Alcohol Abuse, 29*(1), 151–67.

*Padilla, G. V., & Bulcavage, L. M. (1991). Theories used in patient/ health education. *Seminars in Oncology Nursing, 7,* 87–96.

Paehlke, R. C. (1989). *Environmentalism and the future of progressive politics.* New Haven: Yale University Press.

Painter, P. (2003). Exercise for patients with chronic disease: Physician responsibility. *Current Sports Medicine Reports, 2,* 173–80.

*Painter, S. B. (2002). *Community health education and promotion manual.* 2nd ed. New York, Aspen. www.aspenpublishers.com.

*Palti, H., Knishkowy, B., Epstein, Y., et al. (1997). Reported health concerns of Israeli high school students—differences by age and sex. *Israel Journal of Medical Sciences, 33,* 123–28.

*Paluck, E. C. M. (1998). *Pharmacist-client communication: A study of quality and client satisfaction.* Unpublished doctoral dissertation, University of British Columbia, Vancouver, Canada.

*Paluck, E. C., Green, L. W., Frankish, C. J., Fielding, D. W., & Haverkamp, B. (2003). Assessment of communication barriers in community pharmacies. *Evaluation and the Health Professions, 26,* 380–403.

Panter-Brick, C., & Worthman, C. M. (Eds.). (1999). *Hormones, health, and behavior: A socioecological and lifespan perspective.* Cambridge: Cambridge University Press.

*Paradis, G., O'Loughlin, J., Elliott, M., et al. (1995). Coeur en Santé St-Henri: A heart health promotion programme in a low income, low education neighbourhood in Montreal, Canada: Theoretical model and early field experience. *Journal of Epidemiology and Community Health, 49,* 503–12.

*Parcel, G. S. (1984). Theoretical models for application in school health education research. *Journal of School Health, 54,* 39–49.

Parcel, G. S., & Baranowski, T. (1981). Social learning theory and health education. *Health Education, 12*(3), 14–18.

*Parcel, G. S., Eriksen, M. P., Lovato, C. Y., et al. (1989). The diffusion of school-based tobacco-use prevention programs: Project description and baseline data. *Health Education Research, 4,* 111–24.

*Parcel, G. S., Green, L. W., & Bettes, B. (1989). School-based programs to prevent or reduce obesity. In N. A. Krasnagor, G. D. Grave, and N. Kretchmer (Eds.), *Childhood obesity: A biobehavioral perspective,* (pp. 143–57). Caldwell, NJ: Telford Press.

Parcel, G. S., Kelder, S. H., & Basen-Engquist, K. (2000). The school as a setting for health promotion. In B. D. Poland, L. W. Green, & I. Rootman (Eds.), *Settings for health promotion: Linking theory and practice* (pp. 86–120). Thousand Oaks, CA: Sage.

*Parcel, G. S., O'Hara-Tompkins, N. M., Harrist, R. B., et al. (1995). Diffusion of an effective tobacco prevention program: Part II—Evaluation of the adoption phase. *Health Education Research, 10,* 297–307.

*Parcel, G. S., Ross, J. G., Lavin, A. T., et al. (1991). Enhancing implementation of the teenage health teaching modules. *Journal of School Health, 61,* 35–38.

*Parcel, G. S., Simons-Morton, B. G., Brink, S. G., et al. (1987). *Smoking control among women: A CDC community intervention handbook.* Atlanta: Centers for Disease Control.

Parcel, G. S., Simons-Morton, B. G., & Kolbe, L. J. (1988). Health promotion: Integrating organizational change and student learning strategies. *Health Education Quarterly, 15,* 435–50.

*Parcel, G. S., Simons-Morton, B. G., O'Hara, N. M., et al. (1989). School promotion of healthful diet and physical activity: Impact on learning outcomes and self-reported behavior. *Health Education Quarterly, 16,* 181–99.

*Parcel, G. S., Swank, P. R., Mariotto, M. J., et al. (1994). Self-management of cystic-fibrosis: A structural model for educational and behavioral variables. *Social Science and Medicine, 38,* 1307–15.

*Parkinson, R. S. & Associates (Eds.). (1982). *Managing health promotion in the workplace: Guidelines for implementation and evaluation.* Palo Alto: Mayfield.

Parnes, B., Main, D. S., Holcomb, S., & Pace, W. (2002). Tobacco cessation counseling among underserved patients: A report from CaReNet. *Journal of Family Practice, 51,* 65–69.

Parra-Medina, D., Taylor, D., Valois, R. F., et al. (2003). The Program Plan Index: An evaluation tool for assessing the quality of adolescent pregnancy prevention program plans. *Health Promotion Practice, 4,* 375–84.

Parsons, T. (1964). The superego and the theory of social systems. In R. L. Coser (Ed.), *The family: Its structure and functions* (pp. 433–49). New York: St. Martin's Press.

Partin, M. R., & Slater, J. S. (2003). Promoting repeat mammography use: Insights from a systematic needs assessment. *Health Education and Behavior, 30,* 97–112.

*Parvanta, C. F., Gottert, P., Anthony, R., & Parlato, M. (1997). Nutrition promotion in Mali: Highlights of a rural integrated nutrition communication program (1989–1995). *Journal of Nutrition Education, 29,* 274–80.

*Pasick, R. J., D'Onofrio, C. N., & Otero-Sabogal, R. (1996). Similarities and differences across cultures: Questions to inform a third generation for health promotion research. *Health Education Quarterly, 23* (Suppl.), S142–61.

*Paskett, E. D., Tatum, C. M., D'Agostino, R., Jr., et al. (1999). Community-based interventions to improve breast and cervical cancer screening: Results of the Forsyth County Cancer Screening (FoCaS) Project. *Cancer Epidemiology Biomarkers and Prevention, 8,* 453–59.

Pateman, B., Grunbaum, J. A., & Kann L. (1999). Voices from the field A qualitative analysis of classroom, school, district, and state health education policies and programs. *Journal of School Health, 69,* 258–63.

Pateman, B., Irvin, L. H., Nakasato, S., et al.. (2000). Got health? The Hawaii partnership for standards-based school health education. *Journal of School Health, 70,* 311–17.

Patton, C. (1985). *Sex and germs: The politics of AIDS.* Boston: South End Press.

Patton, R. D., & Cissell, W. B. (Eds.). (1989). *Community organization: Traditional principles and modern application.* Johnson City, TN: Latchpins Press.

Pechacek, T. F., Fox, B. H., Murray, D. M., & Luepker, R. V. (1984). Review of techniques for measurement of smoking behaviors. In J. Matarazzo, S. M. Weiss, J. A. Herd, et al. (Eds.), *Behavioral health: A handbook of health enhancement and disease prevention.* New York: Wiley.

Pechacek, T. F., Starr, G. B., Judd, B. T., et al. (1999). *Best practices for comprehensive tobacco control programs, August 1999.* Atlanta, GA: U.S. Department of Health and Human Services, Centers for Disease Control and Prevention, National Center for Chronic Disease Prevention and Health Promotion, Office on Smoking and Health.

Pelletier, K. R. (2001). A review and analysis of the clinical- and cost-effectiveness studies of comprehensive health promotion and disease management programs at the worksite: 1998–2000 update. *American Journal of Health Promotion, 16,* 107–16.

Pelletier, K. R., & Lutz, R. (1988). Healthy people—healthy business: A critical review of stress management programs in the workplace. *American Journal of Health Promotion, 2*(3), 5–12.

Pellmar, T. C., Brandt, E. N., Jr., & Baird, M. A. (2002). Health and behavior: The interplay of biological, behavioral, and social influences: summary of an Institute of Medicine report. *American Journal of Health Promotion, 16,* 206–19.

Perry, C. (2000). Commentary: School as a setting for health promotion. In B. D. Poland, L. W. Green, & I. Rootman (Eds.), *Settings for health promotion: Linking theory to practice.* Thousand Oaks, CA: Sage.

Perry, C. L., Luepker, R. V., Murray, D. M., et al. (1988). Parent involvement with children's health promotion: The Minnesota home team. *American Journal of Public Health, 78,* 1156–60.

Pertchuck, M. (2001). *Smoke in their eyes: Lessons in movement leadership from the tobacco wars.* Nashville, TN: Vanderbilt University Press.

Pertschuk, M., & Erikson, A. (1987). *Smoke fighting: A smoking control movement building guide.* New York: American Cancer Society.

Peterson, A. M., Takiya, L., & Finley, R. (2003). Meta-analysis of trials of interventions to improve medication adherence. *American Journal of Health System Pharmacies, 60,* 657–65.

Petosa, R. L., Suminski, R., & Hortz, B. (2003). Predicting vigorous physical activity using social cognitive theory. *American Journal of Health Behavior, 27,* 301–10.

*Pichora-Fuller, M. K. (1997). Assistive listening devices in accessibility programs for the elderly: A health promotion approach. In R. Lubinski & J. Higginbothan (Eds.), *Communication technologies for the elderly* (pp.161–202). San Diego: Singular Press.

Pickering, T., Clemow, L., Davidson, K., & Gerin, W. (2003). Behavioral cardiology—has its time finally arrived? *Mt Sinai Journal of Medicine, 70,* 101–12.

Pickles T. (2004). What's a man to do? Treatment options for localized prostate cancer. *Canadian Family Physician, 50,* 65–72.

Pierce, J. P., Macaskill, P., & Hill, D. (1990). Long-term effectiveness of mass media led anti-smoking campaigns in Australia. *American Journal of Public Health, 80,* 565–69.

Pietinen, P., Nissinen, A., Vartiainen, E., et al. (1992). Dietary changes in the North Karelia Project (1972–1982). *Preventive Medicine, 17,* 183–93.

Plante, T. G., & Schwartz, G. E. (1990). Defensive and repressive coping styles: Self-presentation, leisure activities, and assessment. *Journal of Research in Personality, 24,* 173–90.

Plough, A., & Olafson, F. (1994). Implementing the Boston healthy start initiative: A case study of community empowerment and public health. *Health Education Quarterly, 21,* 221–34.

Plowden, K. O., & Miller, J. L. (2000). Motivators of health seeking behavior in urban African-American men: An exploration of triggers and barriers. *Journal of the National Black Nurses Association, 11,* 15–20.

Poland, B. D. (2000). Social capital, social cohesion, community capacity, and community empowerment: Variations on a theme? In B. D. Poland, L. W. Green, & I. Rootman (Eds.), *Settings in health promotion: Linking theory and practice* (pp. 301–7). Thousand Oaks, CA: Sage.

Poland, B. D., Green, L. W., & Rootman, I. (Eds.). (2000). *Settings in health promotion: Linking theory and practice.* Thousand Oaks, CA: Sage.

Pollack, M. B., & Middleton, K. (1994). *School health instruction.* 3rd ed. St. Louis: Mosby.

Pollak, K. I., McBride, C. M., Curry, S. J., et al. (2001). Women's perceived and partners' reported support for smoking cessation during pregnancy. *Annals of Behavioral Medicine, 23,* 208–14.

Pomerleau, C. S., Zucker, A. N., Namenek Brouwer, R. J., et al. (2001). Race differences in weight concerns among women smokers: Results from two independent samples. *Addictive Behavior, 26,* 651–63.

Poss, J. E. (2001). Developing a new model for cross-cultural research: Synthesizing the Health Belief Model and the Theory of Reasoned Action. *Advances in Nursing Science, 23,* 1–15.

Potter, M. A., Ley, C. E., Fertman, C. I., Eggleston, M. M., & Duman, S. (2003). Evaluating workforce development: Perspectives, processes, and lessons learned. *Journal of Public Health Management and Practice, 9,* 489–95.

*Potvin, L., Paradis, G., Laurier, D., Masson, P., Pelletier, J., & Lessard, R. (1992). Le cadre d'intervention du projet Québécois de démonstration en Santé du Cœur. *Hygie: Revue Internationale d'Education pour la Santé, 11,* 17–22.

Powell, H., & Gibson, P. G. (2003). Options for self-management education for adults with asthma. *Cochrane Database of Systematic Reviews, 1,* CD004107.

Powell, K. E., Mercy, J. A., Crosby, A. E., et al. (1999) *Public health models of violence and violence prevention. Encyclopaedia of Violence, Peace and Conflict,* Vol 3. Washington, DC: Academic Press.

President's Council on Physical Fitness and Sports Medicine, U.S. Department of Health and Human Services. Online at http://www.fitness.gov/american_att.PDF, accessed September 28, 2003.

Preston, M. A., Baranowski, T., & Higginbotham, J. C. (1988–89). Orchestrating the points of community intervention. *International Quarterly of Community Health Education, 9,* 11–34.

Price, J., Kake, J. A., & Kucharewski, R. (2002). Assessing assets in racially diverse, inner-city youths: Psychometric properties of the Search Institute Asset Questionnaire. *Family and Community Health, 25,* 1–9.

Prochaska, J. M., Prochaska, J. O., & Levesque, D. A. (2001). A transtheoretical approach to changing organizations. *Administration and Policy in Mental Health, 28,* 247–61.

Prochaska, J. O. (1979). *Systems of psychotherapy: A transtheoretical analysis.* Pacific Grove, CA: Brooks-Cole.

Prochaska, J. O. (2001). Treating entire populations for behavior risks for cancer. *Cancer Journal, 7,* 360–68.

Prochaska, J. O., & DiClemente, C. (1983). Stages and processes of self-change in smoking: Towards an integrative model of change. *Journal of Consulting and Clinical Psychology, 5,* 390–95.

Prochaska, J. O., Redding, C. A., & Evers, K. E. (2002). The transtheoretical model and stages of change. In K. Glanz, B. K. Rimer, & F. M. Lewis, *Health behavior and health education: Theory, research, and practice* (pp. 99–120). 3rd ed. San Francisco: Jossey-Bass.

Prochaska, J. O., Velicer, W. F., Fava, J. L., Rossi, J. S., & Tsoh, J. Y. (2001). Evaluating a population-based recruitment approach and a stage-based expert system intervention for smoking cessation. *Addictive Behavior, 26,* 583–602.

Prohaska, T. R., & Lorig, K. (2001). What do we know about what works? The role of theory in patient education. In K. Lorig, *Patient education: A practical approach* (pp. 21–55). 3rd ed. Thousand Oaks CA: Sage.

Proper, K. I., Van Der Beek, A. J., Hildebrandt, V. H., Twisk, J. W., & Van Mechelen, W. (2003). Short term effect of feedback on fitness and health measurements on self reported appraisal of the stage of change. *British Journal of Sports Medicine, 37,* 529–34.

*Proulx, M., Potvin, L., Lehoux, P., Gariépy, E., & Tremblay, M. (1999). L'action structurante de l'utilisation d'un modèle pour la planification de programmes en promotion de la santé (Structuring action from the use of a model for planning programs in health promotion). *Canadian Journal of Public Health, 90,* 23–26.

*Pucci, L. G., & Haglund, B. (1994). "Naturally Smoke Free": A support program for facilitating worksite smoking control policy implementation in Sweden. *Health Promotion International, 9,* 177–87.

*Pujet, J-C., Nejjari, C., Tessier, J-F., Sapene, M., Pasquet, S., & Racineux, J-L . (1997). Diagnostic and education in asthma: A description of the results of a survey by questionnaire. *Revue Des Maladies Respiratoires, 14,* 209–17.

Puntenney, D. (2000). *A guide to building sustainable organizations from the inside out: An organizational capacity building toolbox from the Chicago Foundation for Women.* Chicago: Institute for Policy Research, Northwestern University and Chicago Foundation for Women.

Puska, P. (1992). The North Karelia Project: Nearly 20 years of successful prevention of CVD in Finland. *Hygie: International Journal of Health Education, 11,* 33–35.

Puska, P. (2000a). Do we learn our lessons from the population-based interventions? (Editorial). *Journal of Epidemiology and Community Health, 54,* 562–63.

Puska, P. (2002b). Nutrition and global prevention of non-communicable diseases. *Asia Pacific Journal of Clinical Nutrition, 11* (Suppl. 9), S755–58.

Puska, P., McAlister, A., Pekkola, J., & Koskela, K. (1981). Television in health promotion: Evaluation of a national programme in Finland. *International Journal of Health Education, 24,* 2–14.

Puska, P., Nissinen, A., Tuomilehto, J., et al. (1985). The community-based strategy to prevent coronary heart disease: Conclusions from the ten years of the North Karelia Project. *Annual Review of Public, 6*, 147–93.

Puska, P., & Uutela, A. (2000). Community intervention in cardiovascular health promotion: North Karelia, 1972–1999. In N. Schneiderman, M. A. Speers, J. M. Silva, H. Tomes, J. H. Gentry (Eds.), *Integrating behavioral and social sciences with public health* (pp. 73–96). Baltimore, American Psychological Association: United Book Press, Inc.

Puska, P., Vartiainen, E., Tuomilehto, J., et al. (1998). Changes in premature deaths in Finland: Successful long-term prevention of cardiovascular diseases. *WHO Bulletin, 76*, 416–25.

Putnam, R. D. (2000). *Bowling alone: The collapse and revival of American community.* New York: Simon & Schuster.

Raeburn, J. M., & Rootman, I. (1998). *People centred health promotion.* Chichester, New York, Brisbane, Singapore, Toronto: John Wiley & Sons.

Rafael, A. R. (2000). Watson's philosophy, science, and theory of human caring as a conceptual framework for guiding community health nursing practice. *ANS Advances in Nursing Science, 23*, 34–49.

*Rainey, C. J., Mayo, R. M., Haley-Zitlin, V., Kemper, K. A., & Cason, K. L. (2000). Nutritional beliefs, attitudes and practices of elderly, rural, southern women. *Journal of Nutrition for the Elderly, 20*(2), 3–27.

*Rainey, C. J., & Cason, K. L. (2001). Nutrition interventions for low-income, elderly women. *American Journal of Health Behavior, 25*, 45–51.

Raj, A., & Silverman, J. G. (2002). Intimate partner violence against South Asian women in greater Boston. *Journal of the American Medical Women's Association, 57*, 111–14.

*Ramey, S. L., Shelley, M. C., Welk, G. J., & Franke, W. D. (2004). Cardiovascular disease risk reduction efforts among law enforcement officers: An application of the PRECEDE-PROCEED planning model. *Evidence-Based Preventive Medicine, 1*(1), in press.

*Ramirez, A. G., & McAlister, A. L. (1989). Mass media campaign: *A Su Salud*. *Preventive Medicine, 17*, 608–21.

Ramsey, L. T., & Brownson, R. C. (Eds.). (2002). Increasing physical activity: Recommendations from the Task Force on Community Preventive Services, reviews of evidence, and expert commentary. *American Journal of Preventive Medicine, 22* (Suppl. 4S), 67–108.

*Ransdell, L. B. (2001). Using the PRECEDE-PROCEED Model to increase productivity in health education faculty. *International Electronic Journal of Health Education, 4*(1), 276–82.

Ratner, P., Green, L. W., Frankish, C. J., Chomik, T., & Larson, C. (1997). Setting the stage for health impact assessment. *Journal of Public Health Policy, 18*, 67–79.

Rawl, S. M., Menon, U., & Champion, V. (2002). Colorectal cancer screening: An overview of current trends. *Nursing Clinics of North America, 37*, 225–45.

*Reed, D. B. (1996). Focus groups identify desirable features of nutrition programs for low-income mothers of preschool children. *Journal of the American Dietetic Association, 96*, 501–3.

*Reed, D. B., Meeks, P. M., Nguyen, L., Cross, E. W., & Garrison, M. E. B. (1998). Assessment of nutrition education needs related to increasing dietary calcium intake in low income Vietnamese mothers using focus group discussions. *Journal of Nutrition Education, 30*, 155–63.

Rehse, B., & Pukrop, R. (2003). Effects of psychosocial interventions on quality of life in adult cancer patients: Meta analysis of 37 published controlled outcome studies. *Patient Education and Counselling, 50*, 179–86.

*Reichelt, P. A. (1995). Musculoskeletal injury: Ergonomics and physical fitness in firefighters. *Occupational Medicine: State of the Art Reviews, 10*, 735–47.

*Reid, D., Harris, J., Jacob, M., Davis, A. M., & Randell, J. (1983). Smoking education in the United Kingdom with special reference to England, Wales, and Northern Ireland. In

W. F. Forbes, R. C. Frecker, & D. Nostbakken (Eds.) *Proceedings of the Fifth World Conference on smoking and health, Winnipeg, Canada*, Vol. 1 (pp. 355–60). Ottawa, Ontario, Canada: Canadian Council on Smoking and Health.

Rein, M., & Rabinovitz, F. (1977). Implementation: A theoretical perspective. Cambridge, MA: Joint Center for Urban Studies of MIT and Harvard University, Working Paper no. 43.

Remington, P. L., & Goodman, R. A. (1998). Chronic disease surveillance. In R. C. Brownson, P. L. Remington, & J. R. Davis (Eds.), *Chronic disease epidemiology and control* (pp. 55–76). 2nd ed. Washington, DC: American Public Health Association.

*Renaud, L., & Mannoni, C. (1997). Etude sur la participation des parents dans les activites scolaires ou parascolaires [Study of parental participation in curricular and extracurricular activities]. *Canadian Journal of Public Health, 88,* 184–90.

*Renger, R., Steinfelt, V., & Lazarus, S. (2002). Assessing the effectiveness of a community-based media campaign targeting physical inactivity. *Family and Community Health, 25,* 18–30.

*Renger, R., & Titcomb, A. (2002). A three-step approach to teaching logic models. *American Journal of Evaluation, 23,* 493–503.

Report of the Presidential Commission on the Human Immunodeficiency Virus Epidemic. (1988). Washington, DC: The White House, June 24.

Resnicow, K., Braithwaite, R. L., Dilorio, C., & Glanz, K. (2002). Applying theory to culturally diverse and unique populations. In K. Glanz, B. K. Rimer, & F. M. Lewis (Eds.), *Health behavior and health education: Theory, research, and practice* (pp. 485–509). 3rd ed. San Francisco: Jossey-Bass.

*Resnicow, K., Cohn, L., Reinhardt, J., Cross, D., Futterman, R., Kirschner, E., Wynder, E. L., & Allegrante, J. P. (1992). A three-year evaluation of the Know Your Body program in inner-city schoolchildren. *Health Education Quarterly, 19,* 463–80.

Resnicow, K., Robinson, T., & Frank, E. (1996). Advances and future directions for school-based health promotion research: Commentary on the CATCH intervention trial. *Preventive Medicine, 25,* 378–83.

Ribisl, K. M., Lee, R. E., Henriksen, L., & Haladjian, H. H. (2003). A content analysis of websites promoting smoking culture and lifestyle. *Health Education and Behavior, 30,* 64–78.

*Rice, M., & Green, L. W. (1992). Prevention and education. In D. Kronstadt (Ed.), *Pregnancy and exposure to alcohol and other drug use*, Chap. 7. Washington, DC: The CDM Group, for the Office of Substance Abuse Prevention, U.S. Department of Health and Human Services.

*Richard, L., Gauvin, L., Potvin, L., Denis, J. L., & Kishchuk, N. (2002). Making youth tobacco control programs more ecological: Organizational and professional profiles. *American Journal of Health Promotion, 16*(5), 267–79.

Ricketts, T. (2001). *Community capacity for health: How can we measure it?* (technical report). Research Triangle Park, NC: Research Triangle Institute.

Ridley, M. (1999). *Genome: The autobiography of a species in 23 chapters.* New York: Harper Collins.

Riedel, B. W., Robinson, L. A., Klesges, R. C., & McLain-Allen, B. (2002). What motivates adolescent smokers to make a quit attempt? *Drug and Alcohol Dependence, 68,* 167–74.

Riedel, J. E., Lynch, W., Baase, C., Hymel, P., & Peterson, K. W. (2001). The effect of disease prevention and health promotion on workplace productivity: A literature review. *American Journal of Health Promotion, 15,* 167–91.

Riemsma, R. P., Kirwan, J. R., Taal, E., & Rasker, J. J. (2003). Patient education for adults with rheumatoid arthritis. *Cochrane Database of Systematic Reviews, 2,* CD003688.

Rigby, K. (2003). Consequences of bullying in schools. *Canadian Journal of Psychiatry, 48,* 583–90.

*Rimer, B. K. (1993). Improving the use of cancer screening in older women. *Cancer, 72* (Suppl.), 1084–87.

*Rimer, B. K. (1995). Audience and messages for breast and cervical cancer screenings. *Wellness Perspectives: Research, Theory and Practice, 11*(2), 13–39.

Rimer, B. K. (2002). Perspectives on intrapersonal theories health behavior. In K. Glanz, B. K. Rimer, & F. M. Lewis (Eds.), *Health behavior and health education: Theory, research, and practice* (pp. 144–59). 3rd ed. San Francisco: Jossey-Bass.

*Rimer, B. K., Davis, S. W., Engstrom, P. F., et al. (1988). Some reasons for compliance and noncompliance in a health maintenance organization breast cancer screening program. *Journal of Compliance in Health Care, 3*, 103–14.

*Rimer, B. K., Jones, W., Wilson, C., Bennett, D., & Engstrom, P. (1983). Planning a cancer control program for older citizens. *Gerontologist, 23*, 384–89.

*Rimer, B., Keintz, M. K., & Fleisher, L. (1986). Process and impact of a health communications program. *Health Education Research, 1*, 29–36.

*Rimer, B. K., Keintz, M. K., Kessler, H. B., Engstrom, P. F., & Rosan, J. R. (1989). Why women resist screening mammography: Patient-related barriers. *Radiology, 172*, 243–46.

Rimmer, J. H., Silverman, K., Braunschweig, C., Quinn, L., & Liu, Y. (2002). Feasibility of a health promotion intervention for a group of predominantly African American women with type 2 diabetes. *The Diabetes Educator, 28*, 571–80.

Risser, L. W., Hoffman, H. M., Bellah, G. G., & Green, L. W. (1985). A cost-benefit analysis of preparticipation sports examinations of adolescent athletes. *Journal of School Health, 55*, 270–73.

Rittel, H. J., & Webber, M. M. (1973). Dilemmas in a general theory of planning. *Policy Sciences, 4*, 155–69.

*Rivo, M. L., Gray, K., Whitaker, M., et al. (1991). Implementing PATCH in public housing communities: The District of Columbia experience. *Journal of Health Education, 23*,148–52.

Rizak, S., Cunliffe, D., Sinclair, M., et al. (2003). Drinking water quality management: A holistic approach. *Water Science and Technology, 47*, 31–36.

Robb, K. A., Miles, A., & Wardle, J. (2004). Subjective and objective risk of colorectal cancer (UK). *Cancer Causes and Control, 15*, 21–25.

Roberts, B. J., Mico, P. R., & Clark, E. W. (1963). An experimental study of two approaches to communication. *American Journal of Public Health, 53*, 1361–81.

Robinson, T. N. (2002). Screening. In L. Breslow, B. Goldstein, L. W. Green, C. W. Keck, J. M. Last, & M. McGinnis (Eds.), *Encyclopedia of public health*, Vol. 3 (pp. 1081–83). New York: Macmillan Reference USA.

Rodgers, G. B. (2002). Income and inequality as determinants of mortality: An international cross-section analysis. *International Journal of Epidemiology, 31*, 533–38.

Rogers, E. M. (1995). *Diffusion of innovations*. 4th ed. New York: Free Press.

Rogers, E. S. (1960). *Human ecology and health: An introduction for administrators*. New York: Macmillan Co.

Rogers, R. W. (1975). A protection motivation theory of fear appeals and attitude change. *Journal of Psychology, 91*, 93–114.

Rokeach, M. (1970). *Beliefs, attitudes and values*. San Francisco: Jossey-Bass.

Romm, R. J., Fletcher, S. W., & Hulka, B. S. (1981). The periodic health examination: Comparison of recommendations and internists' performance. *Southern Medical Journal, 74*, 265–71.

Roos, N. P. (1975). Evaluating health programs: Where do we find the data. *Journal of Community Health, 1*, 39–51.

*Rootman, I. (1988). Canada's health promotion survey. In I. Rootman, R. Warren, T. Stephens, & L. Peters (Eds.), *Canada's health promotion survey: Technical report*. Ottawa: Minister of Supply and Services.

Rootman, I. (1997). Continuous quality improvement in health promotion: Some preliminary thoughts from Canada. *Promotion and Education, 4*(2): 23–25.

Rosal, M. C., Ebbeling, C. B., Lofgren, I., Ockene, J. K., Ockene, I. S., & Hebert, J. R. (2001). Facilitating dietary change: The patient-centered counseling model. *Journal of the American Dietetic Association, 101,* 332–38, 341.

Rose, G. (1992). *A strategy of preventive medicine.* Oxford: Oxford University Press.

Rosen, G. (1958, 1993). *A history of public health.* New York: originally copyright by MD Publications; expanded edition copyright by Johns Hopkins University Press.

Rosenblatt, D., & Kabasakalian, L. (1966). Evaluation of venereal disease information campaign for adolescents. *American Journal of Public Health, 56,* 1104–13.

Rosenstock, I. M. (1974). The historical origins of the Health Belief Model. *Health Education Monographs, 2,* 354–95.

Rosenstock, I. M., Derryberry, M., & Carriger, B. (1959). Why people fail to seek poliomyelitis vaccination. *Public Health Reports, 74,* 98–103.

Rosenstock, I. M., Strecher, V., & Becker, M. H. (1988). Social learning theory and the health belief model. *Health Education Quarterly, 15,* 175–83.

Rosner D. (2000). When does a worker's death become murder? *American Journal of Public Health, 90,* 535–40.

*Ross, H. S., & Mico, P. R. (1980). *Theory and practice in health education.* Palo Alto, CA: Mayfield.

Ross, M., & Lappin, B. W. (1967). *Community organization: Theory, principles, and practice.* New York: Harper & Row.

*Ross, M. W., & Simon Rosser, B. R. (1989). Education and AIDS risks: A review. *Health Education Research, 4*(3), 273–84.

Rossi, P. H., Lipsey, M. W., & Freeman, H. E. (2003). *Evaluation: A systematic approach.* 7th ed. Thousand Oaks, CA: Sage.

*Roter, D. L. (1977). Patient participation in the patient-provider interaction: The effects of patient question-asking on the quality of interaction, satisfaction and compliance. *Health Education Monographs, 5,* 281–315.

Roter, D. L. (2003). Observations on methodological and measurement challenges in the assessment of communication during medical exchanges. *Patient Education & Counseling, 50,* 17–21.

Roter, D. L., Hall, J. A., & Aoki, Y. (2002). Physician gender effects in medical communication: A meta-analytic review. *Journal of the American Medical Association, 288,* 756–64.

Roter, D. L., Stewart, M., Putnam, S. M., et al. (1997). Communication patterns of primary care physicians. *Journal of the American Medical Association, 277,* 350–56.

Rothman, J., & Brown, E. R. (1989). Indicators of societal action to promote social health. In S. B. Kar (Ed.), *Health promotion indicators and actions* (pp. 202–20). New York: Springer Publishing Co.

Roussos, S., & Fawcett, S. (2000). A review of collaborative partnerships as a strategy for improving community health. *Annual Review of Public Health, 21,* 369–402.

*Rubinson, L., & Baillie, L. (1981). Planning school based sexuality programs using the PRECEDE Model. *Journal of School Health, 51,* 282–87.

Ruchlin, H. S., Elkin, E. B., & Allegrante, J. P. (2001). The economic impact of a multifactorial intervention to improve postoperative rehabilitation of hip fracture patients. *Arthritis and Rheumatism, 45,* 446–52.

Rudd, R. E., Comings, J. P., & Hyde, J. N. (2003). Leave no one behind: Improving health and risk communication through attention to literacy. *Journal of Health Communications, 8* (Suppl. 1), 104–15.

Rundall T. G., & Phillips, K. A. (1990). Informing and educating the electorate about AIDS. *Medical Care Review, 47,* 3–13.

Russell, E. M., & Iljonforeman, E. L. (1985). Self-care in illness: A review. *Family Practice, 2,* 108–21.

Ryan, A. A. (1998). Medication compliance and older people: A review of the literature. *International Journal of Nursing Studies, 36*, 153–62.

Ryan, B. (1948). A study in technological diffusion. *Rural Sociology, 13,* 273–85.

Ryan, B., & Gross, N. C. (1943). The diffusion of hybrid seed corn in two Iowa communities. *Rural Sociology, 8,* 273–85.

Saelens, B. E., Sallis, J. F., Black, J. B., & Chen, D. (2003). Neighborhood-based differences in physical activity: An environment scale evaluation. *American Journal of Public Health, 93,* 1552–58.

Saelens, B. E., Sallis, J. F., Nader, P. R., et al. (2002). Home environmental influences on children's television watching from early to middle childhood. *Journal of Developmental and Behavioral Pediatrics, 23,* 127–32.

*Salazar, M. K. (1985). Dealing with hypertension: Using theory to promote behavioral change. *AAOHN Journal, 43,* 313–18.

Salk, J. (1973). *The survival of the wisest.* New York: Harper & Row.

Sallis, J. F., Haskell, W. L., Fortmann, S. P., et al. (1986). Predictors of adoption and maintenance of physical activity in a community sample. *Preventive Medicine, 15,* 331–41.

Sallis, J. F., Hovell, M. F., Hoffstetter, C. R., et al. (1990). Distance between homes and exercise facilities related to frequency of exercise among San Diego residents. *Public Health Reports, 105,* 179–85.

Salovey, P., Schneider, T. R., & Apanovitch, A. M. (1999). Persuasion for the purpose of cancer risk reduction: A discussion. *Journal of the National Cancer Institute Monographs, 25,* 119–22.

Saltz, R. (1987). The role of bars and restaurants in preventing alcohol-impaired driving: An evaluation of server intervention. *Evaluation and Health Professions, 10,* 5–27.

Sampson, R. J., Raudenbush, S. W., & Earls, F. (1997). Neighborhoods and violent crime: A multilevel study of collective efficacy. *Science, 277,* 918–24.

*Samuels, S. E. (1990). Project LEAN: A national campaign to reduce dietary fat consumption. *American Journal of Health Promotion, 4,* 435–40.

Samuels, S. E., Green, L. W., & Tarlov, A. R. (1989). Project LEAN. *American Journal of Public Health, 79,* 350.

Sanchez, V. (2000). Reflections of community coalition staff: Research directions from practice. *Health Promotion Practice, 1,* 320–22.

Sandbaek, A., & Kragstrup, J. (1999). Randomized controlled trial of the effect of medical audit on AIDS prevention in general practice. *Family Practice, 16,* 510–14.

Sanders, I. T. (1950). *Preparing a community profile: The methodology of a social reconnaissance.* Lexington, KY: Kentucky Community Series No. 7, Bureau of Community Services, University of Kentucky.

*Sanders-Phillips, K. (1991). A model for health promotion in ethnic minority families. *Wellness Lecture Series.* University of California President's Office, Oakland, CA, Oct. 28.

*Sanders-Phillips, K. (1996). Correlates of health promotion behaviors in low-income black women and Latinas. *American Journal of Preventive Medicine, 12,* 450–58.

Sarkin, J. A., Johnson, S. S., Prochaska, J. O., & Prochaska, J. M. (2001). Applying the transtheoretical model to regular moderate exercise in an overweight population: Validation of a stages of change measure. *Preventive Medicine, 33,* 462–69.

Satariano, W. A., Haight, T. J., & Tager, I. B. (2002). Living arrangements and participation in leisure-time physical activities in an older population. *Journal of Aging and Health, 14,* 427–51.

*Satia-About, A. J., Patterson, R. E., Kristal, A. R., et al. (2002). Psychosocial predictors of diet and acculturation in Chinese American and Chinese Canadian women. *Ethnicity and Health, 7,* 21–39.

Sauter, S. L., & NORA Organization of Work Team Members. (2002). *The changing organization of work and the safety and health of working people: Knowledge gaps and research directions*. Atlanta, GA: U.S. Department of Health and Human Services, Centers for Disease Control and Prevention, National Institute for Occupational Safety and Health.

*Sayegh, J., & Green, L. W. (1976). Family planning education: Program design, training component and cost-effectiveness of a post-partum program in Beirut. *International Journal of Health Education, 19* (suppl.), 1–20.

*Sayegh, J., & Mosley, W. H. (1976). The effectiveness of family planning education on acceptance of contraception by postpartum mothers. *Johns Hopkins Medical Journal, 139* (Dec. suppl.), 31–37.

*Schaalma, H. P., Kok, G ., Bosker, R. J., et al. (1996). Planned development and evaluation of AIDS/STD education for secondary school students in the Netherlands: Short-term effects. *Health Education Quarterly, 23*, 469–87.

Schauffler, H., McMenamin, S., Cubanski, J.,J., & Hanely, H. S. (2001). Differences in the kinds of problems consumers report in staff/group health maintenance organizations, independent practice association/network health maintenance organizations, and preferred provider organizations in California. *Medical Care, 39*, 15–25.

Schechter, J., Green, L. W., Olsen, L., Kruse, K., & Cargo, M. (1997). Application of Karasek's demand/control model a Canadian occupational setting including shift workers during a period of reorganization and downsizing. *American Journal of Health Promotion, 11*, 394–99.

Scheid, T. L. (2003). Managed care and the rationalization of mental health services. *Journal of Health and Social Behavior, 44*, 142–61.

Schellstede, W. P., & Ciszewski, R. L. (1984). Social marketing of contraceptives in Bangladesh. *Studies in Family Planning, 15*(1), 30–39.

Shiffman, S., Mason, K. M., & Henningfield, J. E. (1998). Tobacco dependence treatments: Review and prospectus. *Annual Review of Public Health, 19*, 335–58.

Schill, A. L. (2000). Genetic information in the workplace: Implications for occupational health surveillance. *AAOHN Journal, 48*(2), 80–91.

Schiller, P., Steckler, A., Dawson, L., & Patton, F. (1987). *Participatory planning in community health education: A guide based on the McDowell County, West Virginia experience*. Oakland, CA: Third Party Publishing.

Schoenberg, N. E., Amey, C. H., Stoller, E. P., & Muldoon, S. B. (2003). Lay referral patterns involved in cardiac treatment decision making among middle-aged and older adults. *Gerontologist, 43*, 493–502.

Scholes, D., McBride, C. M., Grothaus, L., et al. (2003). A tailored minimal self-help intervention to promote condom use in young women: Results from a randomized trial. *AIDS, 17*, 1547–56.

Schooler, C., Sundar, S. S., & Flora, J. (1996). Effects of the Stanford five-city project media advocacy program. *Health Education Quarterly, 23*, 346–64.

Schorr, L. B. (1997). *Common purpose: Strengthening families and neighborhoods to rebuild America*. New York: Anchor Books, Doubleday.

Schott, F. W. (1985). WELCOM: The Wellness Council of the Midlands. In *A decade of survival: Past, present, future. Proceedings of the 20th annual meeting*. Washington, DC: Society of Prospective Medicine.

Schroeder, S. A. (2002). Conflicting dispatches from the tobacco wars. *New England Journal of Medicine, 347*, 1106–09.

Schulte, P. A., Okun, A., Stephenson, C. M., et al. (2003). Information dissemination and use: Critical components in occupational safety and health. *American Journal of Industrial Medicine, 44*, 515–31.

Schultz, A. J., Parker, E. A., Israel, B. A., Becker, A. B., Maciak, B. J., & Hollis, R. (1998). Conducting a participatory community-based survey for a community health intervention in Detroit's East Side. *Journal of Public Health Management and Practice, 4*, 10–24.

Schultz, J. A., Fawcett, S. B., Francisco, V. T., & Berkowitz, B. (2003). Using information systems to build capacity: A public health improvement toolbox. In P. O'Carroll, W. A. Yasnoff, et al. (Eds.), *Public health informatics and information systems: A contributed work* (pp. 644–60). Gaithersburg, MD: Aspen.

Schumacher, C. (2000). *The impact of the 1997 tobacco tax rate increase in Alaska: An update.* Juneau: Alaska Department of Revenue and Alaska Department of Health.

Schumann, A., Estabrooks, P. A., Nigg, C. R., & Hill, J. (2003). Validation of the stages of change with mild, moderate, and strenuous physical activity behavior, intentions, and self-efficacy. *International Journal of Sports Medicine, 24*, 363–65.

*Schumann, D. A., & Mosley, W. H. (1994). The household production of health: Introduction. *Social Science and Medicine, 38*, 201–4.

Schuster, M. A., Eastman, K. L., Fielding, J. E., et al. (2001). Promoting adolescent health: Worksite-based interventions with parents of adolescents. *Journal of Public Health Management and Practice, 7*, 41–52.

*Schuurman, J., & de Haes, W. (1980). Sexually transmitted diseases: Health education by telephone. *International Journal of Health Education, 23*, 94–106.

Schwab, M., & Syme. (1997). On paradigms, community participation, and the future of public health. *American Journal of Public Health, 87*, 2049–50.

Schwartz, J. L. (1987). *Review and evaluation of smoking cessation methods: The United States and Canada, 1978–85.* Washington, DC: Department of Health and Human Services, National Institutes of Health, NIH 87–2940.

Scriven, M. (1998). Minimalist theory: The least theory that practice requires. *American Journal of Evaluation, 19*, 57–70.

Secker, J., & Membrey, H. (2003). Promoting mental health through employment and developing healthy workplaces: The potential of natural supports at work. *Health Education Research, 18*, 207–15.

*Secker-Walker, R. H., Flynn, B. S., & Solomon, P. M. (1996). Helping women quit smoking: Baseline observations for a community health education project. *American Journal of Preventive Medicine, 12*, 367–77.

*Secker-Walker, R. H., Solomon, L. J., Flynn, B. S., Skelly, J. M., & Mead, P. B. (1998). Smoking relapse prevention during pregnancy: A trial of coordinated advice from physicians and individual counseling. *American Journal of Preventive Medicine, 15*, 25–31.

*Secker-Walker, R. H., Worden, J. K., Holland, R. R., Flynn, B. S., & Detsky, A. S. (1997). A mass media program to prevent smoking among adolescents: Costs and cost effectiveness. *Tobacco Control, 6*, 207–12.

*Seiden, T. M., & Blonna, R. (1983). A profile of volunteers at the VD National Hotline. Spring '83 *Hotliner* (p. 6). Palo Alto, CA: American Social Health Association, VD National Hotline.

Senge, P. (1994). *The fifth discipline fieldbook: Strategies and tools for building a learning organization.* New York: Doubleday.

Senserrick, T. M. (2003). Graduation from a zero to .05 bac restriction in an Australian graduated licensing system: A difficult transition for young drivers? *Annual Proceedings of the Association of Advanced Automotive Medicine, 47*, 215–31.

Sepúlveda, J. (1998). Origin, direction and destination of the health transition in Mexico and Latin America. International Development Research Centre (IDRC), Canada, July 23. http://www.idrc.ca/index_e.html.

*Shamian, J., & Edgar, L. (1987). Nurses as agents for change in teaching breast self-examination. *Public Health Nursing, 4*, 29–34.

*Sharp, P. C., Dignan, M. B., Blinson, K., et al. (1998). Working with lay health educators in a rural cancer-prevention program. *American Journal of Health Behavior, 22*, 18–27.

*Sharpe, P. A., Greany, M. L., Lee, P. R., & Royce, S. W. (2000). Assets-oriented community assessment. *Public Health Reports, 113*, 205–11.

Shaw, G. B. (1930). *The apple cart: A political extravaganza.* London: Constable and Co.

Shea, S., & Basch, C. E. (1990). A review of five major community-based cardiovascular disease prevention programs. Part I: Rationale, design, and theoretical framework. *American Journal of Health Promotion, 4,* 203–13.

Shea, S., Basch, C. E., Lantiua, R., et al. (1992). The Washington Heights-Inwood Health Heart Program: A third generation cardiovascular disease prevention program in a disadvantaged urban setting. *Preventive Medicine, 21,* 203–17.

Shediac-Rizkallah, M. C., & Bone, L. R. (1998). Planning for the sustainability of community-based health programs: Conceptual frameworks and future directions for research, practice and policy. *Health Education Research, 13,* 87–108.

Shepard, P., Northridge, M. E., Prakash, S., & Stover, G. (2002). Preface: Advancing environmental justice through community-based participatory research. *Environmental Health Perspectives, 110* (Suppl. 2), 139–40.

Shephard, R. J. (2002). Whistler 2001: A Health Canada/CDC conference on communicating physical activity and health messages: Science into practice. *American Journal of Preventive Medicine, 23,* 221–25.

Shepherd, A. L., Smart, L., & Marley, J. (2003). Developing an innovative approach to tackling men's health issues. *Professional Nurse, 19,* 234–37.

Sheridan, S., Pignone, M., & Donahue, K. (2003). Screening for high blood pressure: A review of the evidence for the U.S. Preventive Services Task Force. *American Journal of Preventive Medicine, 25,* 151–58.

Shiffman, S., Mason, K. M., & Henningfield, J. E. (1998). Tobacco dependence treatments: Review and prospectus, *Annual Review of Public Health, 19,* 335–58.

Shimkin, D. (1986–87). Improving rural health: The lessons of Mississippi and Tanzania. *International Quarterly of Community Health Education, 7,* 149–65.

*Shine, M. S., Silva, M. C., & Weed, F. S. (1983). Integrating health education into baccalaureate nursing education. *Journal of Nursing Education, 22,* 22–27.

Shor, I., & Freire, P. (1987). *A pedagogy for liberation.* Boston: Bergin and Garvey Publishers.

Shoveller, J., & Green, L.W. (2002). Decentralization and public health. In L. Breslow, B. D. Goldstein, L. W. Green, C. W. Keck, J. Last, & M. McGinnis (Eds.), *Encyclopedia of public health.* New York: Macmillan Reference USA.

Shoveller, J. A., & Langille, D. B. (1993). Cooperation and collaboration between a public health unit and midsized private industry in health promotion programming: The Polymer Heart Health Program experience. *Canadian Journal of Public Health, 84,* 170–73.

Shoveller, J. A., Lovato, C. Y., Peters, L., & Rivers, J. K. (2000). Canadian National Survey on sun exposure and protective behaviours: Outdoor workers. *Canadian Journal of Public Health, 91,* 34–55.

Shults, R. A., Elder, R. W., Sleet, D. A., et al. (2001). Reviews of evidence regarding interventions to reduce alcohol-impaired driving. *American Journal of Preventive Medicine, 21,* (4 suppl.), 66–88. [Medline]

Shults, R. A., Sleet, D. A., Elder, R. W., Ryan, G. W., & Sehgal, M. (2002). Association between state level drinking and driving countermeasures and self reported alcohol impaired driving. *Injury Prevention, 8,* 106–10.

Siela, D. (2003). Use of self-efficacy and dyspnea perceptions to predict functional performance in people with COPD. *Rehabilitation Nursing, 28,* 197–204.

*Silverfine, E., Brieger, W., & Churchill, R. E. (1990). *Community-based initiatives to eradicate Guinea worm: A manual for Peace Corps Volunteers.* Washington, DC: U.S. Peace Corps and Agency for International Development.

*Simons-Morton, B. G., Brink, S. G., Parcel, G. S., et al. (1991). *Preventing alcohol-related health problems among adolescents and young adults: A CDC intervention handbook.* Atlanta, GA: Centers for Disease Control.

*Simons-Morton, B. G., Brink, S. G., Simons-Morton, D. G., et al. (1989). An ecological approach to the prevention of injuries due to drinking and driving. *Health Education Quarterly, 16*, 397–411.

Simons-Morton, B. G., Greene W. H., & Gottlieb, N. H. (1995). *Introduction to health education and health promotion.* 2nd ed. Prospect Heights, IL: Waveland Press, Inc.

*Simons-Morton, B. G., Parcel, G. S., & O'Hara, N. M. (1988). Implementing organizational changes to promote healthful diet and physical activity at school. *Health Education Quarterly, 15*, 115–30.

*Simons-Morton, D. G., Parcel, G. S., Brink, S. G., et al. (1988). *Promoting physical activity among adults: A CDC community intervention handbook.* Atlanta, GA: Centers for Disease Control.

Simons-Morton, D. G., Simons-Morton, B. G., Parcel, G. S., & Bunker, J. G. (1988). Influencing personal and environmental conditions for community health: A multilevel intervention model. *Family and Community Health, 11*, 25–35.

*Simpson, G. W., & Pruitt, B. E. (1989). The development of health promotion teams as related to wellness programs in Texas schools. *Health Education, 20*, 26–28.

Singer, B. H., & Ryff, C. D. (Eds.). (2001). *New horizons in health: An integrative approach.* Washington, DC: National Academy Press.

*Sjostrom, M., Karlsson, A. B., Kaati, G., Yngve, A., Green, L. W., & Bygren, L. O. (1999). A four week residential program for primary health care patients to control obesity and related heart risk factors: Effective application of principles of learning and lifestyle change. *European Journal of Clinical Nutrition, 53* (suppl. 2), S72–77.

Skender, M. L., Goodrick, G. K., Del Junco, D. J., et al. (1996). Comparison of 2–year weight loss trends in behavioral treatments of obesity: Diet, exercise, and combination interventions. *Journal of the American Dietetic Association, 96*, 342–46.

*Skinner, C. S., & Kreuter, M. W. (1997). Using theories in planning interactive computer programs. In R. L. Street, Jr., W. R. Gold, & T. Manning (Eds.), *Health promotion and interactive technology: Theoretical applications and future directions*, Chap. 3 (pp. 39–65). Mahwah, NJ and London: Lawrence Erlbaum.

*Sleet, D. A. (1987). Health education approaches to motor vehicle injury prevention. *Public Health Reports, 102*, 606–8.

Sloan, R. P., Gruman, J. C., & Allegrante, J. P. (1987). *Investing in employee health: A guide to effective health promotion in the workplace.* San Francisco: Jossey-Bass.

*Sloane, B. C., & Zimmer, C. H. (1992). Health education and health promotion on campus. In H. M. Wallace, K. Patrick & G. S. Parcel (Eds.), *Principles and practices of student health:* Vol. 3, *College Health* (pp. 540–57). Oakland, CA: Third Party Press.

Slovic, P. (1999). Trust, emotion, sex, politics, and science: Surveying the risk-assessment battlefield. *Risk Analysis, 19*, 689–701.

Slovic, P. (2001). The risk game. *Journal of Hazardous Materials, 86*, 17–24.

Smedley, B. D., & Syme, L. S. (2000). *Promoting health: Intervention strategies from social and behavioral research.* Washington, DC: National Academy Press.

*Smith, D. E., & Alpers, M. P. (1984). *Cigarette smoking in Papua New Guinea.* Papua New Guinea Institute of Medical Research Monograph No. 7, Papua New Guinea Institute of Medical Research, Dec., 83 pp.

Smith, H. (1988). *The power game, how Washington works.* New York: Random House.

*Smith, J. A., & Scammon, D. L. (1987). A market segment analysis of adult physical activity: Exercise beliefs, attitudes, intentions and behaviors. *Advances in Nonprofit Marketing*, Vol. 2. Greenwich, CT: JAI Press.

Smith, N., Baugh Littlejohns, L., & Thompson, D. (2001). Shaking out the cobwebs: Insights into community capacity and its relation to health outcomes. *Community Development Journal, 36*, 30–41.

*Smith, P. H., Danis, M., & Helmick, L. (1998). Changing the health care response to battered women: A health education approach. *Family & Community Health, 20,* 1–18.

Smith, T. (1973). Policy roles: An analysis of policy formulators and policy implementors.

*Solomon, D. H., Hashimoto, H., Daltroy, L., & Liang, M. H. (1998). Techniques to improve physicians' use of diagnostic tests. *Journal of the American Medical Association, 280,* 2020–27.

Solomon, M. Z., & DeJong, W. (1986). Recent sexually transmitted disease prevention efforts and their implications for AIDS health education. *Health Education Quarterly, 13,* 301–16.

Soobader, M. J., & LeClere, F. B. (1999). Aggregation and the measurement of income inequality: Effects on morbidity. *Social Science and Medicine, 48,* 733–44.

Sorensen, G., Emmons, K., Hunt, M. K., et al. (2003). Model for incorporating social context in health behavior interventions: Applications for cancer prevention for working-class, multiethnic populations. *Preventative Medicine, 37*(3), 188–97.

Sorensen, G., Glasgow, R. E., Corbett, K., & Topor, M. (1992). Compliance with worksite non-smoking policies: Baseline results from the COMMIT study of worksites. *American Journal of Health Promotion, 7,* 103–9.

Sorensen, G., Stoddard, A. M., LaMontagne, A. D., et al. (2002). A comprehensive worksite cancer prevention intervention: Behavior change results from a randomized controlled trial (United States). *Cancer Causes and Control, 13*(6), 493–502.

Sorensen, G., Stoddard, A., Peterson, K., et al. (1999). Increasing fruit and vegetable consumption through worksites and families in the Treatwell 5–a-Day Study. *American Journal of Public Health, 89,* 54–60.

Soto Mas, F. G., Kane, W. M., Going, S., et al. (2000). *Camine con Nosotros:* Connecting theory and practice for promoting physical activity among Hispanic women. *Health Promotion Practice, 1,* 178–87.

Sowell, R. L. (2003). HIV/AIDS: Mainstream or forgotten? *Journal of the Association of Nurses and AIDS Care, 14,* 16–17.

Speller, V., Evans, D., & Head, M. J. (1997). Developing quality assurance standards for health promotion practice in the UK. *Health Promotion International, 12,* 215–24.

*Spillman, D. A., Harvey, P. W. J., Gillespie, A. M., & Heywood, P. F. (1994). Developing needs assessment for adolescent nutrition education. *Australian Journal of Nutrition and Dietetics, 51,* 9–13.

Spretnak, C., & Capra, F. (1984). *Green politics.* New York: E. P. Dutton.

*Squyres, W. (Ed.). (1980). *Patient education: An inquiry into the state of the art.* New York: Springer.

Stachenko, S. (1996). The Canadian Heart Health Initiative: Dissemination perspectives. *Canadian Journal of Public Health, 87* (Suppl. 2), S57–S59.

*Stanken B. A. (2000). Promoting helmet use among children. *Journal of Community Health Nursing, 17,* 85–92.

Starfield, B., & Budetti, P. (1985). Child health risk factors. *Health Services Research, 19* (6, Pt. II), 817–86.

Staunton, C. E., Hubsmith, D., & Kallins, W. (2003). Promoting safe walking and biking to school: The Marin County success story. *American Journal of Public Health, 93,* 1431–34.

Stead, M., Hastings, G., & Eadie, D. (2002). The challenge of evaluating complex interventions: A framework for evaluating media advocacy. *Health Education Research, 17,* 351–64.

Stebbins, K. R. (2001). Going like gangbusters: Transnational tobacco companies "making a killing" in South America. *Medical Anthropology Quarterly, 15,* 147–70.

Steckler, A., Dawson, L. Goodman, R. M., & Epstein, N. (1987). Policy advocacy: Three emerging roles for health education. In W. B. Ward (Ed.), *Advances in health education and promotion,* Vol. 2 (pp. 5–27). Greenwich, CT: JAI Press.

Steckler, A., Goodman, R. M., & Kegler, M. C. (2002). Mobilizing organizations for health enhancement. In K. Glanz, B. K. Rimer, & F. M. Lewis (Eds.), *Health behavior and health education: Theory, research, and practice* (pp. 335–60). 3rd ed. San Francisco: Jossey-Bass.

*Steckler, A., Orville, K., Eng, E., & Dawson, L. (1992). Summary of a formative evaluation of PATCH. *Journal of Health Education, 23*, 174–48.

Stephenson, M. T. (2003). Mass media strategies targeting high sensation seekers: What works and why. *American Journal of Health Behavior, 27* (Suppl. 3), S233–38.

Stephenson, M. T., Morgan, S. E., Lorch, E. P., et al. (2002). Predictors of exposure from an antimarijuana media campaign: Outcome research assessing sensation seeking targeting. *Health Communication, 14*, 23–43.

Steptoe, A., Feldman, P. J., Kunz, S., et al. (2002). Stress responsivity and socioeconomic status: A mechanism for increased cardiovascular disease risk? *European Heart Journal, 23*, 1757–63.

*Stevenson, M., Iredell, H., Howat, P., Cross, D., & Hall, M. (1999). Measuring community/environmental interventions: The Child Pedestrian Injury Prevention Project. *Injury Prevention, 5*, 26–30.

*Stevenson, M., Jones, S., Cross, D., Howat, P., & Hall, M. (1996). The child pedestrian injury prevention project. *Health Promotion Journal of Australia, 6*, 32–36.

Steuart, G. W. (1965). Health, behavior and planned change: An approach to the professional preparation of the health education specialist. *Health Education Monographs, 1* (No. 20), 3–26.

Stewart, A. L., & Napoles-Springer, A. M. (2003). Advancing health disparities research: Can we afford to ignore measurement issues? *Medical Care, 41*, 1207–20.

Stiell, I., Nichol, G., Wells, G., et al. (2003). Health-related quality of life is better for cardiac arrest survivors who received citizen cardiopulmonary resuscitation. *Circulation, 108*, 1939–44.

Stillman, F. A., Cronin, K. A., Evans, W. G., & Ulasevich, A. (2001). Can media advocacy influence newspaper coverage of tobacco: Measuring the effectiveness of the American stop smoking intervention study's (ASSIST) media advocacy strategies. *Tobacco Control, 10*, 137–44.

*Stivers, C. (1994). Drug prevention in Zuni, New Mexico: Creation of a teen center as an alternative to alcohol and drug use. *Journal of Community Health, 19*, 343–59.

Stokols, D. (2000). Social ecology and behavioral medicine: Implications for training, practice, and policy. *Behavioral Medicine, 26*, 121–30.

Stokols, D., Allen, J., & Bellingham, R. L. (1996). The social ecology of health promotion: Implications for research and practice. *American Journal of Health Promotion, 10*, 247–51.

Stokols, D., Grzywacz, J. G., McMahan, S., & Phillips, K. (2003). Increasing the health promotive capacity of human environments. *American Journal of Health Promotion, 18*, 4–13.

Stone, E. J., Osganian, S. K., McKinlay, S. M., et al. (1996). Operational design and quality control in the CATCH multicenter Trial. *Preventive Medicine, 25*, 384–99.

Stone, E. J., Perry, C. L., & Luepker, R. V. (1989). Synthesis of cardiovascular behavioral research for youth health promotion. *Health Education Quarterly, 16*, 155–69.

Strecher, V. J., DeVellis, B. M., Becker, M. H., & Rosenstock, I. M. (1986). The role of self-efficacy in achieving health behavior change. *Health Education Quarterly, 13*, 73–92.

Strecher, V., Wang, C., Derry, H., Wildenhaus, K., Wildenhaus, K., & Johnson, C. (2002). Tailored interventions for multiple risk behaviors. *Health Education Research, 17*, 619–26.

*Street, R. L., Jr., Gold, W. R., & Manning T. (1997). *Health promotion and interactive technology: Theoretical applications and future directions* (pp. 54–65). Mahwah NJ & London: Lawrence Erlbaum Associates, esp.

Struthers, R., Hodge, F. S., De Cora, L., & Geishirt-Cantrell, B. (2003). The experience of native peer facilitators in the campaign against type 2 diabetes. *Journal of Rural Health, 19*, 174–80.

Stuart, G. L., Moore, T. M., Ramsey, S. E., & Kahler, C. W. (2003). Relationship aggression and substance use among women court-referred to domestic violence intervention programs. *Addictive Behavior, 28*, 1603–10.

Studlar, D. T. (2002). *Tobacco control: Comparative politics in the United States and Canada.* New York: Broadview.

Suchman, E. A. (1967). *Evaluative research: Principles and practice in public service and social action programs.* New York: Russell Sage Foundation.

*Sullivan, T., Allegrante, J. P., Peterson, M. G., Kovar, P. A., & MacKenzie, C. R. (1998). One-year followup of patients with osteoarthritis of the knee who participated in a program of supervised fitness walking and supportive patient education. *Arthritis Care & Research, 11*, 228–33.

Sultz, H. A., & Young, K. M. (2004). *Health care USA: Understanding its organization and delivery.* 4th ed. Sudbury, MA: Jones & Bartlett Publishers.

*Sun, W. Y., & Ling, T. (1997). Smoking behavior among adolescents in the city, suburbs, and rural areas of Shanghai. *American Journal of Health Promotion, 11*, 331–36.

*Sun, W. Y., & Shun, J. (1995). Smoking behavior amongst different socioeconomic groups in the workplace in the People's Republic of China. *Health Promotion International, 10*, 261–66.

Sussman, S. (Ed.). (2001). *Handbook of program development for health behavior research and practice* (pp. 158–203). Thousand Oaks, CA: Sage.

Sussman, S., Dent, C. W., & Stacy, A. W. (2002). Project Towards No Drug Abuse: A review of the findings and future directions. *American Journal of Health Behavior, 26*, 354–65.

Sussman, S., & Sussman, A. N. (2001). Praxis in health behavior program development. In S. Sussman (Ed.), *Handbook of program development for health behavior research and practice* (pp. 79–97). Thousand Oaks: Sage.

*Sutherland, M., Pittman-Sisco, C., Lacher, T., & Watkins, N. (1987). The application of a health education planning model to a school based risk reduction model. *Health Education, 18*(3), 47–51.

*Swannell, R., Steele, J., Harvey, P., et al. (1992). PATCH in Australia: Elements of a successful implementation. *Journal of Health Education, 23*, 171–73.

*Sword, W. (1999). A socio-ecological approach to understanding barriers to prenatal care for women of low income. *Journal of Advanced Nursing, 29*, 1170–77.

Syme, L. W. (1986). Strategies for health promotion. *Preventive Medicine, 15*, 492–507.

Syme, S. L. (1987). Coronary artery disease: A sociocultural perspective. *Circulation, 76* (1 Pt. 2), I112–16.

Syrjala, A. M., Niskanen, M. C., & Knuuttila, M. L. (2002). The theory of reasoned action in describing tooth brushing, dental caries and diabetes adherence among diabetic patients. *Journal of Clinical Periodontology, 29*, 427–32.

*Taggart, V. S., Bush, P. J., Zuckerman, A. E., & Theiss, P. K. (1990). A process evaluation of the District of Columbia "Know Your Body" Project. *Journal of School Health, 60*, 60–66.

*Taggart, V. S., Zuckerman, A. E., Sly, R. M., et al. (1991). You can control asthma: Evaluation of an asthma education program for hospitalized inner-city children. *Patient Education and Counseling, 17*, 35–47.

*Tamblyn, R., & Battista, R. (1993). Changing clinical practice: Which interventions work? *Journal of Continuing Education in the Health Professions, 13*, 273–88.

*Tamez, E. G., & Vacalis, T. D. (1989). Health beliefs, the significant other and compliance with therapeutic regimens among adult Mexican American diabetics. *Health Education, 20*(6), 24–31.

*Taplin, S. H., Taylor, V., Montano, D., Chinn, R., & Urban, N. (1994). Specialty differences and the ordering of screening mammography by primary care physicians. *Journal of the American Board of Family Practice, 7*, 375–86.

Task Force on Community Preventive Services. (2000). Introducing the *Guide to Community Preventive Services:* Methods, first recommendations and expert commentary. *American Journal of Preventive Medicine, 18* (Suppl. 1S), 1–142.

Taylor, J. C., Sterkel, B., Utley, M., et al. (2001). Opinions and experiences in general practice on osteoporosis prevention, diagnosis and management. *Osteoporosis International, 12,* 844–48.

*Taylor, M., Coovadia, H. M., Kvalsvig, J. D., Jinabhai, C. C., & Reddy, P. (1999). Helminth control as an entry point for health-promoting schools in KwaZulu-Natal. *South African Medical Journal, 89,* 273–79.

Taylor, S. G., Geden, E., Isaramalai, S., & Wongvatunyu, S. (2000). Orem's self-care deficit nursing theory: its philosophic foundation and the state of the science. *Nursing Science Quarterly, 13,* 104–110.

*Taylor, S. M., Elliott, S., & Riley, B. (1998). Heart health promotion: Predisposition, capacity and implementation in Ontario public health units, 1994–96. *Canadian Journal of Public Health, 89,* 410–14.

*Taylor, S. M., Elliott, S., Robinson, K., & Taylor, S. (1998). Community-based heart health promotion: Perceptions of facilitators and barriers. *Canadian Journal of Public Health, 89,* 406–9.

Taylor, V., Lessler, D., Mertens, K., et al. (2003). Colorectal cancer screening among African Americans: The importance of physician recommendation. *Journal of the National Medical Association, 95,* 806–12.

*Taylor, V. M., Taplin, S. H., Urban, N., Mahloch, J., & Majer, K. A. (1994). Medical community involvement in a breast cancer screening promotional project. *Public Health Reports, 109,* 491–99.

Tempkin, K., & Rohe, W. (1998). Social capital and neighborhood stability: An empirical investigation. *Housing Policy Debate, 9*(1), 61–88.

*Terry, P. B., Wang, V. L., Flynn, B. S., et al. (1981). A continuing medical education program in chronic obstructive pulmonary diseases: Design and outcome. *American Review of Respiratory Disease, 123,* 42–46.

Teutsch, S. M., & Churchill, R. E. (2000). *Principles and practice of public health surveillance.* 2nd ed. Oxford, New York: Oxford University Press.

*Thamer, M., Ray, N. F., Henderson, S. C., et al. (1998). Influence of the NIH Consensus Conference on *Helicobacter Pylori* on physician prescribing among a Medicaid population. *Medical Care, 36,* 646–60.

Thomas, S. B. (2001). The color line: Race matters in the elimination of health disparities. *American Journal of Public Health, 91,* 1046–48.

Thombs, D. L., Olds, R. S., & Ray-Tomasek, J. (2001). Adolescent perceptions of college student drinking. *American Journal of Health Behavior, 25,* 492–501.

Thompson, M., Minkler, M., Allen, Z., Bell, J. D., Bell, J., Blackwell, A. G., et al. (2000). *Community involvement in the federal Healthy Start Program.* Oakland, CA: PolicyLink.

*Thompson, R. S. (1996). What have HMOs learned about clinical prevention services? An examination of the experience at Group Health Cooperative of Puget Sound. *The Milbank Quarterly, 74,* 469–509.

*Thompson, R. S. (1997). Systems approaches and the delivery of health services (Editorial). *Journal of the American Medical Association, 277,* 670–71.

*Thompson, R. S., Rivara, F. P., Thompson, D. C., et al. (2000). Identification and management of domestic violence: A randomized trial. *American Journal of Preventive Medicine, 19,* 253–62.

*Thompson, R. S., Taplin, S., Carter, A. P., et al. (1988). A risk based breast cancer screening program. *HMO Practice, 2,* 177–91.

*Thompson, R. S., Taplin, S. H., McAfee, T. A., Mandelson, M. T., & Smith, A. E. (1995). Primary and secondary prevention services in clinical practice: Twenty years' experience in development, implementation, and evaluation. *Journal of the American Medical Association, 273,* 1130–35.

Thoresen, C. E., & Kirmil-Gray, K. (1983). Self-management psychology and the treatment of childhood asthma. *Journal of Allergy and Clinical Immunology, 72* (Suppl. Nov.), 596–606.

Thornton, M. A. (1979). Preventive dentistry in the Veterans Administration. *Dental Hygiene, 53,* 121–24.

*Tillgren, P., Haglund, B. J. A., Ainetdin, T., et al. (1995). Effects of different intervention strategies in the implementation of a nationwide tobacco "Quit and Win" contest in Sweden. *Tobacco Control, 4,* 344–50.

*Timmerick, T. C. (1995). *Planning, program development, and evaluation: A handbook for health promotion, aging, and health services.* Sudbury, MA: Jones and Bartlett Publishers.

Timmerick, T. C. (1997). *Health services cyclopedic dictionary.* 3rd ed. Sudbury, MA: Jones and Bartlett Publishers.

*Timmerick, T. C. (1998). *An introduction to epidemiology.* 2nd ed. Boston: Jones & Bartlett.

Tirrell, B., & Hart, L. (1980). The relationship of health beliefs and knowledge to exercise compliance in patients after coronary bypass. *Heart and Lung, 9,* 487–93.

Tones, K., & Tilford, S. (1994). *Health education: Effectiveness, efficiency and equity,* 2nd ed. London: Chapman & Hall.

Torsheim, T., Aaroe, L. E., & Wold, B. (2001). Sense of coherence and school-related stress as predictors of subjective health complaints in early adolescence: Interactive, indirect or direct relationships? *Social Science and Medicine, 53,* 603–14.

Treno, A. J., & Lee, J. P. (2002). Approaching alcohol problems through local environmental interventions. *Alcohol Research and Health, 26,* 35–40.

Trice, H. M., & Beyer, J. M. (1984). Work-related outcomes of the constructive-confrontation strategy in a job-based alcoholism program. *Journal of Studies on Alcohol, 45,* 393–404.

*Tremblay M. S., & Willms, J. D. (2000). Secular trends in the body mass index of Canadian children. *Canadian Medical Association Journal, 163,* 1429–33. Erratum in: *CMAJ, 164,* 970.

Tripp, M. K., Herrmann, N. B., Parcel, G. S., Chamberlain, R. M., & Gritz, E. R. (2000). Sun protection is fun! A skin cancer prevention program for preschools. *Journal of School Health, 70,* 395–401.

Trost, S. G., Pate, R. R., Dowda, M., Ward, D. S., Felton, G., & Saunders R. (2002). Psychosocial correlates of physical activity in white and African-American girls. *Journal of Adolescent Health, 31,* 226–33.

Trotter, C. L., & Edmunds, W. J. (2002). Modelling cost effectiveness of meningococcal serogroup C conjugate vaccination campaign in England and Wales. *British Medical Journal, 324,* 809.

Truchot, D., Maure, G., & Patte, S. (2003). Do attributions change over time when the actor's behavior is hedonically relevant to the perceiver? *Journal of Social Psychology, 143,* 202–8.

*Turner, L. W., Sutherland, M., Harris, G. J., & Barber, M. (1995). Cardiovascular health promotion in North Florida African-American churches. *Health Values: The Journal of Health Behavior, Education & Promotion, 19*(2), 3–9.

Turnidge, J. (2001). Responsible prescribing for upper respiratory tract infections. *Drugs, 61,* 2065–77.

*Ugarte, C. A., Duarte, P., & Wilson, K. M. (1992). PATCH as a model for development of a Hispanic health needs assessment: The El Paso experience. *Journal of Health Education, 23,* 171–56.

U.S. Department of Education, National Center for Education Statistics. (2002). *Statistics of state school systems; Statistics of public elementary and secondary schools; Projections of educational statistics to 2012.* Washington, DC: U.S. Department of Education.

U.S. Department of Health, Education and Welfare. (1979). *Healthy people: Surgeon General's report on health promotion and disease prevention.* Washington, DC: Public Health Service, DHEW-PHS-79–55071.

*U.S. Department of Health and Human Services. (1981). *Promoting health in special populations.* Washington, DC: Office of Disease Prevention and Health Promotion; reprinted (1987), *Journal of Public Health Policy, 8,* 369–423.

*U.S. Department of Health and Human Services. (1988). *CDC and minority communities stopping the spread of HIV infection and AIDS.* Atlanta, GA: Office of the Deputy Director (AIDS), Centers for Disease Control, Public Health Service.

U.S. Department of Health and Human Services. (1991). *Healthy people 2000.* Washington, DC: Office of the Assistant Secretary for Health, Public Health Service. (Also published as *Healthy people 2000: National health promotion and disease prevention objectives, full report, with commentary* (Boston: Jones and Bartlett Publishers, 1992).

U.S. Department of Health and Human Services. (1996). *Healthy people 2000: Midcourse review and 1995 revisions.* Sudbury, MA: Jones and Bartlett Publishers.

U.S. Department of Health and Human Services. (2001). *Healthy people in healthy communities.* Washington, DC: U.S. Government Printing Office.

U.S. Department of Health and Human Services. (2001). *Healthy people 2010.* Washington, DC: Office of the Assistant Secretary for Health, Public Health Service. (www.health.gov/healthypeople)

*U.S. Department of Health and Human Services. (2001). *Healthy people 2010 toolkit: A field guide to health planning.* Washington, DC: The Public Health Foundation. (http://www.health.gov/healthypeople/state/toolkit)

*U.S. Department of Health and Human Services. (1996, Updated 2003). *Planned approach to community health: Guide for the local coordinator.* Atlanta, GA: U.S. Department of Health and Human Services, Centers for Disease Control and Prevention, National Center for Chronic Disease Prevention and Health Promotion. (http://www.cdc.gov/nccdphp/patch/index.htm accessed Nov 26, 2003).

U.S. Preventive Services Task Force. (1989). *Guide to clinical preventive services: An assessment of the effectiveness of 169 interventions.* Baltimore: William & Wilkens.

U.S. Preventive Services Task Force. (1996). *Guide to clinical preventive services.* 2nd ed. Baltimore: Williams & Wilkins.

Urberg, K. A., Luo, Q., Pilgrim, C., & Degirmencioglu, S. M. (2003). A two-stage model of peer influence in adolescent substance use: Individual and relationship-specific differences in susceptibility to influence. *Addictive Behavior, 28,* 1243–56.

Valente, T. W., Hoffman, B. R., Ritt-Olson, A., Lichtman, K., & Johnson, C. A. (2003). Effects of a social-network method for group assignment strategies on peer-led tobacco prevention programs in schools. *American Journal of Public Health, 93,* 1837–43.

Vanden Eng, J., Marcus, R., Hadler, J. L., et al. (2003). Consumer attitudes and use of antibiotics. *Emerging Infectious Diseases, 9,* 1128–35.

van der Pligt, J. (1998). Perceived risk and vulnerability as predictors of precautionary behavior. *British Journal of Health Psychology, 3,* 1–14.

Van Meter, D., & Van Horn, C. (1975). The policy implementation process: A conceptual framework. *Administration and Society, 6,* 445–88.

*van Veenendal, H., Grinspun, D. R., & Adriaanse, H. P. (1996). Educational needs of stroke survivors and their family members, as perceived by themselves and by health professionals. *Patient Education and Counseling, 28,* 265–76.

VanderVoort, D. J., Ragland, D. R., & Syme, S. L. (2001). Anger expression and hypertension in transit workers. *Ethnicity and Disease, 11,* 80–89.

*Vancouver Foundation. (1999). *The social reconnaissance project: Discovering philanthropic leadership opportunities.* Vancouver, BC: Vancouver Foundation.

Vartiainen, E., Paavola, M., McAlister, A., & Puska, P. (1998). Fifteen-year follow-up of smoking prevention effects in the North Karelia Youth Project. *American Journal of Public Health, 88,* 8105.

Vartiainen, E., & Puska, P. (1987). The North Karelia Youth Project 1978–80: Effects of two years of educational intervention on cardiovascular risk factors and health behavior in adolescence. In B. Hetzel & G. S. Berenson (Eds.), *Cardiovascular risk factors in childhood: Epidemiology and prevention* (pp. 183–202). Dublin: Elsevier.

Vartiainen, E., Jousilahti, P., Alfthan, G., Sundvall, J., Pietinen, P., & Puska, P. (2000). Cardio-vascular risk factor changes in Finland, 1972–1997. *International Journal of Epidemiology, 29,* 49–56.

Vartiainen, E., Puska, P., Jousilahti, P., Korhonen, H. J., Toumilehto, J., & Nissinen, A. (1994). Twenty-year trends in coronary risk factors in North Karelia and in other areas of Finland. *International Journal of Epidemiology, 23,* 495–504.

Vass, M., & Walsh-Allis, G. A. (1990). Employee dependents: The future focus of worksite health promotion programs and the potential role of the allied health professional. *Journal of Allied Health, 19,* 39–48.

*Vasse, R. M., Nijhuis, F. J. N., Kok, G., & Kroodsma, A. T. (1997a). Effectiveness of a worksite alcohol program. In R. Vasse (Ed.), *The development, implementation and evaluation of two worksite health programs aimed at preventing alcohol problems* (pp. 43–58). Maastricht: Maastricht University.

*Vasse, R. M., Nijhuis, F. J. N., Kok, G., & Kroodsma, A. T. (1997b). Process evaluation of two worksite alcohol programs. In R. Vasse (Ed.), *The development, implementation and evaluation of two worksite health programs aimed at preventing alcohol problems* (pp. 71–88). Maastricht: Maastricht University.

*Vertinsky, P. A., & Mangham, C. (1991). *Making it fit: Matching substance-abuse prevention strategies.* Victoria, BC: Alcohol and Drug Programs, Ministry of Health, British Columbia.

*Vickery, D. M., H. Kalmer, D. Lowry, et al. (1983). Effect of a self-care education program on medical visits. *Journal of the American Medical Association, 250,* 2952–56.

Villani, S. (2001). Impact of media on children and adolescents: A 10–year review of the research. *Journal of the American Academy of Child and Adolescent Psychiatry, 40,* 392–401.

*Villas, P., Mottinger, S. G., & Cardenas, M. (1996). PRECEDE model utilization in differentiating users and nonusers of alcohol. *Journal of Wellness Perspectives, 12,* 113–22.

*Vincent, M. L., Clearie, A. F., & Schluchter, M. D. (1987). Reducing adolescent pregnancy through school and community based education. *Journal of the American Medical Association, 257,* 3382–86.

Vojtecky, M. A. (1986). Commentary: A unified approach to health promotion and health protection. *Journal of Community Health, 11,* 219–21.

Wakefield, M., Flay, B., Nichter, M., & Giovino, G. (2003). Role of the media in influencing trajectories of youth smoking. *Addiction, 98* (Suppl. 1), 79–103.

Wallace, L. S. (2002). Osteoporosis prevention in college women: Application of the expanded Health Belief Model. *American Journal of Health Behavior, 26,* 163–72.

Wallack, L. M. (1997). Media advocacy: Promoting health through mass communication. In K. Glanz, F. M. Lewis, & B. K. Rimer (Eds.), *Health behavior and health education: Theory, research, and practice,* Chap. 16. 2nd ed. San Francisco: Jossey-Bass.

Wallack, L., Dorfman, L., Jernigan, D., & Themba, M. (1993). *Media advocacy and public health: Power for prevention.* Newbury Park, CA: Sage.

Wallack, L., Woodruff, K., Dorfman, L., & Diaz, I. (1999). *News for a change: An advocate's guide to working with the media.* Thousand Oaks, CA: Sage.

*Wallenius, S. H. (1995). Self-initiated modification of hypertension treatment in response to perceived problems. *The Annals of Pharmacotherapy, 29,* 1213–17.

Wallerstein, N., & Duran, B. M. (2003). The theoretical and historical roots of CBPR. In M. Minkler & N. Wallerstein (Eds.), *Community-based participatory research and health.* San Francisco: Jossey-Bass.

Wallerstein, N., Duran, B. M., Aguilar, J., et al. (2003). Jemez Pueblo: Built and social-cultural environments and health within a rural American Indian community in the Southwest. *American Journal of Public Health, 93,* 1517–18.

Walley, T. (2002). Lifestyle medicines and the elderly. *Drugs and Aging, 19,* 163–68.

Walsh, J. F., Devellis, B. M., & Devellis, R. F. (1997). Date and acquaintance rape. Development and validation of a set of scales. *Violence Against Women, 3,* 46–58.

*Walsh, J. M., & McPhee, S. J. (1992). A systems model of clinical preventive care: An analysis of factors influencing patient and physician. *Health Education Quarterly, 19,* 157–75.

Walsh, J. M., & McPhee, S. J.. (2002). Prevention in the year 2002: Some news, some issues. *Primary Care, 29,* 727–49.

*Walsh, J. F., Devellis, B. M., & Devellis, R. F. (1997). Date and acquaintance rape. Development and validation of a set of scales. *Violence Against Women, 3,* 46–58.

*Walter, H. J., & Connelly, P. A. (1985). Screening for risk factors as a component of a chronic disease prevention program for youth. *Journal of School Health, 55,* 183–88.

*Walter, H. J., Hofman, A., Barrett, L.T., et al. (1987). Primary prevention of cardiovascular disease among children: One-year results of a randomized intervention study. In B.Hetzel & G. S. Berenson (Eds.), *Cardiovascular risk factors in childhood: Epidemiology and prevention* (pp. 161–81). Rotterdam: Elsevier Science.

*Walter, H. J., Hofman, A., Connelly, P. A., Barrett, L. T., & Kost, K. L. (1985). Primary prevention of chronic disease in childhood: Changes in risk factors after one year of intervention. *American Journal of Epidemiology, 122,* 772–81.

*Walter, H. J., Hofman, A., Connelly, P. A., Barrett, L. T., & Kost, K. L. (1986). Coronary heart disease prevention in childhood: One-year results of a randomized intervention study. *American Journal of Preventive Medicine, 2,* 239–45.

*Walter, H. J., & Vaughan, R. D. (1993). AIDS risk reduction among a multiethnic sample of urban high-school students. *Journal of the American Medical Association, 270,* 725–30.

*Walter, H. J., & Wynder, E. L. (1989). The development, implementation, evaluation, and future directions of a chronic disease prevention program for children: The "Know Your Body" studies. *Preventive Medicine, 18,* 59–71.

*Wandersman A. (2003). Community science: bridging the gap between science and practice with community-centered models. *American Journal of Community Psychology, 31,* 227–42.

Wandersman, A., Imm, P., Chinman, M., & Kafterian, S. (2000). Getting to outcomes: A results-based approach to accountability. *Evaluation and Program Planning, 23,* 389–95.

Wandersman, A., & Florin, P. (2000). Citizen participation and community organizations. In J. Rappaport & E. Seidman (Eds.), *Handbook of community psychology* (pp. 247–72). New York: Academic/Plenum.

Wang, C. C. (2003). Using photovoice as a participatory assessment and issue selection tool. In M. Minkler & N. Wallerstein (Eds.), *Community-based participatory research for health* (pp. 179–96). San Francisco: Jossey-Bass.

Wang, C. C., Cash, J. L., & Powers, L. S. (2000). Who knows the streets as well as the homeless? Promoting personal and community action through photovoice. *Health Promotion Practice, 1,* 81–89.

Wang, L. Y., Crossett, L. S., Lowry, R., et al.. (2001). Cost-effectiveness of a school-based tobacco-use prevention program. *Archives of Pediatric Adolescent Medicine, 155,* 1043–50.

Wang, S. C., Tsai, C. C., Huang, S. T., & Hong, Y. J. (2003). Betel nut chewing and related factors in adolescent students in Taiwan. *Public Health, 117,* 339–45.

*Wang, V. L., Ephross, P., & Green, L. W. (1975). The point of diminishing returns in nutrition education through home visits by aides: An evaluation of EFNEP. *Health Education Monographs 3,* 70–88. Also in J. Zapka (Ed.), *The SOPHE heritage collection of health education monographs,* Vol. 3 (pp. 155–73). Oakland, CA: Third Party Publishing Co.

*Wang, V. L., Terry, P., Flynn, B. S., et al. (1979). Multiple indicators of continuing medical education priorities for chronic lung diseases in Appalachia. *Journal of Medical Education, 54,* 803–11.

*Ward, W. B., Levine, D. M., Morisky, D., et al. (1982). Controlling high blood pressure in inner city Baltimore through community health education. In R. W. Carlaw (Ed.), *Perspectives on community health education: A series of case studies. Vol 1: United States* (pp. 73–79). Oakland, CA: Third Party Publishing Co.

Ware, B. G. (1985). Occupational health education: A nontraditional role for a health educator. In H. P. Cleary, J. M. Kichen, & P. G. Ensor (Eds.), *Advancing health through education: A case study approach* (pp. 319–23). Palo Alto, CA: Mayfield.

Ware, J. E., & Kosinski, M. (2001). Interpreting SF-36 summary health measures: A response. *Quality of Life Research, 10,* 405–13; discussion 415–20.

Warner, E. A., Walker, R. M., & Friedmann, P. D. (2003). Should informed consent be required for laboratory testing for drugs of abuse in medical settings? *American Journal of Medicine, 115,* 54–58.

Warner, K. E. (1987). Selling health promotion to corporate America: Uses and abuses of the economic argument. *Health Education Quarterly, 14,* 39–55.

Warner, K. E. (1998). Smoking out the incentives for tobacco control in managed care settings. *Tobbaco Control, 7* (Suppl.), S50–54.

Warner, K. E. (2003). The costs of benefits: Smoking cessation and health care expenditures. *American Journal of Health Promotion, 18,* 123–24, ii.

Warner, K. E., Hodgson, T. A., & Carroll, C. E. (1999). Medical costs of smoking in the United States: Estimates, their validity, and their implications. *Tobacco Control, 8,* 290–300.

Warner, K. E., & Murt, H. A. (1983). Premature deaths avoided by the antismoking campaign. *American Journal of Public Health, 73,* 672–77.

Warner, K. E., Smith, R. J., Smith, D. G., & Fries, B. E. (1996). Health and economic implications of a work-site smoking-cessation program: A simulation analysis. *Journal of Occupational and Environmental Medicine, 38,* 981–92.

Warner, K. E., Wickizer, T. M., Wolfe, R. A., Schildroth, J. E., & Samuelson, M. H. (1987). Economic implications of workplace health promotion programs: Review of the literature. *Journal of Occupational Medicine, 30,* 106–12.

Watson, M. R., Horowitz, A. M., Garcia, I., & Canto, M. T. (2001). A community participatory oral health promotion program in an inner-city Latino community. *Journal of Public Health Dentistry, 61,* 34–41.

Watts, B. G., Vernon, S. W., Myers, R. E., & Tilley, B. C. (2003). Intention to be screened over time for colorectal cancer in male automotive workers. *Cancer and Epidemiologic Biomarkers and Prevention, 12,* 339–49.

Wdowik, M. J., Kendall, P. A., Harris, M. A., & Keim, K. S. (2000). Development and evaluation of an intervention program: Control on campus. *Diabetes Educator, 26,* 95–104.

*Wechsler, H., Basch, C. E., Zybert, P., & Shea, S. (1998). Promoting the selection of low-fat milk in elementary school cafeterias in an inner-city Latino community: Evaluation of an intervention. *American Journal of Public Health, 88,* 427–33.

Wedekind, C., & Milinski, M. (2000). Cooperation through image scoring in humans. *Science, 288,* 850–52.

Weinberg, M., Mazzuca, S. A., Cohen, S. J., & McDonald, C. J. (1982). Physicians' ratings of information sources about their preventive medicine decisions. *Preventive Medicine, 11,* 717–23.

*Weinberger, M., Saunders, A. F., Bearon, L. B., et al. (1992). Physician-related barriers to breast cancer screening in older women. *The Journals of Gerontology, 47* (special issue), 111–17.

Weiss, C. H. (1972). *Evaluation research: Methods of assessing program effectiveness.* Englewood Cliffs, NJ: Prentice-Hall.

Weiss, C. H. (1973). Between the cup and the lip. *Evaluation, 1*(2), 54.

*Weiss, J. R., Wallerstein, N., & MacLean, T. (1995). Organizational development of a university-based interdisciplinary health promotion project. *American Journal of Health Promotion, 10,* 37–48.

Weist, M. D., Goldstein, J., Evans, S. W., et al. (2003). Funding a full continuum of mental health promotion and intervention programs in the schools. *Journal of Adolescent Health, 32* (6 Suppl), 70–78.

Welk, G. J. (1999). The Youth Physical Activity Promotion Model: A conceptual bridge between theory and practice. *Quest, 51,* 5–23.

Wells, B. L., DePue, J. D., Lasater, T. M., & Carleton, R. A. (1988). A report on church site weight control. *Health Education Research, 3,* 305–16.

Werden, P. (1974) Health education for Indian students. *Journal of School Health, 44,* 319–23.

West, R., McEwen, A., Bolling, K., & Owen, L. (2001). Smoking cessation and smoking patterns in the general population: A 1–year follow-up. *Addiction, 96,* 891–902.

Westmaas, J. L., Wild, T. C., & Ferrence, R. (2002). Effects of gender in social control of smoking cessation. *Health Psychology, 21,* 368–76.

Whaley, A. L., & Geller, P. A. (2003). Ethnic/racial differences in psychiatric disorders: A test of four hypotheses. *Ethnicity & Disease, 13,* 499–512.

Whaley, A. L., & Winfield, E. B. (2003). Correlates of African American college students' condom use to prevent pregnancy, STDs, or both outcomes. *Journal of the National Medical Association, 95,* 702–9.

Wharf Higgins, J. (2002). Participation in community health planning. In L. Breslow, et al., *Encyclopedia of public health,* Vol. 5 (pp. 890–91). New York: Macmillan Reference USA.

Wharf Higgins, J., & Green, L. W. (1994). The APHA criteria for development of health promotion programs applied to four healthy community projects in British Columbia. *Health Promotion International, 9,* 311–20.

Wharf Higgins, J., Vertinsky, P., Cutt, J., & Green, L. W. (1999). Using social marketing as a theoretical framework to understand citizen participation in health promotion. *Social Marketing Quarterly, 5,* 42–55.

Whittemore, R., Bak, P. S., Melkus, G. D., & Grey, M. (2003). Promoting lifestyle change in the prevention and management of type 2 diabetes. *Journal of the American Academy of Nurse Practitioners, 15,* 341–49.

Wholey, J. S., Hatry, H. P., & Newcomer, K. E. (1994). *Handbook of practical program evaluation.* San Francisco: Jossey-Bass.

*Whyte, N., & Berland, A. (1993). *The role of hospital nurses in health promotion: A collaborative survey of British Columbia hospital nurses.* Vancouver: Registered Nurses Assn. of British Columbia and Vancouver General Hosp., Pub. 28. [See summary: Health promotion in acute care settings: Redefining a nursing tradition. *Nursing in British Columbia,* March–April, 1994, pp. 21–22.]

*Wickizer, T. M., Wagner, E., & Perrin, E. B. (1998). Implementation of the Henry J. Kaiser Family Foundation's Community Health Promotion Grant Program: A process evaluation. *Milbank Quarterly, 76,* 121–53.

*Wiggers, J. H., & Sanson-Fisher, R. (1994). General practitioners as agents of health risk behaviour change: Opportunities for behavioural science in patient smoking cessation. *Behaviour Change, 11,* 167–76.

Wiggers, L. C., Smets, E. M., de Haes, J. C., Peters, R. J., & Legemate, D. A. (2003). Smoking cessation interventions in cardiovascular patients. *European Journal of Vascular and Endovascular Surgery, 26,* 467–75.

Wilber, K. (1998). Marriage of sense and soul: Integrating science and religion. New York: Random House.

Wilcox, P. (2003). An ecological approach to understanding youth smoking trajectories: Problems and prospects. *Addiction, 98* (Suppl. 1), 57–77. [quotation from p. 57]

Wilkinson, R. G. (1996). *Unhealthy societies: The afflictions of inequality.* London: Routledge.

Wilkinson, R. G., & Marmot, M. (Eds.). (1998). *Social determinants of health: The solid facts.* Geneva: World Health Organization.

Williams, D. R., & Collins, D. (2001). Racial residential segregation: A fundamental cause of racial disparities in health. *Public Health Reports, 116,* 404–16.

Williams, J. M., Chinnis, A. C., & Gutman, D. (2000). Health promotion practices of emergency physicians. *American Journal of Emergency Medicine, 18,* 17–21.

*Williams, P. L., Innis, S. M., Vogel, A. M. P., & Stephen, L. J. (1999). Factors influencing infant feeding practices of mothers in Vancouver. *Canadian Journal of Public Health, 90,* 114–19.

Williams, R. L. (2002). Getting the community into community-oriented primary care. Abstract #49078, American Public Health Association 104th conference, Philadelphia, PA, Nov. 13, online at http://apha.confex.com/apha/130am/techprogram/paper_49078.htm.

*Williams, R. M. (1990). Rx: Social reconnaissance. *Foundation News, 31*(4), 24–29.

Williams, T., & Jones, H. (1993). School health education in the European Community. *Journal of School Health, 63,* 133–35.

*Williamson, N. B., Burton, M. J., Brown, W. B., et al. (1988). Changes in mastitis management practices associated with client education and the effects of adopting recommended mastitis control procedures on herd production. *Preventive Veterinary Medicine, 5,* 213–23.

*Wilson, R. W., & Iverson, D. C. (1982). Federal data bases for health education research. *Health Education, 13*(3), 30–34.

Wilson T. (2001). A bi-state, metropolitan, school-based immunization campaign: Lessons from the Kansas City experience. *Journal of Pediatric Health Care, 15,* 173–78.

Wilson, W. J. (1987). *The truly disadvantaged: The inner city, the underclass, and public policy.* Chicago: The University of Chicago Press.

*Windsor, R. A. (1984). Planning and evaluation of public health education programs in rural settings: Theory into practice. In H. P. Cleary, J. M. Kichen, & P. G. Ensor (Eds.), *Advancing health through education: A case study approach* (pp. 273–84). Palo Alto, CA: Mayfield.

*Windsor, R. A. (1986). An application of the PRECEDE Model for planning and evaluating education methods for pregnant smokers. *Hygie: International Journal of Health Education, 5*(3), 38–43.

Windsor, R. A.. (2000). Counselling smokers in Medicaid maternity care: The SCRIPT project. *Tobacco Control, 9* (Suppl 1), I62.

Windsor R. (2003). Smoking cessation or reduction in pregnancy treatment methods: a meta-evaluation of the impact of dissemination. *American Journal of Medical Science, 326,* 216–22. Review.

Windsor, R. A., Baranowski, T., Clark, N., & Cutter, G. (2004). *Evaluation of health promotion, health education, and disease prevention programs.* 3rd ed. New York: McGraw-Hill.

Windsor, R. A., Cutter, G., Morris, J., Reese, Y., Adams, B., & Bartlett, E. (1985). Effectiveness of self-help smoking cessation interventions for pregnant women in public health maternity clinics: A randomized trial. *American Journal of Public Health, 75,* 1389–92.

Windsor, R. A., Green, L. W., & Roseman, J. M. (1980). Health promotion and maintenance for patients with chronic obstructive pulmonary disease: A review. *Journal of Chronic Disease, 33,* 5–12.

*Windsor, R., Lowe, J., Perkins, L., et al. (1993). Health education methods for pregnant smokers: Behavioral impact and cost-benefit. *American Journal of Public Health, 83,* 201–6.

Windsor, R. A., & Orleans, C. T. (1986). Guidelines and methodological standards for smoking cessation intervention research among pregnant women: Improving the science and art. *Health Education Quarterly, 13*(2), 131–61

*Winett, R. A., Altman, D. G., & King, A. C. (1990). Conceptual and strategic foundations for effective media campaigns for preventing the spread of HIV infection. *Evaluation and Program Planning, 13,* 91–104.

Winnail, S. D., Geiger, B. F., & Nagy, S. (2002). Why don't parents participate in school health education? *American Journal of Health Education, 33,* 10–14.

*Wismer, B. A., Moskowitz, J. M., Chen, A. M., et al. (1998). Rates and independent correlates of pap smear testing among Korean-American women. *American Journal of Public Health, 88,* 656–60.

*Wismer, B. A., Moskowitz, J. M., Min, K., et al. (2001). Interim assessment of a community intervention to improve breast and cervical cancer screening among Korean American Women. *Journal of Public Health Management Practice, 7,* 61–70.

Wojtowicz, G. G. (1990). A secondary analysis of the school health education evaluation data base. *Journal of School Health, 60,* 56–95.

Wolff, T. (2001). Community coalition building: Contemporary practice and research. *American Journal of Community Psychology, 29,* 165–72.

*Wong, M. L., Chan, K. W. R., & Koh, D. (1998). A sustainable behavioral intervention to increase condom use and reduce gonorrhea among sex workers in Singapore: 2–year follow-up. *Preventive Medicine, 27,* 891–900.

*Wong, M. L., Chan, R., Koh, D., Wong, C. M. (1994–95). Theory and action for effective condom promotion: Illustrations from a behavior intervention project for sex workers in Singapore. *International Quarterly of Community Health Education, 15,* 405–21.

*Wong, M. L., Chan, R., & Wee, S. (2000). Sex workers' perspectives on condom use for oral sex with clients: A qualitative study. *Health Education and Behavior, 27,* 502–16.

Wong, R. (2002). The current status of drug testing in the U.S. workforce. *American Clinical Laboratories, 21*(3), 14–17.

*Wong, T. Y., & Seet, B. (1998). A behavioral analysis of eye protection use by soldiers. *Military Medicine, 162,* 744–48.

Woolley, T., Buettner, P. G., & Lowe, J. (2002). Sun-related behaviors of outdoor working men with a history of non-melanoma skin cancer. *Journal of Occupational and Environmental Medicine, 44,* 847–54.

*Worden, J. K., Flynn, B. S., Geller, B. M., et al. (1988). Development of a smoking prevention mass-media program using diagnostic and formative research. *Preventive Medicine, 17,* 531–58.

*Worden, J. K., Flynn, B. S., Solomon, L. J., Secker-Walker, R. H., Badger, G. J., & Carpenter, J. H. (1996). Using mass media to prevent cigarette smoking among adolescent girls. *Health Education Quarterly, 23,* 453–68.

*Worden, J. K., Soloman, L. J., Flynn, B. S., et al. (1990). A community-wide program in breast self-examination training and maintenance. *Preventive Medicine, 19,* 254–69.

World Health Organization. (1983). *Expert committee on new approaches to health education in primary health care* (Tech. Rep. Series 690). Geneva: World Health Organization.

World Health Organization. (1986). *Targets for health for all.* Copenhagen: WHO Regional Office for Europe.

World Health Organization. (1997). *Promoting health through schools: Report of a WHO expert committee on comprehensive school health education and promotion* (pp.1–93). Geneva: WHO Technical Report Services.

World Health Organization. (2001). *International classification of functioning, disability and health.* Geneva: World Health Organization.

World Health Organization. (2002). *The world health report 2002: Reducing risks, promoting healthy life.* Geneva: World Health Organization.

World Health Organization and United Nations Children's Fund. (1986). *Helping a billion children learn about health: Report of the WHO/UNICEF international consultation on health education for school-age hildren, 1985.* Geneva: World Health Organization.

*Wortel, E., deGeus, G. H., Kok, G., & van Woerkum, C. (1994). Injury control in pre-school children: A review of parental safety measures and the behavioural determinants. *Health Education Research, 9,* 201–13.

*Wortel, E., de Vries, H., & de Geus, G. H. (1995). Lessons learned from a community campaign on child safety in The Netherlands. *Family and Community Health, 18,* 60–77.

*Wouters, N., Stadlander, M., Andriaanse, H., Knottnerus, A., De Witte, L., & Kok, G. J. (1986). The use of a health education planning model to design and implement health education interventions concerning AIDS. *AIDS-Forschung (AIFO), 1,* 615–19.

Wright, R. J., & Fischer, E. B. (2003). Putting asthma into context: Community influences on risk, behavior and interventions. In I. Kawachi & L. F. Berkman (Eds.), *Neighborhoods and health* (pp. 222–62). New York: Oxford University Press.

Wright, S. M., & Carrese, J. A. (2003). Serving as a physician role model for a diverse population of medical learners. *Academic Medicine, 78,* 623–28.

*Wu, E. (2000). *Managing health claims effectively.* Singapore: Gerling Global Re.

Wu, J. L., Wang, L. H., Rauyajin, O., et al. (2002). Contraceptive use behavior among never married young women who are seeking pregnancy termination in Beijing. *Chinese Medical Journal-Peking, 115,* 851–55.

Xin-Zhi, W., Zhao-guang, H., & Dan-yang, C. (1987). Smoking prevalence in Chinese aged 15 and above. *Chinese Medical Journal, 100,* 686–92.

Yarzebski, J., Bujor, C. F., Goldberg, R. J., et al. (2002). A community-wide survey of physician practices and attitudes toward cholesterol management in patients with recent acute myocardial infarction. *Archives of Internal Medicine, 162,* 797–804.

Yen, I., & Syme, S. L. (1999). The social environment and health: A discussion of the epidemiologic literature. *Annual Review of Public Health, 20,* 287–308.

Yen, L., McDonald, T., Hirschland, D., & Edington, D. W. (2003). Association between wellness score from a health risk appraisal and prospective medical claims costs. *Journal of Occupational Environmental Medicine, 45,* 1049–57.

*Yeo, M. (1998). *Drug-related illness in older women: Perceptions of factors affecting nonsteroidal anti-inflammatory drug self-management practices.* Unpublished doctoral dissertation, University of Calgary, Alberta.

Yingling, L., & Trocino, L. (1997). Strategies to integrate patient and family education into patient care redesign. *AACN Clinical Issues, 8,* 246–52.

Young, T. L., & Ireson, C. (2003). Effectiveness of school-based telehealth care in urban and rural elementary schools. *Pediatrics, 112,* 1088–94.

*Younoszai, T. M., Lohrmann, D. K., Seefeldt, C. A., & Greene, R. (1999). Trends from 1987 to 1991 in alcohol, tobacco, and other drug (ATOD) use among adolescents exposed to a school district-wide prevention program. *Journal of Drug Education, 29,* 77–94.

Yukl, G. (1994). *Leadership in organizations.* 3rd ed. Englewood Cliffs, NJ: Prentice Hall.

*Zapka, J. G., & Averill, B. W. (1979). Self care for colds: A cost-effective alternative to upper respiratory infection management. *American Journal of Public Health, 69,* 814–16.

*Zapka, J. G., Costanza, M. E., Harris, D. R., et al. (1993). Impact of a breast cancer screening community intervention. *Preventive Medicine, 22,* 34–53.

*Zapka, J. G., & Dorfman, S. (1982). Consumer participation: Case study of the college health setting. *Journal of American College Health, 30,* 197–203.

*Zapka, J. G., Harris, D. R., Hosmer, D., et al. (1993). Effect of a community health center intervention on breast cancer screening among Hispanic American women. *Health Services Research, 28,* 223–35.

*Zapka, J. G., Hosmer, D., Costanza, M. E., Harris, D. R., & Stoddard, A. (1992). Changes in mammography use: Economic, need, and service factors. *American Journal of Public Health, 82,* 1345–51.

*Zapka, J. G., & Mamon, J. A. (1982). Integration of theory, practitioner standards, literature findings and baseline data: A case study in planning breast self-examination education. *Health Education Quarterly, 9,* 330–56.

*Zapka, J. G., & Mamon, J. A. (1986). Breast self-examination in young women. II. Characteristics associated with proficiency. *American Journal of Preventive Medicine, 2,* 70–78.

*Zapka, J. G., Stoddard, A., Barth, R., & Greene, H. L. (1989). Breast cancer screening utilization by Latina community health center clients. *Health Education Research, 4,* 461–68.

*Zapka, J. G., Stoddard, A. M., Costanza, M. E., & Greene, H. L. (1989). Breast cancer screening by mammography: Utilization and associated factors. *American Journal of Public Health, 79,* 1499–1502.

Zaric, G. S., & Brandeau, M. L. (2001). Optimal investment in a portfolio of HIV prevention programs. *Medical Decision Making, 21,* 391–408.

*Zhang, D. &. Qiu, Z. (1993). School-based tobacco-use prevention: People's Republic of China, May 1989–January 1990. *Morbidity and Mortality Weekly Report, 42*(19), 370–77.

Ziff, M. A., Conrad, P., & Lachman, M. E. (1995). The relative effects of perceived personal control and responsibility on health and health-related behaviors in young and middle-aged adults. *Health Education Quarterly, 22,* 127–42.

Zimmerman, M. A. (2000). Empowerment theory: Psychological, organizational and community levels of analysis. In J. Rapporporet & E. Seidman (Eds.), *Handbook of community psychology* (pp. 43–63). New York: Academic/Plenum.

*Zimmerman, R. K., Nowalk, M. P.; Bardella, I. J.; et al. (2004). Physician and practice factors related to influenza vaccination among the elderly. *American Journal of Preventive Medicine, 26,* 1–10.

*Zuckerman, A. E., Olevsky-Peleg, E., Bush, P. J., et al. (1989). Cardiovascular risk factors among black schoolchildren: Comparisons among four Know Your Body Studies. *Preventive Medicine, 18,* 113–32.

*Zuckerman, M. J., Guerra, L. G., Drossman, D. A., Foland, J. A., & Gregory, G. G. (1996). Health-care-seeking behaviors related to bowel complaints: Hispanics versus non-Hispanic whites. *Digestive Diseases and Sciences, 41,* 77–82.

*Zuilhof, W., & Maas Van der, P. (1998). HIV prevention for clients of male sex workers: An experiment in planned action. *International Conference on AIDS, 12,* 918 (abstract no. 29/43367).

Zuvekas, S. H., & Taliaferro, G. S. (2003). Pathways to access: Health insurance, the health care delivery system, and racial/ethnic disparities, 1996–99. *Health Affairs (Millwood), 22,* 139–53.

INDEX